ACKERLEY

Also by Peter Parker

THE OLD LIE (1987)

ACKERLEY

A Life of J. R. Ackerley

Peter Parker

FARRAR · STRAUS · GIROUX

NEW YORK

Library of Congress Cataloging-in-Publication Data
Parker, Peter.
Ackerley : the life of J. R. Ackerley.
1. Ackerley, J. R. (Joe Randolph), 1896–1967—Biography.
2. Authors, English—20th century—Biography.
I. Title.
PR6001.C4Z86   1989   828'.91209   [B]   89-12063

For Christopher

Contents

Illustrations

List of Illustrations

Ackerley abroad, 1920s (*by courtesy of Diana Petre*)
Ackerley, the successful playwright (*by courtesy of Diana Petre*)
Goldsworthy Lowes Dickinson (*by courtesy of the Provost and Scholars of King's College, Cambridge*)
Ackerley and Albert (*by courtesy of Diana Petre*)
Harry Daley and friend (*by courtesy of John Kenny*)
Harry Daley at the Section House, 1920s (*by courtesy of John Kenny*)
Jack Sprott (*by courtesy of P. N. Furbank*)
Ackerley in bed (*by courtesy of P. N. Furbank*)
Ackerley at Lowestoft (*by courtesy of John Kenny*)
Ackerley beside the sea (*by courtesy of Francis King*)
Ackerley at home (*by courtesy of Diana Petre*)
Ackerley at the coast (*by courtesy of Diana Petre*)
Nancy with William Plomer, 1930s (*by courtesy of P. N. Furbank*)
Nancy, Paul, Netta and Leo Charlton (*by courtesy of Diana Petre*)

Between pages 338 and 339
Ackerley and Queenie (*by permission of James Kirkup*)
Queenie at Star and Garter Mansions (*by courtesy of Francis King*)
Ackerley's sketch of Queenie (*by courtesy of Neville Braybrooke*)
Queenie in Putney (*by courtesy of Francis King*)
Aunt Bunny (*by courtesy of Diana Petre*)
May Buckingham with Forster, Ackerley and her son (*by courtesy of P. N. Furbank*)
Ackerley and Jack Sprott in the 1950s (*by courtesy of P. N. Furbank*)
Diana Petre in the 1950s: photograph by Mark Gerson (*by courtesy of Diana Petre*)
Ackerley in Tripoli with Donald Windham (*by courtesy of Donald Windham*)
Ackerley with an Athenian kitten (*by courtesy of Donald Windham*)
Ackerley with Japanese students (*by courtesy of Francis King*)
Ackerley in Nara Park (*by courtesy of Francis King*)
Don Bachardy's drawings of Nancy and Ackerley, 1963 (*by courtesy of Francis King*)
Ackerley at his desk (*by courtesy of Neville Braybrooke*)
Nancy and Ackerley with James Kirkup's mother, 1962, photographed by James Kirkup (*by permission of James Kirkup*)
Ackerley in Villiers David's flat (*by courtesy of Diana Petre*)

Acknowledgements

I AM extremely grateful to all those individuals and institutions who made this book possible, but I must single out several people for particular thanks. Christopher Moore first introduced me to Ackerley's books and subsequently put his house at my disposal during my visits to Cambridge. Alison Hennegan also acted as host, was, as ever, an inexhaustible mine of information, and was one of several people who read the book in draft and made valuable suggestions. P. N. Furbank generously sent me photocopies of his letters from Harry Daley, supplied me with notes he had made during his own researches into the life of E. M. Forster, and loaned me books and photographs. Ian Angus supplied me with a bibliography and photocopies of Ackerley's poetry and journalism. Patric Dickinson of the College of Arms hunted out references in censuses to the Ackerley and Aylward families, and guided me through the complicated lineage of the Dukes of Westminster. Neville Braybrooke's scholarly edition of Ackerley's letters has been a constant source of reference; he also supplied me with numerous addresses, loaned me a suitcaseful of his research material, and read the book in draft.

I must also thank those librarians who assisted me, in particular Dr Michael Halls, Modern Archivist at King's College, Cambridge, whose knowledge of Forster and his circle, and his ability to decipher G. L. Dickinson's handwriting, proved invaluable. I am also much indebted to the efficiency and kindness of: Ms Cathy Henderson (Research Librarian), Ms Patrice Fox, Mr Ken Craven and staff at the Harry Ransom Humanities Research Center, the University of Texas at Austin; Mr David Burnett and staff at the University Library at Durham; Ms Margaret Prythergch, Ms Debbie Butler and Ms Jacqueline Kavanagh of the BBC Written Archives Centre; Mr Martin Taylor, Mr Roderick Suddaby and staff at the Department of Printed Books and the Department of Documents at the Imperial War Museum; Mr John Burt, Mr C. P. Ravilious and Ms Elizabeth Inglis of the University of Sussex Library; Dr Lola Szladits of the Berg Collection at the New York Public Library; Mr Mike Bott and staff at the University of Reading; Mr Philip Reed of the Britten-Pears Library; Mr I. C. Cunningham of the National Library of Scotland; and staff of the British Library at Bloomsbury and Colindale, the India Office, the BBC Tapes and Transcripts Section, the University of London Library, and University College, London, Library.

I am particularly indebted to Mr R. P. Wright on behalf of the Claude Colleer Abbott Estate. Although, under the terms of Abbott's will, the several hundred letters Ackerley wrote to him (now held in the Library of the University of Durham) cannot be published until 1991, I was kindly allowed to read them.

The following answered a host of questions, some of them impertinent, either in person or by letter; loaned or gave me books and original or photocopied material; supplied me with all manner of information; were generous hosts during research trips; or simply took time to answer letters from an inquisitive stranger. I am extremely grateful to them all:

Dr Gerald Abraham; Mr Roger Ackerley; Miss Janet Adam Smith; Mr Ivan Alderman; Mr and Mrs Walter Allen; Dr Peter Alexander; Mr Michael Annals; the late Mr Dennis Arundell; the late Mr David Atkin; Mr Don Bachardy; Mr Paul Bailey; Mr Martin Barron; Professor Quentin Bell; Mr Peter Bennett and Mr J. S. Russ (Rossall School); Mr Anthony Bond (W. P. Nevill Estate); Lady Berkeley; Mr Richard Brain; Ms Virginia Buchan; Mrs May Buckingham; Mr Paul Cadmus; the late Mr Sandy Campbell; Mr Esteban Cerda; the late Mr Douglas Cleverdon; Miss Lettice Cooper; Mr Terence Cooper; Mr Hilary Corke; Mr Eric Crozier; Mr Graeme Cruickshank; the late Mr Adrian Daintrey; the late Mr David Daley; Mr Adrian Dannatt; Mr Timothy d'Arch Smith; Dr P. N. Davies; Mr Michael De-la-Noy; Mr Patric Dickinson; Mrs Carol Dorrington-Ward; Mr John Drumond; Ms Maureen Duffy; Mr Cyril Eland; Mr Geoffrey Elborn; Miss Isobel English; Mr Gavin

Ewart; Mr and Mrs Eric Fletcher; Mr Andrew Forge; Ms Susan Fullilove; Mr Roy Fuller; the Fyffes Group Ltd; Sir John Gielgud; Mr David Godwin; Ms Rachel Gould; Mr K. W. Gransden; Mr Bill Hamilton (A. M. Heath); Sir Stuart Hampshire; Mr Robert Harris; Sir Rupert Hart-Davis; Mr Colin Haycraft; Mr John Haylock; Mr Christopher Hawtree; Mr Philip Hoare; Mr Thurston Hogarth; Mr John Holmstrom; Lord Horder; Mr Miles Huddleston; Mr Jonathan Hunt; Mr Bruce Hunter and Ms Gina Dobbs (David Higham Associates); Mr John Kenny; Mr David Kidd; Professor James Kirkup; Mr Melvin Lasky; Miss Rosamond Lehmann; Mr Jeremy Lewis; Mr Robert Liddell; Mr Colin Mabberley (Mander and Mitcheson Theatre Collection); Mr David Machin; Mr Derwent May; Mr Ian McKelvie; Professor Edward Mendelson; Mr James Michie; Dr Donald Mitchell; Mr Leslie Mitchell (Geoffrey Gorer Estate); Mrs Naomi Mitchison; Mr Charles Monteith; Mr Richard Murphy; Mrs Trekkie Parsons; Mr Tony Peake; Mr Geoffrey Penny; Dr Chris Perriam; Ms Linda Perry; Dr Iain Poplett; Sir Victor Pritchett; Miss Isabel Quigly; Mr Raymond Raikes; Ms Santha Rama Rau; Dr and Mrs Jerome Ravel; Mr Simon Raven; Mr Jonathan Rich; Mr William Roerick; Mrs Margaret Rogers; Mr Alan Ross; Sir Steven Runciman; Mrs Vera Russell; Dr George Rylands; Mr Tony Scotland; Mr Desmond Shawe-Taylor; Mr Richard Shone; Mr Colin Spencer; Sir Stephen Spender; Mr Fred Spotts; Mr Jim Stroud; Mr David Sylvester; Mr Paul Taylor; Mr Christopher Tower; Dr Harish Trivedi; Mr Fred Urquhart; Mr Paul Vaughan; Mr Hugo Vickers; Dr Keith Walker; Mrs Margot Walmsley; Mr Paul West; Sally, Duchess of Westminster; Mr Benjamin Whitrow; Sir Angus Wilson; Mr Donald Windham; Mrs Marjorie Workman; Mr Norman Wright; and the Poetry Book Society.

Extracts from the books, letters, diaries and manuscripts of J. R. Ackerley are quoted by kind permission of Francis King. The majority of Ackerley's letters are owned by, and reproduced by kind permission of, the recipients, with the following exceptions:

E. M. Forster, W. J. H. Sprott, Clive Bell (King's College, Cambridge); Sonia Orwell, Roger Senhouse (Ian Angus); L. P. Hartley, Veronica Jeppe (Ian McKelvie); Geoffrey Gorer, Leonard Woolf (Manuscripts Section of the University of Sussex Library); Frederic

Acknowledgements

Warburg (the University of Reading and Martin Secker and Warburg Ltd); George Barker, Edmund Blunden, Richard Church, G. L. Dickinson, Francis King, David Higham (the Harry Ransom Humanities Research Center, the University of Texas at Austin); William Plomer (University of Durham); Edward Sackville-West, Edward Marsh (Henry W. and Albert A. Berg Collection, The New York Public Library, Astor, Lenox and Tilden Foundations); Benjamin Britten (the Trustees of the Britten-Pears Foundation); The Bodley Head (University of Reading and The Bodley Head Ltd); Chatto and Windus (University of Reading and Chatto and Windus Ltd).

Unpublished and copyright material is quoted by kind permission of the following:

King's College, Cambridge (E. M. Forster and G. L. Dickinson, © 1989 the Provost and Scholars of King's College, Cambridge); John Kenny (Harry Daley); the Society of Authors (Norman Douglas, © 1989 The Estate of Norman Douglas); David Higham Associates Ltd (Gerald Heard, © Michael Barrie, 1989; David Higham, © H. M. Higham, 1989; Edith Sitwell, © Francis Sitwell, 1989); George Sassoon (Siegfried Sassoon); Mr Nigel Nicolson (Harold Nicolson and V. Sackville-West); St John's College Cambridge (H. Festing Jones); the Master and Fellows of Magdalene College, Cambridge (A. C. Benson); Mrs Trekkie Parsons (Leonard Woolf and Ian Parsons); Mr John Tydeman (Henry Reed); Martin Secker and Warburg Ltd (Frederic Warburg); the BBC (material from BBC Written Archives Centre, Caversham Park, Reading).

I have done my best to contact the copyright holders of all the material I have used, but there are a few whom I have not been able to trace. I should be pleased to hear from anyone whose permission to use copyright material has not been obtained.

I am forever indebted to Ackerley's literary executor, Francis King, who agreed to my writing the book, put no restrictions upon me, put me in touch with innumerable people, put up with me as a frequent visitor to his house, entrusted me with photographs, letters, diaries and manuscripts, read the book in draft and gave me help and suggestions throughout. I would also like to pay particular tribute to

Ackerley's half-sister, Diana Petre, who patiently answered questions about her family, loaned me photographs, books and letters and showed remarkable forbearance. I am very grateful to Robin Baird-Smith and Prudence Fay at Constable, and Jonathan Galassi at Farrar, Straus and Giroux for their encouragement, enthusiasm and advice.

Finally, I would like to thank Thomas Blaikie, in whose house I began work on the book; and my parents, who brought me up in the company of animals. Far above and beyond the call of duty, Christopher Potter read the manuscript at several stages and put up with a great deal whilst I was writing it. This book is for him.

Peter Parker
London E17
April 1989

To speak the truth, I think that people *ought* to be upset, and if I had a paper I would upset them all the time; I think that life is so important and, in its workings, so upsetting that nobody should be spared . . .

J. R. Ackerley to Stephen Spender, December 1955

Introduction

'IF there is good to be said of me,' J. R. Ackerley wrote in a notebook for *My Father and Myself*, 'others must report that.' His ruthless, posthumously published, 'Family Memoir' caused considerable dismay amongst his friends for the bleak picture it painted of his life. His oldest and closest friend, E. M. Forster, could hardly bear to read it and complained: 'It seems so ill-tempered, and such a reproach to all his friends . . . I wish I could give him a good smack!' Ackerley received a number of good smacks from Forster over the years and would no doubt have submitted to this final one with good humour. He would have argued that the book was an attempt to get at certain truths and to entertain, rather than an exercise in self-congratulation. 'I think I have managed to make it amusing,' he said, 'but very much at my own expense. I don't cut much of a figure, it seems to me as I try to make myself out dodging about in the mists of the past.'

Those who knew Ackerley certainly felt that he cut much less of a figure in *My Father and Myself* than he did in life. Quite apart from giving the impression that he had no real friends apart from his dog, his book scarcely mentions the fact that for a quarter of a century he had been an important figure on the British literary scene. From 1935 to 1959, Ackerley was literary editor of the BBC's weekly magazine, *The Listener*, where he created some of the liveliest and most authoritative arts pages to be found in any journal of the period. 'The *on dit* of the day was that the best reviewing was in *The Listener*,' the philosopher Stuart Hampshire recalled. When Ackerley died, *The Times* recorded that: 'As an editor Joe Ackerley was incomparable.' This is an opinion that has been frequently repeated and amplified by authorities as diverse (indeed, as antagonistic) as Stephen Spender and Geoffrey Grigson; it is one that remains unchallenged. 'By common consent he was the greatest Literary Editor of his time – perhaps of all time,' wrote the distinguished journalist and editor, Anthony Howard. Nearly all the reviews in *The Listener* were unsigned, except in quarterly Book Supplements, when an impressive array of names was revealed. Along with a vast battery of lesser-known but expert commentators on almost every subject, people of the calibre of Leonard and Virginia Woolf, E. M. Forster, Clive Bell, Herbert Read, C. Day Lewis, Christopher Isherwood, Kenneth Clark and Wyndham Lewis were persuaded by Ackerley to write for him anonymously, unremuneratively and regularly. 'I have been lucky with my team,' Ackerley once reflected, '– in particular with Morgan [Forster] and Virginia Woolf. What they said really did matter. You could feel their impact.' This was characteristically modest; it was less a case of luck than of good judgement and an ability to inspire affection and loyalty. In spite of considerable opposition from his employers, he provided a forum for 'difficult' poems and controversial opinions and, equally importantly, he fostered the talents of successive rising generations. W. H. Auden is merely the most distinguished of those writers who have recorded their indebtedness to Ackerley for providing them with work and space when they were young.

In addition to his editorial work, Ackerley wrote a number of idiosyncratic books which have been widely acclaimed as classics. His reputation has always stood high, particularly amongst fellow writers, who recognize and applaud the sort of perfectionism which led to continual and painstaking revision of manuscripts. (The most extreme example of this process, *My Father and Myself*, was begun in 1933 and was only completed in 1967, the year of his death.) In the course of researching this book I asked a number of people how they would rate Ackerley as a writer and received unanimously favourable answers. 'Oh, very high indeed,' said Stephen Spender, whilst Charles Monteith, for many years senior editor at Faber and Faber, unequivocally described Ackerley as 'one of the best writers of prose of this century'. The general consensus is that Ackerley is a minor master, and he was able to count Elizabeth Bowen, Rosamond Lehmann, Vita Sackville-West, Siegfried Sassoon, Truman Capote, Evelyn Waugh and Cyril Connolly amongst his many admirers. His books continue to be reprinted and to win a new readership, both in Britain and America, and there is little doubt that the best of thcm will last.

In *My Father and Myself* Ackerley barely mentions his considerable literary reputation and achievements; such matters would have distracted him from his principal theme, which is contained in the title. He was always at pains to emphasize that the book was *not* an autobiography and certainly not the last word on his life. 'Curiosity about myself has carried me somewhat further than I meant to go,' he confessed, 'and to small result; however honestly we may wish to examine ourselves we can do no more than scratch the surface.' Even a writer as autobiographical as Ackerley, whose entire output from poetry and drama to fiction and journalism was a mirror held up to his own life, can never tell the whole story. Nor, of course, can a biographer; but this book is an attempt in that direction.

Ackerley often described *My Father and Myself* as a quest for the truth and it is a quest which, as he freely admitted, remained unfulfilled. However, whilst he acknowledged with Wilde that the truth is rarely pure and never simple, he thought it both worthwhile and important to whittle away the evasions and defences with which people surround their lives and to get as near the vital core as possible. He often quoted with approval, and always attempted to uphold, Coventry Patmore's assertion that 'The truth is great and shall prevail.' Amongst his papers are a number of references to 'my biographers', and one suspects that it was his hope that any biography of him would aim to tell the truth where he had been unable to do so. This poses a number of problems, but in so far as I have been able I have told the truth in this account of his life. As Ackerley knew to his own cost, the laws of libel occasionally prevent the truth from prevailing. As he nervously tinkered with his own books, nearly all of which required excisions or alterations on the advice of lawyers, so I have been obliged to suppress the occasional fact or name. Quite apart from the law, there is also the question of tact. As a literary editor Ackerley was remarkably unpartisan and was prepared to publish unfavourable notices of the books of his friends, but, as he wrote when rejecting one particularly brutal review, 'there is a step from not being kind to being actually cruel which I cannot take'. Ackerley himself removed a number of remarks about his sister Nancy from *My Father and Myself*, noting: 'Though never untrue, I thought them unkind.' I too have avoided recording some of his less charitable remarks about friends and acquaintances still living. In all this I hope that I have followed his example, reflecting the spirit rather than the letter of the law.

About Ackerley himself I have felt no such reticence. Ackerley's unflinching frankness about himself sets an example and imposes an unusual obligation. It is perhaps rare to write a biography without ever feeling that one is prying into the subject's sexual life and character, or simply going too far. Ackerley believed that sex was central to his life and central to what might be seen as his failure in human relationships. *My Father and Myself* is scarcely an advertisement for the benefits of homosexuality, but it is very important to stress that, however much unhappiness Ackerley's love-life brought him, he never ascribed his difficulties to homosexuality *per se*. There is no suggestion anywhere in his writing that he ever wished to be heterosexual or thought that his life might have been happier had he been attracted to women rather than men. (That his life might have been easier had the law of the land and the moral climate been different, he never denied.) Neither did he believe, as his friend William Plomer did, that being homosexual hampered him as a writer. His principal subject was himself, a subject he found both intriguing and baffling, but if he never wholly under-stood himself, he certainly accepted what he found with grimly amused resignation. Ackerley himself always complained when biographies failed to provide sufficient sexual details. 'One would think from some of them that their subjects did not possess any manly parts,' he wrote in a draft introduction to *My Father and Myself*, 'and even if they are married and have children, the children are more the result of a conjuring trick than of an act of joyful lust. Considering how import-ant a part sex plays both in us and with us, and how delightful it is, it is odd how industriously it is shuffled out of the way; it played a particularly important part in the lives of my father and his family, and has not therefore been omitted from this memoir.' One ignores such hints at one's peril.

I am conscious that I have been obliged to rely upon Ackerley's own account of many of the episodes in this book. Throughout his life he kept several diaries and wrote a vast number of letters. It is probably true to say that no man writing in a diary or corresponding with friends ever tells the whole truth. However, Ackerley took such pains to be truthful about himself that wherever I have been unable to corroborate his version of events I have taken it to be reliable. I am aware that this raises questions, particularly when Ackerley is writing about his sister. 'I am not a good Press Agent for Nancy I know,' he admitted. The most thorough extant diaries cover a period when Nancy's problems almost entirely took over his life, and much of what he wrote clearly served a therapeutic purpose. Nancy has no voice at this period, apart from a couple of letters, which I reproduce from Ackerley's own transcript of them. Where possible I have checked his account of this troubled period against letters between people who knew both parties. Nancy's illness, which involved extensive amnesia, would cast doubt upon any testimony she might have provided. There are several instances where it is evident that, for whatever reason, she was not telling the truth. Even so, it may be felt that Nancy is condemned unheard. All I can say is that Ackerley himself does not emerge from his own account of their relationship with a great deal of credit either, and I am inclined to accept what he wrote as essentially true.

Although Ackerley suffered very real depression, particularly towards the end of his life, he was a man whose view of life was essentially an amused one. Not everyone understood when he turned his sardonic humour upon life's little ironies, and he frequently grumbled that people took his books far too seriously. In particular, he was annoyed when critics failed to mention how funny they were, for, like some grouchy alchemist, he had laboured hard to turn the dross of his experience to gold. He also put a great deal of energy into writing letters, in which he related the misfortunes which befell him with lugubrious relish, performing selflessly for an appreciative and sympathetic audience of friends. Even so, the melancholy fact remains that this is not a particularly happy story. That does not prevent it from having a rich seam of black comedy running through it and, if at times it seems that in the telling of it there is a certain heartlessness, I can only say that Ackerley would have been the first person to see the joke.

The long-serving (some might argue, long-suffering) editor of *The Listener*, Alan Thomas, wrote that Ackerley was ahead of his time. It is certainly true that many of Ackerley's concerns have become more, not less, relevant. His position on what are now known as 'animal rights' may not have been unassailable (he did not, for instance, become a vegetarian), but in this, as in so much of his life, he went to the basics: he believed that animals had an innate dignity which demanded respect. He also thought that the distinction between what campaigners today would call 'human and non-human animals' was unhelpful and merely served to salve the consciences of those who ignored the needs of birds, beasts and reptiles, and exploited their fellow-creatures for gain. Similarly he deplored the exploitation and destruction of the earth's ecology, in particular the depredations made by Western civilization in the pursuit of financial rewards. Perhaps most importantly, in his work at the BBC he fought a long and hard battle against censorship on political or 'moral' grounds, against members of the Corporation who preferred to keep quiet rather than risk upsetting those in authority: the Director General, the Board of Governors, the Government. He believed that people should be able to conduct themselves in their personal lives, and should be able to express themselves freely, without interference by the state. In this, as in much else, he might be our contemporary.

I

A *chapter of accidents*

J. R. ACKERLEY should not have been born at all. His mother, Netta, disliked sexual intercourse and was frightened of its consequences. She had good reason to be, since Ackerley's father, Roger, was a highly-sexed man who took a cavalier attitude towards contraception. The birth of their first child, Peter, had been extremely traumatic for all concerned. Having failed to take the proper precautions at the proper time, Roger and Netta had made strenuous but amateur attempts to procure a miscarriage. Considerably buffetted from this experience, Peter had emerged backwards into the world in 1895, two months premature, suffering from jaundice and a double rupture. Ackerley's conception was evidence that Roger did not learn from his mistakes.

> Knowing my mother wanted no more children, but once again out of french letters, he deceived her by going through the motions of putting one on, and nine months later I was the result.

Ackerley often wondered whether tardy attempts had been made to prevent his own birth. No doubt painful memories of the 'purges, nostrums and bodily exercises' she had undergone in 1895 deterred Netta from considering this course of action, and her second son emerged unscathed on 4 November 1896. He was registered simply as Joe (the 'Randolph' was added later, as a misguided tribute to his Aunt Bunny's husband, Randolph Payne). Netta did however try to find something to terminate her third pregnancy; to no avail, for in January 1899 she was safely delivered of a baby girl, Nancy Gertrude Louise, after which she went down with a fever and temporarily lost her hair.

7

Like most fathers of the period, Roger believed childbirth and the rearing of infants to be an entirely female preserve. Indeed, there was no proper family home until 1903 when Roger rented a house in Richmond, Surrey. Each child was born in a different house: Peter at the home of his maternal grandmother in Marylebone; Joe in a modest, red-bricked house in South London at 4 Warmington Road, Herne Hill; and Nancy in a house called Rosemead on the front at Herne Bay, on the north Kent coast. A succession of female relations, nursemaids and housekeepers assisted Netta in bringing up the babies, whilst Roger maintained a bachelor flat in central London, putting in the occasional appearance at weekends. In 1900 he packed the entire family off to Bowdon in Cheshire and disappeared on a long business trip to Jamaica.

Roger's business was fruit importing, a venture he had started in 1892 when he offered his services to a friend called Arthur Stockley, who was a manager of fruit shipments for a firm in Covent Garden. The two men gradually built up the celebrated company of Elders & Fyffes, with smart offices at 31 Bow Street and each director drawing a vast annual salary of some £12,000. Roger spent as he earned, and his manner and his largesse earned him the nickname 'the Banana King'. Indeed, in appearance and tastes he bore some resemblance to Edward VII. He was heavily built, favoured top-coat, Homburg and walking-stick, and was rarely seen without a 'Gentleman' cigar in his mouth. He appointed himself 'godfather' to the children of his employees and presented each new infant with a silver christening tankard and spoon. He tipped waiters *before* he dined to ensure the best service and always insisted upon settling the bill himself, occasionally indulging in un-dignified scuffles over the table with those who attempted to pay their share. Ackerley was to recall:

> 'Have whatever you like' – it was the principle on which my Father brought us up. When we went to a restaurant, we might ask perhaps to have oysters, and he would say, 'Of course, old man, have whatever you like.' And it was the same with anything else; I could always have, I could always do, whatever I liked. The good genie could not offer more to Aladdin.

Perhaps Roger was attempting to compensate for his early neglect of his children; perhaps he was simply indulging that commonplace parental desire to give his children what he had never had himself. Whatever the case, the effects of his extravagance were to be far-reaching and disastrous.

Apart from an unfortunate habit of 'scratching himself in an unpleasant way', Roger's manner was so much that of a gentleman that few who met him would have believed that his origins were relatively humble. 'Dad was a self-made man,' Ackerley wrote of his father. 'Remarkable achievement – guardsman to grandee.' This achievement came about as a result of cunning, good fortune and good business sense. Alfred Roger Ackerley was born on April Fool's Day 1863 in Prospect Cottage, a house at Rainhill, the small village near Liverpool which had achieved fame as the site of Stephenson's railway-engine trials of 1829. If the date and place of his birth seem, in retrospect, somewhat propitious, his actual circumstances were not. His father was a share-broker and Roger, as he came to be called, was the seventh of eight children, three boys and five girls (a further daughter had died in infancy).

He learned resilience at an early age, for his mother died when he was two and his father endured a financial crisis in 1875, after which Roger had to leave school and find a job. An early career as an auctioneers' clerk came to an abrupt end when he was obliged to leave home after being caught in bed with a girl. He ran away to London and joined the army. He was a tall and well-built youth and it was therefore easy to convince the Royal Horse Guards that he was older than his sixteen years. He served with the Blues for three and a half years and saw action in Egypt at the Battle of Tel-el-Kebir in the autumn of 1882. Returning with his regiment to England, he purchased his discharge, but nine months later re-enlisted, this time as a trooper in the Second Life Guards. He served only eight months before once again purchasing his discharge, after which he returned to Rainhill to be with his father, who was dying of cancer.

He worked for a time as a traveller for his brother-in-law, John Graham, who had a wine-merchant's business in the region, but trade was poor and Roger left the job to set up a pony farm in Windsor. It was here that he met the woman who was to become his first wife. Louise Burckhardt was the younger daughter of a cultured and wealthy Swiss-American who was a patron of John Singer Sargent. Sargent painted her twice, notably as the *Lady with a Rose*, which was a critical triumph at the Paris Salon of 1882, attracting the notice of

Henry James amongst others.[1] The Burckhardts seem to have been unconcerned that their daughter was to marry an almost penniless former guardsman, and after the marriage, which took place in Paris in September 1889, and an extensive European honeymoon, the couple returned to live at the Burckhardt's apartment on the Boulevard de Courcelles. Louise's father made Roger an allowance of £2,000 a year. Unfortunately the marriage was short-lived, for Louise became ill, probably with some form of tuberculosis, and was submitted to the 'cold water treatment', a primitive form of hydrotherapy which consisted of the patient sitting in a bath whilst cold water was played upon her spine. The result of this was swift and devastating: Louise contracted pneumonia and died early in 1892. Roger commemorated her in 1899 when he gave her name to his daughter Nancy.

Roger returned to England and looked up his old Cheshire friend, Arthur Stockley, who had just returned from a four-year spell in the Canary Islands and now had a third share in Elder Dempster & Co, the fruit importers. Stockley invited Roger to become his partner, appointing him sales manager. The success of the company owed much to Roger's enthusiasm and his common touch. He placed the business on a firm footing by circumventing the rapacious wholesalers and selling his bananas directly to the costermongers. This brought down the retail price and meant that more people could afford the fruit, and the business began to expand in consequence. It was later that year, when on a cross-Channel ferry *en route* for Paris to visit his in-laws, that Roger first saw a pretty young woman vainly attempting to attract the attention of a steward.

Janetta Aylward was a young actress, currently out of work. She was also travelling to Paris, in order to stay with a man called Dick Fijus who had founded the Jockey Club there. Mr Fijus was the brother-in-law of Netta's Uncle Gus. 'It doesn't seem to be a very nice thing to say,' Netta sometimes remarked, 'but actually the breeding came from our side of the family.' Ackerley was intrigued by the theory of inherited family characteristics, and took a particular interest in his mother's family. Although the Aylwards were middle-class, cultured and outwardly respectable, the family tree is a network of illegitimacy

[1] It now hangs in the Metropolitan Museum of Art in New York.

and sexual irregularity. Netta's paternal grandfather was the proprietor of Aylward & Spinney, a music shop in Salisbury, and was twice elected the city's mayor. He had six children by his first wife: Theodore, William (Netta's father), three girls called Leila, Gertrude and Amy, and another boy called Augustus or Gus.

The family was intensely musical, boasting four professors of music. Theodore appears to have been the most respectable; he left Salisbury to become a professor of music in Cardiff. Leila was an Associate of the Royal Academy of Music and also taught music. She was considered 'a great sport': she smoked cigars and had an affair with a Turk who ran the shop next door to her father's premises on the canal. Whether as a result of this liaison – Ackerley, her great-nephew, was to speculate about a venereal infection – or for some other reason, she later lost all her hair, including her eyebrows. She eventually died of an umbilical hernia. Gertie was equally headstrong and fared little better than her sister, marrying a Dr Charles Fuller against her parents' wishes. 'Parental authority had already frustrated an earlier romance in Germany,' Ackerley wrote; 'upon this occasion she brooked no interference. "I will marry him whatever you say!" she cried, breaking in upon the family council.' The parental objection seems to have been to the doctor's nose, which showed signs (and gave off odours) of decay: 'a syphilitic necrosis was alleged'. Whether or not this was true, the marriage proved childless and Dr Fuller took to the bottle. On his deathbed he was observed gesturing feebly to his mouth. Poor Gertie, imagining that a final wifely kiss was being demanded, bent over the bed only to be thrust aside as her husband gasped, 'Whisky! Whisky!' After his death it was discovered that he had defrauded one of his patients, converting for his own use bonds which had been left in his trust.

Of the third daughter, Amy, nothing is known except that she seems not to have married. Gus did marry, but only under duress after he had impregnated a young lady called Fijus, who worked in a Bournemouth hotel. Although 'a notorious old skinflint', Gus's father

had been so upset by this unworthy entanglement that he had gone so far as to offer the Fijus family a large amount of money by way of compensation; but Miss Fijus's father was not to be bought. He threatened to shoot Uncle Gus if he did not marry his daughter, which Gus accordingly did, thereby abandoning another girl to whom he was engaged.

Whether this scandal affected his career as professor of music and organist at St Edmund's Church in Salisbury is not known, but it seems that he inherited the family business when his father died.

Outwardly respectable, Netta's father, William, followed in the family tradition of music, becoming a professor at the Royal College of Music, where he played the cello before the Queen. He was also organist and master at Hawtrey's preparatory school in Slough, where small boys were prepared for entrance to nearby Eton College. It must be assumed that the origins of his wife, Teresa, were not enquired into, for she was one of three illegitimate daughters born to an otherwise respectable and well-bred Miss Buller and a married 'gentleman' named Scott. She presented William with three sons and two daughters, Janetta Katherine and Gertrude Mary (always known as 'Bunny'), before he died at the age of forty-three, when his youngest child was eight. Ackerley was delighted to recall that his grandfather had been 'killed by snobbery':

> He was over-worked and ill in bed with rheumatic fever when he discovered that his son Charlie, aged ten, who had come home late one evening, had not only disobeyed his order that he was not to mix and play with the street boys of Slough, where they lived, but had lied to him about it. He flew into such a rage with the child that he had a stroke and died of it . . . He was obsessed with the notion that his own children, if allowed to mix with the street children, would catch not only their accents but their diseases, vermin and delinquencies.

A snob he may have been, but illegitimacy did not appear to worry him unduly; after his death it was revealed that he had been conducting an affair with the housemaid, 'a very superior girl said to be the bastard of a nobleman'. Teresa was left to fend for herself with very little money and went to live with her three sisters-in-law in Salisbury, where Netta and Gertrude were brought up in a lowering atmosphere of jealousy in which their aunts continually squabbled over them.

Both girls ended up on the stage. Bunny had a fine mezzo-soprano voice, and her early career at the Royal Academy of Music and in opera was extremely promising. She often boasted that she had been cast over the heads of her seniors in spite of being only twenty-one. However, in true Aylward fashion she contracted an unsuitable marriage, to a businessman called Randolph Payne. Her first meeting with this insalubrious character, who was twenty years her senior, was at a private party he was giving at the Café Royal, where the champagne flowed without cease. This vision of extravagance and inebriation should have acted as a warning to Bunny, for Payne lost all his money on the Stock Exchange and ended up a drunkard. Undeterred, she ran away with Payne, married him in 1890 and almost died in giving birth to their stillborn child, an ordeal which she claimed was the ruin of her career. From then on it was operetta and musical comedy rather than *Aïda* and the other masterpieces in which she had built her reputation. She understudied at the famous Gaiety Theatre and toured South America with the D'Oyly Carte Company, and one cannot help feeling that it was here that her real talents lay. Amongst the family photographs is one of Bunny looking very arch and at home in the froggings and epaulettes of Ruritanian costume.

Netta, meanwhile, had had rather more success, working on the 'legitimate' stage and eventually joining Herbert Beerbohm Tree's company in which she made her mark in *Beau Austin*. A scene with Lady Tree in which she was obliged to break down, fetching 'a great sob from her very boots' as she was fond of recalling, was guaranteed to bring the house down. Pretty and slight, she also caused a stir as a ravishing page-boy in Tree's production of *The Merry Wives of Windsor*, playing Robin to Tree's Falstaff. Indeed, so ravishing was she that Tree's interpretation of Falstaff was somewhat compromised, for he insisted upon dandling this Robin on his knee when by rights his attentions should have been concentrated upon Mistress Page and Mistress Ford. Her professional life appears to have been precarious, however, for when she met Roger on the cross-Channel ferry she had been out of work for two years.

The Ackerley children inherited their parents' good looks, as can be seen from contemporary photographs, largely taken in the garden of Apsley House, their first Richmond home. Peter was a dark, thin, rather reserved-looking boy, unlike his brother and sister who were fair and plump. Although he was the eldest child, Peter's traumatic birth, and the medical complications it brought in its wake (he was obliged to wear a truss), made him seem younger than his brother. Joe was an extremely pretty little boy, with blue eyes and straight, blond hair. His mother, with good reason, called him 'Angel Face' and he was accustomed to admiration from an early age. The same went for Nancy, who had long red-gold hair, usually tied up in a bow. One photograph catches the family at a characteristic moment. Roger is absent. Netta is smiling for the camera from under a vast beribboned hat of the period. Next to her, slightly puffy-eyed and unwell-looking, is Peter, his mother's arm draped protectively around his shoulder. At the other end of the bench is Joe, his hands clasped together rather preciously. Between her two brothers, seeking attention by waving her arms about, is Nancy.

In spite of Roger's frequent and extended absences, the family seems to have been a happy one. Even Netta's mother, a rather disapproving figure in black bombazine, is seen to be capable of cutting a caper upon the lawn with her daughter. Although the children got on well together, Nancy later claimed that Peter was her favourite brother. He appears to have been an uncomplicated person, perhaps the most stable member of the entire family, although an unexpectedly anarchic strain occasionally burst out in his passion for amateur dramatics and, later on, for eccentrically theatrical clothes. Ackerley insisted that Roger also favoured Peter and that their relationship had a spontaneous warmth which was lacking in his own relationship with his father, whom he found rather unapproachable. Joe was not effeminate, but he was something of a mother's boy, who shocked Roger by asking for a golliwog at the advanced age of twelve, and he remained sentimentally devoted to Netta throughout his life. His one weakness was enuresis, or bed-wetting, and he later liked to think that this may have been 'a kind of unconscious revenge mechanism . . . pissing upon a world that had not accorded me the whole-hearted welcome my ego required'. Amongst the household staff, two employees left an impression upon him. The first was a boot-boy, and the impression was that of his hand on Joe's bare buttocks in some childishly erotic game; the second a French nurse or governess who, when he 'played with [his] little tassel as children do', took his hands away, told him he was dirty and threatened to cut off his penis with her scissors.

Now that Roger was a member of the prosperous middle classes, he decided that his sons should receive the education of gentlemen. Rossall School had been founded in 1844 as *the* Northern Church of England public school. It was in Fleetwood, a bleak town on the Lancashire coast, and had been recommended to Roger by a business friend called Captain Bacon, one of whose sons, Teddy, was to achieve distinction there as the school tart. Another reason Roger may have chosen the school for Peter and Joe was its 'bracing atmosphere'. A dismal cluster of red-bricked buildings fringed the sand, across which gales blew in from the sea for much of the year. The coastal weather was so appalling that pitches were frequently waterlogged and games often had to be abandoned during the two winter terms, although the beach could be used for hockey. The two boys started at the preparatory school, Peter in 1907 and Joe the following year, his entry delayed by appendicitis. After two relatively protected years, Joe transferred to the senior school.

Rossall had been founded for the sons of clergymen and other parents of modest means. It offered a modern and a classical education and was the first school to have a Rifle Corps. An outbreak of scarlet fever and a shortage of funds plagued the early years, but matters were stabilized with the arrival in 1875 of Dr H. A. James, fresh from Marlborough, which had been founded in 1843 with the same intentions as Rossall, and had endured similar problems. The two young Ackerleys were members of Anchor House, where their diet, and that of their fellows, was supplemented by Roger, who arranged for a crate of bananas to be delivered every week. Joe played hockey for his house, for which he won his colours, and also distinguished himself at shooting. He became captain of the school Shooting VIII, and led Rossall in the competition for the Ashburton Shield at Bisley in 1913 and 1914. He was promoted corporal in the Officers' Training Corps, but although his riflework was excellent, he did poorly in his OTC 'A' Certificate Examinations, passing only one of the papers.

The social life of the school was strictly regimented. One economy exercised by Dr James (long since departed for the more prestigious and comfortable purlieus of Cheltenham and Rugby) had a far-reaching consequence: housemasters were not allowed to marry and were never given early retirement. The result of this policy was that the school was a largely monastic establishment dominated by elderly bachelors. Many of these men were confused, alarmed and obsessed by sexual matters, and rules were formulated to protect both themselves and their pupils from the temptations of the flesh. Amongst the absurd resolutions passed in the Masters' Meetings was a rule that no master was allowed to have an unaccompanied boy in his room for more than ten minutes at a stretch, during which time the door had to remain open, circumstances which must have hindered pastoral work considerably. Older boys were kept apart from younger ones and all pupils were kept under constant surveillance in order to prevent outbreaks of 'immorality', a scheme which was impracticable and ineffectual. Indeed, according to Ackerley, vigilance was so poor that a boy called Jude spent lessons guiding the eager hands of his neighbours into and through his trouser pockets, the seams of which had been unstitched for this purpose. Joe's striking appearance earned him the nickname 'Girlie', but he was very far from following in the footsteps of Teddy Bacon as school tart. Although subjected to advances from older boys, and occasionally obliged to succumb to their sexual blandishments, he kept largely aloof from what he called 'the prevalent depravities of this excellent school'. He was, he confessed,

a chaste, puritanical, priggish, rather narcissistic little boy, more repelled by than attracted to sex, which seemed to me a furtive, guilty, soiling thing, exciting, yes, but nothing whatever to do with those feelings which I had not yet experienced but about which I was already writing a lot of dreadful sentimental verse, called romance and love.

Much of Ackerley's adult energy would be devoted to attempting to reconcile these two impulses: the erotic and the romantic.

His literary ambitions were fostered by S. P. B. Mais, whose influence at Rossall was considerable and benign. Like many young schoolmasters of the period, Mais owed his job to a Rugby Blue rather than academic qualifications. During his interview he had been told by the headmaster that a diploma in education was regarded as a liability: 'We want no theorists here. There's only one Theory of Education. Keep Order. You start with an advantage. Boys always respect a Blue. Keep a tight hand. No fraternizing.' Mais ignored this advice and managed to circumvent most of the Common Room resolutions. Mais was not so much lax as revolutionary, a man who genuinely liked boys (wisely rather than too well) and had a real desire to impart knowledge. He introduced his classes to contemporary literature, insisted that they should act out, rather than merely recite, Shakespeare's plays, encouraged them to read widely and to write their own poetry and prose. Dismayed that pupils were not allowed to use the school's official Debating Society to discuss topics which affected them directly, he set up a private literary and debating society, which met in his rooms every Saturday night. Pupils in any kind of trouble knew that they would receive a sympathetic hearing from Mais and were often to be found, alone, in couples, or in groups in his study. He considered that chaste relationships between older and younger boys could be beneficial rather than harmful. His judgement was not infallible, however, and Joe was piqued to discover that a photograph of Teddy Bacon which Mais kept on his mantelpiece was inscribed with the legend: 'The best boy I have ever known or am ever likely to know.'

Teddy's abrupt departure may have opened Mais's eyes, for in one of his autobiographies he described Joe as his 'closest friend' at Rossall. Mais's rendition of John Masefield's 'The Everlasting Mercy' (complete with 'oaths', a circumstance which nearly led to his dismissal) introduced Ackerley to a poet who was to be an early literary model. Some of his star pupil's Masefield-inspired juvenilia was published by Mais in a collection of literary essays, *From Shakespeare to O. Henry*. 'I've watched the progress of this young poet since he was fourteen,' Mais was to write in 1923, adding without much prescience: 'I have a drawer full of his work, which I am convinced will some day be required at my hands by a discerning public.' One member of Joe's early public who *was* discerning was his housemaster, who required an explanation of a poem his young charge had published in *The Wasp*, a literary magazine which Joe founded and edited at Rossall. Its four verses described a sentimental attachment between two boys and began:

He loved him for his face,
His pretty head and fair complexion,
His natural lissome grace,
But trusted not his own affection.

It was undoubtedly this last line that worried the housemaster; affections were notoriously mistrusted at Rossall. Perhaps Joe had benefited from Mais's instruction in debate, for he pointed out that he had called the poem 'Millstones', a title which saved him from a beating. The poem, worthy of the pen of the Revd E. E. Bradford and the other 'Uranian' poets, had been written as a troubador tribute to a

17

boy called Snook,[1] for whom Joe had conceived a chaste but inordinate passion. Another young master, W. A. Furness, also received the confidences of his pupils, but when Joe told him that he was in love with Snook, Furness was horrified. He reprimanded Joe for squandering his affection upon so heartless a boy, advice which would be proffered by friends repeatedly and fruitlessly throughout Ackerley's life.

[1] Ackerley did not trouble to disguise the identities of his fellow-pupils and fellow-soldiers in *My Father and Myself*. There were two Snooks at Rossall but it is not clear which it was that captured Joe's heart. Both had dazzling careers there, representing the school in football, hockey, cricket and gymnastics, and one of them becoming Captain of School after Joe had left.

2

Prisoner of war

ACKERLEY'S ignominious failing of Little-go, Cambridge's entrance examination, was eclipsed by the outbreak of war in August 1914. Like most boys of his class and education, he applied at once for a commission. Despite his poor results in the OTC examinations, he was successful in his application and on 14 September was gazetted a second lieutenant (temporary) in the 8th Battalion of the East Surrey Regiment. He was a few months short of his eighteenth birthday. The 8th East Surreys were part of Kitchener's New Army and had not existed before the war; and like many other new battalions they combined enthusiasm with an engaging amateurism. Regular soldiers were transferred to the Battalion in order to knock it into some sort of shape. The Battalion's first casualty took place in October when a man fell over a guy-rope in the dark and impaled himself fatally upon a tent-peg.

The East Surreys were part of the 18th Division, which in April 1915 was based in East Anglia. Ackerley was billeted in Colchester with a doctor called Ward, whose hot baths, clean sheets and good food were a relief after army conditions. Dr Ward's other East Surrey guests included a young officer called Nevill. The son of a director of Kelly's Commercial Directories, 'Billie' Nevill was two years older than Ackerley. He had been head boy and captain of cricket at Dover College, before going up to Cambridge. He hoped to be a schoolmaster and had been studying at Jesus College for a year when war broke out. In *My Father and Myself* Ackerley left an unkind picture of Nevill and did not reveal that the two men were quite close friends, soon on first-name terms, as Nevill boasted in a letter to his family in May

1915. The Nevills lived at Twickenham, just up-river from the Ackerleys at Richmond, and the two families were to keep in touch in order to exchange news from the Front when their sons sailed for France. Friendships were born of circumstances throughout the war and it is unlikely that men as dissimilar as Nevill and Ackerley would have been peace-time companions. Nevill was one of those jaunty young officers much loved by the newspapers and the music halls. His letters home were peppered with exclamation marks and such phrases as 'awfully jolly', 'ripping' and 'mon chapeau!', and were usually signed 'Cheer-oh all!'. As keen (as he would no doubt have put it) as mustard, he regarded the war as a combination of splendid lark and sacred mission. In France he was disgusted to find how few religious services were laid on for the men. It is difficult to imagine Ackerley, who delightedly recalled that in Little-go he had been 'defeated by Paley's *Evidences of Christianity*', conducting extra services for the benefit of his troops. Nevertheless, despite characterizing Nevill as a 'buffoon' in his memoir, Ackerley clearly liked the man at the time.

When not at Dr Ward's dinner-table, the young officers spent the long summer days on route marches with their men to Ipswich and other Suffolk towns. On 11 April Ackerley was promoted to lieutenant and at the end of the month the Battalion moved to Hollesley, a small town south of Felixstowe on a part of the coast under threat from Zeppelin raids. Convinced that someone in the area was using lights to guide the Zeppelins, Ackerley and Nevill spent one night out on a hillside armed with loaded revolvers and knobkerries in the hope of catching this 'spy'. Their *Boy's Own Paper* vigilance did not prevent a Zeppelin flying over to Bury St Edmunds and discharging its cargo of bombs.

The entire Division was transferred to Salisbury Plain in May for final training. The regiment went into camp at Codford in Wiltshire and Ackerley and Nevill spent the nights out under the stars, in haystacks. It was at Codford that Ackerley met a fellow officer who was to become his best friend of the war, Bobby Soames.

At last, in June 1915, the East Surreys embarked for France. They saw no action until August when they were sent to Dornacourt, and even here things were quiet, for no large attack had taken place in the section for some time. Nevill set to at once and began editing a 'sprightly Trench Gazette'. It is not known whether Ackerley was a contributor, but, like most well-educated young officers, he kept a notebook and wrote some fairly dreadful poetry, largely about the doomed young men whose good looks attracted his notice. Like much front-line verse of a less controversial nature, three of his poems found their way into the magazine of his old school. Entirely without character or individuality, '*Mort au Champ d'Honneur*', '"R.H." in the Trenches' and the flaccidly chivalric 'Great Heart' are hardly the work of someone who at school had been an avowed disciple of Masefield; but poems written later, after the experience of battle, were to be a great deal stronger.

Ackerley's company was commanded by a man of Hungarian extraction called Theodore Flatau, who left a vivid impression upon the young second lieutenant:

> He was fond of me, unduly I sometimes imagined, for I was a pretty boy and used to being run after. He was short, swart and wiry, little bristly black moustache, long nervous fingers endlessly stubbing out half-finished cigarettes. Green eyes, crinkly black hair, parted down the middle. Strong white teeth with gold fillings. Very animated in conversation, gesticulating, gulping down cigarette smoke and talking it out in rapid, clipped, emphatic speech, rubbing his small moustache upwards all the time with his finger-tips . . . When I reported to him one evening he was in his hip-bath – and I was so astonished by his appearance that I forgot to salute, which was a thing I was good at and liked doing, making a terrific click with my heels, for he had as much body-hair as a chimpanzee. He wasn't a bad chap, but the men hated him. He was determined to have the smartest company in the Brigade, and couldn't leave them in peace for a moment, however tired they were.

At some point Ackerley was persuaded by a fellow officer to visit a brothel. They each selected a whore and retired to their separate rooms. Ackerley lay on the bed beside the girl, fully clothed and at a loss as to what to do.

> Having possessed myself at last of one of her breasts, which I managed to extract from her corsage, I found I did not want it or know what to do with it, so I put it back. I believe she undid my flies, then bothered no further, since nothing stirred within. I stood her a crème de menthe, gave her some money and left. I must have been very innocent to recount, as I did, this gloomy incident to my parents

21

on my next leave; I had no self-knowledge then, nothing to hide, and must have thought it rather a manly joke. So, apparently, did they. Perhaps my father considered it as a step in the right direction. Hardly a reassuring one.

Ackerley's published account of the war in *My Father and Myself* is a masterpiece of cool irony and controlled distaste, but he was profoundly affected by his experience. One legacy was that he underwent a remarkable physical transformation, as if by 1918 knowledge and experience had made their mark upon the *tabula rasa* of the dutifully patriotic youth of 1914. In photographs taken when he enlisted, the studiously adult pose he adopts is at odds with the smooth, unformed face. Within three years that face has taken on character and become rigorously handsome, the fine features for which he was renowned have been revealed. Ackerley now seems to be in collusion with the camera, no longer its passive victim. In particular the eyes and the set of the mouth have become distinctly sardonic.

The other legacy of the war was a feeling of guilt, shame and disgust. Ackerley's only consolation was that he was almost certain that he never killed anyone during it. He felt guilty because he was convinced that he was a coward, and would recall the chill he felt in the 1930s when his friend Herbert Read told him that he had been able to detect cowardice in a man's eyes. Would Read see through him, he wondered? His cowardice, he felt, was exposed by two incidents, the first of which took place on 1 July 1916, the first day on the Somme, during which the British suffered 60,000 casualties. Ackerley was one of these, but, he maintained, an ignoble one. General Haig's disastrous 'Big Push', in which several days of continual bombardment of the German trenches was to be followed by a grand sweep of infantry and cavalry through the line, is well documented. The East Surreys had gone into the trenches on 23 June and were lined up on the extreme right flanks of the 18th Division. Their objective was the small town of Montauban, some five miles east of Albert, which was being pounded to a pinkish dust by the British artillery.

A bad omen had been provided on their last day behind the lines. During a bathing party at Bray a man in a Suffolk regiment had become entangled in weeds and drowned. Further signs that the plan was not running altogether smoothly came during the night of 27 June when British howitzer shells began falling short, so that Ackerley was obliged to withdraw his men from the saps and reposition them in the fire trenches. In spite of a call to the adjutant demanding that the howitzer's ranges should be checked, the shells fell shorter still and the fire trenches had to be evacuated. The saps had been completely destroyed and now shells were beginning to fall in the support trenches, burying two men, who were dug out unhurt. Eventually the fury of the CO, whose dug-out had been shelled, had some effect and the guns were realigned correctly. This self-bombardment had gone on for three and a half hours. Their troubles were not over, however, for an attempt to gas the enemy at stand-to was foiled by the wind which blew the gas straight back into the trenches. Having weathered that, and just as they were congratulating themselves on getting through the night without a single casualty, a British trench mortar fired its bomb backwards instead of forwards so that it landed in a crowded trench, decapitating one man and injuring two others. Ackerley sympathized with one of his men, whom he heard mutter: 'The fucking sooner we get over the fucking top the fucking better!'

This wish was not to be granted, for within hours the assault, which was to have started the following morning, was postponed and the men were marched back into rest behind the lines, where the whole process of anticipation and dread started once again. Some were sanguine about the prospect, and Theo Flatau spent his time writing letters to his family, post-dating them 2 July in order to allay anxiety. Ackerley thought this unwise, as indeed it was, for Flatau was killed on 1 July. Ackerley himself wrote nothing home, seeing little point, but read Conrad's *Lord Jim* for the fifth time. What comfort he drew from this was destroyed by his friend Bobby Soames' quiet announcement that he was convinced he would not survive the attack.

Such was the bombardment that it was fondly supposed that no Germans could have survived it. Unfortunately, like almost everyone else, the Germans had come to hear about it and had taken refuge in their deep, secure dug-outs until the storm of shells had abated. A fatal delay between the end of the bombardment and the beginning of the infantry advance gave the Germans time to scuttle out of their bolt-holes and set up their machine-guns, training them upon the British who now scrambled out of their trenches and sauntered towards the German line as instructed. Although many men shared Ackerley's reservations about what he called 'Sir Douglas Haig's masterly operation', others were convinced that victory was there for the asking.[1] In order to encourage his men Captain Nevill had purchased a number of footballs, inscribed them with fatuous slogans ('The Great European Cup-Tie Finals. East Surreys v. Bavarians. Kick off at zero'), and offered a prize for the first platoon to dribble their ball into the enemy trenches. He did not survive to award the prize, for he was shot dead before he had gone twenty yards, as were many of his men. Only one of the Company's officers survived unscathed, although his entire platoon had been wiped out. Bobby Soames had been detailed to kick off one of the footballs; he almost got as far as the German wire before he was killed, as he had predicted he would be.

Ackerley fared somewhat better, apparently protected by a medallion of St Anthony of Padua blessed by the Pope, which had been given to him by an old woman at Picquigny with whom he had been billeted. His immediate instinct was to run, crouched low in order to protect his genitals. He turned to find his men not yet out of the trench, which was now being shelled. He yelled encouragement and became aware that the air was zipping with bullets; the bombardment, he reflected, had not been the success they had been led to expect. With his 'pet orderly' at his right hand and his servant at his left, he advanced towards Montauban. His orderly was killed almost at once. Ackerley then felt a pain in one arm and saw that he had been shot, but his attention was immediately transferred to his servant, who had fallen to the ground and was 'lying on his back, all twisted, with his arms and legs bent double at the joints and contracted, his face and lips grey.' He had been hit in the spine and was paralysed. It was impossible to do anything and, with hollow reassurances to the dying man, Ackerley urged on the rest of his platoon, which had already been considerably depleted. He was then blown over by a shell and passed out, after which he was dragged into a crater by his platoon-sergeant. The explosion had shattered a bottle of whisky he had been carrying in his haversack in order to celebrate reaching his objective, and fragments of shell and glass had been driven into his side. In all conscience such injuries, if minor, compounded by the concussive effect of the explosion, were enough to put all but the most foolishly brave man *hors de combat*. However, Ackerley was to feel in retrospect that he should have carried on. 'I did not feel ill,' he recalled, 'only frightened and dazed. I

---

[1] In 1965 Ackerley noted that a bottle of Haig whisky was 1s cheaper than any other brand at his local off-licence. He affected to believe that the explanation for this lay in the enduring disgrace the Earl had brought to that name.

could easily have got up, and if I could have got up I should have got up.'

He lay in the shell-hole for six hours, not daring to lift his head, since German snipers were picking off the wounded. Sharing his hole was a sixteen-year-old Londoner, shot in the ankle, and another of his men who brought him the grim news of the heavy casualties amongst the officers. This man assured Ackerley that his servant must by now be dead, adding the unnecessary detail that when he had last seen him ' 'is eyes was all a'goggling'. Whilst waiting for stretcher-bearers Ackerley shared round his cigarettes and was obliged to haul himself up on to the side of the crater in order to urinate. Some time later he looked out to see an ashen-faced man crawling towards the hole on his hands and knees, muttering incoherently. His tunic, shirt and trousers hung open and were saturated in blood. Shot horribly in the stomach, the man tumbled in on top of Ackerley, and died there. Eventually stretcher-bearers arrived and took Ackerley to the first-aid post, where two pieces of metal were removed from his side. Most of the day's casualties had been caused by bullets, and Ackerley's escape was remarkable. His cap had been shot from his head and, apart from the rent in his sleeve, he had four further bullet-holes in his tunic. 'I never want to take men into the "attack abnormal" again,' he wrote to Nevill's aunt, who was a front-line matron. 'I shall never forget the *smell* of it.' However, after a spell of sick-leave, during which his guilt was exacerbated by his family's insistence that he was a hero, he was promoted to the rank of captain and returned to the Front, where he was joined by Peter, by now a second lieutenant in the same Battalion.

Peter, although constitutionally weak, was physically extremely brave, the sort of man, as his brother was very well aware, who would have ignored minor injuries and carried on at the Somme. Indeed, he had undergone surgery in order to cure his rupture so that he could join his brother at the Front. He provided Ackerley with the second test of courage, a test Ackerley was convinced he had failed. In February 1917 Peter's platoon was detailed for a dangerous night-time mission and Ackerley's final glimpse of his brother, swathed in a Burberry, cap at a jaunty angle, hung about with grenades, as he left the dug-out, was characteristically theatrical, like something out of *Journey's End*. Ackerley got permission to watch the start of Peter's 'stunt' from a safe position, but could see very little, so he returned to the dug-out to wait for news.

After some time, Peter's dishevelled sergeant-major returned to report that the mission had failed and that Peter had been wounded. In September 1915 a similar situation had arisen when a young second lieutenant called Thorne had been shot on a night patrol. Thorne's devoted elder brother had won a Military Cross by defying German fire and advancing towards the enemy line in order to retrieve the young officer. The younger Thorne, whose beauty had possessed Ackerley, had in fact been killed outright, but the elder Thorne had brought back the body. The precedent was clear, indeed it had become enshrined in regimental history, but officially Ackerley was not supposed to risk his own life, or the lives of his men, bringing in the wounded. His CO (distancing himself, Ackerley suspected, from what was in essence a family matter) gave no guidance, and Ackerley hesitated, awaited further information, and was then relieved to hear that Peter had managed to crawl back into the trenches, having suffered a wound to his leg, which, although not serious, seemed to Ackerley rather more honourable than those he had himself received the previous summer. Ackerley's guilt over his hesitation to help his brother was compounded when Peter told the family that Joe had behaved 'splendidly'. Ackerley disagreed:

> I needed to have shoves forward. My own nature was not the sort that comes out well in emergency. If I had had a shove from the Major in the Boom Ravine in France I should have acted heroically, though I should not have wished to: his leaving it in my hands or putting obstructions in front of me was fatal to my character.

Whilst on leave at Richmond in the summer of 1916, Ackerley was obliged to perform a duty which fell to many survivors of the Somme. He was contacted by the family of Theo Flatau. Bereaved families everywhere were anxious to be reassured about the last moments of men who had died in the attack: had they died bravely? Had they died instantly and without pain? The meeting was particularly difficult because Ackerley would not be able to use any of the comforting clichés which came to hand when confronting grieving families. Flatau had *not* been 'adored by the men'; indeed, Ackerley affected to believe that there was a strong possibility that Flatau's men had taken the opportunity in those first chaotic moments of the advance to shoot their detested officer themselves, as they had threatened to do. Nonetheless, Ackerley agreed to meet Flatau's brother, Rex, and his sisters, Darota and Hermione. Rex was a more suitable companion for Roger than for his son. 'He was an amiable, boozy, clownish, uncivilized fellow with stick-out ears and rubber features,' Ackerley recalled. 'Rather a cad.' The two sisters he characterized as 'weird, swarthy, handsome, gipsy-like women, strong personalities, rather masculine, tough and "arty". Braided hair, heavy make-up, husky voices, green eyes like Theo, long cigarette-holders, and dabblings in spiritualism and poltergeists.' He liked Hermione, but not Darota, an indifferent novelist who realized that Ackerley was homosexual and disliked him, perhaps because she recognized something of her brother in him. The meeting was a success, however, and the Flataus were frequent visitors to Richmond after the war.

Ackerley also attempted to exorcize the nightmare of the Somme by writing poetry. The formulaic clichés of his *Rossallian* 'Poems from the Trenches' were replaced by a return to the modern values of Masefield. Masefield proved an enormous influence upon young poets at this period, notably Charles Sorley, who had discovered him whilst still a schoolboy at Marlborough, and Siegfried Sassoon and Robert Graves, who discussed him in their war-time letters. In 1913 Sassoon had published a skilful parody of 'The Everlasting Mercy' under the title 'The Daffodil Murderer'. Masefield's famous poem also provided Ackerley with a model and a title. 'The Everlasting Terror' is dated 30 June 1916 and dedicated 'To Bobby'. It is a cleverly conceived monologue which twists and turns in its examination of the meaning of hell. War, which seems to be a rejection of traditional Christian teaching, paradoxically brings out fine qualities in men. The 'gentleman' narrator takes his received 'righteousness' to war and discovers by his appalling experience the true qualities of his caste:

> Oh yes, I've seen it all and more,
> And felt the knocker on Death's door;
> I've been wherever Satan takes you,
> And Hell is good because it makes you.
> As long as you're a man, I say,
> The 'gentle' part will find its way
> And catch you up like all the rest –
> For love I give the Tommy best!

This experience of a real, a living hell disperses notions of Christian damnation:

It's better far than paying shillings
For paper books with rusty fillings
Which say eternal punishment
Is due to those poor men who've spent
Their lives in gambling, drinking, whoring,
As though there were some angel scoring
Black marks against you for your sins
And he who gets the least marks wins.

Hell will not be eternal damnation but that moment when the soul arrives before Christ and receives a sigh instead of a kiss. The poem ends with a memorial to Bobby Soames:

And so through all my life and days,
In all my walks, through all my ways,
The lasting terror of the war
Will live with me for evermore.
Of all the pals whom I have missed
There's one, I know, whom Christ has kissed,
And in his memory I'll find
The sweetness of the bitter rind –
Of lonely life in front of me
And terror's sleepless memory.

This is a highly skilled, controlled and literary poem. Not only Masefield, but Marlowe lies behind the poem, for in its contemplation of the meaning of damnation, and indeed in its title, it also echoes Mephostophilis in *Doctor Faustus*:

Why this is hell, nor am I out of it.
Think'st thou that I, who saw the face of God,
And tasted the eternal joys of heaven,
Am not tormented with ten thousand hells,
In being deprived of everlasting bliss?

The poem was sent to the prestigious *English Review*, founded in 1906 by Ford Madox Hueffer (as he then was), but now under the rather less distinguished editorship of Austin Harrison. It was accepted and appeared in the November 1916 issue. That same month it also made an appearance, above the initials J.R.A. and shorn of its dedication, in the programme of a Grand Concert given by the 3rd East Surreys.

Although it was not listed as such upon this occasion, the poem was probably delivered in the form of a dramatic monologue at similar performances. Certainly Peter, whose theatrical flair was put to good use by the regiment in organizing such events, used other poems by his brother ('the coming "poet laureate"') in this way.

At 3.45 a.m. on 3 May 1917 Ackerley was detailed to lead his men in an attack upon the village of Cérisy, in the Arras region, in order to consolidate recent gains. Ackerley's company went over in the first wave, stumbling from shell-hole to shell-hole towards their objective, some high ground the other side of the village. Although initially successful, the troops were not prepared for the counter-attack which followed and Ackerley's men fled, pursued by their commanding officer vainly shouting at them to stop. He was stopped himself after receiving two wounds in the buttock and thigh. Once again he was obliged to lie in a shell-hole, which he shared with a fellow-officer and two other men, one dead, the other in the process of dying. His wounds were dressed by a German stretcher-bearer, and then he was led off into captivity to the German first-aid post, limping some three-quarters of a mile in considerable pain. He narrowly avoided death when a British aeroplane bombed the Field Dressing Station and was then taken by lorry to a hospital, stripped of all his clothes, and given a nightshirt and a pair of louse-ridden blankets. By stages he made his way from hospital to hospital back behind the German lines to Tournai, then into Germany itself, to a hospital at Hanover. A bullet was cut out of his thigh and he was allowed to send a postcard home (he addressed it to Peter rather than his parents), to say that he had become a prisoner of war. He spent his entire time lying in bed in extreme discomfort, running a temperature and with a draining-tube stuck into a suppurating hole in his buttock. His only solace was the occasional game of bridge and a Russian orderly called Lowkin, who bathed and dressed him and played the mandolin for him in the evenings. Ackerley developed an intense but chaste crush on Lowkin, much as other officers fell for the VADs who nursed them. After several weeks the tube was removed from his wound, but this respite was brief for some bone was syringed out and the pipe then replaced.

Although the hospital was reasonably comfortable, food supplies were uncertain and parcels from home were often held up. Meat in particular was in short supply and often appeared in the form of horse or gelatinous brawn. Ackerley assiduously recorded the meagre and revolting menus on which radish, raw turnip and 'sticklebacks' made frequent appearances. In July he suffered a setback as more bone had to be removed from his wound and the food reached an all-time low with gherkins for breakfast, 'Thin soup (and rice), Meat (leather), Peas (uncooked), Potatoes (old), Gooseberries' for lunch, and eggs in the evening.

Rumours of a projected release of several thousand prisoners into internment in neutral countries briefly cheered him, but when his wound finally healed he was transferred to a POW camp at Karlsruhe. The exchange of prisoners into internment was decided by Swiss and German medical officers. The Swiss visited camp hospitals and made recommendations, but if there was any difference of opinion it was the German doctors whose opinions held. Whilst those who had access to strings pulled them in order to get their relations across the border into a neutral country, many prisoners endured a horrible cat-and-mouse existence, with hopes repeatedly raised and deferred. In spite of Roger's wielding of influence behind the scenes, it was not until 27 December that Ackerley finally arrived in Switzerland, by which time he had been through further POW camps at Heidelberg and Augustabad.

Before the war Mürren had been a fashionable ski-resort. It was spectacularly sited, perched on a high ledge overhanging the Lauterbrunnen Valley, which could be seen a sheer 2,000 feet below by anyone looking out of the back window of his hotel. To the east were the Oberland Mountains with the Eiger, Monch and Jungfrau rearing up out of the Bernese Alps. However, what seemed perfect to the winter sportsman looked rather different to men in captivity. One of the British chaplains described Mürren as 'a prison in paradise'. It consisted of a single street, which took five minutes to walk along, and the town was cut off from the outside world for seven months of the year. The effect of isolation combined with the lowering mountains proved extremely claustrophobic to men suffering the psychological effects of warfare and long periods of imprisonment.

Those whose minds had been affected by their experience were housed in the town's nine hotels alongside those still recuperating from physical injury. Although some attempt was made to keep the men exercised and occupied, there was little opportunity for the games of football which enlivened the war zone and prison camps. The noted sportsman and author Arnold Lunn was on hand to give lessons in ski-ing to the lucky few, and occasional expeditions were made by his pupils into the Alps to practise their slaloms. In spite of well-intended classes where men could learn languages, make clothes and shoes, acquire typewriting and shorthand skills and pursue such crafts as watch-making, carpentry, printing and bookbinding, boredom was a prevalent problem. The YMCA did its best with debates, lectures, concerts and mock trials, but the atmosphere made men listless and unable to concentrate. For much of the time the 600 internees were cooped up in their hotels, virtually confined to billets by the snow.

Ackerley, and the forty or so other officers, some of whom had been there since early in the war, were billeted separately from the men in the Hôtel des Alpes. As in a boarding-school, friendships, factions, passions and jealousies developed. Ackerley focused his attentions upon two unlikely objects of devotion: a man with a glass eye called Carlyon, whose own affections, ominously enough, were lavished upon his Alsatian dog, and a young consumptive who was to be portrayed as the worthless heartbreaker, Grayle, in the play Ackerley wrote about his experience of internment, *The Prisoners of War*.

Ackerley had made several attempts to write an autobiographical novel whilst in the POW camps, but none of these came to much more than a dedication ('To my Mother') and an unresolved chapter or two, largely covering his experiences on the Somme and at Cérisy. One of these, *Walking Round*, which was written at Karlsruhe, has a section indecisively designated 'Introduction' or 'Epilogue', which depicts an evening in the POW camp seen through the eyes of the narrator. He is a solitary young man who hides himself away in his hut, scribbling away at a novel, instead of joining the 'bloods' of the *Lager*, who sit around the canteen drinking 'a peculiarly obnoxious mixture of white wine and bottled lemonade called *Halb-und-halb*'. Whilst getting charcoal from the canteen, the narrator is picked up by a drawlingly effeminate Canadian, who persuades him to come to his quarters, but once there ignores him and starts reading a novel. Thinking that the Canadian might simply be suffering from an excess of *halb-und-halb*, the narrator lights his pipe and gazes meditatively out of the window on to the exercise area. Several pages are ripped out, but on the final page the narrator is woken by someone asking him when he is going to go out to buy the charcoal. Evidently the entire inconclusive encounter has been a dream.

31

Ackerley's attempt to write a play proved a great deal more fruitful, and was perhaps helped on its way by the forthright Arnold Lunn who demanded to know whether Ackerley was 'homo or hetero'. Forced for the first time to confront his own sexuality, Ackerley knew that there could only be one answer to this impertinent enquiry. Lunn, who had become acclimatized to such things at Harrow (about which he had written a characteristically debunking novel), was not in the least shocked, and immediately set Ackerley to read the 'standard works' on the subject, including such classical defenders of the faith as Plutarch as well as the modern, 'scientific' Otto Weininger and the philosophical guru of Sheffield, Edward Carpenter. To Ackerley, who claimed never to have met 'a recognizable or self-confessed adult homosexual' at this point, such writers were a revelation. Able at last to 'place' himself sexually, he was also able to move away from the confused and unfulfilled yearnings of his fragmentary writings towards a mature and considered play.

The first draft of *The Prisoners of War*, which was to undergo a great deal of revision before its eventual performance and publication, was written in its entirety in the Hôtel des Alpes, and is set at Mürren amongst a group of interned officers. The action takes place over a fortnight and is very precisely dated, the first act opening on 20 July 1918, the third act closing on the evening of 3 August. (The significance of these dates has now been lost.) The protagonist, clearly based upon Ackerley himself, is a Captain Jim Conrad (a conflation, presumably, of Conrad's *Lord Jim*), a neurotic and repressed young officer of twenty-four. Although not stated in such direct terms, Conrad is in love with an attractive but shallow young RFC observer of nineteen called Allan Grayle. The other officers are a kindly but melancholy middle-aged lieutenant called Adelby and two young airmen, the Canadian Captain Rickman and the English Lieutenant Tetford. The play follows their shifting relationships and the tensions and jealousies to which their circumstances give rise. Conrad's prickly devotion to the immature but heterosexual Grayle is contrasted with the easy camaraderie of Tetford and Rickman. Grayle is only half aware of the nature of Conrad's feelings towards him, but is quite prepared to exploit the older man, whilst keeping him at a distance. Everyone but Conrad sees through Grayle, whom they tolerate but rather despise. Eventually Conrad is driven mad by a succession of events. He argues with, and strikes out at, Grayle, who has accused him of being rude to a flirtatious Swiss widow called Mme Louis. Shortly afterwards Adelby, who has been refused repatriation on compassionate grounds, learns that his seriously ill wife has died, and consequently commits suicide. Conrad has an epileptic fit, and the play closes with him virtually catatonic, possessively clutching a potted azalea and muttering incoherent apologies to Grayle.

In outline the play sounds preposterous, but although melodramatic, it is both well constructed and psychologically acute. It is scarcely a work of homosexual proselytism, but it presents Conrad sympathetically and gets in a number of entertaining body-blows at conventional heterosexual morality. When Conrad strokes Grayle's head in a gesture of affection, the boy, who (as the stage directions slyly note) 'has been educated at a good Public School', recoils, with the equivocal cry: 'Look out! Someone might come in!' Similarly, when Grayle is asked whether he writes poetry he is 'scandalized' and replies 'Good Lord, no!' The play's most famous exchange is that between Conrad and Mme Louis, who makes an ill-judged attempt to charm him with 'a ravishing smile' as she says: 'I have heard you do not like much the fair sex.' 'The fair sex?' Conrad replies. 'Which sex is that?' There is also a scene in which Adelby borrows Plutarch's *Lives* from Conrad and descants upon the Theban Band, that apparently indestructible army of homosexual partners eventually annihilated at the Battle of Chaeronea in 338 BC. The homosexual theme is reflected in the original title Ackerley gave the play, *The Familiar Friends*, but some of its more outspoken moments were removed at the draft stage. For example, when Conrad's fellow-officers are discussing his moodiness, Grayle suggests: 'He may be in love.' In the original version, Tetford replies: 'You ought to know'; but this was later toned down to: 'Don't you know?' The play was also intended as a critique of the English officer class. Of Grayle, Ackerley wrote:

To love him would be like loving a stone pillar for all the satisfaction one would get out of it. He has never loved anyone in his life with any real affection . . . He has never been intimate with a woman either, and if he could summon up the courage to track one down (as he imagines it) – 'something pretty and clean and young, and so forth' – he would use her in as gentlemanly a manner as possible and doubtless experience afterwards all the best, stereotyped, English remorse, and pity – for himself; not for the girl . . . He is at heart a complete gentleman, correct and dignified and shockingly cold; brainless and self-satisfied; brutally, ruthlessly and undilutedly English.

This was an opinion of the English character which was to change little during Ackerley's life.

Although conditions were comfortable, Ackerley, like his fellow-internees, grumbled and looked forward to the ever-receding day of repatriation. Peter wrote to tell him that he should consider himself lucky, for he was at least out of the war. Peter himself had recovered from his wounds and was back at the Front. In May 1918 he had taken part in another heroic stunt, which he described in modest and jocular detail in a fourteen-page letter clearly written to cheer his younger brother. He had gone into an attack, got tangled in wire, extricated himself and shot dead a German who was emerging from his dug-out. His men took three prisoners and Peter grabbed a handful of important-looking documents. 'Bleeding in many parts', he stumbled back towards the British line and received a small shrapnel wound in his thigh. The punch-line to this anecdote was that the 'important' documents turned out to be 'pages torn out of a German comic song album', which, he added, he 'put to the only possible use, and for which I take it they had been originally meant'. He suggested that after the war ('this "bother"') they might travel abroad together, perhaps to Spain, where the climate was 'bon'. He was now based at the 3rd Corps Infantry School, 'far away from any possibility of participating in any more demonstrations for a period of about five weeks, and so you can let your mind be at rest for a wee while concerning the welfare of your old brother.' Six weeks later his head was blown off by a shell.

As the war dragged into its final phase, the longed-for day of release from the wintry confines of Mürren seemed within the internees' grasp. However, shortly before the Armistice, the town was over-whelmed by *la grippe*, the virulent Spanish influenza which raged destructively through a weary Europe in 1918–19. Some sixty men went down with the infection. For the lucky ones, like Ackerley, this merely meant that repatriation was delayed; but several victims died. Two days before Christmas Ackerley was considered sufficiently fit to make the long journey back to England.

3

Blenheim House

AT Grafton House the family was not united in grief at Peter's death. Netta, who had begged Peter not to go out to the war after he had been wounded the first time, was unable to deal with his death or her own feelings about it. Roger, his dynastic plans blown away with his son, 'was profoundly shaken by a grief he was too proud to share'. Although he spoke of Peter, he could not bear anyone to express sympathy. Nancy had lost her favourite brother. Survivors of major catastrophes often feel an irrational guilt because they have come through whilst others have perished. In Ackerley's case this was compounded by the fact that one of those who did not survive was his brother. Enfeebled by illness and captivity, he found his homecoming to a house shrouded in mourning distinctly muted.

There is little doubt that Ackerley sensed that in some ways the wrong son was returning from the war. Revising the account of his final meeting with Peter for *My Father and Myself*, Ackerley was to write that it 'shows our differences splendidly – and the reason why the better man died'. He even recalled that the letters Roger had written to Peter at Rossall had 'a more intimate note than his letters to me'. It seemed clear to him that Peter was far more his father's son than he would ever be. In 1914 Peter had been travelling in Germany, learning the language as preparation for joining Elders & Fyffes. Roger was sensible enough to recognize that, as he put it when people asked why his surviving son didn't join the family firm, 'Joe isn't interested in bananas.' Indeed, Roger took Peter's jest about Joe becoming the next Laureate with some seriousness. As someone who had grown up without a proper education and had spent his youth in the army, and whose own tastes in literature and the theatre ran to Zane Grey and Florenz Ziegfeld, Roger was profoundly impressed by his son's culture and learning. It is an indication of his faith and his indulgence that he would make no attempt to persuade Joe to get a job and earn a living once he had come down from Cambridge. In spite of his detestation of 'loafers', Roger would pay Joe a substantial allowance, encourage his travels abroad, and become genuinely proud of a son who had poetry published in magazines.

None of this, however, prevented Ackerley's sense of guilt being exacerbated by the notion that he was an inadequate substitute for his dead brother. Roger never deliberately drew comparisons between his two sons, but Armistice Day always proved overwhelming, and he would brood in his study, watching the clock so that he could observe the two minutes' silence at 11 a.m. Later, when he became ill and was attempting to master the shooting pains he suffered in his hands, he would occasionally address his surviving son inadvertently as 'Peter'.

By the time Ackerley came to write his 'Family Memoir', Peter had been dead for decades and had become a rather shadowy figure, capering indistinctly upon the stage of memory. What remained, apart from Peter's few brief appearances in the spotlight, was a sense of the failure of their relationship. Ackerley does not mention his own grief at Peter's death in the memoir, but S. P. B. Mais recalled that Ackerley 'was completely broken up by the death of his older brother' and became reclusive. The news of Peter's death had reached Ackerley at Mürren, and it is likely that his portrait of the bereaved Adelby in *The Prisoners of War* reflected something of his own feelings. He came to feel that he had not paid Peter enough attention, had been unable to return Peter's genuine and uncomplicated brotherly affection, and now it was too late.

Even before his death, Peter had somehow represented everything his younger brother was not, and it is significant that in the minimally fictionalized accounts of his war service which he wrote whilst in POW camps, Ackerley named his *alter ego* 'Peter Saxon' and 'Peter Garvin'. In later notebooks, kept during the early 1920s, there are jottings for short stories and plays in which Peter's presence is also felt, as in the brief fragments of a piece entitled 'The Anniversary'. A young German veteran of the war, Karl Wezel, visits England and sees the photograph of a dead English officer in a shop in Rye. Recognizing the man, he seeks out the family without, it seems, explaining his particular interest in them. The officer's fiancée has transferred her affections to the dead man's younger brother, Jacob. Jacob, who is homosexual, falls in love with the mysterious German. Aware of Jacob's obsession, the girl befriends Karl, who confides in her about his experiences in the war. He tells her that in order to avenge the death of his best friend he murdered an English officer. Another visitor calls, a friend of the dead officer, who has come to give the family the circumstances of the man's death.

> The central link with Karl's story is of course obvious, and it becomes dreadfully clear to the girl, who appears unseen behind, and is the only person who has heard both stories, that it is Karl who slew her fiancé. But her fiancé now is nothing to her but a memory, and, loving Jacob, she realizes that she holds in her hands, not a revenge for the past so much as a solution for the future. Once conveyed to Jacob this knowledge would indeed break down the barrier of his friendship with Karl and leave him free for her. But realizing the danger of betrayal, she is cunning enough to egg Karl on to betray himself . . .

This curious little melodrama was never completed, but what remains gives an intriguing insight into Ackerley's obsessions in the aftermath of the war. Guilt about homosexuality combines queasily with guilt about Peter's death, so that the fictionalized Ackerley, rejecting the love of his brother's girlfriend, embraces his brother's assassin.

Ackerley summed up the effect of the war upon him in November 1921 when he wrote in his diary:

> I am very young. I am so young, I think, as to be quite insensible. For I have been through much; wars, bereavement, starvation – there is no end. But I have felt nothing, and shall never feel anything. And if I die tonight this, I hope, will remain, so long as my memory lasts, as the final word upon my nature.

These might seem the sort of self-dramatizing outpourings to be expected of any sensitive and introspective young man, but it is worth comparing it with 'the final word' of Rolf Gardiner, a fellow undergraduate at Cambridge, who wrote of him to Nancy in 1967:

It is forty-five years since I last saw your brother; and yet I can see him now, and hear his voice . . . Joe made a deep impression on me, his dignified handsomeness as an ex-officer student of twenty-five, masculine yet with a meditative sensitiveness which I described to my mind as 'elegiac' . . . There was a sorrow deep down in his nature, a memory of some hurt.

While convalescing at Richmond, Ackerley completely recast *The Prisoners of War* and then consigned it to a drawer. He attended a crammer and sat the Little-go once again, passing this time. He went up to Magdalene College, Cambridge in the autumn of 1919, initially to read law. After a brief and unenjoyable tussle with legal text-books he decided that his future lay in English letters rather than the law courts, and the ever-indulgent Roger agreed to his changing courses and studying English literature. His flirtation with law was not entirely wasted, however, for it taught him to argue with wit, incisiveness and authority, a skill which was to prove useful in the coming years. He seems to have spent a great deal of his time writing, and by June 1919 claimed to have a sheaf of some 200 poems, but was having no success in publishing them. 'Though none of the papers to which I have sent them think them worthy of publication,' he wrote to Eddie Marsh, 'I cannot bring myself to believe that this opinion is correct.' He enclosed sixteen poems for Marsh's *Georgian Poetry*, but none was accepted. He had more luck locally, and two indifferent, melancholy and vaguely homosexual poems, 'Daedalon' and '9.9.19.', were chosen for the volume of *Cambridge Poets 1914–20*.

No diaries survive of the Cambridge period, which appears to have been rather less of an influence upon him than it had been upon undergraduates before the war. The fact that he had been through the war and was coming to the University at the comparatively advanced age of twenty-three set him apart from the younger undergraduates who matriculated with him. His isolation was emphasized by the fact that he did not live in college, but in digs at 49 Bridge Street, and he felt that he might have missed out on collegiate life because of this. He nonetheless made a considerable impression upon his contemporaries, as one of them recalled:

He always looked distinguished, but in those days his appearance was spectacular. He was a charmer, but at the same time he was somewhat reserved. To those who knew him he was something of a mystery. We knew he had been in a prisoner-of-war camp in Switzerland; we knew he wrote poetry. The Cambridge I knew was in an aesthetical mood, and when we saw handsome Joe riding his bicycle through the streets we looked on him with respect and awe. He was at Magdalene College and had rooms in Magdalene Street [sic]. To these rooms he would retire and his own private preoccupations and, we thought, his poetry, and intruders into his privacy were not welcome . . . I do not recall ever meeting him at a party, though I may be mistaken, but he certainly was a 'figure' and to know Ackerley was something. No one dreamt he was reading law.

This aloofness was misleading, according to Ackerley, who described himself at this period as 'very romantic and talkative; chatty about the Classical Greeks and their ways, inclining to Bohemia, busily acquiring the usual pictures by Flandrin, Tuke, Praxiteles and Glyn Philpot for decorating my room, and ready to respond to understanding and sympathy from any quarter.' His Bohemian inclinations made him a rather dandified figure and this was an element in his character, though not in his dress, which endured. 'I recollect very little about my Cambridge years,' he wrote. 'I felt unsettled, restless, purposeless; I wasted my time.'

Having sorted himself out sexually, it might be thought that Ackerley would have taken advantage of the considerable opportunities Cambridge afforded the young homosexual. That he did not was in part due to his introduction to the homosexual heritage by Arnold Lunn. This had allowed him to see himself as part of a great tradition, but had also encouraged his propensity for idealism. Apart from some unsatisfactory and unenjoyable fumblings at Rossall, Ackerley arrived in Cambridge a virgin. He did not remain one, but sex seemed to get in the way of love, rather than become an expression of it. He was very shocked when he learned of the sexual practices of his more sophisticated and less inhibited contemporaries, but this did not prevent him from making the occasional sexual foray into London's West End, where acquiescent young men could be found lurking in Piccadilly Circus and Leicester Square. He had been told about a 'hotel' in Mayfair's Shepherd Market, an area notorious then as now for prostitution, where rooms could be hired with no questions asked. For a young idealist with aspirations towards the arcadian, such establishments and the transactions which took place within them could seem thoroughly degrading. '11 Half Moon Street. This is the kind of room one kills oneself in,' he wrote in a 1921 notebook.

Nonetheless, he made several friends at Cambridge, amongst them Claude Colleer Abbott, future Professor of English Language and Literature at Durham University and butt of many jokes amongst Ackerley's friends. Some six years older than Ackerley, Abbott was a large, myopic man, whose poor eyesight had debarred him from active service in the war. He had already taken an external London BA in French and English in 1913, and was now working under the supervision of Sir Arthur Quiller-Couch as a research student at Gonville and Caius College, writing a thesis upon Thomas Lovell Beddoes. Abbott and Ackerley became close friends, but there was never any question of a sexual relationship between them. After they had left Cambridge, and Abbott had gone to take up a lectureship in English at Aberdeen University, the two men corresponded regularly and Abbott became a frequent visitor at Richmond. Apart from a distinguished academic career (he discovered a cache of Boswell's papers at Fettercairn House, amongst them the *London Journal*, and edited the letters of Gerard Manley Hopkins), Abbott was a poet whose judgement Ackerley trusted. Abbott's own verses were in the pastoral mode, liberally sprinkled with archaic, rural words and expressions. They were much mocked by people like William Plomer, who conspired with Ackerley in the 1940s to produce an album containing pages torn from Abbott's books, which Plomer 'illustrated' with obscene caricatures of the poet making advances to sailors and agricultural labourers.

Meanwhile Roger and Netta took advantage of their son's absence and got married. It had not occurred to anyone that this distinguished couple, who gave so convincing an impression of bourgeois respectability, were in fact living 'in sin'. In consequence, the ceremony took place 'quietly', indeed obscurely, several miles away from Grafton House, in Pimlico at St Michael's Church, Chester Square. Netta described herself as a spinster and gave her address as 32 Claverton Street, SW, a road running down to the river to the west of Dolphin Square. Roger, modestly describing himself as a 'Fruit Merchant', gave a rather more superior address: 13 Eccleston Street, SW, just off Eaton

Square. They were married by the Revd J. Gough McCormick on 13 October 1919, a date chosen by Netta as 'lucky', the event witnessed by Bunny and her second husband, an alcoholic doctor and gold prospector called Chappell Hodgson Fowler. It was Bunny who had engineered this tardy tying of the marital knot. She wanted Netta to be married less for reasons of morality than for reasons of economics – to make sure that as his wife Netta would be provided for in the event of Roger's death. A few weeks later Roger drew up a brief and prophetically apologetic will: 'I give and bequeath all my property personal or otherwise to my dear wife Netta and only regret that there is not more of it.' Roger's extravagance, which included placing bets of up to £100 on the horses, was beginning to catch up with him. It is not surprising that when he received a letter from his son asking how much he earned he wrote back to say that it was none of his business.

Financial difficulties notwithstanding, in September 1921 the family moved to their final and largest Richmond home, the imposing Blenheim House at 76 Richmond Hill, looking out over the Terrace Gardens down towards the Thames. Next door was Metcalfe's London Hydro, a smart establishment presided over by Dr Harry Wadd, a dirty-minded old fraud who spent as much of the time he could spare from fleecing his wealthy patients exchanging smoking-room stories with Roger. Roger considered Wadd one of his best pals, but the good doctor was looked upon by Ackerley with fastidious distaste.

Ackerley had come down from Cambridge in the summer with 'an inglorious BA degree' (a Third) but little idea of what he was going to do with his life. During his final term he had shown the manuscript of *The Prisoners of War* to the Master of his college, the melancholy (indeed, manic depressive) A. C. Benson. No doubt he suspected that the theme would prove sympathetic, but Benson's reply was dispiriting. Although he admired the piece ('It is full of tense feeling and emotion and moved me painfully'), Benson feared that:

> In spite of its merits, both of idea and of execution, I do not think it could be produced on the stage, as the tragedy & pathos of the whole are so unrelieved and painful. I do not think that any theatre would undertake a play of so harrowing and distressing a character.

41

This was a view of the play that was to become depressingly familiar to its author. Benson even advised against publication:

> I doubt if it would be wise for you, if you have a literary career in view, to begin with a work in so tragic a key. I imagine that it is all unhappily *true* enough; but the fact remains that most people go to a play or a book for beauty and comfort, & for illusion rather than for truth!

Ackerley also sent Benson a poem, which provoked a similar response: 'it goes almost too deep into life & touches a region that it is hardly safe to visit.'

Whilst he pondered fruitlessly upon the future he received a handsome allowance from Roger. In spite of his mild literary successes at Cambridge, Ackerley felt guilty, especially when he spent so much time closeted in his room, gazing into space and producing very little to show for it. He began to cast around for excuses for his creative sterility and decided that the atmosphere of the new house was not conducive, and so, just after Christmas, he took rooms in St John's Wood at 24 Elm Tree Road. He continued to spend much of his time at his parents' house, but the new flat was somewhere he could escape to in order to pursue literature and sex.

Most of his literary energies were engaged in keeping notebooks. He developed a magpie propensity to pick up anything that sparkled, jotting it down so that one can hear the voices years later, with the result that he left a vivid impressionistic picture of Blenheim House at this period. He made use of these notes when working on a number of plays and short stories, since lost or destroyed, and when compiling his family memoir.

By now Roger had taken charge of the marketing of bananas for Elders & Fyffes, organizing extraordinary advertising campaigns in which the health-giving properties of this 'all food fruit' were extolled. A recipe book was compiled, lecturers were hired to tour schools, and all manner of promotions, including 'banana competitions', were sponsored in the press. By extreme good fortune a music-hall artiste called Florrie Forde recorded and performed a new song entitled 'Yes, We Have No Bananas' which became extremely popular. Roger supplied her with hands of bananas for her shows, which were then auctioned for charity. Under Roger's skilful guidance, Britain simply went bananas. When the song 'I've Never Seen A Straight Banana' became popular, Elders & Fyffes offered a £1,000 reward to the first person to discover 'a perfectly straight banana'. No one ever did, but the publicity ensured that sales continued to rise.

In order to maintain this high level of public interest in the fruit, Roger set off from Richmond each morning in a chauffeur-driven car. He left behind him a household which, beneath its unruffled surface, buzzed with jealousies and discontent. Things were not much improved by the fact that the Ackerleys tended to have servants who were incompetent or simply indifferent to the needs of their employers. Netta, ever keen to avoid any manifestation of 'unpleasantness', was always ready to find excuses when the servants disappointed. Some of these were extremely elaborate. One could not blame the maid who broke things because, Netta explained, she 'had double-jointed fingers and I don't suppose they have the same tenacity'. For all his imposing appearance, Roger was equally and endearingly hopeless when it came to reprimanding the staff, particularly Avory, the Ackerleys' young butler.

He came in late again last Sunday night [Roger complained to his son]. Quarter past eleven. I opened the door for him.

'It's a quarter past eleven, Avory,' I said.

'Is it sir?' he said.

'Yes,' I said. 'It is. Get to bed with you – and wake me at quarter past seven tomorrow morning.'

At 7.10 I woke of my own accord. I got up. Came downstairs. Pulled up the blind and opened the curtain in my dressing room. Pulled up the blind and opened the curtains on the landing. Got my own hot water. Turned on the bath. At *twenty-five minutes to eight* I heard a step in the passage and a knock on my door.

'Who's that?' I said. It was the maid.

'Please, sir, what time do you want breakfast?' she said.

'Where's Avory?' I asked.

'He's not up, sir.'

Twenty-five minutes to eight! I tell you the boy's hopeless. He's got no idea, no training. And he won't be taught. It happens over and over again. He simply doesn't care, that's it – and all he thinks of is getting out into the street after the girls.

When Ackerley asked his father what he had done about this lapse, Roger replied:

> Nothing. I didn't do anything. I was too angry; I knew if I said anything at all it would be 'Here's your month's wages and now get out.'
>
> I tell you the boy's no good – oh a decent lad, I daresay – at least Mother's always telling me so – but as a servant, useless. And if I chucked him out Heaven knows what would become of him – there's certainly no-one else in the world who'd give him five hundred and twenty-six pounds a year.

Netta was by now something of a faded beauty, preoccupied with her former theatrical triumphs and bewailing the ravages of time. 'I used to have rather a decent face once,' she would announce as she studied herself in the mirror. 'I had character if nothing else – but of course it's deteriorated. I was thinking to myself the other day I had rather a decent chin once; but now of course my muscles here are all atrophied.' Indeed, her teeth were now rather prominent, giving her a faintly goofy air when she smiled for the camera. She was convinced that her small build prevented her from receiving her proper due from both her family and the servants.

> I wish I were tall and big and imposing [she would complain]. Then people wouldn't laugh at me and the children and servants would respect me. When I tell a story the family laughs at me, not with me. I never have the field to myself. That's why I tell my stories so badly; it makes me so self-conscious. I don't suppose as long as I live I shall ever be treated as anything but a joke. Isn't it awful?

More of a handicap than her size was her almost terminal vagueness. Although she was unaware of the fact, Netta lived largely in a world of her own, only occasionally making contact with the lives of others. She often literally had no idea what day it was. Part of her trouble was that she never quite recovered from her early on-stage success as an *ingénue*, and it was a role she continued to play throughout her life, to increasingly macabre effect. She maintained a girlish zest for life, forever entering rooms as if stepping before the footlights and delivering lines from drawing-room comedies: 'What a beautiful day! The air I should imagine is full of champagne.' Some found this entirely genuine naïvety engaging, but she could be maddeningly distrait, chattering away without any clear notion of what she was saying or what impression she was making. 'A silent tongue means a wise head,' she would say, adding in flagrant contradiction of the facts: 'I'm a woman of few words.' Bridge parties, which formed a staple of Blenheim House evening recreation, saw her at her most disconcerting, scarcely able to deal a hand of cards with any degree of success. 'Now I don't know where I am,' she would exclaim, hovering over the baize. 'Oh, there? I wish you wouldn't talk. How *can* one remember? Is it there? No – this should be there – that's it.' When corrected she would insist: 'No, I left off there . . . I think . . .' Any silence, when another player was concentrating upon his hand for example, would be punctuated by some unnerving observation: 'What a curious smell! What *can* it be? The dogs aren't here.' The dogs were a plump little procession of Sealyham terriers named Tango, Toast, Barbarita, and Carleton-Pearcey.

Netta was also a hypochondriac, who once claimed that she had swallowed her uvula. She suffered from constipation and was forever sucking lozenges to sweeten her breath. She was certain that she had low blood pressure and a weak heart and always slept with a double pillow in the small of her back in an attempt to push out her diaphragm and prevent it pressing on her heart. She was convinced that Death was waiting for her to relax her vigilance for a moment before moving in to claim her. Ackerley recorded one near miss which, incidentally, catches Netta in the full flow of her nervous garrulity:

Joe dear, something really awful happened just now. I sat down in that chair over there to go to sleep – I felt so tired, and I folded my arms like this I don't know why . . . and I was talking to Nancy and bent forward a little like this – d'you see? – so that they pressed on my heart. And do you know I woke up suddenly – I don't know how long I'd been dozing, but it couldn't have been more than a few moments, and simply found I couldn't uncross them. It was simply terrifying. I tried and tried, but I couldn't move them – and I couldn't speak. I tried to call to Nance – she was sitting there reading – to come and move them for me, but I could only just make a faint noise, and when she looked up she saw me going like this [she mouths]. O my dear wasn't it dreadful really? You know I nearly died. Really I did; I'm not exaggerating. I was dreadfully ill, and I'm sure I should have died in another moment. You see I couldn't make Nance understand. She just sat looking at me as though I were demented and saying 'What?' And I was fully conscious all the time and trying to ask her to come and unlock my arms.

You see the pressure of them on my heart had stopped the circulation – stopped it beating. It just shows how careful one has to be. It passed off in a moment – but I'm sure that for one fraction of time anyway I actually was dead.

Nobody took this at all seriously, and indeed Netta lived until she was eighty-two. Her frequent recourse to the chemist to stock up on valerian, cascara, sal volatile and red lavender led to her being mocked by the family as 'a puss in Boots'. She was also concerned for the health of others, forever producing bizarre maxims: 'From high boots one day to silk stockings the next her kidneys will be affected', or 'White wine thins your blood'. She kept Roger, whom she fondly addressed as 'Punch', out of her bedroom on the grounds that sex was 'bad for him'.

Her ideal relationship was the one she had formed with a retired rubber planter called Harold Armstrong, whom the family had met in the course of a seaside holiday. A faintly pathetic creature, who eventually committed suicide in a Reading hotel, Armstrong pursued Netta with the asexual gallantry of a medieval courtly lover. Roger, for reasons of his own, accepted Armstrong and the lonely little man was a frequent visitor to Richmond. He even corresponded with Peter and Joe while they were at boarding school. His nickname for Netta, 'the Rat', was one which was adopted by her children with irreverent glee. Presumably Armstrong was thinking of the sort of white rats people had as pets; Ackerley thought that the name arose from his mother's habit of hoarding things. Clearly she approved of the name for she made a drawing of a rat which Armstrong had engraved upon the backs of her hair-brushes. Netta's children ragged her mercilessly over Armstrong, even after his pitiful end. She often brooded upon this fantasy romance, but was unable to communicate her real feelings about it. Ackerley once met her on the landing and she said:

I've been crying and crying; I thought I should never stop. I've been lying on my bed with a suppository inside me thinking of Harold and saying my prayers. I haven't prayed for years.

Well, I'm on my way downstairs for some Vim.

A rather more concrete concern was Nancy, who was proving extremely difficult at this period. Endlessly indulged by Roger, Nancy spent much of her time out at parties and the rest of it in bed, sulking. She treated Netta like a rather dim servant. 'Go and fill my hot water bottle,' she would command from beneath the sheets; 'Write a note to have me wakened; go and see if there are any letters.' She was extremely beautiful, but without personal grace or modesty. 'Vanity, arrogance, jealousy, wilfulness and a stubborn conceit, a flashing temper,' was how Ackerley recalled his sister at this period.

> My earliest recollections of her are in our dining room . . . standing in front of the mirror above the mantelpiece, smoking, with her coffee cup or a liqueur before her, rowing my mother over her shoulder while she regarded all the time her own face in the glass. She spent much time examining herself in the mirror, and her thought was all for clothes. She treated her young men with the careless inconsiderate indifference of the spoilt beauty sure of her power.

Years later, Ackerley read Edith Wharton's *The Custom of the Country* and was instantly struck by the character of the book's vain, spoilt and extravagant heroine, Undine Spragg. It might almost have been a portrait of Nancy as a young woman, he thought. There is little doubt that at times Netta must have been extremely trying, but Nancy made no allowances at all, and her mother's attempts to jolly her along when she was discontented invariably led to blunt rebuffs and tears. Netta often complained to Joe about Nancy's cruelty and 'peculiar disposition', which she ascribed to the fact that her daughter had reached puberty at the early age of ten. When out of bed, Nancy stalked about the house in black rages which Netta attempted to alleviate without success. She slept badly, but refused to take any soporifics, accusing Netta of attempting to drug her and threatening to throw herself out of a window if Dr Wadd were summoned from next door. This led to farcical scenes, with Netta crawling along the side of the house, under the windows, in order to consult the doctor unobserved. The more Nancy raged the iller Netta became, so that it was she who eventually required the bromides.

It was from this atmosphere that Ackerley escaped to St John's Wood, and in March 1922 he was relieved to be asked to return to Cambridge to take part in a Marlowe Society production of *Troilus and Cressida*. He was a memorable Achilles, particularly in the scene when he summoned his Myrmidons to avenge the death of Patroclus. The future opera-producer Dennis Arundell, who played Ulysses, recalled that the actors were 'encouraged to *be* rather than to perform' and no doubt memories of a more recent war and the death of Peter contributed to the effectiveness of Ackerley's performance. It was altogether a distinguished production, with a cast including Rolf Gardiner as Troilus, George 'Dadie' Rylands as Diomedes and Roland Penrose as Calchas, with Donald Beves and Eric Maschwitz amongst the extras. It was designed by Alec Penrose, and produced by Frank Birch, who took the play to the Everyman Theatre in Hampstead in June, where the women's parts, which had been played by fresh-faced young men at Cambridge, were taken by actresses. Ackerley's Achilles – 'a heroic figure who glamorized all Cambridge' in the memory of Steven Runciman, who was an undergraduate at the time – was less noted in London. As in the case of that other gilded Marlowe player, Rupert Brooke, whose stilted performance as the Attendant Spirit in a pre-war production of *Comus* was more than compensated for by his physical presence, one suspects that it was Ackerley's good looks as much as any theatrical talent which caused a stir.

Meanwhile a long meditative poem, upon which he had been working for some time, was accepted by Jack Squire for the *London Mercury*. Dedicated 'To M.H.O.'[1] and entitled 'Ghosts', it appeared in the April issue. Ackerley was never satisfied with the poem and spent some time attempting to 'iron out its manifest crudities' after it had been published. One reader, however, was impressed enough to write a fan letter. It was dated 26 April and signed: 'Yours sincerely E. M. Forster'.

---

[1] The only one of Ackerley's Cambridge contemporaries to have these initials was Melvill Hayes Oxley, who came up to Trinity College in the Lent Term 1919. There are no references to Oxley amongst Ackerley's papers.

4

Dearest My Morgan

B y 1922 E. M. Forster's literary career had ground to a dispiriting halt. Apart from some journalism and a collection of short
stories, he had published nothing since *Howard's End* in 1910.
He had begun to fear that, at forty-three, his writing life was over. On
the stocks was the 'unpublishable' *Maurice*, the aborted *Arctic Journey*, and part of an Indian novel which he was pessimistic of finishing.
He had recently returned to England after a spell in India as secretary
to the Maharajah of Dewas Senior, by way of Alexandria where
his Egyptian friend Mohammed el Adl was dying of consumption.
Worried by Mohammed's rapid decline, unable to write, and feeling
trapped by his mother, with whom he lived in Weybridge, Forster had
entered a state of deep depression.

It was characteristic that he found his way out of this labyrinth
through an act of disinterested generosity. He had seen and been
stirred by 'Ghosts' and wrote to Ackerley to tell him so. 'He did this
throughout his life,' Ackerley recalled, 'writing to people to thank
them for whatever they did that pleased or moved him; as well as the
pleasure he himself derived he believed in praise and thought that far
too little of it was given compared with the readiness to find fault.' In
retrospect Ackerley described 'Ghosts' as 'a not very worthy midwife'
to a lifelong friendship, but he also felt that it was a 'genuine utterance'
rather than the undergraduate posing of much of his other poetry. It
was perhaps this quality, and the distinct homosexual aura of the
poem, which appealed to Forster.

It also reflected Forster's own concerns at that period. His relationship with Mohammed was very important to him as the only love

affair he had consummated. (A liaison with a court barber at Dewas had been based upon sex rather than true affection.) Now Mohammed lay dying in a far country, beyond any help but the financial, sending a succession of letters which charted the deterioration in his health. Forster was much preoccupied with his feelings about his friend, feelings that were a compound of grief and guilt, the nature of which he was unable to communicate to his mother. In his diary he confessed frankly: 'I want him to tell me that he is dead, and so set me free to make an image of him. Latterly my great love prevents my feeling he is real.' On 6 May Mohammed wrote to say that he was 'very bad' (indeed, he was dead by the time Forster read the letter), and he concluded: 'do not forget your ever friend Moh el adl'. Ackerley's poem, in which a man is depicted sorting through the letters of a dead friend, must have struck a chord:

> Can they still live,
> Beckon and cry
> Over the years
> After they die
> Bringing us grief,
> Bringing us tears?
>
> Those we once set
> With us abreast
> Shielded and cherished,
> Are they distressed
> If we forget
> After they've perished?
>
> So while they sleep
> Do they not trust
> Friendship to keep
> Memory bright
> Lest it fall quite
> Into the dust?
>
> . . .
>
> Then came his eyes
> Shining with truth;
> Then came his voice
> Broken with sighs;

Friend of my choice,
Friend of my youth.

Ah, but I burned
Him to embrace,
Feeling his breath
Hot on my face
So that I yearned
Almost to death;

So that I reeled
Free from sleep's fetters
Out of my chair
Groping to where
I had concealed
Certain old letters.

Holding a candle
Over my head
Thrust I aside
Many a bundle
Labelled and tied
Seeking my dead;

Hearing him yet
Saying 'Good-bye!'
Hearing his sigh,
Murmured so low,
'Ah, but I know . . .
You will forget.'

Forster wrote that he liked the poem's combination of drama and reminiscence, and drew a comparison with Proust, whose *A la Recherche du Temps Perdu* he had been reading.

I don't know whether you and Proust are right in your explanations. 'Out of death lead no ways' is more probably the fact. But being right is of little importance. What you have done is to drive home the strangeness of a creature who is apparently allowed neither to remember nor to forget and who sees in the stream of his daily life, piteously disordered, the recurrence of something that was once beautiful and that passes as inevitably away now as it did then. No –

of course you don't quite do this, because your poem ends in unalloyed remembrance, if such a condition exists: but I don't suppose that you – i.e. the narrator – supposes that the remembrance is permanent. The moment a memory is registered by the intellect is its last moment.

The poem, he wrote, had 'set me feeling about, and thinking'.

Ackerley's reply has not survived and it is not altogether clear how the friendship developed over the next two years. For much of 1922 Ackerley was abroad, supposedly writing a play and visiting Nancy who was working as a mannequin with a small fashion house in Paris. An unknown twenty-five-year-old, Ackerley was no doubt immensely flattered to receive such considered praise from a man as eminent as Forster, but if Forster wrote further letters during the year, they have been lost or destroyed, for the next surviving letter is dated 4 January 1923.

Ackerley's excuse for foreign travel was 'research', soaking up the atmosphere of Italy and gathering the raw material of experience to transform into poetry, fiction and drama. He set out out for Italy in August; possibly made optimistic by the fact that Squire had published another poem, a nostalgic and narcissistic study in lost innocence entitled 'On a Photograph of Myself as a Boy', and that several of his poems were about to be published in a book, *Poems by Four Authors*. But more than anything he wanted to escape from the expectations of family and friends, expectations he felt he was failing to realize. He might not get much work done abroad, but at least he would no longer have to face the eager enquiries of those who believed in him as a diligent young writer whose name would shortly be known to the world through the masterpieces he was concocting behind closed doors. He would also be able to broaden his sexual experience, taking advantage of the more relaxed attitude towards such matters which prevailed on the Continent.

He was accompanied by the unidentified 'lisping little artist' mentioned in *My Father and Myself* and referred to as 'T.' in letters and diaries. They stayed in Rome and Florence, and went to the Balkan port of Ragusa (now the Yugoslavian Dubrovnik), presumably at the suggestion of T., who wanted to paint Slav youth there. As so often happens on holidays, the two friends gradually discovered their basic incompatibility, or rather Ackerley discovered it, for T. seems to have been volubly happy, a circumstance which added to his companion's irritation:

> He 'adored' things; that was the kind of person he was. He 'adored' salame and macaroni and olives and sour German bread; he 'adored' Serbians and Turks, and shiny tight black hair, cats, trees, and the vulgar shades of pink; he 'adored' jugged hare and Japanese women; he 'adored' the sun because it made him brown, but he did not 'adore' the wind because it blew his hair about.

Ackerley had agreed to pose as the figure of Christ his companion was painting for a canvas entitled *Christ Leaving the Home of his Mother*; after some days sketching Ackerley, T. was obliged to retitle the painting *The Prodigal Son Leaving Home*. Ackerley was happiest when T. packed up his easel and paints and went off on his own, for then he could sit in cafés, scribbling in his notebooks and observing life around him – a life gradually becoming darkened by the black shirts of the *fascisti* – and occasionally being distracted by a passing youth whose glance suggested that some assignation might be made. He would also 'stand for hours, almost in a trance, watching the pale-coffee-coloured boys with their jet-black hair bathing in the Arno and standing quite naked on the little white island of shingle between the Alle Grazie and the Richio, or swimming about in the dull olive-green water, the sunlight turning blue on their wet black heads.' All too often T., who preferred company and chatter, would abandon his easel and sit with Ackerley, who vented his frustration in a notebook, gradually transforming the experience into a short story, 'Estlin' – the name he gave to his friend. He depicted himself as 'Revel', but was able, in fiction, to present an even-handed analysis of their relationship:

> They never seemed to agree upon any point, and I think their incompatibility was deep-rooted, Revel being the kind of person who is happier alone, Estlin in company. While the former was thoughtful and uncommunicative, the latter was excitable and enthusiastic. Both were observant – the one with the journalist's, the other with the painter's eye – but whereas Revel could pleasurably observe in silence, Estlin was obliged to communicate his observations to others. He needed sympathy and expression.

Here was a stumbling block to begin with, for Revel disliked having his silences intruded upon and his attention redrawn to things he had already observed and, as it usually happened, passed over as of little interest. But what chance of readjustment was there? These things are matters of temperament, and the best will in the world cannot alter that.

Estlin did his best; of that I am certain, but his pride as a painter would not permit him to praise as beautiful things which gave a grim sardonic pleasure to Revel's tragic morbid eye; and Revel on his part not only refused to agree with but actually sneered at Estlin's enthusiasms. It is true as I have said that he did not see eye to eye with his friend, but had he pretended every now and then to coincide with him their companionship might have been simpler. As it was, his repeated disagreements took on at last the colour of cantankerousness, and so Estlin began unhappily to see it.

Rather more congenial company was to be found in Florence with an old admirer, Norman Douglas, who had left England under a cloud he memorably described as 'No bigger than a small boy's hand'. Indeed, the cloud had nearly been cast by Ackerley, who later confessed: 'Norman Douglas stalked me for a time, but he didn't stand a chance.' The two men had met when Ackerley had just left school. It seems that Ackerley had sent the author some of his poetry and asked for comments. Douglas was encouraging and when his young protégé had gone to the trenches, the older man had entered a rather one-sided correspondence.

> Did you get my last letter, by the way? [he asked in October 1915] No matter if you didn't; there was nothing of interest and importance in it – merely a sign of life, on my part, conveying a breath of sympathy . . . are there any books you would like me to send out to you?
>
> I hope you have got over the influenza by this time, and, what is more important, that you are otherwise all right. A postcard from you, to that effect, would do me good; a letter would do me better (is that all right?) . . . If I weren't shy, I would send you a book of mine called 'Old Calabria' – rather stodgy, but quite readable on the whole . . .

Ackerley sent poems from the trenches, but failed to answer letters. This caused Douglas a great deal of concern, particularly during the dangerous summer of the Somme in 1916:

> I got your last (?) letter from France [Douglas complained in September] and wrote you *twice* afterwards, but got no answer. A friend saw your name among the casualties. I went to Richmond but failed to find Grafton House the first time. I wandered about aimlessly, asking here and there where it was; the second time I captured [?] a policeman, who said he knew where it was. He didn't! He said Ararat Road. I enquired all over the place and, when it got dark, rang a number of bells – in vain. This only to show you I had not forgotten you.

Shortly afterwards Douglas had been arrested and charged with gross indecency with a sixteen-year-old boy whom he had picked up whilst loitering in the Natural History Museum in Kensington. After further charges and a number of court appearances Douglas hastily boarded the Channel packet and went into exile in Florence. He had kept in touch with Ackerley without any real intimacy developing, but each was glad to see a familiar face in the Florentine streets. Douglas's frank hedonism shocked the idealistic Ackerley. Whilst lunching at a café Douglas had gestured to the youthful waiter and said to Ackerley: 'Hasn't got a hair on his body, Joe. It slips into him like a knife in butter. When are you coming out here to join us?'

Ackerley was introduced to Douglas's friend, the publisher Giuseppe 'Pino' Orioli, who became his unofficial guide, telling him about the aphrodisiacal properties of truffles and oysters, introducing him to men, and proffering advice at every turn. He claimed that the young Florentines had gaberdine trousers especially tailored to display their genitals, and one of his favourite pastimes was to wander the streets of Florence ogling youths and attempting to induce erections merely by gazing in turn at their trousers and their faces, up and down, up and down. He would have bets with Ackerley upon his success rate. More seriously, he understood something of Ackerley's predicament: young Italians, although often sexually compliant, were not necessarily available for any more serious relationship. He explained how once, after spending the evening making love to a boyfriend, during which the young man swore eternal fidelity, Orioli had followed him from the house straight to a brothel. 'There is no love to be found that way,' Orioli said philosophically:

> You will discover that for yourself after a time. Everyone does. Why should a boy of seventeen or eighteen love you when he can love someone of his own age? Youth is everything to him. No, that is a thing separate from friendship. I take great pleasure, I set great value on my friends – they are the stable, enduring bonds; all the rest passes.

Nonetheless, whilst Ackerley was learning, Orioli had no objection to lending him his rooms in which to conduct his temporary romances. On one such occasion Ackerley emerged from Orioli's flat to find his host waiting for him in the street outside. Orioli explained that Bruno, the young man with whom Ackerley had been spending the evening, had been known to rob his pick-ups. He had not wanted to spoil Ackerley's fun but felt that he ought to mount guard in case of difficulties. Ackerley's luck did not hold and he later got into a number of scrapes. He met an Italian count, wealthy and charming, who seemed to know everyone. They booked into a grand hotel, but after two days the 'count' disappeared, taking Ackerley's luggage with him. On another occasion he picked up a young Frenchman on a beach and was led to a cliff-top, where another young man appeared. Under the threat of pushing him over the edge, the two youths robbed Ackerley of everything he had. 'When they came to his trousers,' a friend reported, 'they hesitated about the quality, but eventually decided they were not good enough and left them for him to walk back to the town in.'

In spite of such distractions, Ackerley managed to do some work. In the Uffizi he had been impressed by a portrait of Galeazzo Maria Sforza by Piero Pollaiuolo and set about discovering something about the life of this fifteenth-century despot, whose cruelty and depravities had led to his assassination in the porch of Milan Cathedral. The result was to be a melodrama in blank verse, entitled *Oligati* or *Girolamo*, which was never completed and none of which has survived. Although it was Pollaiuolo's portrait of Sforza which had inspired the play, it was the (no doubt sentimental) friendship of the young assassins, the Girolamo of the title and a cathedral stone-mason, which was to be at the heart of the drama. Ackerley also began a short story, which was

completed but never published, entitled *The Bench of Renunciation*.
Set in Florence, it is a portrait of the expatriate Miss Mitchell, a
dilapidated fellow-guest in the *pensione* of an unnamed young man.
'Mitchy' is a former artist who one day came to the conclusion that she
would never succeed in her life and simply laid down her paintbrush,
never to take it up again. Almost at once her eyesight began to fade,
and now, purblind, impoverished and unheeded, she sits alone in the
dining-room of the *pensione* or on the bench of the title on the banks of
the Arno. The young man is drawn to this curious creature and
befriends her. She is rather deaf and forgetful, and is a perfect
sounding-board for him as he discourses upon his own ambitions and
failings, which are of course those of Ackerley himself:

> He traced for her the gradual evolution of his literary aspirations
> from the moment of his discovery and encouragement by one of the
> masters at his school to this day; a rush of activity it had been, he
> told her, up to a point, and from that point on a gradual decline, a
> long period of continual disappointment and distrust. He told her of
> the atmosphere of England, among his family and those friends who
> had watched his progress at Cambridge, of patient loyalty and
> rather drooping expectation – an atmosphere which had operated
> to drive him away, not once but many times, to find some quiet place
> where he could be unknown, and could work out his own problems
> alone (those strange, insubstantial problems that occupied so much
> of his time) . . . It couldn't altogether be said to be lack of ideas; he
> was full of ideas; not very big ones perhaps, but ideas nevertheless,
> and had quantities of notebooks crammed with phrases and isolated
> dramatic scenes, imaginary conversations and the results of
> observation. He was sure his psychological powers were above the
> normal – his insight into other people's minds, his faculty for clear
> and penetrative analysis; but perhaps it was the synthetic power
> which was lacking in him – the power of welding things together in a
> perfect whole, or, rather, perhaps of being able to see things as a
> perfect whole. No, this was going too deep; it went down to essence,
> to fundamental disabilities, whereas mere synthesis could be
> patiently acquired; one could learn to build up scenes as a man
> knocked together a pair of boots – given the bits and pieces. But he
> would not admit to any weakness that was irremediable. It was too
> late for such an admission now. It would be the same thing as giving

in altogether as she had given in, and that he would never do. He would never acknowledge defeat.

In October 1922 Ackerley eventually left Florence for Paris, where he was plunged into despair by some sort of romantic disaster, which could not be resolved because of the imminent arrival of Netta and Nancy who were on an extended shopping spree. He was obliged to accompany them to innumerable dressmakers and felt unable to write in their presence. Colleer Abbott's estimation of him as a sensitive, talented Bohemian (an estimation he shared to some degree) was beginning to seem increasingly bogus, since all he had to show for it was a handful of poems and five bad stories. His only solace was a waiter at the Café de la Paix.

In December he accompanied his mother and sister back to Richmond, feeling that he had achieved little during his four and a half months abroad. After a few weeks back in London looking for new rooms in Chelsea, Sloane Square, Soho, Shepherd Market and other suitably artistic quarters, he set off for Italy once again. More work was done on the Sforza play, both there and, when he returned a month or so later, in rooms he acquired in Earls Court. The play was getting nowhere and he no longer felt that such work as he was doing justified the expense of this bolt-hole. In June he reluctantly moved back to Blenheim House.

Now that he was back in London to stay, Ackerley re-established contact with Forster, who proposed that they should meet to discuss Ackerley's poems. *Poems by Four Authors* had been published in Cambridge by Bowes and Bowes during the previous summer, and contained 'four independent books of verse which the authors did not consider suitable for separate publication'. One of the three other poets, A. Y. Campbell, was already established, whilst the other two, Edward Davison and Frank Kendon, were Cambridge contemporaries of Ackerley. Most of the poetry had been gleaned from assorted magazines. Ackerley's contributions were 'Ghosts'; 'On a Photograph of Myself as a Boy'; 'The Portrait of a Mother', an impression of Netta rendered unrecognizable by filial homosexual guilt; five very old-fashioned 'Sonnets' on the theme of unrequited love; 'Among the Tombs', a graveyard meditation upon the absence of love; and 'The Conjuror on Hammersmith Bridge', a disturbingly laconic account of a suicide. Several of these poems were to rise up and haunt him throughout his life, since they were often reprinted in anthologies.[1]

Although he might have been pleased to be in print at the time, Ackerley later described the book, which sold extremely slowly and was eventually remaindered, as 'a wretched compilation'. Jack Squire, who had been the original publisher of several of the poems, commended the book to his *London Mercury* readers, in particular the poems of Ackerley, Davison and Kendon: 'one would be surprised were any other three young men of their generation to get together a collection as good, or as promising as this.' The *Spectator* judged 'Ghosts' 'the most completely successful poem in the book ... its metre is interesting, its sentiment delicately handled, and its unity neatly contrived', but suggested that Ackerley was 'not too happy' in the sonnet form. *The Times Literary Supplement* described his 'meditations' as 'honest but prosaic'.

By now Ackerley was more concerned with plays and short stories than with poetry. When he and Forster lunched at the 1917 Club[2] shortly after Ackerley's return from the Continent, Forster came away with the prose 'sketch' 'Estlin'. More importantly, Ackerley came away with Forster's suggestion that he should consider applying for the post of 'secretary' to the 'fantastic and endearing' Maharajah of Chhatarpur.

Forster had been introduced to the Maharajah through a Weybridge neighbour, Sir Theodore Morison, who had been His Highness's personal tutor in the 1880s.[3] During his two visits to India in 1912–13

[1] 'On a Photograph of Myself as a Boy' was chosen by Thomas Moult for his *Best Poems of 1922*, whilst 'Ghosts' would resurface over twenty years later in *Poems of Our Time 1900–42*, an anthology in which 'The Portrait of a Mother' might have appeared had it not been for the blushing author's personal intervention [*see* Chapter 12 p. 239]. This 'ghastly' poem was reprinted by Jack Squire in his *Second Selections from Modern Poets* (1924). 'The Conjuror on Hammersmith Bridge' appeared in St John Adcock's *Bookman Treasury of Living Poets* (1926).

[2] The 1917 Club was in Soho's Gerrard Street and had been founded in honour of the Russian Revolution. It became a meeting-place for left-wing politicians, intellectuals, conscientious objectors and the like. Leonard Woolf was on the committee and it was much frequented by members of the Bloomsbury Group who delivered papers on pacifist and other topics there, or simply dropped in for tea. Forster used to refer to it as 'my anarchist club'.

[3] Morison had a distinguished career, later becoming Principal of the Muslim Anglo-Oriental College at Aligarh, a Member of the Council of India and adviser to the Secretary of State for India.

and 1921 Forster had spent some time at Chhatarpur as the Maharajah's guest. His Highness had a thirst for the wisdom of Western civilization, and he always welcomed English intellectuals, particularly if, like Forster, they shared his homosexual tastes. When he heard that Forster had gone to be the Maharajah of Dewas Senior's secretary, His Highness was extremely jealous and attempted to bribe Forster to defect. He had employed a succession of English 'secretaries', few of whom had proved satisfactory. The only qualification he demanded was that the applicant should resemble Olaf, the hero of H. Rider Haggard's *The Wanderer's Necklace*. He had gone so far as to apply to Haggard himself, then badgered Morison, but without success. Forster rightly judged that Ackerley would please His Highness, and that it would give his young friend a chance to escape from the confines of England and provide him with new material for his writing. Privately, he also thought that Ackerley and His Highness would be 'well suited or rather matched', because the Maharajah was 'the Prince of Muddlers, even of Indian muddlers' and he had come to much the same conclusion about Ackerley.

Correspondence with His Highness was an elaborate procedure, and the protracted negotiations which ensued confirmed Forster's view of his two friends. Much of the Maharajah's energy was devoted to arguments with a succession of Political Agents, the British officials with responsibility for the Native States. His Highness had to persuade these men that he needed a 'secretary' and this was to take some time, perhaps because he was unable exactly to define the duties of the post. His habits of prevarication and flattery led Forster to dub him 'the royal flirt', and once Forster had instigated negotiations between the Maharajah and Ackerley, he sat to one side, offering advice, but declining to act as go-between.

It was necessary for Ackerley to keep his head and be both clear and firm about the salary, since His Highness was already outlining a fantastical and glittering career which moved progressively from private secretary to secretary to the cabinet, culminating in the combined roles of Prime Minister and tutor to the royal children. However, by May it looked as though the whole idea was off, since His Highness had been unimpressed both by Ackerley's terms and his photograph. He maintained that he could not afford Ackerley and that he had decided that he wanted someone who was experienced (in what, he did not say) and who would take the post permanently.

Forster dismissed His Highness's letter as 'parsimónious and havering', and suggested Ackerley send a copy of *Poems by Four Authors* to entice the indecisive Maharajah. Further hitches ensued and at one point Forster advised Ackerley to give up the whole idea. His Highness used the Political Agent as an excuse, even though the PA had no jurisdiction over the royal household. It was not until December that Ackerley eventually set off for Chhatarpur.

Meanwhile his friendship with Forster had grown apace, and the two men were meeting regularly. Forster may well have been attracted by Ackerley's spectacular good looks, but their relationship was comradely rather than erotic. Ackerley's recklessness, particularly in sexual matters, attracted Forster who enjoyed hearing about the antics of those less timid and circumspect than himself. Forster was also grateful to find someone in whom he could confide without reservation. Too many of his friends had fallen at the sexual hurdle, unable or unwilling to take on board Forster's revelations about himself. Bloomsbury had no such qualms, but equally few scruples, and he feared and disapproved of Garsington gossip. At one time Forster had thought that he would be able to confide in Siegfried Sassoon, but Sassoon was a difficult, introverted character, his mind preoccupied with the war as he scratched away at his voluminous diary. Although the two men remained on friendly terms, their intimacy withered almost as soon as it flourished. Sassoon stopped consulting Forster about his homosexual difficulties, sending him instead strenuously jocular letters addressed to 'Old Tomato Face'. Florence Barger, the wife of a Cambridge contemporary, had been the recipient of many letters about Forster's sexual awakening in Alexandria, but even she was not quite what Forster was looking for. Forster confessed to her, shortly after writing to Ackerley, that Mohammed el Adl's death had been 'a misfortune for me as well as a grief for at my age I need someone of another generation to speed me up and divert me from the *pottering* kindness which is naturally required by my life.' Ackerley was to provide a great deal of diversion over the years and was to have a liberating influence upon his older friend. 'One deeply cherished and lifelong daydream', P. N. Furbank has written of Forster, 'was to have a loving brother with whom he could share his secrets'; this was the role that Ackerley was to play.

Ackerley's apparent worldliness impressed Forster who saw his new friend as something of a dashing Town Mouse to his own dowdy

Country Mouse. Ackerley knew his way around London, particularly around its more disreputable areas, and was happy to act as raffish cicerone. Forster would write touching letters detailing his own inconclusive encounters and wondering what might have happened had Ackerley been him. A typical incident was when Forster, emboldened by the festive atmosphere of Trafalgar Square on New Year's Eve 1924, saw a man in evening dress standing at his open door and bade him 'Happy New Year'. Unfortunately, his voice failed to carry and he was obliged to go home alone. Similarly he once went to Bird Cage Walk, where guardsmen from the nearby Wellington Barracks were to be found, but was unromantically overcome by an attack of diarrhoea. Ackerley could also be relied upon to provide the necessities of sophisticated metropolitan life, whether it was a dinner-jacket at short notice or ointment for pubic lice. (Ackerley was instructed to send the bottle suitably disguised, perhaps in a flat manuscript box, so that Mrs Forster would not ask awkward questions when the post arrived.) Ackerley, like Forster himself, could also be relied upon in a crisis. When Forster became involved with a young man he had met on a Channel packet and things went wrong, Ackerley volunteered to act as intermediary, and earned Forster's deep gratitude. In his late seventies Forster would look back to these years and thank Ackerley in a rather squiffy letter, written after consuming a large whisky:

> It occurred to me suddenly that you and old Arthur Barnet[1] have done more than any others to confirm me in the lower portions of my stability. I am not of course referring to friendship, though that enters, and no doubt Arthur has done most, because he took, and I desired him to take, personal action in those portions. But I think that, but for you both, I should have passed a much more uncertain and disquieted old age. So much nonsense has been cut away, and oh so much gaiety and spunk has been admitted . . .

Forster may also have been delighted to have a disciple. If Ackerley had been flattered by the older man's interest in his poetry, Forster was no doubt touched by Ackerley's deference. 'I was always one of life's natural vassals,' Ackerley confessed, 'a voluntary subordinate to minds or personalities stronger than my own.' Forster was a case in point, and friends of the two men were amused when they heard

[1] See below, page 83.

Ackerley repeating Forster's opinions as his own. This is not to say that Ackerley was insincere; he was merely learning. But Forster remained wary for some time. 'It is difficult to make real intimacies at my age,' he complained, and he confessed in his diary in October 1923: 'I don't quite like A. though he has intelligence and charm. I suspect him of cruelty, but perhaps it's merely that I suspect all young men. I have no friend under thirty now.' Then he added, almost as a maternally prompted afterthought: 'Also I remember his ill bred ancestry.'

This is a reference to Ackerley's great-grandfather, William Aylward, whose marriage into Forster's family had caused a great scandal because he was *in trade*. The fact that he had twice been Mayor of Salisbury counted as nothing beside the social disgrace of his being proprietor of a music shop. The family connection was rather remote, in fact, for he had married (*en secondes noces*) 'Maimie' Synnot, the widow of a first cousin of Forster's father. In any case the marriage had been a success and Maimie, who was a close friend of Forster and his mother, had been forgiven. Indeed, Forster greeted the news that he and Ackerley were 'cousins' with great excitement, jocularly addressing the young man as 'Dear Cousin Joe'. Forster's mother, who had 'interviewed' the unfortunate Aylward on behalf of the clan and been impressed enough to promote the match against considerable opposition, appears to have been equally pleased. 'My mother liked your great-grandfather so much, I remember,' Forster told Ackerley, not entirely truthfully:[1] 'we often stopped at Holmleigh.' This was the Aylwards' house, usually pronounced by the Forsters as 'Olmleigh' in imitation of its aitch-dropping owner. In his 'Domestic Biography', *Marianne Thornton* (1956), Forster was to write that Aylward had 'a further claim on my gratitude for becoming, by his first wife, the great-grandfather of my friend Joe Ackerly.' This gracious tribute was spoiled by Forster's customary misspelling of Ackerley's name. 'I've often thought that the final "e" was quite unnecessary,' Ackerley remarked generously. Before long Forster had devised a form of address which the two men were to use, with variations, throughout their lives, a form Forster 'copyrighted' as 'Dear My© Joe'. Ackerley returned the compliment and most of his letters are addressed to 'D.M.M.', Dear (or Dearest) My Morgan.

---

[1] Mrs Forster disapproved of the match almost as much as her relations, but, in her son's words: 'If Maimie really wanted to marry him, she must; it was a mistake, but her mistake; nothing to do with her in-laws.'

Meanwhile Forster introduced Ackerley to his Bloomsbury friends, urging him to drop in on Leonard and Virginia Woolf who also lived at Richmond. He was very good at bullying Ackerley about his work and this was the push Ackerley needed. He rightly praised the 'Estlin' sketch as amusing and psychologically sound, but rather lacking in direction, and took a keen interest in *The Prisoners of War*, which he had been told by A. C. Benson was unpublishable because of its treatment of homosexuality. When he persuaded Ackerley to lend him the manuscript he was very impressed by the play, 'much moved and interested', and he gave encouragement and made suggestions as to how it might be improved, not all of them serious. (He imagined a version in which Grayle was 'converted . . . and assists Conrad to murder Mme Louis in a back bedroom, off'.) Forster's close friend, Goldsworthy Lowes Dickinson, a Fellow of King's College, Cambridge and writer on philosophical, social and political matters, was shown the play and asked for his comments, and further revisions were made.

Unfortunately Ackerley had been sidetracked from *The Prisoners of War* by the Sforza play. By June 1923 he had completed sixteen scenes, but was dissatisfied; a rape scene was causing him particular difficulties. He returned to *The Prisoners of War*, which he sent to the theatrical producer, Theodore Komisarjevsky, in August. It was returned promptly as insufficiently dramatic, a criticism Dickinson had also made. Ackerley fiddled at both plays, bored and depressed, resisting Forster's request to see *Girolamo*. Forster offered his own Balkan farrago, *The Heart of Bosnia*, in return, but Ackerley was still wary of showing unfinished work to anyone and prevaricated until he was saved by the Maharajah of Chhatarpur, who had overcome all his objections, and those of the Political Agent, and was ready to offer Ackerley the job of secretary for six months.

Forster was delighted and at once set about providing Ackerley with contacts and advice. With the relish of a nanny brought out of retirement, he instructed his young friend about bed-linen, underwear, medicines and inoculations. Dear Joe must remember to keep his stomach warm at all times and must be particularly careful to avoid snakes and the 'rapacious, detestable and incompetent' natives of Bombay. Indians, Forster said, did not mind being hated, but they could not bear to be despised: 'The manners of Anglo-Indians, which are still appalling, spring from contempt, and as long as it persists, everything goes wrong.' Armed with this advice, several letters of introduction, and a Hindustani phrasebook ('chiefly composed . . . of a translation from some poem by Kipling and part of the Lord's Prayer'), Ackerley set forth upon his long, arduous journey, stopping off in Venice where an encounter with a *ragazzo* provided him with material for a wistful story, never completed, in which the narrator falls for a boy prostitute, but fails to reform him by love.

From Venice he took the SS *Tevore* to Bombay. Amongst the crew of this ship was a young sailor called Giorgio with whom Ackerley rapidly made friends. Giorgio came from a well-to-do Italian family and had been at university, studying medicine, when his father had died unexpectedly. The family was left very badly off and Giorgio, the oldest of four children, had abandoned his education in order to support his mother and siblings. His father had been a *commandante* in the Lloyd Triestino service and Giorgio had hoped that this connection would help him rise quickly if he worked in shipping. Ackerley was much taken both by Giorgio and his story, gave him ten shillings to send to his mother and suggested they should meet up in Bombay, which they did, spending several nights together in Green's Hotel. They parted with promises to reunite in Turin the following autumn. When not occupied with Giorgio and writing his Venetian story, Ackerley went in search of the people Forster had urged him to see. Forster's friend, Syed Ross Masood,[1] was away, but his absence was more than compensated for by an ever-proliferating family called Tyabji, assorted members of which Ackerley met. He was taken sightseeing by them and they lent him their car.

The heat in Bombay was intense, the hotel expensive, his trousers had been scorched and his cufflinks stolen, so it was with some relief that Ackerley, 'almost penniless', boarded the train for Jhansi, travelling second class. The official at Cook's had suggested that in first class Ackerley would not have to travel with natives, a consideration which 'didn't weigh with me, of course,' he reported to his mother, very much the Forsterian, '– indeed I'd sooner travel with natives than Europeans'. In the event he had a compartment to himself, with two berths and its own lavatory, and so he spent the journey in some comfort, writing letters and preparing himself to meet his royal employer.

---

[1] The dedicatee of *A Passage to India*, Masood was the ward of Theodore Morison. Forster had been his tutor before the Great War and had fallen unrequitedly in love with him.

5

In the service of the Maharajah

CHHATARPUR, a minor Native State and part of the Bundelkhand in Central India, came into being in the latter part of the eighteenth century. It was founded by Kunwar Sone Shah Panwar, a relative of the Maharajah of Panna, who was confirmed as ruler by the British in 1806. On his death the State passed to his son, Raja Pratap Singh Bahadur. When, in 1854, Pratap Singh died without issue (poisoned by his own mother, according to Ackerley's employer), the State was forfeited to the British Government, which allowed his adopted son, Jagat Raj Bahadur, to reign 'in consideration of the loyalty and fidelity of the family'. In fact the State was administered by the late Pratap Singh's Rani, under British supervision, until Jagat Raj came of age on his twenty-fifth birthday in 1867. Almost immediately the new Raja died, leaving Ackerley's Maharajah, aged fourteen months, as his heir. The Dowager Rani once more took the reins of state, acting as Regent under British supervision. The little Maharajah was educated at the Raj-Kumar College at Nowgong and then privately by Theodore Morison. In 1884 he married the daughter of the Maharajah of Orchha and three years later he was given full powers of administration and the full title His Highness the Maharajah Vishwa Nath Singh Bahadur, entitled to a salute of eleven guns and a return visit by the Viceroy. His first wife died in 1921, without issue, but the year before he had taken a second wife, the daughter of a local Jagirdar, or landowner-administrator, who had borne him a son.

The State was low-lying and temperate, although in summer a hot wind dried most of the tributaries of the principal river, the Ken. Much had to be imported, and scarcities and famine visited the State, and indeed the whole of the Bundelkhand, every five or so years. There was no railway at Chhatarpur, because of inter-state rivalry, and the nearest a traveller could get to the capital by train was Harpalpur, some thirty-four miles away; the remainder of the journey was usually accomplished by tonga. The entire area was backward, but the Maharajah was unusual amongst the native rulers in being well educated and able to speak English. The affairs of state were overseen by the Dewan, or Prime Minister, Pandit Shukdeo Behari Misra MA, who made tours of inspection throughout the State, worked in an office at the palace and wrote an annual report for his ruler, compounded of optimism, flattery, mock-humility and pages of appendices devoted to tables explaining income, expenditure, law and order, and the like.

By the time Ackerley came to Chhatarpur, the Maharajah was a bent little figure of fifty-seven. Short, bow-legged and pug-nosed, his grotesque appearance was accentuated by a certain femininity of gesture and a taste for regal finery: embroidered frock-coats, extravagant hats and flashing jewels. He combined a considerable, if wayward, intellect with a deep-rooted superstition. Accounts of conversation with him give the impression of a demanding child, constantly demanding Why? Who? or How? His thirst for knowledge led him to a widely differing number of largely undifferentiated sources, for he was as anxious to discuss Marie Corelli as he was to discuss George Moore. He was far more interested in literature and philosophy than in the affairs of state and his reign was characterized by financial mismanagement and sexual misdemeanour, these two elements combining in the immensely expensive productions of Hindu plays written by himself and performed for his pleasure by an unruly company of boy actors. He was constantly at odds with the Political Agents, who could scarcely approve his extravagance, his morals, or such dynastic ambitions as marrying off his niece to a local Rajput chief who had taken his fancy, in the hope of enticing the man to his palace. His experience of both the English ruling caste and the internecine rivalries of Indian royalty had made the Maharajah very suspicious of any communication which took place in his absence or without his knowledge. In particular, he was convinced that 'matters of the greatest interest, diplomatic or scandalous, [were] discussed in any conversation, especially between Europeans, in which he [had] no part'. He imagined plots being hatched behind every screen, issued grave warnings about the danger of being poisoned by one's enemies, and kept a careful eye on the mail, often having letters opened before they left the palace to make sure that nobody was reporting upon his movements to the PA. When in 1921 one of the letters he sent to Forster at Dewas Senior went astray, he wrote in high dudgeon, regally issuing orders for punishments like the Queen of Hearts:

> Please get a thorough search made in the post office there [i.e. at Dewas] & get the post master punished for his carelessness – I am also following the same here. It is serious that letters are unsafe! It was never before so. What is the reason?

Ackerley was met at Jhansi by Captain Stoney of the Indian Medical Service who was acting as the Maharajah's envoy (and who appears with his wife as 'Captain and Mrs Montgomery' in Ackerley's account of his Indian jaunt, *Hindoo Holiday*). Accompanying him was one of His Highness's servants bearing a letter of welcome from the king. The journey continued to the terminus at Harpalpur, where 'an antique and dingy' Belsize car awaited him. The Kothi Palace Guest House was filled with Christmas visitors, and Ackerley was shown to the small two-room bungalow with a verandah where he was to live during his stay. It had a living-room and a bedroom, the latter almost entirely filled by a 'quadruple bed' which no mosquito-net would fit; the bathroom was situated in an outhouse. Ackerley was wearing his newly acquired biscuit-coloured suit, knowing that whoever greeted him at Jhansi would be asked by His Highness for a full report. Now he was intending to wash and change, but just as he was doing this a messenger arrived to announce the imminent arrival of the king.

> Had he teeth in your time? [Ackerley asked Forster] He has none now. He was clad in a round green velvet hat, thickly embroidered with gold; a kind of drab mauve tweed frock-coat with velveteen cuffs and collar of elephant grey, white linen trousers, purple socks of a vivid hue, and dancing pumps. He is now a sufferer from rheumatism (a favourite topic of conversation) and walks *péniblement*, his feet pointing one East, one West, like a decrepit man. But I do not think he is ugly – praps [sic] because I dislike misusing the word. If a pekinese is ugly; then also is the Maharajah. But he has a nice expression – childish – rather pathetic . . .

The similarity to a pekinese was emphasized when the Maharajah laughed and his tongue, stained nasturtium by betel-chewing, poked in and out of his mouth. His Highness was accompanied by his private secretary, an equally unprepossessing figure, fat and pockmarked, called Babu Gulab Rai (the 'Babaji Rao' of *Hindoo Holiday* and a distinguished Hindi writer). Almost immediately the Maharajah began questioning his guest about his reading. His Highness, somewhat sceptical about Hinduism's ability to assist him in his eternal quest to discover 'the ultimate meaning of meaning', was certain that Western philosophers possessed this knowledge. Impatient of the niceties of dialectic, His Highness wanted straight answers. Had Ackerley read the works of G. H. Lewes and Herbert Spencer? No? In that case he must do so at once: 'Spencer says there *is* a God, Lewes says no. So you must read them, Mr Ackerley, and tell me which of them is right.'

The following day a rather more temporal but nonetheless vital question preoccupied the king: what was he to wear for the Christmas Eve concert at Rajhagar? He wanted to look his best, but his finest clothes were rather flimsy. Unless he was to risk catching cold, he would have to wear an overcoat, which would spoil the effect. Could Mr Ackerley advise him? Perhaps Mrs Stoney, who was staying at the Guest House for Christmas, could help? Mrs Stoney pooh-poohed the Maharajah's fears for his health and was more concerned that his elaborate dresses should not clash with her own evening gown. The Secretary Sahib was despatched to fetch a selection of garments which were then displayed before the ladies, and so the afternoon passed in these sartorial arrangements.

Ackerley was not very impressed by his fellow guests, most of whom seemed to bear out Forster's strictures about the Anglo-Indians, that breed Forster was shortly to immortalize as the Chandrapore Club's 'Turtons and Burtons' in *A Passage to India*. One lady, the 'Miss Gibbins' of *Hindoo Holiday*, was indeed called Burton. A preposterous spinster who imagined herself emancipated, she once remarked: 'I only know one swear word, and I use it for all it's worth.' Ackerley did not find it easy to adapt to the social life of these people and had to be taken aside and lectured by Mrs Stoney because he had not immediately 'placed' himself with them by giving details of his background and education. Ackerley was so astonished by their conversation, which largely concerned dogs, hunting and the disgraceful manners of the natives, and which was liberally sprinkled with such Bright-

Young-Things adjectives as 'putrid' and 'lethal', that he spent much of his time surreptitiously scribbling on the backs of envelopes beneath the tea-table.

Christmas dinner was not a success. The unfortunate Gulab Rai had been delegated by His Highness to attend, no doubt to report back anything the guests might say, but since he was a devout Hindu he was unable to eat or drink with Christians and so sat there glumly, contributing one long anecdote which nobody appeared to understand. Matters were not improved by Mrs Stoney's determined attempts to enliven the proceedings with charades and a paper-chase. 'It was all pretty ghastly,' Ackerley noted in his diary.

A few days later the Political Agent arrived, earlier than expected and bringing with him his brother. Major D. G. Wilson was not a popular figure, for he was much feared by His Highness and for some reason despised by the Anglo-Indians: 'A horrid man and a fool,' was Mrs Stoney's verdict. The PA dumped his luggage and whisked some of the guests off on a hunt. News of his arrival reached the palace and His Highness was very alarmed, principally because he feared that Ackerley would have introduced himself and might have said something untoward. The king came rushing down to the Guest House and was greatly relieved that Wilson had not yet met his new 'secretary'. Ackerley was told that it would not be necessary to mention the fact that he was receiving a wage in addition to his passage and his board and lodging. The PA was constantly on the look-out for unnecessary expenditure and treated the king as a child who could not be trusted with much pocket-money. He was tactless, impatient and intolerant, and made no attempt to conceal the fact that he found the king boring and exasperating, even slipping away from social functions the moment the Maharajah was announced. He was supposed to act merely as an adviser, but as His Highness observed sadly: 'What sort of advice is that when I am obliged to take it?' Ackerley and Wilson did eventually sit next to each other at dinner, which was held after a ceremonial fireworks display, and got on surprisingly well. When Wilson left Ackerley was questioned closely by the suspicious Maharajah.

It soon became clear that Ackerley's duties were negligible. Apart from his Dewan and his private secretary, the Maharajah kept a large retinue of servants, apparently employing one man, a cousin, solely for the purpose of lighting cigarettes. Books were sent to Ackerley's bungalow, with instructions for him to read them and deliver his verdict. In order to stem the growth of this 'considerable and dismal library', which had been founded with a copy of Hall Caine's *Eternal City*, Ackerley pretended that he was more widely read than was in fact the case. He was also worried that His Highness would think him scarcely qualified for his duties if he admitted to never having read the eclectic books which formed the basis of the king's search for truth. His other principal job was to assist the Maharajah in composing letters to the Acting Governor General of the province. His Highness's innumerable titles, his picturesque state processions with umbrella, *Chour*, flag, coat-of-arms and heralds, his entitlement to gun-salutes and Viceregal tea-parties, all these were as nothing compared with the KCSI or KCIE he craved from the King Emperor, George V. No flattery was too egregious in the pursuit of this end and Ackerley's chief task was to eliminate from His Highness's letters whole paragraphs of praise for the personal attributes of the AGG and his equally illustrious wife. Privately Ackerley considered that the Maharajah was scarcely a suitable candidate for such honours, since he was 'an entirely medieval figure and cares not a fig for his subjects unless they are male, good-looking, and entertaining'.

Ackerley was also expected to accompany His Highness on car journeys in search of various animals which would bring good fortune. The Maharajah's superstition was tempered by pragmatism, for if a creature was encountered upon the 'wrong', ill-omened side of the road, His Highness would order the chauffeur to turn the car round so that the animal could be re-encountered on the 'right', well-favoured side. But the reason for his presence at Chhatarpur was best put by Ackerley himself in the touching 'Explanation' to *Hindoo Holiday*:

> He wanted someone to love him – His Highness, I mean; that was his real need, I think. He alleged other reasons, of course – an English private secretary, a tutor for his son; for he wasn't really a bit like the Roman Emperors, and he had to make excuses . . .
>
> He wanted a friend. He wanted understanding, and sympathy, and philosophic comfort; and he sent to England for them.

The post turned out to be less that of a 'secretary' than that of a paid companion of the sort bullied by grand old ladies at that period.

Ackerley's sexual credentials had already been established and the

Maharajah was keen to impress his secretary with his plays, and in particular with the 'Gods', as he dubbed the boy actors who performed them. Would Mr Ackerley agree that such-and-such a boy was really beautiful? Or did this one seem to him more appealing? His Highness's classical education had left him with a desire to Hellenize his kingdom. More like a child with a dolls' house than the hereditary ruler of some 167,000 souls, he envisaged a picturesque Greek state for his subjects in which they would stroll around in togas. He even commissioned an architect to design a classical temple which he hoped would be like the Parthenon, although he was not altogether clear what the Parthenon was.[1] On car journeys the passing landscape would put him in mind of pastoral eclogues: 'If there were Greeks and Romans on that,' he would remark wistfully of a grassy hill, 'I would play hide and go seek with them.'

Such innocent-seeming dreams were somewhat at odds with the sexual despotism which reigned in the palace. Ackerley had been particularly struck by a young 'valet' who waited upon the Maharajah, and told his employer that the boy was far more beautiful than any of the company of actors. This boy, the 'Sharma' of *Hindoo Holiday*, was called Rāghunāndi. He was attractive but unintelligent and had become the royal favourite. His Highness seemed to have little affection for the boy whose principal duty was to sodomize his master, an act he performed unwillingly and under the threat of beatings. Another service he was obliged to perform, one which indeed suggested the Roman emperors, was to have sex with the Rani whilst His Highness watched from a discreet distance. Since Rāghunāndi was the son of a barber and the member of a lowly caste, this liaison breached religious and social as well as sexual barriers. Worse still, there was some suggestion that Rāghunāndi was in fact the father of the Rani's two children, the young heir to the throne and his sister. There may well have been some truth in this allegation, for His Highness was not

---

[1] The Political Agent soon put a stop to this particular fantasy, suggesting that the money would be better spent on road-improvement schemes. This was merely the most grandiose and least practical of the many building projects under way at the time. His Highness was also busy constructing a shrine to his mother, a 'small compact building of red stone, with a central dome and four corner *chhatris*'. Unfortunately this was sited 'a few paces behind the monument to His Highness's wife, so close that neither shrine has any chance of effect'. The cost of erecting this shrine was Rs 21,635-8-7, some £1,422 at the 1924 exchange rate.

the most likely of procreators. At this time in India a man's sexual potency was deemed to have been exhausted by the time he was in his early forties; the king was fifty-seven ('and looks it', Ackerley noted). His shuffling gait and stooped posture were in fact less due to rheumatism than locomotor ataxia, a common symptom of advanced syphilis. Rumours that he was not the father of the heir to the throne may have had something to do with the repeated omission of the Maharajah's name from the Birthday Honours List, and the birth of a second child had fuelled speculation that someone else had fathered it. Ackerley noted that:

> Captain Drood, of the RAMC, is clearly though decently doubtful; but though he sometimes prescribes medicines for His Highness, he has never had an opportunity to examine him — and the little king will no doubt see to it that he never will have.
> Nor is His Highness likely to consult Captain Drood on a point which interests himself. An Indian doctor has told him, he says, that human semen is excellent for the voice, it makes it very sweet.

Ackerley's demands upon Rāghunāndi were rather more moderate, restricted to the occasional kiss and holding of hands. His Highness once remonstrated with Ackerley for attempting to kiss Rāghunāndi, and when Ackerley protested, 'I must kiss *somebody*!', the king merely giggled up his sleeve.

Rāghunāndi had a friend called Mahadeo Nayak, an altogether superior young man whom both Ackerley and His Highness also found attractive. The 'Narayan' of *Hindoo Holiday*, he was employed as Clerk of the Guest House, and soon became devoted to Ackerley, spending much time loitering outside the bungalow, accompanied by Rāghunāndi, whom he treated with affectionate condescension. Like his friend, Mahadeo was subjected to the Maharajah's sexual demands, but he was not prepared to submit to the royal blandishments and thus made himself unpopular. If he would not have sex with the king, perhaps he would order Rāghunāndi to do so and witness the proceedings? Mahadeo remained obdurate and Ackerley was frequently obliged to defend the young Indian against trumped-up charges and other marks of royal disfavour.

Although he disapproved of homosexuality (and indeed both he and Rāghunāndi were married), Mahadeo was sufficiently besotted with

Ackerley to put up with some gentle wooing. He was an exceedingly graceful boy, both in appearance and manner, and his behaviour did much to encourage Ackerley. When he made some foolish remark and Ackerley called him a *bēwākūf* or 'fool' ('more for the pleasure of pronouncing a newly learnt Indian word than with the intention of rebuking him'), Mahadeo was deeply upset. 'Now I have much sorrow,' he said, 'now I do not speak again unless you ask me questions, until you say I am good boy, your lover boy.' He even permitted Ackerley to kiss him on the mouth in spite of a religious horror of the lips of a meat-eater. It may well have been that Ackerley, disillusioned by the easy but unsatisfactory assignations he had made in England and Europe, found such relationships refreshing.

> I like to see the men and boys holding hands as they walk along, or with their arms about each other's shoulders. I have seen it too in Egypt and other Mediterranean countries. But how 'unmanly' the English would think it – if not worse! Oh, the English! the English! And even more so, the Scotch! Outside the Delhi walls yesterday I saw two workmen following their carts, walking together with their hands lightly linked. Oh, the English! What a rubbishy lot!

If he had sexual relations whilst in India, he left no record of the fact.

Devotion of a less welcome kind was exercised by 'the insupportable Habib', a gormless child who attached himself to Ackerley as a personal servant.

> I didn't engage him [Ackerley wrote in *Hindoo Holiday*]. I didn't want him. And I don't know whether he just took me over of his own accord, or was detailed to do so, or, being denser than the other dozen or so servants, was left behind by them as a piece of wood is left by an ebbing tide upon the shore, in their languid withdrawal, after the first fuss and excitement of my arrival had subsided.

'A small, dusky boy of about twelve, with thick brown lips, eyes like wet toffee, and very dirty feet', Habib was a constant and irritating presence. Even worse was the man appointed as Ackerley's tutor in Hindustani, a twenty-two-year-old Muhammadan called Abdul Haq. Preoccupied with his Venetian story, the Tyabji family and Giorgio,

74

Ackerley had had little time during the journey to Chhatarpur to learn the language, and now welcomed the opportunity to do so. However, becoming Ackerley's tutor was little more than a stepping-stone in Abdul's scheme of self-advancement. A Muhammadan in a Hindu state, he used his acquaintance with Ackerley to demonstrate to anyone who would take notice that he was a person of substance. Not satisfied to have the Sahib simply as a pupil, he insisted that Ackerley should be his friend. He used all his powers of emotional blackmail to get Ackerley to accept invitations to his house, and attempted to persuade his pupil to influence the Maharajah and get him a better job.

Ackerley resisted, for he found Abdul an intolerable bore, 'stiff, self-conscious, humourless.' He paid one visit to Abdul's house, finding his room 'very like his mind, small, mean, tidy, uncomfortable, and full of rubbishy things'. In desperation Ackerley attempted to dismiss his tutor, but without success, for Abdul kept coming back, insisting that no payment would be expected. Apart from the sort of phrases to do with sex that all schoolboys want to learn and with which Abdul had hoped to ingratiate himself with his pupil, it seems that Ackerley acquired very little Hindustani during his lessons. He had hoped to be able to converse with the boys who, drawn there by curiosity, came and sat outside his bungalow, but feared that he never would with Abdul for a teacher.

His Highness's terror of spies was perhaps justified, since Ackerley spent much of his time observing life at the court and noting it down in his diary. He also sent long and vivid letters to England. One of these, describing the celebrations surrounding the birth of His Highness's daughter, had so impressed Theodore Morison that he had asked Roger for permission to broadcast extracts on the Newcastle 'Ladies' Hour'. Others were less suitable for transmission. It must be assumed that those written to Forster escaped the palace censor, for they were crammed with highly scabrous accounts of the Maharajah's sexual antics. Forster was much amused by what he called the 'crafty-ebbing' details, but was also impressed by Ackerley's observations upon other matters:

You sound awfully understanding of those people: indeed your letters are all those of one who has lived in the country for years; not Anglo Indian years, but the years of reality that seldom get lived anywhere and scarcely ever in India.

He also claimed that Ackerley's letters 'were a godsend to my etiolated novel [*A Passage to India*]. I copied in passages and it became ripe for publication promptly.'

In March Ackerley persuaded His Highness to allow him some time off to travel, and he visited Delhi, Agra, Jaipur and Gwalior. At St John's College in Agra he visited Gulab Rai's brother. The students had hung a banner out of a window inscribed with the word 'Welcome'. Once inside Ackerley was obliged to answer some searching questions about how Indian students would be treated if they came to an English university. (Not well, he thought.) In Jaipur he was serenaded during dinner by one of the court musicians who sat on a verandah playing 'Yip-i-addy-i-ay' in the mistaken belief that this would impress and please a Western guest. Elsewhere time seemed to have stopped, and he was deeply moved by the beauty of the landscape, its buildings and the people who appeared in it:

> In Fatehpur Sikri I drew into the shadow of the Elephant Gate, as the sun rose, to watch a man pass. I didn't want to break the spell. I was there all alone, until this man suddenly appeared on a horse beneath the walls, at the bottom of the slope by the Karawan Sarai, and came riding up the rough, cobbled, weedy approach to the gate – a beautiful steep road three hundred and fifty years old and for three hundred years almost unused. The rider was a peasant boy. He rode a brown horse and wore a long cloak of the brightest blue which draped his shoulder and his horse's rump, brilliant against the red sandstone of the deserted town. He passed without seeing me, going perhaps from one village to another along this ancient road. He and I were the only people in this great empty town which Akbar built in 1569 and which was then abandoned forever with all its great palaces and mosques, courts and terraces, fifty years later – and only I was an anachronism. Time had stood still in India, it seemed to me, and this boy on his horse in his flowing bright blue cloak was one of Akbar's men returning home.

Naturally, it was the boys and young men who most held his attention, but he was also delighted by the wildlife, in particular the buffaloes:

> There is something very ecclesiastical about the appearance of the buffaloes. The thatch of glossy black hair, often parted in the

middle, between the laid-back horns, and their rather foolish expressions of mild disapproval always puts me in mind of clergymen. The young ones have an eggy look as though they had been hatched.

There was a herd of them at the Shah Tank outside the Amjer Gate this evening and a lot of beautiful bullocks and cows. Many of the buffaloes had advanced into the middle of the shallow tank and were lying there immersed in the cool water, while the bullocks stood about round the rim, pale and statuesque, motionless, some of them garlanded with necklaces of pink flowers. It was a lovely scene.

Other scenes were less attractive, particularly to someone as fastidious as the young Ackerley. In Delhi he saw a female sweeper going to work in front of a sweetmeat shop:

> It was in a poor, squalid quarter of the city, and the sweets, which can be attractive in India, were already positively disgusting to look at, slabs and balls of some grey, greasy, dough-like substance, piled up on dirty shelves in the interior of the shop and swarming with flies. The sweeper swept. She swept lustily, right into the shop. Clouds of dust filled the air and the shop itself was momentarily invisible. When the dust subsided, there was the proprietor, still squatting on his ledge, puffing at his hookah, not in the least disturbed.

Once the novelty had worn off, he also became disenchanted with many of the Hindu customs, 'all this preserved fruit' which governed everyone's life. It seemed absurd that a Hindu went through all manner of ceremonial ablutions, recoiled from physical intimacy with non-Hindus and would not eat at the same table as a meat-eater, and yet patronized food shops buzzing with flies and smothered in the filthy dust from the streets.

> What does my friend, the Dewan, think of all that, I wonder with his squeamishness about dirt and germs, his disgust with other people's mouths, his dread of sputum in the tea-cup, his repugnance to the kiss upon the lips? With all his shrill prejudices against European customs, how does he fare in his own land? Indians are great expectorators. Hawked-up phlegm, streams of red betel-juice

saliva, are shot about incessantly as they walk . . . And there the sweepers were in Delhi churning it about, whirling it all up in one's face, the dried sputum in the dust, anonymous coughings; one could not help but have it in one's nose, in one's mouth. Give me the unhygienic customs of Europe! Give me the loving-cup! Give me the kiss!

He suspected that many of the religious rites and observances were practised more from a sense of social duty than from any profound belief. 'His Highness observes and disbelieves in them all,' he noted. Social customs began to look like so much 'faded red tape'.

Perhaps they think it makes them more interesting to tourist and anthropologist, and I do see that, as a subject race, they are in need of self-esteem. But irritated by so much traditional rubbish, for which the dustman should have called long ago, I find myself regarding it with scepticism . . .

However, attention and sympathy are at once unwittingly re-stored by the Dewan, who mentions another custom with which I am less disposed to find fault. When a young Hindu boy is fond of another, he says to the parents of his friend:

'Give him to me. I want him for my brother.'

'Take him,' the parents reply, if they approve of the applicant. 'We give him to you.'

Nonetheless, such customs did not apply to visiting foreigners, and Ackerley's stay was drawing to its close. In spite of the blandishments of His Highness (' "If I give you land," he cried, "will you come with all your family and live here?" ') and the tears and lamentations of Rāghunāndi and Mahadeo, Ackerley announced that he would be returning to England in May. Now that Ackerley was determined to leave, His Highness was determined that he should stay. At times he had appeared bored with Ackerley, giving the impression that their meetings and excursions were keeping him from more important and interesting things, such as the 'Gods' and his innumerable and ruin-ously expensive building projects. However, the poor Maharajah had been dealt a sad blow by the death of Marie Corelli, and now began thinking up excuses to keep Ackerley in India. He needed a biographer, he claimed, a biographer whom he could trust.

'I will not leave you, Mr Ackerley,' he said; 'I will not leave you now. How can I keep you with me? Will it be possible for you to come back every year for six months? I will pay your passage money and give you a thousand rupees a month. Will it be enough? And I will give you a bond binding my son also to keep you in a sum of money all your life.'

Ackerley remained obdurate. Much as he had enjoyed his stay, five months had been enough. He had grown weary of the 'endless little mummified items of ceremony and procedure and social custom', and told Forster that he wanted 'to get back to reason and will power and stout common sense'. However, as soon as he boarded the SS *Aquileja* in Bombay he was brutally reminded that England was not always a repository of such virtues.

The man in my cabin said he was vastly relieved to find that I wasn't a 'Dago' or 'Babu'. The blasted passenger list was stiff with them, he said; nothing but 'Dagos'. It was bad enough to have had to live and work among them for five years, without finding them over-running the ship that was taking one home on leave.

I did not say anything; but wondered why he had chosen an Italian steamer instead of a P & O, where the Company understands and sympathizes with the Englishman's abhorrence of his Indian subjects, segregates the latter at meals at a table by themselves, and would never dare to put an Indian into a white man's cabin.

6

Theatricals

BACK in England, Ackerley attempted to make good the inefficiencies of Abdul Haq and continued with his Hindustani studies. He thought that he might apply for a job with the Bombay Education Service. This arose less from a sense of missionary zeal than from the feeling that he had returned from his trip merely to fall back into the rut he had been trying to escape. Forster was determined that his original plan in sending his friend to Chhatarpur should not be thwarted by enervation and insisted that Ackerley should submit to him all his diaries and letters. 'Morgan was already my mentor,' Ackerley noted, 'and had upon me the effect of keeping me up to the mark and making me feel that I had a best and should look to it.' Forster, who had a truffle-hound's nose for indelicacies in the works of others less reserved than himself, complained about erasures in the manuscript of Ackerley's diary, but was assured that only passages which the author had considered jejune or showed his own character in a bad light, had been obliterated. Forster pronounced the journal 'a great work', but Ackerley was determined to submit the manuscript to considerable revision and the scrutiny of others before offering it to a publisher.

His days of independence seemed to have come to an end, for he was once more installed in the family home, shut away in his room, where he spent most of July unproductively tinkering with his unfinished plays. He was also distracted by thoughts of his sailor friend, Giorgio, with whom he had kept in touch by letter, although he must have realized that there was little future in such an affair. He had a brief fling with his dentist and went to visit Edward Carpenter in Sheffield, an

80

almost obligatory pilgrimage for homosexual literary types at that period.

An interview with the Director of Bombay Education proved inconclusive, but in the summer of 1924 his literary fortunes began to improve. Although critical of the scene in *The Prisoners of War* in which Conrad has an epileptic fit, Colleer Abbott had offered to approach his own publishers, Chatto and Windus, on Ackerley's behalf with a view to their publishing the as yet unperformed and seemingly unperformable text of the play. Ackerley agreed about the fit, but felt unable to do anything about it. He promised to put the finishing touches to the play and he sent it off on 9 July. To his astonishment and delight Charles Prentice, senior partner of Chatto and Windus, replied within the month, accepting the book for publication. Having checked with Abbott that he was being offered standard terms, he accepted, regarding the publication as a reward for his father's patient indulgence.

Ackerley was extremely fortunate to find an editor like Prentice, who numbered Norman Douglas, Aldous Huxley, Richard Aldington, Lytton Strachey and Wyndham Lewis amongst his authors. Prentice, who designed all the firm's books, managed to perform a remarkable balancing act between generosity and financial prudence, earning the love of his authors whilst maintaining the respect of his colleagues. His passion was for all things Greek – he had studied classics at Oxford – but he was also prepared to take a risk on modern and controversial authors, as his impressive list shows. He was a genuine patron, who not only commissioned difficult and financially unrewarding books because he admired them, but also had paintings by Wyndham Lewis on his walls. He rarely pressed his authors when the delivery of a manuscript was delayed, preferring that a book should be absolutely right than be on time. Invariably described as Pickwickian, he led a solitary but comfortable bachelor's existence in Kensington, and he and Ackerley soon became friends.

Prentice personally liked *The Prisoners of War* and encouraged Ackerley to continue in his attempts to find a manager willing to mount a production. Ackerley took the play to the London Play Company, but Aubrey Blackburn, who ran the agency, was away and the manuscript had to be left with a reader. This woman's report was both frank and pessimistic in the extreme. She told Ackerley that the play was unrelievedly gloomy, without the slightest glimmer of humour; that it was pathological and undramatic; and that every character was either neurotic or unpleasant. She did concede that the play could be improved if Ackerley brought in the Armistice at the end – 'an obvious solution which really hadn't occurred to me,' Ackerley remarked sardonically. She would, however, keep the manuscript for Blackburn himself to read. This turned out to be no more than a stay of execution, for Blackburn approved and indeed amplified his assistant's remarks. He admitted that the play was remarkable, but said that it was without commercial possibilities.

The enormous interest in the war, which was to produce a plethora of memoirs, novels, plays and collections of poetry, had not yet started. People were still attempting to forget its horrors and such reminiscences as there were tended to be gently elegiac rather than bitterly critical, as they would eventually be by the end of the decade. It was to be another four years before the 'first' war play, R. C. Sherriff's record-breaking *Journey's End*, was produced. One of the reasons Blackburn gave for rejecting *The Prisoners of War* was that the play lacked 'feminine interest'. When Ackerley complained to his parents about this, Roger appeared to be much amused, glancing up briefly from the *Evening Standard* to suggest that such a remark would puzzle his son. Ackerley seemed to think this a good anecdote, but failed to recognize its significance. There is little doubt that Roger was perfectly aware of his son's sexual proclivities.

Ackerley was bitterly disappointed by Blackburn's verdict and went to spend some time in Ilfracombe, working on the intractable *Girolamo*. He was making little progress with the play and, as usual, blamed this on the stultifying atmosphere at Blenheim House, which involved him in elaborate ploys whenever he wanted to be alone or seek company. Colleer Abbott was frequently used as his 'Bunbury'. Ackerley was twenty-seven years old and it was high time he left home; he began looking for rooms in central London. It had become clear by now that he would not be returning to India. Not even a heartfelt letter from Chhatarpur persuaded him:

Sorry.
My dear Sahib,
    I am extremely sorry to write you that your beautiful *bachcha* [baby; i.e. Rāghunāndi] after the serious illness of two month lost his breath 12 October. He was suffering by thysis. At first he was

under Treatment of Doctor and after that of Vaid Raj. No doubt his death is always piercing and pinching my poor heart.

May God rest his gentle soul.

Oh! my dear sahib *now I am alone* in this world (or in Bundelkhand, Chhatarpur). I have nothing; and I have no lovely friend except *you*. So you are not here, what can I do. Now I am in *Great trouble* or (in danger). I have nobody to love me. If you love me *you must come here. I want to cry to meet you with both hands in your neck.*

My hand was could not write you this sorryful letter. Why I always write you pleaserful letter. How can I write you such . . . letter.

Now I want to finish my letter. Now I am crying.

I am your unfortunate and
Bad luck
Mahadeo Nayak.

At the beginning of September he found new accommodation at 76 Charlotte Street, behind the Tottenham Court Road. The flat had an impressive Bohemian pedigree, for Augustus John had lived in (and been evicted from) it before the Great War, and earlier still John Constable had been a tenant. Apart from a gas-stove and some ancient linoleum, it was unfurnished and consisted of two rooms, one of them a spacious studio. It was perfectly situated, with a brothel in the flat above and a church next door, and the rent was thirty shillings a week. Ackerley was triumphant, and celebrated by looking up accounts of Constable's life, which, he heard, had been promisingly disreputable,[1] and by buying a table and chair and inviting Charles Prentice to tea.

Another visitor was E. M. Forster, who was embroiled in a complicated and clandestine romance. Whilst he and his mother were preparing for the move from Weybridge to their new home, West Hackhurst at Abinger Hammer, Forster had met and befriended a bus-driver called Arthur Barnet. He was married and had a child, but seemed very friendly and Forster had thought the relationship worth pursuing. Arthur would visit the Forsters' Weybridge house — for French lessons, Forster's mother was informed. To Forster's surprised

---

[1] This was based upon a misconception, perhaps upon the case of some brothel-keepers in the 1820s who ran premises opposite. Constable had been shocked by this and had brought a successful prosecution to have the establishment closed.

delight, the friendship had developed and been consummated one day whilst Mrs Forster was out of the way at Abinger. It was clear that this highly enjoyable affair could not last, since Arthur's wife, Madge, although unaware of the nature of the friendship, was jealous. Forster had no wish to cause problems in the Barnets' marriage and so gradually, but reluctantly, disengaged himself, thus remaining friends with the family. Forster had chosen Ackerley to be his confidant in these fraught and painful manoeuvres: 'It may cause him to despise me,' he wrote in his diary, but such fears were groundless.

A further complication in Ackerley's own affairs had arisen during the summer. Forster had taken him to dinner at Edward Arnold's house, with some idea that the publisher could help Ackerley to join the Indian Education Service. Although the dinner was informal, Ackerley arrived in immaculate evening dress and made a great impression upon a fellow-guest, Goldsworthy Lowes Dickinson. Dickinson had already been struck by Ackerley's looks when he saw *Troilus and Cressida* at Cambridge, and the young man cut as glamorous a figure in a dinner jacket as he had done in Greek armour. Ackerley was resisting Arnold's attempts to renew his interest in India and happened to glance across at Dickinson and smile in complicity. 'He had a lovely smile,' Dickinson confided to his diary. 'His whole face shines. Something passed to me.'

They arranged to lunch the following day in Pall Mall and were so engrossed in conversation, which largely concerned what Dickinson termed '"the" subject', that they sat there into the afternoon. Dickinson then went to Northumberland for the summer to stay with one of his sisters, although the two men met again at West Hackhurst during the August bank holiday. When Dickinson returned to town in the autumn, he visited Charlotte Street and Ackerley paid a return visit to Dickinson's home in Hanover Terrace. In November Ackerley went to Cambridge and stayed with Dickinson at King's, claiming that he enjoyed the town as he never had when an undergraduate. At the end of the visit he kissed his host in affectionate gratitude. 'His kiss finished the business,' Dickinson wrote, 'and since he left, a week ago, I have not been able to get him out of my mind.'

This was no new sensation for Dickinson, but it was one invariably hedged about by guilt and frustration, since the objects of his desire had previously always been heterosexual. They might link arms on walks, might permit an embrace, even a kiss, but they gradually disengaged themselves as they acquired wives and children. Forster was very good at adapting to such circumstances, but Dickinson was less successful, and his affairs were obsessive and torturing. Ackerley was not one of Dickinson's great loves; of these there were five: Roger Fry, Ferdinand Schiller, Oscar Eckhard, Peter Savary and Dennis Proctor. The first two relationships had been with contemporaries, the next two with men much younger. Dickinson had met Savary during the Great War when the latter was a schoolboy of sixteen. They had kept in touch and in the spring of 1922 Savary had contracted influenza and Dickinson had taken him to the Isle of Wight to convalesce. Dickinson confessed his love and Savary had allowed the occasional kiss and embrace, but no more. The following year Savary had gone to the French Alps as a tourist guide, and Dickinson, who had been at the League of Nations in nearby Geneva, joined him for a fortnight's holiday. '61', he noted in a birthday diary entry, 'older, but it seems not wiser'. He later wrote of the holiday: 'Excitement, worry, delight, peace, torment, and all the rest of it.' There was clearly no future in such a relationship, apart from a paternal friendship.

With Ackerley, although there was an equally large difference in age, the case was different. He was at least homosexual and Dickinson, in spite of his customary pessimism about such relationships, may have felt that for once there would be a chance of reciprocation. Forster, to whom Dickinson wrote after Ackerley's Cambridge visit, was not encouraging:

My Dear Goldie,

Have received your letter and like answering it. I *acknowledge* the charm yet don't exactly *bow*, so that it is possible I may help you. I know that he likes you very much – he said so – and though I have not seen him since he stayed with you, a letter I have suggests no change. Yes, indeed, I will be awfully careful in all shades of the word. What I think about his character is this: kindness as well as curiosity – I thought once it was only curiosity, but I am wrong. The drawback, both for himself and others, is that when he makes a gesture of encouragement, he is sometimes scared when it is responded to. The nervous reaction goes wrong. On this account one has to be rather careful, and I also think it accounts for him having had less than what seems obvious in the way of happiness.

He has never done to me what you mention as occurring at the end of his visit. I did it – sketchily – once to him, and did not think I had been wise. He wrote afterwards to me about the contrast in his mind between the 'embodied' and the 'disembodied', myself clearly belonging to the latter.

I hope the above is plain. No mysteries are concealed in my words, yet it is not quite convenient to write straight out. I have burnt your letter. No more for the present. I have to take my mother out and wish to catch the post. With love, also hopefulness,

Morgan.

Ackerley may not have ranked with the five men of Dickinson's *Autobiography*,[1] but there is no doubt that this new friendship affected the older man profoundly:

He has upset the structure I was living in [Dickinson wrote in his diary, 23 November 1924], and revived the mood of thirty years ago, with Ferdinand, but, rather oddly, not the mood I had so distressingly with Oscar. I read and re-read my own poems, because they seem once more to express what I am feeling. I have also given them to him ... I am rather afraid about this business, for a relationship with passion on one side and not on the other has always been my trouble; and Joe, of course, could not have passion, nor what one calls 'love', for me. One can but 'wait and see'. Joe is kind and without any conventional fears or restraints. Since he is so handsome and so attractive, he ought to be happy, but he is not. He has not found the response one would think it would be easy for him to find.

One would suppose that at my age, this kind of thing would not happen; and one might hope that, at least, one could not behave stupidly. But alas! I don't trust myself, even now.

[1] His two typescript notes concerning Ackerley may have been intended as part of the *Autobiography*. Dickinson's typing was notoriously bad, so much so that his typescript is frequently as problematical to decipher as his handwriting; but the typing of these pages is good enough to suggest that he had carefully copied them from an original manuscript note. As his literary executor, Forster inherited all Dickinson's papers and it seems clear that he passed on these pages, along with a letter of Ackerley's that Dickinson had kept and annotated, to Ackerley. Detached from the (in any case dismembered) body of Dickinson's 'Recollections', they passed with assorted other papers to the University of Texas, and so were not amongst the manuscripts from which Sir Dennis Proctor put together Dickinson's *Autobiography*.

Quite apart from being physically extremely attractive, Ackerley was also a charmer, and his genuine 'curiosity and kindness', allied to a propensity for flattery, often led people to imagine that he cared for them more deeply than he did. Some people thought that his charm was unconscious, as much a part of him, and as inescapable (both for Ackerley and his admirers) as his fair hair and his piercingly sympathetic blue eyes. Others suspected that he was unable to resist exercising this charm, fascinated by the effect it had. This was partly true, for there was a distinct and conscious streak of narcissism in his character. But the exercise of charm was also his way of compensating for a basic insecurity, one which had increased after he had met Forster and begun mixing in intellectual and literary circles.

> I have often been called a diffident man; I am not sure what 'diffident' means, but I doubt if it is quite the right word. 'Modest' is certainly unsuitable. Modesty, I take it, need not lack self-confidence but, out of deference or politeness, does not push forward. I had little, if any, confidence in myself, rather a sense of inadequacy, my 'diffidence' was nervousness or fear, the fear of giving myself away, of being caught out or seen through. It seems to me, looking back, that I was always pretending, especially to my friends who were far cleverer, better read, in their various ways more brilliant, than I – pretending to be different from what I was, more like them or as they believed me to be, more thoughtful, intelligent, attentive, better educated, more interesting, considerate, affectionate. I was generally liked and I wanted to be liked, it may be true to say that I was afraid of *not* being liked. Probably it is for this reason that I was very susceptible to criticism.

Ackerley used charm as a pre-emptive strike, disarming potential critics and getting away with remarks and opinions which in other circumstances might have caused grave offence. Few people could resist this onslaught, as he well knew, and many of them gladly surrendered, only to find that their victor had marched onwards in search of other conquests. 'I fear that in my life I have disappointed a great many people,' he confessed; 'having been attractive there were more to disappoint than would otherwise have been the case.' Amongst the disappointed was Dickinson. As Ackerley explained to James Kirkup in 1963: 'I had to disengage myself from an emotional relationship I did not want. He managed to sublimate it, as he sublimated all his unreciprocated passions.' Dickinson recognized the signs, and bowed to them gracefully, contenting himself with taking a friendly interest in his young friend's literary endeavours. He was very impressed with Ackerley's Indian journal, but felt unable to judge it objectively because of 'the peculiar interest I take in [its author], and also in Chhatarpur' (which he had visited with Forster in 1912).

Dickinson was also very interested in *The Prisoners of War*. By now the proofs had arrived and thrown Ackerley into a panic. Whilst the ending was better than he had remembered, the first scene of Act Three, in which the sympathetic Englishwoman, Mrs Prendergast, attempts to console Conrad for the defection of Grayle, and which ends with Conrad's problematical fit, seemed impossibly bad. Roger had offered to read the play for proof-errors, but Ackerley disagreed with all his father's corrections. Friends were asked for their opinions and eventually the proofs were returned to the publishers.

Meanwhile the Hampstead Everyman had turned down the play, but Geoffrey Whitworth, a theatre critic, founder and Director of the British Drama League, and art editor at Chatto and Windus, suggested that the script should be shown to his wife, Phyllis, who ran a private theatre club. The aim of Mrs Whitworth's Three Hundred Club was to put on plays which, because of a difficult theme or lack of popular appeal, could find no commercial backing, all of which applied to *The Prisoners of War*. This may have seemed something of a last resort, for Ackerley insisted that the play should be shown to the Stage Society first, which it was, without success. Mrs Whitworth invited him to tea and told him that she was very impressed by the play and that she wanted it to form part of the Club's new season at the Court Theatre. Ackerley had slight reservations – Mrs Whitworth thought equally well of *Guilty Souls* by Robert Nichols – but accepted her offer, and Chatto and Windus decided to postpone publication of the text so that it would coincide with the opening in March 1925.

Encouraged by this success, and by a visit to London Zoo where he was reminded of the face of Girolamo's father by the eagles, Ackerley returned to his Sforza play with renewed but short-lived confidence. He was by now on the twentieth draft and the whole thing seemed to be getting sillier and sillier, opening with the young conspirators up on the scaffolding of Milan Cathedral. He realized that, for all his time in Italy, he was really grossly ignorant about the background of the play.

The entire project had begun to bore him. However, thoughts of Italy reminded him of his Italian sailor, Giorgio, with whom he had continued to correspond, and it occurred to him that he might escape to Turin for their planned reunion. He dithered for a while until, stung by Forster who penetratingly suggested that Ackerley was 'scared or bored by response' in his affairs, he decided to take a chance.

This was to be the cause of the sort of hopeless muddle into which Ackerley's love-affairs invariably tumbled. He did not want to tell his family where he was going, and therefore asked Forster to be his Bunbury. Forster had been uncomfortable about deceiving his own mother about his affair with Arthur Barnet, but after his little lecture and Ackerley's good offices over that episode, he was in no position to refuse, and so reluctantly agreed to cover up for his friend. All would have been well had not Roger suffered a serious heart attack whilst his son was absent. In a surprising display of medical proficiency, Dr Wadd had saved Roger's life by rushing in from next door with a syringeful of digitalis which he jabbed into a vein in Roger's hand, raising a large lump which never subsided. Netta sent a wire to Weybridge and Forster decided that the only thing to do was to go to Richmond and admit to the deception. Another wire was then sent to Turin, but by this time Ackerley had remembered that his twenty-eighth birthday was due and that attempts would be made by his parents to contact him at Weybridge, and so he was already on his way home. He was therefore totally unprepared for the scenes that greeted his return, and in the ensuing confusion gave the game away to Roger, who had been kept in the dark about his son's whereabouts. Ackerley, 'perhaps through some guilty need to confess', attempted to tell his father where he had been, but Roger, not liking the sound of this preamble, said: 'It's all right old boy. I prefer not to know. So long as you enjoyed yourself, that's the main thing.'

In December 1924 Ackerley went with Dickinson to see the opening play in the Three Hundred Club's season, and was alarmed to find that it was very poorly produced. Furthermore, Mrs Whitworth's assertion that the play was about jealousy turned out to be something of a misconception: quite clearly the theme was sadism. Ackerley reflected that if the first play was sadistic, the second (W. J. Turner's *Smaragda's Love*) androgynous, and the third (his own play) homosexual, then Mrs Whitworth was certainly breaking new ground; but he also wondered whether this was by accident rather than design.

His suspicions were confirmed in January when Mrs Whitworth summoned him to a meeting. Word had come to her that *The Prisoners of War* was being talked about in London clubs as 'the new homosexual play'. As a consequence she had been inundated with requests for tickets from unknown people. She had reread the play and realized that it was open to misconstruction, and so wondered whether cuts could be made to avoid this. In particular she wanted revisions of the scene when Conrad strokes Grayle's head, provoking the cry: 'Look out! Someone might come in!' Mrs Whitworth thought that both Conrad's gesture and Grayle's response would be better omitted and she was sure that Ackerley would agree. Ackerley did not. He told her that the whole point of the play was that Conrad was in love with Grayle, an announcement which caused pandemonium. In that case, the gesture would certainly have to go, and perhaps the play should be submitted to the censor; Mrs Whitworth was convinced that she would end up in gaol.

Ackerley stood firm against the cut, especially when Mrs Whitworth made an ill-judged appeal to his chivalry. She explained that the majority of her subscribers were women, and whilst a man might tolerate the suggestion of homosexuality, a woman could not, for it struck at her very being. This was not an argument Ackerley found persuasive. He insisted that since Mrs Whitworth had read the play several times without recognizing its homosexual element until someone pointed it out to her, then it was safe to assume that her lady subscribers would be similarly insulated by their innocence. Ackerley's old Marlowe Society friend Frank Birch, who had been engaged as producer, undertook to discuss the matter with Ackerley and, although somewhat concerned for the effect such a production might have upon the morals of her seventeen-year-old Etonian son, Mrs Whitworth was pacified. The production was to be delayed until the summer, when Birch would be free.

Chatto and Windus could not rearrange their schedule and so *The Prisoners of War* was published as planned on 26 March 1925. It was dedicated 'To My Father', not merely in acknowledgement of Roger's financial support over the years, but also perhaps as a sort of recompense for the death of Peter. Roger, clearly moved after reading it, had said: 'Anyone should be proud to have written it.' Ackerley was delighted with the book, particularly the Chatto and Windus colophon of two cupids, which he thought very appropriate. The book was well reviewed, although many people regarded it as 'morbid'. The character of Conrad struck an immediate chord with one of the play's readers. Siegfried Sassoon had none of Mrs Whitworth's hesitation in recognizing Conrad as 'a tormented homosexual officer', whose experiences were similar to his own during the war:

> I so seldom read anything remotely connected with 'the subject nearest my heart' that almost any work of that kind causes a peculiar emotional disturbance in me. And all to-day I have carried about with me an inward sense of home-sickness for that land where I would be – that Elysium, forever deluding me with its mirage in the desert of my frustrated and distorted desires.

Meanwhile, whilst hanging around the Court Theatre attending rehearsals of *Smaragda's Love*, Ackerley had been spotted by a producer, who thought that his profile would look well in a production of Shaw's *Caesar and Cleopatra* to be mounted at the Aldwych Theatre. He duly appeared in a walk-on part, making as great an impression as he had as Achilles in Cambridge.

It was during this period that Ackerley met the 'good-natured normal Richmond tradesboy' mentioned in *My Father and Myself*.[1] They met when the boy delivered groceries to Blenheim House; his name was Jack Jones and he was Ackerley's entrée into working-class life.

Many of Ackerley's homosexual friends suffered from what Quentin Crisp memorably diagnosed as 'the Cophetua complex'. Middle-class themselves, they were attracted almost exclusively to working-class men, a phenomenon which was and is widespread. What had shocked people as much as anything at the Wilde trials, which took place the year before Ackerley was born, was that the playwright had transgressed social as well as sexual codes. A friendship with a young aristocrat like Lord Alfred Douglas was explicable, but Wilde's association with members of the working classes was seen as extremely suspect. 'What was their occupation?' Edward Carson had asked whenever a young man's name was mentioned during his famous cross-examination of Wilde at the Old Bailey. In one damaging exchange Carson asked Wilde:

---

[1] Where Ackerley incorrectly places the affair prior to 1923.

'Did you know that one [young man], Parker, was a gentleman's valet, and the other a groom?'
'I did not know it, but if I had I should not have cared. I didn't care twopence what they were. I liked them. I have a passion to civilize the community.'

Wilde's (admittedly disingenuous) passion for civilization was not one comprehensible to Carson or the jury. The simple truth was that Wilde got a kick out of associating with young working-class men, particularly if they were also amateur criminals. 'Feasting with panthers' was his grandiose phrase for such sexual slumming. This was certainly not an exclusively homosexual preserve, as the innumerable Victorian heterosexuals who pursued working-class women knew perfectly well. Various elaborate theories have been produced to explain this passion for 'the lower orders' amongst both heterosexual and homosexual men. Patterns are said to have been established in childhood with the sexual initiation of young gentlemen at the hands (as it were) of domestic servants, perhaps followed by further experience at public school. Here, within the fagging system, small boys often held a position roughly equivalent to a skivvy in the outside world, in service (domestically and sexually) to their seniors. The truth of the matter probably has more to do with availability than with nursery high-jinks and closed study doors.

Whilst some men, heterosexual and homosexual, pursued long-term relationships with working-class partners, the majority put down their money, had their sex, and departed. The advantages of such transactions were evident: variety without complications, and indulgence without responsibility. In the Victorian era prostitution was a thriving industry, with almost anything available for a price to the sexually adventurous. Given the choice of starving or submitting to the sometimes complicated embraces of the moneyed, it is unsurprising that the virtue of so many young men and women became 'easy'.

Some two decades after the fall of Wilde the classes were to mix in circumstances far less propitious than the bar of the Alhambra Theatre in Leicester Square and the incense-laden rooms of Wilde's co-defendant, Alfred Taylor. For many middle-class men the Great War provided their first close encounter with the working classes, and the trenches were to show these men at their very best. A new community where the classes co-operated closely and forged passionate alliances gave some young officers an unexpected glimpse of Utopia amidst the horrors. The men often idolized their public-school officers and in turn the officers grew to love, and sometimes to romanticize, their men. The pre-war years had seen considerable industrial unrest and many officers were consequently surprised by the resilience, good humour and common decency of the ranker. For the most part, the bonds formed between officers and men, although intense, were paternalistic and platonic. However, for young homosexuals like Ackerley (and Owen and Sassoon and many others), these relationships were tinged with the erotic. Many unthinking young Tory squires had their eyes opened by the experience and learned, like Sassoon, 'that life, for the majority of the population, is an unlovely struggle against unfair odds, culminating in a cheap funeral'. Many emerged from it as committed, if romantic, socialists. As with Wilde, the socialism of many homosexuals was created – and some might say compromised – by their sexuality.

An overly rosy view of working-class family life also played its part. Many homosexuals, contrasting the constraints of a middle-class upbringing with the apparent emotional freedom in which Tom, Dick and Harry were reared and lived, often seem like children out in the cold, pressing their faces to the windows of tenements and cottages, in awe of the cosy glow within. It was this contrast which appealed to Ackerley, and the notebook he kept when he first met Jack Jones is crammed with contrasting glimpses of life amongst the grandees and life amongst the tradesmen. He was, however, intelligent enough not to be entirely taken in by his romanticism:

> I try to remember, when Jack recounts those domestic scenes and situations that shed upon his house a light of such solidarity, such sensitive kindness and sensibility, so that when, in my enthusiasm, I compare it with any other house I know, I find it so much better – I try to remember that he is not taking me across the level ground of his ordinary life but up to the hills of joy or down into the valleys of sadness. It is not of the level of our life that we're aware, but only of the peaks that bring us suddenly to a view, or of the depressions into which we fall.

Nonetheless, working-class peaks and valleys often seemed rather more inspiriting than those of Blenheim House. Part of his reason for keeping the notebook was that he was gathering material for another play with a homosexual theme, provisionally entitled *Judcote*. He gives a dismissive outline of the play, of which a mere page and a few notes survive, in *My Father and Myself*:

A young, upper-middle-class, intellectual homosexual (myself of course), lonely, frustrated, and sick of his family, especially the women, his feckless chatterbox of a mother, his vain, quarrelsome and extravagant sister, and the general emptiness and futility of their richly upholstered life, becomes emotionally involved with a handsome young workman. This workman and his mate come to repair the french windows of the Judes' sitting-room, the catch of which has broken, so that they are always drifting open, being irritably closed, drifting open again (symbolism, you see, the invitation to escape), and the young Jude catches envious sight of the two young men affectionately larking at their work. The larking ends in a small disaster, for the handsome boy's chisel accidently wounds the hand of his mate. But Jude has a vision of the happy companionship he lacks. Months later the window starts drifting open again, manual labour is once more summoned, only the handsome boy turns up. Where is his mate? asks Jude. Dead of course, the cut in his hand turned septic and he died of septicaemia. Jude bursts into tears. The boy puts his arm round him and comforts him. Jude falls in love with him and, after various other happenings which I never got right, runs away with him into working-class life and they live happily together as mates ever after.

In order to make his working-class characters authentic, Ackerley made lists of 'Jackisms', such as 'I didn't 'arf give 'im a length (bit of my mind) I didn't! Oo dear!'; 'He wasn't 'arf a case 'e wasn't'; and 'If you 'ad Mrs Jones for yer mother she wouldn't put up with none of your back answers'.

Although Jack was heterosexual, and had a girlfriend called Jean (whom, much to Ackerley's delight, he addressed as 'mate'), Ackerley fell in love with him, and was to be caused much heartache. Forster was consulted in numerous letters over the next two years, and frequently lost patience with Ackerley, begging him to give up this fruitless liaison.

Ackerley's heart might have been caught up with Jack, but this did not prevent his seeking sexual encounters elsewhere, since Jack was 'physically unresponsive'. Richmond was very much a weekend playground during the summers of the 1920s and 1930s, where Londoners came in their Sunday summer best to meet friends and take the air in the Park or to picnic on the banks or boat upon the waters of the River Thames. Like Roger – often to be seen standing on the steps of Blenheim House in a light suit and Panama hat, smoking his cigar and watching the 'wonderful old world' go by – Ackerley took full advantage of the house's commanding view. The part of the world which interested him was that inhabited by young men, frequently to be seen toiling up the hill towards the Park, or strolling along the Terrace, famed in its day as a parade ground for picking up both men and women.

One summer afternoon in 1925 he caught the eye of two teenage boys whose demeanour clearly suggested that whatever they might lack in experience they made up for in curiosity. Ackerley followed them through the Terrace Gardens into Richmond Park and engaged them in conversation. One boy, an attractive Polish Jew, son of a Richmond furrier, was rather more sophisticated than his fellow and well used to the approaches of strange men. He realized at once what Ackerley wanted but, being heterosexual, was not particularly interested in supplying it. The other boy, a fifteen-year-old called Ivan Alderman who was just about to enter art school, was nervous but already knew that he was homosexual and, fascinated by the strikingly handsome man, agreed to meet him again. They did so, some evenings later, under the portico of Wick House at the top of Nightingale Lane, the short road which runs through the Terrace. They walked into the Park and repaired to some concealing bracken under the trees.

For Ackerley, this was a pleasurable interlude, one of many, but the effect upon the young and impressionable boy, whose first sexual encounter with an adult this had been, was enormous. Sixty years later he was to regard the ensuing affair as the most significant of his life, perhaps because it was the first but also because he had fallen in love with Ackerley at first sight. At this period Ackerley often drove around Richmond in Nancy's green MG, an open, sporty model with wire wheels, and the smitten boy always kept a look out for it, his heart leaping as it came into view. The following Saturday Ackerley agreed to take Ivan to his flat, well away from Blenheim House and from the Kew Road, where Ivan lived with his strict and puritanical mother.

Each Saturday thereafter over the next year or so, whenever both were free, Ivan would spend the afternoon with Ackerley. It must have been very pleasant to have an adoring fifteen-year-old on tap, but it was not long before Ackerley was regretting that what had been planned as a brief encounter in the bushes was rapidly turning into an affair. He was not in love with Ivan, for his heart was engaged with Jack Jones, and he did his best, in the kindest possible way, to disengage himself. Ivan, although aware of Ackerley's intentions, proved tenacious. Less kind methods were then employed. Ivan was once delighted to be asked out on a Sunday afternoon, but instead of the jaunt *à deux* he had imagined, he was taken to a homosexual tea-party at Petersham where Ackerley attempted to palm him off on an associate, without success.

Meanwhile poor Goldie Dickinson was still smitten with Ackerley, but was having to content himself with sublimation. What Dickinson *really* wanted was to be firmly trampled upon by the shiny boots or shoes of a young man. This fetish is confessed in some detail in Dickinson's *Autobiography*, and in his poetic dialogue 'Body and Soul', which he was to write in about 1928–9. Ackerley does not figure in this poem, described by Dennis Proctor as 'an extraordinary summation of [Dickinson's] whole sex life' in which his relationships with four of the five friends (he had not met Proctor when he wrote it) can be discerned. Savary represents the end of Dickinson's romantic endeavours in the poem:

> *Body* He was the last; the *next* remains untold.
> *Soul* Why should there be one? You are growing old.
> *Body* Oh don't deceive yourself! I shall not tire!
> After the frost will always come the fire.

*   *   *

> *Soul* It never can be, and I'll tell you why,
> Since we are bent on candour, you and I.
> The trouble is, in honesty and truth,
> You never had a charm for any youth.
> *Body* I! Not?
> *Soul* No, never! No one ever drew
> Nearer to me because he cared for you.
> I was the magnet, and in your despite,

96

For sake of me, they gave you your delight.
How could you, so supremely misendowed,
Hope to attract the sensitive and proud?

Since the poem was written whilst he was still, to some extent, in Ackerley's thrall, the distinction made between the 'embodied' and the 'disembodied' may owe something to the friendship and to Dickinson's discussions of Ackerley with Forster. Although Ackerley could not respond to Dickinson's love, there is no doubt that he remained very fond of the older man, whose name appears in a diary entry in November 1948, heading a short list of the 'dear dead' whom Ackerley commemorates during a walk on Wimbledon Common. They saw each other quite often, occasions which Dickinson sometimes found painful, and exchanged affectionate letters in which this pain is quite evident:

> I liked seeing you, Joe dear, though at tea yesterday everything seemed impossible, and I suppose that was my fault and no one else's. I'm sorry. This I write for my comfort and solace, not for you to reply to.

By now *The Prisoners of War* had been cast and rehearsals were under way at the Court Theatre. In the cast of Turner's *Smaragda's Love* had been a young actor who had caught Ackerley's attention. It was rumoured that this actor had heard about the theme of *Prisoners* and was keen to audition, but Ackerley had been informed that the young man was 'undesirable'. Ackerley's interest was further whetted by this news, but in spite of his attempts to insinuate this actor into the cast, presumably as Grayle (which would have been casting to type), the Club stood firm. The young man was Godfrey Winn, who played the part of Sylvester Snodgrass in Turner's play. Now remembered as the gushing popular journalist and royal commentator, in the 1920s Winn divided his time between the stage and assorted louche bars. He later became an ornament of the bridge table at Blenheim House until one day, emboldened by his social success, he asked which of his profiles was the best, a question which Roger did not care to answer, or indeed have asked. Ackerley might not have been able to get Winn into *The Prisoners of War*, but he did eventually get him into bed one night at Blenheim House, whilst Winn's unsuspecting lover was asleep in another room.

The part of Grayle eventually went to Robert Harris, in a cast which included Raymond Massey and Carleton Hobbs, with George Hayes playing Conrad. Ackerley attended the rehearsals, as did Mrs Whitworth who one day saw Nancy arrive and sit next to her brother in the stalls, draping an arm affectionately across his shoulder. Mrs Whitworth turned to Robert Harris in horror and breathed: '*Incest*, as well!' Meanwhile Ackerley's friends were being encouraged to buy tickets for the first night, 5 July; amongst them was another rising star of the theatre, John Gielgud, an acquaintance through Cambridge friends. Colleer Abbott had been enrolled as a Club subscriber by Ackerley, and Forster was looking forward to going, partly because it would give him a chance to meet Jack Jones. In the event he was critical of both the play and the young man. His remarks about the play – that the relationship between Tetford and Rickman showed more sentimentality than camaraderie – were mitigated by his overall judgement that: 'The play is much more moving and bigger than I thought.' No such mitigation coloured Forster's view of Jack who, he complained, did not appear to care sufficiently for Ackerley.

The play went extremely well, 'received with great enthusiasm' according to the *Nation*, and there was a party after the performance, from which Roger, who had sat by himself at the back of the dress circle, tactfully slipped away. Robert Harris described the reviews as amongst the best he ever received in a long and distinguished career. 'The success was not surprising,' wrote the *Nation*'s critic, 'as it is one of the most interesting English plays to be discovered for some time.' Jack Squire in his *London Mercury* was clearly delighted to hail the success of a protégé: 'It is the best play I have seen for a long time. It also happened to be magnificently produced and acted . . . its faithfulness and fine feeling left one with something of that exaltation that the great tragedies leave.' Hugh Walpole wrote an equally flattering notice of it in the *Evening Standard*. The *New Statesman* thought it 'the most important new play produced this year' and hailed Ackerley as a true disciple of Ibsen. 'A piece of which one would not miss moment, incident, or personage,' wrote the celebrated critic James Agate. He was rather more alert than Mrs Whitworth to Conrad's nature ('the least understood of abnormalities'): 'It is an arresting and dreadful story . . . It jumps to the eyes that the problem is one not of depression but of repression.' The *New Statesman* and *The Spectator* also recognized the play as a psychological study, the latter reviewing it with

Michael Arlen's adaptation of his own *The Green Hat* and the improbably named Mordaunt Shairp's *The Offence* under the headline: 'A Few Special Cases'. Without explicitly describing Conrad's affection for Grayle as homosexual, the critic had clearly understood the situation, and neatly nailed Grayle as 'the male equivalent of an exasperating "flapper"', adding perceptively: 'And the worst of it is that, like so many men of his temperament, [Conrad] cheats himself into the belief that he likes Grayle because he is "clean".'

The critical response to the play encouraged Nigel Playfair to transfer the production to the Playhouse Theatre at Charing Cross. It opened there on 1 September and once again Forster and Dickinson were in attendance. They had come up from Cambridge the day before, and poor Dickinson endured a frustrating tea-party at the Charlotte Street flat, dinner at L'Étoile, just down the road, and an outing to see the modern-dress *Hamlet* at the Kingsway Theatre. 'Dear Joe tried to be nice, & took my arm,' he wrote. 'Think, on the whole, I behaved decently, & well. It appears that no age preserves one from these things.' There is little doubt that part of the success of *The Prisoners of War* had been due to its reputation as 'the new homosexual play'. Indeed, it was one of the first plays to deal with this topic in a contemporary setting that had ever been produced on the London stage. Stephen Spender recalls his excitement as he and Christopher Isherwood, sunning themselves on Reugen Island, speculated about the author of this bold piece of theatre. Dickinson's response, if rather more aware than that of some people, highlights this aspect of the play's success. It 'moved and appealed' to him, he told the author:

> But that might be a subjective matter; and the same interest might be merely a lack of interest for those who are not *anders als die andern* [i.e. homosexual]. So I endeavoured to regard it objectively. Well I thought that the dialogue was plainly very good, nothing superfluous and nothing flat; that the action did move on in a way that I had not realized in reading it, so that there was a sense of climax. Also that it was all fresh and based on your observations . . . In fact, your play and Morgan's novel [i.e. *Maurice*] are the only things I know in literature in which the theme is handled so as not to be merely sentimental and trivial, if not worse. Tetford [Carleton Hobbs] was delightful. My mind was distracted from its objectivity by an irrelevant attraction to him . . .

Not all homosexual members of the audience were impressed. Brian Howard, fresh from the aesthetic and avant-garde hothouse of Oxford, thought it 'dreary'. However, those of Ackerley's own generation, like Siegfried Sassoon, were moved, and T. E. Lawrence described the play as 'first rate psychology. The people in it were our very selves.' These responses were in contrast to that of Arnold Bennett, who, less susceptible to the play's theme, dismissed it as 'no good at all, quite untrue to life', when lunching with Forster at the Reform. 'I wonder how it will hold the public,' Dickinson wrote, adding (in a phrase lifted from or adapted for *Maurice*): 'No people I believe are so recalcitrant to reality as the English.'[1]

His pessimism was justified; *The Prisoners of War* ran for a mere twenty-four performances at the Playhouse, replaced by a play appropriately entitled *The Desire for Change*. Ackerley blamed those reviews which, although good, described *The Prisoners of War* as 'morbid'. He suspected that this 'infectious word' was responsible for poor audiences; 'and the theatre itself in its poverty of outside lighting and desolate, windy situation always reminded me uncomfortably of a tomb, confirming the rumour of death and disease.' Robert Harris blamed Playfair for merely transferring the play without making sufficient efforts to capitalize upon its excellent notices and publicize it properly. In contrast, Chatto and Windus used the *New Statesman*'s review to boost sales and keep up interest. In June 1927 a second, corrected impression was published, in both hard and paper covers.

---

[1] When Maurice asks Dr Lasker Jones whether England would adopt the Code Napoléon which had legalized homosexuality in France, the hypnotherapist replies: 'I doubt it. England has always been disinclined to accept human nature.'

7

Promising young man

WITH the success of *The Prisoners of War* Ackerley was seen very much as a coming dramatist. He was hailed as a recruit to *Vogue*'s 'Hall of Fame' in the distinguished company of Viscount Haldane, André Derain, Léonide Massine and the young medievalist, Eileen Power. Bearing a striking resemblance to the American actor Montgomery Clift, Ackerley poses anxiously for his *Vogue* photo, his hands clasped before him, beneath a fulsome explanation of his credentials for admittance to the Hall:

> Because he is one of the most interesting of our younger dramatists: because his play, 'Prisoners of War', has recently been acted with great applause: because he has written a play which is neither melodramatic nor sentimental: because he acted in 'Caesar and Cleopatra' at the Aldwych Theatre, and at Cambridge took the part of Achilles in Shakespeare's 'Troilus and Cressida': and because he is equally good as an actor and a dramatist.

In fact, promising or not, he was never again to attempt another play. The wretched *Girolamo* was finally abandoned and although much work of a dilatory nature was done upon *Judcote*, the play was never completed to his satisfaction and was subsequently destroyed. According to S. P. B. Mais, there were other plays which have simply disappeared, most of them written before *The Prisoners of War*:

> He has a sense of the dramatic which is all his own; he is clever enough to see this and his plays (of which there are many) have not

been acted in London theatres solely because of the weird plots he persists in using: a Cabinet minister throwing a Cornish labourer over a cliff in one instance, and a tobacconist with a Swiftean sense of humour frightening the life out of a lady customer in his shop by pretending to be mad.

It is hard to believe that the disappearance of these manuscripts represents much loss to British theatre. But, if Ackerley failed to produce any further works for the stage, he had served an apprenticeship that was to prove useful in the future. The success of *The Prisoners of War* impressed Forster deeply, and thereafter he would defer to Ackerley on dramatic questions, seeking his advice over the libretto of *Billy Budd* and calling him in to help with the stage adaptations of his own novels. More immediately, Jack Squire commissioned him to review books of *belles lettres* and volumes on drama for the *London Mercury*.

The play's success also meant that Ackerley began to mix freely in theatrical circles during the 1920s, enjoying a number of affairs. Forster was amused by Ackerley's sexual conquests there, but had a distinctly Edwardian view of theatre people:

> As for them nactor [sic] chaps, Joe, as many as you like, but *many* – take no one of them seriously for you will then be asking for what they can't give. So either many or none!

Ackerley was to be found hanging around the film studios, watching Ivor Novello basking in the expressionist lighting of his new film, an adaptation of Mrs Belloc Lowndes' Jack the Ripper saga, *The Lodger*, directed by the young Alfred Hitchcock. The two glamorous young men ended up in bed where, Ackerley was to tell Simon Raven decades later, Novello's equipment turned out to be disappointingly substandard.

By this time, January 1926, Ackerley had moved once more, finding new accommodation in a curious Hammersmith household. Hammersmith Terrace is a row of attractive eighteenth-century houses at the river's edge, and at No. 6, a tall narrow building of four storeys, lived a family of three elderly siblings called Needham. Their father had been an inventor, noted for the mechanism by which spent cartridges were ejected from shotguns. His two sons, Arthur and Cecil, pursued a life of shabby eccentricity, looked after by their sister Louie. They followed their father's profession, and had invented and patented a number of comparatively useless objects such as automatic cigarette cases and perpetual table fountains. This decrepit trio had a suite of rooms to let at the top of the house and Ackerley took it without hesitation. Arthur, a somewhat faded old queen, must have been delighted when the glamorous young man presented himself, but this would have been followed by disappointment, since Ackerley was stand-offish and remote, forever scuttling to the top floor in order to write. Later, he would be found conducting numerous young men to his room, and Arthur, delighted by the flow of working-class youth up and down his ancient staircase, was inclined in consequence to wear his dentures more frequently. He was also intrigued by Ackerley's name, for it stirred up memories of an old friend of his, a certain Count de Gallatin.

One of Forster's working-class friends remarked that Ackerley would be able to tell friends: 'Now I am living by the river I shall be glad to see you drop in any time!' Indeed, Hammersmith Terrace soon became quite a meeting place. The accommodation was not particularly comfortable. John Gielgud, who paid the occasional visit, recalled a 'rather spartan flat . . . I only remember a statue of a Greek youth, a large bunch of bananas on the dining table, and a rather anonymous young disciple ironing shirts in the kitchen.' However, the garden ran down to the Thames and the Needhams allowed their new lodger to make use of this, since none of them ventured out of doors very often. The novelist Naomi Mitchison had moved to Hammersmith in 1923 and found 'neighbours with similar tastes and standards all along the river right up to Chiswick and round St Peter's Square; many were more or less in the arts, writers, painters and sculptors'. Ackerley found much the same and the atmosphere was extremely convivial with innumerable parties spilling out into the gardens and terraces during the summer months. Some of the most notable parties were given by the author A. P. Herbert and his wife Gwen at 12 Hammersmith Terrace, where guests and gatecrashers dived into the Thames to refresh themselves. Mrs Herbert was an artist and several young men, having spent an hour or two behind closed curtains with Ackerley, were despatched along the Terrace to No. 12 to earn some money as models. Stephen Spender was once invited into the studio to inspect Mrs Herbert's work and recalls being shown 'dozens of nudes

– young men with enormous cocks, which were supplied for her by Joe'.

One Sunday morning Ackerley was approached by a genial-looking young police constable who got into conversation with him. When Ackerley confessed to being a writer and the author of *The Prisoners of War*, the policeman was very interested since he had seen and much enjoyed the play. Harry Daley was the son of a Lowestoft fisherman who had died in the great September Gale of 1911, when Harry was nine. Daley *père* had been an orphan from Poplar apprenticed to a Suffolk fishing-smack whilst still a child. The skipper had virtually adopted the boy, but this sense of being part of the family did not prevent the young Cockney from falling in love with, and eventually marrying, one of the skipper's six daughters, Emily, who worked as a parlour-maid in Great Yarmouth. The young couple had five children, Annie, Janet, Joey, Harry and David, and although life was hard and impoverished, the family grew up in an atmosphere of love, fun and innocent ribaldry. The children were encouraged to read, and thus began a lifetime of self-improvement which more than compensated for the rudimentary lessons they received at the local school. Harry received education of a different sort at the hands of local boys and soon realized that this was where his sexual interests lay.

His mother was determined to keep the family together after the death of her husband, and took in lodgers in order to supplement a tiny donation from the Shipwrecked Mariners' Society. As soon as they were able, the children went out to work, and Harry eventually became a telegraph boy, a job with both prospects and a pension. When the First World War broke out, Joey marched away, never to return, and Harry gazed up at those same Zeppelins for which Ackerley and his fellow-officers had lain in watch in the south of the county. Annie had married and moved to Dorking and, alarmed by newspaper reports of Zeppelin raids, urged her mother to join her. Mrs Daley held out until rumours of an invasion of the East Coast began to circulate. In the spring of 1916, finally unnerved by the naval bombardment of Lowestoft, she removed the entire family to Dorking. Harry's future in the Post Office came to an abrupt end and he took a job as a delivery boy for Kingham's, a local grocer. He drove a pony and trap around the outlying villages and estates, collecting orders

from the households of Marie Stopes, Mrs Ronnie Greville, Lord
Beaverbrook and, at Abinger Hammer, E. M. Forster's Aunt Laura.
He saved his wages to further his education, buying books and records
and going up to London to visit the theatres, concert halls and art
galleries. Realizing that he could not be a delivery boy for ever, he
decided without much enthusiasm to become a policeman.

A less likely or suitable recruit to the Metropolitan Police Force
would be difficult to imagine. At twenty-four he was, he admitted,
'uneducated, but possibly slightly above average intelligence for the
period; well below average plain common sense; sexually both innocent and deplorable; honourable if not exactly honest; trusting;
truthful; romantic and sentimental to the point of sloppiness.' A
further disqualification was that he was 'always and automatically on
the side of the loser or lonely, whether male or female, human or
animal, weak or strong, attractive or unattractive, right or wrong,'
(although it was the male, human, strong, attractive and wrong who
usually engaged his heart). Nonetheless it was decided that if he lost a
little weight he would be just the sort of person the Force was looking
for, and so he was enrolled at Peel House for training. He passed his
examinations and was posted to the West London district of 'T'
Division.

His beat was in Chiswick, but, like all the Division's single policemen, he lived at the Section House in Hammersmith. This was a sort of
spartan boarding-house (in the scholastic rather than the seaside
sense), with a fatherly older sergeant acting as housemaster to a
hundred fledgling coppers. They slept in cubicles, shared bathrooms,
ate communally in a mess hall (for a weekly charge of 12s out of a wage
of £3 6s), and sought recreation in the billiards room and an Army hut
in the yard which was used as a gymnasium. A roll-call for those not on
duty was held every night at midnight. Police Eights skimmed up and
down the river, training for fiercely contested competitions, and
further amusement (one of particular appeal to the susceptible Daley)
was provided when local professional boxers were allowed to use the
'gym' for practice bouts. After the Great War the police had recruited
amongst the returning soldiers, and many of Daley's fellow constables
were demobbed, tough and unruly guardsmen. There was much
rowdiness and practical joking, drinking, gambling, and even petty
theft amongst the Section House inmates. The gentle, soppy Daley,
who never bothered to disguise his homosexuality, cut an unusual

figure amongst these colossi, and was teased a great deal but rarely persecuted with any real viciousness. Amongst the later influx of civilian recruits he found many friends, and 'in this cramped world of cubicles we lounged on one another's beds to talk and conduct our affectionate Platonic friendships . . . It was like camping out and was heavenly.'

Sex aside, it is quite clear why Daley and Ackerley took to each other at once. They had several characteristics in common: both were somewhat naïve idealists; although promiscuous, they were basically romantic in their attitude towards sex; they were also romantic in their attitude towards the more feckless members of the working classes, Daley as a sympathetic insider, Ackerley as an admiring outsider. They were by nature outrageous, reckless and wildly indiscreet (Daley described 'Safety First' as a 'contemptible slogan'); they were also, in Forster's term, born 'muddlers'. Daley was fascinated by the world of the arts, Ackerley by the world of the criminal; each was the perfect guide to the other.

Whilst there is little doubt that they went to bed together, there is some confusion as to whether they were ever lovers in a more permanent sense. Unusually, Ackerley kept all Daley's letters, but this may have been for their intrinsic rather than their sentimental value, for Daley was an extremely vivid writer. When Ackerley died, Nancy returned these letters to Daley who burned them all, ashamed, he said, by their literary naïvety. This is probably true, since Daley, for all his bluster, remained a modest man. The only surviving record of his friendship with Ackerley is contained in letters he wrote to P. N. Furbank in the late 1960s shortly before he died, frank letters in which deep affection for and gratitude towards Ackerley are evident, but which contain nothing to suggest a grand passion. His sexual tastes, like Ackerley's, were for working-class, heterosexual men, although he had affairs with people who were neither, and over the next few years he was much in demand amongst Forster's friends. During the 1920s and 1930s both men were having (by their standards) long-standing relationships elsewhere. For a time they 'shared' a guardsman, whose loyalties were further divided since he also had a regular girlfriend. Nonetheless, David Daley admitted to raking a sheet out of the bonfire of letters and reading a fragment in which his brother had written: 'I don't care who you go with as long as you don't love *them* more than you love *me*.' Other people who knew both men at this period think it unlikely that any really serious affair took place.

Perhaps the truth of the matter is that their relationship was like that of Auden and Isherwood: sex was a natural, pleasurable but not very serious expression of a deep and lasting friendship. As Daley wrote in his memoirs: 'a good sexy life . . . is essential to happiness. I don't mean moping about and falling in love, which often has nothing to do with love, but a high-spirited romp with someone you like – if you love them, all the better.'

By this time, under the influence of Forster and his widening circle of working-class friends, Ackerley had become socialist in attitude and habit. The atmosphere of Hammersmith no doubt contributed to this, for it was just around the curve of the river at Kelmscott House on Upper Mall that William Morris had founded the Hammersmith Socialist Society in 1890. Such traditions were kept alive by the Mitchisons and their left-wing friends. Ackerley told Daley that he liked his parents but did not approve of them, and instructed his father that he could no longer accept so large an allowance. Henceforth he would manage to live on £6 a week. (Nancy, still living at Blenheim House, received £500 a year.) Forster may have agreed with the attitude, but thought the resultant self-sacrifice nonsensical and often urged Ackerley to take full advantage of Roger's largesse, advice Ackerley would have done well to heed. Of course, if ever he ran really short of funds he could rely upon Roger's help, and he was always welcome at, and indeed frequently visited, Blenheim House when the New Socialism proved too uncomfortable. However, he took his new role in society with some seriousness, casting off the finery of his youth (blazer, fedora and cloak) for the sort of shabby costume which would become his hallmark. In imitation of the Section House, he ate at a bare table and dispensed with his milk jug, but still managed to finance what Daley described as an 'overwhelmingly generous life'.

The socialism of Ackerley and his friends needs to be qualified, for the conversion was not always an easy one. Intellectual conviction often struggled with emotional doubt. The consciousness of the difference between themselves and the apparently uncomplicated young men with whom they had affairs was a large part of the attraction for middle-class homosexuals. In bed, or in the abstract, the working classes were splendid. Unfortunately, however fond one might be of them as individuals or an idea, prolonged exposure to their apparent defects often caused the candle of the faith to gutter alarmingly in the chill draughts of experience. 'How irritating and unsatisfactory the so-called working classes are seen to be, with their irrationalities, and superstitions, and opinionatedness, and stubbornness, and food foibles, and laziness, and selfishness, the more one knows of them,' Ackerley moaned during one particularly low point in his life. Whenever anything went wrong the barriers of class were hastily re-erected by way of explanation. There was nothing really *wrong* with the young man that could not be regretfully ascribed to his background and education, or lack of same. If the beloved turned out to be ignorant, feckless, idle, mercenary, or touchy, then this was hardly surprising given his upbringing (working-class women were, by and large, beyond the pale). Forster once complained that he had been put to considerable expense by Ackerley's troubles with a current boyfriend; he had been so put off the lower classes that he had been obliged to travel first rather than third class on a railway journey. It was not easy to jettison class-consciousness in the first half of the twentieth century.

But the generosity, and the genuine affection recognized by Harry Daley should be set against these disenchantments. Both Forster and Ackerley were always willing to do something practical to help out their working-class friends and often remained loyal friends long after any sexual relationship had ended. For example, one young man, Jim, had been discovered by Ackerley sleeping rough in Hyde Park. His girlfriend was pregnant and he had no money. Ackerley disapproved of the relationship but nonetheless gave the couple some money so that they could get a room. They subsequently married and had children. Jim was constantly out of work, but every time Ackerley and Forster met him, they slipped him some cash, and he became devoted to them. Ackerley would have his old suits cut down to fit Jim and also gave him Nancy's old bicycle, which he rode for years. The correct balance was often difficult to achieve and considerable tact was required in order not to offend the dignity of such friends. Ackerley was furious when he discovered that James Agate had dressed Jim as a waiter and employed him to serve drinks at a smart party in Swiss Cottage. 'Never go putting a friend of mine in a white coat again,' he warned. Although they saw little of each other after the war, Jim remained very fond of Ackerley, and after Ackerley's death became very friendly with Nancy, largely, she thought, because she reminded him of her brother.

Ackerley continued to castigate successive governments which failed to improve the lot of the working classes and, as he put it in a poem, 'contrived to keep them poor'. He would have argued that his case was strengthened by the fact that to some extent he remained socialist in spite of, rather than because of, his knowledge of working-class life and attitudes.

Ackerley was also mixing with a number of people whom he had met through Forster and who were to become close friends, notably W. J. H. Sprott, Gerald Heard, Christopher Wood, L.E.O. ('Leo') Charlton and Tom Wichelo. Sprott had been a Cambridge contemporary of Ackerley, but had found him somewhat aloof. A member of the Apostles, Sprott had formed most of his friendships there, and soon became a satellite of the Bloomsbury Group, amongst whom he discarded the Walter, John and Herbert bestowed upon him at his christening and became known as 'Sebastian'. He was at one time the lover of Maynard Keynes, and was a frequent but platonic travelling-companion of Lytton Strachey in numerous walking holidays on the Continent. Strachey, apparently unaware of the sort of figure he cut himself, reported that Sprott had turned heads during a holiday in Venice and looked far from reputable. Indeed he was something of a Firbankian exquisite, tall, slender and sinuous with expressive hands and a taste for casually outlandish clothes. This appearance was exaggerated when he appeared, as he often did, with his sister Velda, who favoured severely masculine attire. After graduating he remained in Cambridge, working as a demonstrator in the Psychological Laboratory there, and in 1926 he was appointed Lecturer in Psychology at the University of Nottingham. Here he became plain 'Jack' and lived in a poor district, gradually accumulating a circle of working-class friends and lovers. Professor E. A. Thompson, in a supplementary note to Sprott's obituary in *The Times*, recalled 'a slum street of gruesome squalor. Of the amenities of the house you could say little more than at least the lavatory was indoors and not at the end of the yard.' Thompson added that as well as his many distinguished visitors, Sprott also received

unabashed persons of a different type. I have myself heard his quick footsteps hurry to the hall door in answer to a ring, and his warm greeting, 'Come in, dear boy, I *knew* you were to be released this afternoon.'

Sprott amused Forster with long letters detailing his sexual escapades amongst the rural and industrial workers of Nottinghamshire. Although based in Nottingham, he also shared a house with his sister in Norfolk, and was a frequent visitor to London. He became one of Ackerley's most loyal friends, the two men forming with Forster a close-knit and intimate triumvirate.

One of Sprott's devoted admirers was Gerald Heard, the omnivorous scientific and religious philosopher, memorably dubbed by Naomi Mitchison 'a kind of prophet'. He was secretary to Sir Horace Plunkett of the Irish Co-operative Movement, and worked from his employer's house in Weybridge. The Forsters had met Heard through Sir Horace, whom they knew as a neighbour. When not working for Sir Horace, or accompanying him to the motor-racing circuit at Brooklands to admire 'the strange and attractive clothes worn by the race-goers', Heard spent his time reading. Such was his rate of consumption that it was popularly believed that he read some two thousand volumes a year. One result of this diet, and his speculative curiosity on all matters, was a number of books, influential in their time but now mostly forgotten, with such imposing titles as *The Ascent of Humanity* (1929), *The Emergence of Man* (1931) and *The Source of Civilisation* (1935). These books made his reputation amongst his contemporaries, whom he was eventually to abandon when he took off with Aldous Huxley on the wings of Buddhist mysticism, perhaps influenced by his belief that nearly all Tibetan saints were homosexual. He came to land in California, where he really did become a guru, much fêted by the devout.[1]

His striking appearance at the Blenheim House dinner-table in purple suede shoes and a leather jacket with a leopardskin collar was recalled in *My Father and Myself*. No less striking was his manner, for he spoke much as he thought, words and notions cascading forth as he pursued his various and interrelated ideas. This interrelation was not always apparent to his listeners but his breadth of reference and allusion gave authority to his sometimes crackpot notions. Some impression of his manner can be gained from his letters, evidently written at speed in an elegantly calligraphic, but frequently illegible,

---

[1] His friend and disciple, Christopher Isherwood, provides a touching portrait of Heard in California in *Down There on a Visit* (1962), where he appears as 'Augustus Parr'.

hand. Studded with puns, private allusions, obscure literary and classical references, they rattle along in a Shandian progression until their sudden and often unheralded conclusion. In spite of his encyclopaedic knowledge and apparent self-assurance, he diagnosed himself as having a considerable inferiority complex, referring to himself in letters as 'infy com' or sometimes plain 'infy'.

At this period Heard was particularly interested in homosexuality and spent much energy attempting to discover the psychological impulse behind buggery. Homosexual himself, he was also much taken up with the phenomenon of promiscuity and carried out an *ad hoc* field study amongst his friends, finding in Ackerley's circle a rich source of primary material. Was there 'any psychological explanation of promiscuity & its unsatisfactoriness?' he asked Jack Sprott. 'If it's an exorganic urge why the sense of bafflement & tedium which seems general?' He was much taken by Daley, whom he referred to with characteristic obscurity as 'Our Great Harry, the Harmodius of Hammersmith, P.C.'. He introduced him to Jack Sprott, who instantly fell in love with him. Daley thought this 'an awful nuisance', but Sprott, egged on by Forster and Heard, was not to be rebuffed so easily.

At about this time Heard had met a wealthy young dilettante called Christopher Wood, with whom he was to spend the remainder of his life. Wood's money came from the family firm Petty, Wood & Co., which made jams and canned and bottled products that were sold in grand emporia such as Selfridges, Harrods and Fortnum and Mason under their own labels. He had a fascination for mechanical objects and at Cambridge used special electrical tools imported from America to break into the Post Office and steal all the stamps, returning them by the same method some days later. He was a gifted pianist of concert standing whose proudest moment was when he had been praised by Sir Thomas Beecham, but he never played professionally or pursued any sort of career. Wood was immensely generous, forever lavishing gifts upon his friends: clocks, electric razors, musical boxes, bicycles, even cars. He was so impressed by a recording of Rachmaninov's Second Piano Concerto, played by the composer with Stokowski conducting, that he bought fifty sets to distribute amongst his (in every sense) musical acquaintances. Ackerley was given a Salmson sports car but when he went to collect it from the garage in Hammersmith, he reversed out into the road straight into a tram. Wood merely laughed and paid for the car to be repaired.[1] When Sir Horace Plunkett died, Heard became 'secretary' to Chris Wood and moved in with him. He was appointed literary editor of *The Realist* (a 'Journal of Scientific Humanism') and also did work for the Howard League for Penal Reform.

Very different indeed was Lionel Evelyn Oswald ('Leo') Charlton, a distinguished military man of Catholic aristocratic background who had served as a general in the Great War and then become an air commodore, working in the Middle East. He had courageously resigned from his post as Chief of Air Staff in Iraq in protest at the bombing of unarmed villages, and had retired to the Thames Valley with a younger former RAF man called Tom Wichelo. Apart from their unorthodox relationship (more easily accepted as avuncular or comradely at that period), they pursued a blameless Home Counties life, their chief recreations being gardening and bridge. 'The General' was a frequent and welcome visitor at Blenheim House, where he made up a hand at cards, drank whisky with Roger and was gravely courteous to Netta, who was very fond of him. He later embarked upon a literary career, producing two volumes of rather ponderous memoirs written in the third person,[2] and becoming air correspondent of the *New Statesman*. He also wrote a number of successful books for boys, which featured healthy young lads and exotic aircraft. *The Mystery of Cowsole Wood* (1948) is a characteristic example, in which Walter Selby and Bobby Measham ('bosom friends, in their middle teens') capture Martin Bormann and learn a great deal about helicopters. Although kindly, Charlton was something of a snob, once describing Harry Daley as 'the sort of chap you give orders to, not sit down to dinner with'. Daley, who often discerned slights where none were intended, claimed that Charlton had cut him dead in the Café Royal one day. Charlton insisted that he had not seen him, but it was never satisfactorily decided whether his myopia had been physical or social.

---

[1] In spite of practice in Nancy's car, driving was something Ackerley had never mastered and friends were terrified when travelling with him, only doing so under duress or in cases of emergency. Bowling along at top speed (thirty miles per hour), or crawling along in a cautious low gear, he was equally dangerous. When he collected the repaired Salmson he got no further than the Broadway before crashing it once again.

[2] *Charlton* (dedicated to Wichelo, Forster and Ackerley) and *More Charlton*.

This group, along with such satellites as Raymond Mortimer, Eddy Sackville-West, Francis Birrell, Lionel Fielden, Duncan Grant and a number of theatre people – John Gielgud, Robert Harris, Robert Helpmann – formed a raffish and intellectual circle that racketed around London, visiting cinemas, theatres, concerts, the zoo and the Ring in Blackfriars Road, where Harry Daley's beloved boxers took part in competitions. They had their favourite pubs, notably the York Minster in Soho's Old Compton Street, and their favourite restaurants: the Café Royal; the Criterion, which did a good three-and-sixpenny lunch; the Isola Bella in Greek Street; and Gennaro's in New Compton Street, famous for its beautiful waiters, who were carefully selected by the flamboyant old proprietor during holidays back in his native Italy.

But perhaps the highlight of the social calendar was the Boat Race. All along Hammersmith Terrace garden-parties would be in progress, held by such riverside dwellers as the A. P. Herberts and the Mitchisons. The view of the Oxford v. Cambridge race was magnificent, but at No. 6 there was usually so much drink laid on (bottles of champagne for the intellectuals, crates of beer for the working classes) that little attention was paid to the strenuous proceedings on the river. One veteran recalled Aunt Bunny sitting in the garden, glassy-eyed, vainly attempting to smell a daffodil. At the end of the day someone, usually Leo Charlton, would telephone to discover who had won. Regular guests were Forster, Colleer Abbott, Charlton and Wichelo, Harry Daley and his brother David, accompanied by their current boyfriends, Bunny, Netta, a clutch of Section House constables, soldiers, sailors and the odd petty criminal or two. A photograph taken by David Daley, a skilled amateur photographer, shows Syed Ross Masood's two sons joining in the festivities.[1]

A passion for uniforms, or rather for the men who wore them, was noticeable amongst this group of friends, 'all sorts of uniforms right down to bus conductors,' Daley recalled. Although there were few policemen as obliging as Daley ('his kindness is as comprehensive as Semiramis',' Heard commented), blue serge was much admired; but this was as nothing to the scarlet jackets and gold epaulettes of His

---

[1] Masood had been appointed Vice-Chancellor of the Muslim Anglo-Oriental University in 1929, and Forster and his mother had looked after the boys who were at school in England.

Majesty's Brigade of Guards. Gerald Heard described a party given by Eddie Gathorne-Hardy as 'garnished with Guardsmen' and Naomi Mitchison recalled another one at which the host was given a guards-man as a present, a scene which she felt recalled the Roman Empire.

The guardsmen were not necessarily, or primarily, homosexual, but in a time-honoured tradition they combined ceremonial duties and casual prostitution. For generations, soldiers wishing to supplement the King's Shilling had only to lurk enticingly in Hyde Park's Monkey Walk (conveniently close to the barracks), or loll on the bars of the West End's pubs. Perhaps without passion, but equally without shame, guardsmen submitted to the embraces of gentlemen for a fixed sum which they would spend on drink or female prostitutes. There was very little 'exploitation' or 'corruption' about such liaisons, whatever choleric judges may have pronounced on the occasions when gentle-men were caught with their pants down. Indeed it appears that young recruits were frequently 'broken in' by their elders when they joined the colours. Guardsmen usually referred to their clients as 'twanks', but 'steamers' and 'fitter's mates' were two further colourful synonyms much in use at the period. A good twank was something to be valued, indeed occasionally to be bequeathed. Ackerley once received a letter informing him that a soldier he had seen several times had died. The letter came from one of the man's fellow troopers who offered himself as a replacement.

> It would be the blackest ingratitude to disparage the guards [Acker-ley wrote after receiving the letter] – these brave soldiers are of incalculable use to a great many lonely bachelors in London – but it must be said that the usual disadvantage attaches to them that attaches to all prostitutes, they are mercenary.

He also complained that, in spite of barrack-room initiations, these 'dumb pumphandlers' were frequently inexperienced and perfunc-tory, 'surely the most inefficient prostitutes that any wretched man had to fall back on'. Guards often accepted invitations to parties only to find themselves unsociably isolated amidst the grander guests and were piqued at being ignored. Heard once complained of guardsmen that: 'You can never get the l.o.s [lower orders] to realize that business is business, they will confuse the issue with fancies about breeding.' However, it was more often the middle-class clients who forgot the nature of their sexual transactions and became emotionally involved

Roger Ackerley and Arthur Stockley in 1885 – sparring partners who founded Elders & Fyffes.

New Brighton, 1885. Arthur Stockley, Roger Ackerley, the Count de Gallatin and Dudley Sykes.

Charlotte Louise Burckhardt, Roger Ackerley's first wife.
Janetta Aylward as Robin in H. Beerbohm Tree's production of
The Merry Wives of Windsor.

Ackerley's mother and grandmother cut a caper on the lawn.
The three Ackerley children. In descending order: Peter, Nancy and Joe.

The extended family at Apsley House, Richmond:
Harold Armstrong, Joe, Peter, Granny Aylward, Roger, Nancy, Netta.

Ackerley aged twelve. 'I was a chaste, puritanical, priggish, rather narcissistic little boy,' he recalled. His mother called him 'Angel Face'.

Peter

Nancy

Joe

Father and son: Roger and Joe, 1913.

Roger undergoing the cure at
Bad Gastein, 1920s.

Netta at home in Richmond, 1920s.

Muriel Perry, Quartermaster of the
Soldiers' and Sailors' Free Buffet at Victoria
Station, 1915.

Muriel (left) at the wheel of a Red Cross
Motor Kitchen *en route* for Italy, 1918.

The three Perry girls with ponies in Richmond Park, about 1924:
Diana, Elizabeth, Sally.

The model for Allan Grayle in *The Prisoners of War*, with Ackerley beneath and the Oberland Mountains behind.

Ackerley taking tea on the balcony of his room in the Hôtel des Alpes.

with their mercenary partners, upon which followed many a sorrowful tale similar to those told by Dumas and, perhaps more significantly, by Proust. Ackerley was to endure much Swann-like anguish over the years, failing to heed Forster's salutary warning: 'Joe, you *must* give up looking for gold in coal mines – it merely prevents you from getting amusement out of a nice piece of coal.'

Ackerley's decision to have his allowance reduced must have been something of a relief for his father, who was about to incur enormous expense by marrying off Nancy to a fellow-fruiterer. Paul West was an American who worked for the United Fruit Company and there is some suggestion that the marriage was founded upon dynastic ambition rather than true love. Nancy was later to claim that the match was 'arranged', but she was not entirely reliable, particularly where her marriage was concerned. The fact remains, however, that the couple met whilst Nancy was on an extended holiday in the West Indies and Panama, visiting countries where Elders & Fyffes had considerable business interests. She was chaperoned by one of Roger's cousins-by-marriage and met her future husband at a 'bathing party'. The newspapers insisted that it was a case of 'Love at First Sight in Swimming Pool' and there is no doubt that Paul fell in love with the beautiful English girl. However, the United Fruit Company had a long-standing interest in Elders & Fyffes and had taken over the smaller company in 1913 after protracted negotiations with the shareholders. Their promise that Elders & Fyffes would continue to operate independently had been honoured, but it is conceivable that a marriage between the Panamanian manager of UFC and the daughter of one of E & F's directors would be thought no bad thing. Whatever the motives of the principals, the press certainly thought the match a romantic one, and much was made of the fact that West, who was based in Cristóbal at the mouth of the Panama Canal, travelled 4,500 miles to collect his bride.

Ackerley rather dreaded the entire prospect of the wedding, but was pleased that Colleer Abbott, who was jocularly supposed to aspire to Nancy's hand himself, would be coming to lend moral support. Nancy had always been spoiled by her father, but never more so than in the spectacular wedding reception which he arranged for her at the Hotel Cecil. The service was held at Corpus Christi Church in Maiden Lane on the afternoon of 24 August 1926, after which the guests repaired to the hotel for champagne and dancing. From the Canary Islands and Belgium, from England, Scotland, Wales and Ireland, from offices at Bristol and freighters at sea, the respectful employees of Elders & Fyffes sent 'purely nominal' donations totalling 'well over £100', with which a platinum bracelet wrist-watch set with diamonds and engraved with good wishes was bought for the bride. Most of an edition of the *Banana Budget* (Elders & Fyffes' weekly house magazine) was devoted to the occasion. 'We are bound to say that the happy expression borne by Mr West on the eventful day in question indicated that his long journey was indeed amply rewarded,' the magazine reported. By the evening Mr West may have been having his doubts, since Nancy had already begun to quarrel with him. He spent his wedding night on the sofa.

Rather more romantic circumstances, meanwhile, attended the relationship of E. M. Forster and Harry Daley, who had embarked upon an affair. 'Daley's sensitive mind, pudgy face, and attractive limbs gave me between them a very pleasant evening,' Forster reported. Whilst the affair brought Forster a great deal of happiness and much incidental entertainment, particularly when he accompanied Daley on his beat and got to know the seedier parts of Hammersmith and Chiswick, it also caused him a great deal of worry. They were not well-matched, for Daley, as he candidly admitted in old age, was 'vulgar, indiscreet, a security risk, quick-tempered and as unfaithful as an old tomcat'. Furthermore, whatever his spiritual qualities, the stooped and shambling Forster hardly conformed to Daley's preferred sexual type of tough, gymnasium-trained, working-class heterosexuals. Although Forster could take vicarious pleasure in the reckless exploits of his friends, he felt that Daley, like Ackerley, sometimes Went Too Far. For his part, Daley resented the lectures Forster liked to deliver to his friends and lovers, particularly those concerning money. He was also made to feel uneasy and self-conscious because he knew that whatever he did would be discussed by Forster and Ackerley in his absence. However, in spite of their basic incompatibilities the affair flourished.

Meanwhile, Ackerley's long, muddled and expensive search for the elusive person he designated 'the Ideal Friend' was continuing. This chimera:

should not be effeminate, indeed preferably normal; I did not exclude education but did not want it, I could supply all that myself and in the loved one it had always seemed to get in the way; he should admit me but no-one else; he should be physically attractive to me and younger than myself – the younger the better, as closer to innocence; finally he should be on the small side, lusty, circumcised, physically healthy and clean: no phimosis, halitosis, bromidrosis.

Ackerley admitted that such criteria might suggest that he was deliberately consigning himself to disappointment, but for all his self-analysis, he stopped short of really confronting the issue in *My Father and Myself*. The men amongst whom he sought the Ideal Friend were almost by definition unlikely to meet many of the requirements. For example, the fact that they were chosen from the working classes meant that there was a high probability that they would be uncircumcised. Unless religious belief or medical complications intervened, working-class boys tended to escape the knife at this period. Similarly, at a time when dentistry was only available at a price, halitosis would have been prevalent amongst his working-class partners.[1] Some of them did not have bathrooms in their houses and so personal cleanliness was not always easy to achieve. And as he acknowledged, if he had really been looking for men 'on the small side' it might be asked why he spent so much time patronizing the Brigade of Guards.

This frank catalogue of physical requirements, and indeed the unabashed sexual details of *My Father and Myself*, tend to obscure what is perhaps the most important aspect of Ackerley's character: his romanticism. Throughout the book he disparages his 'sentimental' crushes upon boys and men, and the 'nauseous verses' he wrote about them, but this strand in his character persisted. Perhaps the most significant statement in the chapters dealing with his sex life is the 'neat sentence': 'Unable, it seemed, to reach sex through love, I started upon a long quest in pursuit of love through sex.' Ackerley wondered whether this was true. It seems that to a certain extent it was. Paradoxically, the impulse behind his relentless promiscuity was a

---

[1] Indeed Ackerley paid for a couple of his lovers, amongst them Harry Daley, to have dental work carried out. 'To be a dentist, always peering into people's mouths, seems to me to be the most revolting job in the world,' he noted in later life, 'incomprehensible that anyone should choose it'.

romantic one. Although Ackerley did not study classics at Cambridge, the 'syllabus' provided in Mürren by Arnold Lunn included texts which idealized homosexuality. Furthermore, Ackerley's friendship with Lowes Dickinson would no doubt have led him to that author's *The Greek View of Life*, with its section on 'Friendship'. The tension between physical desire and romantic aspiration is found in the *Phaedrus* of Plato, with its image of the charioteer attempting to master his two horses. Certainly the desire for a partner who was younger and willing to be educated has its Greek model, and the dislike of effeminacy is one the Greeks shared. This is not to say that such choices were learned from classical literature and philosophy, but that such texts would have confirmed and validated Ackerley's feelings. Similarly he seems to have looked upon his promiscuity as a genuinely Platonic search for the 'other half' of his soul.

Harry Daley was unkindly but justifiably sceptical, and one wonders how far Ackerley really wished to succeed in his quest. For all his intellectual conviction about the 'naturalness' of homosexuality, Ackerley had a residual feeling that his fellow homosexuals were not 'real men' and were therefore, by definition, undesirable. The very fact that heterosexual men were not likely to be sexually interested in him made their conquest all the more significant: if they were making an exception for him then there must be something more to the relationship than mere sex. Ackerley's undoubted vanity, endlessly fuelled by men and women who told him how good-looking he was, would have made him particularly susceptible to such a delusion. For delusion it was, since it failed to take into account that in certain circumstances – prison, the army and other all-male enclaves – or for certain rewards, heterosexual men would indulge in homosexual acts without being temperamentally or psychologically homosexual. Most of Ackerley's affairs were with men who were married or had girlfriends, and who later settled down to conventional family lives. They might enjoy the sexual release without complications that a relationship with Ackerley would provide, and they might well grow genuinely fond of him, but they were extremely unlikely to be *in love* with him. Indeed, the emotional demands he made of his lovers were likely to cause them to beat a hasty retreat. He had romantic notions about sex, but by seeking it amongst men whose romantic inclinations were towards women he was cheating himself. Forster's remark about looking for gold in coal mines was echoed rather more bluntly by Daley:

When one wants to give normal young men lingering kisses on the mouth (ugh!) and endless romantic talk about eternal friendship (with thee beneath the bough O my love etc) one must know that a soldier offering himself in a pub for a quick wank at ten shillings a time is unlikely to be suitable.

There were plenty of young men like Ivan Alderman who would have been very happy to have played the role of Ideal Friend, but whose very willingness proved a disqualification. As Ackerley himself observed ruefully: 'Far more people have gone out of my life than have stayed in it – like a hotel. And the rooms are mostly bedrooms.'

In the last years of his life, Ackerley attempted to analyse his sexuality. At ease with his own body, he was wary of the bodies of others. 'I have never been able to enjoy other people's smells – farts, feet, armpits, semen, unwashed cocks – as I enjoy mine,' he admitted. Although *My Father and Myself* was quite graphic enough for most readers, W. H. Auden complained that: 'Frank as he is, Mr Ackerley is never quite explicit about what he *really* preferred to do in bed.' Auden wanted to know because he took a strictly Freudian view of homosexual practices and their symbolic meanings. Was Ackerley, like Auden himself, 'oral', acting out 'Son-and/or-Mother', or 'anal', playing 'Wife-and/or-Husband'? 'My own guess', Auden continued, 'is that at the back of [Ackerley's] mind, lay a daydream of an innocent Eden where children play "Doctor", so that the acts he really preferred were the most "brotherly", Plain-Sewing and Princeton-First-Year.' Whether one agrees with Auden that fellatio, sodomy, mutual masturbation and intercrural intercourse are 'rites of symbolic magic' or merely ingenious variations upon the theme of sexual release, his analysis remains acute.[1]

When revising *My Father and Myself* in the last years of his life, Ackerley made notes cataloguing various sexual practices he found faintly ridiculous or frankly repellent, and it seems clear that he much preferred 'brotherly' methods. One regular partner recalled that

[1] Auden may well have been proud to be the first person to use the term 'Princeton-First-Year' in print, but it is not altogether clear what he meant. His biographer, Humphrey Carpenter, suggests that the term is 'a variation of "Princeton Rub"', a term for *coitus contra ventrem*', or, in plainer terms, rubbing off on a partner's chest. However, Bruce Rodger's exhaustive (and occasionally fanciful) *The Queen's Vernacular: A Gay Lexicon* bluntly defines 'Princeton style' as 'fucking the thighs'. 'Plain-Sewing' is mutual masturbation.

Ackerley invariably kept his clothes on during sex, whilst insisting that his partner should be naked. He had assumed that Ackerley was simply voyeuristic, but there was good reason for remaining clothed. Ackerley recognized that many of his friends did not object to, indeed enjoyed, other forms of sex and wondered whether his 'squeamishness' was somehow inherited from his mother. Perhaps some sense of the physical incompatibility of his parents, of his mother's distaste for sex, had subliminally affected him. In spite of what was to be an extremely promiscuous life (some 'two or three hundred' partners, according to his own calculations), Ackerley remained sexually fastidious. This fastidiousness was considerably compromised by the fact that Ackerley suffered from *ejaculatio praecox*, or sexual incontinence. This condition is generally caused by psychological rather than physiological circumstances and is responsive to psycho-sexual counselling. However, at a period when the majority of doctors were more likely to want to 'cure' homosexual men rather than help them to enjoy a full sex life, there was little hope of seeking professional help.

Ackerley's vicarious experience of medical attitudes towards homosexuality would certainly have prevented his approaching anyone for help. One of his lovers at this period was a Danish medical student called Johannes. This young man had been very unhappy about his homosexuality and had sought help in Copenhagen. It was seriously believed that homosexuality could be 'cured' by removing one testicle and replacing it with the testicle of a heterosexual man. His professor at the medical school was prepared to carry out this extraordinary procedure, but whilst they were waiting for a donor – difficult to find, one imagines – Johannes met Ackerley, became a great deal happier about his sexuality, and so decided against surgery. Unfortunately, he also met a sixteen-year-old youth with whom he had an affair. Danish law was comparatively advanced, and homosexual acts were permitted between men over eighteen, but this liberalism was offset by severe penalties for those who had sex with under-age partners. Johannes was arrested and would have been imprisoned, but was allowed to go free (having paid a considerable fine of £100) on condition that he agreed to undergo the transplantation. This judgement was passed in spite of the fact that considerable doubt had by now been expressed about the 'success' of such an operation. Johannes viewed this astonishing collusion between the law and medicine with the sort of detachment only a true scientist would feel:

I think that the outcome of an operation is very problematical (do you know anything about it?) but now I'm obliged to submit to operation, although I do not want it now. It will be very interesting to see the outcome – if I will be able to feel the same for women as now for men! – I doubt, and you need not be jealous of one or another girl. *You* I'll never be able to forget – 10 operations, I feel sure, were not able to alter my love to you.

Ackerley was horrified and he and Forster tried to find out as much as they could about such experimentation. Forster discovered a book on the subject and reported that, although the evidence about the success of such an operation was conflicting, the author had little faith in it. Exactly what happened in the end is not altogether clear. Ackerley lost touch with the young Dane and the note he made on Johannes's letters, which he carefully kept, was rather ambiguous: 'By now all the experiments had failed, but to satisfy the Law and get Johannes off a perfunctory operation was performed.' How perfunctory, one wonders? It is scarcely surprising that Ackerley's view of doctors and 'medical science' remained sceptical throughout his life.

Unable, therefore, to find any help, Ackerley simply had to cope with premature ejaculation and its consequences. The constant fear of achieving orgasm before one's partner has even achieved erection, the fear no doubt exacerbating the condition, would have been devastating to sexual confidence. Ackerley also believed that premature ejaculation caused him to be sexually inconsiderate for, having achieved release himself (albeit unsatisfactorily) he was disinclined to continue love-making. Guilt, disgust and shame were catastrophically anaphrodisiac. His subsequent manoeuvres in order to disengage himself from further sexual activity, manoeuvres which frequently included deception, merely increased the sense of failure.

None of this prevented Ackerley from pursuing sex with an abandon which alarmed some of his more discreet friends. 'Joe I am worried by,' Forster confessed guiltily to his diary when summing up 1926, 'for I and his other friends are inclined to be critical of him, having first encouraged him to be what he is.' One of the false impressions given in *My Father and Myself* is that Ackerley's promiscuity at this period was a hopeless, miserable and degrading quest. In fact he turned many of his adventures into splendid anecdotes for the amusement of Forster and others, and Harry Daley remembered him

as being at his happiest at this time. This is not to say that the quest for
the Ideal Friend was without its painful or glum moments, but it seems
that much of the sexual activity was good-humoured and light-
hearted. The chance encounters, hasty unbuttonings and snatched
pleasures might be amusing to hear about, but the quest could be
tiresome when it became obsessive. Ackerley once went to Lowestoft
with Daley for a weekend. At the station Ackerley spotted a young
Indian whom he tracked to the staff entrance of a hotel. Thereafter,
apart from meals which he condescended to return to the lodgings to
consume, he spent the entire weekend hanging around the back of the
hotel in the vain hope of seeing the waiter again. Apart from being
boorish, he could occasionally go too far even by Bloomsbury
standards. He once visited Mr Philip and Lady Ottoline Morrell at
Garsington and failed to appear at luncheon. A footman was also
found to be missing and a search party was sent out. The two men were
eventually discovered enjoying a romantic moment in a summerhouse.
Gerald Heard and Christopher Wood, who were fellow guests, were
embarrassed and angry, perhaps because, like Forster, this was the sort
of escapade in which they had encouraged their friend.

The concern felt by Ackerley's friends about his recklessness in
sexual matters was increased when in 1928 he applied for a job with
the British Broadcasting Corporation. He had been recommended for
the job of Assistant Talks Producer by one of his circle, Lionel Fielden,
who was already employed in that department and had just been
promoted in the General Talks division. Ackerley accepted the job on a
three-month trial at £400 p.a. in May, and was to continue in the
Corporation's employ for the next thirty-one years.

8

Talks Department

BEFORE the arrival of Hilda Matheson in January 1927, there had been no Talks Department as such at the BBC. 'Talks' had been part of a General division, which included news, education and, of course, religion. Talks were divided into two categories, 'News' and 'Topical', but in both any hint of the controversial had to be avoided. In 1927 what had been the British Broadcasting Company became the British Broadcasting Corporation and Sir John Reith's title was changed from Managing Director to Director General. The Corporation's licence was renewed by the Postmaster General with the reminder that absolute neutrality should guide all pronouncements over the air. On no account were there to be any comments broadcast upon public policy, neither should any opinions be voiced upon political, religious or industrial controversies. The inevitable result was that the Corporation's critics accused it of being drearily bland. Reith pleaded that the rules should be relaxed, insisting that the Corporation's integrity could be trusted, and in March 1928 the Postmaster General relented.

Hilda Matheson was just the sort of person to test this agreement, and the staff she appointed were intensely loyal, frequently called upon to give her much-needed support. She was very popular with women in the Corporation, seen as giving a lead and showing what women could achieve. This 'glamour' was much enhanced by having two attractive young men working as her assistants, Lionel Fielden, very much the dapper Old Etonian, and now Ackerley, rather more casual but nonetheless striking. Unknown to the majority of their colleagues, all three were homosexual. Matheson was to be one of Vita

Sackville-West's many conquests, affectionately but unflatteringly dubbed 'Stoker'. The two met when the swashbuckling Mrs Nicolson was employed to broadcast on poetry, and by the end of 1928 they had embarked upon a passionate affair. The atmosphere at Savoy Hill the following June when Matheson and her team produced a radio discussion between Sackville-West and her homosexual husband, Harold Nicolson, on the topic of marriage, must have been piquant, to say the least of it.

The department was to go through many changes, most of them controversial, but when Ackerley joined on 30 May 1928 it was divided into three sections, headed by Matheson: Women's, General and News. It was in General that Ackerley was employed, working alongside Fielden in the Corporation's offices on Savoy Hill, tucked between the famous hotel and the Thames. The job was an onerous one, with only two people in the Division. Speakers had to be found and then trained to use the microphone, and all scripts had to be read, discussed with the speakers, revised and sometimes censored. In particular it was vital that no product brand-names should be mentioned on the air. Notes had to be written for the BBC announcers and extracts from the talks circulated to the press for publicity purposes. Once the talk had been broadcast, Ackerley and Fielden made confidential reports of the speakers' suitability, which entered BBC records. The method of choosing speakers for this brave new enterprise had been fairly haphazard in the early days. *Who's Who* was scanned and letters were sent to anyone who might appear to have something to say and might be persuaded to do so. No fee was offered since it was considered a privilege to be taking part in such pioneering work. A great deal of time was wasted, since many people deemed 'suitable' appeared to regard the radio with alarm or abhorrence and wrote stiff letters of refusal in reply to the Department's enquiries.

By the time Ackerley joined the staff things were managed rather better and a battery of regular broadcasters who were paid for their work had emerged from the ranks of art, education and commerce. Ackerley's many contacts in intellectual and literary circles had impressed the BBC and several of his friends became frequent broadcasters. Forster had already made one broadcast by the time Ackerley joined the Corporation, but he now became frequently in demand. He also offered Ackerley much practical advice, making suggestions for broadcasts about India and telling his friend to steer clear of certain

here as introducer of the series and I have no qualifications without it'. The rather louche photograph of himself which he provided for an illustration further emphasized his apartness from the book's real heroes, most of whom had supplied portraits of themselves in uniform. In contrast Ackerley wears a smart flat cap and looks more like a man of the theatre than a man of action. Like the series, the book was a considerable success, boosted in *The Listener* by Forster and reprinted shortly after publication.

As well as editing submitted talks, Ackerley was occasionally called upon to reject them. This required tact and firmness, two qualities for which he was to become celebrated. He was thus able to bring back broadcasters who had been miffed by earlier producers. Forster told him shortly after he joined the Department that David Garnett had boycotted the BBC after being 'underpaid and insulted' by Lance Sieveking, but would now be prepared to do talks once again. 'One has to be very careful with institutions which are gentlemanly,' Forster had warned; and the BBC in those days was exceedingly gentlemanly, its high standards maintained by such practices as unseen radio broad-casters clambering into evening dress before confronting the micro-phone. It was therefore necessary for any employee of the Corporation to deal with broadcasters and other members of the public with the utmost civility. Occasionally this led to difficulties, as when the popular author and cricketing enthusiast A. G. Macdonell appeared to be submitting scripts which were not up to scratch. One talk, entitled 'A Scotsman looks at England', was so poor that Ackerley returned it. Unable, by the conventions of the Corporation, to say that the script was no good, Ackerley was obliged to create a fiction in order to placate Macdonell. 'Our new syllabus starts very shortly,' he wrote, 'and leaves us practically no spaces to play with. The few there are have chiefly to be reserved for talks of topical or national importance.' Macdonell was unconvinced. 'Does the return of the manuscript I sent you, and the rather guarded wording of your letter, mean that my dazzling career as a broadcaster has come to an abrupt conclusion?' he asked. Ackerley was now obliged to be rather more frank:

> I hope your dashing career as a broadcaster has not come to an abrupt end, but we have all felt here that there has been a slight progressive deterioration in the manuscripts you have been sending us. You started off gaily enough, but the standard of your first talk

has not, in our opinion, been kept up and your later manuscripts have had the air of having been rather 'knocked off'. That is really the truth of the matter. We do not usually tell the truth in this office if we can possibly avoid doing so, but I gather from your letter that my excuse did not take you in. The same criticism applies to your broadcasting manner.

This new breath of frankness, usually only to be found in the Corporation's internal memos, was to grow to gale force in the coming years of Ackerley's employment.

When Ackerley had been given the job at the BBC, Forster had counselled him to work hard there, partly to take his mind off problems in his personal life. The chief of these was a young man he had met through Harry Daley and who was to engross him for some four or so years. Daley was having an affair with a boxer called Fred Burton, who was introduced to Ackerley. Before long Ackerley had become friend and benefactor to the entire Burton family, all of whom were out of work, apart from one brother, Albert, who was a deep-sea diver in the Navy. Ackerley employed members of the family as chars at Hammersmith Terrace, had crates of bananas delivered to their home and made the occasional cash hand-out. He also attempted to procure employment for Fred through his father. Roger was very keen on boxing, for there was a gym beneath his offices in Bow Street and he enjoyed watching the men spar there. He was about to give Fred a job with Elders & Fyffes, but then heard that the young man had once gone on strike whilst working at Lyons. For Roger, strikers came into the same category as 'idlers', 'loafers' and other 'five-letter men',[1] and nothing would persuade him to make an exception and take Fred on. Ackerley retreated to socialist Hammersmith and relieved his frustration with a vigorous bout of spring cleaning. 'You see, Harry —' he explained to Daley, shaking a doormat out over the river, 'he is a different *sort* of person from you and me.'

There was much talk in the family of Albert, who was away at sea on a two-year cruise, and it seems that Ackerley had decided to fall in love

[1] Five because the word in question was 'shite', in Roger's terms an even worse insult than 'shit'.

with the young man before he even saw him. On Albert's return from his tour of duty Ackerley drove Daley and Fred to Waterloo station and paid their fares to Portsmouth so that they could greet him off the ship. When Albert appeared in London and was introduced to Ackerley, he lived up to all expectations:

> Small in stature and a lightweight boxer quite famous in the Navy, his silken-skinned, muscular, perfect body was a delight to behold, like the Ephebe of Kritios. His brown-eyed, slightly simian face, with its flattened nose and full thick lips, attracted me at once. If he smelt of anything it was the salt of the sea.

Forster was understandably sceptical about this new affair, for he had seen his friend chasing a good many rainbows over the years. Along with the innumerable soldiers, sailors, waiters and so on who, quite literally, came and went, there had been several young men who had engaged Ackerley's heart for rather longer than one night. There had been Jacks and Jims and Bills and Roberts and Ernests and Georges. Forster disapproved of this *embarras de richesses* and drew a parallel with the 'indecent' stories he had destroyed in order to clear the way towards completing his masterpiece, *A Passage to India*:

> You have to make some such sacrifice now. I feel convinced that what distracts your vitality now is that you are keeping Ernest and about a dozen others on the simmer on the chance of their being useful or exciting some time. An enormous part of your energies go not in lust nor love but in the equivalent of my destroyed mss. It is complicated by the fact that you make most of the simmerers fond of you by taking enough bother – but they've got to go all the same and if this advice is too vague I will go through the names when next we meet, and say who must be dropped.

Whether this cull ever took place is in some doubt. Two who seemed to Forster obvious candidates for dismissal were the Burton brothers, but by this time Ackerley was far too involved and this advice was ignored. Ackerley had recognized the danger of falling in love with Albert and had had plenty of opportunity of retreating before things became serious, but he reflected ruefully that love, however painful and unsatisfactory it was likely to be, should not be rejected. Regardless of whether his advice was taken, Forster continued to give it and was in constant correspondence, offering encouragement at one moment and advising caution the next. 'I feel so inadequate as soon as Albert's touched,' he confessed, 'but I do want to talk to you and do love you.'

Kind, modest and sexually inexperienced, Albert seemed to fulfil all Ackerley's exacting criteria. However, his frequent trips abroad caused endless anxiety for Ackerley who expected his lover to keep faith, write regularly and behave as any middle-class husband or wife might. In fact, the young sailor cancelled appointments at short notice or turned up late or not at all for long-anticipated meetings. Because he was so close to the ideal, Albert's falling short was a constant source of disappointment. Harry Daley, who recognized an element of exhibitionism in Ackerley's character, a theatricality derived perhaps from Netta, referred to the affairs that dominated Ackerley's life as 'his three big set pieces'. Certainly, much public mopping and mowing went on as Ackerley struggled in the toils of this protracted and unsatisfactory affair. Friends were consulted, amongst them the Belfast novelist Forrest Reid, whom he had met through Forster and who was taken to Battersea Park when visiting London to discuss the problem of Albert. Reid, undergoing similar difficulties with someone not his social or intellectual equal, was very sympathetic:

> My youngster met me at the boat and I was rejoiced to find that the sight of him awakened only a feeling of ordinary friendliness . . . At any rate I've given up trying to persuade myself that something exists when I really know it doesn't. Unfortunately it took me eight months to discover what should have been obvious in a week — What it amounts to, I suppose, is that we are idealists, and the others are realists if they are anything at all.

Others took a rather more callous line. 'Joe strives protagonistically with his Albertine,' Gerald Heard reported unkindly. This was just the sort of remark from which Ackerley wanted to protect Albert, feeling that the camp banter of his intellectual friends would alienate his beloved. In spite of his apparent shyness, Albert was scarcely in need of Ackerley's protection. Although the Burtons were a respectable family, they had many friends in Hammersmith who were on the fringes of the criminal world and amongst whom Albert enjoyed gambling when on leave. Forster warned Ackerley against possessiveness:

If you want a permanent relationship with him or anyone, you must give up this idea of ownership, and even the idea of being owned. Relationships based on ownership may be the best (I have never known or tried to know them), but I am certain they never last.

Ackerley's idealization of Albert caused Forster much irritation, partly because in spite of being 'a charming straight creature' (high Forsterian praise), Albert was unresponsive to the finer feelings Ackerley bestowed upon him, was in fact 'a bollard'. Forster felt that the affair would progress rather better if Ackerley could bring himself to brutalize it a little. Ackerley was forever firing off long, emotional letters and being disappointed when he did not receive equally fervent replies. 'Brief notes of affection' or a firm 'torpedo' now and again were what was needed, Forster insisted. His principal feeling was that the relationship was disastrously unequal, not because of social differences as such, but because Ackerley failed to recognize these differences or make provision for them. Forster thought it a mistake to attempt to treat Albert as an equal:

> The standards which are so obvious to you are very remote to him and his class [he wrote after one disappointment], and he was bound to lapse from them sooner or later. And by standards I mean not only conventions but methods of feeling. He can quite well be deeply attached to you and yet suddenly find the journey up [from Ports-mouth] too much of a fag. It is difficult for us with our middle-class training to realize, but it is so.

Whatever Forster's personal feelings about Albert, he was prepared to use him as raw material for his work. *Maurice* was undergoing one of its many revisions and Forster was having difficulty with a scene in which Maurice and his working-class lover, Alec, are in bed together. 'How do you think Albert would talk in such circumstances?' he asked Ackerley. 'Properly, improperly or not at all? I can't hear his voice in the dark.'

When, in the summer of 1928, Albert announced that he was to be sent on a two-year commission, Ackerley vainly suggested that his friend should leave the Navy altogether. Forster was later to recall Ackerley at this period staggering through the streets, blind with misery and influenza, literally bumping into people. Further anxieties were caused by the fact that, frustrated by Albert's absences, Ackerley had continued to pursue a promiscuous sex-life in London and was still to be found prowling around Bird Cage Walk and Hyde Park Corner in search of 'love'. What he got was a dose of clap, caught from a guardsman whom he had unwisely allowed to bugger him. His main concern was that Albert would turn up and that he would be *hors de combat*, or, worse still, might infect his beloved. Fortunately, he managed to see a doctor and get a cure before Albert returned. This happened sooner than expected, for Albert was recalled after ten months abroad in order to spend two years ashore on a training programme. He was based at Portsmouth, where Ackerley instantly rented a flat so that they could spend more time together. It seemed that their relationship could now continue on a much firmer footing.

Ackerley's happiness was almost immediately extinguished, however, by a sharp decline in his father's health. The heart attack Roger had suffered at the end of 1924 was a warning which he had studiously ignored, and his health had been in a poor state for some time. His penchant for good living had begun to catch up with him. When told by Dr Wadd that if he gave up claret he could be guaranteed an extra ten years of life, he had memorably replied: 'Thanks. I'd sooner have the claret.' He took little exercise, drank and smoked heavily, and ate richly and well. His only attempt to remedy these excesses was a yearly trip to Bad Gastein in Austria where he spent a month taking the 'cure'. These month-long holidays appeared to be lonely and cheerless excursions, from which he would return little improved. Ackerley once offered to accompany him but was brusquely rebuffed. Roger also suffered badly from what he called his 'jumps', shooting pains in his hands supposedly caused by neuritis. The frequency and severity of these attacks increased over the years, with Roger interrupting his own dirty stories, or leaping up from the dining-table, in order to rub or shake his fingers and admonish the pain personally: 'Ah! damn you! Why can't you let up?' Dr Wadd prescribed pain-relieving capsules, which Roger dissolved in whisky. This combination of drugs and alcohol may have relieved his immediate symptoms but can scarcely have done his general health much good. According to Ackerley the 'jumps' were in fact caused by syphilis which Roger had contracted during his tour of duty in Egypt. Insufficiently treated, the disease was now in its tertiary stage. Early in 1929, Roger noticed a patch on his tongue and at once recognized the symptoms of the cancer which had killed his own father. Wadd took him into the Hydro and he embarked upon the unpleasant course of treatment which involved having radium needles stuck into his tongue. This remedy worked and within weeks the cancer, caught at an early stage, was clearing up. His neuritis was also being treated and he was obliged to wear a neck-brace for five hours every day. The regime at the Hydro seems to have been far from spartan, however. After the needles had been removed, Roger was lunching on asparagus and caviare, and was drinking whisky and smoking his cigars once more. It is not altogether surprising that whilst there he suffered a slight stroke, which left him very weak on his legs.

Cured of cancer, but otherwise in a worse state than when he entered, Roger left the Hydro at the end of June in order to convalesce on the coast. He went down to Southsea and booked into the Queen's Hotel, after which it was hoped he would have sufficiently recovered his strength to make his annual trip to Bad Gastein. He took with him an envelope which contained a note from Dr Wadd to a Southsea colleague giving Roger's medical history and adding that the patient was able to pay substantial fees. Once there, he settled into a routine of massages, check-ups and excursions in a bath chair along the promenade. The specialists had told him that his heart and pulse were good, but they told his son that Roger was a dying man. He might survive for another two years; certainly no more, probably less.

Netta was quite incapable of coping with the situation and had no intention of accompanying her husband. It was therefore left to Ackerley to deal with this family crisis. Matters were little helped by the presence of Nancy, who had returned to England the previous October, ostensibly to introduce her two-month-old baby, Paul, to his grandparents and uncle. There was, in fact, a more worrying reason for her return: her marriage was in difficulties. Paul Snr's job as manager of the Panamanian branch of the United Fruit Company was extremely important since it was a key to the United States' involvement in South America and was considered by many to be almost as crucial a position as that of the Governor. There were endless functions and a large household of servants, but Nancy had been bored. Her baby had been a brief distraction, but after his birth Nancy's boredom had given way to acute depression. She became listless and started to lose weight. Whether she was suffering from the then unrecognized condition of post-natal depression or simply exhibiting the symptoms of what amounted to a constitutional dissatisfaction with life, is unclear, but her husband was worried enough to send her to England and to ask Dr Wadd to keep an eye on her and send him bulletins about her progress. It gradually emerged that Nancy hated Panama and was virtually indifferent to her husband. Her father's illness provided her with the perfect excuse to remain in England. Far from being a support to her mother, she sat around the house, unwilling to help, and soon fell back into the familiar routine of bickering and sulking. Paul Snr did not receive a single bulletin from Wadd, and in her infrequent letters Nancy failed to report any improvement in her condition. In April 1929 she finally cabled to say that she would return to Panama in May, but within a few weeks she had changed her mind. By now Paul had lost faith in Dr Wadd, and complained to Ackerley:

> Instead of the weekly bulletin I was to receive from him I've had one report in eight months which I had to write for. It contained absolutely no information – and Nancy now tells me she dictated the letter herself!

He asked his brother-in-law to engage a proper 'nerve-specialist' who could examine Nancy and provide a reliable report. Ackerley was the only person in whom he could confide:

> Nancy's letters have indicated, very clearly that even the thought of coming back here has scared her. I could understand it, of course, for a while, but she's been continually worrying over the idea of coming back. Her letters have shown it. For that reason I couldn't even tell her how much I've missed her and how much I've missed seeing our youngster grow up – for fear she might jump on a ship and arrive here, sick, miserable and hating it. And this God Damned five thousand miles separating us makes it impossible to know what's going on, or in fact get news of anything until it's all over.

By now it had become clear to everyone except Paul that there was more than mere geography separating him from his wife.

Although ill, Nancy was far from inactive. She battened on her already overburdened brother and relied on him to provide her with a social life. She went to Section House dances, where it seems she was as much taken by policemen as her brother, and was given a rather livelier and more raffish time than she was used to in Panama. In old age Nancy would claim that she had slept with Albert, but whether or not this is true is impossible to say. She certainly met Albert and liked him, but it seems that if any affair, however brief, took place, Ackerley was unaware of it. Nonetheless, Forster viewed Nancy's acceptance within the circle with alarm and warned Ackerley against allowing her to become too dependent. 'She is so charming but an accredited vampire,' he diagnosed acutely, 'who would have no scruple in destroying your life as she has destroyed Paul's.'

The choice of Southsea for Roger's supposed convalescence was a fortunate one, for it was just along the coast from Portsmouth and Ackerley was able to combine visiting his father and spending time with Albert. Indeed, Albert often accompanied him to the Queen's Hotel and Roger, by now accustomed to his son's democratic choice of friends, seemed to get on well with the young sailor. During July Ackerley, sometimes accompanied by Nancy, visited his father every other night and had dinner with him:

> I've often thought it rather a triumph for all concerned, my Father the great businessman, with his £12,000 a year and capitalist standards laying himself out to be nice to the sailor, and the sailor with nothing but his strength, inarticulate, expressing himself with his hands, awed by the hotel, etc., and myself getting the best of both worlds.

After dinner Ackerley would drive back to Portsmouth and take the first train to London in order to be at Savoy Hill in time for work. This must have been an enervating routine, but since Netta could rarely be persuaded to visit Roger, there seemed to be no one else to keep the old boy's spirits up. Apart, that is, from a mysterious person known as 'the lady from the Pier Hotel'. The existence of this woman was revealed one day when Ackerley and Albert had been with Roger and a lift operator had brought a message that the lady wanted her suitcase. There was an awkward pause before Roger collected himself and told the man to fetch it from his room. No explanation was forthcoming and so Ackerley thought no more about it. Then some time later, when the whole family had gathered, another message was delivered: the woman was on the telephone and wished to speak to Roger. Her name was Muriel and Roger reminded his family that she was an old friend.

In fact my father had mentioned this lady to us, but not often and not for many years; she had been actively engaged, we dimly recalled, in some ambulance or hospital service, of patriotic interest to him, during the war, and he had occasionally alluded to her in laudatory terms as a splendid woman who had done wonderful work for the sick and wounded in various countries and received for it sundry foreign decorations.

Nothing more had been heard of her, but it appeared that she had now brought her medical skills to Roger's aid. Ackerley bumped into her on several occasions after this, once with one of her daughters, an attractive teenager who bore an ominous resemblance to Nancy.

Roger's health, so far from improving in the bracing atmosphere of Southsea, was now beginning to deteriorate rapidly. He had further minor strokes, the last of which left him considerably incapacitated. On 3 September Ackerley received a message at the BBC that his father was dying. By the time he reached Southsea, Roger was already dead. He had been laid out in the hotel bedroom and a sprig of heather and a photograph of his family had been placed between his hands. The lady from the Pier Hotel was in attendance.

9

House of cards

BACK in London, Ackerley discovered a sealed envelope in his father's desk, addressed to him in Roger's hand. It carried the warning: 'Only in case of my death'. Inside were two letters which could hardly have come as a total surprise. The first, dated 21 October 1920, revealed that 'the lady from the Pier Hotel' (whose full name, Muriel Perry, was now disclosed) had three daughters by Roger: twins, Sally and Elizabeth, born in 1910 and another girl, Diana, born two years later. Roger asked that financial provision should be made for them:

> I am not going to make any excuses, old man. I have done my duty towards everybody as far as my nature would allow and I hope people generally will be kind to my memory. All my men pals know of my second family and of their mother, so you won't find it difficult to get on their track.

Indeed, their tracks had already crossed, and the two young Ackerleys had already suspected that the pretty young girl they had met in the lobby of the Queen's Hotel would turn out to be a half-sister. It is an index of their own self-absorption that they had barely given the matter another thought. Ackerley had even taken Diana out to a pub in his car and had failed to ask her a single searching question about herself or her mother, but had spent the time chatting to the barman. It may also have been that Joe and Nancy were concerned more about their father's immediate health than about whatever he had been up to in the past. The family had always been unconventional and neither of them was in the least perturbed by this initial disclosure. Ackerley's immediate reaction to the confirmation of his suspicions was to regret that his father had not managed to provide him with three half-brothers; if Nancy was an example of a sister, one was quite enough. It was the second letter, dated 1927, which provided the worse shock, for it showed that these new siblings had proved expensive in their upkeep.

> I opened the envelope enclosing this other document just now to refresh my mind. Seven years have passed since I wrote it and seven years of expensive education for the three girls etc. etc. It means that my estate has dwindled to almost vanishing point and my latest effort viz. buying a house in Castelnau for them has about put finishing touches.

These letters showed Roger at his most nonchalant, and he had good reason to be self-satisfied. He had pulled off what must at times have seemed almost impossible and had kept his 'secret orchard', as he put it, hidden until the end. This had required considerable social ma-noeuvring, especially since he had set up his second family in Barnes, which was only about three miles away from Blenheim House. Until the final few weeks of his life, he had been very careful to keep the two families apart whilst being as even-handed with them as he could. The Ackerleys, of course, took precedence: it was they who accompanied Roger to the first day of the annual Richmond Horse Show when he presented the prize for the best turned-out costermonger; the Perry children would merely be given tickets for the second day. There had been some difficult moments, as when Joe and Nancy bumped into their half-sister in the Southsea hotel and when the porter had tactlessly asked about Muriel's suitcase in front of Netta. Fortunately Netta was so vague that she would probably have had to be introduced to Muriel for anything to have registered. Ackerley considered his father's two letters naïve but characteristic, and felt that Roger had managed to carry off his double-life as much by luck as by judgement:

> I see him as an easy-going, tolerant, rather careless man, simple and boyish, whose motto might have been 'Live and let live', and who got out of 'this wonderful old world' as much as he could, blunder-ing about after pleasure and hoping for the best.

It has never been satisfactorily explained how, where and when Roger and Muriel met. In spite of years of persistent and perceptive questioning by her daughter Diana, Muriel remained stubbornly evasive about her life before Roger, going so far as to lose or destroy birth certificates and mutilate her passport. Her birth was never registered, but she claimed that it took place on 5 March 1890, which made her twenty-seven years Roger's junior. It is possible that they met on one of Roger's many trips to Bristol, a port which saw much Elders & Fyffes traffic. What is certain is that at some point Muriel was employed as a barmaid at the Tavistock Hotel on Long Acre in Covent Garden, just around the corner from the Elders & Fyffes offices. This would have been around 1908, when Roger's sons, a mere six or so years younger than Muriel, were at school in Lancashire. Ackerley described Muriel as 'a tall rather coarse-looking woman', and in 1929, when he met her at Southsea, she might well have been, since by then unhappiness and alcohol had taken their toll. But when Roger first saw her she was an attractive woman, strikingly tall and long-limbed, with a mass of dark hair, centrally parted and loosely gathered up at the nape.

Whatever the circumstances of their meeting, the consequences were inevitable: Muriel became pregnant. Muriel was delighted, but Roger can scarcely have shared in this. He already had three illegitimate children by Netta and may have felt some relief when the child, a boy, was stillborn. Muriel had a sentimental regard for children – until, that is, she actually produced some – and was deeply distressed. No doubt she had envisaged the child as her stake in Roger, something which would give her security. However, by the end of 1909 she was pregnant again, and in June, after a near-fatal labour, she produced twin girls, Sally and Elizabeth. Roger, by now accustomed to deceiving the General Registrar, acquired birth certificates for them on which their father was recorded as a certain and fictitious 'George Perry'. He never acknowledged his relationship to his daughters and they grew up in the belief that he was some beneficent but remote relative, whom they always addressed as 'Uncle Bodger'. When he wrote to them, he signed himself 'Unks'.

All Roger's plans had gone awry, thwarted once again by his own contraceptive carelessness. As his letters to her amply demonstrate, Roger was in love with Muriel, and she adored him in return, regarding him as 'father, lover and friend all in one'. Roger also loved Netta, but Muriel was someone with whom he could enjoy sex without feeling that he was imposing upon her. He regarded Muriel as a mistress rather than as a wife, and that relationship was considerably complicated by the appearance of children. Roger hired a nursemaid, but was annoyed to discover that at first Muriel was keen to act as mother, more interested in her babies than in becoming his lover once more. Nonetheless, it was not long before she was again pregnant, and the entire household was moved to a flat in Chelsea. By now Muriel had begun to realize that her babies were in danger of estranging her from her lover and a difficult decision was taken. Roger bought a house in Woodlands Road at the edge of Barnes Common and it seems (the sequence of events has never been established) that shortly after the birth of Diana in April 1912 all three children were installed in this new home, where they were joined by a Miss Coutts, the sister of one of Roger's Scots acquaintances. Muriel did not go with them.

The terrible story of the childhood of these daughters, abandoned to the loving but parsimonious care of an elderly spinster, was later recorded by Diana.[1] Free of maternal ties, Muriel found a new lease of life doing remarkable work in the Great War. She ran a canteen for the troops at Victoria Station, lavishing upon battle-weary Tommies the love and attention she denied her own children. This charitable work was advertised in the press and funded by benevolent individuals and companies such as Elders & Fyffes.[2] The enterprise grew until it was clearly in need of some proper administration, whereupon the Red Cross adopted it, appointing Muriel Quartermaster. Her self-confidence boosted by the astonishing success of the Soldiers' and Sailors' Free Buffet, Muriel teamed up with a Mrs Mouse McCalmont, the lively widow of a racing millionaire and sister of a man with whom Muriel had enjoyed a brief relationship. Mouse donated a motor kitchen to the Italian Red Cross and Muriel took it to the Front in the spring of 1918. Her war effort and feminine charms impressed the Duke of Aosta, who fell in love with her. She received a chestful of medals, Belgian, British and Italian, survived a severe bout of dysentery and serious abdominal surgery, but decided to remain with the Red Cross after the war had ended. She had not, however, forgotten

---

[1] See *The Secret Orchard of Roger Ackerley* (1975) by Diana Petre.

[2] Roger must have experienced a considerable *frisson* in 1926 when he read an account of Nancy's wedding in the *Evening News*. In the course of the report reference was made to the 'very prominent part' he had taken in 'organising the provision of refreshments for the Service men at Victoria Station'.

Roger, and they were often reunited during the latter's post-war business trips to the Continent.

Meanwhile her three daughters had developed rickets as a result of neglect. It seems extraordinary that Roger, who occasionally visited them during the war, failed to notice the state of the house or the condition of his daughters. It may have been that his eye was so undomesticated that he simply didn't see the shabby furniture in the stuffy gloom created by Miss Coutts. In the excitement of his un-heralded appearances, the chauffeur-driven car piled high with gifts, the true state of affairs may not have been apparent. Roger's mind was no doubt preoccupied with the fate of his two sons at the Front. Miss Coutts received an entirely adequate allowance, but with true Scots carefulness spent only a fraction of this, determined not to spoil her charges.

When Muriel finally returned in the spring of 1922 she was aghast at the trio of 'slum children' who greeted her. She had intended only to look in upon her daughters before pursuing a career in London, but realized at once that she could desert them no longer and so came to live with them and with Miss Coutts, whom she disliked and mis-trusted. She was no better a mother when in the company of her children than she had been when separated from them, and, after a brief flurry of redecorating had momentarily lightened the Barnes house, the atmosphere there became dark and embittered. Sally was the only one of her children to whom Muriel became devoted, and that obsessively and destructively. Sally had been allotted the place left blank by the death of Muriel's stillborn first child and Muriel always referred to her as her 'son' and addressed her as 'Sam'. This drove a wedge between the twins, and the dependent Elizabeth never entirely recovered or managed to function separately from her beloved sister. Diana, now aged ten, had never known her mother at all and Muriel seemed little interested in making up for this. Miss Coutts gradually faded from their lives, withdrawing to her own room in which she shortly died. The children were packed off to school. Muriel began to drink. The only bright moments were occasioned by visits from, or outings with, Roger.

In 1927 Roger bought a new house in Muriel's name a little over a mile north of Woodlands Road in Castelnau, a road which the chauffeur took every day on the journeys between Blenheim House and Bow Street. In spite of this auspicious move, Muriel was by now a serious and secret drinker and there were appalling nocturnal scenes as she staggered around the house like a wraith, stark-eyed and weeping. One afternoon, whilst Muriel was at the hairdresser, Sally organized her sisters to make a thorough search of the house, collecting up and throwing away all the hidden empty bottles and pouring the contents of the full ones down the kitchen sink. She told Roger of her discovery and her action and insisted that he should stop sending Muriel his customary gifts of wine and spirits, advice he weakly ignored. As soon as they possibly could the twins left home and it fell to Diana to cope with her increasingly unhappy and incoherent mother. The worsening of Roger's health and the defection of Sally took their heavy toll on Muriel. 'I hardly ever saw her drinking,' Diana recalled, 'but I don't think she was ever quite sober.'

School terms were something of a relief. In 1929 when Diana was packed off to the latest in a long line of boarding-schools, Muriel went into a nursing home to be dried out, emerging in June just in time to take charge of Roger at Southsea. She shut up the Castelnau house and booked into the Pier Hotel, and thus began the final manoeuvrings of Roger's life, a grim farce in which various members of his two families popped in and out of hotel rooms, occasionally and embarrassingly coinciding.

Faced with the financial realities of the situation his father had bequeathed him, Ackerley began to economize at once. His socialist sensibilities were outraged by the quotation given to him by the undertakers, and he asked them how the poor could possibly afford to bury their dead. The undertaker delicately outlined economies, explaining that there were four grades of coffin. The cheapest was something called 'the Violet Shell', but that could hardly be seen being carried out of somewhere as grand as Blenheim House. Oh couldn't it, Ackerley replied.

Violet Shell or not, the funeral was an extremely grand affair. According to *The Times*:

> Nearly a thousand business men from all over the British Isles as well as from the Continent attended the funeral at Richmond Cemetery . . . and the wreaths were so numerous that four men were specially engaged to load and unload them. The procession of

mourners reached the length of the largest part of the cemetery, and two police officers experienced difficulty in regulating the long stream of private motor-cars. The small chapel in the cemetery, where a brief service was held, was totally inadequate for the occasion, and quite two-thirds of the mourners were unable to enter.

Neither Netta nor Muriel attended, which was perhaps as well. Muriel followed the hearse when Roger's body was driven from Southsea back to Richmond, tactfully branching off for Castelnau at the appropriate moment. Netta simply refused to countenance death and would not read any of the letters of condolence. She announced that the funeral would only upset her and that Roger would have understood her absence. She had not, of course, been informed of the reasons for the dramatic decline in her husband's financial fortunes and presumably put it down to her dear old Punch's celebrated generosity. Ackerley described her as 'like a character in Tchehov – moving gaily through her heaving, tottering world as though nothing whatever was happening, surrounded by her joblot servants and joblot dogs.'

Forster was out of reach in Africa when Roger died, so that Ackerley called upon the support of friends like Leo Charlton and Tom Wichelo, Colleer Abbott, Gerald Heard, Frank Birch, Harry Daley and 'sweet old Albert'. Nonetheless, he was greatly relieved when Forster returned, characteristically cutting short his holiday to do so. Ackerley had merely informed Forster of Roger's death, not wishing to spoil his friend's fun (with a French sailor named Achille) with details of his own crisis. 'The house of cards has indeed come tumbling about my ears,' he reported now. 'There isn't really – I'd better forewarn you – a chink of sky to be seen; the wreckage is so overwhelming and complete.'

The family's financial position was grave indeed. When Roger had made his will in 1919 he already knew that his finances were in a poor way, and did well to regret that there was so little to leave to Netta. The Banana King had less than a year's salary to bequeath: £11,382 8s 5d. He had assumed that Elders & Fyffes would automatically give Netta a pension, thus releasing a £2,000 life insurance policy for the benefit of Muriel and her daughters. Unfortunately, Roger's extravagance had brought the company to the brink of bankruptcy and Arthur

Stockley had neither the funds nor the inclination to maintain his late partner's families. He seems to have disliked Muriel intensely. It is possible that there had been some rivalry between the two men over her when they used to see her at the Tavistock Hotel, and that, as usual, Roger had won.[1] Stockley told Ackerley bluntly that the company would only give Netta a pension – and one far smaller than Roger had anticipated: £500 rather than £3,000 a year – on condition that no money whatsoever went to Muriel.

Apart from the parlous state of the company's finances, Stockley may have had personal reasons for thwarting his late partner's post-humous wishes. Although he was supposed to be Roger's oldest and best friend, he had not troubled himself to visit his partner when it became clear that he was extremely ill. He had, after all, plenty of reasons to resent Roger. It had been he, Stockley, who had started the firm, but it was Roger who strutted around in Covent Garden, hailed by everyone as the Banana King. Whilst Stockley had been financially and personally prudent, Roger had been spectacularly extravagant and imprudent, and yet he had managed to outwit them all. Whilst Roger had a charming, doting wife who was blissfully unaware of the existence of his mistress, poor Stockley had a wife who was considered 'a drone', and from whom he had been unable to hide his ill-managed liaisons with other women. Ackerley detected a note of jealousy in Stockley's attitude to his partner:

> Dad was popular, Arthur was not. Also while we were a spectacular family, the Stockleys were not. Though decent sorts of fellows, they were nothing to look at, did not write books or have their heads blown off in war. They were unaccomplished and commonplace.

Certainly, in the pompous and preposterously titled book Stockley was to write about Elders & Fyffes, *Consciousness of Effort: The Romance of the Banana* (privately printed in 1938 in an edition of fifty copies), he played down Roger's role in the company's success. He

---

[1] Another theory is that Muriel was the illegitimate daughter of a member of the Stockley family, possibly the daughter of Harold Moore, the much younger brother of Arthur Stockley's mother. Considerable research by a number of people has failed to prove or dispose of this intriguing idea. If it *were* true, it might explain how Roger and Muriel met. It might also explain the strained relationship between Stockley and Roger.

must have resented the way in which Roger had 'got away with it' in life and was determined that he should not do so from the grave.

Stockley's obstinacy put Ackerley in the unenviable position of having either to disregard his father's wishes or to follow them and see his mother still further reduced in circumstances. 'Even now I don't know what else I could have done,' he wrote in *My Father and Myself* in justification of disinheriting Muriel. She had, after all, done well out of Roger, and she at least owned the house at Castelnau, whilst Blenheim House was rented. Anyone less valiant for truth might simply have told Muriel that no provision had been made for her, but Ackerley insisted upon telling her of his dilemma and how he intended to resolve it. Muriel, who did not like Ackerley, partly because he was the representative of Roger's other life and partly because she recognized him as homosexual, must have bitterly resented him as he told her. She had a further reason to do so, since money that Roger had put aside for her daughters had been spent on Nancy's wedding and was never replaced. And what a waste of money that seemed, now that Nancy was back with her mother, the marriage collapsing after a couple of years. Ackerley was to remember nothing of this painful interview, apart from a promise to pay Diana's school fees. He and Muriel never saw each other again.

Having disposed of the mistress, Ackerley now had to deal with his mother. The first thing to do was to dismiss the servants, and friends who came to visit were warned that they would have to fend for themselves. (Leo Charlton was much resented when he continued to polish off a 12s 6d bottle of whisky each visit.) Netta could no longer afford the upkeep of Blenheim House and somewhere much smaller would have to be found.

Something would also have to be done about Nancy. Briefly united by Roger's death, mother and daughter soon began to bicker once again and Ackerley spent a great deal of time attempting to adjudicate between them. Forster advised him to threaten to go to Hammersmith Terrace and not return until they behaved themselves. Quite apart from the expense of Nancy and her child, there was also the question of finding her somewhere to live. Blenheim House contained enough rooms for Nancy and Netta to keep to their own domains; in a smaller house there would be less room for manoeuvre and their 'jealous warfare' would get worse. Paul wrote to Nancy frequently, asking when she would be returning, but Nancy's replies were evasive and unsympathetic. Exasperated, he announced that he would institute proceedings for divorce, a challenge which alarmed Ackerley and reduced Nancy to a state of incoherent rage. Various friends, like Forster, Colleer Abbott and Leo Charlton, offered advice and acted as intermediaries between the estranged couple. The Wests and the Ackerleys arranged meetings and the luckless Charlton was despatched to New York to plead with Paul to take Nancy back. Once he met Paul, however, he was far too sympathetic to put his case with any conviction and returned empty-handed, to be branded a turncoat by Nancy.

It was not until the following July that Nancy was persuaded to return to Panama with her baby in order to make one last attempt to patch things up. She had been placed in lodgings on Richmond Hill whilst preparations were made to clear Blenheim House, which Harry Wadd was to take over as an annexe to the Hydro. He astutely offered to buy any furniture and fittings that Netta did not want to take with her; one wonders whether the £514 he owed Roger was added to the small price he paid for these. Netta gradually retreated into the top floor of Blenheim House, finally occupying two small rooms, whilst beds, screens and other nursing paraphernalia were moved in below her. Meanwhile Ackerley had found a small house for her in a less select area of Richmond at 159a Sheen Road, where she was eventually to retire with a maid, her Sealyham, and several padlocked trunks, cases and boxes.

10

His father's son

ACKERLEY later claimed that the disclosure of his father's double life made him 'confused and muddled about the nature of truth'. What shocked him was the fact that Roger had never confided in him, and he was determined to understand this failure of communication. He recognized the irony that though father and son had had much in common – each going about his secret life, each unwilling to confide in the other – they had failed to capitalize upon this: 'We never really knew each other; he was no real use to me nor I to him.' Ackerley might have been much closer to his father if only they had not let the opportunities for truth-telling slip away in mutual embarrassment. He acknowledged that both his parents 'were afraid of emotion' and this he ascribed to 'well-developed instincts for self-preservation'. Roger 'didn't like prying into other people's affairs because he didn't like people prying into his.' One of Roger's other children, Diana, agreed with Ackerley that for all his bountiful jollity their father had seemed somehow unapproachable. Roger may have given the world a convincing impression of a gregarious and popular man, but the oppressive life of secrecy he had been obliged to live had resulted in considerable loneliness. He had no real friends, no one he could really trust, apart from his business cronies and his wily medical neighbour. His friendship with Stockley had been undermined by his partner's jealousy and contempt, whilst that with Dr Wadd amounted to little more than exchanging a whisky-and-soda for the latest dirty joke. Roger had been obliged to lie not only to friends and associates, but to both his wife and his mistress, keeping Muriel a secret from Netta, and excusing himself from marrying Muriel by

149

saying that he was already married, which at the time he was not.

If, as Roger claimed in his first posthumous letter, he had seen Joe as 'a grown man, with every sign of great intelligence and a kindly nature towards human frailties', why had he not confided in him? Ackerley accused himself of being too interested in his own life to take any notice of his father's. 'Between my Father and myself it was too late,' he wrote. 'He died, so to speak, as I turned to look at him; the conversation we should have had never took place.' In notebooks he rehearsed those lost conversations in which each was forced to confront the truth about the other. He thought that Roger would have been only too pleased to have helped a son get rid of 'troublesome women' or illegitimate children, but might have been less enthusiastic about homosexual problems. Certainly, Ackerley's attempts to introduce the topic had been firmly rebuffed, but he felt that had he been braver and less quick to take offence, he could have persisted and become a true son and friend.

This question of the relationship between his father and himself had one very important legacy. It provided Ackerley with a lesson for life, a lesson he was to take very seriously. In the words of Coventry Patmore, which Ackerley repeatedly copied into diaries and notebooks as the new year's epigraph:

> When all its work is done, the lie shall rot;
> The truth is great, and shall prevail,
> When none cares whether it prevail or not.

Ackerley's insistence upon telling the truth in both life and art was an obsession whose roots were buried deep in the lies which had surrounded his childhood. It had been intellectually nurtured by the guru-like figure of Gerald Heard, who had impressed upon all his friends the importance of truth. Ackerley's belief that the truth should be told whatever the cost was buttressed by the fact that the cost of *not* telling the truth lay all about him in the financial and psychological ruination of his family.

Although Ackerley no longer relied upon the small allowance his father had paid him, the collapse of the family's fortunes meant that he was obliged to make economies himself. Forster advised him to leave Hammersmith Terrace, and upon discovering that Ackerley was broke and owed the Needhams money promptly offered to settle the debt himself. 'You are only at the beginning of your trials with me as a moneyed man,' he warned prophetically. He remarked that the Ackerleys would not realize how little money they had until the tradespeople started refusing to send them supplies. The real reason Forster wanted Ackerley to leave Hammersmith was because he wanted to remove him from the influence of Harry Daley. The affair between Forster and Daley had come to an end, bringing disenchantment in its wake. Daley himself had felt rejected and his relationship with Fred Burton was in difficulties. Like Ackerley, Daley was far from monogamous, but was by now a deal less idealistic. His exhilarating life amidst the criminal fraternity of Hammersmith continued and Ackerley, whilst disapproving of Daley's casual affairs, gave him a key to the Hammersmith Terrace flat and often left out wine and food for him and whoever it was he had picked up. Forster, who was convinced that Daley's recklessness would land all of them in the dock, cautioned Ackerley against Daley, enlisting Leo Charlton's support, but to little avail. In spite of Daley's devotion to Ackerley (he had been chided by Gerald Heard for regarding Ackerley as above criticism), the two friends began to have disagreements, which developed into rows. On one intemperate occasion Daley called Forster and his friends 'pimps', not entirely without justification when one recalls how Daley, a not unwilling parcel, had been handed round the circle. Reconciliations between Daley and Ackerley became fewer and briefer, and Forster was much relieved.

Another relationship that was disintegrating was Ackerley's affair with Albert. The cosy domesticity in the Portsmouth flat, with Ackerley driving down to prepare dinner, was not a great success. Now that he was stationed in England for some time, Albert was less inclined to be at Ackerley's beck and call. Ackerley's claim in *My Father and Myself* that the relationship eventually unravelled because Albert was disgusted when Ackerley performed fellatio upon him is disputed by Harry Daley. It is clear that the friendship was in difficulties, and, considerably reduced in means himself, Ackerley strongly disapproved of what he saw as Albert's extravagance at gambling. According to Daley 'meanness and deceit' were unjustly alleged by Ackerley and the friendship came to an end. Whatever the case, Ackerley was extremely miserable and worked off some of his despair in a series of poems. He described them as 'a small sad collection . . . sad in execution and much else, besides their story – for I fear they tell a story.'[1] He also described them as 'personal and old-fashioned', as indeed they were, especially a sequence of six sonnets, one of which opened:

How often, with my every need contained
In this one thought, that soon *you* would appear
And self-forgetful Eden be regained –
How often have I waited for you here!

Far better was a poem written as a pastiche of A. E. Housman, whose simple language and mood of ironic resignation suited him. 'The Jacket' describes a poignant encounter in the streets of Hammersmith:

I met your brother out today
Returning from some job or other
In working clothes. We always stay
    And talk to one another.

He always hails me heartily
With vague, impulsive friendliness;
His aimless amiability
    Dejects me, I confess.

And so we passed the time of day
With 'Pleased to meet you! 'Ope you're fit.'
His jacket was a lightish grey,
    And I remembered it.

The cloth was faded, pockets torn
And bulging with his plumber's kit,
And stained it was, and old and worn;
    But I remembered it.

---

[1] The last phrase echoes Forster's famous lament about the novel: 'Yes – oh dear yes – the novel tells a story.' This comes from the Clark Lectures Forster had delivered at Cambridge in 1927, which won him a three-year fellowship at King's College and were published that year as *Aspects of the Novel*. Ackerley declared that *Aspects* was his favourite book and often quoted from it.

His father's son

It sagged about him like a sack —
I had to look; I had to stare,
For once it clothed another back,
    And not for working wear.

I bought it for you years ago,
When first I fell in love with you,
And you were proud of it, I know,
    When it and I were new.

And how I worried over it,
Considering in loving pride
The colour first, and then the fit,
    And were you satisfied.

Ah, I remembered many things;
Yes, many things did I recall;
They beat me down with heavy wings;
    I sank beneath them all.

The way you stood; the way you stept;
Your shoulder-muscles' lift and swell;
The simple things the pockets kept —
    I knew them all so well.

How often round those shoulders lay
My fond protecting arm at rest,
And years of darkness fell away
    Against that jacket's breast.

Once more I lay upon your lips,
And knew your body's feel afresh,
And, savouring of sea and ships,
    The flavour of your flesh.

But all my love and all my care
Through years of mingled hope and pain
To keep the heart that wearied there
    Were dedicate in vain.

You turned away. 'Ah, stay!' I cried;
But nothing could your coldness move . . .
And now outworn and cast aside,
 The jacket and my love.

   * * *

Your brother greets me cheerfully
With 'Pleased to meet you! 'Ope you're fit.'
 His hazy geniality
 Depresses me a bit.

This charming and affecting little poem underwent some revision, but never satisfied its author, who later pencilled a line through every verse. He also continued writing a poem he had begun when first in love with Albert, 'Notes for a Portrait of a Sailor', which ran to 118 lines and was 'of a somewhat Whitmanesque nature'. One section of it had been published in November 1928 in the first issue of *The Venture*, a literary magazine edited from Ackerley's old Cambridge college by Anthony Blunt, H. Romilly Fedden and Michael Redgrave. 'Salute One Another in Passing!' is some considerable way after Whitman, but it was declared 'lovely' by Forster. Redgrave was less delighted, later describing it as 'enough to sink any literary magazine'. 'There was a great deal more of it which I have destroyed,' Ackerley told a friend, 'and it was going to be an epic (whatever an epic might be), but life started to bang me on the head soon after, and it turned, as you will notice, into a kind of aspic.'

One of the things which banged him on the head was the return of Nancy from Panama in the autumn of 1932. She had failed to patch up the marriage and now threw herself and her child upon Ackerley's mercy. It was a position she was to adopt for the remainder of her brother's life. Against her son's advice, Netta insisted upon Nancy coming to live with her at Sheen Road. She appeared to have forgotten the rows of the past and had convinced herself that her daughter had been cruelly discarded by her errant husband. Paul had in fact behaved impeccably and was allowing Nancy to divorce him. Forster had warned Ackerley that firmness was required and that Nancy should be put into lodgings near her mother, but firmness was not a quality that Ackerley ever exercised when dealing with personal relations. He vacillated, worried, prowled round and round the problem, sought and disregarded advice, and eventually allowed his mother to have her own way. Before long he was being summoned once or twice a week to settle differences between mother and daughter.

Young Paul was packed off to boarding-school, clutching a model yacht, the only present he ever received from his mother, he claimed. He was far too young to be sent away and before long got into trouble. One day two ten-year-olds (boys twice his age) grabbed his sailboat and pissed on it. Paul, who had by now learned to stand up for himself, laid into both these bullies, who then complained to the headmaster who demanded that the little boy should be removed. Another school was found for him, which he endured for some years in spite of being the victim of unwelcome attention from older boys. Unable to speak about this to his remote and distracted mother or his Uncle Joe, he set about defending himself and those juniors less able to cope with the situation.

Back at Sheen Road, the pleasant life Netta had led, enlivened by a succession of Sealyhams and visits from her son's friends, had come to an abrupt end. Part of Ackerley's problem in dealing with the violent arguments which formed a staple of daily life there was that although common sense required him to be neutral, he was far more sympathetic towards his mother than he was towards his sister.

> My mother was a consistently sweet, gay, playful, friendly little creature, whom nobody had ever disliked or could possibly dislike [he wrote in 1949], though with her endless loquacity, for which she did not really require an audience, she might have bored them. But she was warm, kind, charming, sweet natured and friendly, and everyone took to her always, from the domestics upwards. My sister was a very different cup of tea – cold tea. She is a woman of whom I think it is true to say that she lacks all the middle registers of human feelings; her relationships, such as they are, have all been of a nature in which the emotions are involved, love, hatred, jealousy and so on; she has scarcely ever made any friends or acquaintances, and such as she has made she has lost either through quarrels or neglect.

Although this analysis should be placed in context – it was written after Netta's death and during the latest and most serious in a long succession of Nancy crises – it was one shared not only by Ackerley's friends (whose views of women in general were far from reliable), but by others who came into contact with Nancy. A female doctor who once attended her said to Ackerley: 'You know what the trouble with your sister is, don't you?' ('I know a number,' Ackerley replied. 'Which have you in mind?') 'She doesn't fit in.' As Ackerley recognized: 'It was a brilliant diagnosis; it was absolutely right.' Nancy herself, who was not given to self-analysis, admitted as much, recalling that she had hated boarding-school and not made any friends there. She had preferred to be with her two brothers than to mix with a lot of girls with whom she felt she had nothing in common.

The ruination of Nancy had begun very early on and she had failed to grow up. Indulged and, quite literally, spoiled by her father, she was accustomed to getting her own way and had developed little from the small girl who stamped her foot and screamed until her desires were met. 'I never liked being told what to do,' she confessed late in life. She was not stupid and had quite enjoyed the lessons at school, but her mind had lain fallow ever since. Having few intellectual resources, she was constantly a prey to boredom. What she lacked in mental and emotional maturity she made up for in great physical beauty. Her clear blue eyes and red-gold hair had attracted the attentions of many young men before she met Paul West. It is likely that part of his appeal for her had been the implacable opposition to the match of his mother, a formidable Catholic widow of Irish origins who disapproved of the marriages of all her children, but of this one in particular, since there was a religious difference. Had the young couple lived in England rather than Panama the relationship might have survived, but now, at the age of thirty-four, the bad behaviour of a spoilt young beauty was being superseded by signs of extreme emotional instability. 'Rejected' by her husband, unable to cope with a young son who was himself showing signs of disturbance, and at war with her mother, Nancy saw her brother as a lifeline and she clung to him with all the tenacity of someone who was drowning.

Anyone less suitable to cling to would be difficult to imagine. If Ackerley was a misogynist, it should in fairness be said that his experience of women might well have given rise to, or confirmed, his poor opinion of them. This is to explain, rather than to excuse him, and of course, like Forster, there were women in his life of whom he was extremely fond. However, there is no doubt that the homosexual world in which he moved, emotionally detached from the sex, was inclined to be dismissive or critical of women. It was a world in which the word 'feminine' was almost invariably used pejoratively: it meant possessive, jealous, interfering, domineering – all of which, it must be admitted, applied to Forster's mother and Ackerley's sister. If they agreed with little else that Kipling wrote, Ackerley and his friends certainly concurred in the assertion that 'the female of the species is more deadly than the male.' At best, women might contribute to 'one's comfort and stability':

> Although my mother has been intermittently tiresome for the last thirty years [Forster was obliged to confess to Ackerley], cramped and warped my genius, hindered my career, blocked and buggered up my house, and boycotted my beloved, I have to admit that she has provided a sort of rich subsoil where I have been able to rest and grow. That, rather than sex or wifiness, seems to be women's special gift to men.

This complacent view of women as compost was one shared by many of Forster's friends and those women who failed in their allotted role were severely criticized. 'Is it not the woman's part artfully to serve the man,' Ackerley asked, 'to consider and fit in with him, however tiresome and difficult he may be.' What these men required were women who would fulfil the traditional domestic duties, but would not fuss, would not interfere, would not make demands, and would be content with dutiful family affection. In this – sex apart – they were not so different in their expectations from many heterosexual men of the period.

However inclined Ackerley was to involve himself in 'messy' emotional entanglements with his lovers, he was psychologically unprepared to deal with the similar demands of his sister. It is not without significance that his mother always wiped her mouth before kissing her children and was unable to ask whether they 'loved' her, taking refuge in the coy 'luff', making a joke of this urgent and anxious question. Netta's relationships with her husband, with Harold Armstrong, indeed with the entire world, were evasive. She shrank from unpalatable truths and took refuge in a fantasy world unsullied by any of the awkward, unpleasant and inescapable aspects of humanity. 'I had been brought up to suppose that people controlled their emotions,' Ackerley wrote, 'and did not spill them about like piss or shit.' Nancy's psychological incontinence disgusted and frightened him: he was, he admitted, 'afraid of her possessiveness, her emotionalism, her dependence and her resentful temper'.

He soon became so alarmed by the continual warfare being waged at Sheen Road, however, that he made a New Year's resolution to separate the two women. He wrote to Nancy to tell her that he was determined to find her a flat or room near him and that she should pack in readiness to move. Upon receiving this letter Nancy took to her bed and announced that she was having a nervous breakdown. If people didn't stop being nasty to her she would throw herself in the river. Since Ackerley had always been a prey to remorse, this tactic proved very successful and Nancy employed it frequently, indeed whenever it looked as if her brother was going to take a firm stand, a holiday, or anything else that upset her. On this occasion Ackerley persisted, and managed to find alternative accommodation for her. Whether or not Nancy's behaviour triggered her mother's alarming decline in mental and physical health, as Ackerley claimed, is impossible to say. Forster had seen the danger signs shortly after Roger's death and had advised Ackerley to give his mother Brazil nuts rather than champagne for Christmas. Whatever the case, the seventy-year-old woman had been badly shaken by the experience of living with Nancy and thereafter drank heavily and became eccentric and slovenly.

Since his return from India, Ackerley had done a considerable amount of work upon his Chhatarpur diary and it had been circulating in manuscript amongst his friends for some time. Nearly everyone had praised it, although some were wary about publication, largely because of Ackerley's frankness over the sexual atmosphere of His Highness's court. Forster advised Ackerley which passages might cause offence, using his mother as a touchstone of public opinion. Such details, however, found great favour elsewhere. 'I want to see your snapshots of all your people, and to ask you lots of questions the answers to which are, I daresay, unpublishable,' wrote Henry Festing Jones.[1] 'But perhaps you are not thinking of publication. I'll come and see you and have lunch and talk it over and all that as soon as I can.'

---

[1] 1851–1928. Friend, executor and biographer of Samuel Butler and for Ackerley's generation a link with that iconoclast of Victorian family values. He was affectionately known as 'Enrico', less so as 'Festering Bones'.

Harold Nicolson thought the manuscript 'so excellent that it must certainly be published regardless of all questions of taste and risk.' It was the most amusing thing he'd read since Norman Douglas's *South Wind* and he felt that it gave the reader 'a better understanding of the oriental mentality than any study I know with the possible exception of *A Passage to India*.' Ackerley sent the manuscript to Charles Prentice at Chatto and Windus, 'for your private eye – and I trust it won't bore you beyond all words of criticism.'

Prentice was certainly not bored, but was understandably cautious about handling a book which, in the terms of the period, was both libellous and obscene. Nonetheless, he was very keen to publish the book in some form and so asked whether Ackerley would be willing to make some alterations to the manuscript so that the book could be sent to the printers. Names were changed throughout and Chhatarpur became 'Chhokrapur'. This half-hearted and sly disguise ('Chhokrapur' translates as 'city of boys') was bolstered by an introductory 'Explanation' which concluded:

> This journal, then, which developed day by day out of almost complete ignorance, and for whose accuracy of fact, since I was depending solely upon my memory, I cannot therefore vouch – this journal, then, concerns itself exclusively with the small Hindoo native state of Chhokrapur (a name for which, since I have just invented it, it will be idle to explore the map) – and it docs not pretend to have cxhausted even that.

Chatto and Windus still insisted that Ackerley make a number of large cuts before the book could be passed for publication. The Maharajah of Chhatarpur was still alive, as were his children, therefore an obvious excision, which was both libellous *and* obscene, was the reported conversation in the journal in which Mahadeo tells Ackerley that Rāghunāndi had been obliged to have sex with the Rani and might well be the father of His Highness's heirs. When Roger had been shown the manuscript Ackerley had already taken the precaution of removing this passage, but nonetheless his father had asked: 'Was the Maharajah a bugger?' Prentice felt that anyone reading the book was likely to ask the same question, and this was particularly disturbing since the book was likely to fall foul of the powerful and prudish circulating libraries. Equally worrying were scenes in which Ackerley portrayed himself wooing 'Narayan' and 'Sharma'. 'I want Narayan to be presented with a kiss,' Ackerley told Prentice, 'but I'll make it more of an avuncular peck.' He agreed to modify the book further 'in such a way that there'll really be nothing, I hope you'll agree, for Boots and Smiths to seize upon.' He also provided some accomplished line caricatures of several of the characters, four of which were used to illustrate the book.

Hindoo Holiday was published in April 1932 to great acclaim and large sales, in spite of the fact that it was launched without the assistance either of Forster or the BBC. Forster had declined to write an introduction when publication was first proposed in 1929. The reasons he gave in a letter to Ackerley were scarcely compelling: 'I don't expect I could introduce it, partly because it sounds a good book, partly because it's about him [i.e. His Highness].' A far more likely reason was that, however much Forster may have enjoyed Ackerley's 'crafty-ebbing' details in private, he did not greatly care to see them in print, or to be in any way connected with their publication. (What, after all, might his mother think?) It was another example of Joe Going Too Far. This might be the reason that in spite of instructions issued to the publishers at Christmas 1931 that the book should carry the cryptic but appropriate dedication '*To D.M.M.*', when the book was published the following spring it was dedicated '*To My Mother*'. Any hope that the book would be recommended on the radio was firmly quashed by Sir John Reith. Vita Sackville-West had agreed with her husband about the book's merits, but had been prevented from including it in the weekly review of fiction she presented for the BBC by the DG himself 'on the grounds of indecency':

> I was sorry not to be able to make a trumpet-blast about 'Hindoo Holiday'. You know how I love it. I have done as much private propaganda about it as I possibly could, and everyone I meet is raving about it. No wonder. It really is a gem, and I read it again and again with renewed delight. (This isn't a polite phrase; it is true. I take it out of my shelf and read a few pages whenever I want to cheer myself up, and to believe again that books *ought* to be written and *ought* to be published.) Do please set about writing more books.

The silenced Sackville-West trumpet was more than compensated for by a fanfare in the *Spectator* from Evelyn Waugh:

Mr J. R. Ackerley's Indian journal leaves the reviewer in some embarrassment as to the terms in which he must praise it. For praise it certainly demands; the difficulty is to control one's enthusiasm and to praise it temperately, for it is certainly one of those books of rare occurrence which stand upon a superior and totally distinct plane of artistic achievement above the ordinary trade-market, high-grade competence of contemporary literature. The danger is one of overstatement. It does not qualify for the epithets 'great', 'stupendous', 'epoch-making', &c., so generously flung about by critics, but it is a work of high literary skill and very delicate aesthetic perception and it deals with a character and a milieu which are novel and radiantly delightful. What more, in an imperfect world, has one the right to expect?

Reith's distaste did not prevent *Hindoo Holiday* from receiving praise in the pages of the Corporation's magazine, *The Listener*, although in searching amongst the gaily indecorous pages of the book for that essential Reithian ingredient, moral value, T. Earle Welby somewhat misinterpreted Ackerley's intentions:

If a moral is to be pointed it is not that the systems of rule in these States produce such odd and unseemly results but that certain characteristics of India find expression in such ways when not hampered by an alien civilization . . . Here, in what professes to be no more than an entertainment, is an exhibition, remorseless for all that it is in its queer way affectionate, of the childishness and intellectual muddlement and moral anarchy of certain kinds of Indians . . . It must be taken into account in any settlement made with India.

The notion of *Hindoo Holiday* being seriously adduced in Independence negotiations was clearly absurd, and Ackerley was alarmed that the book was being taken far too seriously in some quarters. He had aimed, he complained, at providing a mischievous, scandalous romp and was dismayed by references in reviews to Socrates and what he dismissed as 'all this balls about Plato'. Far more to his taste was the notice in the *Week-end Review* by Edward Thompson, the novelist and historian of India, which described the book as 'a lark' and which ended: 'I think this book is in for a big success.' How big a success surprised everyone. Published on 7 April, the second impression was exhausted by the end of the month and it went through two further printings that year. Since Ackerley intended to leave the BBC ('this damned lunatic asylum' as he described it to Prentice), sales were as important to him as prestige. It was, and remains, his most successful book, and shortly achieved cult status. Ackerley joined Ronald Firbank and Lord Rochester as 'authors of the moment' in Cyril Connolly's 1934 journal, for instance. The book's popularity made Ackerley regret that he had not been firmer with Chatto and Windus, for he felt that he had been made to take out 'the guts of the book' unnecessarily. Regardless of the praise of Waugh, who was as much as Ackerley a literary craftsman, Ackerley complained to L. P. Hartley that the cuts he had made to the book had 'left it without shape and unity'. In spite of such bowdlerization, *Hindoo Holiday* was to be found in 'specialist' shops in Soho, where inflammatory books fought for space on the shelves with rubber goods.

The Aga Khan, who had known the Maharajah, was so impressed by the book that he named one of his racehorses 'Hindoo Holiday'. Ackerley, who was too poor and, after the example of his father, too wary to bet on the horses, nonetheless backed this one, which lost, repeatedly. He wrote to the Aga Khan to ask about the horse and received a reply from Deauville in which His Highness confessed that he had been given the opportunity of buying either Windsor Lad or the horse he had named after Ackerley's book. 'The great goose had chosen the wrong horse,' Ackerley later complained. 'Windsor Lad, who became a very famous horse, might have been called Hindoo Holiday and made my fortune . . . As it was the real Hindoo Holiday, wretched animal, which I felt obliged to back whenever it ran, never won a race in its life.' The Aga Khan said that *had* Hindoo Holiday won the Derby he would have asked the public who had backed it to invest part of their winnings in buying the book, which, he said, he preferred 'to any other work of imagination about India written by one of your countrymen, including Kipling'. He hoped to see the book translated into French, with its expurgations restored and offered to write an introduction for a French edition if the publishers thought it would help to promote and sell the book. Ackerley held him to this promise and when in 1935 the book was published (on the recommendation of André Gide) by Gallimard in a translation by Marie

Mavraud, *Intermède Hindou* carried a fulsome *Préface* by the Islamic spiritual leader. Although the Maharajah of Chhatarpur died almost as soon as the book was published ('a stroke of Providence, which you certainly don't deserve from that Power,' Lowes Dickinson observed), no Indian edition of the book appeared until 1979. It carried an introduction by the Indian academic and Raj expert, Saros Cowasjee, who described it as 'the only book about India by an Englishman in which I have not been conscious of the author's nationality while reading it. To me, this in itself speaks of the book's triumph.'

Throughout the troubles he had been having with his family and Albert, Ackerley had been guided by Forster, but it was now his turn to offer solace and counsel. Bob Buckingham announced that he had met a young nurse called May Hockey and that they intended to get married. Forster realized that the only thing to be done was to accept this new situation. However, he was determined that May should conform to his dim view of women as possessive and destructive creatures, and when Bob began to postpone or cancel meetings he felt that his worst fears were realized. In fact May was getting rather less than her due as a newly married woman, for Forster insisted that Bob should spend his one day off a week with him and thought nothing of whisking him off for weekends, leaving May at home. However, in the autumn of 1932 crisis point had been reached: 'If he fails me again I *feel* I shall smash,' Forster told Ackerley. A conspiracy to estrange the young couple was launched, headed by Forster and Jack Sprott. Sprott loaned his car so that Forster and Bob could make a two-week tour of Devon and Cornwall, leaving May behind in London. She was very fond of Harry Daley, and he of her, and, never able to resist stirring up trouble, he decided to tell her what was going on. May was well aware of what was being attempted, but had resolutely decided to do nothing, feeling sure of Bob's affection for her.

Ackerley had had no part in this conspiracy, largely because he was still in the confidence of Daley. Furthermore, he had met and liked May, whose forthright atheism and disdain for make-up endeared her to him. Indeed, she was to become one of the few women he liked and the two became firm friends, Ackerley making good the few gaps left by Harry Daley in May's education in the ways of the homosexual world. Unshockable, unflappable, efficient and kind, 'Darling May' became Ackerley's feminine ideal,[1] so much so that she later destroyed most of his effusive letters for fear that a later generation might misinterpret them. May was right to make no protest at Forster's monopolizing her husband, for the scheme to unseat her came to nothing. Indeed, Forster accepted Bob's new circumstances, and, after this false start, grew very close to May. The young couple were affectionately referred to as 'the Bucks' and 'the Maybobs', and their home in Shepherd's Bush became a gathering place for most of Forster's circle.

Ackerley had been looking for somewhere else to live ever since Roger's death and eventually moved to 13 Upper Mall, a select enclave a little further round the curve of the river from Hammersmith Terrace, and centred upon the famous 'Dove' pub, where many of his artistic neighbours congregated. Ackerley stayed there for a mere nine months before moving out of the area altogether, exchanging the River Thames for the Regent's Canal, and acquiring a flat at 44 Clifton Gardens, in the part of Maida Vale known as Little Venice. The area, like the Italian city after which it was named, exhaled an air of decayed grandeur. Its large stucco houses, now peeling to reveal the crumbling brickwork beneath, were reflected blearily in the waters of the canal. In the 1930s Maida Vale was acquiring quite a reputation, for several writers and artists, most of them homosexual, had recently begun to colonize the area which, like neighbouring but rather smarter St John's Wood, had previously been celebrated as a place where gentlemen secreted their mistresses. Although prostitutes still thronged the pavements, Maida Vale now acquired a distinctly homosexual atmosphere and Virginia Woolf did not allow her fondness for 'the Bugger Boys' to stand in the way of a good quip when she coined the generic term 'the Lilies of the Valley'. Leo Charlton and Tom Wichelo lived there, as did Stephen Spender with his guardsman boyfriend Tony Hyndman, and William Plomer, who spoke of the 'Canal School of English Literature'.

Plomer was to become one of Ackerley's closest friends. Born in South Africa in 1903 and educated at Rugby during the Great War,

---

[1] Rosamond Lehmann was the only woman he admitted to finding *sexually* attractive, although there was a definite spark between him and Sonia Orwell which, in spite of her best efforts, failed to ignite.

Plomer had returned to his native land and, 'with a hard pencil on thin paper', written *Turbott Wolfe*, described by the *Natal Advertiser* as 'A Nasty Book on a Nasty Subject'. That subject was miscegenation and the book caused a furore when published by the Woolfs at the Hogarth Press in 1925. Undeterred by the controversy surrounding the book, Plomer joined forces with the poet Roy Campbell to found and edit a satirical magazine called *Voorslag* or 'Whiplash'. He then left Africa for good, travelling to Japan, where he spent two years working as a tutor, and finally arriving in London 'a young man of English origins and Afro-Asian conditionings'. His literary reputation was consolidated by his Japanese novel *Sado*, published in 1929. It was a discreet account of a homosexual relationship, and discretion was very much part of Plomer's character. In this he differed from Ackerley, but in spite of this and of his assertion that 'the word "circle" is distasteful, with its suggestion of clique or coterie, and I have a disinclination of hunting in a pack', he was soon mixing with Ackerley's set. The two men had originally met at the BBC in 1929, but it was only when they became neighbours that their intimacy thrived. Plomer was a tall, rather dapper figure, with owlish spectacles. His bland exterior, like his beautiful, stylish handwriting, had been adopted as a mask, largely to conceal the fact that he was homosexual. Unlike Ackerley, Plomer never fully came to terms with his homosexuality, although this did not prevent him from leading an equally promiscuous love-life. Ackerley became extremely fond of Plomer and dubbed him 'Sweet William' and 'D.L.B.' (or 'Dear Little Bird').

Once he had settled into his new home, Ackerley began work on a new literary project. By this time he had become interested in discovering more about his father. He realized that the story of Roger's two families had the makings of an interesting book, one which might be used to capitalize upon the success of *Hindoo Holiday*. There was the problem, of course, that Netta was still alive and, although drinking too much, was in reasonable health. No book could be published until after her death. However, he had already found that the books he wrote took several years to mature and that this one would involve a great deal of research. A further reason for delving into the past was that in Ackerley the self-obsession which sometimes characterizes the writer (and which he felt was characteristic of the homosexual) was developed to a high degree. In particular, he was interested to learn how his own sexual character had been moulded by family history. The discoveries he made were to surprise even him.

Whilst it was impossible to talk to his mother about his father's life, he realized that Aunt Bunny was an excellent source of gossip. Exceedingly worldly, a splendid anecdotalist with an excellent memory, and, it had to be said, somewhat 'coarse-grained', Bunny would not allow considerations of decency or tact to stand in the way of the truth, or at any rate her perception of the truth. It was she who supplied the information that, far from being part of a legitimate, planned family, Peter, Joe and Nancy were quite as much 'mistakes' as their three half-sisters. She also supplied the less honourable details about her own family, the Aylwards.

Another source of information was one of his Hammersmith landlords, Arthur Needham. At some point during Ackerley's tenancy Arthur had pointed out an oil painting on the staircase of 6 Hammersmith Terrace. It depicted 'a pompous old gentleman dressed in ceremonial attire and seated on a kind of throne', and was identified by Arthur as Count James Francis de Gallatin. The name was familiar to Ackerley, for the Count had been mentioned as a former acquaintance of Roger. He recalled that some sort of falling-out had occurred, but had taken little interest in the matter. Needham explained that the Count had been a friend of his and both men mused upon this coincidence. Ackerley was introduced to a Miss Emily Lenfant, who had been employed by the Count and his mother before him, and she supplied further information about the Count's association with Roger. It became apparent that in his dotage the Count (who had died in 1915) had been actively, indeed notoriously, homosexual. He had been an *habitué* of the Paxton pub where guardsmen from nearby Knightsbridge Barracks were to be found, as Ackerley, himself a latter-day patron, was well aware. It occurred to Ackerley that there might have been more to the relationship between his father and the Count than had thus far been revealed. When questioned, old Arthur Needham became giggly and evasive. Ackerley's curiosity was largely idle and his questions mischievous, for at this time his father was still alive, in every sense a solidly heterosexual presence at Blenheim House.

Nevertheless, Ackerley was now rather more serious in his interest and he began mulling over the stories he had heard at Hammersmith Terrace. He recalled that when his father had died, Stockley had offered to dispose of the large roll-top desk Roger had kept in his office at Bow Street. Astonishingly, Ackerley had agreed to this, perhaps feeling that he had quite enough to do without sorting through papers which were probably all concerned with the marketing of bananas. The desk and its contents had been burned. Now Ackerley bitterly regretted giving Stockley permission to carry out such wholesale destruction and was suspicious of Stockley's motives in making the suggestion in the first place. Stockley had also known de Gallatin. Ackerley wrote to him, and to Roger's youngest brother, Denton, who lived in South Africa, asking for information about Roger's early life. Neither man was inclined to give much away, but they did supply some photographs and a little general information about Roger's youth and his connection with both the Count and a barrister called Ashmore.

Fitzmore Paley Ashmore had met Roger in 1879 when the latter first came to London aged sixteen. He was in his thirties, married, and lived at Radnor Place, between Paddington and Hyde Park. It is not known how Ashmore met Roger, but his indifference to his wife and children and the fact that he purchased Roger's discharge from the Blues and left him £500 when he died, all suggest that Hyde Park or one of its adjacent pubs were likely venues for their first encounter. Unfortunately, scarcely had Roger returned from the Egyptian campaign, left the army and become Ashmore's 'secretary', when his protector unexpectedly dropped dead. It was then that Roger re-enlisted with the Second Life Guards where, as 1228 Trooper A. Ackerley, he served eight months before once again purchasing his discharge in February 1884. In April of that year he came into Ashmore's legacy which had been left in trust with his father. This money was handed over as a 'loan' to de Gallatin, who undertook to pay the young man 20 per cent interest per annum.

De Gallatin was a Swiss-American Count of the Holy Roman Empire (hence the fancy dress of Arthur Needham's painting), a rather grotesque figure with staring eyes and a walrus moustache. Once again it is not known how this eminent personage came to befriend a young guardsman; once again, the inevitable conclusion must be drawn. When Roger returned to Rainhill to work for his wine-merchant brother-in-law, de Gallatin frequently accompanied him on his travels. The Count hired a house at nearby New Brighton for the summer and weekends, and holidays were spent there with Arthur Stockley and another young man called Dudley Sykes, about whom nothing is known.[1] Working on commission, Roger was earning very little to supplement the £100 a year interest on his legacy, and it was de Gallatin who suggested that Roger's cavalry experience could be invested in a pony farm. De Gallatin already rented a disused farm near his family home in Windsor and now bought it in order to establish the enterprise. Unfortunately, Roger then fell seriously ill and was obliged to convalesce abroad, at the Count's expense. The two men travelled in style, lost heavily at the tables of Monte Carlo, and ended up in a Neapolitan villa. It was not until the spring of 1887 that Roger was fit enough to travel to Ireland in order to buy stock for the farm. At the Fairhill Fair in Galway he found ten ponies at £5 each, but, being unable to transport them to England immediately, he had been obliged to leave them on the estate of Lord Wallescourt. By the time he had paid for their keep, his lordship's grooms and transportation, he had spent another £200. In spite of this financial setback, Roger was soon doing well, breaking in and selling on the ponies, as well as riding in local point-to-point races.

All went well for eighteen months, but some time late in 1888 Louise Burckhardt came to stay at the invitation of de Gallatin's mother. There is some suggestion that Mme de Gallatin had hoped that Louise would prove a suitable wife for her son, but Louise was more interested in the younger man and before long they had fallen in love. Aware that this would cause an upset in the de Gallatin house, Roger announced his intention of marrying Louise one evening and left the house early the next morning. The Count and his mother were, for different reasons, furious.

The Burckhardts appear to have grown very fond of Roger, perhaps succumbing to the celebrated Ackerley charm, and after Louise's death, the grieving father assured the widower that he would continue to receive his allowance. Whatever his intentions, Burckhardt failed to make a legal record of them, for when he died, within months of his

---

[1] Looking through some family photographs when Roger was still alive, Ackerley had discovered a group portrait taken at New Brighton, which, to use a word Roger favoured, was distinctly 'rum' (see picture opposite p. 110). Ackerley asked what had happened to Sykes. 'He married and died,' was Roger's suspiciously brusque reply. It may have been in this company that Roger acquired the mysterious nickname with which he sometimes signed his letters to Stockley, even when they became business partners. 'Coney' seems a curiously inappropriate name for a strapping former guardsman.

daughter, no will was discovered. Without a job and without an allowance, Roger had returned to England, widowed and penniless. He approached his former benefactor and asked whether the loan of £500 could now be repaid. Understandably piqued by Roger's behaviour, de Gallatin refused to return the money, claiming that it had been invested in the pony farm and that he had himself lost money in this venture. Roger unwisely decided to take the matter to court, whereupon the Count put in a counter-claim for £600. It was a sordid and dismal affair in which Roger came off badly, for the court took into account the interest paid by de Gallatin as well as the free board and lodging Roger had enjoyed, and eventually found in favour of the Count. From then on de Gallatin would not allow Roger's name to be mentioned in his presence.

Such details fascinated Ackerley, but he was greatly frustrated that he was unable, as he put it, 'to drag [Roger] captive into the homosexual fold'. One of the reasons he wanted to do this may have been to reclaim his father from Peter, his dead brother. If he could prove that Roger had been homosexual, it would make Ackerley quite as much his father's son as Peter had appeared to be. The long shadow Peter had cast across his life might at last be lifted. Ackerley never did find any proof that Roger had, like so many of his fellow-guardsmen, supplemented the Queen's Shilling in the time-honoured way. Whilst it seems unlikely that the interest Ashmore and de Gallatin had taken in Roger was innocently paternal, this does not necessarily mean that either of them ever actually went to bed with him. But if they did not, one wonders how they struck up an acquaintance with him in the first place. The question has little to do with Roger's own sexuality. Even if he had been the paid partner of a whole barful of late-Victorian twanks, there is no reason to suppose that he was, in any real or permanent sense, homosexual. There was, after all, an embarrassing abundance of evidence of his heterosexual proclivities. The fascination for Ackerley was that he had begun by exploring the gap between his father and himself and had ended by discovering that, psychologically viewed, their relationship was potentially closer than those between most parents and their children. Given a slight shift in time, any one of those fine young men whom Ackerley propositioned in the shadows at Hyde Park Corner or at the bars of the Knightsbridge pubs might have turned out to be his own father.

In spite of its success, *Hindoo Holiday* did not provide its author with sufficient funds to abandon his career with the BBC. He had already weathered one storm with the Corporation when, in despair about Albert, he insisted upon taking leave and was threatened with the sack. Forster had cautioned him, since it was clear that in the financial aftermath of Roger's death Ackerley needed full-time employment. Matters were not improved by serious ructions in the Talks Department. Hilda Matheson's choice of speakers continued to cause concern and, in spite of pained memos despatched from the Director General's office, she refused to compromise. Before long she and Reith had reached a point where communication between them had moved almost imperceptibly from frigid politeness to outright contempt. Reith suggested that certain figures should not broadcast and Matheson suggested that Reith was insufficiently informed culturally to advise her. Perhaps in order to curb Matheson's excesses, or even to force her towards resignation, the Talks Department was reorganized in December 1929 and was merged with the Adult Education Department. To everyone's disgust but his own, the ambitious and unpopular Charles Siepmann, who had been head of Adult Education, was put in charge of the new department, over Hilda Matheson. According to the internal 'History' of the department:

> Miss Matheson was in normal [i.e. nominal] charge of the new Talks Department, but she was not given a categorical mandate over all its affairs, Mr Siepmann being autonymous [sic] in regard to his own talks and speakers; joint affairs being conducted on a basis of colleagueship.

It was hardly to be expected that Matheson would be content with what amounted to a demotion and after a difficult year the department was reorganized once more and a General Talks Department, dealing with topical talks, poetry readings and book reviews, was formed, headed by Matheson, with Fielden and Ackerley as her assistants. The department staggered on until February 1932, when Matheson eventually resigned, in protest, it was said, at Reith's refusal to allow Harold Nicolson to broadcast upon Joyce's *Ulysses*. However, it is more likely that the real reason for her departure was Siepmann's usurpation of her department. The departmental history records that she resigned partly in protest at the 'change of policy with regard to the

Talks programme' and partly because of 'difficulties with regard to staff (see her personal file)'. Because BBC personal files remain closed even after the subject has died it is not possible to discover what these difficulties were, but it seems unlikely that they involved Ackerley or Fielden. The prospect of being answerable to Siepmann without Matheson as a buffer appalled them both and they determined to resign with her. Matheson herself dissuaded them before departing to become 'secretary' to the Nicolsons.

Siepmann was very keen that Lionel Fielden should stay, for he needed his expertise in order to establish his reign, but he was less concerned about Ackerley. The two were temperamentally anti-pathetic and Siepmann did little to recommend himself by his habit of disparaging the achievements of Matheson. There was further trouble about a series of debates which Ackerley produced, on such topics as public schools (Bertrand Russell v. F. B. Malim, Master of Wellington, both of whom Siepmann found 'disappointing') and the press. Ackerley appears to have flouted the BBC's policy of causing no offence during a 'Debate on Newspapers' in 1933, because he allowed 'indirect references' to be made to a current example of journalistic invasion of privacy. Siepmann wrote a stiff rebuke:

> I thought I made it quite plain that we could have no allusions to these specific cases but that, on the contrary, we wanted some hard-hitting, in general terms without particular instances, at the intrusion of newspaper correspondents into the people's private lives. As it was this passage was either so cryptic as to be so much a waste of time, or so obvious as to be doubly offensive to those concerned.

There was also an occasion when J. B. Priestley, one of the most popular and highly regarded of the Corporation's broadcasters, ar-rived at the microphone in the studio and was waiting to be handed the script when he heard his talk announced. The live broadcast had to be hastily abandoned and an investigation was launched. The announcer thought that Priestley had the script, Priestley thought the announcer had it. In fact it was in Ackerley's office, which was locked, its occupant having forgotten all about it and gone home. Reith was furious and made abject apologies to Priestley, but the novelist had been rather amused and no doubt it was this reaction which saved Ackerley from being further disciplined.

Ackerley had briefly considered a job with the *Evening News*, but since it paid a great deal less than the £600 p.a. he was now getting from the Corporation, this was never really a serious option. Forster felt that Ackerley should only leave the BBC if Fielden also resigned, but in the event Fielden allowed himself to be persuaded to stay on and soon succumbed to shingles and 'a nervous breakdown of madhouse proportions'. Ackerley continued in the department until 1935, when Janet Adam Smith announced that she was getting married and would therefore be resigning from her post as literary editor of the BBC's magazine, *The Listener*.

11

Inside the machine

THE announcement in December 1928 that the BBC was to publish a new magazine had caused an unexpected outcry. The press release prepared by the editor-elect, R. S. Lambert, who had made his reputation in the Corporation's Adult Education Department, seemed innocuous enough:

> The BBC will shortly commence publication of a new illustrated weekly journal, entitled *The Listener*, to be devoted to the extension and improvement of its Adult Educational work . . . It is intended that *The Listener* shall stand for much more than the mere reproduction of talks. The journal will be educational in the broad sense of the word: that is, it will take cognizance of all the serious interest[s] of the listening public in such a way as to provide a paper which the intelligent man or woman will wish to buy for its own sake for entertainment and information.

Some sections of the press, notably those who feared the competition, complained that the BBC were 'invading' the field of publishing. The principal objections were that the new magazine represented further empire-building on behalf of the Corporation ('an illegitimate stretching of official activity', as the *Financial News* put it); that its BBC backing would give *The Listener* an unfair advantage over similar magazines (the *New Statesman* was particularly vociferous about this 'thoroughly objectionable' project); and that, most importantly, in the scramble for advertising revenue 'the BBC was diverting trade from legitimate trade channels'. Representatives of these channels, a delegation of newspaper proprietors, were determined to halt publication and sought an audience with the Postmaster-General, who oversaw the BBC on behalf of the government. The PMG refused to receive them, so they appealed direct to the Prime Minister, Stanley Baldwin. By this time Reith had returned from his Christmas holiday in Switzerland much invigorated by alpine air, and he got on to Baldwin immediately, suggesting that the proprietors should meet the BBC before trespassing upon the valuable time of the head of government. A meeting between the Governors and the proprietors was arranged which lasted a mere ten minutes and from which the BBC emerged triumphant. A few concessions were agreed upon, notably that only as much advertising as was 'strictly necessary' would be taken, since the magazine was not intended to be profit-making. Another concession, released to the press on 14 January 1929, was that:

> The BBC states that it is not intended that 'The Listener' should contain more than 10% original contributed material not related to broadcasting. The rest of the paper will consist of talks which have been broadcast, and comments thereon, articles relating to broadcast programmes, and programme personalities, and news of broadcast service generally.

Lambert, whose true ambition was to produce a journal of general culture ('something on the lines of a twopenny *Spectator*'), later admitted in a confidential memo that:

> To some extent the working out of this clause in practice has depended upon the interpretation of the phrase 'original contributed material not related to broadcasting'. Editorially, we have always reckoned that anything published in the paper which could be in any way related to broadcasting, or any part of the broadcast programmes, would not rank as part of the 10%.

To ensure that they got away with this Lambert decided early on to stop the practice of printing footnotes informing the reader when each talk had been broadcast. In this way the paper's rivals would be unable to work out what percentage of an issue was 'original contributed material not related to broadcasting' and so accuse the Corporation of violating the agreement.

Two days after this agreement had been published the first issue of the magazine appeared, priced at threepence, half the cost of its nearest potential rivals, the *Nation* and *Spectator*. Its weekly net sales during the first year averaged 27,773 copies.

The Listener did not have a literary editor at first, this part of the magazine being handled by the deputy editor, Janet Adam Smith. As the paper moved closer to Lambert's ideal it was decided to create a separate post of literary editor and Adam Smith was appointed, gladly relinquishing the less interesting aspects of her previous job. It was she who created the magazine's high literary reputation, particularly with regard to the poetry which it regularly published from February 1931 onwards. An anthology of poems which had originally appeared in *The Listener* was edited by her and published a few months after she had left the staff to marry the poet and mountaineer Michael Roberts. Its title, *Poems of Tomorrow*, was intended to reflect the magazine's discernment in publishing the poetry of young writers whose names had subsequently become familiar. Indeed, the contents page is a distinguished roll-call of the period: W. H. Auden, C. Day Lewis, Louis MacNeice, Stephen Spender, David Gascoyne, John Lehmann, George Barker, Roy Campbell, Gavin Ewart, Julian Bell, Charles Madge, William Plomer, Kathleen Raine, Herbert Read, Michael Roberts, Dylan Thomas, Edwin Muir, and so on. Her departure was a blow to the magazine and it was necessary to find a replacement who could capitalize upon and continue her excellent groundwork.

A BBC memo dated 17 January 1935 noted that there had been 'a long-standing promise' to Ackerley to consider him for any vacancy which arose at *The Listener*. Lambert apparently regarded the thirty-eight-year-old Ackerley as something of a catch, partly because he had a literary reputation of his own and also because of his wide circle of acquaintance, which had already proved useful in the Talks Department. It may also have been felt that an appointment from the Talks Department would help to heal the breach that had risen between it and the magazine. Talks tended to think that the main purpose of *The Listener* was to provide a verbatim record of the best of their output, and they objected when Lambert edited their material for reasons of space or because talks which broadcast well sometimes read awkwardly. Whatever the case, Ackerley's promise was honoured and he was appointed to begin work on 15 April. It was in many ways a brave appointment, since Ackerley's record in the Talks Department was far from spotless and he was the very opposite of a Corporation

Man as envisaged by Reith. Lambert frequently had occasion to wonder whether the appointment had been a wise one, as it soon became clear that Ackerley was not a man likely to mellow with age and experience.

Towards the end of his life Ackerley was to claim that he was entirely unsuited to the job. He would claim that he was insufficiently intellectual and had no breadth of interest. This was not true. When reviewing his relationship with his father, he had discovered the penalties of inattentiveness and self-obsession, and had mended his ways a little. Those who knew him in the 1930s remarked upon his lively curiosity in the lives and opinions of others. Friends were unable to make a casual judgement without being challenged: 'Why do you say that? What do you mean by that?' It is possible to see the influence of Forster here. Ackerley admitted that in spite of their long friendship he often felt uneasy in Forster's company: 'It is because he *listens*, he listens not only to what one is saying but to the motive behind.' If, in old age, Ackerley once more became inattentive, his face adopting a suitably engaged expression whilst his mind drifted elsewhere, at this period, and throughout his career, he had a genuinely enquiring mind. He once told Neville Braybrooke that curiosity was the key to being a successful literary editor: 'I read everything in sight – histories of the Ottoman Empire, instructions on patent medicines, bus-tickets, anything.' It was a quality regular contributors such as Geoffrey Grigson recognized and applauded:

> He was unrelentingly curious. Literature wasn't everything. His book pages had to cover a width of interest . . . Little or nothing he found alien, this cultured man doing a journalist's job.

The post of literary editor was, more accurately, that of an arts or review editor. When he joined the magazine, Ackerley was responsible each issue for commissioning eight pages on the arts (excluding music). Usually there would be three pages of short, unsigned book reviews ('*The Listener*'s Book Chronicle'); a full-page signed review of the latest novels every fortnight; the occasional longer, signed literary article or review of 'specially important, or controversial books'; and some two to three pages on art, including a page of photographs of works currently on show, chosen and captioned by a critic and entitled 'Round the Art Exhibitions'. Ackerley also chose one or more poems for each issue and a short story 'whenever possible', this being circumscribed by lack of space and (according to Lambert) the lack of good stories available. 'With regard to the short stories,' Lambert reported to his superiors in October 1935, 'we have set ourselves the highest possible standard, that is, only to publish something which is definitely above the level of ordinary interest and merit.' In addition Ackerley had to prepare quarterly Book Numbers, which contained signed reviews, and the occasional extra supplement for travel books. In the early years priority was given to broadcast material supplied by the Talks Department, where suitable or possible (Desmond MacCarthy, for example, refused to sign a contract allowing his talks to be published). However, by early 1937 the department's Book Talks changed character when they abandoned reviewing current titles and began broadcasting general literary talks 'mainly of an elementary character, dealing with out-of-date publications'.

Any sense of security provided by the BBC was far outweighed by a lack of freedom in the job and Ackerley frequently felt oppressed by the weight of the Corporation. Many opinions, and even words, which passed without comment in comparable magazines were not permitted to sully the pages of *The Listener*. Every review, poem or story which Ackerley wanted to publish had to be passed by Lambert. When Ackerley first arrived *The Listener* was under the control of D (IP), the Director of Information and Publications, who was in turn answerable to C (P), the Controller of Programmes. The outlook of these men can be gathered from a private memo sent by D (IP) to C (P) concerning the choice of a new deputy editor when Janet Adam Smith had become literary editor. The candidate 'should be a man of distinctly conservative leanings in thought, both political and artistic'. The initial letter of 'conservative' was originally written in upper case. From 1935 to 1936 the structure of the Corporation underwent a change. The post of D (IP) was abolished and the new post of C (PR), Controller of Public Relations, was created, taking over responsibility for all BBC publications from C (P). In theory C (PR) was answerable to the Director General and the Board of Governors, but their role as far as *The Listener* was concerned was that of post-publication admonition rather than pre-publication interference. To avoid such Directorial raps across the knuckles, C (PR) maintained a wary eye upon the contents of the magazine, an eye that was to become warier still once Ackerley took over the arts pages. The job of C (PR) was given to

Sir Stephen Tallents, late of the Empire Marketing Board, whose assistant, AC (PR), was the equally obstructive A. P. Ryan, late of the same organization. Both men were to occupy prominent places upon Ackerley's black list. After a distinguished career in assorted ministries (Munitions, Food and the Board of Trade), Tallents had cut his Public Relations teeth at the Post Office. Ackerley was to recall that Tallents' 'vigilance over and interference with' the magazine earned him the title of 'the highest paid proof-reader in the country'.

Lambert's first attempt to capitalize upon Ackerley's literary connections was unsuccessful. On his very first day in the office Ackerley was asked to write a 'personal' letter to Norman Douglas in an attempt to procure a contribution to the magazine's projected series of a modern version of the Grand Tour. Perhaps embarrassed by the task, Ackerley made little effort to recommend the commission to Douglas:

> My dear Norman,
> I expect this letter will be a surprise to you, and I wish that I could think that it would be a pleasant one. Its main object, however, is to try to persuade you to do an article for *The Listener*, which, as you probably don't know, is the British Broadcasting Corporation's journal.

After outlining the concept of the series, he ended by confessing:

> The length of the article would not be less than 2,000 words; and then we come to the question of fee. I am afraid that you are likely to be far too expensive for us, but I have no knowledge at this point, and can only tell you that the fee we are thinking of offering all round is twelve guineas.

Unsurprisingly, Douglas declined to contribute. Others did, however, and the series was popular enough to be issued as a book later in the year. Ackerley was more successful with other friends, and a number of distinguished people agreed to review books for him in spite of his offering them no byline, little space and a meagre fee. People like Forster and Colleer Abbott, who had helped him in the Talks Department, were joined by Jack Sprott and members of the Bloomsbury Group, notably Clive Bell, Maynard Keynes and Leonard and Virginia Woolf, and representatives of the younger generation such as W. H. Auden, C. Day Lewis, Louis MacNeice, Christopher Isherwood and

Stephen Spender. Auden later recorded the indebtedness of his generation to Ackerley: 'Those of us . . . who were starting our literary careers at the time have very good cause to remember how much he did for us; *The Listener* was one of our main outlets.' Ackerley had already attempted to recruit Isherwood to cover the May Day celebrations in Berlin for the Talks Department in 1933, describing him to Siepmann as 'an intelligent and serious-minded young man'. This came to nothing, but Isherwood wrote a number of reviews for *The Listener* and Ackerley was to describe him as 'the most consistently brilliant' of the magazine's contributors in the 1930s period.

Many writers who had submitted poems or short stories were later asked to review books, but great pains were taken to ensure that books went to people who were specially qualified to offer an opinion on them. Indeed, books were often 'sent out to specialist reviewers, with a request that they judge whether the book be worth review at all'. Space was so tight and books so numerous that Ackerley preferred not to review indifferent books, 'unless some public interest is served, for example, by exposing the faults of a book which has gained a fictitious reputation by unskilful reviewing elsewhere'. Such policies, formulated in February 1937, were maintained throughout Ackerley's time at the magazine, with the result that *The Listener*'s arts pages developed a very high reputation.

Ackerley valued controversy, since he believed it made the paper lively. Certainly, had it been left to the editors of the 1930s and 1940s *The Listener* would have been singularly inert. Ackerley always encouraged provocative views and would fight to keep them in despite considerable editorial faint-heartedness. 'Delighted with your bad-tempered, outspoken script,' begins one of his letters to Douglas Cooper. 'You will no doubt realize that Lambert is exceedingly unlikely to pass it as it stands.' Cooper had made some 'wounding' remarks about the Royal Academy and this, along with certain other institutions like public schools, the monarchy and J. B Priestley, was regarded as a protected species. 'I won't have all this cocking snooks at the big wigs,' Tallents would complain. 'I don't want misunderstandings with the big wigs.' This remark was made after Ackerley had sent a book entitled *The Headmaster Speaks: A Symposium by twelve famous public school headmasters* to A. S. Neill, the radical educationalist and founder of Summerhill, with predictable results. The piece had been spiked.

Nonetheless, Ackerley continued to send out books to people who held strong views and had the knowledge and experience to back them up if challenged. For example, Colleer Abbott's vitriolic assault upon the Society of Jesus in the course of a review of John Pick's *Gerard Manley Hopkins: Priest and Poet* caused considerable alarm in the editorial offices. Abbott had dismissed Pick's defence of the Jesuits at the expense of Hopkins' friends as a 'monstrous lie', an expression considered unsuitable in a BBC publication. 'Gross misstatement' was suggested as a substitute, but after much wrangling 'monstrous lie' was allowed through because Ackerley's (anonymous) reviewer was a leading Hopkins scholar and therefore entirely qualified to make such a remark.

Whilst there is no doubt that Ackerley, a natural rebel, enjoyed cocking snooks for the sheer fun of it, much of the criticism he encouraged had a more serious purpose, opening up subjects for debate, and exposing dishonesty and hypocrisy. He insisted that his own standards, and those of his contributors, should, therefore, be beyond reproach, and he became renowned for conducting himself at *The Listener* without any regard to personal feelings. 'As for the *New Writing and Daylight*,' he told Roy Fuller, who was reviewing the latest venture of their mutual friend John Lehmann, 'please give it its due, without fear or favour. Personal relationships cannot enter into these matters.' Indeed, Fuller's review turned out to be a case in point. The issue of *New Writing and Daylight* in question contained a number of tributes to Demetrios Capetanakis, the Greek poet and critic who had recently died of leukemia aged only thirty-two. Ackerley was shocked and saddened by this death, for he had been very fond of 'little Demetrios', listing him four years later as one of the 'dear dead' whom he thought of when out walking. Even so, he permitted Fuller to write that the memorial contribution by Edith Sitwell was 'quite remarkable for its overstatement, and rather predisposes one against' the other tributes. This review deeply offended not only Sitwell, but also Lehmann, who refused to speak to Fuller for some months when the young man confessed to being the author of the anonymous piece.

Sitwell had already been extremely angry with Ackerley for publishing an unfavourable review of her latest volume of poems – a review, as it happened, also by Fuller, who claimed to have no particular animosity towards her, but happened to think she was greatly overrated. In fact he had done his best to be generous towards her and the only really adverse comment was a reference to 'a lifetime's work which can hardly be said to be other than minor verse of a limited kind'. This was just the sort of judgement to enrage Sitwell, and she fired off a letter, characteristically *de haut en bas*, which might have alarmed most literary editors. The letter itself does not survive, but a draft (apparently written in high temper and in places illegible) gives some idea of the onslaught:

> I expect to be treated with the respect that is due to my poetry, & to which (after many years of the insults to which all important artists are subjected at the beginning of their careers) I am now accustomed. You permitted an entirely disgusting and denigrating anonymous [?] attack to be made on my last book of poems in the Listener. I shall therefore allow no future [book?] of mine to be sent to . . . Although the attack was anonymous, [?] I am perfectly aware of the identity of the writer, and of the circumstances [of] the attack . . .

And so on and so forth. Never someone to deal in understatement, she now wrote to Lehmann to announce that: 'The dregs of the literary population have risen as one worm to insult me.' One need hardly add that some time later this breach was healed and it was 'Dear Joe' and 'Edith, dear' once again. Ackerley knew perfectly well how to handle such people ('There was a great deal of "Dear Edith . . ." and all that about Joe,' a friend recalled; 'it became a sort of literary curlicue'), and the letters he wrote when she once again offered poems for publication in *The Listener* were so buttery they would not have put the Maharajah of Chhatarpur to shame.

Whilst he valued candour, he believed that there was a difference between being frank in criticism and being cruel. When Hilary Corke, a regular reviewer of poetry and fiction, submitted a particularly savage review of Herbert Read's *Moon's Farm*, Ackerley rejected it, explaining:

> The fact that H. is an old friend of mine does not place him beyond criticism, by any means, and he has often been taken to task in my paper on the Art side; but the tone of your review is not a tone I can use to him, or could wish to use. I expect the book is just as bad as you say, but he has written some much better poems in the past, many of which I have published, and that, I think, is the kind of

thing that should have been said when the present vol. was regretfully written off as a disappointment. I take pains always, as you
know, not to be 'kind' to my friends, and go to trouble to obtain
objective reviews of their works; but there is a step from being kind
to being actually cruel which I cannot take. So I would prefer not to
review the book at all. So sorry.

This letter is an excellent example of his ability to reject work firmly
but politely, a quality which earned him considerable respect, as
Geoffrey Grigson recalled:

> Did I ever know a virtuous literary editor? Did I ever know one with
> an unfaltering conscience, a literary editor, a single literary editor,
> not given to compromise or betrayal? One. Joe Ackerley of *The
> Listener*, whom some of his elder colleagues in the BBC did their
> best now and again, to get rid of, in part, I imagine, because they
> knew him to be homosexual.[1] . . . If Joe was prejudiced, his pre-
> judice was against the shoddy, the shoddy book or a shoddiness in
> his reviewer's account of it. If he was gentle, he was also unrelenting.
> If in some ways or to some degree he lived the often sad life of a
> lonely homosexual in days when you had to be on public and private
> guard in your homosexuality, what mattered to Joe was quality,
> irrespective of the sexual keeping of author or contributor.

Ackerley managed to combine tact with a fearless honesty, never
discriminating between the wary novice and the old friend when work
he considered substandard earned its author a severe but well-
intentioned rap across the knuckles. As with short stories, his suggestions for alteration were often radical. He once suggested that Clive
Bell should remove the first two paragraphs of an article about the

---

[1] Grigson was not the only person to make this assertion, and others have spoken of
an attempted purge of homosexual members of BBC staff in the 1950s. Indeed,
Grigson goes on to claim that Ackerley was once 'saved only by E. M. Forster's direct
intervention with the Director-General of the Corporation'. Evidence of this may of
course exist in the Corporation's personal files, but nothing has emerged elsewhere. In
the wake of the defection to the Soviet Union of Guy Burgess in 1951, there may well
have been some panic at Broadcasting House. Burgess had worked as a BBC journalist
in the 1930s and 1940s and certainly knew Ackerley, though how well is uncertain.
Burgess's name appears in a list of addresses in a pocket diary, but nowhere else in any
correspondence or notebooks.

National Gallery. If, however, Bell disagreed, then the paragraphs must remain.

Although he would often make suggestions for improvement, he always preferred a contributor to make his or her own alterations:

> I think you had better have another look at this before it goes in [he told Roy Fuller in a letter accompanying a proof], for I have tinkered with a word or two, not because of your opinions I need hardly say, but because they did not seem to me expressed with your usual crystal clearness. I like the *exact* word always, and the exact meaning, but whether my changes are on or off the mark only you who know what was in your mind can say.

When a contribution *was* bad, he said so. Adriana Tyrkova Williams was left in no doubt as to Ackerley's view of her article on Pushkin, which, he wrote in a long letter:

> seems to me to contain nothing except the few biographical facts about his life that I think anyone could have supplied; your general remarks about him, his place in literature, the Russian view of him and the general significance of his work, seem to me to have turned into little more than an uninformative and superlative eulogy which might equally well have been written about any great man. Moreover, I must say that the writing itself is not at all satisfactory and a good deal more work would need to be done on that alone. The effect of the whole is quite the opposite of what you intended. I feel that it will not interest readers in Pushkin in the least and, indeed, your opening pages and final paragraphs seem to be almost unreadable.

Mrs Williams meekly rewrote the article, which Ackerley then passed and published. In spite of editorial bluntness, remarkably few people took offence. Roy Fuller recalls that as a reviewer one was always on one's mettle with *The Listener*. Andrew Forge, who contributed to the art pages, concurred: 'He was the most marvellous editor, very appreciative. One felt one was writing *for Joe* and one's reviews were directed to him personally.' As the letter to Fuller shows, his suggestions were presented tentatively, and he never altered copy without consulting the contributor, as he was later to boast: 'In all my twenty-five years as Lit Ed. of *The Listener* . . . I never published a signed article by anyone without sending a proof. I would have considered it the greatest impertinence to do otherwise.' His perfectionism and good manners sometimes went to extremes. Forge recalls one occasion when he had to clamber out of bed at midnight to answer the telephone. It was Ackerley, calling from the printers. 'I'm sorry to call so late, dear boy. Have you got your galley?' Stark naked, Forge went off in search of the proof. 'Second paragraph from the end, penultimate sentence,' Ackerley continued. 'I've been worrying about that comma. Could we drop it? Would that be all right?'

Since he was at such pains to treat his contributors, as contributors, dispassionately, any attempt to curry favour was frowned upon, as one distinguished writer found to his cost. Ackerley had very strong views about degrees in personal relations and although he gave some people an impression of immediate intimacy and warmth, he could be chillingly formal on occasion. He recalled that he had once inadvertently addressed Geoffrey Grigson, whom he did not at that stage know well, by his first name and had been gruffly corrected. He thought this entirely dignified and deplored the way people addressed total strangers as if they were close friends. Part of his objection was that in doing so some people were

> often seeking some advantage from familiarity or hoping to disarm criticism; it is felt to be more difficult to be unkind to Billy Graham or Danny Kaye than to Dr William Graham or Mr Daniel Kaye.[1] Attempts were often made to get at me by such means when I was Literary Editor of *The Listener*. [—] affords a good example. He used to send me his poems, which generally I did not care for and returned. Then he wrote to ask whether we could drop formalities in our correspondence and, although I had never met the man, we became 'Dear Ackerley' and 'Dear [—]'. This was not enough; soon he was addressing me as 'Dear Joe Ackerley', to which I replied 'Dear [initials]' for I did not know what his given names were. I continued to reject his poems and at last he lost his temper and

[1] In 1954 Ackerley accompanied Rose Macaulay to the greyhound stadium at Harringay where Billy Graham was holding one of his evangelical rallies. They went in a spirit of curiosity, Macaulay as a devout but troubled Anglo-Catholic, Ackerley as a convinced atheist. They were duly appalled by the vulgarity of the proceedings, though Macaulay thought Graham 'sincere'. Ackerley thought him a 'dreadful creature' and reported that the atmosphere of the rally was fascist.

attacked me in a furious letter in which he said I had no taste and therefore no right to be a Literary Editor.

At first Ackerley failed to match Janet Adam Smith's pioneering work in the poetry pages, a fact which may have commended itself to the BBC hierarchy. In a report on the first six months of Ackerley's incumbency, Lambert wrote:

> I would point out that the poems which have been printed since Mr Ackerley took over will show that they are very much nearer the conventional and traditional idea of poetic form than those published previously. By this change I think we have lost something in the form of the inclusion of a few rather daring poetic experiments; on the other hand we have gained in stability and general coherence of style.

The attitude of the British Broadcasting Corporation to 'experimental' poetry might be compared with that of the British Board of Film Censors to 'experimental' film. In 1930 the BBFC had remarked of Dulac's *The Seashell and the Clergyman*: 'This film is apparently meaningless, but if it has any meaning it is doubtless objectionable.' Reith had been disturbed by Adam Smith's bold 1933 poetry supplement, complaining that many poems struck him as 'odd', 'uncouth' and 'puzzling'. That they had been published in the first place was entirely due to Adam Smith's editorial sleight of hand. Knowing that Lambert was as likely as Reith to be suspicious of poems like Auden's 'The Witnesses', she waited until he had returned from a good lunch, then presented him with a sheet of poems, at the top of which was the most innocuous and easily understandable of the batch. As Lambert cast a woozy eye over the page, Adam Smith would engage him in conversation so that he rarely bothered to read the entire sheet before passing the poems for publication. What counted as 'objectionable' may be judged from a row which Ackerley had with his superiors over a poem by Henry Reed about sailors in Cape Town, which he was obliged to return because it contained the lines:

> We watch the sea daily, finish our daily tasks
> By ten in the morning, and with the day to waste,
> Wander through the suburbs, with quiet thoughts of brothels.
> And sometimes thoughts of churches.

A. P. Ryan suggested that if Ackerley wanted to publish the poem, he could ask the author to change 'brothels' to 'movies'. When Ackerley had pointed out that the word 'brothel' had appeared in *The Listener* on a previous occasion. Ryan replied that 'it had only been used in prose, a poem was different.' He asked Ackerley whether he would ever use the word in conversation with a lady at the luncheon-table.

Ackerley was insecure about his judgement of poetry, claiming to know nothing about the art, but this had the beneficial effect of making him extremely conscientious. He outlined the qualities he was looking for in poems submitted to the magazine in a letter to Herbert Read, who had recommended a poem by Rayner Heppenstall in November 1935:

> Do you, or do you not, agree that a different kind of mind is brought to a weekly journal from that which is brought to a volume of poems, and that therefore certain qualifications are needed for the former? For want, perhaps, of better words I would call these qualifications clarity and edge – the poem should cut a little and pretty sharply, intellectually or emotionally, and it should be clear. Heppenstall's poem doesn't seem to me to have either of these qualifications. I hope I'm not being obtuse over this.

With experience, he revised these guidelines, admitting in 1939 that he did not believe that it was necessary for a poem to be instantly assimilable: 'if one gets something out of them that is interesting or agreeable, that is enough.' Unfortunately, as he explained to Roy Fuller, whose work he began publishing in the war, 'it is not enough for the Editor, so would you like to let me know briefly how to explain your poem to him if he should require me to do so.'[1] Frequently he would carry manuscripts about with him for days, delving into his pockets at odd moments to take another look and 'see whether familiarity puts me into any closer touch with it.' Consequently manuscripts sometimes went astray, and he was once obliged to confess to Fuller that he had mislaid an entire sheaf of poems.

> I expect they will turn up [he wrote], for I am not a loser, but at the moment I can't put my hands on them . . . I suppose you will have

---

[1] In this case Fuller's 'interesting letter of explanation' did not prove successful and the poem was rejected.

copies of the poems. The one I liked and wanted was that long one —
was it called Night Piece? . . . Could you send me another copy of it
— though I am sure I shall come upon the collection soon, probably
in my flat.

He also showed contributions to poet friends, like Fuller and Spender,
asking their opinion, or even for suggestions as to how the work might
be improved. In fact, his own experience as a poet, however inglorious
he might have thought it, had taught him a great deal and Walter Allen
recalls being both impressed and delighted to have a poem returned
much improved by Ackerley, who had altered just one word. A
craftsman himself, he regarded such skills as important, as he explained
to Richard Church when disagreeing about the merits of A. L. Rowse:

> I have always regarded Rowse as *not* a poet, in the true sense of the
> term, whatever else he may be; and I confess to being slightly
> surprised that you, who have that admirable craftsmanship which
> was what C.D.L. [C. Day Lewis, who had criticized Rowse's poetry
> in *The Listener*] so particularly admired, should praise him so high.
> For craftsmanship, at any rate, is what Rowse has not got; though
> he may sometimes bring off a passably well-made piece, as in his
> Housmanish moments (and that phase soon became mechanical),
> he seems to me to know little or nothing about poetry-making, to
> disregard form altogether, and to have no feel for words or sounds.
> Yet, at the same time, I sometimes like the things he has to say, and
> accept them for that reason, while disapproving mostly of the way in
> which he says them — that is to say, as poems. But this, you may say, is
> just a question of a 'name', and yes that is all it is. Rowse may,
> indeed does, sometimes have poetic feelings, but does he express
> them in poetry? is he a poet? I agree with John Lehmann that he is
> not.

However, if he liked a poem or the poet, he was prepared to offer
extremely detailed suggestions for improving work submitted to the
magazine:

> I do not care for 'The Ruins' [he wrote to Fuller], but 'Defending the
> Harbour' has the makings of a good poem, I think. The last 3 lines of
> verse 2 for instance almost persuade me to take it as it stands. But at

present it seems to me untidy; like your grey gun, and not altogether digested. It wants a little more time spent on it I feel sure, and then I should be very happy to renew its acquaintance if you cared to submit it again.

Having renewed its acquaintance, Ackerley did indeed publish the poem. James Kirkup, who had been recommended to Ackerley by William Plomer, was given similarly detailed advice, not only at the beginning of his career, but also when he was established, as Ackerley's suggestions for Kirkup's 'A Correct Compassion' in 1951 demonstrate. Ackerley believed that part of his job was to foster new talent, and in both Fuller and Kirkup he saw, and was determined to help realize, their potential. 'He had a kind of personal genius as editor of poetry,' Frances Bellerby recalled.

As with reviews, Ackerley favoured short poems, since there was never enough space. He was obliged to confer with the people who pasted-up the magazine's pages and often kept poems until there was part of a column to fill. He would set up several galleys of poems 'of all shapes and sizes, so that the ladies of *The Listener* can always be sure of having something handy to plug up every crack and cranny.' It was not only the poem itself which should be short, but also its individual lines, and he was often obliged to return poems which would not fit on to the page. He regretted that poems had to be treated like pieces of a jigsaw puzzle but knew that there was no way round this particular problem.

However, if poets were annoyed to have their work returned late and in less than pristine condition, they could at least be sure that it had been very thoroughly considered. Under his literary editorship *The Listener* retained its reputation as a forum for the best contemporary verse. As well as the work of Auden (including 'The Unknown Citizen', 'Matthew Arnold', 'Voltaire at Ferney', 'Song for the New Year' and 'Oxford'), Spender, Day Lewis and MacNeice, Ackerley published Larkin's 'Ultimatum' (the first of his poems to appear in print outside a school magazine), Betjeman's 'Cheltenham', and poems by Ruthven Todd, Clifford Dyment, Walter de la Mare, Kathleen Raine, H. B. Mallalieu, Michael Roberts, George Barker, Lilian Bowes Lyon, Edmund Blunden, Siegfried Sassoon, Henry Reed, Laurence Whistler, Hal Summers, Frances Bellerby, Sidney Keyes, Edith Sitwell, Edwin Muir, William Plomer, C. P. Cavafy, Maureen

Duffy, Francis King, Vernon Watkins, R. S. Thomas, David Jones, Paul Dehn, Demetrios Capetanakis, John Lehmann, Laurie Lee, Dylan Thomas, Norman MacCaig, Elizabeth Jennings, D. J. Enright, Roy Fuller, Alan Ross, Robert Conquest, Alex Comfort, Herbert Read, Richard Church, James Kirkup, Ruth Pitter, C. C. Abbott, John Fuller, James Michie, Geoffrey Grigson, Stevie Smith, James Reeves, Anne Ridler, John Wain, Brian Hill, Charles Causley, Jocelyn Brooke, Michael Hamburger, E. J. Scovell, Robin Skelton, F. T. Prince, Patricia Beer and Marianne Moore.

Ackerley claimed to know even less about art than he did about poetry. Fortunately, *The Listener* had an excellent regular critic in Herbert Read, to whom Janet Adam Smith introduced Ackerley before she left. The two men took to each other at once and became lifelong friends. Read undertook to give Ackerley tuition in art history, conducted at the Corporation's expense over long lunches. After one such 'lesson', Lambert found Ackerley sneaking back into the office at half-past three. When Ackerley explained that he had been receiving instruction from Read, Lambert replied: 'Yes – but is it necessary to lunch him five times a week at the Café Royal?' 'It's not only modern art,' Ackerley retorted. 'It's Korean art, Chinese art, Japanese art and Red Indian art.'

If *The Listener* did not noticeably benefit from this particular course in ethnic art, Ackerley was soon in a position to commission entire series on modern painting and sculpture, the first of which, entitled 'Art and the Social Crisis', he proposed in April 1936. Ackerley also widened his knowledge about art by visiting exhibitions, always in BBC time. Once, when he should have been at his desk, he bumped into Reith in a gallery. He was not in the least embarrassed by this unfortunate encounter, nor by the fact that he had a cauliflower under his arm, but marched straight up to Reith and, before the DG had time to say anything, thrust the vegetable under the venerable nose and said: 'I've just bought this for my supper. Do you think it's fresh?'

Because the BBC's opinion of what made a good painting was very similar to its idea of what made a good poem, the arts pages were frequently the cause of rumblings from above. Within months of Ackerley's appointment, the Controller of Programmes was horrified to find reproductions of paintings by Rousseau and Klee disfiguring the 'Round the Art Exhibitions' page. He wrote at once to Gladstone Murray, who as D (IP) was responsible for *The Listener* at this period:

I feel you must be distressed, and annoyed, as I am, by the selection of illustrations on Pages 1001 and 1002; in particular the ridiculous caricature of a portrait by Henri Rousseau on Page 1001, and the still more fantastic absurdity by Paul Klee on Page 1002. These are the kind of things which cannot fail to bring ridicule upon 'The Listener', and through it upon the Corporation. The paper is so good as a rule that it is a pity that it should damage its reputation by such absurd extravagances from time to time.

This was passed to Lambert, whose reply was conciliatory and duplicitous in a way Ackerley despised. He explained that the feature was merely intended to reflect, rather than recommend, what was currently on show at 'the most reputable art galleries'. He defended Rousseau, but contradicted his earlier statement that the feature was not committed to any judgement of the work reproduced by pretending that a point was being made by reproducing Klee's *Portrait with Foliage* next to Cranach's *Portrait of the Baroness von Schenck-Winterstein*:

I suggest that the majority of people will consider how contemptible Paul Klee's work is, as compared with that of an old master such as Cranach, when both are engaged on the same kind of subject. Actually you will see therefore that our purpose in putting in the Klee was to show it in its true light by comparison with an old master.

One wonders what Herbert Read would have made of this 'defence'.

The difference in attitude between Lambert and Ackerley may be seen by comparing the Klee upset with the first major controversy Ackerley experienced at *The Listener*. For once he and the BBC were fighting on the same side. The decorations which Cunard had commissioned for their new luxury liner, the *Queen Mary*, had aroused considerable interest, and Ackerley decided to commission an article about them. Kenneth Clark, who wrote regularly for the magazine, was approached, but declined on the grounds that he had been consulted as to which artists Cunard should employ and his advice had been ignored. Clive Bell had no such qualms about impartiality and was indeed delighted to have an opportunity to puff the work of two of the artists involved, his wife Vanessa and friend Duncan Grant. However, when Cunard were asked for photographs of Grant's decorative panels to illustrate the projected article, they refused. The reason they gave was that they had been disappointed with Grant's work and did not want it to receive advance publicity in favour of work with which they were more satisfied. Ackerley was not to be fobbed off and suggested that pressure should be brought to bear by the BBC, pointing out to Cunard that they were extremely fortunate to be given the opportunity of free publicity. His instinct for a row also prompted him to begin compiling a file on the affair.

Cunard now said that they were not yet sure whether they would even use Grant's panels, and, understandably nervous, added a post-script asking to see Bell's article in proof before they co-operated. Lambert asked Tallents to reply, which he did in best BBC style, as one great organization to another, or rather, as one public relations man to another. In a letter to F. A. Derry, Cunard's publicity manager, Tallents suavely suggested that the postscript had been 'added under a misunderstanding': 'I cannot think that you yourself can have in-tended to suggest that either a distinguished critic like Mr Clive Bell, or a periodical of the standing of "The Listener" would consent to submit the text of an article on such a subject for approval to your Company.' Derry disingenuously replied that he merely wanted to ensure that the article avoided factual inaccuracies. Worried that the BBC might fall for this, Ackerley wrote a memo in which he hoped 'we shall remain absolutely steadfast in the line we have already adopted of not allowing the Cunard people to interfere in the slightest.' He suggested the letter should be ignored and that the article should go ahead without the shipbuilders' co-operation. He then wrote to Derry in order to arrange for Bell to visit the ship in dock in Glasgow. Derry agreed to this 'under the mistaken belief', Ackerley told Bell, 'that he will be allowed to see your script before we publish it.'

By this time Cunard had decided to reject Grant's panels, a decision that had already provoked letters to *The Times*. Bell was despatched to Glasgow where he found his worst fears confirmed. He wrote his article and Ackerley submitted it for approval, remarking that the Director of the National Gallery (i.e. Clark) had seen it and said that the 'expression of Bell's opinion is polite in comparison with what his own would have been.' For good measure he added that the *New Statesman* would take the piece if *The Listener* refused to print it.

In the event the highly critical article, ambiguously titled 'Inside the "Queen Mary" – A Business Man's Dream', was passed and published, much to the displeasure of Cunard, who attempted to claim that the magazine had not been granted permission to use the photographs. Thanks to Ackerley's decision to create a file, the letter in which permission had been given early in the proceedings had been kept. Tallents intended to offer Cunard space to reply, a prospect that Ackerley at first thought would provide 'some fun'. On reflection, however, he decided that this would be a mistake, and sent Tallents a stiff memo, which showed, amongst other things, how far he had benefited from Read's lunchtime tuition:

> Do we really engage to publish, with the full dignity of an article, any criticism of Bell and appreciation of their ship, which they can quite easily procure some hireling second-rate critic to write – someone like Stanley Casson, who is known to have no taste in modern art, in which he constantly interferes; who thinks that Paul Manship, for instance, is a heaven-sent genius?[1]

Ackerley suggested that the correspondence columns were open to Cunard, as they were to anyone, and that the shipbuilders would be welcome to use them. Tallents meekly accepted his advice and Cunard were not invited to reply.

This affair shows Ackerley shaping up for the furores ahead, in which it would be the BBC rather than a hapless outsider who would be the enemy. His tactics were those he was to use again and again in his battle against censorship and obstruction. He often solicited the endorsement of his views from acknowledged experts in order to bamboozle the BBC bureaucrats; he was prepared to be totally unscrupulous working behind the scenes but could be bravely confrontational if necessary; and in the last resort he would tell the

---

[1] Stanley Casson (1889–1944) was an archaeologist who also lectured in, and wrote books about, sculpture, including the reactionary *Some Modern Sculptors* (1928) and *Twentieth Century Sculpture* (1930). Paul Manship (1885–1966) was the award-winning American sculptor, winner of innumerable medals at International Fairs and Exhibitions.

Corporation that if *The Listener* was too timid to print something, there was always the *Spectator* or the *New Statesman*, which was now under the literary editorship of his friend Raymond Mortimer.

The pre-war BBC was just the sort of organization to bring out the best in Ackerley. Hand in hand, Prudery and Philistinism stalked the corridors of Broadcasting House, and there was a continual struggle between the desire to educate the Corporation's audience and a determination to protect it from the 'indecent' and the innovative, a form of censorship Sir John Reith dignified by the term 'moral responsibility'. In many ways Reith was an admirable man, but his strongest tastes, like those of Evelyn Waugh's Gilbert Pinfold, were negative, and like Pinfold, he reserved a particular detestation for Picasso and jazz:

> Are you quite happy about *The Listener*'s dealings with art matters [he asked Tallents in 1936], e.g. this week's article on Picasso? I think his style is quite dreadful, and as you know, there are many who have strong views about *The Listener*'s art attitude and articles.

Herbert Read was a staunch ally in Ackerley's battles with such philistinism, often indeed the instigator of them. 'I think the Delvaux are lovely,' Read wrote, hoping to insinuate a reproduction of the Belgian Surrealist's nudes on to the 'Round the Art Exhibitions' page, 'but I suppose it would give the D.G. a fit.' When writing about Toulouse-Lautrec he felt obliged to ask whether the word 'prostitute' was permissible in a BBC publication. (It was.) In 1938 Read wrote a scathing account of the Royal Fine Art Commission, which Tallents vetoed. Ryan sent a curt note to Lambert: 'C (PR), who is absent on sick leave today, asked me on the telephone to let you have this article back. He feels that it should not be published.' Lambert handed this to Ackerley, who was infuriated by its high-handed manner and its lack of any explanation for the decision:

> I do not understand this. This article was commissioned by us, and seems a reasonable criticism of a matter of public interest and importance, in general conformity with the directions we gave Mr Read. A paragraph which seemed to us too strongly worded has already been removed by him at our request.
>
> I do not see how I can undertake to reject the manuscript without

a good reason. The fact that people are nevertheless paid for their work is by no means always considered by them as compensatory for such actions. If, as I understand it, the reason for the rejection of this script is that the Chairman of the Corporation is also a member of the Fine Arts Commission, I doubt if this will seem to Mr Read an adequate reason from a journal which lays claim to the virtue of impartiality.

Ackerley was not above stirring and there is little doubt that he was very well aware that the article would prove unacceptable. This is not to say that he did not genuinely believe that the RFAC was a matter of public interest which ought to be written about, nor that he did not commission the article in good faith. But one suspects that there was a certain amount of gleeful rubbing of the hands in his office when Read's copy was delivered. It must have been extremely satisfying to be able to catch out his high-minded masters. Such became Read's reputation that, asking him to review a book, Ackerley felt obliged to add: 'if you are able to do so without getting me the sack.'

Occasionally, in the 'summer holiday season', *The Listener* launched series of articles on art and these were to cause Ackerley a great deal of difficulty, largely because they were extremely ambitious. In April 1936 he proposed a topical series of six articles looking at art under different political regimes, which involved commissioning articles from foreign critics, who failed to answer letters, submitted texts in their own language and – in the case of the Italian and German contributors – used the series as a platform for political propaganda.

Undaunted by such problems, Ackerley was already proposing another logistically complex series whilst 'Art and the State' was still appearing in *The Listener*. In October 1936 he suggested that a number of leading artists should be asked to contribute to a series entitled 'The Artist Speaks', in which each could write a short essay and provide reproductions of his or her work and one original, unpublished and unexhibited illustration. He drew up a list of people who might be approached: Picasso, Matisse, Braque, Léger, Rouault, Dufy, André Masson, Marie Laurencin, Le Corbusier, Paul Nash, Walter Sickert, Jacob Epstein, Henry Moore, Winifred Nicholson, Edward Burra, Duncan Grant and Eric Kennington. Georges Duthuit, a close friend of Ackerley and former lover of Nancy, who was to become *The Listener*'s French connection, was enlisted to approach the French artists since, being married to Matisse's daughter, he was in a unique position to use personal influence. Douglas Cooper, the combative collector and promoter of Cubist art, and a regular contributor to *The Listener* ('the Queen of Art Historians' as Ackerley dubbed him), was also asked to help since he was in France. In England Ackerley consulted Kenneth Clark, Herbert Read, J. B. Manson (Director of the Tate Gallery), the secretary of the Royal Academy, and the art critic Roger Hinks.

There were only two problems. The first, soon resolved, was the fee, for, as Ackerley noted, 'I suppose we cannot expect well-known artists to do special illustrations for *The Listener* without adequate reward'. To his surprise a fee of ten guineas proved sufficient. The second difficulty, tentatively mentioned in Ackerley's submission, was rather more intractable:

> People who paint cannot always write. My own view, however, is that if I can find some particular subject specially suited to each artist – some problem which occupies his mind and attention, about which he is enthusiastic, that it may be possible with a little persuasion to get more out of him than I should be likely to get if, for instance, I had a general formula for all.

He was to regret this latitude.

By the following March he confessed that he had 'failed to secure any of the real giants, for Sickert, Epstein, Picasso, Matisse and Braque have all either refused or neglected to reply to my letters.' He had, however, secured Georges Rouault, who had been asked to provide a feature on his work in stained glass. Unfortunately, the copy that arrived on Ackerley's desk hardly fulfilled this commission, as he explained to Lambert:

> The script he has already sent, which is made up from a great collection he appears to have, of what he calls 'Soliloquies on Art, and so on' was so incomprehensible to me and, in parts, so remote from matters of art, that I have asked him to supply some more jottings for me to select from, and this he has consented to do; but he is a man in any case, I understand, who is famed for the obscurity of his writing, and he writes all the time that he is not painting; and

since he is without doubt the most important contributor in the whole collection, I think we must take from him what we can get – especially as he is sending an original drawing.

His fears that whatever Rouault produced was 'likely to be almost unintelligible' were confirmed in July when he received another batch of Rouault's 'outpourings', these ones about Cézanne. However, Rouault had also sent a small painting of a clown's head which Ackerley very much liked and so he told the artist that he would submit the manuscript to *'notre meilleur traducteur de français'*, Vyvyan Holland, who confessed that he could make very little of Rouault's confused and ill-written text. Determined at any cost to use Rouault's illustrations, Ackerley decided that the only possible course of action was 'to conceal from the general reader the rubbish of this writing by publishing one of the articles . . . in the more decent obscurity of its difficult French'. He had the 'Soliloquies' set up and despatched the proofs to Rouault, tactfully pointing out *'un certain nombre de passages obscurs, résultant . . . de l'omission de quelques mots'* and asking for corrections and clarifications by return. However, Lambert was disinclined to hoodwink his readers and refused to 'publish rubbish – even by Rouault, and even in French'. Ackerley next sent both articles, with translations, to Douglas Cooper (who had already secured and translated an article by Léger) begging him to make something of them, perhaps 'something in the way of a dialogue between Rouault and another, or it could be a straight article somehow framing the meditations and observations of this important and somewhat mystically-minded French painter'. Cooper obliged and an article eventually appeared in the series. Ackerley gave it the title 'The Wisdom of Georges Rouault'.

Other contributors included Marie Laurencin, Jack Yeats, Henry Moore and William Coldstream, whose original illustration was a pencil drawing of Ackerley, looking understandably grim. Nonetheless, in spite of complaints from the Royal Academy that too few of its members were represented – they had in fact been invited, but had declined or failed to reply to letters – the series was adjudged a great success, and in 1939 a further series was launched on 'Art in Education'. Although all the contributors were English, some were so muddled as to make little more sense of their subject than Rouault.

Finding short stories suitable for the pages of *The Listener* was no easy task. A number of criteria had to be fulfilled before valuable space could be given to fiction. Stories had to be very short indeed, 3,500 words, usually taking up a page and a half at most. As with the poetry, writers were not permitted to use words and expressions or deal with themes which might shock the BBC hierarchy. Some stories came to Ackerley direct from his Corporation colleagues, having already been broadcast on the Third Programme, and thus constituted the magical ninety per cent of broadcast material which the magazine was supposed to contain. This was a reciprocal policy and Ackerley sometimes sent on stories which had been submitted to *The Listener* but which he had been unable to use. A similar arrangement obtained with some of his 'rival' editors, notably John Lehmann, who founded *Penguin New Writing* in 1940. Lehmann and Ackerley were friends of long standing and had many friends in common, so they frequently passed to each other stories or poems they did not want to publish in their respective magazines. Ackerley would also send circular letters to well known writers, such as Lehmann's sister Rosamond, V. S. Pritchett, Elizabeth Bowen, Sean O'Faolain and James Hanley, asking whether they had anything that they would care to submit.

Over the years Ackerley managed to acquire stories from all these but Rosamond Lehmann, as well as stories by Walter de la Mare, Stephen Spender, John Betjeman, William Plomer, A. E. Coppard, A. H. Teece, P. H. Newby, Arthur Calder-Marshall, Angus Wilson, Francis King and Donald Windham. Perhaps his greatest scoop, however, was when he published Forster's 'Entrance to an Unwritten Novel' in the Christmas 1948 edition of the magazine. This was the first new fiction Forster had published since *A Passage to India* in 1924. Forster gave the piece – in fact the entrance to an 'unpublishable' (i.e. homosexual) short story which appeared posthumously as 'The Other Boat' – to Ackerley largely because he appreciated the help his younger friend had given him with the manuscript over the years. This was one of several stories which Ackerley read for Forster, often making suggestions which Forster took up.

As with poetry, Ackerley was also keen to publish the work of less familiar names, and occasionally unsolicited manuscripts would prove publishable, as for example when G. F. Green submitted his story 'A Summer Night' in 1938. Ackerley liked to follow up such successes, and when he heard no more from Green he wrote to him a year later asking whether he could see other stories. Whilst he tried to encourage younger writers he never made excuses for them, as the Scottish writer Fred Urquhart discovered. The first stories he sent Ackerley in 1936 were unsuitable for publication in *The Listener*, but Ackerley enjoyed them and asked to see anything else that Urquhart might have. No doubt he had been attracted by their subject matter: 'No Fields of Amaranth', Urquhart recalls, was 'about a young homo and the man he'd picked up on holiday'. Urquhart immediately sent another story, which Ackerley promised to attempt to get past Lambert, but without much hope of success:

> It calls a spade a spade, which is so badly needed; but as you no doubt realize if you listen to the wireless at all, broadcasting does not consider it can go in for such plain speaking, and its publications are similarly limited. I get what I can into my art and literary pages – *The Listener*'s so called independent side, but apart from the somewhat fruity conversational passages in your story, which I think will also be jibbed at, they would never put up with a story which set out to make army recruiting prospects even worse than, thank God, they are at present.

He asked for further stories and said he would look out for Urquhart's 'I Fell for a Sailor' in the *London Mercury* ('it sounds very much up my street').

Urquhart next sent a story called 'Début', which was returned with a long letter of advice as being 'too undigested, inconsequent and too long'.

> Art and life are not the same; the writer must use the former to present the latter. There seems no reason why the story should end when it does; and if the whisky was life, art should, I think, have eliminated it. The seeds of disappointment are already in the situation, in the young man's character and high ambition; art does not require the whisky . . . You must excuse these, probably impertinent, remarks: they only come from interest.

Further stories were sent and returned with long and detailed criticism, some of it quite drastic, as for example, the suggestion that the last five pages of one story should be discarded. He offered to pass on stories he could not use, either to his old stand-by Raymond Mortimer at the *New Statesman* or to the *London Mercury*. He also recommended Urquhart's work to Roger Senhouse, who was a director of Secker and Warburg, and gave the young writer advice about literary agents. After some ten months of correspondence, Ackerley had still not accepted any of Urquhart's stories:

> I am always sending your stories back. I feel very unhappy about it and expect you will soon be losing patience with me. However, I always think there is something about them, though they fail to leave me with a satisfied feeling when I reach the end.

Urquhart was having better luck elsewhere, with stories appearing in *Penguin New Writing*, *The Adelphi*, *Left Review* and *Fact*, and a novel being issued by Duckworth. Ackerley was pleased, but unimpressed. He found the novel *Time Will Knit* 'unreadable, by which I mean that it seems to me to fail completely to pull the reader along'. A story published in *Penguin Parade* was dismissed as 'definitely bad', an example of the way Urquhart's work was becoming 'experimental in the wrong sort of way'. Ever resilient, Urquhart replied, defending his work, causing Ackerley some pangs of guilt:

> Your letter was very civil and decent and made me ashamed of my own which I had in any case regretted as soon as it was irrevocably in the box – and you are quite right, I was too harsh altogether and did not do sufficient justice to the fact that your heart is in the right place.

Nonetheless, further advice and criticism was offered: Urquhart should read the novels of John Hampson and Forster's *Aspects of the Novel*. 'As for the "canons of art" I really don't know what they are, and I bet you don't either.' Urquhart's 'The Christ Child' was dismissed in a brutal postscript as 'nothing':

> so say I, and so says the Professor of English at Cairo University, an exceedingly cultivated man, far more than I, for I made him read it on the Alex. to Rhodes boat, and, when I heard his comments, read it myself. I'm sorry, but that is what we both felt, that it was cheap and nothing.

Ackerley suspected that Urquhart submitted stories he knew perfectly well to be below par and administered further jolts to the unfortunate young man.

> I think ['No Experience'] is awfully thin and superficial, and wish you would give up writing this kind of propaganda stuff. Also I find your mixture of facetiousness and fretfulness unacceptable; again I expect it is the effect of your politics on your work.
>
> Both stories seem to me to be aimed at the same target, and the second seems to me even wider of the mark. A really boring story, I think – can't imagine what you see in it – absolutely flat.

It was now two years since Urquhart first submitted stories to *The Listener* and Ackerley was clearly dismayed by what he considered a falling off. A postcard despatched in December 1936 shows a mounting irritation:

> No, no, a thousand times no. This is a magazine story, sentimental, with bright chatter and a 'surprise ending': its epitaph is, 'Makes you think, don't it?' – or would be if one had not foreseen from somewhere about the middle the end you are so busily preparing behind your screen of patter. As soon as one knows the end, the story's over: it's one of that kind. I'm sorry, but there's nothing else to be said for it: the story's obvious; the patter poor; yourself, as usual, all over the page (your work's frightfully selfconscious) and in your most sentimental mood. Why your cancered hero should be thought to be any more sympathetic because he bores us with laughter instead of with tears it would be hard to say.

By the beginning of the next year Ackerley was obliged to concede defeat:

> No, I've dried up over your stories. It's time we heard the counsel for the defence instead of the prosecution – so if you think I ought to like this story you'd better put up a case for it – why you wrote it and why I should publish it.

Undaunted, Urquhart continued to submit work despite the fact that encouragement was no longer forthcoming:

No, I think nothing of these two stories. What a lot you do write. They seem to pour in from all directions. I too am just recovering from 'flu. It quite knocked me out.

It was not until July 1949, almost thirteen years after Urquhart first sent work to Ackerley that a story, 'Alicky's Watch', was accepted for publication. The letter of acceptance came not from Ackerley, who was on leave, but from Maurice Ashley, the deputy editor, an irony which Urquhart duly acknowledged. However, when Ackerley returned from his holiday he bumped up the fee from twelve to fifteen guineas. Urquhart submitted further stories, but none was ever accepted. In retrospect Urquhart was grateful for Ackerley's advice, but felt that he was being treated rather like a schoolboy handing in essays for correction. When the two men finally met, it was not a success. Urquhart found Ackerley 'a cold fish . . . there was the same cold attitude about him that I also found in John Lehmann when I eventually met him.' Since it had been made perfectly plain that Urquhart was homosexual, he expected a rather less formal reception. 'I don't think I intended him to make a pass at me,' Urquhart recalls, 'but I feel he should have made a greater effort to treat me as a fellow member of the tribe.'

Looking back from the embattled days of 1937, during which professional difficulties were compounded by private crises, Ackerley was to regard his first year or so at *The Listener* with pleasure and affection, since interference from above was minimal. This was an extremely brief honeymoon in what was to be a long and embittered marriage. The appointment of H. A. L. Fisher to the Board of Governors in 1935 ushered in a new era of interference, more particularly since Fisher had the ear of Reith. As Warden of New College, Oxford, a former Minister for Education and chief architect of the 1918 Education Act, Fisher took a particular interest in the 'educational' side of the Corporation, notably *The Listener*, which he considered 'in every way an admirable production', a phrase which in his correspondence was usually followed by the word 'but'. The first big 'but' came in the autumn of 1936, when Fisher told Reith that the poetry in the magazine was 'almost uniformly mediocre: in general, much too precious; angular and contorted. No doubt it will encourage young talent, but I have seen much decent verse which is less abstruse than that which prevailingly finds its way into the columns of *The Listener*.' These rumblings continued intermittently like a circling storm. Much discussion of slipping standards went on over dinners at High Table in assorted Oxford colleges, as Fisher sought the opinions of colleagues. The President of Magdalen was canvassed and gratifyingly described the magazine's poetry as 'very poor'. However, when challenged by R. S. Lambert, he admitted that these were lean times and that he 'could not say that better poetry was in fact available.'

Fisher also supported Reith's criticisms of the book reviews which he considered 'intelligently done and generally competent', *but* he wondered whether the otherwise admirable Edwin Muir should really be recommending Aldous Huxley's 'inconceivably disgusting' *Eyeless in Gaza?* Reith thought not and wrote to Tallents:

> I don't think I ever mentioned my concern about book reviews in *The Listener* – books of all kinds.
>
> When we stopped reviewing books by wireless, *The Listener* carried on with criticisms of its own, but it was always understood that *The Listener*'s standard, for all kinds of books, was to be high. There was a particular point to be kept in mind (about which trouble had been experienced when novels were reviewed by wireless) – that of moral tone . . . There are few activities fallen into such low repute as that of criticism in general, and there is certainly little recognition of moral responsibility anywhere.
>
> I am sure you have been giving consideration to this generally, but it does come to hand through a protest from Mr H. A. L. Fisher against the laudation of Aldous Huxley's *Eyeless in Gaza*. He thought it the most disgusting book he had ever read (and having struggled through it myself I more or less agree with him). At least, he says, if we review, still more recommend such a book, the reviewer should make it plain that it is in parts quite disgusting.

By the beginning of 1937 Reith was looking for further ways of improving the books pages. He suggested that 'literary reviews run as a comprehensive guide to reading, e.g. for country rectories, would be a good circulation point.'

Ackerley was aiming rather higher than country rectories, as his list of reviewers shows. Apart from the New Novels column and the quarterly Book Supplement, all reviews appeared unsigned. This was perhaps as well, for Reith might have regarded many of the contributors as entirely lacking in moral responsibility. Socialists, pacifists, anarchists, homosexuals, contributors to the *New Statesman* and other subversives made the books pages both lively and often controversial. There were frequent complaints that the magazine favoured Bloomsbury, but as Lambert replied to Tallents shortly after Ackerley had been appointed:

> I wonder whether there is any other weekly paper using, in proportion to the number of books reviewed, a larger and more varied list of reviewers? . . . There are now few subjects for which we have not a specialist reviewer available. Consequently the number of 'general' reviewers is very small. This fact is the principal safeguard against the possible growth of 'clique-ism'. We cannot, of course, expect to be a 'Times Literary Supplement', since we have about one-tenth of their space, but in our own way we do try to ensure that every single review comes from the pen of a reviewer who, if his name were published, would be admitted to be a person fully qualified to do the book.[1]

The alleged Bloomsbury bias was one of Fisher's most ridden hobbyhorses, and Reith, with his suspicion of modernism, was prepared to back it. Fisher's criticisms of the arts and literary pages reached such a pitch by the end of 1937 that Ackerley sent a tart note to Lambert:

> In view of the continual official criticisms which are made upon the art features in 'The Listener', I find it increasingly difficult to know

---

[1] Ackerley later compiled a directory of reviewers which bears this out and shows the wide range of books the magazine attempted to cover. He listed page upon page of names under subject headings: Administration, Africa, America (North and South), Anthropology, Archaeology, Architecture, Art, Asia, Asia Minor, Australia, Ballet, Biography, Biology, Book Production, British Isles and Ireland, Broadcasting, Children, Cinema, Crime, Drama, Economics, Education, Empire, Europe (broken down into individual countries), History, International Affairs, Law, Literature, Classics, Medicine and Health, Music, Natural History, Navy, Philosophy, Political Science, Psychology, Religion, Science, Sociology and Social Science, Sport, Travel, War, Witchcraft and Magic. Some of these lists were extremely long – 90 reviewers listed under Art, 130 under History, 194 under Literature – and against each name specialist subjects within the categories were noted.

how to make a choice of subjects for articles which may avoid displeasure – I do not say give satisfaction, for messages of appreciation from above seldom reach this office, possibly because they are never sent.

Art exhibitions are now beginning, and we usually find in them material for some of our articles, so as to keep the public *au courant* with what is going on. So far they have not been particularly good, but the most outstanding exhibition at the present moment is that of Miss Frances Hodgkins' work at the Lefevre Galleries.[1] I went to see the show, but at once rejected any idea of using it for an article, believing, rightly or wrongly, that, with the rest of advanced modern art, abstract, constructivist, surrealist and so on, it was the kind of exhibition which would receive official disapproval, and not now being sure in my mind whether my job is the negative one of avoiding this, or the positive one of upholding the standards of taste set by such pundits as Kenneth Clark, Sir Eric Maclagan [Director of the Victoria and Albert Museum], J. B. Manson, Herbert Read and the other experts on art and architectural matters whose opinion I always seek before committing myself to any art feature at all.

In view, however, of the attached letter from Reid and Lefevre [now detached and lost], and the additional fact that Mr Herbert Read thinks Miss Hodgkins' exhibition worth an article, and that Mr Kenneth Clark has reserved one of her pictures for his own collection, I would be glad of official direction in this matter. Some photographs of the most photographable of her works are also attached in case her particular brand of painting should be unfamiliar.

Eventually a general review was demanded. For the defence, letters were sent to the Directors of the Tate, the V & A and the National Gallery, asking whether they thought that the magazine's 'art articles and art features are on the right lines and hold a fair balance between modernistic and traditional schools of artistic criticism and expression.' Both J. B. Manson and Sir Eric Maclagan prevaricated,

[1] Frances Hodgkins (1869–1947) is considered New Zealand's most important twentieth-century painter, although she spent most of her life in England and Europe. She worked in oils and water-colours and was influenced in her use of colour by French artists such as Dufy. Her work was figurative: portraits, still lifes and landscapes.

explaining that they were rather busy but would reply in due course, but Kenneth Clark, an intermittent and somewhat reluctant contributor, replied that the arts pages 'show a very high level – so high that I can make hardly any constructive criticisms'. He made a few, but concluded: 'I think that the arts are better treated in your paper than in any other, and no editor can get away from the fundamental difficulty that good writers on art hardly exist.'

In fact the contributors to the arts pages were extremely distinguished: apart from Clark himself, Ackerley was commissioning articles and reviews from Herbert Read, Clive Bell, Douglas Cooper, John Pope-Hennessy, Anthony Blunt and Paul Nash. He also liked to have unacademic views in the magazine and would commission poets and novelists (notably Elizabeth Bowen, Stephen Spender and William Plomer) to review exhibitions which particularly interested them. Testimonies to the wide range, distinction and impartiality of the magazine's contributors were collected and sent to Reith, who remained obstinately unconvinced. He wrote to Tallents:

> I read those papers about *The Listener*, and of course found them interesting. The Chairman read them too, and he found them interesting, but he asked me whether I could explain why he and so many others (despite what was said in these papers) felt as they did – particularly with regard to cliquishness. I do not know whether you can answer this question better than I. All I could say was that it frequently happened that one remained of an opinion despite the production of facts and figures which should lead to a different conclusion; and I do not know that you are quite happy about it either.

Tallents could take a hint and, abetted by his assistant, Ryan, stepped up his persecution of the magazine.

Of course the BBC had forged links with Bloomsbury long before Ackerley joined *The Listener*, and was constantly inviting people like Forster, Desmond MacCarthy, Harold Nicolson and Vita Sackville-West to broadcast for them. It was Ackerley's connections with such people that had recommended him to the Corporation in the first place and it would have been a poor literary editor who did not commission work from them during the 1930s. However, there is little doubt that part of the attraction for Ackerley of someone like Leonard Woolf, who was a regular contributor of unsigned book reviews, was that he could be relied upon to stir things up with his outspoken views. For instance, whilst Fisher was grumbling to Reith, Woolf was writing a review of the first volume of Frederick Maurice's biography of Viscount Haldane of Cloan and Herbert Asquith's *Moments of Memory*. Some of his unflattering comments about politicians were blue-pencilled by Ryan. Woolf had commented that: 'Haldane's character was too solid and serious to win him the kind of popularity which many modern politicians struggle for in competition with film stars and little princesses.' The last two words had been marked for excision since they constituted a disgraceful slur upon the royal family. Woolf had gone on to repeat:

> the well-known fact that politics is a dirty business. The underworld of politics is a treacherous and dangerous place, inhabited by persons who would not disgrace the underworld of Chicago, and it extends far beyond the frontiers of politics proper into such places as the Army and the Army Council, as Sir Henry Wilson's confessions show.

If Sir Henry Wilson was entitled to his opinion, Mr Leonard Woolf was not, and Ryan returned the proof with this passage marked for alteration or excision. He attempted to offset editorial indignation with a little jest:

> Taken literally the passage I've underlined is, I suppose, alright. You, I and Ackerley would not 'disgrace the underworld of Chicago'. On the contrary we should (I hope) raise its moral tone. But the plain meaning is, of course, that some politicians and soldiers in England are as bad as Al Capone. And that's surely too strong. It should be deleted, I'm sure you'll both agree, and this whole passage toned down.

Lambert stood firm, and the second passage remained unaltered. However, the reference to the 'little princesses' was removed. Leonard Woolf was furious:

> I feel I must say that the under-housemaid snobbery of the BBC makes me queasy. I note that one is not allowed to say that a

politician cannot compete with the popularity of little princesses, though you may say that it cannot compete with that of film stars. Are reviewers expected to remember to write with the standards of the underhousemaid in mind; if so, it would be better to add it to the instructions on the slip included with review books.

Ackerley recognized a kindred spirit in Woolf and replied:

Your deservedly acid note is very timely and welcome – though God knows, it will not shame them, I fear. I am in the very thick of battle, and have passed it on to Lambert and Ryan (Tallents' shadow) with this remark. 'When you tell me that I am being unduly sensitive about the increasing petty censoring which I complain of here, this example of how it seems to the intellectual world outside is perhaps timely.' But I don't expect any result, except that you may not in any case wish to review again for me, or even that an attempt may be made to prevent me sending to you again.

Lambert disloyally added a note to Ackerley's memo before passing it on to Ryan: 'It seems to me Mr Woolf is being silly.' Ryan sent the memo back with a characteristically facetious comment:

Sorry, but I'm on the side of the underhousemaids. If we may not hope for the honour of entertaining Mr Woolf below stairs, still I think some members of the intellectual world will sit round the kitchen fire with us in agreement that royalty deserves special treatment not accorded to film stars.

Ackerley had been going through a particularly difficult period with his employers, as he explained to Woolf:

The place is becoming insufferable, Fascist; and I am constantly in the dock for everything I do – modernism in art and poetry, leftism in literature . . . I begin to feel dirty here, and hardly know what to do. It is only money that keeps me to the wretched place, and yet I do not feel I can stand it much more, though I hope to stagger on to next year when I complete my term and get a present of 3 months' leave and a month's salary.

Woolf was sympathetic to Ackerley's position, which confirmed his worst suspicions about the BBC:

> I am glad that you did not mind my writing as I did and that you even found it timely. It must be torture to be inside the machine. That the BBC should be reactionary and politically and intellectually dishonest is what one would expect and forgive, knowing the kind of people who always get into control of those kind of machines, but what makes them so contemptible is that, even according to their own servants' hall standards, they habitually choose the tenth rate in everything, from their musichall programmes and social lick-spitlers and royal bumsuckers right down their scale to the singers of Schubert songs, the conductors of their classical concerts and the writers of their reviews.

Ackerley was delighted but felt that Woolf was in a position to do something about it:

> The most I can do is to resign, which I dare say will happen soon, but as my editor points out that would be utterly ineffective . . . I long to do the dirty on them and my disloyalty and ungentlemanliness are at anyone's disposal.

Nobody took up this offer, and Ackerley was to remain with the magazine for another twenty-two years, during which time he continued to challenge complacency, provide a platform for controversy, campaign against censorship, and pursue and promote excellence.

12

The dark ages

A CKERLEY'S personal affairs were a good deal less orderly than his desk in Broadcasting House. However, the perfectionism Ackerley brought to his work was echoed in his search for a lover, and involved an equal amount of sifting and rejecting. He was an admirer of craftsmanship: he liked the well-constructed poem and the well-made play, the review which summed up a book in an exact number of words. In his own books, like most writers, he wanted to impose patterns upon life, to order experience and so create art. Unfortunately, he applied similar criteria to his love-life, hoping to find perfect balance in the heart's affections.

In spite of Forster's lectures, Ackerley remained an idealist, unwilling to accept that most human relationships are based upon adjustment and negotiation, adaptation and making do. His good looks and easy charm had accustomed him to admiration, but admiration was not the same thing as love. He discovered that beauty, like money, was not altogether an advantage. As he entered his forties, he was still a strikingly handsome man, but he became increasingly aware of the difference in age between himself and the young men to whom he was attracted. All his life he had been the one whom others had approached, and he found it difficult and humiliating to make the transition from prey to predator. One effect of this was that he had developed what one friend described as a 'come-and-get-me marmoreal quality'. For all his social friendliness some people noticed a certain chilliness in his character, even a frigidity. Wishing to be approached rather than do the approaching, he appeared to be someone who absorbed, rather than radiated, emotion. Once that approach had been made, he could be very sympathetic and responsive, but he disliked making the first gesture.

Now that Albert had disappeared from his life, Ackerley set about finding the Ideal Friend once again. In the winter of 1935–36 he nearly found him, but he only realized this too late, and in retrospect, for the young man did not entirely fill the role Ackerley allotted him. Born 'one too many' in a Welsh slum, Frank Harris had, like Ackerley's father, escaped from his family by joining the Guards. Ackerley picked him up at Marble Arch and took him back to Clifton Gardens. Ever fastidious about the bodies of others, Ackerley was rather put off by the fact that Frank suffered from bromidrosis, or smelly feet. There seems no reason why this small matter could not have been overcome with baths before bedtime, but Frank's solution was to keep his boots on in bed. Ackerley had seen Frank as a one-night-stand and in a diary he kept at that time, had described him as 'a dull chap, quite nice-looking, but physically unrewarding'. However, whenever Ackerley went on further prowls he would see Frank, pale-faced in the lamplight at Marble Arch. Sometimes they would go home, but often Ackerley would merely exchange a word or two before going on his way in the hope of meeting someone better. Sometimes, seeing Frank loitering like a ghost, Ackerley would head off in the opposite direction, hoping that he had not been recognized.

Frank was immensely good-natured and patient, making very few demands upon Ackerley, but thus unwittingly causing pangs of guilt. At some point he got a girl pregnant and agreed to marry her. He left the Army in order to support her and took on a number of part-time and short-lived jobs, ending up as a commissionaire in the City. He lived on a 'squalid fourth floor' in Camden with his wife and baby son, but continued to hang about Hyde Park, looking rather lost. Unlike most of the guardsmen Ackerley encountered, Frank was genuinely affectionate and, in spite of the repeated efforts Ackerley made to get rid of him,

> He came again, and he stuck. He was a sweet boy, and that . . . I recognized in course of time. He became, at last, the person in my life whose kindness and constancy I valued most.

Frank adored his small son and his marriage seems to have been reasonably successful. His wife appears to have been very understanding and tolerant, or, as Ackerley suggested, was simply under 'control'.

Frank was devoted to Ackerley, often refusing money when he had done odd jobs, even nursing his friend when he was ill. The relationship was a sunny one, but was also fraught with disappointments. For all Frank's gentleness and affection, and the fact that he was the only one of Ackerley's lovers who took the initiative in love-making, he was not sexually Ackerley's ideal. Few people were. In spite of Frank's devotion, Ackerley still spent much of his time prowling the streets, lurking in bars and bushes, attempting to pay his way to fulfilment. For six months he kept a diary in which his encounters were obsessively recorded in great detail. Fifteen years later he was to discover this diary, read it and destroy it. He was appalled by what he had written, particularly about Frank:

> It contained one of the nastiest things of all, my irritable disenchanted comments, after my first meeting with him, of [Frank], his loutishness and smelly feet, this boy who was to become . . . the most constant and sweetest of my friends.

In order to broaden the field of his activities from Hyde Park, Bird Cage Walk, the pubs of Soho and the 'meat rack' at Piccadilly underground station, Ackerley decided to follow William Plomer's lead and take rooms in Dover. In the 1920s Portsmouth had been the place to go, and such luminaries as Raymond Mortimer and Eddy Sackville-West could be seen dancing with sailors in some of the more louche pubs. Unfortunately, one pub became so crowded that a balcony gave way and someone was killed, after which the London literati had been obliged to make do with Limehouse. Portsmouth, of course, also held unhappy memories for Ackerley of Albert. Dover was already well known as the place to see off or welcome back friends travelling between cold and stuffy England and the warmer and more liberated atmosphere of Europe, but it was Plomer who first set up residence there in June 1936.

Unlike other seaside towns within easy reach of London, Dover was not a haven for trippers. People who came to Dover were generally on their way somewhere else, across the Channel, and the port had the transient air, at once gay and melancholy, of some vast hotel. Furthermore, it was home base and port of call for ships which disgorged innumerable sailors into the streets and pubs, all out for a good time. To this tidal swell was added the soldiers from the garrison and the nearby military camps of the hinterland, those soldiers who exercised so strong an influence upon the imagination of Jocelyn Brooke (one of the few writers who was indigenous), and who were immortalized by Auden and Spender in their poems, 'Dover' and 'The Port'. In Auden's poem he lists the Lion, the Rose and the Crown as the pubs where soldiers foregathered, but this owed more to scansion than fact. As with all such meeting-places, the pubs moved in and out of favour, but those most 'fruitful', as Ackerley put it, were the British Queen near the post office, where the Seaforth Highlanders lolled in their kilts, the Invicta, which was on the Front, the Granville and, 'noisiest and most disreputable of them all', the Prince Regent in the corner of Market Square. If all else failed there was the Clarendon near the old harbour along the coast at Folkestone.

In the summer of 1936 Ackerley decided to take rooms at 33 Marine Parade, a house belonging to a pair of pious spinsters called Miss Phillips and Miss Hughes. The landladies were at first very pleased to have a distinguished literary gentleman as their lodger, and even offered to nurse him when he was ill. Forster was also delighted to have somewhere to convalesce after his second operation for prostate. Having spent some time there in July, he offered to pay half the rent (which was £1 a week) throughout August and September.

Ackerley arranged for various friends and relations to spend time in Dover and over the next couple of years the town was alive with literary homosexuals, becoming a sort of Maida Vale sur Mer. Visitors included Jack Sprott, John Hampson, T. C. Worsley and a painter friend Graham Bell, who stayed at the Hotel de Paris, Auden and Isherwood ('a pair of scamps' according to their landlady), and Stephen Spender. Leo Charlton and Tom Wichelo liked the town so much that they settled there permanently. Forster remarked that if a bomb fell on the town it would wipe out almost all the country's undesirables. Despite sitting in the Granville consuming numerous pints of beer, Forster had little luck sexually, but he liked the atmosphere and recommended the sea air to May Buckingham, who was also recuperating from an operation. She and Bob were frequent visitors, as were several of Forster's working-class friends and their wives. Somewhat incongruously amidst all the feverish sexual activity, Forster's mother paid the occasional visit, sometimes bringing a friend and inviting over relations from nearby Sandgate. Mothers were not necessarily a problem and the presence of Mrs Sprott, Ackerley suggested, should not deter her son from missing out on the fun to be had at the British Queen when the Fleet was in. She could be introduced to Gladys, the barmaid, whom she would like.

For the next few years most of Ackerley's spare time was spent in Dover combing the pubs and conducting 'love affairs' with assorted members of the forces. Some of these affairs lasted no more than a night, if that, and most involved the exchange of money. (Ten shillings appears to have been the going rate.) Discretion was necessary at Marine Parade, but it seems that for a while the 'Holy Ladies' remained in ignorance of their lodger's activities. Occasionally Ackerley would become more involved with his pick-ups, far too involved some of his friends thought. One sailor, whom Forster thought pleasant enough but 'too trashy to deserve serious attention', was to cause considerable trouble. As so often happened, Ackerley allowed what should have been a one-night-stand to develop into a bogus relationship which involved him in considerable emotional and financial expenditure. Most of the men spent the money they gained from sex with their twanks on drink and women, often amateur tarts like themselves. Jo-Jo was no exception, and, like many before him, he slipped up over contraception and got a girl pregnant. Ackerley had to be dissuaded by Forster from helping the couple to procure an abortion. Ackerley's association with the petty criminals of Hammersmith had fuelled his natural recklessness. He admired the fact that they, like him, were living outside the law, and he was frequently becoming involved as what might have been regarded in the courts as 'an accessory'. Smitten with Jo-Jo, in spite of the boy's involvement with women, Ackerley continued to see him and to lavish money upon him. Seven months later, Forster was still counselling: 'Jo-Jo is certainly underweight & the better you can realize this, the better for your comfort and your purse.'

Although sexually extremely active, Ackerley was not sexually fulfilled, as he noted in the margin of one of the drafts of *My Father and Myself*:

> Pleasure of orgasms. But constant mismanagement, unable to arrange things to my own satisfaction, sex too late at night, other person coming first. Unable to be myself. Incontinence improved.

Such anxieties contributed to a new problem. He began to experience bouts of impotence. Like his former incontinence, this was psychological, prompted by

213

the smallest worry or discomfort: why had I let him [i.e. his partner] have an orgasm first? he would be bored now; we had left it all so late, could I manage after all that beer? Was I lying too long or too heavily upon him? He never came himself, why not? He took hold of me in the wrong place and was too rough, it hurt. It was all done for money. Oh God, let me manage.

This miserable situation did not prevent Ackerley from picking up innumerable soldiers and sailors and, in spite of such complications, he enjoyed the time he spent in Dover. Before long, however, Ackerley took unwise risks and became involved with men who, even by the standards of the casual prostitute, were dishonest and dangerous. One such was a soldier with the unlikely name of Catkin, whom Ackerley had met at Marble Arch 'in full regalia, with no money'. The man was based at Shorncliffe and claimed that he had been given two days' leave as a reward for 'proficiency at tent-pegging'. A warier customer than Ackerley might have wondered at the soldier's story and circumstances, but the man was 'young (about nineteen), well favoured, uninhibited & obliging, well spoken, lively, reasonably priced (7s 6d), non-grasping, and acts affectionateness quite passably. Also he enjoys it.' Ackerley recommended him to Jack Sprott, who was visiting Dover, but added a final warning: 'he fibs . . .' Sprott was unable to avail himself of Catkin's services, because, Ackerley reported in a letter, Catkin 'was one of the first people to ring me up when I reached here [i.e. Clifton Gardens] and is presently asleep in my other room.' Ackerley was already rather disillusioned with the young man, who clearly knew a good thing when he saw one. Life for Catkin, Ackerley reported,

> is merely a rather jolly scene, set mainly for him, in which he has only to put on his uniform and stand about, whereupon (like Aladdin rubbing his lamp) a queer genie will appear who will be prepared for the minimum amount of gratitude or even attention, to house and feed him and give him pocket money so that he will be able to run about after other people, mainly girls.

Worse was to follow, for Catkin disappeared one morning, taking one of Ackerley's suits and leaving behind his uniform. There was no question of attempting to apply to the military authorities for the return of the suit, since questions were bound to be asked. Forster consulted Leo Charlton, whilst Ackerley went to Harry Daley to seek advice. Charlton's first instinct was to return the uniform to Catkin at Shorncliffe, but enquiries established that the trooper had gone AWOL. It was quite possible that if it were discovered that the suit was Ackerley's, he might be accused of assisting, or even inciting, a member of the forces to desert, a very serious offence. If Catkin were caught no doubt questions would be asked about the owner of the suit. Catkin might keep quiet, but had not proved at all trustworthy in the past – 'a regular Ratkin' is how Ackerley now described him. If the suit were traced back to Ackerley and it were discovered that he had destroyed the uniform, this might confirm suspicions that he had abetted Catkin in his desertion. Eventually it was decided to post the uniform back to the barracks anonymously.

However, by this time Ackerley's indiscretions had come to the notice of his landladies and he had been obliged to depart. The Holy Ladies didn't expect ever to hear from or see Ackerley again, Forster reported crossly, and he should consider himself lucky that matters were no worse. Ackerley should realize that 'to the average person, this sort of thing is disgusting, especially when it obtrudes its creaks-and-sheets end first upon their notice.'

In common with many members of his generation Ackerley had watched the rise of Fascism in Europe with mounting despair. In particular he dreaded the prospect of a period in which civil liberties would be seriously curtailed. As early as November 1937 he was complaining to Leonard Woolf of the restrictions being imposed by 'Dame Dora[1] and Mrs Grundy who (I suppose inevitably with the return of militarism) are back with us again.' A veteran of the Great War, he had no illusions about the attitudes and actions of the armed forces, the Church and Parliament in a national emergency, and he regarded them all with almost equal loathing. Memories of the Great War were further rekindled in January 1939 when *The Prisoners of*

---

[1] The much-hated Defence of the Realm Act (DORA) was a piece of emergency legislation which came into effect during the first week of the First World War. It gave the government wide-ranging powers to restrict any activity which might be regarded as prejudicial to national security.

War was revived by Raymond Raikes at the Tavistock Little Theatre. Ackerley took a keen interest in the production, attending rehearsals, proffering advice and writing a programme note about the background to the play.

As, throughout that year, the outbreak of war began to seem inevitable, so Ackerley's unhappiness increased. There would be no question of his fighting, since he was in his mid-forties, but there were other skins to save than his own. In particular he had to decide what to do with his nephew, Paul Jnr, who was now aged twelve. It was decided that Paul should sit out the war in America with his father, who had left the United Fruit Company, remarried and settled in New York as an advertising manager for the Time-Life Corporation. It was felt that Paul needed a father-figure, since although Ackerley did his best he was not considered a suitable role model for the young boy. Ackerley was fond of his nephew, but had little idea of how to treat a child. He would bring him review copies from the office, usually of books which turned out to be entirely unsuitable for a schoolboy. What Paul really liked were Leo Charlton's adventure stories and he was very proud to be presented with copies of the books by the author himself. Another reason for sending Paul to America was that relations between Netta and Nancy continued to be bad and the atmosphere in their respective homes tended to be rather lowering. In spite of this, Paul was comparatively happy, largely because of Aunt Bunny, who had been living with Netta since the death of her second husband, 'Doc' Fowler, in 1935. Paul recalls that Bunny appeared to be the only sane member of the family.

Although he had little inclination for travelling across the Atlantic to live with a father he scarcely knew, Paul relinquished his gas-mask and was put on a boat for New York. 'You were like a dad to me, and you always will be,' he told Ackerley in one of a bleak procession of homesick letters he would send his uncle throughout the war. 'How can I love Dad as much as you, when I have only just seen him?' Paul wrote regularly and as each new letter arrived, Ackerley must have wondered whether they had made the right decision in sending the boy to America:

Dear Joe
Ho do I wish I was with you this christmas. It is not nice not being with you and Mum at 159A Sheen Road. You are the only man I can

reliy on, please give me your word that I will be at home for Christmas before *1941*, please Joe. I do hope that I will be at 159A, at 6pm Dec 5 1940, lots and lots of *love*
Paul x x x x x x x x x x x x x x x
PS Keep Mum well. Paul

The war turned out to be a period of almost unrelieved gloom for Ackerley, during which the darkness which had descended upon the world was mirrored by a series of disasters in his own private and professional life. His original philosophy, much approved by Forster, that everyone should destroy Hitler by determinedly enjoying themselves, did not survive very long, and his dismal forebodings about wartime restrictions were amply fulfilled. Friends who spoke of the 'special circumstances' in order to excuse the infringement of liberty were sternly rebuked and sent newspaper clippings for comment. He took grim pleasure in the accidents of war, exposing as they did the folly and wickedness which such emergencies produced. After dining with 'someone high up in the Ministry of Information' during the second week of the war, he was able to report to Stephen Spender that 'our achievement so far . . . was to have bombed a Danish village, shot down two Belgian planes, shot down one British plane during the last air-raid alarm, and lost five other planes which simply dived into the sea during the raid on the Canal.' When, later in the war, a bomb fell on the Guards Chapel during divine service, Ackerley blamed the incident upon a deplorable BBC broadcast in which George VI had implied that God was on the side of the British.

News that R. S. Lambert was to retire as editor of *The Listener* was welcome, but any relief Ackerley may have felt was almost instantly extinguished by the announcement that the deputy editor, Alan Thomas, was to be appointed in Lambert's place. The recommendation of Thomas for the job came from Lambert himself, who described his deputy as 'a very shrewd, business-like and likeable man who would be a sound appointment'. A great deal sounder, in Lambert's opinion, than Ackerley. In the same BBC memo it was recorded that Lambert had 'expressed the view strongly that Ackerley could not be considered as Editor or Deputy Editor as he lacked the necessary business-like qualities and width of interest, and there was a streak of irresponsibility in him.' It is doubtful whether Ackerley had ever considered himself in the running for the job; there are certainly no references to such hopes in any of his letters at this period (although Forster urged him to push to be made the new deputy editor). He was not in any sense a Corporation Man and although the increased salary would have been welcome, it is unlikely that he would have wanted the responsibility that came with the job. In 1952 he would remark that the only advantage of being editor would be that he could publish what he wanted: 'otherwise I should hate the job, committees and all that, so boring'. Because of the 'impertinent' laws which governed England, his sexual life had to be one of subterfuge and risk-taking, and he regarded the unwritten laws which governed the BBC with similar disdain, to be flouted whenever possible in the cause of Truth and Freedom. He was by nature a *franc-tireur*, who was happiest when waging an inspiriting undercover operation against the forces of 'decency' (which he saw as prudery) and 'restraint' (which he saw as repression). However, there were to be many occasions during Thomas's editorship when Ackerley would have liked to have wielded more power.

When Ackerley described Thomas as 'the best of Editors', he was being rather less gracious than at first appears, his opinion of editors not being of the highest. Later in life the two men came to like and respect each other, but their early years together were extremely acrimonious. 'Joe came yesterday, very gloomy,' Forster reported to the Buckinghams shortly after Thomas's appointment, '– trouble with the new editor and muddle with the new guardsman.' Over the years trouble with the editor was to occupy as much of Ackerley's time as muddles with guardsmen, and Thomas was to cause him as much irritation as his predecessor had done. Worse still, whereas Lambert often backed up his literary editor, Thomas was a Corporation lackey. Ackerley had no respect whatever for Thomas, whose persistent kow-towing to Tallents and Ryan was the cause of many disagreements. By January 1941 (in a letter to Edward Sackville-West) Ackerley could describe his relationship with his editor as:

one long series of [rows]. He is a *little* man, a person of no mental stature at all, and should never have been given the job. His appointment is a real tragedy. He is what is called 'nice' (which Lambert wasn't), but is quite lacking in taste, judgement, imagination, or courage. His friends are people like Robert and Sylvia

Lynd, the Farjeons, E. C. Bentley, Ivor Brown,[1] dull, second rate people like himself, and if he had his way the paper would be full of them. He is a funk and a prude, and thinks of nothing but his blue pencil and dreams of it at night. The result can be seen in the correspondence columns which used to be lively and have now fallen away to nothing. There is nothing now in the paper ever to write about.

As Thomas recalled in *The Times* after Ackerley's death:

The going, particularly in the early days of his literary editorship, was not invariably easy, mainly, I think, because in many respects Joe was in advance of his time. The 'climate of opinion' 30 years ago, both in the BBC and outside it, was very different from what it is in the 1960s.

If Ackerley was ahead of the times, Thomas appeared to be a symptom of them and relations between the two men rapidly deteriorated. Matters had not been helped by the appointment in the summer of 1938 of F. W. Ogilvie as the new DG. What Ackerley referred to with distaste as 'the Ogilvie-Tallents regime' was quite as repressive as that of Reith, 'the erstwhile Dictator of Broadcasting', as Ackerley called him. In the winter of 1940–41 matters reached a head and the ensuing row saw Ackerley defining and defending his position as literary editor. In December he was rebuked by Ogilvie for publishing Sidney Keyes' poem 'Remember Your Lovers'. The DG thought it indecent, largely because it contained the word 'lust'. Ackerley later admitted that he had not thought the poem particularly good, but – as in the case of Henry Reed's poem – he had decided to publish it in order to encourage a young writer, an attitude for which Keyes was very grateful. Ackerley complained about the rebuke to Herbert Read, who

[1] Robert Lynd was the long-serving literary editor of the *Daily News*, which became the *News Chronicle* in 1930. He was a regular contributor of whimsical essays in the *New Statesman* under the pen-name 'Y.Y.'. With his wife, Sylvia, a poet and novelist, he held a Hampstead salon for publishers, editors and authors. Herbert Farjeon was a theatrical manager and drama critic. He was *The Listener*'s radio critic, 1943–45, and wrote and produced a number of revues. His sister, Eleanor, was a prolific and prize-winning author of children's books. Ivor Brown was an author and journalist, a drama critic and leader writer for the *Manchester Guardian*, and editor of the *Observer*.

sent a letter of protest at the DG's action and suggested that other poets might do the same. As a result of Ogilvie's rap across the editorial knuckles, Ackerley was also obliged to return a poem to Alex Comfort since it contained the words 'harlotry' and 'randy'.

Then Thomas objected to the use of the word 'homosexual' in a review by Eddy Sackville-West of Derrick Leon's *Introduction to Proust,* a book which failed to take account of the writer's sexuality. The BBC's refusal to countenance this stung Ackerley both professionally and personally. Three years earlier he had written to Richard Church about a review of Laurence Housman's *A.E.H.: Some Poems, Some Letters, and a Personal Memoir,* suggesting that reference should be made to the poet's long-standing attachment to a Venetian gondolier.

> I don't want to 'claim' Housman unwarrantably for the homo-sexuals, but I don't, also, see why facts thought proper by his very correct brother to mention should not be alluded to in any review – even in our respectable 'Listener' . . . Will you not add this small item of information, without any remark, in its appropriate place? I very much dislike the idea that the 'Listener', more than any other paper, should suppress such matters . . .

Church inserted a reference to the gondolier, without comment, and the review was published. It was presumably Sackville-West's comments that caused the problem (the review has vanished both from the BBC archives and Sackville-West's own papers), and a violent argument ensued. 'I feel very angry and militant about this business', Ackerley told Sackville-West, 'and I want to pursue it – to Ogilvie if necessary.' He even declared that he would resign as soon as possible rather than work under such an editor.

> The whole thing is disgraceful. Here is a book which purports to be a biographical sketch of the greatest novelist of our time and an examination of his novel. A published work which will be bought and read. It is based on a misconception – or a deliberate lie. How can any reputable journal that sets out to review it escape the duty of correcting that misconception or exposing that lie?

He then wrote an official letter to Sackville-West which (as he explained to Sackville-West in an *unofficial* letter) he made 'as wounding and shaming to the editor as possible, for he will later be obliged to read the carbon of it'. The 'official' letter, accompanying the galley, ran as follows:

I am sorry, but the statements of fact in this review about Proust's homosexuality are too strong for the editor. He wishes to use the review as he has cut it on one of these galleys, on the pretext that the omitted statements are sufficiently implied in what remains and will be read between the lines by our perspicacious readers. I take it, however, that your reference to Proust's 'theory of love' has nothing to do with his homosexuality, and since the latter fundamental point still remains uncovered, and the book cannot, as the *Spectator* also realizes, be properly examined without reference to it, you may well wish to offer an alternative version.

It must, however, be less honestly worded. It is not our policy to call a spade a spade: I fear I do not know to what extent it may be called a shovel. The *Spectator*, I know, calls it an unmistakable shovel, and it was not long ago that cultivated people turned to our reviews before those of any other journal, because, as Professor Furness put it, they told the truth; but now we have a policy which appears to be that though we still like to be thought a cultural and educational paper, we are nevertheless more 'popular' than the *Spectator* (? i.e. we have a larger circulation), and the more popular one is the more obscurantist it is necessary to be. For the sophisticated know already, and the ignorant are better left in ignorance where knowledge is liable to shock or offend.

I make these observations so that you may try to word your revisions in such a way as to avoid any further puritanical blue pencilling.

Thomas was not at all pleased by this letter, but would have been wounded further had he seen the series of 'unofficial' letters his literary editor was writing to Sackville-West, in which he was described as 'a rabbit'. Ackerley asked Sackville-West to write Thomas

a *sensible* but firm letter – it may be taken up to the DG, but he is an even worse puritan – pointing out that it is a reviewer's duty to review a book adequately and that this book cannot be reviewed without a certain allusion to a discussion of the homosexual theme.

The more reasonable and firm your letter is the better. I want to put him in as difficult a dilemma as possible.

Sackville-West was concerned that the whole affair might blow up in Ackerley's face, but was reassured in another private letter. By this point Thomas had taken to his bed with a chill, 'caught I hope from the frostiness of my manner to him,' Ackerley remarked. Ackerley took advantage of his editor's absence to draft a long memorandum in which he used the Proust row as the basis of a wide-ranging attack upon 'general "Listener" policy':

What is vaguely termed the 'special position of *The Listener*' has always been with you a convenient excuse for pursuing what I can only call a dilutionist policy, and on this particular occasion you attached the word 'popular' to our paper. Your argument was that since *The Listener* has a larger circulation than the *Spectator*, it is therefore more popular, and cannot therefore be so outspoken. Apart from the fact that I do not follow the sequence of this argument, it seems to me that to attach the word 'popular' to our journal in such a crippling sense is entirely to ignore its history and tradition. *The Listener* has a larger circulation than the *Spectator* only because of the former's connection with broadcasting and broadcasting's connection with education. To call it popular is, to my mind, to do it a disservice. Far from being 'popular', *The Listener*'s reputation is surely that of an advanced journal of culture and education; its position (never a popular position) has been in the vanguard of contemporary thought, the forefront of the battle. Stronger rather than weaker for having no editorial policy, it seems to me both invidious and false to suggest that it has lagged behind other weekly journals in any way; indeed, so far as *The Listener*'s book reviews are concerned, it is their pride that they have been preferred by cultivated readers above those of the other journals for their honesty and detachment. I am speaking mainly of the independent literary side; the fluctuation in weight and quality on the broadcast side has been beyond the Editor's control, but I do not believe that an examination of it would reveal a large percentage of what could justly be called 'popular' material. Though untrue, it would surely be truer to call *The Listener* 'high-brow', for the names which have been associated with its origins and development –

Herbert Read, Edwin Muir, the Coles, Stanley Casson[1] – just as names like Y.Y. and Sagittarius are inseparably associated with the *New Statesman* – are anything but 'popular' names. I don't want to labour the point, which the high standard of *The Listener* verse and the journal's strong and fearless protection and encouragement of the young and experimental artist confirm, as do also the constant battles that have raged around these features between the editor and the philistines outside the building and on the board of governors; nor do I want to come out as an opponent of the word 'popular', excepting in the strange muzzling sense in which you used [it].

He went on to outline the 'Position of the Reviewer', over which, he believed, *The Listener* was singularly muddle-headed, and which he characterized:

An anonymous reviewer may not express a personal opinion. Owing to his anonymity, his opinions are, or are taken to be, the opinions of *The Listener*. Impersonal though we consider him to be we nevertheless recognize him as an individual in so far as (i) we put an official restriction on him that he must not undertake a review for us if he has already undertaken one of the same book for any other paper and (ii) his opinions are defended, if necessary, in our correspondence columns by himself as 'Your reviewer' and not editorially by 'The Editor'.

Ackerley thought this 'somewhat paradoxical' and pointed out that, signed or unsigned, reviews 'express the reviewer's opinion, and that opinion must necessarily be personal, unless he has cribbed it from someone else.' Furthermore, the fact that a review is anonymous does not give the editor the right to 'maul [it] as he chooses', for

sensitive and distinguished writers (as we usually employ) . . . will by no means consider themselves as impersonal as all that, and will quite rightly protest against alterations made without their per-

[1] Cf. page 192 for Ackerley's earlier opinion of Casson. G. D. H. Cole and his wife, Margaret, were leading Fabians, who lectured and wrote books on social theory and labour history, in particular the Trade Union movement. They also wrote detective novels, which were published by Penguin, and were friends of Ackerley's former neighbour, Naomi Mitchison.

mission . . . Signed or unsigned they have pride in their writings, their judgement and taste, and will certainly cease (as Woolf did for some time) to contribute to *The Listener* if their contributions are, in their own opinion, improperly tampered with.

This outburst was not the sort of welcome Thomas required on his return to the office. He suggested Ackerley took the matter up with Sir Richard Maconachie, who was Controller (Home) – a wartime appointment, replacing C (PR) – but Ackerley declined to do so, probably because he realized that he simply could not afford a confrontation which might put his job in jeopardy. 'I shan't resign unless I am absolutely forced out,' he told George Barker. He often complained that he was compromised by his lack of funds, with the result that he was obliged to wage guerilla rather than open warfare with the Corporation. It might be argued that this was in the long run more effective, since Ackerley kept his job and maintained standards, rather than resigning and allowing the BBC to replace him with someone more tailored to their reactionary values. There seems little doubt that Thomas saw in this memorandum an opportunity to get Ackerley disciplined, for he sent it, along with the 'official' correspondence with Sackville-West, to Maconachie, with a covering note explaining his position and stating that the memorandum showed:

(i) that there was evidently a deep misunderstanding between him and me as to what was suitable for publication in *The Listener* and what was not, and
(ii) that this memorandum, and particularly his letter to Sackville-West, seemed to me to call in question his attitude to the editor of *The Listener*.

Nothing appears to have come of this incident, but clearly neither Thomas nor Ackerley was satisfied with the outcome. Ackerley's guerilla tactics continued, as may be seen from a letter he wrote in September 1941 (from his home address) to his old ally Leonard Woolf:

I thought I had better draw your attention to the fact that your review of Priestley's book [*Out of the People*] has been mutilated, for it would have to be such a very idle moment for any intelligent man to open the paper of his own accord. If you are curious, and can be bothered to make a fuss, I wish you would write to the Editor and ask for an explanation. It would interest me very much to see what he says. I will give you the truth if he doesn't, and see that he knows, too, that you have got it. I should start your enquiry firmly but without immediate anger. There will be plenty of opportunity for wrath later. I will see to that. But I should much like to see what explanation he offers first. Begin 'Dear Sir' and address it to The Editor.

Woolf's observation that 'There is just a tinge, a fragrance, of the great Mr Pecksniff in [Priestley's] attitude and his diction,' had caused Thomas to complain: 'O dear, old Jack won't like that! I don't know how I shall ever face him again.' Ackerley felt that these were insufficient grounds for censorship, but Thomas refused to budge. 'Well, it's your bloody paper,' Ackerley had said, 'so you can do as you like; but if [Woolf] comes back at you I will only say that I think he has entirely proper and justifiable grounds for complaint.' Woolf obliged with a letter, but if Thomas provided an explanation it has since been lost.

In 1942 economic measures prompted by the war provided Thomas with another opportunity to rid himself of his turbulent literary editor. A report on staffing levels was drafted and passed to Thomas for his comments. He made several significant alterations. Sir Richard Maconachie's original draft read:

> *Editor, Deputy Editor and Literary Editor*: It would be possible, in case of absolute necessity, to carry on with two out of these three. Mr Ackerley's duties could, at a pinch, be distributed between Mr Thomas, Mr Abraham [the deputy editor] and Miss Scott-Johnston [sub-editor]; but his departure would mean *a very definite loss to the paper, and some lowering of its standards, particularly* as regards book reviews, art page, poetry, short stories and contacts with the world of literature and art.

Thomas altered the words in italics for the more ambiguous, and certainly less warm, 'a change in the paper's standards'. It seems fairly clear, and owing to the more public disagreements between editor and literary editor the Corporation would have been aware of this, that Thomas believed that the 'change in standards' occasioned by

Ackerley's departure might be welcome. Even with this alteration the DG felt 'justified in leaving the position as it is.'

During his correspondence with Woolf about the Priestley review, Ackerley had asked: 'Is it not true that they are the mild respectable little men like Thomas who are the real obstructors of that liberty and progress which they strut around in battle dress to defend?' Examples of such behaviour abounded during the war and one such was furnished by a letter published in the *Daily Telegraph*, headlined 'The Evil of Stage "Undress": Defenceless Youth Endangered', in which Douglas Reed, an authority on European Fascism, expressed concern about such places as the famous and innocuous Windmill Theatre, home of decorous *poses plastiques*. Reed had been dining with a man who had lived in Berlin during the Weimar Republic:

> He remarked to me, and I thoroughly agreed with him, in deep foreboding, that 'it is appalling to see this thing beginning in England, in exactly the same way – first, a few nude shows, then more and more nude shows, all camouflaged as "art" or as "physical culture"; then pornography, and "smut" of all kinds in "literature"'.
>
> Are we going to tread the whole path that Berlin trod, and have palaces of sexual perversion, with electric signs outside advertising the wares? To anybody who remembers the appalling conditions in Berlin between 1918 and 1930 the present trend of affairs in London is terrifying.

This despite being 'a hardened "Bummler" in Europe ... beyond being shocked'. Reed's complaint was made on the grounds that the girls in question were being exploited, but he concluded:

> Is this the 'freedom' we are fighting for? In Berlin 'freedom' meant just that – freedom for the exploiter of youth. A young girl, even a young man, coming inexperienced to Berlin in those days, had hardly a chance of escaping corruption. A whole generation was corrupted in this way. The first duty of patriotism, of which we hear so much, should be to protect the youth of Britain against this exploitation.

In a subsequent letter Reed commented upon communications he had received as the result of his original letter, and concluded:

The one thing that National Socialism did, which even its most inveterate enemies, including myself, were unanimous in praising, was to stamp out the revolting conditions which the Weimar Republic allowed to develop in Germany. If, in this of all matters, we allow the Berlin of 1918–1933 to enjoy a second lease of life in London, we shall make our invocation of the cause of Freedom ridiculous and repulsive.

Appalled by these letters, Ackerley wrote to Reed, who occasionally reviewed for him, to protest and shortly received four pages of typescript in reply. Reed felt that he had been misunderstood and protested that his abhorrence had nothing to do with sex *per se*, but with the circumstances in which young British girls who wanted to get into the film business went to Berlin and were obliged to sleep with every employee of the film studio before being allowed to participate in crowd scenes. This vision of hordes of innocent Sally Bowles figures did not impress Ackerley, neither did Reed's appeal to his patriotism. In an equally lengthy reply Ackerley wrote:

I think I had better say to you at once that I really can't have you appealing to me as a 'Britisher'. It is an appeal to the emotions, and it is most important that the emotions should be kept firmly out of any discussion of this subject. 'You, as a Britisher' is the emotional clan call to arms, and I am too old to respond to it. I am an Englishman, and I love my country and do not wish to live anywhere else. But if I am asked to say that it is better than any other country I shall not say so, for I don't believe it. Indeed, like all other countries, I believe it has faults, and that the sexual suppression we are corresponding about is one of them, and that it could learn a lot, if it chose, from its neighbours. So I must at once reject the 'Britisher' appeal and also the 'patriotic' one. I don't believe in patriotism either, and if this war does not knock the national out of 'democracy' as well as out of socialism, and lead us towards some international order then I do not believe that any good can come of it.

His distaste for the England of Mrs Grundy and other spoilsports was apparent when he compared his own country with the rest of Europe, the freedom of which he had taken advantage of when younger.

Sex and fun. Sex and gaiety. The conjunction of these words, which fall naturally together in the minds of all other Europeans, would never for an instant be permitted by our governors and governesses here where the good old word 'unwholesome' is at once trotted out to join the word 'nudity' (cf. 'Janus' in last week's *Spectator*[1]), where everything is driven underground and there is always some-one on the alert to stamp on it the moment the dreadful beast raises its head.

A rather more public debate was instigated by Ackerley in November 1942, when he was appalled to read of a group of men in Abergavenny who were being tried for homosexual offences. This particularly grim case was brought about when a fifteen-year-old page-boy complained of the 'improper conduct' of a cinema manager in the course of fire-watching duties. Police inquiries uncovered 'an orgy of perversion' in the sleepy Border town, involving a number of youths who, one suspects, were no better than they ought to be, and a sorry parade of hairdressers, hotel chefs, clerks, window-dressers and out-of-work actors. The cinema manager took poison and attempted to hang himself, but survived to have 'attempted suicide' added to the other charges against him. Another man suffered a stroke after being arrested and, paralysed down one side, had to be dragged into the dock and supported there by officers. Much was made of the evidence that one of the accused had been known to put on drag and had written an unpublished novel under the name Miss Amanda Flame, that another had committed offences with Indian soldiers, whilst a third had been a conscientious objector and a member of the Peace Pledge Union ('a timid, undersized, pathetic person' was the prosecution's predict-able description). Sentences ranged from one to twelve years imprisonment.

---

[1] Wilson Harris, editor of the *Spectator*, has asked 'whether, particularly in wartime, it is a wholesome thing' to encourage young soldiers, deprived of female company, to go to nude revues. Ackerley was later to castigate Harry Daley for his use of the phrase 'clean and wholesome' in his memoirs to describe people he liked. 'Are such words allowed? I thought they belonged exclusively to the language of those persons – reformers, head-masters, scout-masters etc. – who wish to stamp out vice (which includes you and me) and generally disinfect the country.' He may also have been guiltily recalling Conrad's use of the word 'clean' in *The Prisoners of War* to describe the attractions of Grayle.

Ackerley was determined to make a public issue of this case and canvassed opinion amongst his friends. He hoped to get a letter published in *The Times* or *Sunday Times* and wrote to the latter's chief book reviewer, Desmond MacCarthy, for advice. He wanted other people to write letters or add their signatures to his own, and sent drafts to a number of people including Forster, who, like MacCarthy, offered suggestions for making the letter more effective. Forster felt the same about the proposed letter as he had about the one to Douglas Reed, which he thought quite as emotional as Reed's own letter ('though your emotions happen to be decent ones'). It was 'much too long and vigorous ... You have to choose between relieving your feelings and effecting (possibly) a little good. If you want to do good you must write differently.' In particular, he cautioned Ackerley against attacking the judge, who was obliged to administer the law. Eventually, a calm, reasonable draft was put together and sent to the *Spectator*, where it was published under the cautious heading 'A Subject for Thought'. The only signatory was Ackerley:

> Sir,
>
> Is it considered that educated thought and scientific progress are not yet sufficiently advanced to permit ventilation on a subject which, although it may be freely and objectively discussed in psychological, anthropological, biographical works, &c., seems still to be regarded in contemporary life as almost unmentionable anywhere except in the *News of the World*? I refer to homosexuality. During the course of legal proceedings against twenty men recently concluded at Abergavenny, one youth of nineteen committed suicide on the railway lines, and two others [*sic*] attempted unsuccessfully to do away with themselves by hanging and poison, to avoid the shame of exposure. The reports from which these facts are gathered were published on August 23rd and November 8th in the newspaper referred to above.
>
> It would be interesting to know whether public opinion today regards such suffering as merited, and the savage sentences, up to and including ten years' penal servitude, allowed by the law and imposed by the judge, as the most enlightened method of dealing with this matter.

One of the places where homosexuality was considered unmentionable, of course, was the pages of *The Listener* as overseen by Alan

Thomas. However, in the *Spectator* the word was permitted (even if it sprouted an unwarranted hyphen), and several letters concerning public attitudes to 'homo-sexuality' were published there. Opinion was divided as to whether the laws were 'one hundred years behind informed public opinion', as a Bournemouth correspondent thought, or whether, as a Shoreham-by-Sea correspondent feared, public opinion considered the punishment insufficiently severe. Dr Kenneth Walker, who was one of Ackerley's valued contributors at *The Listener* and a personal friend, wrote from Harley Street with the advanced view that psychologists could never 'cure' homosexuality, only help people come to terms with it, but feared, from his experiences of a committee under the last Labour Government, which had intended to introduce a bill to *increase* penalties, that 'there is little evidence that any reform of the existing laws is likely to be demanded'. The controversy widened with the rebuttal from a Wiltshire vicarage of Walker's 'sweeping statement' that homosexuality was incurable, but at this point Wilson Harris hastily closed the correspondence. Ackerley was not entirely satisfied:

> My own letter is dreadfully dry, but it would never have seen the light of day if it had not been. As it was, the one unrestrained remark, in which I said that the matter had been prosecuted 'with the zeal of a medieval witch-hunt', was removed.

The news that it was a Labour government which had attempted to impose further curbs upon individual freedom, and which had failed only because it fell from power, must have been disillusioning for Ackerley, who always voted for this party. It was further proof that England had returned to the dark ages. The only good that came of the war was the flood of servicemen and the increased sexual opportunities they afforded. Soldiers, sailors and airmen of all the Allied nations thronged the London streets, and homosexual activity thrived in the black-out. Ackerley had affairs with a number of Jamaicans, his 'sable fiddlesticks' as Forster dubbed them, including a steward on a cargo boat whom he continued to see for several years. In different circumstances, he also met several American servicemen, including the actor William Roerick, who had come to England with a forces show and was given an introduction to Forster through Christopher Isherwood. Roerick was to be a link with several young Americans with whom Ackerley and Forster became friends in the post-war years. Ackerley particularly admired Roerick's Army fatigues, with their many and capacious pockets into which manuscripts could be thrust. Roerick supplied Ackerley with several pairs of trousers and blue 'Homesteader' shirts, which he adopted, along with a beret, as his everyday wear.

Such spoils apart, Ackerley's attitude to the prevailing ethos of the war years was summed up in glum poems such as his 'Christmas Carol, 1940', an indignant and rather incoherent assault upon the hypocritical attitude of the State, which was now delighted to recruit to the forces those it customarily regarded as negligible underclasses: the poor, petty criminals and members of the Commonwealth. Colleer Abbott, to whom Ackerley sent the poem for comment, thought the verses about hanging looters were too strong, and was sent by return an item in the *Daily Telegraph* reporting that the Parliamentary Secretary to the Home Office had issued a circular pointing out 'that people convicted of indictment of offences against the Defence Regulations are liable to sentence of death or penal servitude'. Ackerley was disgusted that the death penalty, which he deplored in any case, might now be implemented for crimes against property as well as against the person. His anger and concern were not unconnected with the problems he was experiencing with his most recent lover, a feckless young Irishman called Paddy. William Plomer thought that the boy was a gold-digger; in fact the route Paddy took to other people's property was rather more direct. The affair followed the customary course of rows, disappearances, reconciliations and recriminations, with Paddy vanishing for days and refusing to answer Ackerley's impassioned letters. As in the case of Albert, Forster had advised Ackerley against making more of Paddy than there was, to no avail.

Hanging had also been much on Ackerley's mind ever since he had read *The Village Labourer, 1760–1832* by J.L. and Barbara Hammond. This book, originally published in 1911, contained an account of the death of an illiterate nineteen-year-old ploughboy from Micheldever in Hampshire called Henry Cook. Cook had been involved in the agricultural riots of 1830, had been convicted of striking a magistrate and had gone to the gallows at Winchester. The correspondent of *The Times* had commented: 'The fate of Henry Cook excites no commiseration. From everything I have heard of him, justice has seldom met with a more appropriate sacrifice. He shed some tears shortly after hearing his doom, but has since relapsed into a brutal insensibility to his fate.' This was an example of the sort of smug and barbarous complacency which Ackerley particularly loathed and which he saw returning with the war. In spite of the fact that Cook had been described by the sympathetic Hammonds as 'a heavy, stolid, unattractive boy', Cook became a symbol for Ackerley of all society's victims, in particular those working-class youths who were persecuted in the courts and callously sacrificed by the ruling classes in wars. In the final section of 'Micheldever', a long poem he wrote about Cook, Ackerley makes the parallel clear:

Does that forgotten army march again?

It marches, yes, but stones are turned to shot;
Now uniformed, more formidable, faster
Your army has not ceased to march, but not,
Not now, not yet again, against its masters.

For still the fight continues. That astounds
You, doesn't it? Illiterate country chaps,
No doubt you thought an extra half-a-crown
Was all the stake at issue. But the traps

Were set for more than yokels. Ruthless eyes
Looked further than your petty fields for power.
Big business had begun, and other skies
Drew blood up with the dew. The greed and fear,

The struggle still goes on. We give it names
You'd never comprehend and we defend
What you contested, but the fight's the same;
You fought at the beginning, we at the end.

And all are in it now; across the world
The dikes are down; in intricate dismay
Gainer and loser both in the flood are hurled:
Those tears you shed, we drown in them today.

The poem touched on the same themes as the dismal 'Christmas Carol', but with a great deal more skill and conviction. Ackerley decided to submit it to Stephen Spender at the recently founded

Horizon, where it was published in August 1940. As so often in Ackerley's experience, there were problems with the printers, who refused to countenance his forthright view of the Church's collusion with the landowners:

And all the while before your famished view
The sacred pheasant flashed his jewelled ruff,
The rich the richer and the grander grew,
And parson licked their arse. You'd had enough.

The final line, which would certainly have failed to get past Alan Thomas, had to be altered to the unsatisfactory 'And parson toadied after them. Enough!', which H. B. Mallalieu, a regular contributor of poetry to *The Listener*, criticized. Ackerley replied:

I don't consider myself a poet, and don't really know anything about these things. Ordinarily I tinker at my work endlessly, but am never convinced that it gets any better – or worse. Harold Monro[1] once said to me of a poem I showed him: 'It's all right, except that every word is wrong': I accepted that as a likely verdict on my poetry.

I didn't tinker as much with 'Micheldever' as I would have done if we'd been peaceful. The war depresses me too much.

The whole of the second section bored me, but I couldn't work at it any more. The last sections seemed to me to have some virtue, so I let Stephen have it. If it makes a small contribution to the general undermining of our plutocratic constitution, I ask for nothing more.

Elsewhere, Ackerley described 'Micheldever' as 'overlong, and clumsy and dull in parts . . . It is rather doubtfully digested communism.' It is indeed rather doubtful communism, since although he briefly flirted with the idea of joining the Communist Party in the 1950s (largely as a response to fears for world peace in the wake of the Korean War), it is unlikely that any organization which sacrificed the individual, for

---

[1] Poet, publisher and editor (1879–1932) who founded the Poetry Bookshop in Bloomsbury's Devonshire Street in 1913. He published Edward Marsh's series of *Georgian Poetry* and was a friend and adviser of several of the poets of the Great War, notably Wilfred Owen. Although married, he became entangled with a number of worthless youths. He and Ackerley met in the 1920s.

however good a cause, was likely to win his support. He remained a lifelong Labour voter, but was essentially, in party terms at least, apolitical.

On top of all his other problems, in May 1941 Ackerley lost his home. There was a severe air-raid during the evening, with incendiary bombs falling all over Maida Vale setting many properties alight. Just before midnight Ackerley went round the corner to Randolph Crescent to see how William Plomer was surviving. This act of charity was justly rewarded, for as he helped Plomer extinguish fires in the garden a bomb fell on Clifton Gardens. Plomer's casements were blown in by the blast, but at Ackerley's flat there was utter devastation. It was not a direct hit, for the bomb had landed on the opposite side of the street, destroying three houses, but it is doubtful whether Ackerley would have survived had he been at home, for all the ceilings came down and all the doors and windows were blown in. He lost all his crockery and much of his furniture, and the entire flat was covered in filth. A heavy bronze statue of a Greek boy, one of his favourite possessions, had toppled from its shelf and landed on the sofa where Ackerley usually sat. Thus he had escaped a fate which would have had a certain poetic justice: to be killed by Narcissus. Those less lucky than Ackerley were laid out on the pavement beneath sheets.

Several of Ackerley's working-class friends helped him to salvage his remaining possessions and he went to stay at Forster's flat in Chiswick whilst he looked for somewhere new to live. Forster was pleased with this arrangement since he freely admitted that he did not like to be alone in the flat during air raids. He was less pleased by his guest's inability to decide upon somewhere new to live. Ackerley was distracted by worry over Paddy. The day after the bomb, Plomer's flat was burgled and everyone assumed that Paddy was responsible, especially since he had once again disappeared from the scene. 'The magpie in Paddy is a nuisance,' Forster remarked, rather mildly in the circumstances. There was little that could be done about such incidents since, in their promiscuous pursuits, Ackerley and Plomer were living outside the law quite as much as petty criminals. The occasional theft was an occupational hazard, which they grew to accept, and Ackerley was more worried by Paddy's disappearance than by his crime. Forster patiently offered pragmatic advice:

You *know* he's a thief, a crime-boy and a dramatizer, and you will only tire yourself out and bewilder him if you inflict lengthy confessions and emotional appeals. *Do* write simply and shortly to him if at all. He'll come back to you again all right. When he does, lock up your valuables and be nice to him.

But to Plomer he complained: 'Paddy, coming on top of the blitz, seems to have got [Joe] down much more than did similar rubbish in the past. I wish he would either keep on in my flat or take one of his own.'

Eventually, in July, Ackerley did take a flat of his own, on the south bank of the Thames at Star and Garter Mansions on the Lower Richmond Road, a few hundred yards upstream of Putney Bridge. The ornate, French-style, red-brick block had been built in the late nineteenth century on the site of the old Star and Garter Hotel. One half of it was taken up by a pub, with four storeys of bedrooms above it. The other half contained seventeen flats, reached through a dingy entrance hall and, when the lift failed, up a flight of dark stairs. No. 17 was on the fourth floor, beyond the reach of the lift, and was an irregularly shaped flat, smaller than its neighbours since one third of its floor-space contained the block's water tanks and the lift's winching mechanism. The accommodation was limited, and consisted of a narrow passage which widened at one end to form a dining area, off which were a dark, poky kitchen and bathroom to the right and two further rooms, right and left, at the far end. One room Ackerley used as his bedroom, the other as his study and sitting-room.

The whole flat was very dingy, but its gloomy interior was more than compensated for by a large open-air terrace, reached up some steps and through french windows at the end of the hall. This terrace, which comprised most of the roof space of the whole mansion block, was ideally suited to summer boozing, Ackerley reported to friends, and commanded perfect views across the river to Fulham Palace, set amidst plane trees in the Bishop's Park. Ironically, its 'perfect' position was what made the rent so reasonable, £6 a month. German aircraft on their bombing raids used the river to navigate by, and a flat at the top of a large block at the river's edge was deemed rather too inviting a target by most prospective tenants. Ackerley spent the summer days out on the terrace, dressed in beret and shorts, restoring his salvaged furniture by painting it cream and green. A further attraction was the tow-path which ran along the embankment all the way to Hammer-smith and was a perfect place for strolling and for casual encounters. During his twenty-six-year tenancy Ackerley was to show little regard for clause (ix) of his lease: 'The Tenant hereby covenants with the Landlord not to permit the Flat to be used for any unlawful or improper purpose but on the contrary so far as is possible to contribute to the respectability of the building.'

Ackerley was very contented with his new home, but scarcely had he settled in than his mother was made homeless. In mid-September a land-mine exploded in Peldon Avenue, a cul-de-sac which ran off Sheen Road just by Netta's house. Bunny was away at the time, and Netta was sleeping with her maid, Robina, on mattresses on the ground floor. The house was cracked open and ceilings and windows fell in. Robina rushed into the streets to call for help, abandoning Netta, much to the latter's disgust. When Robina returned, she was scolded for being inconsiderate: she had not swept up the glass before departing and Netta might have cut her feet. In spite of the fact that Netta was seventy-seven and had been reported eighteen months before as being fit only for an institution, all she suffered was a ruptured blood-vessel in one eye. It was necessary to rehouse the two old ladies at once, even though this meant putting them in a flat next door to Nancy at Lichfield Court in Richmond. Their furniture was placed in a depository, which was shortly hit by an incendiary bomb.

Ackerley continued to receive letters from his nephew, who was longing for the war to end so that he could return to England. Nancy wrote to her son every week, but her letters, although entertaining and well-written, were not always very reassuring and Paul would write to his uncle asking for explanations:

I would like to tell you something I can't write to Mum about because she doesn't seem to have any sense left. I asked her if she would put my mind at rest on my going back to England at once after the war even if England lost it. Well she said that she wanted me back but that just because I have had to live with dad two years he has a right to keep me. Well I only came over here for a short time anyway. Before I came over here I asked her if I might have to stay over here a year and she nearly fainted. Now after being here *two years* she writes me that I should stay at school here and maybe come home for the summer. Well she writes as if the schools over here were better than the ones are in England. Well the ones in England are so much better that it seems silly to go to school at all over here. She says the country will be poor. I don't care how poor it is. I would rather be in a German England than a free and rich America. As soon as this war ends I am coming back if I have to run away and live by myself when I get back. I hope Mum was having a touch of madness when she wrote that letter. She certainly couldn't have been sane not my *own mother?!!!*

Ackerley was only too aware of Nancy's inability to deal with her son and was now having to negotiate with Paul's stepmother, since Paul Snr had enlisted when America joined the war. Geographical distance and the war confused communications and Ackerley and Nancy were perhaps less worried than they might have been because they believed that Paul Jnr got on well with his stepmother. This was not the case and it is unsurprising that the boy was so homesick. The American education system thought as little of Paul as he did of it and his school reports complained of 'an extreme lack of co-operation'. That this was a result of desperate unhappiness seems not to have occurred to his teachers or his stepmother.

A further disaster had occurred just before Ackerley had been bombed out of Clifton Gardens. His loyal guardsman friend, Frank Harris, had re-enlisted when war broke out and had gone to France where he apparently shot down a bomber with a bren-gun. He and Ackerley continued to correspond quite regularly. Frank survived the evacuation from Dunkirk, and was at Tunbridge Wells in October 1940, where Ackerley visited him. Six months after Dunkirk he was once more posted overseas to the Middle East as a driver. In April 1941, during the evacuation of troops from Greece, the transport ship he was on was bombed and set on fire in the Gulf of Nauplia. The troops were transferred on to two British destroyers, the *Wryneck* and the *Diamond*, but the following morning, 27 April, both ships were dive-bombed by the *Luftwaffe*, and sank. Of the 950 men on the two ships only fifty were saved. Frank was not among them.

In Star and Garter Mansions Ackerley began to write a long poem in memory of Frank. Entitled 'Destination D' (one of the official addresses of the British Expeditionary Force to the Middle East), it exists in several versions and is perhaps in both terms of quantity and quality his most substantial poem. Only two small extracts from it have been published: the first 'December (To F.H.)' in the *Spectator* in 1942,[1] the second posthumously in *Micheldever & Other Poems* as 'After the blitz, 1941'. The poem was cast in the form of a letter to Frank, and opens with an account of the bombing of Clifton Gardens ('That house you called your second home'), followed by a description of Star and Garter Mansions. In the second section Ackerley recalls a letter Frank had sent him describing his 'perilous long journey' to unknown countries. The next section charts Ackerley's growing anxiety in the knowledge that Frank had been posted as missing. Once again the new house is described ('this conducted tour/Is specially for you'), and Ackerley, recalling the delightful letters he had received, muses upon the two sides to Frank's character: the dumb, obedient soldier and the childlike, mischievous young man. The former belonged to the Army and the war, which had swallowed up his individuality, reducing him first to a number, then to a casualty and finally to a statistic; the latter belonged to Ackerley. He recalls Frank's generosity of spirit when rejected at Hyde Park Corner for other men, 'other faces, other fancies,/The constant search for new romances . . .' Ackerley watches seagulls on the river from his flat and recalls hearing how at sea these birds hover above battles and swoop down to peck out the eyes of the drowning. The next section is set in November, when the letters Ackerley had written to Frank find their way back to him. Ackerley still does not know exactly how Frank died and imagines him in his lorry. In Housmanic mood, he wonders who will miss or recollect this young life so casually stubbed out by the war, a young life that left nothing behind. Ackerley tells Frank that his widow and child visit Star and Garter Mansions and talk about him. He recalls his past failures with Frank, how, because of the inequity of their backgrounds and education there had been 'blunders' over money, but how in the end they had reached an understanding. Ackerley concludes by dedicating the finished poem to 'my friend Frank'.

Ackerley found the poem very difficult to write partly because he was motivated by fondness for Frank rather than by any profounder emotion and partly because whilst he wrote it he was still unsure of Frank's fate (he had been posted as missing and official notification of his death did not reach England until August 1942). The poem had

---

[1] Published in a slightly different version, probably a later draft, as 'Missing' in *Micheldever & Other Poems*.

gone quite well until William Plomer suggested, on some unspecified inside information he had gained during his work in the Naval Intelligence Division, that Frank might well be still alive. However, Ackerley worked away at it for a whole year until it was complete, whereupon he had a very striking and disturbing dream about Frank:

> He looked very ill, pale with yellow streaks in his face, and had an injury to his foot. He was dressed in a very nice new lounge suit of grey-blue worsted and when he pulled up his trouser leg to show me the place the cloth of the trouser had stuck to the wound and had to be pulled out of it. The wound itself was very curious, a deep neat round hole in his ankle bone, as though the centre of the bone had been cut out as one cuts a hole in an orange. It was about the size of an egg cup. It was a frighteningly nasty-looking wound, with a patch of gangrene at the bottom of it. The mood of the whole dream was anxiety, anxiety for his welfare, blood-poisoning, amputation. He seemed calm and unworried: I do not recollect that he smiled. He did look smart. The dream faded out in a muddle of doctors and medicine.

Ackerley was puzzled by the dream. It was clear that the new suit represented the poem he had just completed for Frank, but he was mystified by the location and the very vivid detail of the wound. He was wary of showing the poem to anyone since he saw it essentially as a private meditation rather than a public utterance; he described it as 'a poem of reclamation from the darkness'. He had tentatively offered a section of the poem to Roger Senhouse, who had written to him asking for permission to include 'The Portrait of a Mother' in an anthology of *Poems in Our Time, 1900–1942*, which Richard Church and M. M. Bozman were editing for the Everyman Library. Ackerley had long since disowned this poem as 'shameful': 'Excuse me, but it says that love is guilty,' he told Demetrios Capetenakis who had, for some reason, praised it: 'I am very sorry I ever published it.' Instead he offered Senhouse 'Ghosts' and six stanzas of 'Destination D': 'I doubt if you'll want it, or whether really I want you to want it,' he wrote. 'Since I haven't yet shown it to William [Plomer], or indeed anyone, and don't know if it's any good or putrid.' In the event, 'Ghosts' (in a slightly different version to the one Forster read) was selected for the anthology.

239

When official confirmation of Frank's death came through, Ackerley decided to offer another extract from 'Destination D' to Alan Thomas for the Christmas edition of *The Listener*. Both Forster and Henry Reed (who had become a friend and a regular contributor since the row over his sailor poem) had seen these lines and made suggestions, some of which Ackerley had incorporated. Thomas confirmed Ackerley's own view of the poem by rejecting the lines as 'too personal'. Whilst one might understand Ackerley's reservations, Thomas's are curious. How personal is personal? How impersonal were most of the poems published in the magazine? Perhaps he felt nervous about the elegy of a non-combatant for another man? However, the *Spectator* had no such qualms and published the poem in their Christmas 1942 issue. Ackerley copied out the whole of 'Destination D' and sent a copy in a ring-binder to William Plomer as a gift. However, by this time Ackerley had met another guardsman, a young man who was, in the eyes of many of Ackerley's friends, the agent of his doom.

13

A young man marred

FREDDIE Doyle was fairly typical of Ackerley's pick-ups, but his circumstances were rather more dangerous. He was in the Guards, but had deserted and was on the run in London, paying his way by prostitution and mixing in an outcasts' underworld of tarts and petty criminals. He saw Ackerley fairly frequently and what began as a commercial transaction soon blossomed into a more substantial relationship. Freddie was tall and fair and very vain, with naturally wavy hair which he insisted upon smarming into place, and puffing up into a quiff at the front. In spite of the milieu in which he moved, he was essentially a conventional and self-conscious young man, who would never go out in shirt-sleeves or be seen running in the street. Unfortunately he contracted gonorrhoea from a female prostitute. When he confessed to this infection, unbuttoning to display the gruesome symptoms, Ackerley regarded it as 'one of the highest compliments I had ever been paid'. It showed, of course, that Ackerley had become more to Freddie than just another twank. Had Freddie remained in the Army, such an infection would have been treated as a matter of course; finding a civilian doctor who would not ask awkward questions of his 'civilian' patient was rather trickier. Matters were not helped by Freddie's own reluctance to seek medical help. His understandable nervousness was compounded by constitutional fecklessness, and he failed to keep any of the appointments Ackerley made for him.

By now Ackerley had convinced himself that he had fallen deeply in love with Freddie, a state of affairs his friends both disbelieved and deplored. 'In the face of all the evidence,' Harry Daley recalled, 'Joe had decided [Freddie] was a magnificent man of great charm and sensibility.' It seems that Freddie was indeed an engaging character, who was weak rather than actively vicious, easily dominated and led astray. Even Forster had to admit that Freddie was a great deal nicer than he had feared. Despairing of ever getting Freddie to see a doctor, Ackerley eventually decided that the only course of action left to him was to shop him. He approached a detective (probably through Daley) and told him where Freddie was living. Freddie was promptly arrested, whereupon Ackerley attempted, through John Sparrow, who was working as Assistant Adjutant General in the War Office, to get him punished lightly. This was unsuccessful: Freddie was court-martialled and sent to 'the Glasshouse' at Aldershot, where he served a six-month sentence.

Ackerley was racked with remorse over his 'betrayal' of Freddie, but instead of keeping quiet about it, he confessed both to the soldier and the soldier's doting mother. Unsurprisingly both were furious and cut off all relations with Ackerley, who went into a deep depression, becoming a prey to guilt and fear. The fear arose from the fact that once deserters had served their sentence they were usually sent straight off to the front line under military escort. 'Having saved Freddie from venereal disease, was I now to be responsible for his death?' Ackerley asked. 'I lived at this time in constant torment.' The betrayal was to haunt Ackerley, and he recorded its anniversary in his pocket diaries for many years, transferring it at the beginning of each new year along with telephone numbers and other enduring information. This is an example of how Ackerley fuelled his remorse, and a further interesting psychological sidelight is provided by the fact that after Netta's death, Ackerley confused dates and convinced himself that he had betrayed Freddie on his mother's birthday, 6 June. This final twist of the knife was unjustified, however, for he had shopped Freddie two days later, on 8 June.

Recalling his own experiences as a prisoner of war, Ackerley felt Freddie's deprivations keenly. He continued to petition Sparrow, relating (and exaggerating) Freddie's grievances and asking for concessions. One, which Sparrow implemented, was to stop the 'monstrous' practice of depriving prisoners of books at night. Thanks to Ackerley's intervention, books no longer had to be returned to the library each evening and prisoners were allowed to finish them in peace.

Ackerley in India, 1924, with students from St John's College at Agra.

His Highness the Maharajah Vishwa Nath Singh Bahadur of Chhatarpur. A studio portrait (1912).

Ackerley's caricature (1924).

The Guest House Clerk,
Mahadeo Nayak ('Narayan').

Ackerley's child-servant,
'the insupportable' Habib Khan.

Ackerley's sketch of his
Chhatarpur tutor, Abdul Haq.

His Highness's 'valet',
Rāghunāndi ('Sharma').

Dandy at large: Ackerley on a continen-
tal jaunt in the 1920s.

The successful playwright: the author of
The Prisoners of War in the 1920s.

Goldsworthy Lowes Dickinson, who succumbed to Ackerley's charm in
1924. 'He has upset the structure I was living in,' Dickinson confessed.
'I have not been able to get him out of my mind.'

'The Ideal Friend', almost. Ackerley with Albert at the river's edge
in Hammersmith, late 1920s.

The long arm of the law:
Harry Daley and friend.

Harry Daley loading 'criminals' into a
Black Maria; one of a number of care-
fully posed photographs taken at the
Section House in Hammersmith, 1920s.

Jack Sprott: lecturer in social psychology,
Daley devotee and lifelong friend of
Ackerley.

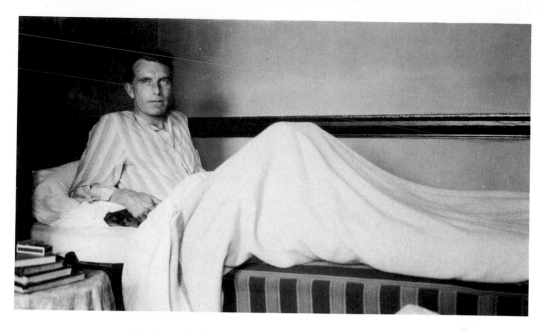

Ackerley in bed at 6 Hammersmith Terrace, late 1920s.

Ackerley in the rigging at Lowestoft,
while on holiday with Harry Daley.

Ackerley beside the sea.

The literary editor of *The Listener* working at home.

The literary editor of *The Listener* relaxing at the coast.

Nancy with William Plomer, 1930s.

Family portrait: Nancy with Paul and Netta, late 1930s, an avuncular Leo Charlton in attendance.

As soon as Freddie was released, Ackerley persuaded him to desert all over again, paying him £100 'in compensation for my interference in his life and for the hardships he had suffered'. Failing to learn by his experiences at Dover with Trooper Catkin, Ackerley also offered Freddie civilian clothes and put the spare room at Star and Garter Mansions at his disposal. Freddie's mother, seeing a way of protecting her son, forgave Ackerley his treachery and colluded with him. Inciting a soldier to desert was a serious criminal offence, as indeed was acquiring forged identity documents, which Ackerley immediately set about doing. Harry Daley was approached and agreed to help, using his underworld connections. Daley was put in an extremely difficult position: he had only recently made his peace with Ackerley after a 'final' quarrel (one of many during the course of their forty-year relationship) and a period of estrangement. Furthermore, he loathed Freddie, describing him as 'a horrid man, a great sloppy cissy with a lisp'. In the event Daley never managed to get the cards, which was no doubt just as well.

Forster was very alarmed that Daley had become involved. He was also disturbed by the possibility that police other than Daley might become embroiled in the muddle; apart from anything else the whole affair might have made things very awkward for Bob Buckingham. Forster may have recalled the affair with Paddy and seen history repeating itself. The dangers they had all been courting had recently been brought home to them very forcefully when William Plomer was arrested for soliciting near Paddington station. A sailor had objected to Plomer's advances and had summoned a military policeman. Fortunately, Plomer's employers at the Naval Intelligence Division had somehow sorted things out with the authorities and no charges were brought, but for Forster and others, the message was clear: discretion and common sense were called for. Plomer withdrew further into his shell and set about destroying a lot of papers; Forster suggested that Ackerley, who was running similar risks, should do the same. Amongst these papers, the ones causing Forster deepest concern were letters he himself had written to Ackerley, since they contained details of his affairs which incriminated others as well as himself.

Eventually Ackerley did remove his papers from the flat to the security of his office in Broadcasting House, no doubt in response to a salutary shock delivered by the impatient and concerned Forster. As upon many previous occasions, Ackerley had become exclusively preoccupied with his affair and consequently neglectful of his friends. Forster was fearful that this obsession signalled a definite and perhaps permanent change in his friend's character: 'Such a story of woe, weakness and muddle,' he complained to Plomer, 'and so ardently claimed by him as such! In some ways it must have been worse for me than for him, since he cannot realize how much he has altered.' The frank advice, which Forster saw it as a duty of friendship to give, had been rebuffed, indeed, hardly listened to, and he sensed that Ackerley was no longer confiding in him. Eventually he was stung to write: 'As for my other news, I don't think I shall be telling you any more of it unless it is arrestingly good or bad, and this letter is, in a limited sense, a farewell.' On top of all Ackerley's other troubles, this letter must have come as a terrible blow, but matters were patched up within a couple of days when Forster sent a letter apologizing for this loss of temper, generously pretending that it had been caused by the lack of response his own 'trivialities' were receiving.

Feeling unable, or unwilling, to take any direct action, and suspicious that Ackerley was still keeping things from him ('I saw from his muddled guilty manner that he wondered whether I knew about the £100,' he wrote to John Morris), Forster began working behind the scenes, doing his best to avert what must have seemed inevitable nemesis. Morris was well chosen as Forster's ambassador in these matters. The same age as Ackerley, he was an old Far East hand who had served with the Gurkhas , a body of men for whom he retained a passionate, indeed almost obsessive, admiration. Upon retiring from the Army he had joined the BBC and been appointed Head of the Far Eastern Service. He became a Corporation Man in a way Ackerley never would, and endured tickings-off from Forster when he toed the BBC line too slavishly. Very much the punctilious military gent, he was, in Francis King's suggestive phrase, 'a believer in discipline, both for himself and for others', and he occasionally lacked perception and humour, as when he described Harry Daley as 'a very sinister homosexual policeman'. 'He might have been so much more interesting to us had he chosen,' Forster complained of Morris in retrospect. 'He did not choose. He chose to be torpid and pedestrian, and the loss is ours.' He was commonly referred to as 'Pudding', a reflection no doubt upon his stolidity.

In spite of such reservations, Forster knew that Morris was reliable, and admired him for his later frankness about his homosexuality in his autobiographical writings. He no doubt felt that Morris was just the right man to bring Ackerley to his senses, or at least to heel. Morris had several meetings with Ackerley, all of which were reported back to Forster. 'You have been awfully good to him and done what mortal man could,' Forster told Morris, 'and I feel very grateful to you. He has been for so many years a sensitive faithful friend, and it is sad that you should, so to speak, only come in at his death.' Forster was genuinely grieved at what he often referred to as Ackerley's 'death'. As he wrote to Plomer:

> It is so disconcerting, at my age, to find that younger people are dropping out, are finding the road too strong or too dull. Joe has been such a support and a chum for the last 20 years that I assumed his affection would outlast me, and cannot get used to his indifference. Well, it is just another example of 'Nothing Lasts', the truth of which none of us will accept, though some of us pretend we have.

'I love and have loved you,' he wrote to Ackerley himself, 'but none of that means anything to you, I'm afraid.' 'It is shy-making to write such a thing to someone whose face is turned away,' he told Morris. Such protestations of enduring affection did not mean that Forster had given up in his attempts to secure the return of his letters. He told Ackerley that he was glad that the letters were now at the BBC, but added:

> If you'll let me, I could come along and cast away anything specially relating to myself and to those about whom I must have written to you. You can't now want it, and it is no good letting it lie about.

Ackerley was having none of this, and a week later Forster was obliged to write once more:

> As for the letters, I should be grateful if they could be posted in a packet down to me, and I will undertake not to look at them or destroy them, since that is your desire. I must seem selfish and timorous over this, but it is the only corner of a very large affair which I feel competent to touch. If I was in a position to trouble you more extensively, no doubt I should do so . . .

Ackerley was not taken in by this for a moment and the letters remained in his office. Perhaps as a consequence of this he received comparatively few letters from Forster over the next couple of years.

Forster was not alone in considering Ackerley's relationship with Freddie a disaster. Other friends felt that Ackerley's outlook became more pessimistic as a result of the affair. They recalled that the spring literally went out of his walk and that he no longer bounced along as he used to do. The blue eyes which he brought to bear upon people became distinctly melancholy, and the vaguely troubled expression with which he viewed the world now became one of pained puzzlement. He tended to keep Freddie away from his friends, but those who looked on became convinced that, unlike Albert, this new lover was very far from being a charming, straight creature.

Evidence of this was provided when Ackerley discovered that Freddie had been living with a woman called Eileen and that the couple had a baby. In spite of Eileen's claims, Freddie was not altogether convinced that the baby was his. However, when Eileen once again became pregnant, he was determined to do his duty and marry her. Several of Ackerley's working-class friends had got women pregnant in the past and he had always counselled them against marriage. Ackerley's attitude to such marriages was, once again, summed up by Kipling: 'You may carve it on his tombstone, you may cut it on his card,/That a young man married is a young man marred.' As so often in the past, Ackerley's advice went unheeded and the weak-willed Freddie found himself married to an extremely determined young woman. Ackerley found the family a flat near Olympia, which he considered within walking distance of Star and Garter Mansions, but Freddie appeared to live in terror of his wife, and made little effort to meet his friend. It is hardly surprising that Eileen did not much care for Ackerley, any more than he cared for her. However, she was a shrewd woman ('sly' was Ackerley's word for her) and her antipathy did not prevent her from accepting and spending the allowance which Ackerley settled upon the family.

In order to finance the new family, Ackerley sold off several of his valuable possessions, including the small painting by Rouault of a clown's head, which he had been given by the artist for *The Listener*'s 'The Artist Speaks' series.[1] He spent all his clothing coupons on them

[1] It is not altogether clear how Ackerley acquired this painting, which officially belonged to the BBC, since they had paid the ten guineas to secure it for reproduction purposes. Presumably it should have been returned to the artist, but perhaps Rouault had given it to Ackerley as a reward for all the trouble he had been to with the article.

and also decided to take on extra work. Herbert Read had told him that the actor Robert Donat, who had recently become manager of the Westminster Theatre, was looking for script-readers. For the next three years Ackerley conscientiously ploughed through innumerable plays and novels which might be made into plays, few of which he could recommend and most of which were distinctly low-brow. Many of his reports were written on BBC paper and, no doubt, in BBC time. Hackwork this may have been, but Ackerley brought to it all his customary wit, care and impartiality. His old Hammersmith neighbour A. P. Herbert, who had unwisely submitted a patriotic play entitled *No Quarrel*, was shown no mercy. Ackerley complained that the play's

> most convincing aspects are the lavish nautical terms that render much of the dialogue incomprehensible. The characters ... are incredibly stock, and speak frequently in the Lyceum melo-drama tradition of 1900. The play is structurally and dramatically incompetent ... Two 'humorous' *Punch* articles (1000-word speeches of remarkable ineptitude) are inserted arbitrarily in the text. The argument of the play (if there can be said to be one) does not, of course, bear the briefest scrutiny, although Mr Herbert, with intellectual dishonesty, rigs it all he can ... The Chapman Bell (whatever that may be) rings throughout.

After he had sent off the report he was concerned that some of his notes had gone astray and hastily wrote to Donat's secretary asking her to make sure that they were not returned to the author with the script, in which case Gwen Herbert would certainly have recognized Ackerley's handwriting.

Similar disdain was brought to bear upon the works of Patrick Hamilton ('piffle'), Clifford Bax ('Dreadful cheap stuff. Reject without hesitation.'), Lloyd C. Douglas ('stodgy'), and H. E. Bates ('madden-ingly written in the repetitious tradition of Mr Patrick Hamilton'). Donat had asked for 'only the UNVARNISHED TRUTH', a request Ackerley always found hard to resist. Indeed, Donat and his secretary were occasionally obliged to report back to authors and agents in more conciliatory tones than those employed by their reader. Thus Donat claimed to find John Drinkwater's *Garibaldi* (which he had not of course read himself) full of the sort of distinction he would expect from such an author, whereas Ackerley (who had read it) found it 'sketchy . . . misleading . . . thin . . . Not much of a play.' Nonetheless Ackerley gave praise where it was due, not only to Louis MacNeice's *Eureka*, but also to the work of less distinguished authors such as Ferencz Molnar, Paul Vincent Carroll and Margaret Kennedy. Indeed, in the case of Kennedy's *Sigh No More*, Ackerley felt that he had not done the play justice in his first report. He re-called and reread the play, then produced a new and much more favourable report on it.

The proceeds of this hard labour were squandered on Freddie and his burgeoning family, who showed little gratitude or co-operation in return. It seemed that they could get by on Ackerley's money and made no attempt to find work in order to support themselves. Even without his cards, Freddie could have found casual or part-time work with employers who asked no questions. In the autumn of 1944 Ackerley decided to reduce Freddie's 'allowance' in the hope that this might spur him to find work. Instead, Freddie joined forces with an acquaintance called Mac, who was a successful professional burglar. Harry Daley maintained that Mac was part of a 'really dangerous' gang, but Ackerley seems not to have realized this at first, largely because Freddie's accounts of their exploits suggested considerable amateurism. Ackerley noted down Freddie's stories, perhaps hoping to make use of them in the future. Freddie and Mac would break into pubs and in the excitement not know what to take away with them:

> We found £20 in the till in that place, so we was all right. We was satisfied with that. If you find money in the till you don't want to trouble about the drink. That's being greedy . . . That's the mistake a lot of fellows make. They're greedy. They want too much. And that's 'ow they get pinched. If you just satisfy yourself, you're all right.
>
> But we went mad sometimes with all the stuff lying about and not bein' able to take it all and not knowin'. You don't know what to take for the best – whisky, gin, champagne, brandy – and there was about £20 in coppers, we 'ad to leave it all behind. Well you can't carry all them coppers, can you, I ask you. We 'ad our pockets filled with 'em as it was. There was a big tin box too, full up with threepenny bits. 'Undreds there was. Easy. We 'ad to leave that, too. Funny the things people collect.

Ackerley was fascinated by this life of petty theft, for it appealed to his sentimental notions about society's outlaws, amongst whom he counted himself. He jotted down details of how to break in through the leaded-glass windows of a mock-Tudor pub, of how to tell whether people were asleep by the sound of their breathing, how to wait until a train rumbled past before breaking glass. 'It's not an easy life, y'know,' Freddie would complain, much to Ackerley's amusement. 'If we 'ad someone who knew the value of things it'd be different, but we don't know what champagne's worth, or cognac.' Or, indeed, jewellery:

They hoped that I, with my higher education, could inform them. Pearls they hit with a hammer; if they were genuine they were expected to withstand the blows. It also occurred to Freddie that I, with my higher education, would excite less suspicion than he in selling the stuff. I allowed myself to be cajoled into selling a diamond ring. He stood well away from the shop in Fulham while I went in. When I came out I smiled at him and nodded. He was careful not to join me until I had turned the corner.

'Ow much?'

'Ten pounds.'

'Is that all?' It had been a large diamond.

I said, 'That you'll never know, Freddie, since you haven't the nerve to go in and check on me. Perhaps I got fifty or a hundred pounds and have pocketed the rest.'

He grinned at me, slightly bewildered, searching my face.

'That's all right,' he said at last. 'I know you wouldn't twist me.'

In spite of his fascination with Freddie's new career, many of the stories he heard were far from reassuring. 'You'd be surprised how floors creak,' Freddie would say nonchalantly as he boasted about creeping about 'one of them big houses, belongs to Lords you know.' He was, after all, in bad enough trouble as it was, as a deserter. Increasingly worried, Ackerley determined to save Freddie from a life, or at any rate the penalties, of crime and so increased his allowance to £6 a week. Eileen had given up work owing to her pregnancy, and Ackerley agreed to pay this sum until two months after the baby was born, that is until the end of April 1945. Eileen insisted that she would be quite happy to resume work, but by mid-May had failed to make any attempt to find a job. Ackerley reduced his payments once more to less than £5, but neither of the Doyles showed any signs of attempting to make up the difference by working, apparently preferring to visit the pawnbroker. In June, on Shepherd's Bush Green, Freddie bumped into Mac who had returned to London from Ireland 'where he had been wintering with his parents after a successful London season of "screwing" pubs and private houses.' He and his wife had nowhere to stay and Freddie had offered to put them up.

Ackerley was worried that Freddie, his income now reduced, would turn once again to burglary, and hastened to Olympia for a 'family conference'. Unfortunately Mac was not at 'work' (he usually spent the days wandering the streets sizing up likely establishments to break into), and a stilted half hour or so of conversation ensued. Ackerley was convinced that the two men had been discussing 'business' when he arrived and that they were waiting for him to leave. When Mac left the room for a moment, Ackerley seized his chance:

> 'Freddie dear, you're not lining up with him again, are you?'
> 'No, Joe. I knew you was thinking that.'
> 'Promise?'
> 'Of course I promise. After all, 'e's a mate of mine and you 'ave to show a bit of 'ospitality, now don't you?'

Freddie agreed to visit Star and Garter Mansions the following week and Ackerley went home naïvely reassured.

Freddie did turn up, as promised, but two hours late and protesting that he could only stay a couple of hours since he had agreed to meet Eileen later in the evening. 'He was gentle, charming, friendly and obstinate as ever,' Ackerley wrote in his diary. 'I was cross and irritable. I spoilt his evening and my own.' Ashamed of his behaviour Ackerley went round the following evening to apologize, but he was instantly put out of humour by a fresh instance of the family's thoughtlessness. It had been arranged that the eldest child was to be sent over to Ireland to stay with Eileen's mother, thus easing Freddie's financial burden. However, in an unexpected access of paternal feeling Freddie had decided that he could not bear the child to be away for more than a fortnight. 'You miss 'em when they ain't 'ere,' he explained. 'This charming sentiment failed to charm me,' Ackerley noted. Furthermore Eileen announced that she had accepted a part-time job, the proceeds of which were to pay for her to have a holiday in Ireland.

Both these items of information seemed to me bloody cheek. It irritated me that Freddie, who hasn't a penny except what I give him, should decide on the child's return when he can't keep her himself and has no prospect of doing so, and although it would suit me in one way to have Eileen in Ireland, for then I could get Freddie more to myself, it enraged me to hear her calmly planning to save for her own pleasure out of a small wage the whole purpose of which was that it should go to the urgent relief of Freddie's situation and my own. If anyone deserved a holiday it was I who had kept them entirely for a year, taking on extra work to do so; but I was the last person to be considered.

Incensed by Eileen's attitude, Ackerley wrote a letter to Freddie in which he said he was overdrawn at the bank and in consequence would have to halve the allowance.

Inevitably, as soon as he had posted the letter he regretted it. He was not, in fact, overdrawn, and since Freddie would be coming to see him the following week, it would have been more civilized to deliver the bad news in person. He had lied in the letter and, however conciliatory its tone might have been, Freddie would no doubt recognize that it had been written in anger. Ackerley therefore decided that he must retrieve the letter before it reached his friend. This posed a problem since by law a letter, once posted, became the property of the General Post Office until it was delivered, when it became the property of the recipient. Legally, the moment Ackerley put the letter in the post-box, he relinquished all claim to it. Several plans suggested themselves, none of them very sensible. The only one that seemed at all feasible was to intercept the postman, somehow cause a diversion, and in the ensuing confusion, substitute another letter.

With no very clear idea of how to do this, Ackerley got up early, went round to Freddie's house and lay in wait for the postman. As the postman turned in at Freddie's gate, Ackerley pretended that he was thrusting a copy of the *News of the World* through the front door. 'Anything for Doyle?' he enquired innocently. As the postman handed him the letter, Ackerley dropped a book. While the postman fumbled to retrieve it, Ackerley effected a swap and hastily pushed the substitute letter through the door. The postman was very suspicious. Why would Mr Doyle be posting letters through his own front door? Ackerley insisted there had been a misunderstanding and that he was merely a friend of Mr Doyle and was delivering a newspaper. Although he spent the rest of the day worrying that his ruse would somehow be exposed, all was well. This characteristically farcical incident was later put to good use, when Ackerley adapted his diary to make a story which he sent to *Encounter* in the 1960s, giving it the title 'Robbing the Mail'. The editors turned it down on the grounds that it described how to do just that; although it seems likely that any potential criminal amongst the readership would have been able to devise some more foolproof method of cheating the GPO.

Although Ackerley's threat to reduce the Doyles' allowance seems not to have been carried out, relations between him and the family deteriorated over the next few weeks. Eileen was by now so jealous that she would not allow her husband to leave the house without telling her where he was going. Freddie became more and more unreliable and Ackerley wasted entire evenings waiting patiently in pubs for him to turn up. Freddie's excuses were lame, his apologies off-hand, but there was little that Ackerley could do. A state of cold war existed between Ackerley and Eileen, and they deployed whatever forces they could in the struggle for possession of Freddie. Ackerley attempted to impose financial sanctions, insisting that Freddie could only have his money if he came to get it personally, but Eileen was less and less prepared to put up with her husband's protector. One day Freddie called at Star and Garter Mansions and Ackerley took him to the neighbouring pub, the Duke's Head. As they were drinking in the public bar there was a tremendous commotion and in burst Eileen, screaming vengeance, bawling them out in front of everyone as 'a couple of sods', and threatening to call the police unless Freddie came straight home with her.

Fortunately within a week or so of this alarming incident, Freddie found himself a job with a builder at £5 a week. Ackerley agreed that if Freddie could get hold of new cards he would pay for them, no matter what they cost. In the event they cost £3 10s and the two men arranged to meet so that Ackerley could hand over the money. It was 15 August, the day the war ended.

> I met him and gave him £4 10s. He was very happy. So was I. We had won through. The war was over (it was the first victory day), he had got right through, and had what looked like a good permanent job.

We had won through. He said he would come and spend the next day 16 August with me; nice and early he said.

Needless to say Freddie did not turn up. Neither did he telephone. After two weeks of agonized waiting, much of it spent going over Freddie's past unreliability and brooding upon his unsatisfactory nature, Ackerley went to the coast for a few days' holiday, sending Freddie a brief, uncomplaining note to say where he was if Freddie was in trouble or needed help. He heard nothing. He sent further letters, which went unanswered. He took to travelling to the BBC via Olympia and lurking outside the flat, not daring to knock and risk confronting Eileen, but hoping to catch Freddie on his way to work. There was no sign of his friend. By this time he had not heard from Freddie for almost a month and was so worried that he steeled himself to visit the flat at the weekend.

By an uncharacteristic stroke of good luck, when Ackerley got there Freddie was in the process of storming out of the house after a row provoked by Eileen who insisted that he should hand over his entire pay-packet and had threatened to shop him to the military authorities unless he did so. She had also decided that since Freddie now had a proper job there was no need for him to see any more of his former benefactor. Freddie insisted that he had only received the last of Ackerley's letters; they deduced that Eileen had got to the post first on the other occasions and, recognizing Ackerley's distinctive hand, had opened and, having ascertained that they contained no money, destroyed the letters. Freddie explained that he had not turned up when he said he would spend the day with Ackerley because his mother had called unexpectedly. By now Ackerley knew better than to ask why Freddie could not have telephoned him to let him know of this change of plan, or to challenge Freddie over any other of his claims. 'I noticed,' Ackerley noted bleakly, 'not for the first time, that I had gone through the most appalling time of worry and disappointment, but that he had not troubled at all.' Instead he asked how the job was going and whether it brought in enough money. When Freddie said that they just about managed to scrape by, Ackerley offered to supplement his wage by £2 a week.

In spite of this bribe, which he accepted, Freddie continued to disappoint. Ackerley knew perfectly well that Freddie was constitutionally unreliable, lacking in will power and infirm of intent, but this appears to have increased rather than diminished his attractions. As a deserter, criminal, married man and member of the oppressed working classes, Freddie was just the sort of victim-figure Ackerley found irresistible. He was at the mercy of Militarism, the Law, Women and the Class-system. No amount of feebleness, fecklessness, indecisiveness or ingratitude could entirely tarnish the romantic lustre of the outcast. Furthermore, Freddie knew perfectly well how to play Ackerley, and play up to him. When challenged, Freddie would always insist that he wanted to see Ackerley, but was unable to because of Eileen. Her jealousy was such, he complained, that he couldn't even go out to the pub in the evening; she claimed he was only going to look at other women. Sometimes he wondered how much longer he could put up with her jealous rages. These protestations chimed very nicely with Ackerley's ingrained view of women. If Freddie's will had been sapped, then clearly some vampiric woman was to blame, and Eileen had left no one in any doubt that she was out for blood. Together the two men plotted ways to trick Eileen into loosening her grip upon her husband.

> We . . . discussed the idea of my writing a letter to him for him to open and show to Eileen – a letter saying that 'I did not want to make trouble between man and wife, saw that for some reason she was against me, felt I'd better withdraw altogether, but in that case could not help if they got in difficulties etc.' He was then to throw it over to her and say: 'There you are you see. Joe's clearing out and no wonder. And he 'ad us in his will too for £100, and another £100 for Patrick [the baby].'

Freddie would agree to all sorts of plans Ackerley devised to circumvent Eileen's jealousy, but when it came to the point nothing ever happened.

Apart from money, there was one further weapon in Ackerley's armoury, a secret weapon which he never used. Some years later he wrote in his diary:

> I recollected how I still had in one of my drawers the police document I had kept for years and funked ever using, which contained the secret of Eileen's past, known only to myself and the police, pure dynamite, which in my rage and anger I had once

thought of showing Freddie, when he himself was fed up with his wife to expose her and destroy his marriage.

This document was the record of Eileen's conviction for prostitution. How Ackerley came to have this is a mystery, but it may be safe to assume that Harry Daley had a hand in the matter, since he had been stationed at Vine Street at the beginning of the war, spending much of his time on West End vice cases. Daley would have done almost anything for Ackerley, might even have acquired confidential police documents for him. Why Ackerley failed to use this piece of paper is a matter of speculation. It may well have been that, like the nervous player with the trump card, he hesitated too long and so lost to his opponent. He may also have felt that the plan would backfire and that Freddie would be appalled that Ackerley should stoop to such tactics.

After another couple of weeks of silence, during which Ackerley once again travelled to work by Olympia, where he spent three or more hours each morning waiting in vain in the cold streets, hoping to see Freddie, Ackerley became very concerned. He could not understand how the family was managing to support itself if, as seemed likely, Freddie was not going to work. Eventually he spent an evening combing the pubs and in one of them found Freddie, drinking alone. He had been ill, he said.

> I asked him if he'd tried to see me and he said he'd tried that Monday, but as soon as he'd said he was coming she'd gone off the deep end, running out of the pub they were in and shouting Police! He volunteered the information that he'd put 10s on the dogs and won a fiver and that was what they'd been living on that week. He had money on him and stood me a drink.

Freddie agreed to meet Ackerley at the same pub the following day and spend the afternoon with him. To Ackerley's surprise Freddie was indeed waiting for him, but he had brought unwelcome news. He and Mac had been seen by detectives attempting to pawn a clock which, Freddie insisted, genuinely belonged to Mac. They had been followed, questioned and searched. The detectives had been suspicious that Freddie had a pound note in his pocket, but had released them.

> We had a few drinks at our local and a game of shove-halfpenny, and he broke into his pound. Then we went back and he had a bath

and we had a nice afternoon. While he had his bath, I looked in his wallet to be sure, and there was the 10s note. I did not therefore put anything in. How could I? Although I knew he had no money and no wages for the next week, if I'd stuffed in £6 or so I put myself at once in Eileen's power: she would say 'You've got plenty of money so no need to go over to Joe's.' That was what had happened after I gave him £4 10s in the Live and Let Live: I hadn't seen him for a month. In nearly 8 weeks I'd had his company twice only, and both times I'd had to go and get him myself, standing for hours, morning after morning, in the cold and rain, to find him. No more of that. From what he'd told me he'd had enough money all this time, and I'd had to fight to see him; my only chance clearly was when he was broke, like now; my chance of seeing him and for him to see me if he really wanted to had come. He only had to say to Eileen – as I'd told him: 'Well I've *got* to go and see Joe now, haven't I?' So I did nothing.

He reasoned that Freddie had enough money to see him through the weekend and that he would be bound to telephone on the Monday since that was when the rent was due.

Freddie did telephone on the Monday, but only to arrange a meeting on the Wednesday; he did not ask for money. This was puzzling, since by then the rent would have been overdue. Ackerley assumed that once again Freddie had been lucky with the dogs. On Tuesday morning the telephone rang. It was not Freddie, but Eileen. She explained that her husband had been out with Mac the previous night and had been arrested. She wondered whether Ackerley could settle the rent.

As Forster had feared, Bob Buckingham was indeed involved: as arresting officer. Bob had never met Freddie and it was only when he went to the Olympia flat and recognized Ackerley's gramophone there that he realized who it was he had taken into custody. He was very upset, as indeed was Ackerley, who of course blamed himself. Had he given Freddie some money at the weekend then there would have been no need for his friend to go out housebreaking. He was determined to do everything in his power to prevent Freddie from being sent to gaol. He thought that he should enter the witness box as a character witness at Freddie's trial, but fortunately was dissuaded from this absurd idea by Harry Daley:

I said by all means appear if you want your picture in the *Mirror* sobbing on the steps and the report that your screams as you ran

256

through the corridors could be heard all over the Old Bailey. That his beloved would certainly get an extra twelve months from any reasonable judge never entered his head.

Nor did it enter his head that such an appearance might have landed him in gaol himself, not only for perjury but also for homosexual offences. Freddie was sent down for nine months.

Visiting hours and letters were restricted and naturally Eileen had precedence. She failed to communicate any news to Ackerley, claiming when challenged that she had forgotten. Ackerley was finally driven to the extreme measure of contemplating her murder. It would be easy to dismiss the preposterous plot he hatched as mere fantasy, but it is important to emphasize that he was by now both desperate and deeply depressed. His relationship with Freddie, constantly frustrated by law, circumstances and Eileen, had become completely obsessive, and his behaviour compulsive and irrational. Jack Sprott, a lecturer in psychology, had warned Ackerley that his hatred of Eileen was bad for him; not as bad, however, as it might have been for Eileen. The problem, as Ackerley saw it, was a practical rather than a moral one: how to despatch the woman undetected. He had read about blood-poisoning and tetanus, and it occurred to him that he might rid himself of Eileen by inducing one or other of these potentially fatal infections. Lockjaw, he felt, would have a certain poetic justice. His plan was to infect some drawing-pins and then scatter them on the bedroom floor. Freddie was safely in prison and Ackerley had no sentimental notions about the children being accidentally afflicted: 'good riddance to the lot of them,' he wrote. He imagined Eileen blearily stumbling from her bed one morning and treading on one of the tacks. Grimacing with pain and puzzlement, she would examine her foot, remove the offending pin, but not before its bacteria-laden point had sown the fatal seeds of infection. More like the prank of a schoolboy than the machinations of a master criminal, this plot never got much beyond the planning stage and Ackerley later wondered how serious he had really been. He had, however, gone so far as to stud a piece of rotting liver with drawing-pins, keeping this gruesome object, wrapped in cloth, at the bottom of a drawer.

14

A dog's life

SOME time before he had been arrested, Freddie had arrived at Star and Garter Mansions with a young Alsatian bitch called Queenie. Freddie had bought the dog as an investment, since he hoped to breed from her, but he had also become extremely fond of her and was concerned about what would happen to her whilst he was in prison. Eileen, with her brood of children, could not cope with the dog on her own, and he wondered whether Ackerley could take Queenie on? Ackerley refused and so the dog was sent to Walthamstow where Freddie's much-married mother, Molly, lived with her latest husband, Ron. Much as he detested Eileen, Ackerley had always got on well with Molly, whose devotion to her son almost exceeded his own. United in their dislike of Eileen, they had long since forgotten their brief estrangement when Ackerley had shopped Freddie to the military authorities, and there is even some suggestion that Molly was sentimentally in love with her son's protector, thus arousing Ron's jealousy. Ackerley agreed to visit Molly and keep an eye on Queenie, and was disturbed to find that the young dog had been banished to a small back yard because she had proved destructive in the house.

Like her master, Queenie was beautiful but unreliable, and there is no doubt that her 'imprisonment' in the yard made the image of man and dog further coalesce in Ackerley's mind. He rapidly discovered that Freddie's family had little idea about how to keep a dog and little inclination to give her the exercise she needed. He volunteered to take her on walks and these excursions were the first steps in what turned out to be a rescue mission.

Few photographs seem to do Queenie justice, for even those people who came to loathe the dog agreed that she was a beauty. As with many potential lovers, her immediate appeal for Ackerley was an aesthetic one. Ackerley wrote countless descriptions of her, the most evocative in *My Dog Tulip*:

Her ears are tall and pointed, like the ears of Anubis. How she manages to hold them constantly erect, as though starched, I do not know, for with their fine covering of mouse-grey fur they are soft and flimsy; when she stands with her back to the sun it shines through the delicate tissue, so that they glow shell-pink as though incandescent. Her face also is long and pointed, basically stone-grey but the snout and lower jaw are jet black. Jet, too, are the rims of her amber eyes, as though heavily mascara'd, and the tiny mobile eyebrow tufts are set like accents above them. And in the midst of her forehead is a kind of Indian caste-mark, a black diamond suspended there, like the jewel on the brow of Pegasus in Mantegna's 'Parnassus', by a fine dark thread, no more than a pencilled line, which is drawn from it right over the poll midway between the tall ears. A shadow extends across her forehead from either side of this caste-mark, so that, in certain lights, the diamond looks like the body of a bird with its wings spread, a bird in flight.

These dark markings symmetrically divide up her face into zones of pale pastel colours, like a mosaic, or a stained-glass window; her skull, bisected by the thread, is two primrose pools, the centre of her face light grey, the bridge of her nose above the long, black lips fawn, her cheeks white, and upon each a *patte de mouche* has been tastefully set. A delicate white ruff, frilling out from the lobes of her ears, frames this strange, clownish face, with its heavily leaded features, and covers the whole of her throat and chest with a snowy shirt front.

For the rest, her official description is sable-grey: she is a grey dog wearing a sable tunic. Her grey is the grey of birch bark; her sable tunic is of the texture of satin and clasps her long body like a saddle-cloth. No tailor could have shaped it more elegantly; it is cut round the joints of her shoulders and thighs and in a straight line along the points of her ribs, lying open at the chest and stomach. Over her rump it fits like a cap, and then extends on in a thin strip over the top of her long tail down to the tip. Viewed from above, therefore, she is a black dog; but when she rolls over on her back she is a grey one. Two dark ribbons of fur, descending from her tunic over her shoulders, fasten it at her sternum, which seems to clip the ribbons together as with an ivory brooch.

Unsurprisingly, she was a nervous dog, for she had endured beatings and an unsettled upbringing in Freddie's house, where more often than not voices had been raised. Because she was an Alsatian, this nervousness was sometimes mistaken for aggression. Now the most popular breed in the country, Alsatians have always had a reputation for ferocity, partly because they have been used by the police and the Army. In fact, they are traditionally German shepherd dogs, originally bred to herd sheep rather than give chase to escaped criminals and prisoners. But in the wake of the Second World War, German dogs were suspect and insular prejudice was further fuelled by images of such creatures patrolling prisoner-of-war camps. Ackerley could hardly have chosen a breed more likely to arouse comment and involve him in arguments.

Apart from her beauty, not at this stage fully developed in the gambolling puppy, Queenie was attractive to Ackerley as being a link with Freddie. It was clearly impossible for Ackerley to have much to do with Eileen, but by performing this service for his imprisoned friend, and by keeping in with Freddie's devoted mother, Ackerley was able to keep the relationship alive. Whenever he could, Ackerley went to visit the prison, but since Eileen always had precedence, such visits were rare. Freddie was grateful to Ackerley for looking after his dog, but the family became suspicious of Ackerley's motives. Queenie was always delighted to see Ackerley, since he represented freedom, and Ackerley himself was becoming fond of her. He offered to look after her at weekends and was then accused of attempting to alienate her affections. Unable to understand the psychological complexities behind Ackerley's burgeoning feelings for the dog, the family suspected that he wanted to breed from her himself in order to make money. Freddie was incommunicado in Wormwood Scrubs, only allowed infrequent visits and letters, and many misunderstandings and arguments took place. Appalled by the conditions in which Queenie was living, Ackerley even offered to buy her, but Freddie refused, insisting that he was devoted to the dog, thought, indeed, the world of her.

When Freddie was eventually released (he gained three months' remission for good behaviour) Eileen expected him to spend time with her, and objected to his taking Queenie out when he got home from work. Before long Queenie was getting almost as little exercise in Olympia as she had in Walthamstow. Gradually a system was worked out whereby each afternoon Ackerley collected the dog on his way back from *The Listener*, returning her on his way to work the next day. She spent her weekends with Freddie and occasionally the two friends met at Star and Garter Mansions and took her out together. Eileen's jealousy was aroused once more, and now that Freddie was in full-time employment as a roofer, she saw little reason why the two men should continue to meet. The same old pattern of missed and cancelled appointments started all over again. Preoccupied with leading an honest family life, Freddie had less and less time to devote to the dog. Furthermore, he had failed to mate Queenie and there was some suggestion that she might be barren. Eventually, in the summer of 1946, he agreed to sell her to Ackerley.

When Ackerley came to write *We Think the World of You*, a novel which told the extraordinary story of how Queenie came into his life, he described it very accurately as 'a fairy story for adults'. Queenie was cast in the role of a beautiful princess, imprisoned by unsympathetic step-parents, until rescued one day by a shabby and tetchy prince. Ackerley had become, quite literally, enchanted by this beautiful creature and she held him, spellbound.

> I came late in life into the domestic pet world [Ackerley later told readers of the *New Statesman*], and I had no intention of entering it at all. I desired neither cat nor canary; and, as for dogs, my sympathies lay, if anywhere, with that liberal but ruffled school of thought (William Macaulay, Henry Orwell, Lord Forster, Rose Reed, George Plomer, E. M. Berners) which felt that a firm stand should be made against British sentimentality over dogs – dirty, noisy creatures – or disliked having the pavements fouled. But I chanced to do some kindness to Queenie when she was very young and in need of help, and from that moment she marked me as her own. I knew little about dogs and had no means of maintaining one; but to be wooed by the most beautiful dog in the world was difficult to resist, and, like Mignonne the panther in the Balzac story [*Une Passion dans le Désert*], she had her way in the end.

Being wooed suited Ackerley's psychology very well. Although he still
turned heads when he entered a room, he was now almost fifty and
what one friend described as 'slightly a faded beauty'. Ackerley
admitted as much: 'I saw ... that I was becoming what guardsmen
called an "old pouff", an "old twank", and that my chance of finding
the Ideal Friend was, like my hair, thinning and receding.' The
experience of Freddie, a culmination of a lifetime's frenetic devotion to
a lost cause, had reduced him to a state of abject misery. Freddie had
been a sort of Guardsman Everyman, the ultimate incarnation of everything Ackerley had found alluring and unsatisfactory about his lovers.
Queenie was at once part of and entirely different from Freddie, and,
by degrees, she usurped the position that her former owner had held
for so long in Ackerley's heart. For fifteen years she was to provide him
with the 'constant, single-hearted, incorruptible, uncritical devotion,
which it is the nature of dogs to offer', and which had been so
conspicuously lacking in Freddie or any of his predecessors. Ackerley's
absorption in Queenie excluded the harrowing and time-consuming
quest for a human partner and he would later claim that his interest in
sex fell away as his love for Queenie grew. A diary entry made in June
1950, whilst he was staying with Siegfried Sassoon, demonstrates how
Queenie changed his life.

A great red lorry farts and groans among the trees at the edge of
Siegfried's wood. Some workmen move about here putting chain
tackle round the trunk of a felled tree. I think to myself as I watch
Queenie roaming about after a rabbit in vain, 'The cunts! They have
frightened all the rabbits to earth; they are spoiling her sport!' Then
I think to myself, 'Dear me! A few years back when there was no
Queenie you would have put down your books and strolled (earlier
still you would have hurried) up to that lorry to inspect the
workmen; incurably romantic then, or so your intimates thought,
you could not have rested until you had satisfied yourself that that
small gathering of workmen, of country chaps, did not perhaps
include the One, the Charmer, the Long Sought-For & Never Found
Perfect Friend to Be, instantly recognizable, instantly responsive, the
Destined Mate.' I smile to myself sadly, recollecting that discarded
and almost forgotten past, those (were they not wasted?) twenty-
five years of emotional fidget, when I could scarcely ever conclude or
even start a journey, but must always be impulsively leaping off the

bus as it went, or leaving the train at some intermediate station, or getting on to a train that was going heavens knows where, to follow, to get a closer look at, to make myself known to, that sailor, that soldier, that young workman, whom I had seen pass in the street below, or glimpsed on the station platform, or seated in some other train. Twenty-five years, at least . . . Now I do not move, I do not care, nor trouble: 'The cunts! They are spoiling Queenie's sport!' Is that then the epitaph upon my sex life? Yes. What has happened? It is a question I must ask myself I suppose, though the answer scarcely matters. Old age? I am fifty-four. That is not the age of the body's death. Wisdom? Alas, no, I cannot claim that. Is it Queenie? I am not sure. I think so. I mean I know that it is Queenie at present. But if she dies, what then? Should I revert to my old ways? I tell myself that I should – if I financially could (no more dogs anyway) – that I would pack up this life and go to some Mediterranean country, where friendship is easy, and pick up a boy. But would I? Questions, questions, which only time can answer.

Not everyone shared Ackerley's enthusiasm for Queenie, and he was obliged to acknowledge that the majority of his friends were dismayed that he appeared to have ended up with a dog rather than a boy. In particular Forster, with his belief in the primacy of human relations, could hardly see this development as anything but an admission of defeat. Early in their friendship, Forster had written: 'I think love is beautiful and important – anyhow I have found it so in spite of all the pain – and it will sadden me if you fail in this particular way.' It now seemed that Ackerley *had* failed. Forster may also have recalled, as Ackerley clearly did, his observations about human and animal relationships in an article he wrote in 1934. Forster admitted that he partly subscribed to the psychological theory 'that people love animals because of sex-repression, and that our civilization, which was until lately full of sex-taboo, has consequently become a happy hunting-ground for parrots and pekingese and for the ageing hearts upon which they trample.' Whilst Ackerley was scarcely an example of sexual repression, the diagnosis stood. Unwilling to accept this turn of events, Forster (out of Ackerley's hearing) often referred to Queenie as 'that unnecessary bitch'. Ackerley stoically reflected that few people had approved of his choice in human partners either and merely asked:

'what could be sillier than denying or questioning other people's love affairs?'

Few people, least of all Ackerley himself, failed to recognize the central irony of the situation, which was that Queenie exemplified all the 'feminine' traits that Ackerley had so disliked in humans. She was ferociously jealous, barking at anyone who dared make any physical overture to Ackerley, even merely shaking his hand. She was demanding and interfering, constantly seeking attention and preventing him from getting on with things. She dominated and circumscribed his life quite as much as any female relation would have done. And he loved it.

Having effected her rescue, Ackerley was very conscientious over Queenie, lavishing hours of attention upon her care. He swiftly discovered that she did not like vets, an opinion Ackerley was to come to share. She had to be dragged to the surgery and heaved into the consulting-room, whereupon she cowered under the table, barked threateningly and resisted any attempts at examination. Having exhausted the patience of several vets, Ackerley telephoned a woman who bred Alsatians to ask what he should do. 'Shoot her,' was the unequivocal reply. More sensible advice came from Miss Woodyear (the 'Miss Canvey' of *My Dog Tulip*), a vet who was to join May Buckingham in Ackerley's rather exclusive pantheon of Excellent Women. Miss Woodyear provided a compelling diagnosis of the problem:

> She's in love with you, that's obvious. And so life's full of worries for her. She has to protect you to begin with; that's why she's upset when people approach you: I expect she's a bit jealous too. But in order to protect you she's naturally got to be free; that's why she doesn't like other people touching her; she's afraid, you see, that they may take hold of her and deprive her of her freedom to guard you . . . Dogs aren't difficult to understand. One has to put oneself in their position.

This was what Ackerley was to do, with very great thoroughness, throughout Queenie's life. Rosamond Lehmann went straight to the heart of the relationship between Ackerley and Queenie when she described *My Dog Tulip* as 'the only "dog book" I know to record a human–animal love in terms of *absolute equality* between the protagonists.' It was less a matter of sympathy on Ackerley's part than of empathy. He would reflect sadly that communication between dogs and humans was a very inadequate thing since dogs, unable to put their desires into words, were obliged to rely upon a sign-system which inattentive human beings all too often missed.

Ackerley was delighted to hear from Miss Woodyear that Queenie was a healthy bitch and he was determined that she should remain so. The only problem was that her digestion was poor: in-breeding had apparently deprived her of the important gastric juices with which dogs can digest bone. If by any chance she managed to eat a bone, she would pay for it later when she attempted to excrete the sharp little fragments undissolved by her inadequate enzymes. Yelping with pain, she would have to be bundled off to a vet for an enema, an ordeal for everyone concerned, with the dog squirming and yelping, Ackerley hovering anxiously and the vet attempting to keep his temper. Ackerley had learned that much could be told about a dog's health by examining its faeces, advice he took with some seriousness. People wandering along the Putney towpath grew accustomed to the bent figure of a distinguished middle-aged man prodding and peering at the steaming mounds, or more often the slurry-puddles, which obstructed their way. Ackerley no longer had any time for those fastidious beings who complained about dogs fouling pavements and parks, and once drafted a letter to a local newspaper in reply to an alderman who had complained about the nuisance caused by dogs in open spaces:

Sir – Should not Alderman Rowe (your issue of August 13) be more specific? To what 'commons' and 'parks' does he refer? Wimbledon Common? Putney Common? Richmond Park? Or has he the smaller variety in mind, and if so where does he draw the line? Is he really telling us that we are under any obligation, legal or moral, to prevent our dogs defecating on *any* common or park land where they are permitted to scamper about free? If he is telling us this, perhaps he will also tell us *how* to prevent it? Dogs do not hold up their paws and say 'May I?'; they simply squat and begin. What would he recommend us to do if our free-running dog squats on the grass in the middle of Putney Common, far from any road? Train it? Train it to go where? It is possible to train some dogs (not all, for dogs vary in intelligence as we do) to move a yard or so, off the pavement into the gutter, though they must hate it, so close to dangerous and stink-ing traffic. What is the Alderman's notion of a suitable lavatory

for a dog on Putney or Wimbledon Commons, or any other
Common, and will he also tell us how we are to inform our dogs of
its whereabouts? I wonder if he minds the birds, the squirrels, the
Richmond Park deer defecating? They do, you know. He and his
complainants should be awfully careful about sitting on the grass in
Kew Gardens anywhere near the lake where the large waterfowl
wander about.

This was in the days before scientists discovered that dogs' faeces can
contain the eggs of the parasite *Toxocara canis*, which, if swallowed,
can cause blindess in children, but it is unlikely that this argument
would have swayed Ackerley much. He disliked children, regarding
them as noisy and violent, and would no doubt have argued that it was
up to parents to keep their offspring under control, a rather easier task
than preventing a dog from defecating when and where it wanted.[1]
Those casual enough to allow their brats to crawl about unattended
would have to take the consequences. When defending the rights of
dogs, his arguments were always presented with ruthless logic, and
he could be quite as bloody-minded as he was in his dealings with *The
Listener*.

One way to regulate Queenie's bowels and to keep her well and fit
was to make sure that she ate properly. Recalling his mother's
Sealyhams, most of which had been grossly fat and subject to eczema,
Ackerley consulted numerous books on pet-care in order to work out a
balanced diet for her. He was astonished to find the advice he found
there 'vague and inconsistent' and it was not until someone suggested
that he should proceed by trial and error that he was satisfied. One
thing he soon decided that she must have was plenty of fresh meat.
In those days of post-war rationing, he would devote his entire
lunch-hour to queueing at the butcher's for horsemeat, which he

---

[1] So careful to avoid sentimentality in his attitude towards dogs, Ackerley deplored
it in the attitude of others towards children. Harry Daley recalled an incident in the
1920s when he and Ackerley were having tea in Kensington Gardens. A small,
beribboned child was running from table to table much to the delight of most of the
patrons, who patted her and gave her biscuits. 'Her parents, smug, smiling and proud,
watched the pretty scene. When the little girl at last ran to our table with pudgy arms
outstretched, Joe, with genuine distaste, cried out in a shrill voice: "Go away – you
horrid child!". The indignant parents gathered the child into their arms and Joe was
quite unaware of their hostility, and that of the other customers.'

buttoned into the capacious leg-pockets of the army fatigue trousers he favoured, or bundled into his rucksack amongst manuscripts and proofs. Several of *The Listener*'s contributors were alarmed to have work returned to them nastily foxed with dried bloodstains. Such trouble was worthwhile because Queenie appeared to like horsemeat. However, Ackerley's attempts to infiltrate roughage into her diet met with some resistance, since she was a pernickety feeder:

> Was it a year or two years that we spent at cross purposes, I concocting for her elaborate meals, and she contriving, with gentle patience and unerring skill, to extract her horse flesh, cooked or raw, from the midst of cabbage, and carrot, cooked or raw, cauliflower, sprouts, turnips, swedes, spring greens, runner beans, parsnips, onions, lettuce, wholemeal bread, rusks and Melba toast, leaving everything else behind? Of all these, to her, superfluous adjuncts, she occasionally managed, without visible repugnance, to swallow a little carrot or cabbage (the tender heart, not the outside leaves), but only if they were finished with butter (margarine would not do); spinach was such an abomination to her that she would not even eat the meat that had come into contact with it, and I had to throw it all away and start again . . .
>
> Fish was an even greater trial to us both . . .

Herrings, haddock and cod were all purchased at considerable expense, prepared with considerable pains and rejected without hesitation, as were tripe and whale-meat. Chicken and rabbit were almost unobtainable at this period, but Ackerley used his meat ration to buy lamb and beef for her, which she condescended to eat. None of the proprietary brands of dog biscuit appealed to her and in addition to the hours spent cooking delicious food which Queenie sniffed at with unvarying disdain, Ackerley now spent evenings baking his own biscuits for her.

Exercise was also important in order to keep Queenie in peak condition. Ackerley took her for long walks on Wimbledon and Putney Commons, where he could remove her lead and let her gambol through the bushes and bracken in pursuit of rabbits and squirrels. Such expeditions were fraught with hazards, the first of which was actually reaching these open spaces. Ackerley discovered that bus conductors tended to eye Queenie with suspicion, often refusing to carry her at all. When they did allow her on she would be forbidden to sit on the seats, even if there were plenty to spare and Ackerley placed his mackintosh under her. When asked why she should have to sit on the floor, Ackerley would usually be told: 'It's the rules.' Such intransigence infuriated him. 'Rules! Rules!' he would exclaim crossly. 'How the English love them!'

Other rules forbade Queenie to be let off her lead in certain parks and Ackerley was constantly arguing with park-keepers about such regulations. No one, it seemed, could ever provide a satisfactory answer when he challenged them to substantiate or explain these restrictions: it was simply The Rules. He affected to believe that the councils employed only psychologically disturbed or sexually repressed people to oversee their green spaces. It seemed that on the commons, rangers spent their entire time upbraiding dog-owners or attempting to maintain standards of 'decency', ensuring that no couples were copulating in the bushes and that everyone who used the ponds was properly clad in a bathing-costume. Ackerley believed that they would have been better employed cleaning up the broken glass which littered the commons, and which posed a threat to the delicate pads of Queenie's paws. She cut herself on a number of occasions and Ackerley was to devote much of his time during walks to picking up sharp fragments in order to dispose of them safely. He was aware that he sometimes must have seemed an absurd figure, and commented resignedly in his diary:

> Once upon a time I was a handsome young man, regarded as one of the most promising writers of the day, much sought after by everyone, involved in countless exciting love affairs – and now look at me, grey haired and going deaf, a dog lover and grovelling about after glass in a public park.

The fact that most of the glass came from bottles which boys had smashed for their entertainment did little to improve his regard for children. 'I have devised a number of exquisite tortures for little boys who break bottles,' he wrote, 'such as circumcising them with the jagged fragments, if they haven't been circumcised already, or even if they have . . .'

Gradually he began to regard park rules as part of a general infringement of liberty, imposed by the same sort of people who declared homosexual acts illegal:

This business of obedience is deeply ingrained in the English character; I find it one of their most repulsive traits. I obey no rules myself,
unless I think they are good ones, I bring my reason to bear; having
been born with homosexual tendencies, a pleasant life I should have
led if I had obeyed the laws of this country into which I had the
misfortune to arrive.

Ackerley believed that life should be led off the leash by humans and
animals alike, and he regarded the proud owners of obedient dogs with
the suspicious eye of a libertarian. All too often dogs he met on walks
appeared to have been cowed into submission by their power-hungry
owners. Queenie's obedience, such as it was, resulted from a mutually
respectful relationship, he argued, founded upon love rather than fear.
Far too many dogs appeared to be the victims of their owners' warped
psychology:

> Dogs – it is the general view – have to obey. Dogs, poor dogs, are the
> great makeshift and substitutes for human frustration, they provide
> a target for the working-off of all human emotion. The power-
> loving fellow who has never been able to rule his family or rise in the
> world, he can always buy a dog and stop him doing anything he
> wants just for the pleasure of feeling important. The frustrated in
> love, they can always have a dog and lavish upon it, whether it wants
> it or not, the human love they have been denied.

What he had in mind was 'the poor little dog, scented, pampered,
overfed and kissed to death' by domineering women, but it has to be
asked how far Ackerley belonged to the category of people who make
a dog substitute for humans in their emotional lives. 'Unable to love
each other,' he once wrote, 'the English turn naturally to dogs.' Whilst
freely admitting that Queenie had all the attributes he found missing in
his lovers, he would argue that, unlike the 'dog-lovers' he distrusted,
he was aware of this and to some extent rejoiced in it. ' "Never a dull
moment," I think to myself when I look back over my four years with
Queenie,' he wrote in 1949. 'What a rare thing to be able to say of any
relationship.' It was his consuming interest in the dog which put this
relationship on so sure and equal a footing. Ackerley was determined,
in so far as he was able, to discern and fulfil Queenie's needs. He
accused himself in the past of thoughtlessness in his relationships, of
thinking only of himself. All this was to change with Queenie. Some of

his friends saw this devotion to Queenie's every need as the culmination of a lifetime's self-abasement before his lovers, but unlike the
young men in the past, Queenie was responsive to Ackerley's devotion.
She both needed and adored his attention and remained ferociously
loyal in return.

It was inevitable that people would speculate about the exact nature
of Ackerley's relationship with Queenie. When Ackerley claimed that
all desire for sex fell away from him when he was with Queenie,
eyebrows were raised in scepticism and inquiry. It was the novelist
Olivia Manning who eventually put the question that had been in
the minds of several of Ackerley's friends. With characteristic forthrightness she asked whether he ever had sex with Queenie. 'Just a little
finger-work,' he is supposed to have replied, a phrase perhaps
deliberately open to interpretation.

A former victim of sexual frustration himself, Ackerley wondered
what effect similar deprivation would have upon a bitch. None of the
books he consulted was any help at all; they might contain a discreet
chapter on 'Breeding', but the concept of relieving sexual desire
without pregnancy was clearly alien to the so-called experts. What else
could one expect in a country where the reaction of human beings to
the sexual antics of animals (and indeed humans) was that it was 'not
nice'? Unless profit could be engendered, the standard response to the
sight of dogs copulating was a bucket of cold water. When the dogs
they met on walks frisked around Queenie sniffing at her bottom,
Ackerley would be very annoyed by any owners who attempted to
interfere. Apart from anything else, their reaction betrayed ignorance.
It was not that dogs were 'dirty' and liked the smell of excrement; they
were investigating the secretions of two anal glands with which dogs
mark their way in the world, just as they do by those frequent brief
sprinklings of urine, which Ackerley likened to the calling-cards left by
Victorian ladies. Ackerley believed that there were quite enough
killjoys meddling in human affairs without encouraging puritanism in
the world of animals. He composed a little song, which he sang to
Queenie as they walked along:

Piddle piddle seal and sign,
I'll smell your arse, you smell mine;
Human beings are prudes and bores,
You smell my arse, I'll smell yours.

The problem still remained as to how Queenie could be allowed to pursue a satisfactory sex-life. In spite of Freddie's suspicion that she was barren, Queenie came into heat regularly and her sexual desire became quite apparent. She would gaze at Ackerley and then turn round to present him with her swollen vulva. She shuddered with pleasure even when he stroked her back and tail. What was he to do to help her through these intense weeks? In *My Father and Myself* he tells us:

> In truth, her love and beauty when I kissed her, as I often did, sometimes stirred me physically; but although I had to cope with her own sexual life and the frustrations I imposed upon it for some years, the thought of attempting to console her myself, even with my finger, never seriously entered my head. What little I did for her in her burning heats – slightly more than I admitted in *My Dog Tulip* – worried me in my ignorance of animal psychology, in case, by gratifying her clear desires, which were all addressed to me, I might excite and upset her more than she was already excited and upset. The most I ever did for her was to press my hand against the hot swollen vulva she was always pushing at me at these times, taking her liquids upon my palm. This small easement was, of course, nearer the thing she wanted than to have her back, tail and nipples stroked.

Quite apart from pacifying Queenie, Ackerley was also assuaging his own guilt at not allowing her to have sexual experience with other dogs. He did not want to subject her to spaying, but neither would he be able to cope with a litter of puppies. Further insight into Ackerley's attitude to physical contact with Queenie is provided by a note he made on the back of a letter. It also provides a footnote to Ackerley's own sexual psychology:

> I am more and more convinced that with animals, as with humans (at any rate with men, I have no experience of women) the closer and the sooner you get to them sexually the better – and the sooner – you understand them. To get a man's balls into one's hand – generally speaking one has his whole psychology there at one's mercy; if it is something that he himself actually wants, physically or psychologically, and most men want or are open to homosexual practices at some moment in their lives, the hand upon the genitals lays them

completely open. They are in one's power and will tell one anything about anything, their most private thoughts. I believe that this is the same with animals too, even more so, that love, devotion and confidence is got by attending in a tender manual way to their genital organs.

Ackerley also developed a philosophy concerning Queenie's transformation from a cowed and nervous puppy to a mature and intelligent bitch:

> The only training I ever gave Queenie was to set her free . . . I did not want a performing dog, I did not want an obedient dog, I did not want a led dog, and I did not want to hurt my dog. I wanted a dog of character, not a slave. I wanted to see Queenie's full personality. Animals have individual characters, like ourselves; I wanted Queenie to develop hers, and character, I believe, can be developed only in an atmosphere of freedom . . . I was the first person ever to release Queenie in the streets, her then owners . . . were afraid she would run away. They had treated her stupidly and sometimes even brutally, but I don't believe she would have run away even from them. Dogs are wonderfully faithful, even to fools and brutes. These people would have gained from her what I gained when I set her free, her reciprocal confidence and respect, her gratitude.

Not everyone approved of the character Queenie developed. Harry Daley hated Queenie, and blamed Ackerley for turning her 'into a noisy, dangerous creature that rushed about barking and made conversation impossible, and was too hysterical to stand still for even one hundredth of a second for me to take the photograph Joe so much wanted.' She was extremely territorial, regarding Ackerley's room as her preserve, to be guarded against all comers who might distract his attention from her. Bill Roerick recalls:

> She acted quite wolf-like if one looked in – baring teeth, snarling, raising ruff. Actually, a wolf would probably have been more reasonable, unless protecting her young. But perhaps Joe was Queenie's young . . . His method of discipline when discipline was called for was to smile at Queenie and say in a tone of intense affection and delight, 'Queenie, I'll murder you.' Queenie would wriggle with pleasure and wag her tail, and do just what she wanted.

What she wanted to do included standing on the terrace and barking at the building opposite, regardless of whether or not the tenants were to be seen at the windows. There were complaints, which Ackerley met with courteous apologies, but the barking went on. Eventually the police were summoned and Ackerley was given a warning which he disregarded.

Those of Ackerley's friends who kindly invited Queenie to social occasions usually regretted it, for she rarely behaved well. At a party given by the Buckinghams in their Shepherd's Bush garden, she took up a position under a table and snapped at all those who attempted to help themselves to food. In spite of this May Buckingham was one of the few people who did not disapprove of Queenie and her influence upon Ackerley's life. When people complained that Ackerley made a fool of himself over the dog, May reproved them, insisting that 'love is never wasted'. She further strengthened her position in Ackerley's heart by not only inviting Queenie for Christmas, but even preparing a stocking for her. Such kindness was ill-rewarded, for during dinner, Queenie would nag endlessly, wandering in and out of the door demanding attention, or would slump in front of the fire keeping the heat off a disgruntled Forster. Her magnificent tail was a further hazard as it swept drinks glasses and ornaments from occasional tables. Ackerley often attempted to cover up for such accidents, pretending that it was he and not the dog who had clumsily knocked something to the ground.

When people complained that the dog was insufficiently disciplined, Ackerley would ask them to watch him when he took her for a walk. He would carry the lead clipped around his own neck (a suitable symbol of his enslavement, some thought), whilst Queenie paced obediently beside him as they processed along Putney High Street in perfect array. He insisted that her discipline had nothing to do with obedience but everything to do with love. She simply refused to leave his side.

The only time Queenie failed him in this respect was when Guy Fawkes' Night began to be celebrated once more after its wartime suspension. Queenie was terrified of noisy fireworks and one bang would send her pelting home, heedless of traffic and terrifying her master. He liked reversing the Biblical notion that 'Perfect love casteth out fear'; in the case of Queenie, 'Perfect fear casteth out love' and this explained her desertion. He wrote a long letter to *The Times*, which had often accused dogs of causing road accidents, to point out that 'bangers' were enough to make the most well-disciplined dog bolt into the road, and wondering whether their sale should be confined to the first week of November. To his intense displeasure 'some interfering official [on the newspaper], unable to let well alone' ignored his suggestion that the letter should be headed 'Bangers' and it was published under the title of 'Fireworks'. Ackerley liked decorative fireworks and had been very careful to confine his criticisms to those fireworks whose 'function is simply to make a large bang'. Unsurprisingly, other correspondents accused him of being a killjoy. He also made complaints to the local town clerk, who was sympathetic, and the Putney police, who were not. There was in fact a law which forbade the letting off of fireworks in the street, but the police were too busy to enforce this. Eventually, Queenie became 'so demoralized' during the firework season that Ackerley was obliged to take her off to the country each year, staying with sympathetic friends. It was not until she grew deaf that Queenie was able to endure 5 November with any equanimity.

In spite of such problems and the alienation of many of his friends, Ackerley was extremely happy with his new life. At first his charwoman refused to stay in the flat with Queenie unless Ackerley was there as well, informing an acquaintance: 'First it's niggers, now it's a wolf!' However, eventually she got used to Queenie's manner and grew quite fond of the dog. Each morning Ackerley got up early in order to take her for a long walk before setting off for the office. They would go to Wimbledon Common where Queenie could roam in complete freedom and Ackerley could watch men bathing naked (as they were permitted to do in the early hours) in Queen's Mere, a large secluded pool set in a valley amongst chestnut and beech trees. These expeditions were Queenie's chief delight:

> Knowing that she may not bark and shout with joy for fear of disturbing the other residents, but unable to restrain muted and contralto ejaculations of excitement and impatience as the too-slow lift descends, Queenie sallies forth in the morning, her tail high like a sail, her ears cocked, to greet each new day with the utmost eagerness and anticipation of pleasure.

Each afternoon he looked forward to coming home, to be greeted by Queenie, and to sit in his study and read or work, her beautiful eyes constantly upon him.

Before long this domestic idyll was destroyed by the irruption of human concerns in the shape of Nancy. The flats at Lichfield Court were proving very expensive and when the rates went up after the war it was decided that the three women could no longer afford to live there. Netta and Bunny were packed off to a house in Carshalton on the southern outskirts of London, and it was arranged that Nancy would go to live in Hampshire with a woman friend who had a cottage there. Unfortunately, the cottage was not yet ready to receive Nancy and the only place for her to live in the meantime was Star and Garter Mansions. 'It was far from a happy experience for either of us,' Ackerley noted mildly. The only way for two people to live in the flat was to convert the bedroom and the study into two bed-sittingrooms. Ackerley and Queenie relinquished their bedroom for Nancy and, since the divan in the study was single, were obliged to sleep apart: Ackerley in the bed and Queenie, who disdained the thick black rug in front of the gas fire and the blanket placed in a corner by the window for her, in an armchair. Any attempt by Nancy to enter this preserve was greeted by warning barks from Queenie, a challenge which delighted Ackerley. He admitted:

> If Queenie got to like Nancy as much as me, if she went to sleep in Nancy's room instead of mine, or failed to growl at her when she came into mine, I should like Queenie less. I could not share a lover, human or canine, who actually lived with me. The more Queenie liked Nancy the less, I think, she would mean to me, her single-hearted devotion to me is the whole point, and if she began to love and devote herself to Nancy too, equally with or more so than me, she would leave off being 'my' dog, and become 'everyone's' dog.

Nancy was a great deal happier with her new circumstances than her brother, since she had been angling to come and live with him for some time, protesting that it was mere selfishness which prevented him from sharing his home with her. Ackerley had to make it very clear to her that the arrangement was a temporary one, but when the original fortnight was up Nancy showed no signs of departing. Neither sibling made any concession to the habits and character of the other. Nancy could not understand that her brother was set in his bachelor ways, which he had no intention of changing to suit her, for fear of inadvertently encouraging her to prolong her stay.

There is no doubt that Nancy was desperately lonely, separated now from her mother and aunt, skirmishes with whom had provided some diversion in her empty life. With little else to occupy her mind, she became obsessed with her alimony and her bowels, both of which were proving irregular. Now that Paul was with his father in America, Paul Snr was less inclined to send money to his former wife. Ackerley was ceaselessly petitioned to write to Paul Snr or to solicitors in order to extract further funds. Anxiety over this and other matters had played havoc with Nancy's alimentary canal and in an attempt to help her digestion, she had become a devotee of 'food-reform', and was now semi-vegetarian. These two preoccupations appeared to furnish her with hours of conversation, which Ackerley combated by bringing books to the dinner-table and pointedly reading as he ate. Eventually Ackerley was more or less obliged to send her on her way.

Then, in the autumn of 1946, news came that Paul Jnr, who had by now adapted to life in America, was coming to London on a visit. He was staying in London and Nancy seemed disinclined to have him at her Hampshire cottage, so once again Ackerley foolishly invited her to spend a few weeks at Star and Garter Mansions. This time things were worse than ever. The long-anticipated reunion between mother and son was anticlimactic and awkward, since when they had last met Paul had been a boy of eleven and he was now an adult of eighteen. There was embarrassment and disillusion on both sides. Although she had previously discouraged him, Nancy now entertained the vague hope that Paul would be coming 'home' forever, rather than stopping over. She was incapable of hiding her disappointment, criticizing him and his father and claiming that he no longer loved her. Paul had the distinct impression that his uncle was also entertaining a vague hope: perhaps Paul could be persuaded to take Nancy back to America with him? The young man was unemployed and in no position to support her; furthermore, it seemed unlikely that Nancy, at forty-eight, would be able to adjust to life in New York. When Paul firmly stated his intention of returning to America, Nancy took to her bed. Ackerley recognized the symptoms at once:

> It was one of those undiagnosable temperature illnesses – taken seriously by medicos, true, O yes, genuine enough – which hysterics are always able to induce in themselves when they can't get their own way. If the boy had suddenly returned, cast himself at Nancy's

feet and said 'I repent. I will live with you forever', her temperature would have vanished in 24 hours.

Paul, however, departed and Nancy was carted off to hospital with pleurisy:

> She was there, rather expensively, for nearly two months – complaining as usual, and trying to food-reform the hospital ('a difficult patient' said her doctor) . . .

Meanwhile, Netta's health, which had been in decline for some years now, collapsed entirely. She had continued to drink heavily and had become senile, spending her time placing crumbs around the rim of the bath in her house at Carshalton in order to feed a house-fly she had befriended. On 2 December 1946, at the age of eighty-two, she died. Now it was Bunny who was suddenly homeless. She was seventy-eight and entirely without funds; as a temporary measure and as a reward for looking after Netta for so long, Ackerley offered her the room Nancy had occupied.

Although her nephew often grumbled about her, Bunny was a colourful addition to the Star and Garter household. Small in stature, she nonetheless seemed larger than life, 'a figure entirely out of fiction'. Although long-since retired from the stage, Bunny remained highly theatrical in appearance and manner, 'very dyed-looking' and always dressed up to the nines. She reminded one visitor of a character out of 'a somewhat crude representation of the Edwardian age, the Spirit of Cockney in a rather straightforward play'. Sipping her pink gins, slightly red in the face, she gave the impression that she had 'seen life' and that nothing could ever shock or surprise her. The most unsuitable anecdotes about the sexual lives of her nephew's friends were greeted by her 'saloon-bar laugh'. Although Ackerley became bored with Bunny's long stories about her theatrical past and the exploits of her second husband, 'Doc' Fowler, to whose memory she was devoted, she often astonished and delighted him with her unexpected flashes of erudition and her stout common sense. For her part, Bunny was devoted to her nephew, and was popular amongst his friends. Unlike Nancy, she was cheerful and helpful and did her best to fit in with Ackerley's life. When Ackerley wanted her room for friends who came to stay, she would pack a bag and depart for Thornton Heath on the southern edge of London, where a friend called Ann, who had once been one of Netta's maids, had a flat. It was hoped that eventually Bunny would go to live in the Thornton Heath flat, but unfortunately Ann broke her leg and had to spend a year in hospital. Consequently Bunny became a permanent fixture at Star and Garter Mansions.

Nancy, meanwhile, had left hospital for a convalescent home in Brighton, where she complained so much that she was eventually removed to a food-reform hotel. From there she moved along the south coast to lodgings in Hove, where she underwent a course of herbs and fresh air with a naturopath, and then went to lodge with 'a fellow-thinker on the Littlehampton Road'. Although Bunny had been installed at Star and Garter Mansions as a matter of necessity, for at her age she could hardly be expected to live alone, Nancy saw it as favouritism. She would not rest until she too could live with her brother.

It was not long before Nancy fell out with the friend with whom she was living, but she seemed to have become attached to the south coast and, to everyone's surprise, announced one day that she had taken a winter lease on a bungalow in Beehive Lane, Ferring. She later claimed that she had intended to set herself up as a seaside landlady in 'Wendy', as the bungalow was unfortunately called. Even Ackerley conceded that Nancy was an accomplished vegetarian cook, but it seems rather unlikely that she could have managed the financial or practical aspects of such a venture. Almost as soon as she rented Wendy she regretted it. It was all very well for Ackerley, she complained, who had a nice flat, a job, a dog and Aunt Bunny for company. She had nothing. This was one of those unassailable truths to which there can be no glibly reassuring answer. Ackerley recognized, deplored and feared the desolation he was forced to confront whenever he and Nancy met. Alarmed by her depression, he arranged for Bunny and Queenie to stay at Wendy until the lease expired, and visited them every weekend. Predictably, this arrangement was a disaster. Bunny was not used to living in the country and missed the social life she still pursued in London. The pubs and shops were too far for her to totter to in the high heels she insisted upon wearing for any sort of outing, and she soon got bored with Nancy's dietary regime. She was obliged to spend most of her time grating nuts and raw vegetables in the kitchen whilst Nancy did all the shopping and took Queenie for her walks.

Now that she had Bunny in her power, Nancy exacted her revenge, bullying the poor old woman, reading her letters and not allowing her to drink, except at weekends, when Ackerley arrived loaded up with gin and wine. Drink always had a disastrous effect upon Nancy, and most of the weekends disintegrated into terrible rows with Nancy slamming in and out of rooms, accusing her brother and aunt of plotting against her and repeatedly threatening to kill herself. 'No wonder Mother died if you were looking after her,' she raged at Bunny. 'We only have your word for it that you looked after the Doc so well before he died.' On one particularly dreadful occasion she tore off all her clothes and ran out naked into the garden in the hope, she said, of catching pneumonia. 'It was the most neurotic six months I've ever spent,' Ackerley recalled.

The only respite he had during this period was when he went to Italy to spend ten days with his old BBC colleague, Lionel Fielden, who now lived in a villa outside Florence. Although the two men had remained friends since the early days at Savoy Hill, Fielden had spent much time abroad, first in India and then in Europe, and they had seen little of each other since the early 1930s.[1]

Because Ackerley had written a highly successful travel book and spent much of his youth holidaying in Europe, it was often assumed that he was by nature a traveller. Forster, who was always urging him to take a proper holiday on the Continent, and supplying him with funds to do so, was frequently irritated by the prevarications which attended any proposed trip. In fact Ackerley disliked travel intensely, or, rather, he disliked the means by which the traveller was conveyed from his native island. His love of the sea was largely confined to the men whose life was spent upon it, for he was himself a very bad sailor, obliged to take all sorts of pills before venturing upon the water. Memories of the transport ships awash with vomit during the Great War were all too easily revived when he took cross-Channel ferries. A further disincentive was Queenie, whom he disliked leaving behind, fearful that some accident would befall her in his absence or that she would pine away. He was extremely conscious of the short life of a dog, so that what might be a mere fortnight in human terms was the equivalent of some three or four months out of a dog's life. He often wondered whether Queenie had any sense of time, whether she was

[1] Ackerley is notable by his absence in Fielden's otherwise frank and full autobiography, *The Natural Bent* (1960).

able to differentiate between an absence of three days and one of three weeks. This problem intrigued him, but even if Queenie was unable to tell the difference, he was still aware that weeks away from her were weeks irrecoverably lost.

After the usual postponements and panics, however, Ackerley summoned up courage and at the end of October 1947 booked himself on to an aeroplane. If boats were bad, they were as nothing compared to planes, as he wrote to William Plomer:

> Flying seems to me the most alarming experience, and as for shortness – I thought the journey would never end. A know-all sitting beside me accurately foresaw and foretold all the dangers as they approached. 'I hope I am not boring you,' he kept saying, for, occupied in swallowing Veganin tablets and sips of brandy I made scarcely any response. If the window through which he was peering had been open, I would cheerfully have pushed him out.

This alarming experience set the tone of the whole holiday, which got off to a bad start even before he reached the airport.

> In a moment of panic over Queenie's safety I had cancelled the whole trip, which was all neatly fixed up for going on the 21st [October] and returning on the 31st. Then I repented, letting Lionel down and all that, and refixed it untidily for the 23rd, plunging thereby all his arrangements in confusion. A bad start, from which we never wholly recovered, though it was luckily typical of his own conduct in life, and therefore, though irritating, understood.

The holiday was further dampened by Ackerley's lack of money, the poor weather and Fielden's car. This last was a Rolls-Royce and Fielden was very concerned that its tyres, already thin, should not be 'worn out'. 'It became', Ackerley told Plomer, 'an object of dreadful solicitude, like a relation with an aneurism.' Promised trips to Siena and Pisa failed to materialize and Ackerley was left to make his own way into Florence, either on foot or by train, where he wandered penniless around the Pitti. Fielden seemed disinclined to do anything much and lost patience when Ackerley failed to catch what he was saying. He suggested that his guest might be growing deaf and Ackerley thought that this was a distinct possibility.

On the other hand, it might be the last result of that defensive mechanism I have acquired for shutting out family noises; from having wanted not to hear so much, it may have become difficult for me to listen at all.

His altered plans meant that he failed to get a return air passage and although this was something of a relief, he was obliged to borrow money from his host. Shortly afterwards he came upon Fielden's diary, which had been left lying around and read: 'Gave Joe ten thousand lire today for his ticket back, miserable me.' 'One saw that one was not by any means as a guest a one hundred per cent success,' Ackerley told Plomer. 'I have brought back a heavy cough and cold, but I suppose it was all worth it.'

Back in England, Ackerley's main preoccupation, apart from his troublesome family, was to get Queenie mated. He decided that if he allowed the dog to experience motherhood once, he would be contributing significantly to her well-being. The problem of where she could whelp and what he could do with the puppies would have to be dealt with when the time came. He had never believed that she was barren; she was merely difficult, and this was no doubt attributable to her nervous nature. The saga of attempting to mate Queenie was later recounted with considerable relish and not a little caricature in *My Dog Tulip*. It was hard to distinguish which were the more inadequate: Queenie's 'suitors' or their owners. Nonetheless, Ackerley found plenty of copy in the dog world and kept voluminous notes of his canine and human encounters there. He was also working upon a 'novelette' in which he would give an account of the means by which he became involved with Queenie, and this took up nearly all the time he could spare from *The Listener* and walks on Wimbledon and Putney Commons. Meanwhile Queenie's heats came and went without success. It seems that, like her master, she preferred the local strays to the impressively pedigreed creatures he arranged for her to meet. In the spring of 1948, however, she came on heat whilst staying at Wendy, and had her democratic way with one of the innumerable mongrels which had laid siege to the bungalow. Ackerley had endured so many wasted journeys with her in search of a Kennel Club registered dog that he stood back and watched this *mésalliance* with amused resignation. Unfortunately, Queenie had run the same risks as her master in his own dealings with rough trade and picked up a venereal infection, but this condition was cleared up without causing any complications to the pregnancy.

Queenie's offspring were anticipated with a great deal more plea-sure than Freddie's ever had been and, in spite of some half-hearted resolution that the expectant mother would have her accouchement at a kennels, she eventually gave birth to eight puppies in a box in the bedroom of Star and Garter Mansions. Entranced, Ackerley watched this event and later described it in one of the finest passages of *My Dog Tulip*. He had been advised to drown some of the litter (he intended to single out the bitches for destruction in deference, he claimed, to 'Hindoo social philosophy' and the notion that dog pups were easier to sell than their sisters), but his courage failed him and he was to spend many hours dealing with these new additions to the flat's already cramped quarters. He found homes for them all, but later regretted that he had not vetted the buyers more carefully.

The main thing was that Queenie had been sexually and maternally fulfilled. Indeed, there were plans for her to be mated again, this time with a pedigree Alsatian and involving an arrangement whereby the whelping would take place at a kennel and the puppies would be disposed of by the sire's owner, but nothing ever came of this. If Queenie was up to it, Ackerley was not. In any case, such plans were swiftly overtaken by an event even more traumatic than Queenie's confinement.

The lease on Wendy ran out before alternative accommodation could be found and Nancy took to her bed once more. Ackerley found temporary rooms for her in Wimbledon, whereupon she informed him that she had found somewhere on the coast. Bunny returned to Star and Garter Mansions and begged her nephew to 'put her in a poor house rather than in Nancy's power again'. In spite of entreaties to come to London and get rooms near Putney, Nancy refused, saying she could not bear to see Bunny installed at the flat. Eventually she found a room in Worthing.

For a while it seemed as if Nancy had settled into her new home quite happily. After the storms which had battered Wendy, tranquil-lity seemed to have descended. Before long, however, news came that she had had a row with her landlady over blankets, which Nancy had claimed were damp. The landlady took umbrage, but supplied another blanket, whereupon Nancy complained to the woman's husband. Upon hearing this, the landlady gave Nancy notice to quit. Terrified by this (to her) unexpected development, Nancy apologized and was allowed to stay.

In October Ackerley went to visit her and there were the usual arguments and complaints – in particular, that he did not put himself out sufficiently to secure her alimony. In fact, he had spent a great deal of time writing to lawyers, eventually dispensing with their services in order to save money and coming to a personal agreement with Paul that he should pay his former wife £20 a month. By now the marriage had been over for some twenty years and her son was independent. 'What a law to make a man support a discarded wife forever!' Ackerley exclaimed. 'A specified number of years would be the juster thing, time for a woman to find another man or get some occupation.' Nancy had failed to do either of these things. Lovers had come and gone and the idea of getting a job had been raised and dropped innumerable times. The truth of the matter was that Nancy was virtually unemployable. The only job she had ever had was in the 1920s when she had gone to Paris and worked as a model.

> For the last twenty years she has been talking about getting a job [Ackerley wrote in his diary] – with no intention of getting one! If people want jobs they go off and get them without talking endlessly about it to relatives. The moment Nancy gets anywhere near a job she has a nervous breakdown. There is not a job that has ever been invented that would suit her – or the person who attempted to employ her. Nor any job that I know of that a woman so unedu-cated, uninterested, vain, self-centred, hypochondriac, idle-minded, irresponsible, left-handed, ignorant and untalented could hold for a week.

Allowing for Ackerley's exasperation, this character reference was not entirely inaccurate. Completely unworldly, Nancy often gave the impression of imbecility and there are many stories concerning her misapprehensions about things most people took for granted. Whilst dancing to music on the radio, she once asked Leo Charlton whether he could turn one of the knobs to adjust the tempo. On another occasion, informed by a charwoman that a table would come up nicely with a little elbow-grease, Nancy set out for the shops in order to purchase a tin of this remarkable commodity.

Any job Ackerley suggested was instantly rejected by Nancy as being beneath her. Employment with the GPO, sorting letters, was dismissed as 'the sort of work that skivvies, prostitutes and little brainless girls did'. It was in Ackerley's interests for Nancy to get a job, since he was himself maintaining her at £30 a month, as well as providing for Bunny. His BBC salary was inadequate, and he was gradually using up his capital in order to support his sister. She now suggested that she should find a job suited to what she thought of as 'her "organizing" talents and looks: a receptionist, for instance, in a hotel, looking after the engagement book of some professional man, or running some flatlets.' Ackerley applauded these suggestions, whilst fearing for 'the fate of any hotel, professional man or block of flatlets that Nancy, with her ignorance, laziness and lack of tact, had the managing of.' Nothing ever came of these suggestions and the only evidence of any attempt at procuring employment is a draft of an advertisement which Nancy wrote on the back of an envelope: 'Wanted by lady part time job any capacity – morning or afternoon'.

She did, however, move to a new room in Worthing and urged her brother to come to visit her. He wrote a rather tactless letter, explaining that he was very busy. In an attempt to prove this, he unwisely listed all his social obligations as well as his BBC ones and this catalogue of engagements was in stark contrast to Nancy's life, for she had no real friends, no real home, nothing to occupy her at all. Christmas arrangements always called for tricky manoeuvres, since Ackerley was torn between desire (spending it with friends) and duty (spending it with Nancy and Bunny). In 1948, a plan to join Jack Sprott in Nottingham had fallen through, but Ackerley and Queenie had been invited to have Christmas lunch with Forster at the Buckinghams' home. Bunny had asked her friend Ann to come to Star and Garter Mansions to share her Christmas lunch and stay a night or two. Ackerley was worried that Nancy would be spending Christmas Day alone, but counted upon the fact that she would not mind so much if she knew that he would not be with Bunny.

He invited himself down to Worthing on the Saturday before Christmas, but had forgotten a prior engagement, so changed the visit to the Sunday. He then fell ill and so postponed the meeting to Boxing

Day. They agreed to meet at Haywards Heath, half-way between London and Worthing. The minute he saw Nancy, Ackerley realized that she had been very upset by the Christmas arrangements. In particular she felt that Bunny should have invited her to the flat. She had refused all invitations from her fellow lodgers and had spent the day alone. The weather on Boxing Day was horrible and Nancy complained that she was cold, as well she might be, since she had not worn her fur coat because she felt that it did not go with her much-darned old slacks. This pathetic clinging to the few remnants of her former style struck Ackerley as little more than the vanity and irrationality that characterized her sex. She began weeping and they hastily retired to a pub, where she drank too much.

The afternoon passed in bleak misery as, hunched against the bitter cold, they staggered around Haywards Heath, Nancy weeping hysterically and making all the old accusations: Ackerley and Bunny hated her, plotted against her and were determined to keep her out of Star and Garter Mansions at whatever cost. As usual when voices were raised, Queenie became agitated and joined in by barking. Whilst attempting to pacify both his sister and his dog, Ackerley was accused by Nancy of being more interested in Queenie than in her, as indeed he was. She wanted to come to London, but only on the condition that she lived with Bunny or with Ackerley; what she could not bear was for her brother to live with her aunt rather than with her. She calmed down slightly whilst they had tea, but this cheerless day ended with her threatening suicide if she were forced to return to her room alone. Ackerley was firm, promising to do something about her situation when he got back to London. 'No, no, it's got to happen now, now,' she pleaded. 'You're only fobbing me off as you always do.' There was some truth in this accusation, as Ackerley acknowledged, but the reason he made vague promises was that there really was no solution to Nancy's problems.

However, as soon as he got back to Putney, he sent her £50 in order to buy some warm clothes, and offered to come down to Worthing to see her in a few days' time. He was torn between a genuine love for Nancy, which was rapidly curdling into pity and guilt, and an equally felt hatred. He loathed scenes and emotional blackmail, loathed what they did to Nancy and what they did to him.

What, in his anxiety, he failed to realize was that by now Nancy had become very disturbed indeed. As long as he could remember there had been scenes and sulks and crises, even when Nancy had been a wealthy, beautiful and popular young woman in a large house in Richmond rather than an impoverished, friendless divorcee approaching her fiftieth birthday and confined to a shabby room in Worthing. Ackerley was aware of this decline, but not of its serious-ness. He too had been brought up in comfort and some style and had been obliged to adjust to new and straitened circumstances. However, he had already rejected the standard of living offered by his parents when, in an access of youthful socialist zeal, he had embraced the spartan life of Hammersmith. Although his life was now genuinely circumscribed by his lack of means, he was acclimatized to this. In contrast, Nancy's loss of money and social prestige had been an appalling shock. She had taken far greater advantage of it than her brother, living like the daughter of a millionaire, never wanting for anything. Her beauty had brought her a glamorous husband, but when her marriage failed to match up to Blenheim House expectations, she had run away from it. She had returned to the security of her home only to have it fall about her ears when her father died and left her without any money at all. Unlike her brother, she had no inner resources, nothing to fall back upon when wealth and beauty receded. The losses had been devastating.

Every step Ackerley took to help Nancy was a stop-gap measure, a doomed attempt to shore up her rapidly crumbling life. In spite of past experiences, Ackerley determined to ask Nancy to come to London for a holiday and stay at Star and Garter Mansions. Her fiftieth birthday would be a perfect opportunity to give her a holiday. Bunny had agreed to stay with Ann, who, although incapacitated by a leg-brace, was out of hospital and living once again at her flat. The question was how long the holiday should last. It was necessary to put a firm limit to it in order to prevent Nancy outstaying her welcome as she had on previous occasions. These well-intentioned plans were interrupted by a letter from Nancy, returning Ackerley's cheque and telling him not to come to see her:

I knew it would be no good going to Haywards Heath and having salt rubbed into my wounds but you made me. I couldn't stand any more of that – and of course I don't want this money you've sent me this morning for clothes or anything else.

I told you on Sunday that this has all been too much for me. I shall never get over it and I can't stop thinking about it. It's been going on so long you see — month after month I've tried to shove it away, to fill my life with other things when there was so little to fill it with, to keep on hoping and not believing the worst — it has been wearing me down for a long time. It was bad enough to be forced back into the life which both you and Bunny know I dreaded, but you didn't even stop at that. You have both gone out of your way to make me feel like an exile, no welcome in the only home left to me to go to. I keep thinking of that ultimate cruelty which I got news of for the first time on Xmas morning — that you have asked Ann instead of me. You could never have me in the flat because there wasn't room, but you make room for Ann. Do you suppose I haven't thought of that alternative over and over again and longed for you to say come up and sleep on the floor or a couch, or that you would borrow or hire another bed as so many people do at Xmas. You see none of your reasons for not having me have been the sort of reasons that one couldn't get over if one had really wanted to.

It is all too much for my poor brain to cope with. I know you keep saying that you didn't think I minded about Xmas. Perhaps you didn't, although actually I mind very much and dread it more and more as the years go on and my life gets emptier than ever, but you did know that I was lonely and wretched and had been longing for you to have me to stay, so surely you must have realized that to leave me alone at Xmas and ask someone else instead was the most frightfully cruel thing to do. How can one believe in affection or kindly feelings in the face of such treatment.

I know there is nothing to be done now and I have nothing left to hope for — I might have spared myself the last humiliation of begging you to help me on Sunday.

Please don't ring up here any more, or try to come here. I would much rather be left alone.

In her misery Nancy had misrepresented the facts, as she often did. Ackerley had indeed asked her to come for Christmas, suggesting that she could be put up in comfort in the Star and Garter Hotel, in the same block as the flat. She had declined. She would only come if Bunny was ousted and packed off to Ann. There was no question of sending Bunny to Ann's unheated flat, so Ackerley told Nancy that since she had declined to come, Ann would be spending Christmas at the flat with Bunny. He did not point out, as he might well have done, that Ann could stay in the flat because she would share Bunny's room without causing a row. Bunny had not yet recovered from her experiences at Wendy. In his diary Ackerley wondered how Nancy could 'suppose that Bunny would invite her to the flat – an old woman of eighty whom she had persecuted with her jealousy and pulled from her bed at nine o'clock at night, pulled from her bed twice, throwing the clothes about, trampling on her things, and threatened with a knife until four o'clock in the morning.'

Upon receiving this letter, Ackerley sent Nancy a wire telling her that he was writing with an invitation for her to stay at Star and Garter Mansions. He showed Nancy's letter to Forster, who said that it did not display any signs of actual mental instability, merely 'unfocussed hatred', and that there was no need for Ackerley to dash to Worthing. After a day at *The Listener* spent worrying about Nancy, Ackerley decided to ignore Forster's advice, and took a train. As usual, he was prevented from taking any forthright action by indecision. He could not even decide whether, when he got to Worthing, he could face a confrontation or whether Nancy would agree to see him at all. Perhaps it would be better to leave a note, or post one. In the event, he telephoned her from a pub and was surprised to find her quite amenable to seeing him. That he *was* surprised shows how little he really understood Nancy's tactics.

Apart from a rather desolating absence of any photographs on the mantelpiece, her new room seemed comfortable and attractive. Nancy herself seemed calm and had clearly been thinking about her behaviour. She recognized that she was by nature hysterical, but denied that she was really capable of inflicting physical injury upon people. Constipated since before Christmas, she was concerned about her health and said that she had been brooding too much on her problems. Ackerley gave her the note he had written on the train in which he had said that of course he needed her quite as much as she needed him, that in the end they would certainly live together, and that in the meantime she must come to stay in Putney for 'two or three weeks'. Nancy read the letter, began to weep, and embraced her brother. All seemed to be going well, but having established that she was delighted with the prospect of a visit to London, Nancy began to criticize Bunny. Ackerley wisely kept his counsel whilst this went on, then said that he must return to London. He used *The Listener* as an excuse, although concern for Queenie was his real reason. Nancy accompanied him to the station and asked whether he could spend the following evening, New Year's Eve, with her. He agreed, but said that he would have to return to London on New Year's Day in order to prepare for Forster's seventieth birthday party. She then told him not to bother and to come some other day. She didn't mind seeing in the New Year without him.

In the event he went down on the evening of 2 January 1949, a Sunday, feeling somewhat the worse for the 'rather sweet sherry, rather sharp champagne and brandy' he had consumed the previous evening in honour of Forster. A room had been booked in the house for him, since he had agreed to stay to dinner and leave early the following morning for the office. On the way to Nancy's room he unwisely stopped at an off-licence and bought a half-bottle of gin. The evening began well, with Nancy, apparently in good spirits, telling her brother all about her fellow lodgers. However, too much was drunk, making Ackerley drowsily inattentive and Nancy reminiscent. She began to talk about 'past grievances, future prospects', and Ackerley attempted to deflect her by pleading tiredness. A bottle of wine had also been opened and neither of them was now fit to discuss Nancy's prospective holiday. She complained that nothing had been solved, but Ackerley remained firm and suggested she should come to bid him good-night when he'd got prepared for bed. Tired of waiting for her, he turned out the light and was almost asleep, when the door opened and the light switched on to reveal Nancy bearing a huge slab of cheese. 'Here's some cheese for you,' she announced. 'I knew it would be like this. You don't mean anything, do you, just placating me somehow.' Ackerley firmly sent her to bed.

At half-past six the following morning Ackerley was awakened as arranged by Nancy's landlady knocking on his door. As he stumbled blearily out of his bedroom he noticed a letter which had been left on the threshold:

> I thought you were going to help me, Joe – what did your letter mean – just nothing. You know I am utterly miserable and frightened living by myself like this and you keep promising me things will be different and pretending you are fond of me – then when I see you again you are quite different and I know you were only trying to lull me into a sense of false serenity – it will always be like this I know. I can't stand it any longer. This awful lonely life and a succession of

bed sitting rooms. I have wanted to die for a long time. Now I am going to. I never wanted to hurt anyone – you least of all. I wanted so little – only to be near you and feel that I had something left to live for, to be able to do all the little things to help you that I did at Wendy which kept me busy and happy and not interfere with your life in any way – but you don't want me, and I can't go on alone. I thought you knew that, and have only pulled myself together these last few days, because your letter and visit gave me hope – But how many times have you raised my hopes lately and in the end it means nothing – You only want to go on as you are – leaving me here to be lonely – ill – frightened – all the things I have been for years – and would go on being for the rest of my life –

I can't do it – even for you – my nerve and my spirit is broken.

Ackerley wondered whether he should find Mrs Gray, the landlady, or go to Nancy's room. He fumbled about in the dark, but could not remember the layout of the large house. 'O hell, I thought, why bother? And I shall miss my train. I slipped out of the side door, and by hurrying caught it.'

15

My Sisters and Myself

WHEN Ackerley got back to London he showed the letter to Bunny and telephoned Forster. The latter now decided that perhaps there were signs of mental illness after all, but he did not take the suicide threat seriously. Neither had Ackerley when he re-read the letter on the train:

> I did not really suppose that she could have carried out her threat, any more than she did when she returned from Haywards Heath, and added in my mind irritably that anyway if she killed herself last night she killed herself, and is now dead, and if she didn't she didn't and is now alive, and one can't upset a household of old ladies at 6.30 in the morning to find out which.

He went to the office, did his morning's work and then went out to lunch. When he returned to the office he decided to telephone Nancy, but was told by the switchboard that a message had been left for him to telephone the police: 'Would I go at once to Worthing Hospital where my sister Mrs Nancy West was lying dangerously ill from gas poisoning, and would I please call in at Worthing police station on the way.'

He took the next train and spent the journey torn between hoping that Nancy was dead and dreading that this might indeed be the case. At that period suicide was a criminal offence and one of the policemen who interviewed him at Worthing was 'extremely hostile and unpleasant, severe and moralizing, watchful and suspicious'. It occurred to him that he was under suspicion of attempting to murder Nancy, or at least conniving in her suicide bid. He was told that one of the residents at Winchester House had smelled gas at ten a.m. and this had been traced to Nancy's room. Her milk had not been collected, so the landlady had entered the room. Nancy was lying on the floor unconscious, her head covered by the fur coat she had disdained to wear with slacks, the tube of the gas fire and an empty bottle of Veganin beside her. The police asked Ackerley whether he had had any idea that Nancy might try to commit suicide. He had already decided not to mention Nancy's letter and said 'No'. However, the police had found another letter, 'a long letter, which began with firm writing, and then straggled off into incoherency'. This letter was not produced, but the constable said: 'She seems to have been jealous of your wife as well as your aunt.' When Ackerley protested that he was not married, he said: 'Well another woman is mentioned. Someone called Queenie.'

After he had made his statement, he was taken to the hospital where he found Nancy, still unconscious but out of danger, lying behind screens. A woman police constable was in attendance, mounting a twenty-four-hour guard to prevent the patient making another attempt upon her life. She would be taking a statement as soon as Nancy was fit to make one. Ackerley returned to London, arranged to take time off work and prepared to travel to Worthing the following day. He was a prey to remorse, feeling that he could have prevented this episode if he had really wanted to.

Friends reassured him, telling him that there was nothing he could have done to help Nancy more than he had. They told him that he tended to forget what he had had to put up with from Nancy in the past: her rages, her jealousy, her refusal to respond to his offers of help. Jack Sprott told him he had always done everything he could for Nancy, and Leo Charlton and Bunny agreed. Forster remarked: 'I feel ashamed of having been critical of Joe. Which of us could have stood up to what he has to bear?' He pronounced Nancy an 'awful woman', whose behaviour had renewed his doubts about the fair sex. 'Even if you'd committed incest with her, do you suppose that would have made her happy?' he asked. Ackerley believed that, whether or not she was wholly aware of it, this was indeed what Nancy wanted. Certainly the relationship between them was far stronger, both positively and negatively, than that usually found between brother and sister. Nancy often demanded some sort of physical show of affection, hugging and kissing, but Ackerley dreaded such intimacy, fearful of what it might mean, and did his utmost to avoid 'slobbering reconciliations' after they had argued. He found them both alarming and physically distasteful.

Ackerley was little mollified by his friends' testimonials, and even began to blame himself because he would not be at Nancy's bedside when she came round, to welcome her back to the world. Could the doctors be persuaded to give her an opiate, he wondered, so that her return to consciousness could be replayed with him in attendance? Then, gradually, a genuine fear ousted these fantasies. What if Nancy asked after the letter she had left under his door? How could he admit to having ignored it? Worse still, what would happen if Nancy had mentioned the letter when making her statement? He had told the police that he had no inkling that Nancy intended to kill herself; he could hardly claim that the existence of the letter had slipped his mind. Well, if Nancy did mention the letter, he could deny its existence: it would be his word against that of a drunk, drugged and traumatized woman. But there still remained the problem of convincing Nancy. Perhaps he could go back to the house and tell Mrs Gray that he was looking for the missing letter? He would secrete the letter about him somewhere and then pretend to find it in the room. He placed the letter in his sock in readiness for this plan.

At the hospital Nancy had regained consciousness. 'I ran to her, and knelt beside her, and put my arms round her, and, luckily I suppose, burst into tears. I sobbed and sobbed on her breast and arms.' To his surprise Nancy seemed very composed, not at all the desperate, wild-eyed woman dragged back from the brink that he had expected.

> When I realized that she was in a perfectly normal state of mind [Ackerley wrote in his diary], I remember feeling self-conscious and thinking, 'I needn't have done this at all.' But now I found it easy to go on, and thought it would be better for her perhaps if I went on crying as long as possible . . . She was pleased with me crying, I think, and though I hated doing it, and resent being made to do it, and saw this even, in its way, as the last gasp of emotional blackmail, I was glad I had been able to cry so naturally and spontaneously, and let it go on since it was now easy . . .

Not only was Nancy calm, she had also remembered the letter. Ackerley attempted to bamboozle her, pretending she was talking about the letter the police had found, but she insisted that she had left another letter outside his door. He said that he would ask Mrs Gray when he went round to pack up her belongings. He urged her to keep her statement to the police short and to the point: drink, muddle and amnesia should be the impression. He then went to see the police-woman:

I said 'She doesn't seem to remember much, she's all mixed up. She says she never turned on the gas.' The policewoman smiled: 'She did that alright.' I said, 'I don't think she knew what she was doing. She also says she put a letter under my door saying she was going to do it.' The policewoman said 'Delusions.' So that finished the letter, I hoped; I'd taken it to the end. Yet if Nancy asks me later whether I got the letter or not, I'm quite able to say 'Of course I did; I just thought it better for both of us if I didn't admit it then.'

The police said that if he and Nancy signed a paper to say that she would not attempt suicide again and that he would take responsibility for her future behaviour, then the case would not need to go before the courts.

After a few days Nancy was moved to Graylingwell, a place she later described as 'a sort of loony bin near Chichester'. Worthing Hospital's resident psychiatrist, who recommended it, preferred to call it a 'nerve hospital'. As Nancy's next of kin, Ackerley was asked to sign a form giving the hospital permission to treat her with ECT, or electroconvulsive therapy. This vividly named and controversial treatment consisted of attaching electrodes to the patient's head and administering strong electrical charges. It was widely applied at the time for mental disorders and considered very effective. The psychiatrist explained to Ackerley that 'it was a wonderful treatment and gave magnificent results', but that it was necessary for both the patient and next of kin to sign a release form because there was a remote chance that the treatment could result in 'the fracture of small bones'. 'I said that I would sign anything he liked,' Ackerley wrote: 'a few powerful electric shocks might do Nancy the world of good, I thought.'

Graylingwell turned out to be nearer Nancy's estimation of it than the psychiatrist's, 'full of neurotics and cranks and hysterics and, in other buildings, the insane'. However, in spite of complaints about the vegetarian diet (no brown bread), Nancy seemed quite happy. Her doctors had decided against ECT, relying instead upon a rest-cure, and after a couple of weeks she was transferred to a convalescent home in Worthing.

Ackerley now had to make plans for her to come to Star and Garter Mansions, a prospect he was dreading. Bunny was packed off to Ann's and all was in readiness for Nancy's arrival: furniture was moved around, tulips were put in Nancy's room and a celebratory bottle of sherry was purchased. Ackerley set off for the station with rather mixed feelings. Unlike Bunny, Nancy would be able to help look after Queenie, but on the other hand, he could hardly forget the previous occasions she had shared the flat with him. In fact Nancy was not on the train. He telephoned the convalescent home and was told that she had suffered a relapse and had been returned to Graylingwell. He then telephoned Graylingwell and was told that for some reason Nancy had lost her physical coordination, had had hysteria and collapsed. Her condition was not particularly serious and she was now undergoing treatment.

In fact Nancy's condition was a great deal more serious than the doctors first admitted. They were giving her deep insulin treatment and ECT, and they advised Ackerley not to visit her for the present. Unsure of the exact nature of her setback, Ackerley was racked by anxiety and guilt, blaming himself for not going in person to Worthing to bring her back to London. The doctor assured him that this had nothing whatever to do with her relapse, but still he fretted. He was further upset by James Kirkup's assertion that ECT was 'a dreadful thing and a mistake'. He confided his dark fears to a voluminous diary, accusing himself of hating Nancy and driving her out of her mind by his cruelty.

> Once again through these wretched days and nights, unable to sleep, tramping with my self-torturing thoughts over Wimbledon Common, without joy, without noticing any longer the branches of the woods or the happiness of my dog, my wretched mind, as it had done so often before, turned right round once more: the problem now, as in Worthing Hospital, was how to get the poor woman to me – to get her now to Putney, to have her in my place, to care for her and help her with kindness and love, to make reparation somehow for the unkindness of the past and give her back her self-confidence in the last thing, me, she had lost – that was now my one desire and preoccupation.

He even telephoned the hospital and asked whether he could remove Nancy immediately to Putney. The doctors were firm and reassuring, insisting that she should remain in the hospital but that there was really nothing to worry about.

When he finally visited Nancy, he was led along corridors by a nurse, who unlocked and relocked doors as they went. Nancy was in bed, looking quite plump and well, but extremely vague and dazed-seeming. He noticed that one of the magazines she was reading was upside-down. He attempted to make desultory conversation with her, but really got nowhere. He saw her collapse as 'a second attempt at self-destruction, a psychological form of suicide . . . a second effort to escape from an intolerable burden of thought, and the hateful problems of her life'. He recognized that whatever treatment Nancy received, there was always the problem of what was to happen when she was discharged from the hospital. The basic situation of her life could not really be altered, so how could the old patterns of behaviour be prevented from re-forming? He wrote to her doctor, giving a brief synopsis of Nancy's life.

> What I am so afraid of is, that as soon as my sister begins to 'think' once more, if ever she does, she will find herself so beset by the same despairs that she will either collapse again, or start to take up permanent residence at Graylingwell under psychiatric control.

The doctors remained evasive but reassuring.

When he next went to visit her, Nancy was led into a dayroom, tottering between two nurses, her head sunk in her shoulders, her eyes not entirely focused. She reminded Ackerley of Netta in her final decline: 'This was my sister, destroyed by me.' Although out of bed, she seemed no better than when last he had seen her. Ackerley had another interview with her doctor who was forced to admit that, if anything, she had regressed slightly, but he was convinced that within six weeks she would be fit to come to Putney. Ackerley was beginning to find the doctor very unsatisfactory and lacking in imagination. He had stopped believing what the man told him. He described what had happened to one of his contributors at *The Listener*, a doctor who reviewed books for him. This man offered to write to Nancy's doctor and, at last, received a frank, but alarming reply. In the convalescent home Nancy had become completely withdrawn and very difficult to contact. She sat about in a lost fashion and seemed to take no interest. We had to bring her back to the main hospital where she deteriorated still further. She became incontinent of both urine and faeces and developed a crude hysterical gait, in fact she had to be assisted to stand and walk. She takes no interest whatever, neglects herself, is untidy, and at meal times has displayed degraded behaviour. When one talks to her she answers briefly and to the point, but she is unable or unwilling to sustain a conversation.

The 'very grave twilight state' which Nancy had entered suggested schizophrenia, but the doctor was unwilling to make this diagnosis:

In all my conversations and correspondence with Mr Ackerley I have studiously avoided the word schizophrenic as I feared this might give him the idea that the prognosis is worse than I really believe it to be. At the same time I must confess that I am not as pleased with her response to treatment as I would like to be.

What was undeniable, however, was that Nancy's illness was the result of 'a long-standing personality disorder'.

Ackerley attempted to forget his troubles by taking Queenie for long walks on Wimbledon Common, but nothing could put off the moment when Nancy would be sufficiently recovered to leave Graylingwell. His diary entries at this period, whether self-recriminatory or describing Queenie and the Common, usually ran to several pages, but the one for 15 April is chillingly succinct:

Bunny and Ann go to Thornton Heath tomorrow, and I go to Chichester to bring Nancy up. She is to live with me from now on.

In spite of the fact that Nancy's return was complicated by Queenie's being on heat (a circumstance which always made Ackerley alter his routine, having to get up early in order to take her to Putney Heath at six a.m. when it would be deserted), things went well for a while. Nancy was 'quiet, dull, acquiescent, vague, slow, dragging', but seemed reasonably content. Ackerley consulted his GP who was unwilling to take Nancy on because he felt that she needed specialist attention. Ackerley suspected that it was the doctor's past experience of Nancy as a patient that was the real cause of his hesitation. The doctor was not encouraging. Her Graylingwell psychiatrist was still reluctant to confirm a diagnosis of schizophrenia, as was the GP, who suggested that Nancy should become an out-patient at the Maudsley Hospital in South London, where a further opinion could be sought. If Nancy did have schizophrenia, the GP warned, Ackerley was in for a difficult and unrewarding time: there was little he could do to prevent Nancy's condition deteriorating, and the first signs of decline would be when the patient appeared to find whatever he or she tried to do too much trouble. Ackerley was horrified, since Nancy appeared to have reached this stage already. The doctor at the Maudsley was rather more optimistic, diagnosing Nancy as 'an environmental case'.

The rows that Ackerley had feared did not materialize, partly because Nancy was still convalescent and too lethargic to do much. This did not prevent her from voicing the occasional criticism, particularly when she saw Ackerley's devotion to his dog. Bunny had been ejected, but still Nancy did not have her brother to herself. She began to complain that Queenie should not be sleeping on blankets, but on straw; she should not be allowed a fresh egg (still rationed at this period); Ackerley should pay less attention to her. Ackerley was determined to take his walks with Queenie alone, for it gave him time to think, away from the world, and he wanted to study and make notes upon Queenie's behaviour in preparation for *My Dog Tulip*. In any case the walks were too long and arduous for Nancy, sometimes lasting as long as three hours. When Nancy did accompany her brother and his dog, she refused to adopt sensible footwear and gingerly picked her slow way through the long grass in high-heels or sandals. As Ackerley observed: 'Unhappily my sister is a woman who has never made a practice of listening to reason, which she has, indeed, an inadequate equipment to receive, and is certainly impervious to it when so much as she is able to understand conflicts with her own desires.'

He attempted to entice Nancy to exhibitions, without success, and urged her to go out to the cinema whilst he was at the office. Apart from some desultory shopping and housework, Nancy did nothing. Within a fortnight of her arrival at Star and Garter Mansions she announced: 'I don't mind telling you I'm fed up with this place already.' Nancy never minded telling anyone, particularly when she had something disagreeable to impart, but Ackerley did his best not to lose patience with her. The situation was impossible, since neither sibling was at all adapted to living with anyone else, least of all with each other. Nancy appeared to have no interest in people and was unable to relate to them, as past experience had shown. Those who attempted to invite her anywhere were soon rebuffed and Nancy may have felt that most people were making an effort out of a sense of pity or duty and that few people really wanted to spend any time with her. She appeared to have only one friend, a former lover called Geoffrey, and did not really want to see much of him, writing him off as a bore. It was not long before arguments began in earnest. Her desperate loneliness was an unbreachable wall around her and her attempts to relieve the condition almost always took an aggressive form. She was also almost incapable of apology, insisting that she was right even in the face of evidence to the contrary. She saw herself as a victim of the world, which was to a certain extent true. She was at any rate a victim of her upbringing and her psychology. She was fifty years old and had made a mess of her life, and she seemed to have neither the energy nor the resolve to attempt to remedy the situation. She was, in a word, defeated.

Ackerley was equally poorly adapted to sharing his home and his life with another person. In spite of his many friendships, he was essentially a solitary man, set in his ways with his own routine, and had become even more so since the arrival of Queenie. Unlike Forster, he was very resistant to cosseting and even the kindly attentions of Aunt Bunny would irritate him. Nancy could not look after her brother without at the same time smothering him, behaving as if she were a lover or wife rather than a sister who performed housekeeping duties in reparation for being given a home and financial support. She could never be content with merely sharing a flat with him. She was jealous of his friends and jealous of his dog: any attention he paid to anyone or anything other than herself she interpreted as a rejection.

Ackerley knew very well that his reassuring protestations that he needed Nancy as much as she needed him were untrue. But he also knew that their joint fate was inescapable:

Near the Telegraph Inn is a curious old hawthorn tree. Starting from one stem, it has split near the ground into two, and these two limbs, growing independently upwards side by side, have become later intricately and intimately involved. One stem has divided again and has locked round the neck of the other in an embrace so close that the touching surfaces have fused. Its twin column, which has grown up straight from the ground, has the effect of being possessed, throttled and imprisoned by these passionate, tight, enwrapping arms, which, where they bend so to speak in their joints, have small lines or folds in their bark like the wrinkles in our own flesh when our limbs flex. The torment of these two self-suffocating stems from the same tree does not end with this embrace, for the two boughs continue to divide and grip each other all the way up.

In the event, Nancy's role was further relegated to that of cook-housekeeper, since Ann's unheated and uncomfortable flat in Thornton Heath was entirely unsuitable for Bunny during the winter. The final solution was one that Ackerley had urged upon Nancy whenever she had complained of loneliness on the south coast: lodgings were found for her in Putney. The same objections still applied, but Nancy must have realized that this was the best that could be done for her. She may also have taken her aunt's age into consideration. Bunny was now eighty; she was in reasonable health but she could not go on forever, and then her room would be free. In fact Nancy virtually lived at Star and Garter Mansions, arriving every morning and staying until after dinner when she returned to her lodgings to sleep. Aunt and niece appeared to get on reasonably well and Nancy may have realized that this truce was necessary to her own survival.

Ackerley still attempted to keep to his perfect routine, which began with a pot of tea in bed at seven a.m. Drinking his tea, he would lie in bed reading until eight, when he would get up and have a swift breakfast with Bunny, before taking Queenie for her morning walk, returning at ten-thirty. He then went to the office, where he worked until about four p.m. His hours at *The Listener* were flexible, since he was trusted to take work home with him and work out of office hours when necessary, as for example when preparing the quarterly Book Supplements. He would work in his room until drinks at six-thirty, followed by dinner. He would then retire to his own room once more, leaving the table in the corridor dining-room as soon as was decently possible and shutting the door firmly behind him. He would use the time until bed to read or write. The sacrosanct parts of this routine, which he jealously guarded, were Queenie's morning walk and his period of work between tea and drinks – hours of uninterrupted solitude. The arrangement appears to have worked reasonably well, but domestic irritations and arguments were a constant reminder of the freedom he had lost.

Occasionally, he would escape on brief holidays or pack his 'human bitches' off to the south coast to a cheap hotel for a fortnight. It was now possible to leave Queenie in the care of his aunt and sister if he needed to, but the best holidays were those spent with friends who lived in the country. Queenie would be invited as well and would find new countryside to explore and new rabbits to chase. One such friend was Siegfried Sassoon who lived in melancholy grandeur at Heytesbury House, the large stone manor near Warminster which he had acquired in 1934. Sassoon had surprised many of his friends by marrying in 1933 at the age of forty-seven. He had met his wife, Hester Gatty, at the Wilton Pageant, shortly after the collapse of a long-standing but painful affair with the aristocrat-aesthete Stephen Tennant. In spite of confiding in his friends about the homosexual relationships which had dominated his life and his complete lack of experience with women, Sassoon was convinced that he had fallen in love. Apart from the birth of a much-loved son, George, in October 1936, the marriage had not been a success, and the couple, although still married, had decided to live apart.

As far as anyone could be a friend of Sassoon, Ackerley was, and had been so for some time. He was intrigued to recognize something of himself in Sassoon's self-absorption, his passion for his son and his persecution at the hands of his wife. By 1949, when Ackerley paid his first visit to Heytesbury, Sassoon could hardly bring himself to be polite to Hester when she came to see him. She lived nearby, and, in spite of being told by her husband's doctors that she should leave him alone (Sassoon was recovering from an ulcer), she was a frequent and upsetting visitor. Ackerley's visit, and a further one the following summer, gave each man an opportunity to consider the other's character and note similarities. Their respective diaries provide intriguing analyses of their personalities.

In July 1949, Sassoon was very glad of company and he found Ackerley the perfect guest. The same could not, alas, be said for Queenie, who disgraced herself on the first night.

Not in my room, of course [Ackerley noted], but in the best bedroom that communicates with it. The door was open unfortunately. I should never have known it if Miss Benn, Siegfried's housekeeper, not understanding whether I wanted breakfast in my room or down stairs brought it up to this adjacent room and setting the tray down on a table, stepped in Queenie's very loose shit which Queenie, I must praise her, such an intelligent dog, had deposited on a dark mat by this table instead of on the beautiful thick white pile carpet which covers the floors of most of the rooms in the house. However her forethought was of no avail, for Miss Benn, having unwittingly stood in it, then walked over the white carpet of my room and wondered how she came to leave brown stains everywhere. Coming upstairs after breakfast I found the poor woman trying to clean up the mess with ammoniated water – and Queenie outraged to find a stranger in her bedroom, menaced her and even nipped her ankle as a warning. But Miss B. has been a kennel maid luckily and understands dogs, and forgave Queenie both her shit and her nip, explaining, and quite rightly, both away as excitement, and jealousy respectively. I debated whether or not to tell S. of this mishap. Was inclined to do so, then decided against; it seemed like sneaking on my dear doggie.

When, some years later, Sassoon heard that Ackerley was writing a book about Queenie, he asked Forster whether her visit to Heytesbury would feature. It did, but in a considerably disguised form, with Sassoon caricatured as 'Captain Pugh', a Kentish farmer who had served with Ackerley in the Great War.

Sassoon regarded Ackerley's visit as a convalescent one. 'He was desperately in need of a holiday and peace,' he noted in his diary, 'owing to a bad time he's had with his sister, who is a prize fanatic, and is making his life intolerable . . . It has bucked me up, having someone to talk to, with whom I can really discuss things that interest me . . . I have asked J.A. to stay as long as he likes, as it is doing him so much good.' Ackerley, whilst enjoying Heytesbury's amenities, which included a fine cellar and 230 acres of park and woodland, felt that it was Sassoon who was the chief beneficiary of the visit.

Siegfried sweet, kind, loquacious, absent-minded, lonely, dreadfully self-centred and self-absorbed. I like him very much, there is some-

thing very touching about his aged, beautiful worn face, the light in
the eyes dimmed from constant looking inwards. He scarcely ever
meets one's eye – he never has I think, – but talks, talks away from
one, from side to side, or into his lap or over one's head, always
about himself, his life, his past fame, his present neglect, his
unhappy marriage, his passionate love for his son. It is all intensely
subjective (he scarcely ever asks about oneself – a flash or two of
effortful interest, but always reminding him about himself) and
threnodic, it is a man who has spent years and years of loneliness
talking his thoughts at last aloud to an ear.

This self-communing had, of course, led to Sassoon's masterpiece, his
double-trilogy of memoirs which had been published to great acclaim
between the two wars. However, the sixth and final volume,
Siegfried's Journey, had been published in 1945 and the task was now
complete. He had achieved literary fame with his poetry during the
First World War, but had failed to find a voice with which to greet the
Second, and was temporarily out of fashion. Even so, Ackerley
thought highly of him and had published several of his poems in *The
Listener*. Ackerley was convinced that his friend's work would endure
and his reassurances, if they had been listened to in the twilight of
Heytesbury's drawing-room, might have cheered Sassoon. Although
fond of him, Ackerley also saw his host as an awful warning, in
particular in his brooding and in his obsession with George, who was
then attending a local preparatory school:

Dear Siegfried, he has taken a wrong turning somewhere. There is
no happiness in self, self as a permanent diet is melancholic and
poisonous, it kills, one dies, as he is dying, talking talking away
about his lost fame, his loneliness, his domestic affairs – his aged
worn fine face turned sideways, sightless, towards the window . . .

He is not yet a permanent deaf recluse, as he might very well be. I
must help him. Indeed he is a lesson and a warning I must profit by,
for I myself could easily become like him. He with his son George, I
with my dog Queenie – we both of us run for a fall. All our eggs are
in these baskets. He would go mad, I think, if anything happened to
his son. And what will happen to me if Queenie dies! These are
wrong roads, they lead only to disaster, to death. Even if George
survives, the happiness and closeness, and present intensity of

Siegfried's present relationship with him can't last, this schoolboy love. And Siegfried has nothing to put in its place – he is fixated upon the child. Alas, these passionate attachments, how little they are.

Another point of similarity between the two men was that they both saw themselves as victims of jealous and possessive women. Sassoon had managed to detach himself from Hester rather more successfully than Ackerley had done from Nancy, but they both treated these women in much the same way. When friends came round to Star and Garter Mansions, they would be briefly allowed to exchange a word or two with Nancy before being led off into Ackerley's room. The door was closed upon her firmly as it might have been upon a servant. Bored and exasperated with her himself, Ackerley assumed others would feel the same. Many did, but even those with some claim to Nancy's attention saw no more of her than her brother considered absolutely necessary. This customarily meant a brief drink before Ackerley withdrew to his room, taking both the discomfited guest and the bottle with him. At Heytesbury there was similar awkwardness for the guest when Hester descended upon her husband. 'You'd better come and do the polite tea-table stuff,' Sassoon told his guest gloomily. 'Besides it will be a help to me not to have her to myself.'

The battle, the fifteen years' battle, was still on; I belonged in S's camp, to S's side, and must not traffic with the enemy. Not that I had any wish to do so. Constitutionally wary and critical of women, and with Nancy's troubles still upon me, it is hardly likely that a sex which has never attracted me and seemed to me an inferior and troublesome gender, should have produced a specimen in this particular situation which would have seduced my allegiance in this my fifty-fourth year. And Hester, even more than Nancy, seemed to me at once visible as the embodiment of all the emotional vices S. attributed to her. Nevertheless I am a polite person by nature, and would not have known how to be rude to her nor cared to be rude to her if I had known. Nor was it suitable that I should be anything but polite, never having met the woman before and having nothing personal against her. Yet politeness must be formal and limited, I saw, no overstepping the mark; a difficult situation. I confess I could not help feeling sorry for her, sorry without sympathy. She had alienated her husband and her son in the same way, according to S's account, that Nancy had alienated all the people who were fond of her, or of whom she was fond, and one could not help a sad feeling for this woman trying to hold on still to something she had lost through emotions beyond her control, making tea table conversation to a husband in whose face and manner aversion and distaste were only too plainly writ, and who made not the slightest effort to help her carry this social situation off, and to me, a visitor, whom she must slightly suspect of having already been put against her. Her manner was therefore nervous, ingratiating, squirming – a painful exhibition to watch.

There was a rather grim fête held in the park and opened, much to Sassoon's disgust, by Hester, who had been invited by the tactless vicar to do so. Eventually, Sassoon informed his guest of the times of trains and Ackerley wondered whether he had in some way fallen out of favour.

He had not, for he was invited again the following year, 1950. Both men noted a distinct deterioration in the other. Sassoon was delighted to see Ackerley at first: 'You don't know what it's like to come down here in the morning and have nothing in front of one for the day – and day after day –' he said, 'no one to talk to, nothing to do. It's awful, and very bad for me.' Ackerley brought news of literary London and Sassoon was briefly cheered by the fates that had overtaken his younger rivals: Day Lewis was worn out and aged, Dylan Thomas rarely sober and finished.

> I like having him here [Sassoon wrote], though he is a vaguely devitalizing friend to be with. Ten years younger than me, he is old and disillusioned. Slightly deaf, he doesn't hear me well, and I often have to repeat my remarks – feeling at the same time that I might just as well not have uttered them.

Ackerley was indeed growing slightly deaf, but Sassoon's ruminative monologues, muttered almost to himself, would have been difficult for someone with very acute hearing to catch. Ackerley often felt himself to be a sounding-board for his host, who seemed even lonelier and more self-obsessed than the previous year. Whilst Sassoon, in his room, confided to his diary that Ackerley's 'outlook on life is sad and used up. No enthusiasm for anything. No forward view.', his guest was in *his* room, noting:

S.S. is still as complaining and egotistic as ever, poor chap. It is surprising in a lover of FitzGerald[1] but we cannot be rid of ourselves whatever our objective models may be . . .

He gets no joy out of life and therefore gives none, for you cannot give what you have not. The tone of his voice is always as it were complaining, moody, weary and resentful. Gaiety there is none. This is not to say that he does not joke and laugh, he does; but the jokes are mostly wry and the laughter sardonic or bitter. He never sings or hums or even whistles. Though he can play the piano he never does . . . What a sorry and dreary figure he is, this strange lean man, moving about his beautiful estate with rather short staccato steps, slovenly dressed in unbecoming clothes, with a rent more than likely in the seat of his trousers through which a patch of white buttock shows, a loose short-sleeved yellow pullover draped almost like a blouse over his long-sleeved blue flannel shirt, and on his head, with its brim turned down all round, a thirty or forty year old felt hat only held together in its decayed, faded and greasy parts with safety pins. His hat, of course, besides being a joke is a symbol; it is the past, his old life when he was famous and young and sought-after, before he grew old and forgotten and was put to moulder and gather dust upon the shelf. He clings to it therefore – making of it a sardonic joke.

The two men were too alike to be really close friends, and perhaps the feeling of each being the other's tarnished mirror proved too uncomfortable, for this appears to have been the last time Ackerley visited Heytesbury. The similarity between Ackerley's circumstances and Sassoon's was not apparent to everyone, however:

When I told Nancy about Mrs Sassoon phoning up S. every night from Mull [where she had a family house], with nothing but

[1] Edward FitzGerald (1809–83) is chiefly remembered for his translation of *The Rubáiyát of Omar Khayyám*. He also translated plays, one of which Ackerley had read for Robert Donat in 1945. FitzGerald spent most of his life in Suffolk, his emotional life centred upon a young fisherman called 'Posh' Fletcher. He had edited the poems of another Suffolk writer, George Crabbe, whom Forster had written about for *The Listener* in 1941. Benjamin Britten had read the article and was inspired to write his opera, *Peter Grimes* (1945). When Britten and his partner, Peter Pears, set up the annual Festival of Music and the Arts at Aldeburgh in 1948 they invited Forster to deliver a lecture on Crabbe and William Plomer to deliver one on Fitzgerald.

trumped-up things to say, and knowing that he could not bear her and hated the telephone, but unable to accept defeat of her marriage, Nancy said, 'I don't know how women can behave like that, forcing themselves where they aren't wanted; it's so undignified.'

Ackerley had given little or no thought to his three half-sisters since the final painful interview with Muriel at the end of 1929. When he had returned, after that, to his mother in Richmond, Muriel and her youngest daughter, Diana, had gone to Austria on Roger's tickets. There, the traumas of Diana's childhood had erupted in an alarming psychosomatic illness: she was unable to eat or sleep, her throat became swollen and she had fainting fits. After a brief spell alongside her mother in an alpine health resort, they were obliged to return to England. The twins were at an unorthodox art school in Sussex, run by their former art mistress, and they invited the seventeen-year-old Diana to join them. She took a number of jobs, working as a cinema usherette and a house parlourmaid. When Muriel heard of this last appointment, which she considered unspeakably 'common', she insisted that Diana should not besmirch the family name and so Diana 'Perry' became Diana 'Bryn'.

In 1930 Muriel married a man she had met during the Great War. She opened the paper one morning and read an obituary of the man's wife, who had committed suicide; she wrote to him, and he asked her to come to stay with him and his teenage son, and stay she did. After the wedding they lived on Dartmoor for a while and then moved to Weybridge in Surrey. By this time Diana had also married. Her husband, some thirty years her senior, was Louis Wilkinson, who wrote novels under the name of Louis Marlow. He had embarked upon a literary career as a schoolboy at Radley, when he had begun a correspondence with the disgraced Oscar Wilde, recently emerged from Reading Gaol. At Cambridge, Wilkinson had become involved with the Powys brothers and wrote several books about them. He had never met Ackerley, but knew of him through literary acquaintances and so suggested that Diana should re-establish contact with her half-brother. She wrote to Ackerley at the BBC, proposing that they should meet, and was bitterly disappointed by his curt reply, in which he said that he could see no point in such an idea.

Diana's life with Wilkinson revolved around literary parties and holidays abroad, during which she drank too much and took pills in order to sleep. Although still ill and unstable, she had become more confident and had even written (and destroyed) a novel. After three years the marriage came to an end, although the parting was amicable and she and Wilkinson continued to meet. However, she was obliged to return to her mother, where she was joined by her sisters and Muriel's stepson. Before long she and Elizabeth moved to a room in London, where Diana worked for a film company. Sally got a job as a governess in Hungary and Elizabeth went out to join her there. In 1939 Diana remarried. Her second husband was a young man called Edward Petre. Almost at once war broke out and her new husband marched out of her life and into the services. She spent the war living with her in-laws, but the marriage did not survive the enforced separation.

Elizabeth's life was similarly disrupted by the war. In Budapest she had met and become engaged to an extremely wealthy Hungarian. They planned to live in America, and Elizabeth went on ahead to France, leaving her fiancé to sort out his business affairs. War broke out before he could join her and they were not able to marry until it was over. Sally left Hungary for Cairo, where she met Gerald Grosvenor, a professional soldier who was rather remotely related to the Duke of Westminster (his father had been the sixth son of the first Duke). Gerald was badly wounded and was invalided out of the Army. He married Sally in 1945 and began a new life as a gentleman farmer.

Just after the end of the war, Louis Wilkinson was in a restaurant when someone pointed across the room and said: 'Do you know Joe Ackerley?' 'I feel I ought to,' Wilkinson replied; 'I was married to his half-sister.' Introductions were made, and when Wilkinson said that he would be seeing Diana the following weekend, Ackerley sent a message that she should telephone him. Diana was very excited: she had hero-worshipped her half-brother from afar, ever since she first bumped into him in the 1920s, attracted by his charm, his looks and now his literary *éclat*.

> I couldn't wait to get out of the house, and I remember running down the street – *running!* – thinking: Where can I ring up? Where can I ring up? I got into a call-box, and he was in, he was there . . .

He invited her to lunch at a restaurant in Charlotte Street. She arrived 'shaking all over' and found that her hero lived up to all expectations:

'He was divine to me – absolutely lovely.' Ackerley appeared to be delighted with Diana and began taking her round London with him and introducing her to his literary friends. All this stopped when Nancy attempted suicide. Ackerley had not introduced Diana to Nancy, although he had talked about her a great deal, complaining about the problems she caused him.

Now that Nancy was living at Star and Garter Mansions and frequently complaining that she never saw anyone, Ackerley wondered whether he should invite Diana to meet her. His motives for this were not entirely honourable. On the one hand, he hoped that they would take to each other, since Nancy was always complaining that she had no friends of her own. But he would be almost equally pleased if they did not get on. He was fascinated to see how two women, both of whom, in their different ways, were devoted to him, would react when brought together. His experience as unwilling referee between his sister, aunt and mother had combined with his misogyny to convince him that no two women could ever be introduced without becoming critical and jealous of each other. He had given Nancy such a bad press that he assumed that Diana could only have one reason for wishing to meet her half-sister:

> Of course Diana only wants to meet Nancy because she wants to see me, and fears she won't now Nancy is here unless she sees her too. And of course Nancy is jealous. I do feel mischievous, I must say, the two cats. They'll soon tear each other to pieces – and perhaps me too!

In the event, the two women seemed to like each other,

> though God knows how long that will last. At any rate, I expect Diana will invite her out, and even without me, to please me if for no other reason, so something may evolve out of that.

Inevitably, however, it was not long before Nancy began to show signs of jealousy. 'Why don't you have Diana to live with you, since you obviously like her better than me?' she asked after one evening when she felt that she had been ignored. 'How natural that Diana should have been more interested in me than in her,' Ackerley remarked complacently in his diary. 'I am a man and a prominent and cultivated one. Nancy has nothing to offer at all, she is uneducated and ignorant. Of course Diana, or any other cultivated guest, would turn to me more than to her.' This was only too true, for Nancy simply had no conversation at all, and had been very stand-offish all evening.

> Maddening woman! What does she want? How is it possible to please her? I have given her roof, money, and much of my life. I have spent the last two months in entertaining and helping her. Through this kind of behaviour – fault-finding, jealousy, row-making – she has alienated everyone in her life until, entirely friendless and penniless, she had nothing left but the gas oven. I rescued her from that and have given her asylum, a new life. And such is my reward.

What Ackerley had not given Nancy, and what he never could give her, was love.

Love was entirely absorbed by Queenie, about whom Ackerley continued to make copious notes in the same journals in which he analysed his relationship with Nancy. He recalled that Gerald Heard had once said that love and curiosity were the two most important things in life, and these two qualities combined in Ackerley's relationship with his dog. They also illuminated what he wrote about her. He began extracting journal entries and adapting them into tentative sketches of Queenie. This was his usual method of composition, gradually and painstakingly working up an entire manuscript from brief notes jotted down in small pocket-books which he carried around with him. He would try out a chapter on loose-leaf paper, perhaps produce three or so pages, then start again. His surviving manuscript drafts have new sheets interleaved throughout, reworking a page, adding a paragraph, all in his immaculately neat, faintly dandyish, hand. He almost always wrote with a fountain pen, and rarely typed anything before he got to the final draft stage. He believed that there was a right word for everything and would not rest until he had found that word. Although he was often self-deprecating about his writing, he took it very seriously and complained when things were not going well. He once asked David Sylvester how the painter, Francis Bacon, worked:

I think writers (and it certainly applies to me) live often in a state of emotional overflow as they work, tears (perhaps maudlin), self-hugs of delight, grins of satisfied hatred: these pleasures are partly psychological, partly artistic – the exact right phrase or word, the inalterably perfect passage.

Any interruption was deeply resented, particularly if it came from Nancy asking some unnecessary question about how much meat she should buy at the butcher's or other queries she could answer herself. Ackerley thought his books, and not *The Listener*, were his real work, and their composition, one friend recalled, was accompanied by 'a kind of Flaubert-like noise'.

It was particularly important to get Queenie right, partly because he was aware that many people were bored by what he referred to as 'doggery'. It would also be his first piece of serious writing since *Hindoo Holiday* and expectations would be high. He decided to try out one of his pieces about Queenie on Stephen Spender, who was now co-editor of *Encounter*. Henry Reed had pointed out that Queenie's name was something of a drawback and likely to arouse titters amongst the literati. Ackerley eventually decided upon the pseudonym 'Tulip', and called his essay 'The Two Tulips', referring to the different sides of her character as displayed during walks with her master and visits to the vet. Spender accepted the piece, but the title was changed, presumably to avoid an impression of horticulture, and appeared in the March 1954 issue as 'My Dog, Tulip'. Ackerley was delighted to receive £60 for it. It was an amusing and beautifully written account of human and canine eccentricities, in which Ackerley himself appears as the hapless victim of his wilful dog. It is full of characteristic Ackerley touches, notably a sly attack upon the military in the depiction of the tactics adopted by the least satisfactory vet, who is a colonel, some proselytism on behalf of the breed, and a few teasingly 'upsetting' details. Only Ackerley, one feels, would walk into a surgery and discover the vet 'busily engaged in extracting a tintack from the anus of a hen'. The essay received praise from a wide variety of readers, including Forster, Arthur Waley and Rose Macaulay, which encouraged Ackerley to return to the novel he had been engaged upon since 1948, which charted the shifting relationships between himself, Freddie and Queenie. Forster, who had thought that Ackerley would be concentrating upon his Queenie essays, was not pleased:

'Queenie could not bring a libel action, Freddie could, so I am not sure the change is for the better.'

Amongst those delighted to see Ackerley producing new work were his publishers, who had done very well with *Hindoo Holiday*, but had seen little of Ackerley except when they attempted to reissue the book in 1951. After its initial success, *Hindoo Holiday* had continued to sell on, and plans had been mooted to film it and to turn His Highness's playlets into a ballet for Constant Lambert and Robert Helpmann. Nothing came of either of these projects, but the book went into several Chatto and Windus editions, including their cheap pocket 'Phoenix Library' and their rather grand 'Golden Library'. The Penguin edition had come out in 1940 and sold over 47,000 copies within the first six months. Assorted foreign rights had been sold, and Viking acquired the book for America, where it sold out but was not reprinted, much to Ackerley's displeasure.

In spite, or because, of his comparative lack of funds, Ackerley could be an astute businessman, as his dealings with publishers and agents demonstrate. Viking asked whether Alexander Woollcott could include a condensed version of the book in one of his popular series of *Readers*, which they published. This would have involved the text's being cut by some twenty or twenty-five per cent, and Ackerley suspected that it was Viking's roundabout way of renewing their licence without actually reissuing the book intact. 'I am very much against cutting books,' he told his publishers, 'so if Woollcott does not care to include the whole of *Hindoo Holiday* in his Reader, he cannot have it at all . . . since [Viking] show so little interest in it, I don't see why they should have it any more . . . Well, if they still want it now they can buy it all over again; and this time it will be considerably more expensive.' Indeed, he was more concerned to restore passages removed from the original text than to mutilate the book further. He had hoped that the Penguin edition would be an opportunity to do this, since the Maharajah was now dead, but Penguin refused on the absurd grounds that their books were advertised as 'unabridged' and should therefore contain nothing more nor less than the regular publisher's editions.

However, in 1951 Chatto and Windus decided to reissue the book themselves and Ian Parsons, who was now Ackerley's editor there, agreed to the restoration of all the material the company had been too faint-hearted to print in the original edition. Ackerley was delighted to restore not only the sections which might have shocked 'the James Douglases of this world',[1] but also some observations of animals and a shocking recollection from the Great War in which his orderly kills a wounded German officer and takes several souvenirs. He also prepared a new preface. Then, in October, John Murray sent a copy of the memoirs of Sir Arthur Cunningham Lothian to *The Listener*. Lothian had been an Indian civil servant and so Ackerley was interested to read his account of the Native States. This interest turned to horror when he found a reference to himself in the second chapter: 'Another of the larger states was Chhatarpur, whose Ruler was subsequently the hero of that curious and somewhat cruel book, *Hindu* [sic] *Holiday*, by Ackerley.'

Ackerley had always believed that he had sufficiently 'faked' the book to avoid any danger of libel. He had been delighted when members of the Indian High Commissioner's entourage had assured him that everyone knew the real identity of 'Chhokrapur' and had then named another state altogether. Since the books were to be published the same week, Ackerley foresaw that they were likely to be reviewed together and that his cover would be very publicly blown. He even thought that one of his colleagues might offer *Hindoo Holiday* to Lothian for review. It was quite clear that part of the reason the 'brute' Lothian had blown the gaff was that he strongly disapproved of *Hindoo Holiday*. Chatto and Windus suggested that they might delay publication, but Ackerley was still concerned and wondered whether they ought to attempt to trace His Highness's son, who might consider himself libelled if it were suggested that his father was a barber rather than a king. 'One hopes that he is a moronic country squire in C. India, unable to read,' Ackerley told his publishers; 'but of course he may be round the corner in the Far Eastern department of the BBC.'

It was eventually decided to postpone publication to the following year and sample copies which had already been despatched to Bombay, Calcutta, Poona, Ceylon and Toronto were hastily recalled.

[1] Douglas was responsible for a hysterical *Sunday Express* article in 1928 in which he demanded that Radclyffe Hall's lesbian novel *The Well of Loneliness* be withdrawn from circulation. His assertion that he 'would rather put a phial of prussic acid in the hands of a healthy girl or boy than the book in question' earned him a notable place in the annals of British puritanism.

There was some suggestion that writs could be issued against both books, but John Murray said that he was prepared to take the risk and go ahead with Lothian's. Eventually both books had to be withdrawn and altered: Lothian's would have the reference to Ackerley and his entry in the index expunged and *Hindoo Holiday* would lose the scene in which Ackerley discusses the possible parentage of the baby rajah with Narayan. Ackerley was not prepared to excise this passage without making certain that it was absolutely necessary to do so, and he approached the Indian High Commission in an attempt to trace His Highness's widow and son. 'Expectation of life is not so great in the East as it is in the West,' he told Parsons, 'and tho' I wish them no harm, if it should turn out that the Reaper has had both in the last thirty years, we shall not be put to the bother of altering my book at all.' The Reaper had not in fact called, and so the passage had to be deleted, a task to which Ackerley brought his editorial skills, cutting and pasting so as to cause the printers the least trouble. The new preface was scrapped altogether. Ackerley would write out the missing passage by hand and send it to friends to insert in their copies of the book, but it was never restored in print, nor indeed published until it appeared as an appendix to Neville Braybrooke's edition of Ackerley's *Letters*.

Although Ackerley had felt guilty about the trouble to which Chatto and Windus had been put on his behalf, they appeared to be relatively unbruised by the experience. A few months after the publication of 'My Dog, Tulip' Ackerley received a 'heart-rending appeal' from Ian Parsons, who was 'anxious to have a really distinguished list of books' with which to celebrate Chatto and Windus's centenary the following year. 'Is there any chance of your book about Queenie being ready in time for us to publish it during the course of 1955?' he asked. Ackerley sent his only typescript of the novel which was to become *We Think the World of You*, commenting:

I am *not* really offering it for publication, my mind is not made up upon its readiness for that, but it would help me to have your views . . . Do you think that dear Leonard [Woolf], friend and dog-lover, could be persuaded to offer an opinion?

Parsons replied that it was 'immensely exciting to have a new ms of yours in the house'; quite how exciting he was yet to discover.

Ackerley described the novel as: 'Homosexuality and bestiality mixed, and largely recorded in dialogue: the figure of Freud suspended gleefully above.' Woolf duly delivered his reader's report, which was cautiously favourable. He admired the novel, but wondered whether Ackerley or Parsons would risk publication. He also wrote personally to Ackerley saying that he thought the book 'a work of art. I enjoyed it and your skill immensely – it is a work of great fascination.' He outlined his objections under three headings: decency, which he thought could be got round with a few alterations 'even with the present furor puritannicus'; libel, which was a greater obstacle, since any alteration would destroy the book; and Ackerley himself: 'whether you could really from your point of view publish. No one except you can really be the final judge of this, but for what it is worth my opinion would be – no.'

Unsurprisingly, the threat of proceedings for libel and obscenity alarmed Parsons. The company had, after all, only recently sailed fairly close to the wind with *Hindoo Holiday*. It was abundantly clear that in its present form the book was unpublishable, and Parsons went to see Ackerley to tell him so personally over dinner. Ackerley had realized that the homosexual element would prove a stumbling block, particularly since the book is narrated in the first person, but he had not really considered the libel aspect.

> I am rather naïve in such matters [he wrote to Woolf], as I was explaining, rather tipsily, to Ian. It had not occurred to me that the working classes brought actions, even if they ever read books, and the only thing that worried me a little in the matter of publication was that the real Johnny might, by chance, come upon it and be hurt in his feelings.[1] For unfortunately he turns out rather nastier in the story than in fact he was or than I intended. That was the only hesitancy that troubled my innocent little mind.

Taking up Woolf's third point, Ackerley wrote:

[1] In the novel Ackerley becomes 'Frank', Freddie becomes 'Johnny', Eileen becomes 'Megan' (having at one stage been 'Maureen'), Queenie becomes 'Evie', Molly and Ron become 'Millie and Tom Winder', and Nancy appears as Frank's cousin, 'Margaret'.

As for myself, if the story is to be taken as a confession, as you seem to think it would be, I don't care a rap – but, further naïvety, I am not quite clear in my mind as to the grounds on which your advice would go against publication, and wish you had been more explicit. I mean that autobiographically there are two 'embarrassing' situations in the book, the overt homosexuality and relationship with the dog, and I am not sure whether your view is that I should be regarded askance for admitting the former, or pitied for the latter. Perhaps you mean both.

'Yes, I do mean both,' Woolf replied with the sort of forthrightness Ackerley was accustomed to use himself. 'Askance for the homosexuality and contempt for your own naïvety.' This was a blow, but Ackerley conceded that Woolf and Parsons were right, and he offered 'some bits and pieces (still canine I fear)', which included 'My Dog, Tulip' and a number of other essays about Queenie. 'I don't think they contain any libel,' he wrote cheerfully, 'though some of them are not in the best of taste.' Blithely unsuspecting of what was to come, Parsons said that he was delighted by the suggestion.

Of all Ackerley's books *My Dog Tulip* is the one which still shocks people, often provoking an instinctive response of embarrassment or disgust. This was part of his strategy, of course, in providing chapters which discuss Queenie's sex-life and bowels in unabashed detail. As in *Hindoo Holiday* and *My Father and Myself*, in *My Dog Tulip* Ackerley unobtrusively employs the literary device of posing as an innocent narrator who blandly reveals the most surprising and shocking things, and with the professional insouciance of a showman, pulls aside curtains normally left drawn. Thus the Maharajah's sexual tastes are presented as entirely natural, rather eccentric perhaps, amusing even, but nothing to get excited about. Similarly the famous opening sentence of *My Father and Myself* – 'I was born in 1896 and my parents were married in 1919.' – is studiedly casual, its elaboration almost world-weary: 'Nearly a quarter of a century may seem rather procrastinatory for making up one's mind, but I expect that the longer such rites are postponed the less indispensable they appear and that, as the years rolled by, my parents gradually forgot the anomaly of their situation.' In each book Ackerley has an extraordinary tale to tell and the surprises are all the stronger for being presented with such calm. Each of the three books is a voyage of discovery, in which the innocent abroad, the inexperienced pet-owner, and the family historian (three standard 'types' usually to be avoided) set out to have their expectations hilariously confounded. In *My Dog Tulip* Ackerley is at pains to take the reader with him, not lecture him or provide a stuffy 'users' manual'. He wanted it 'to be firmly planted (as it is) upon inexperience and personal adventure – I don't want anyone to have the opportunity of saying, "Bloody cheek! Telling us how to treat our dogs when we know far more about them than he does."'

There is no doubt at all that Ackerley thoroughly enjoyed shocking people,[1] but his evident delight in doing so risked obscuring the serious motive behind this impulse. 'I am not anxious to spare the feelings of the philistines,' he told Stephen Spender when discussing *We Think the World of You*; but he hoped to provoke something more than mere fury.

> To speak the truth, I think that people *ought* to be upset, and if I had a paper I would upset them all the time; I think that life is so important and, in its workings, so upsetting, that nobody should be spared, but that it should [be] rammed down their throats from morning to night. And may those who cannot take it die of it; it is what we want.

The crux of that notorious pronouncement is Ackerley's belief in the *importance* of life. He had no real belief in any after-life and so thought that people had to make the most of the temporal one they undeniably had. He was fond of quoting a line from Sophocles' *Antigone*: 'We have only a little time to please the living, but all eternity to love the dead.'[2] Most of *My Dog Tulip* had been written against the background of Nancy's suicide attempt and Ackerley had no illusions

---

[1] One draft of *My Father and Myself* apparently began: 'My father's penis was twelve inches long.' Several people claim to have seen this draft, but it has since disappeared.

[2] This, in fact, amounts to misquotation, since Ackerley takes it to mean the exact opposite of what Sophocles intended. In the play, Antigone is justifying her determination to defy King Creon, who has decreed that her brother, Polynices, should remain unburied outside the gates of Thebes. When her sister, Ismene, warns her that her actions will result in the death penalty, Antigone replies: 'I will bury my brother; / And if I die for it, what happiness! / Convicted of reverence – I shall be content / To lie beside the brother whom I love. / We have only a little time to please the living, / But all eternity to love the dead.'

about how upsetting life could be. But he also felt that life should be celebrated and it is this sense which permeates the pages of the book. It was his answer to those, like Forster, who failed to see the point of Queenie. Ackerley wrote of her that she possessed 'the art of life' and greeted 'each new day with the utmost eagerness and anticipation of pleasure. That is how life should be lived, this adventure of life; she provides me with my lesson . . .' In celebrating Queenie Ackerley is celebrating life, in all its mess and muddle, and mourning its transience.

It was the mess and muddle, of course, which caused all the problems. Lyrical descriptions of Queenie breasting the bracken on Wimbledon Common were evidently and attractively celebratory; descriptions of her sexual and excretory activities were not. He wanted to tread the fine line between shocking people and merely disgusting them: 'It is the wrinkled nose, not the lifted brow that I fear,' he confessed. 'If people are disgusted they won't read.' *Encounter* had in fact turned down the chapter about Queenie's sex-life and this had rather unnerved him. He tried out his essays on friends to test their reactions and was encouraged by their response. He particularly valued the opinion of the anthropologist Geoffrey Gorer, a regular contributor to *The Listener* who owned a golden labrador bitch called Meg. Gorer was a difficult man, much disliked in some quarters for his spikiness and his obsessive enmities in the anthropological world, and his friendship with Ackerley was at once intimate and uneasy. Ackerley disliked many aspects of Gorer's personality and often found his behaviour intolerable, but he also thought him highly intelligent, which he was, and respected his judgement. Even Forster, an inveterate cat man, was enthusiastic about the chapters Ackerley had sent him:

> Your book [i.e. manuscript], besides impressing me enormously, made me realize my own make-up in a way I never have before – my repulsion I mean from all excretions from snot to shit, which must be more than normal. I am rather humiliated, still it's interesting. No washing in the blood of the Lamb for me thank you.

Ian Parsons seems to have shared Forster's squeamishness and may have regretted the encouragement he had given. He said that Chatto and Windus could not accept 'Liquids and Solids', as Ackerley had graphically titled the chapter on Queenie's bowels, and that in the sex chapters they would have 'to cut out *every* dirty joke, every reference to vulvas, vaseline and penises.' The decision was not the publishers' alone, since if a prosecution were brought against the book the printers would also end up in court, and it now seemed unlikely that they would handle the offending pages.

Ackerley was dismayed by Parsons' decision. He spent the greater part of his job at *The Listener* trying to avoid euphemism and challenge censorship, and he had no intention of being thwarted over his own work. Furthermore, the advance Chatto and Windus were offering would not be sufficient to give him enough spare money to go on a much-needed holiday. Forster suggested that Ackerley should be very firm with his publishers, and should bargain for an improved advance. He thought that no publisher would handle 'the shit chapter', but that some compromise could be reached over the sex one. He added that if the printers refused to print 'kit and shunt' and the whole deal fell through, he would *give* Ackerley £200.

It soon became clear that Chatto and Windus were going to demand 'ruthless excisions' which Ackerley felt would 'destroy the "beastliness" which I wished to restore to the life of beasts'. He had always resented the fact that the cuts imposed upon *Hindoo Holiday* by Chatto and Windus had spoilt the book for him, and so he decided to approach another publisher. He offered the book to Frederic Warburg, enticing him with the assertion that the subject of canine anal glands had 'never been aired before, so you have a scoop'. He was particularly proud of his investigation of this matter, in which he surpassed Konrad Lorenz, doyen of animal behaviourists. Letters were written to the Professor of Zoology at Nottingham University, telephone calls made to the Director of London Zoo, and veterinary surgeons were taken out to lunch so that his observations about anal glands could be discussed and confirmed. Warburg replied, offering much improved terms and promising as few cuts as possible. 'I am quite delighted to think that we shall have this most exceptional book for publication,' he wrote, 'and look forward to a rather lively time with it.'

16

Last years at The Listener

IN order to avoid too much liveliness, and 'in view of the most unusual and, indeed, unique, character' of *My Dog Tulip*, Warburg decided to submit the typescript to lawyers, perhaps the first time that such a step had been taken over an 'animal book'. Secker and Warburg asked Thurston Hogarth, a solicitor who worked for the company of Oswald Hickson, Collier and Co in the Strand, to give an opinion as to whether the book could be prosecuted for obscene libel, whether it 'would tend to deprave and corrupt even minds open to such an influence'. Hogarth thought that 'since dogs cannot read, no section of the public is open to corruption' and no 'rational judge and jury' would convict the book on such grounds.

> I have, of course, not the slightest doubt that there would be broad sections of the pekinese owning public who would be shocked to the core by the detailed description of a bitch and her love life, but this can hardly constitute an invitation to sodomy, even for the most depraved. While, therefore, passages from 'Tulip' might not normally be found outside a technical publication, on the other hand 'Tulip' is an equally serious work, if in a lighter vein.
>
> There are, of course, words in the text that seldom find themselves in print; in particular, for example, Part 2, page 2 where there is a splendid exchange of gutter English.[1] I think, however, mere coarse-

[1] Between Ackerley and a bicyclist who complains that Tulip is fouling the pavement:
'What's the bleeding road for?'
'For turds like you!' I retorted.
'Bleeding dogs!' he screamed, almost falling off his bicycle in his rage and excitement as he swivelled his body round to hurl denunciation at me.
'Arseholes!' I replied.

ness is unlikely to occasion a prosecution since, taking some liberty with Mr Justice Stable's Judgement, we are entitled to know that cyclists by the 'Star and Garter Hotel' do not necessarily talk like debutantes at Queen Charlotte's Ball.

He suggested that any modifications of language would be a matter for the editor rather than the law. This good news was undermined by Hogarth's concern that certain passages might invite a civil libel action, in particular from the dog-owners Ackerley pillories in the course of the book. He wondered how far the author had disguised these people and their circumstances, and suggested that further deletions or disguise might be necessary to avoid any action for defamation of character.

Ackerley was now keen to see the book in print and agreed to most of the suggestions, but there was one further obstacle to overcome: the printers. 'It is not a foregone conclusion that the b.f.s will agree to print it,' Warburg warned, 'but all being well they will.' They didn't. Whilst they were prepared to print such oaths as 'Arseholes!', they balked at the words 'by his penis' in a passage describing 'Tulip' dragging her still tumescent lover across the lawn at Wendy. Further alterations ('for "my leg and overcoat" substitute "me"'; 'for "a poke" read "some sex"') were made and the book was finally accepted. There had also been trouble over some of the footnotes, in particular one in which Ackerley speculated about the psychological damage done to both dogs and humans by sexual continence. Another loss – at what stage it is unclear – was a footnote to the passage where 'Tulip' finally mates outside Mon Repos (as Ackerley had rechristened Wendy). In the published version Ackerley annotates his observation that Dusty's detumescence took 'a full half-hour' with a note: 'It could have been an ˥ore.' In one manuscript version of this page, the footnote

ˎeen longer. Dogs, foxes and wolves are the only
ˎwe know whom Nature locks together in this way
ˎicular determination to preserve them. Other
ˎuickly. With cats, lions and monkeys it is all
ˎ the elephant, according to Ford, takes
ˎElephant Bill, five to ten minutes; the
ˎᴣulls, stallions, rams and stags ˎ

ejaculate and withdraw soon after penetration. Hen Stick-fast fleas, it is true, remain in conjunction for twenty-five minutes, but the Honourable Miriam Rothschild, who has not yet elucidated the mystery of the construction of the flea's penis, is still unable to inform us what they are doing all that time. Among human beings, the British have not been so thoroughly investigated as the Americans, but my mother once told me that she surprised the butler embracing the under-housemaid one evening, and heard him say, in a wheedling voice, 'Come on, it won't take a second.'

It may be that this was jettisoned at the same time as Ackerley's plans to illustrate his text with snapshots he had taken of Queenie flirting with local mongrels and fouling assorted Putney footpaths. Instead he submitted some sketches he had made of Queenie which he thought might serve for the dust-jacket, but these were not considered strong enough. The young artist Lucian Freud was invited to Star and Garter Mansions to make some drawings of Queenie, but the afternoon was not a success, since the dog would not settle, and eventually this idea was abandoned in favour of a letter-press design.

The book was now arranged in six chapters and an appendix. Joining 'My Dog, Tulip', 'Liquids and Solids' and the three chapters covering Ackerley's attempts to get 'Tulip' mated and to dispose of her puppies, was a section entitled 'The Turn of the Screw'. Ackerley had been very unsure about this chapter, which, he explained to Geoffrey Gorer, was 'a kind of prose poem about the passage of time and the frustrations of life'. Whilst he considered this beautifully wrought meditation 'the main point of the book', he feared that others might dismiss it as 'a piece of sentimental whimsy'. In particular, he was concerned about a reference he had inserted to 'young Holland', a fifteen-year-old schoolboy who had been found dead on Wimbledon Common in 1926.

Michael Holland had been a brilliant pupil at Lancing College, studying for a scholarship to Oxford. However, his school reports had commented upon his effeminacy. His housemaster had insisted that there was 'nothing vicious' about Holland's behaviour, but that he used perfume and avoided games. He had been mocked by schoolfellows about his 'curious habits', and although they insisted that he had not been bullied, he ran away. His guardian had decided to keep him at home, but Holland he wanted to return to school. He was told that he would probably be caned. He then disappeared and was found two days later face downward in a swampy part of the Common. Although death had been caused by asphyxiation, the autopsy appears to have been rather confused. The doctor had said that there were faint traces of what might be potassium cyanide in the body, but also thought that death could have been caused by an epileptic fit. An open verdict was brought in, but the implication was that the boy, who had been remarkably healthy, had committed suicide. An account of this wasteful death had been published in *The Times* and Ackerley had cut it out and kept it, as he often did with items that interested him. He told Gorer:

> It made a strong mark upon my young crusading homosexual mind and, one day, I thought, I will do something for young Holland, though possibly he was an odious youth. So you see he is, like the rest, part of the true furniture of Wimbledon Common.

He incorporated it in his meditation and referred the reader, in a footnote which much moved Forster, to the original report. Gorer approved the chapter and Ackerley was very relieved. As he later told Roy Fuller:

> I was pleased with the last chapter when at last I saw how to do it, how to do a portrait of Wimbledon Common and to convey, within its setting, an impression of the passage of time, the rise and fall of the seasons, the pressures of life and death and the impossibility of escape from responsibility and the sorrows of the world; but when I got it it was rather fun, like playing an organ.

The appendix contained a short dissertation upon the sexual needs of dogs and upon the human race's disinclination to consider these seriously because of 'embarrassment, fear, snobbery'. The addition of an appendix was not entirely satisfactory, but Ackerley was obliged to use this device again when he came to write *My Father and Myself*. He would have preferred to work such addenda into the main body of the text, but when they would not fit, or made the text overlong, he decided that it was better that they should be retained in a postscript rather than be discarded or allowed to spoil the shape and structure of his books.

My Dog Tulip was scheduled for publication in the summer of 1956, but before this happened Ackerley was obliged to go into hospital. As Lionel Fielden had predicted, Ackerley was becoming deaf. His left ear was still functioning clearly, but he could hear almost nothing with his right and an operation was to be performed to repair his eardrum with a graft taken from his thigh. Although he dreaded the prospect, he was not pleased when the operation was delayed because Nancy chose (as he saw it) to fall ill with pleurisy and pneumonia and had to be nursed back to health. In April he booked into a public ward at St Thomas's Hospital. He affected still to believe that his deafness was partially self-inflicted, brought about by a habit of blocking out the chatter of people who bored or annoyed him, and insisted that he was going into hospital merely to satisfy those who complained that conversation with him was becoming difficult. As he wrote to May Buckingham after the operation:

> Since I am the most arrant physical coward that ever walked, I rather preen myself now on having endured it all. Excepting for Jonathan who laid down his life for his friend, few people can have behaved as considerately as myself in laying down my ear.

The surgeon discovered that Ackerley's deafness had not been caused by a defective eardrum after all, but by several exostoses, or growths of bone, which he removed. The operation became one of Ackerley's grand set pieces and whilst he was recuperating he regaled several of his friends with accounts of his experience. As a former nurse, May Buckingham (on holiday at the time) was teased about the horrors of hospital:

> There were moments, when you perhaps with ravished eyes were regarding the wonders of Olympia or Delphi and I was observing my neighbours who preceded me to the slaughter house being wheeled off in their nasty little shroud-like shifts and wheeled back, hours later, insensible, bandaged, groaning and sometimes bleeding, that I said to myself with astonishment and terror 'What in the world possessed me?' and wondered whether I could not still send for my clothes and take to my heels – even though the side of my head had already been shaved.

He was indeed wheeled back into the ward bleeding, his ear plugged with cotton wool, but was told that the operation had been a success.

True I nearly died afterwards [he told Forster]: it seemed I liked the state of anaesthesia so much that I would not emerge from it, and six hours later it took four nurses, two doctors and a heart specialist to slap me back to life, tipping my bed up as they once did yours, when you had your second prostate. I had turned an unbecoming shade of citron . . .

He told Spender that his last memory before the anaesthetic took effect was 'of green linen trousers stretched over the bottom of a student' and that it was *eight* hours before consciousness was regained:

I daresay that in a person like myself who has no very passionate grip on life, the soul is liable to try to slip away when it finds a chance. My only sub-conscious memory of those fifteen hours is that something very unpleasant was happening to my penis. I must ask the doctors about this. I felt I screamed and struggled as though it were being cut off. Yet why should I mind? I seldom use it, except to pee.

He suggested that someone should set a ballet in an operating theatre, with surgeon and students pirouetting in their green linen and masks like Picasso figures.

In fact the operation was less of a success than had been predicted and he was to grow increasingly deaf over the years.

Meanwhile Fred Warburg was still rather nervous about the public reaction to *My Dog Tulip* and asked Ackerley whether a bouquet of 'puffs' could be gathered to print on the book's dust-jacket in order 'to off-set the storm of indignation that is expected'. William Plomer submitted 'A revolutionary book', and Julian Huxley offered 'most entertaining and sometimes instructive.' As with *Hindoo Holiday*, Forster prevaricated, one minute prepared to write something, the next minute recanting. He eventually came up with: 'However much readers dislike or like this book, they will be obliged to agree that it is unlike any other book that they have read.' Unsurprisingly, Warburg was 'not much thrilled' by this and so Forster told him that he need not feel obliged to use it. Ackerley, who had thought Forster had in fact withdrawn permission to use the quotation, was appalled to see it on the finished copies and took Warburg to task. Eventually this mis-understanding was sorted out and Forster wrote a letter to Ackerley that might have proved rather more useful than his distinctly bet-hedging public pronouncement:

I am re-reading with increased intensity, *more* admiration and amusement, *more* disgust and gust, *more* gusto and disgusto, more *certainty* that it is one of the most important books to come out during my life time. It compels a re-examination which reaches far beyond bow-wows. It makes me realize that I have specialized lasciviously on the human male, and not taken account of what lies outside. Your own specialization – perhaps because it is not lascivious, certainly because it is unusual, has opened my eyes.

. . . I am delighted with the excellence of the writing, from the nice use of words upwards, but it is the re-awakening power that I find so remarkable.

'So having provided me with an under-statement before,' Ackerley remarked to Warburg, 'he now provides me with an over-statement.'

Forster's reticence, understandable in the case of *Hindoo Holiday*, is difficult to explain in this instance. His 'mouldy old mother', as Ackerley dubbed the redoubtable spanner in Forster's works, had been dead for some years. He seems to have had no particular aversion to helping to launch the books of friends, for a few years later he was to write a laudatory introduction to *The Warm Country*, a collection of short stories by Donald Windham. It may simply have been a fear of making a pronouncement on a book he felt uneasy about. He need not have worried, for the book was well received. It is telling that he was later to choose *My Dog Tulip* as his 'Book of the Year' for the *Sunday Times*, to which he contributed a far warmer salute than he had when one was urgently needed. ('I fancy it was the only book he read last year,' Ackerley told Francis King, 'so it wasn't too difficult for him to call it the best.')

As well as the 'puffs', a blurb was concocted which warned parents not to

present [the book] to their children without a previous careful reading themselves. For here at last is the truth about dogs and bitches, not a pretty picture sentimentalized but a down-to-earth study, a book likely to offend those who care more for themselves than their dogs.

For the most part this calculated defiance paid off and when the book was published on 16 July 1956 the reaction of both friends and critics was gratifying. In particular, Ackerley was very pleased with a review by Richard Price which appeared in *Punch* and struck exactly the right note. Indeed, so pleased was he that he went to the library to copy it out by hand:

> This is the first highbrow dog-book ever written, highbrow not in the sense of relating the keeping of a dog to a general theory, but of striking the note of the solemn highbrow joke that is essentially serious. It will, one hopes, infuriate the stupid dog-lover. It may make non-owners queasy by its scatological and gynaecological detail, for it is, among other things, a beautiful plea for the understanding of the sexual nature of bitches.

His own critic, in an unsigned review, described it as 'a remarkable and unusual book: one that the reader may very well throw down but will certainly not put down'. The more squeamish reviewers admired the manner but deplored the matter, regretting, in the words of the *Spectator*'s Virginia Graham, that Ackerley had 'plant[ed] the beautiful Tulip in a redolent manure heap'. Some people felt that Ackerley had made the mistake of rubbing the reader's nose in it rather than the dog's. Ackerley was once again disappointed that few people realized or admitted how funny the book was. He would have liked someone to write that *My Dog Tulip* was the most indecent book he or she had read, but also one of the funniest, something, indeed, along the lines of a letter written to him by Roy Fuller:

> The reviews have given but a pale and garbled idea of *Tulip* as you must know. First of all, it is tremendously funny. In bed last night I tried to read aloud to Kate [Fuller's wife] the episode of Max and the matches, but couldn't get it out for laughing. And then all is wonderfully observed and put together: the sense of *time* I thought particularly skilfully done. But most important of all and what moved me most was the great courage about, and pity and love for, physical life – man's not merely Tulip's.

Ackerley replied:

> I too was disappointed that the blessed booklet was taken so
> seriously. It's the trouble, I suppose, with having A Reputation;
> oracular utterances are then expected. Scarcely anyone has said it
> affords a good laugh, even a little cry for the more serious – selling
> remarks – Naomi Lewis poking about for a prevailing 'mood'
> thought I had a horror of organic life and was writing a last chapter
> to Gulliver. Still, give her her due she cracked a very amusing joke
> herself. But you are one of the few people who have understood
> what I was trying to convey.

Not all Ackerley's friends were as enthusiastic as Fuller. Warburg had
apparently miscalculated when he sent Harold Nicolson a copy of the
book. Nicolson informed his wife:

> I think Joe Ackerley must have gone off his head. His book *Tulip* is
> disgusting.
>   I could hardly read it and shall certainly not review it. I was so
> shocked that I thought it must be Victorian inhibitions, so I asked
> Colin [Fenton, with whom he shared his Albany flat] to read it. He
> was equally revolted. You see it is all about the functions of the body
> and spares us no detail at all.

Edith Sitwell agreed, privately dismissing the book as 'meaningless
filth about a dog', and Richard Church lamented his friend's development of 'interests that struck me as being a calculated defiance of
normal good taste'. Others did their best to promote the book, none
more entertainingly than the novelist Julia Strachey, who wrote to
Frances Partridge:

> Another excitement in this house has been reading Joe Ackerley's
> little book *My Dog Tulip*, which though entirely about dogs and
> bitches is a veritable little marvel of brilliance and shockingness. I
> don't know when I read anything so indecent, disgusting, touching,
> beautiful and stylish; I do fervently recommend it. Now I am telling
> all the tweedy philistine old crabs up here [in Newcastle] to read this
> sweet book about a man and his loyal doggy, and revelling in the
> idea of their scarification as they proceed.

Meanwhile, both the subject and the author of the book were beginning to feel their ages, which were eleven and sixty respectively. Deafness worried Ackerley more than it did Queenie, who was now able to go about her business unaware of sudden and frightening noises. Both she and her master were suffering from rheumatism and were obliged to embark upon a course of Bemax and vitamins which neither much liked. Whilst Queenie appeared to benefit from her innumerable tablets and supplements, Ackerley was obliged to take pain-killers and buy a new Sleepsounda mattress, thus discarding the horsehair one which had 'supported my ancient body, and many other bodies too in its time, for at least thirty years'. They increasingly came to resemble a Darby-and-Joan couple as they toyed with their health foods and tottered around on their walks.

In the early summer of 1957 Ackerley's teeth began to give way and Queenie developed a septic womb. This distressing infection, heralded by a high temperature and an alarming flux 'like pink toothpaste pressed out of a tube', had already caused problems some years previously. On that occasion the vet had told Ackerley that he could administer a course of injections which would clear up the infection, but that he personally advised a hysterectomy. When Ackerley had nervously asked whether the operation was dangerous, the vet's reply was not entirely reassuring. He had performed the operation hundreds of times:

Matter of fact I did two only yesterday, both in the owners' flats. Took my anaesthetist with me. One was a very old bitch, she could scarcely walk she was so blown. I whipped out her womb on the kitchen table and she's as good as new. The other was a young Boxer and – funny thing – she came out of the anaesthetic all right; we gave her a dish of tea, which she drank, then she laid her cheek down on the arm of the chair where she was sitting, gave a sigh and died.

Ackerley had decided upon the injections. After a few days of improvement, Queenie had had a relapse. Clearly she should have had the operation, but the question was, who was to perform it? His own vet's record did not seem entirely satisfactory, added to which he wore suede shoes, he spelt his forename 'Denys', and his female assistants were suspiciously glamorous. A second vet, when consulted, decided to administer another course of injections and this had cleared up the infection, so that there had been no trouble for two and a half years.

This time Ackerley insisted that Queenie should have the operation, but when told that this could not be performed for some ten days began to worry that she might not survive that long. However, she was given an injection and began to improve, so he then wondered whether it was right to subject her to major surgery. He arrived at the Royal Veterinary College and, after a consultation with the surgeon, cancelled the operation and went back to his own vet to resume the course of injections. Queenie appeared to improve once again. The account he wrote of this farce should, he suggested, have been given the title 'Infirmity of Purpose'.

By now Ackerley had become interested in the entire animal kingdom, and in man's relation to it which he regarded as almost entirely malign. He read a great deal about birds, beasts and reptiles, acquiring vast amounts of arcane material with which he attempted to entertain and interest his friends. Not everyone was receptive to his enthusiastic exclamations about the number of teeth to be found in the mouth of a tadpole (640 apparently), but his interest in natural history led to his being employed as an occasional reviewer by Janet Adam Smith, now literary editor of the *New Statesman*. A review published in December 1957 took several pot-shots at a couple of big-game hunters who had written their memoirs. It opened:

> Colonel Meinertzhagen and Mr von Rogister are both big-game hunters. Fifty years separate their activities. During that period ninety per cent of the wild life of Africa has been destroyed, some species are in danger of extinction, and the sportsman-hunter has become a controversial figure. People tend to look at him askance and wonder what went wrong with his childhood. Awkward questions pop: 'Why not stalk with a camera instead of a rifle?' Both our authors are conscious of criticism; both return lame answers.

Ackerley suggested that Meinertzhagen, who had served in Kenya during the White settlement in the early years of the century, was a pathological case ('there is evidence of father-trouble') who simply enjoyed killing and did not particularly care whether he looked down the barrel of his gun at a lion or a troublesome native so long as blood was spilled. Ackerley also made a mock-innocent diagnosis of von Rogister's passion for bagging rhinos:

> His delight in hunting, which he, too, fails to elucidate ('that inexpressible bond that unites the hunter and the hunted'), seems to be the horn. He is obsessed by the out-size. The large horn, larger and larger horns, he cannot resist them and, when he gets them home, stands 'gazing at them in wonder for hours on end, and touching them reflectively!'

In fact both men got off lightly, as may be judged by earlier drafts of this review, which was to have included further books 'drenched in animal blood'. One draft is headed 'Dangerous Animals, or, Some Nasty People', amongst whom Ackerley counts William Bazé, author of *Tiger! Tiger!*, bracketed with Meinertzhagen as a conscienceless psychopath who has 'wrought much havoc among the tigers of Indo-China in his time'. Ackerley quotes at length from Bazé's gloating descriptions of the beasts he has shot whilst they were eating or 'in the middle of a romance', and of the death agonies of those he has poisoned or caught in traps.

> In his preface [Bazé] says: 'If, as they say, there is a deity that protects drunks, there is certainly another that watches over big-game hunters!'. It is indeed the melancholy reflection that has haunted us throughout his book.

In another draft Ackerley wrote:

> Colonel Meinertzhagen says he has never seen animals copulating. Would he have shot them if he had? No, unofficial conduct. But M. Bazé would, and would have moralized about it afterwards . . . Can animals copulate now in any kind of privacy? What a life they lead, the animals! With native warriors [armed] with spears and European hunters looking for sport, in an ever dwindling kingdom, how do they manage their private affairs? Where do they go to have their babies? Colonel Meinertzhagen did not see that either, I fancy, though he shot some beasts that were on the point of giving birth.

The animals . . . who thinks of them in their hardships, who cares?
Animals, persecuted for their tusks, their hides, their meat, their
tails, their horns (aphrodisiac for the Chinese! What a filthy notion!
Propping up the flabby old pricks, as though there were not enough
humans already) – and on top of all else to be persecuted by rich
European [sic] psychopaths like Hemingway, to [solve] some
psychological problem, to prove how brave and manly they are –
when we know that almost all the animals are only too happy to get
out of humans' ways. Should we not send all big-game hunters to
psychoanalysts?

The battle Ackerley had been conducting in private, in Putney and on
Wimbledon Common, was now in the public domain. He also began
writing to the newspapers in response to things he had read. His
interest in the Guards was now confined to their headgear: was it really
necessary, he wondered, to use real bearskins? He also had an
entertaining skirmish with John Sparrow who, with William Plomer,
had formed a mock Anti-Dog League. The two men scoured newspapers for 'horror stories' (dogs devouring babies and so on) which
they would clip out and send each other. Sparrow had written to *The
Times* complaining that a man who had kicked and trampled a puppy
which had annoyed him in a park was jailed for six weeks whereas a
motorist who had injured a woman wheeling a pram had only received
a sentence of four weeks. Ackerley rose to the bait and wrote a reply in
which he said that had Sparrow trampled on *his* puppy, 'I would fell
him to the ground and trample upon him – that is to say, if the law was
not prepared to trample upon him for me.' He claimed that the letter
was intended as a private joke, but a friend to whom he had sent it
(almost certainly Plomer) had posted it to the newspaper. Nonetheless,
he was not entirely displeased when it was published, for it drew public
attention to a topic which was to preoccupy his old age: the rights of
animals.

Meanwhile, at *The Listener*, Ackerley and Alan Thomas had achieved
some kind of *modus vivendi* by the 1950s, although an incident
recalled by Lettice Cooper suggests that the old enmities had not
entirely died out. Cooper was reviewing novels for the magazine
during this period and found Ackerley 'unhappy, rather dull, and a bit

hard on people'. When Thomas's indifferent novel, *The Director*, was sent to her, Ackerley made it clear that he would be delighted if she 'gave it hell'. This small revenge was one of the very few examples of Ackerley's attempting to influence his reviewers, and suggests a deep-seated resentment. 'Ackerley was vicious about Thomas,' Cooper recalled. She ignored Ackerley's suggestion and managed to steer a middle course in her review, describing the book as 'sober'.

Although he claimed to be bored with the job, Ackerley was now doing it without too much interference from the authorities. After some fifteen years at *The Listener* he had become very much a grand old man of the BBC, a position he found uncomfortable. He detested the idea that he 'belonged' to such an organization or that he should be seen as some sort of respectable pillar of the Establishment. (Unlike most of his friends, he was never listed in *Who's Who*.) He continued to search the ranks of the young and talented in order to find new reviewers. His method of recruitment may have been unorthodox, but he had a sure eye. Quentin Bell was enlisted to replace Wyndham Lewis as art critic largely as a reward for driving Ackerley to the station after he had been lunching at Charleston with Bell's parents.[1] Bell recalled:

> I needed an excuse and a free ticket for London [from Sussex, where he lived] in order to see my future wife. It seemed fearful cheek to ask for the job but [Joe] was very kind, he always was, and I wrote criticism for him until he retired.

Another unusual but rewarding recruitment had taken place in 1949 when Forster, who was by then living at King's College, Cambridge as an Honorary Fellow, invited Ackerley to meet a 'naughty under-graduate', the future novelist Simon Raven. According to Raven, he and Ackerley found themselves standing together at a college urinal, where, 'as we buttoned our flies', they struck a bargain: Ackerley would supply Raven with reviewing in exchange for 'Morganiana', or disobliging stories about Forster's Cambridge behaviour. 'I thought it would be a beginning,' Raven recalled:

---

[1] Lewis had been obliged to retire because he was going blind, his sight affected by the brain tumour which would eventually kill him. His farewell piece, entitled 'The Sea-Mists of Winter', was published in May 1951.

333

In fact it was a jolly good one, for which I have been most grateful to Joe ever since; for while we were both as good as our word, Joe was much better: whereas I could only supply Morgan stories up to the time I left Cambridge, Joe supplied me with work, when I needed it, for long afterwards, and twice let me have three months stint at the fatly paid and fully signed novel column.

One perk of this particular reviewing task was that all novels that came into *The Listener*'s office would be sent to the critic who could supplement his fee by selling them. Raven recalls sending 'sackloads' of books to Gaston's, the second-hand book dealers. When Raven went into the Army, Ackerley continued to send him books for review, so that he could keep his hand in. In return Ackerley was rewarded by scabrous stories of life at the King's Shropshire Light Infantry barracks at Shrewsbury, where, Raven assured him, the majority of the officers were rampantly homosexual.

It was from amongst his contributors that Ackerley continued to make his friends, inviting them to lunch or dine 'at the Corporation's expense', a phrase which many recall with pleasure. Stuart Hampshire almost always met Ackerley at lunch, usually at Chez Victor in Wardour Street. Ackerley had established a friendly relationship with the proprietor and would tease him about the quality of his wine. 'Monsieur Victor,' he would say grandly, 'you have the sourest wine in London.' He would also exercise his charm on the waiters there and elsewhere, expecting them to take an interest in which soup he should choose from the menu.

Other younger writers Ackerley met and befriended through *The Listener* in the late 1940s and the 1950s included his future literary executor, Francis King, who contributed reviews and poetry, both his own and translations from the Greek; David Sylvester and Andrew Forge, who wrote for the art pages; and the poets James Kirkup and Richard Murphy. The younger generation appeared to be more outspoken and so provided new ammunition in the long battle against Mrs Grundy. Another new friend, Donald Windham, had been 'discovered' by Forster during a trip to America. Forster had encouraged Windham to send some of his stories to *The Listener*. Several of these had a homosexual theme, which Thomas, in spite of his improved regard for Ackerley, still regarded as taboo:

I would have published ['Servants with Torches'] without hesitation if I had been Editor of *The Listener* [Ackerley told Windham in 1952], but my editor won't have it. It's awfully depressing and annoying to be frustrated over it. He's nervous, that's the trouble. I reminded him that the subject is quite commonplace now in novel writing (one of our reviewers indeed remarked about a novel the other day that it would probably be hailed as 'the best homosexual novel of the year'), and if it is acceptable in novels, why not in short stories; but he shook his head.

Oddly enough, the BBC itself did not share Thomas's caution, for when Ackerley offered the story to P. H. Newby for broadcasting on the Third Programme, it was turned down on the grounds of length rather than subject matter. When Windham published the story three years later, Ackerley wrote:

What wretched cowardice and feebleness on my Editor's part to have rejected it. I was so mortified when I read it again, so beautifully done, so exactly right; it would have adorned this paper. Since then he has rejected the picture of a female nude by Delvaux because it had pubic hair, and a poem by Kirkup about a public lavatory. It is no pleasure working for such a paper; one can get nothing at all outré in.

James Kirkup, who had been put forward to Ackerley by William Plomer, was a flamboyant young man from a northern working-class background. A conscientious objector during the war, he may well have recommended himself to Ackerley by his claim to have been responsible for the death of H. A. L. Fisher. Kirkup had come up before Fisher at a military tribunal and had been treated with unseemly disdain by the great man. This was unwise, since Kirkup claims to possess 'the evil eye', which he vindictively flashed upon Fisher. On leaving the hall, Fisher was mown down by a bus. Another attraction was that Kirkup was unashamedly, indeed exhibitionistically, homosexual and was to provide Ackerley with much amusement during their friendship. He also provided him with some fine poems and became something of a protégé, whose talent Ackerley nurtured.

Kirkup was almost from birth a controversialist, and Ackerley was delighted in the early 1950s to be sent a poem entitled 'The Convenience'. Ackerley had worried that an earlier poem, 'A Correct Compassion', would meet with editorial objections on the grounds that open-heart surgery was not a 'nice' subject. In fact there had been no trouble and the poem, one of Kirkup's best-known, was duly published in *The Listener*. 'The Convenience' was also accepted and set up in proof, but Marjorie Redman, the long-serving chief sub-editor of the magazine (and hitherto a supporter of 'difficult' material), was revolted by it, as was 'every female member of the staff'. For once, Thomas supported Ackerley, but Redman insisted that the poem should not be published. 'Do you *want* to read a poem about the smell coming out of a women's lavatory?' she asked. She told Thomas that 'as probably 50% of *The Listener*'s readers were female, probably 50% wouldn't care for Kirkup's poem.' This, at least, was Redman's recollection of events in 1973. In fact the poem was clearly, indeed graphically, about a men's urinal, and Ackerley explained to Kirkup that the 'real' reason the female staff objected was because they 'all felt a deep-seated resentment against men's lavatories because in their own they had to pay a penny to pee'. Whatever the case, the poem was rejected.

Ackerley's younger friends were also useful guides to the homosexual subculture of the 1950s. Although he claimed to be entirely absorbed in Queenie, Ackerley nonetheless continued to take a keen academic interest in such matters. Homosexuality was much in the news during this period as a result of the Wolfenden Committee, a parliamentary commission appointed in 1954 to consider the law relating to homosexual offences. The defection to Russia in 1951 of the two spies, Burgess and Maclean, had alerted the government to the supposed 'dangers' of homosexuality, and in consequence there had followed an unseemly hounding of homosexual men. A pack of uniformed police and *agents provocateurs*, led by the Metropolitan Police Commissioner, Sir John Nott-Bower, and the Home Secretary, Sir David Maxwell-Fyfe, wasted large amounts of public money harrying otherwise law-abiding citizens, hallooed on by the 'popular press' and several baying peers. This 'purge' resulted in a number of highly publicized court cases. Sir John Wolfenden made his report in 1957 and recommended that homosexual acts between consenting adults should be decriminalized. This suggestion encountered fierce opposition and it took another ten years to change the law.[1]

Meanwhile, homosexual meeting-places continued to open and close like umbrellas in showery weather, and in the post-war years Francis King and Simon Raven introduced Ackerley to several clubs and coffee-houses. The Rockingham was rather grand, 'piss-elegant and full of queens who thought they were in the Athenaeum', according to one *habitué*. Much more to Ackerley's taste was the Mousehole, an extremely popular coffee-house in Swallow Street, just off Piccadilly Circus. This was 'a perfectly respectable little place', according to Ackerley, full of rather flamboyant types, who sometimes wore make-up and addressed each other as 'darling', but were otherwise orderly in their conduct. Its name became enshrined in homosexual slang of the period: 'queuing for the Mousehole' was used to denote 'a really squalid and hopeless situation'. At the end of 1957, the police raided the Mousehole on the grounds that it was dangerously overcrowded, full of homosexual men and the haunt of male prostitutes. The raid was set in motion by a P. C. Heaver who had entered the premises in plain clothes and been complimented upon his haircut by a forward young man who also placed a hand upon the constable's sturdy knee.

Fortunately, Forster, who was sometimes to be seen sipping coffee amidst this colourful crowd, was not there at the time. Ackerley was alarmed at the prospect of his distinguished friend's being splashed all

---

[1] One of the few books Ackerley reviewed in *The Listener* was Roger Gellert's *Quaint Honour*, a play about homosexuality in public schools which had caused something of a stir when mounted in a club performance (thus avoiding the wrath of the Lord Chamberlain) at the Arts Theatre. Ackerley had asked Forster to review it, but although Forster admired the 'marvellous superplay', which he felt 'completely abolished morality, society and discipline, and leaves nothing but milk boiling over as the result of affection', he felt unable to review it and asked to be excused. Ackerley used his signed review to attack what he considered the feebleness of the Wolfenden Report which proposed twenty-one as the age of homosexual consent. He opened the review: 'In the present state of our society in which the right of the law to interfere in people's sexual relations is being disputed, it is important that works such as this should be read.' He remarked that the play was 'about the young whom the Report seeks to protect, boys of fifteen to eighteen at a public school, and however "immature" the Report may consider them to be, they are presented here as perfectly in command of their senses and situations and as little likely to be grateful for legislation on their behalf as they are for their house master's pi-jaw – or "set piece", as he calls it – with which the play opens.'

over the *News of the World*, but Forster was more concerned for Ackerley, who might have lost his job had he been involved in a prosecution. In the past Ackerley had sometimes criticized Forster's reluctance to be more open about his homosexuality, pointing to the fine example set by André Gide, to which Forster would reply: 'But Gide hasn't got a mother!' Now that Forster was an orphan, he was prepared to be rather less guarded, and eagerly transferred his custom to Bobbie's, an 'afternoon club' in Soho. This was 'a single rather dingy little room' off Dean Street with a rather more robust, predominantly working-class clientele. There was a bar and a juke-box, and dancing took place upon the crowded floor. Forster liked Bobbie's, although he thought that 'the entrance arrangements were culpably slack' and suggested that in the wake of the Mousehole raid, Ackerley should have a quiet word with the club's secretary in order to tighten security. He also encouraged Ackerley to make a public issue of the Mousehole raid, which had resulted in a prosecution for 'disorderly conduct'. Ackerley regarded the whole incident as yet 'another piece of unnecessary interference in people's private lives' and drafted an indignant letter to send to the papers. Forster thought that he had got the tone wrong:

> Be frisky, but not 'we homosexuals' nor so much about yourself, lest it humourlessly be brought against you. 'I have occasionally drawn a cup of coffee in the Mousehole myself little knowing of my peril, or that a policeman might be observing me and might demand my name and address because my taste in clothes differed from his' – is about the level.

Ackerley wanted the law properly defined so that it could be made clear whether men were breaking the law if they wore jewels, painted their faces or addressed each other as 'darling': 'Could we have some ruling on such matters, I wanted to ask.' However, he soon became discouraged and never finished the letter.

> I wanted to be tiresome to the Home Office and rather wish I'd gone through with it; but I've written and published similar protests before, and one gets bored after the mounting surge of indignation. One feels that nothing will ever be done in this country, and that whenever people are observed uninhibitedly enjoying themselves, public opinion and the police will always step in.

One man and his dog: Ackerley and Queenie taken by James Kirkup at his Wiltshire cottage.

'The most admired dog in Putney': Queenie, with Star and Garter Mansions in the background.

Queenie fouling a footway in Putney. One of a series of photographs with which Ackerley had hoped to illustrate *My Dog Tulip*.

One of Ackerley's sketches of Queenie, made in the 1950s.

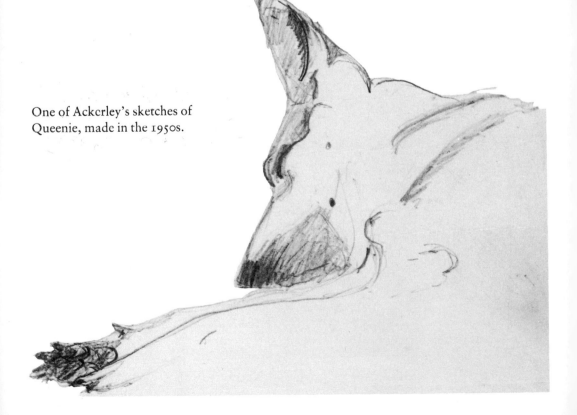

Mrs Gertrude Fowler, Ackerley's Aunt Bunny, who lived with him from 1946 until her death in 1961. A former star of the musical stage, she was once described as 'a figure entirely out of fiction'.

'You have always reigned in my heart as the dearest and wisest of women,' Ackerley told May Buckingham, seen here in the garden of her house at Shepherd's Bush in the 1950s, with E. M. Forster, Ackerley, and her son, Robin.

Ackerley and Jack Sprott in the 1950s.

Diana Petre in the 1950s.

ACKERLEY ABROAD, 1960
'Strong feeling, for the first time in my life,
of not ever having to return. Go anywhere but back.'

In the courtyard of a museum in
Tripoli with Donald Windham.

With a stray Athenian kitten: 'Considering
how neglectful they are of cats, it is a good
thing the Greeks have no dogs,' Ackerley
commented.

In Japan with Francis King's students.

Feeding deer in Nara Park.

My Sister and Myself: Nancy (65) and Ackerley (67),
drawn by Don Bachardy in the summer of 1963.

Ackerley at his desk.

Nancy and Ackerley in Bath with James Kirkup's mother, October 1962. 'She is not the most interesting companion in the world,' Ackerley complained of his sister.

Ackerley in Villiers David's flat in St James's, where there was access to a well-stocked bar.

Ackerley's pessimism was to some extent justified. The Sexual Offences Act did not become law until 27 July 1967, which was rather too late for Ackerley, who had died some seven weeks previously. His impatience with British sexual attitudes is scarcely surprising in view of the fact that, throughout his entire life, every time Ackerley had sex with someone he was committing a criminal offence, punishable by a term of imprisonment.

Other friends Ackerley made during the 1950s included George Orwell's widow, Sonia, who subsequently married one of the most prominent victims of the current homosexual witch-hunt, Michael Pitt-Rivers. Ackerley was very fond of both Sonia and her new husband (and their labrador, Larmer) and often visited them in Dorset. Ackerley believed that Sonia was unhappy because she suffered from an excess of intellect, and he occasionally grumbled that she talked too much. However, they had dogs and (latterly) drink and depression in common, and became close friends, exchanging frank letters about their disappointments and despair. Another curious figure was Villiers David, a wealthy painter and writer of Parsee origins. He wrote a number of comic novels, which did not sell in any great numbers but which drew praise from Evelyn Waugh and John Betjeman. He also had several one-man shows of his paintings in London galleries, but he was essentially a dilettante. He lived in a flat on the top floor of a block in St James's with commanding views across London and, more importantly, a well-stocked bar. He rarely rose before eleven in the morning and spent much of the day drunk. Although an excellent cook, he appeared to live off Fernet Branca. He was a clever, witty, charming and generous man, but, unfortunately, extremely unattractive; Ackerley felt that he had not had much in the way of sexual fulfilment, and would encourage him to go abroad in pursuit of boys, which he occasionally did.

Ackerley had an enormous number of contacts in the literary and artistic world and some of his friendships began when he was called upon for advice. For example, when Forster collaborated with Benjamin Britten on the opera *Billy Budd*, Ackerley was consulted about which painters might be approached to design the sets. Ackerley was at the opera's opening night and occasionally visited Britten and Peter Pears at their home in Aldeburgh. In the summer of 1951 Britten asked

Ackerley to recommend a librettist for an opera he hoped to compose based on one of Beatrix Potter's children's books. Britten had thought Paul Dehn might be suitable, but Ackerley had been to see a revue to which Dehn had contributed, which he thought

> so flat and silly I could have smacked him. I find it awfully hard to reconcile Paul the poet of five years ago with Paul the scenario and feature-writer of today. Or indeed with Paul the person. So bright and amusing and inventive in his conversation; so puerile, simple minded in his productions – that film, those sketches. Still, there *were* those poems, many of which were lovely, though I sometimes feel they may belong to the past (the last poem of his I published was really not up to scratch). And there *is*, I believe, still that serious feeling he has for birds, which informed the early poems with much of their charm and provided their most sensitive images. If you could catch him on that 'hop' . . .

If Dehn was no good, Ackerley would suggest other *Listener* poets. 'Tell me more of what you want, what book or books, how much libretto.' Britten wondered whether William Plomer could be persuaded to collaborate with him on an opera based on *The Tale of Mr Tod*. 'How nice if William did,' Ackerley wrote.

> But it does not strike me as probable. He seems to write hardly anything now, poetry least of all. Nor, I think, since he was quite a young man, has he been considered, or considered himself, a lyricist. Ask him though by all means; he'd be flattered, for I think he's much neglected as a writer all round.

Plomer was delighted and, although *Mr Tod* fell through because of copyright difficulties, he wrote the libretto for Britten's *Gloriana* (1953) and for the three Parables for Church Performance, based on Japanese Noh plays. Ackerley continued to take an interest in Britten's work and was particularly pleased when, some years later, Britten began work on the *War Requiem*. He sent Britten his own copy of Wilfred Owen's *Collected Poems* since, unlike Britten's edition, it contained a photograph of the poet: 'Here is Owen with his beautiful face . . . I would be so happy for you to have this copy if you would prefer it to yours. Do take, I would like to think of it being an inspiration to you.' The *Requiem* appealed to Ackerley's anti-militarist beliefs and although he could not attend the first perform-ance, he listened to it on the wireless and told the composer: 'The whole thing was one of the greatest experiences of a longish lifetime.' When it was performed at the Albert Hall Britten sent Ackerley tickets.

> I was deeply moved [Ackerley wrote afterwards] not only by your beautiful and stirring message but by the sight of that vast crowd of hushed listeners that crammed the enormous hall. Besides the pleasure you gave, what a good you have done, what an effect you have had upon poor troubled humanity . . . I hope it may be heard in every country of this distracted world.

Privately, he felt that the *Requiem* got rather lost in the Hall: ' "Not noisy enough," as Morgan remarked.'

Such new friendships were particularly important because some of his old friends were less close than they had been. After William Plomer's nasty brush with the authorities during the war, he had become a great deal more circumspect, and his relentless promiscuity had been given a further check when he met and set up house with Charles Erdmann, who was to be his companion for the remainder of his life. Ackerley may have been suspicious of Plomer's war work for the Admiralty, since it smacked of secrecy and the State, two things he deeply mistrusted. Indeed, Plomer gradually became something of an Establishment figure, serving on the board of the Society of Authors, becoming a Fellow of the Royal Society of Literature and, worst of all in Ackerley's view, drifting back to re-embrace the Christianity of his childhood. He became more and more secretive – installing a tele-phone without telling the majority of his friends, for example. He and Ackerley remained fond of each other, but to some extent dis-approved of each other's lives and beliefs. Plomer hated dogs and deeply resented the influence Queenie exerted upon Ackerley. The two friends saw much less of each other when in 1953 Plomer and Erdmann moved out of London to a bungalow at Rustington on the Sussex coast. Plomer referred to himself, with good humour, but half-seriously, as 'the Hermit of Rustington'.

A further disenchantment occurred in 1953, when John Morris, who was the head of the BBC's Third Programme, 'banned' a broad-cast by Jack Sprott. Sprott had visited China as part of one of the first

Western delegations allowed in to inspect Mao Tse-Tung's recently established People's Republic. Sprott had been impressed by the prisons he was shown, and wanted to give a talk on the radio about them. Morris believed that Sprott had had the wool pulled over his eyes and accused him of gullibility. He therefore turned down the broadcast. Sprott complained to Forster, who was extremely displeased and wrote to Morris calling him a Fascist. Forster's displeasure was increased when Ackerley told him that Sir Ian Jacob, who had been appointed Director General of the BBC in 1952, had been nominated for the job by Churchill with the intention of making the Corporation 'a mouthpiece of the Foreign Office'.[1] Forster intervened personally and had 'an hour's hammer and tongs' at Broadcasting House. 'They complained that [Sprott] hadn't given a "general picture" of China,' Forster reported. 'I replied, "Give me a general picture of England." There was silence.' But there was no change in the decision to 'ban' Sprott's talk. Relations between Forster and Morris were strained for several years as a result of this incident, and it took all Plomer's diplomatic skills to heal the breach. Although Forster eventually relented, the battle-lines had been drawn: the repressive forces of the Establishment were represented by Morris, seconded by Plomer; Freedom of Expression was represented by Jack Sprott, seconded by Ackerley. Forster remained friends with all four men, but Morris and Plomer disliked Sprott and in their letters grumbled about his being Forster's literary executor.

---

[1] Ackerley had good reason to imagine a conspiracy. Jacob, like Morris, was a former soldier who had been recruited to overseas broadcasting. He had also been 'seconded from the BBC to be deputy secretary of the Cabinet during 1952'. Jacob was one of those whom Ackerley delighted in imagining at stool when he passed lavatory stalls:

> I like to think that in the shut-up shit-house boxes respectable people are behaving in a way of which they are slightly ashamed . . . Who are occupying all those shit-houses? I think to myself gleefully, and populate them, in my imagination, with all the people I most despise, the eminently respectable and blimpish, the black-coated high-ups, let us say, of the BBC.
>
> Possibly Sir John Reith is shitting there, I think to myself, and Sir Basil Nicholls [Controller of Programmes], Sir Ian Jacob, Jack Hulbert [the popular comedian]. I like to think of them all with their trousers down, sitting with their pale legs apart, having a GOOD SHIT, and I like it because I know they would not like me to think of it.

In 1957 Ackerley was asked by the Poetry Book Society to serve on their 1958 panel with Roy Fuller and Patric Dickinson. The judges were expected to choose two volumes of poetry a quarter, which would then be given the imprimaturs of a 'Poetry Book Society Choice' or a 'Poetry Book Society Recommendation'. These selections were made from the forty or so books published that year and the judges were paid fifty guineas each. Ackerley had been choosing poetry for *The Listener* for over twenty years and had published the work of many fine poets, not least that of his fellow panellists. Indeed, the BBC had been impressed enough by his record to appoint him poetry selector for the Third Programme in 1950, a job that Dickinson had previously done (when poetry had been broadcast on the Home Service). Nonetheless, he viewed this new task with considerable apprehension. He was delighted to be working with Fuller, who had become a close friend, but was rather alarmed by Dickinson, 'because I make so little always out of *his* poetry'. He confessed to Fuller:

> The thing is that although I read and choose poetry for *The Listener*, I am not used to reading it with such wide critical judgement as this task demands. Away from my desk, I seldom pick up a book of poems to read with interest and attention, unless it is by a personal friend, and confronted with all these books, I find my mind in a state of confusion in which, I imagine, you and Patric do not share, since you are both poets, and perceptive critics.

His own tentative first choices for the Spring award were books by Thomas Kinsella, Michael Hamburger and Michael Roberts, but he insisted that he was willing to be guided. Fuller had very strong views, most of which chimed with Ackerley's own. 'I am delighted to find myself less stupid than I thought I was,' Ackerley wrote, 'delighted also to see you smacking your cards on the table with such a splendid bang of conviction. I agree with every word you say, though I would not have ventured to say them myself, especially the disrespectful ones to Mr [—], of whom I made neither head nor tale [sic].' Dickinson had other ideas and, foreseeing a wrangle over the luncheon table, Ackerley asked the PBS whether it would be 'unprecedented to have no quarter's choice'. He was told it would be. In the event, he was content, as he told William Plomer, 'to leave the contest to these clever, oh far cleverer, little game cocks [i.e. Fuller and Dickinson], and to throw in

343

my own vote with theirs,' and Thomas Kinsella's *Another September* was made the 1958 Spring Choice of the Poetry Book Society, with Michael Hamburger's *The Dual Site* given a Recommendation.

The Summer submissions were disappointing; 'so poor,' Ackerley told Fuller, 'that I find myself without any strong preference, and would readily agree with you or Patric if you have warmer feelings.' Fuller's feelings were not particularly warm, but a decision had to be reached, and Ackerley fell in with his suggestion: 'If Patric agrees, then, and presumably he will, [Patrick] MacDonogh shall be recommended, or "chosen" I should say. And I take it we leave the matter at that. No recommend.' Dickinson, it appears, did not agree, and the Summer Choice was John Smith's *Excursus in Autumn*. MacDonogh's *One Landscape Still* became the Recommendation. 'O dear!' Ackerley exclaimed, 'I do hope that next time we shall find something that will knock us all down into a glorious heap. This business of going over the poets' heads with a fine tooth comb to find a louse or two – which are at least LIFE – is very boring.'

Dickinson made the first suggestions for the Autumn Choice, which Ackerley broadly agreed with, although two of the poets, both of whom regularly submitted their work to *The Listener*, did not inspire him. One was rejected out of hand, since Ackerley always refused his poems and so 'could hardly be expected to enjoy his book'. He occasionally published the work of the other poet, but without much enthusiasm, greeting the 'constant crammed envelopes with a sinking heart'. The panel eventually picked two other *Listener* contributors, A. S. J. Tessimond and R. S. Thomas, a decision Ackerley confirmed in a characteristic postcard to Fuller: 'Okay baby, it shall be Tess. & Thos. in that order. Love Joe.' 1958 was a far from vintage year, it seems, since the submissions for the Christmas Choice were so dismal that the panel was obliged to choose an anthology, *New Poems 1958*, rather than an individual poet's collection. However, Ackerley had enjoyed working with the two poets and had been able to wangle an extra lunch or two at the Corporation's expense.

Such perks were shortly to be denied him since 1959 was his last year at *The Listener*. Retirement from the BBC was usually enforced at sixty, but Ackerley had been given a three-year extension. Any thoughts about a comfortable retirement were brutally dispelled when he discovered the financial arrangement the BBC had made for him. He had hoped for a 'nice fat long-service cheque' in recognition of his 'thirty years' hard labour', but the Corporation was inclined to give him a standard pension and the usual Security Pay of half-a-year's salary in a lump sum. He registered his disgust and was eventually given Security Pay of a whole year's salary (which had recently been increased to £1900), spread over five years and subject to taxation. The pension would remain at £468 a year, which Ackerley considered 'stingy'. This, added to unemployment benefit and the return upon his few investments, would produce an annual income of, at best, some £1200. As he told Plomer, 'This would be serviceable if I were alone: with my three women it will be tight, to say the least.' He was already overdrawn at the bank and was getting almost no income at all from his published books. Indeed he had endured several disappointments over both *My Dog Tulip* and *We Think the World of You.*

My Dog Tulip sold less than half its first edition and by this time Secker and Warburg were about to remainder it. Furthermore there had been a major row in January 1958 between Ackerley and Warburg, who had handled American and foreign rights. American publishers had been less than enthusiastic, and the book had been turned down by Harper's, Knopf, Farrar Straus, Harcourt Brace, Random House, Macmillan, Viking, Putnam and Bobbs-Merrill. Eventually Warburg had secured a contract with a small Boston firm, the Beacon Press. Ackerley's muted delight was entirely extinguished when Warburg wrote to him to say that since the English edition had earned only £113 10s 2d of its £200 advance, the first half of the US advance would have to be set against the unearned balance:

> I am afraid you are not going to be very pleased about this [Warburg wrote], but there it is. If you feel harshly about it, please bear in mind that we spent a great deal of money investigating the possibility of publishing your other masterpiece [i.e. *We Think the World of You*] without result.

Ackerley was indeed displeased, and sent the letter and a draft reply to Forster, who castigated the unfortunate Warburg as a shit, but advised his friend to tone down his reply since, although not actually libellous, it was certainly intemperate. The draft has disappeared, but the letter Ackerley eventually sent could scarcely be described as pussyfooting:

Dear Fred Warburg,

I would have answered your letter earlier but have been too busy with my Travel Books Number and bothering my head over the critical fate of other publications of yours to attend to the legal fate of my own. You are perfectly right in your nervous apprehension that I would not be pleased with your letter and that 'harshly' is what I would be likely to think of it. It is all too clear that I have been a proper pigeon. My contract was always a stiff one, allowing you higher percentages which, one would have thought, would have gratified the greediest publisher's heart; your clever little phrase in Clause 17 escaped my innocent eye. It is doubtless true that if the book sells in America it will mean money for me 'in the end'; if it means money to me it also means money to you, for you have 15% of it, which would repay my English 'over advance' in time; there is no equitable reason why it should be the author who has to wait, for authors are generally poorer than publishers. My £80 odd cannot matter a jot to the prosperity of Secker & Warburg; to me they spell the difference between a holiday abroad and no holiday this year. If you had felt so very sore about my debt to you of £80 and could not wait to get it all back in percentages, you might have suggested some compromise like annexing perhaps £30 and no more of the U.S. advance towards its repayment; to swipe practically the lot, especially on top of the high percentages, seems to me an unseemly piece of rapacity.
Yours sincerely,
J. R. Ackerley
    P.S. And pray do spare me those little winning flatteries with which you seek to sugar-coat your nasty pills.

Forster, who semi-regretfully acknowledged that he had never had any trouble with his own publisher, was very pleased with this version of the letter. Warburg was not. He described it to Ackerley as 'exceptionally nasty and, considering what we have done for your book, uncalled for'. When he refused to reconsider, Ackerley approached the Society of Authors. They 'disapproved' of Ackerley's behaviour and told him that Warburg was within his rights. There, for a while, the matter seems to have ended, but Forster had much enjoyed this skirmish and was delighted to be given the opportunity to continue it. A month later Warburg's partner, Roger Senhouse, sent Forster a copy of Tibor Dery's *Niki*, hoping that he would provide a 'puff'. The book was ostensibly about a dog but was in fact a critique of the communist regime in the author's native Hungary. Dery had been prosecuted for writing the book and other subversive activities and had been given a long prison sentence. Forster was unmoved: this was a case in which a cause had to be sacrificed to personal relationships, and he wrote to Senhouse in his most feline manner:

> What a to do over Joe's royalties last month! He showed me Warburg's letter. I must say I thought it most unsympathetic and irritating – the references to masterpieces particularly so – and I am not surprised that Joe blew up. Since he did, I'm afraid I can't consider doing anything over Secker's present dog.
>
> To turn to pleasanter matters . . .

Warburg was furious, but wrote a reasonable letter to Forster, explaining his position and pointing out that according to the contract he was quite within his rights.

> We have not made money on *My Dog Tulip*, indeed we have lost quite a bit. This is our affair and we do not blame anybody for it except ourselves and the bad taste of the public. But this is not a case where a publisher who has done extremely well out of an author is refusing to go beyond the bounds of his contract to help an author in a jam – quite the contrary.
>
> I regret that your irritation with me and with this firm, which I think is uncalled for, should have resulted in harm to Dery. Joe may miss his holiday; Dery is now spending nine years in prison.

Forster did not feel in the least repentant and, summing up the year, listed Warburg amongst those he had 'ticked off' during 1958. Tempers eventually cooled, largely because the Beacon Press underwent a change of director and cancelled the contract, so that neither Ackerley nor Warburg ever received any money from Boston, and the two men were soon once again on good terms.

Warburg was keen to take another look at *We Think the World of You*, which Ackerley had been revising – a matter, largely, of removing a scene in which Frank and Johnny go to bed, and attempting other changes to avoid libelling Freddie and his family. Ackerley had sent the manuscript to a number of friends, including Forster, Roy Fuller, Stuart Hampshire, Hilary Corke and Stephen Spender. He was particularly interested to have the views of Fuller and Hampshire as representatives of a heterosexual readership and frequently consulted both men about his work. He was now very pleased with the book, as he told Spender:

> I don't often have a feeling about what I write, but I believe in this. It has a kind of structural perfection, like an eighteenth-century cabinet, everything sliding nicely and full of secret drawers.

This was just the sort of structural perfection he had found lacking in his life, particularly in that part of his life upon which the book was based. But, in spite of his art, he insisted that the book was like life: the ending was anti-sentimental and not happy. He had worked extremely hard to write a book that would stand up to the closest scrutiny and be re-read with renewed pleasure. What particularly pleased him was that he had managed to conceal his art so as not to lose the naïve and embarrassing quality of the story, a quality he felt necessary for the book's impact. There was a further purpose in concealing the book's pattern from the casual reader: like Frank, the reader would plough blindly on until the final page, and only then realize that Frank's fate was predestined and quite clearly signalled. A second reading would reveal verbal and imagistic echoes which increase the central irony, which is that Megan and Evie are (in Ackerley's terms) essentially the same: jealous, possessive bitches. Frank is constantly bewailing the fate of Johnny at the hands of his wife, without realizing that his own fate at the paws of the dog is exactly the same.[1] This was ambitious and sophisticated, and Ackerley wrote letters to a number of friends drawing their attention to his ploys.

Since there seemed little prospect of the book's being published in full in England, he had allowed Spender to attempt to sell it in America, which he eventually did to another independent publisher,

---

[1] A clear verbal prefiguring of the book's last paragraph is found on pp. 13–14, and the jokey confusion between Megan and Evie during Frank and Johnny's conversation on p. 10 instantly establishes a parallel which becomes more obvious as the book progresses. Ackerley further amused himself by giving Megan and Evie the same 'costume', to Megan's distinct disadvantage: cf. p. 46 and p. 110. (All page references are to the first English edition.)

the Cummington Press in Iowa City. It was to be published in a de luxe limited edition of 300 copies, illustrated and retailing at $15. However, the Press collapsed, quite literally, the machinery toppling over and smashing, swiftly followed by the company itself. Ackerley then sent the book to Maurice Girodias of the notorious Olympia Press, who returned it as 'not nearly dirty enough'. He now decided to try the 'purified' version on Warburg, who had been obliged to reject it in its original version on the advice of his lawyers. The Obscenity Act, 1959 had been rather more liberal and Warburg was optimistic. However, in May 1959 he once again rejected the novel, telling Ackerley that nobody thought that there was any chance of its achieving sufficient sales to justify publication. In fact, Warburg would have gone ahead had it not been for the implacable opposition of his partners, Roger Senhouse and David Farrer, who were 'absolutely adamant against our publishing it, more fools they'. Senhouse's opposition is surprising, since he had been a friend of the author and was also homosexual. Farrer's opposition was not, since he had greatly disliked *My Dog Tulip*, an opinion which poor sales appeared to have justified.

News of this latest setback reached Hamish Hamilton who asked to see the manuscript. Three people read it before it was regretfully returned. Hamilton quoted a reader's report in his accompanying letter:

Frank's pathos too soon turns to futility and one finds oneself sympathizing first with Johnny's relations for being bored by him and then with the unfortunate dog for being put on such a pedestal.

Ackerley marked this passage and scribbled in the margin:

Then 'one finds oneself' doing precisely what the book intended one to do. Frank is an unstable, maladjusted man, obsessed and frustrated, and the story is subtly contrived to turn completely over so that his 'persecutors' can be viewed in a sympathetic light. And why is Evie [the dog] 'unfortunate'? She (with [Megan] and Margaret [the Nancy character]) is the most formidable character in the book and gets her way in the end. She is Eve, the prototype, Shaw's tigress. The book is about the human predicament, and is meant to be amusing, in a wry sort of way. This duffer has missed all its points.

The duffer was not the only person to misunderstand the book, and if it has a flaw, it is that which frequently attends the unsympathetically intended first-person narrator. The reader is automatically, and sometimes inattentively, predisposed towards the person telling the story, particularly, as in this case, when the other characters remain resolutely unattractive. However, Ackerley's remarks also show what he frequently attempted to emphasize: although the book is autobiographically based, it is a *novel*. Indeed, part of the reason that he was surprised when the manuscript was criticized by Leonard Woolf and assorted lawyers was that he had become so bound up in the characters that he had almost forgotten that they were recognizable portraits of real people. Fortunately, another employee of Hamish Hamilton, Richard Brain, was interested enough in the novel to alert a friend at The Bodley Head, where it was declared to be a small masterpiece and eventually accepted by that publisher, subject to further alterations. These alterations were considerable and were to occupy much of Ackerley's time.

Exhausted by correspondence and disappointments, Ackerley decided to ask David Higham to be his literary agent. He also began soliciting anyone he knew about possible part-time employment, possibly as a publisher's reader (clearly feeling that such firms as Hamish Hamilton required new blood in that department). He applied to Chatto and Windus, Secker and Warburg, The Bodley Head, Methuen, *The Times*, John Lehmann and Stephen Spender, all without success. An anthology of poems from his years at *The Listener*, similar to Janet Adam Smith's *Poems of Today*, was suggested, but came to nothing. There were also some half-hearted schemes to take the whole BBC pension at once and invest it in property. He did not much relish the prospect of 'squatting in my flat all day with an aged dog, an aged aunt, and a numskull sister', and one alternative was to go to Japan. Francis King and James Kirkup lived there, in Kyoto and Sendai respectively, and had been urging him to join them, perhaps lecturing for the British Council, studying the country in order to produce a Japanese equivalent of *Hindoo Holiday*, or merely to recuperate after twenty-five years of literary editorship. The chief objection was financial. He had asked whether Fred Warburg would sponsor him in return for a book, but since the rejection of *We Think the World of You*, this seemed an unlikely prospect. When Ackerley had been having his row with Warburg, Forster, increasingly worried over his friend's parlous financial state, had attempted to do something practical. As he explained to Plomer:

> I am the only bugger of us all who has any money, and instantly wonder whether you could be persuaded to start a fund on his behalf. I see three objections (perhaps there are 4, 5, 6): (1) he might refuse, still I think he wouldn't if you did it: (2) the purchasing power of money is certain to decrease further: but who can stay that?: (3) gifts given within 5 years of one's death might be taxable – here £5 notes are an assistance, if not a final solution.

He offered to start the fund with £1000, 'just conveniently released by Cousin Dolly's decision, last month, to be certified'. Nothing ever came of this remarkable scheme, the necessity of which Forster regarded as a sign of the times.

> If literary ability, scholarship and military nobility were adequately rewarded [he told Ackerley], neither you nor William nor Francis[1] nor Leo nor others I could think of would be scrabbling and worrying towards the end of their lives. It's part of the drift away from culture and integrity towards the worship of the Golden Calf – an animal never censured in these days, and why? Because Big Business including the newspapers have invested in him.

Ackerley's displeasure with the BBC was further increased when he discovered that there was a plan to give him a tea-party as a send-off, rather than drinks. Whilst there was time, he took as many people out to lunch as he could. 'Let us chew and swig away another chunk of the Corporation's wealth before they ditch me,' he wrote to Fuller. Similar invitations were issued to other contributors. He planned his final issue of *The Listener* to be 'a sweet end to my career', containing reviews and articles by Plomer, Sprott, Stuart Hampshire and, of

---

[1] E. K. 'Francis' Bennett (1887–1958) had met Forster before the First War, when he had been a student at the Working Men's Club. He went to Cambridge on a scholarship and eventually became a Fellow of Caius College. He wrote a number of books under the *nom de plume* 'Francis Keppel'. He became a close friend of Forster and subsequently met Ackerley in the 1920s and grew fond of him. Simon Raven remembers him as a 'motherly old don' who held treasure hunts for his favourite undergraduates, hiding the prize in his pockets.

course, Forster. In the event, his farewell party was not a tea-party at all, but a rather grand affair of cocktails held on 29 October 1959 at the Langham Hotel, opposite Broadcasting House. There were a few disappointments and absences. Marjorie Redman was unable to attend, as were Edith Sitwell and Kenneth Clark ('sudden colds were alleged'). L. P. Hartley turned up on the wrong day and Forster, displeased with the way Ackerley had been treated by the Corporation, boycotted the occasion altogether. 'We missed you at the funeral party,' Ackerley wrote to David Sylvester:

but never mind, it was jollier than expected and went on until 8.30. The ebbing tide of distinguished guests had left behind them only a Corke and a Reed, and those I took off to dine. It was my last expenses sheet.

A fairer young bitch there never was seen,
My old dog is grey that used to be black.

And so on.

Rather more interesting was a review of three books about the
ecological havoc wreaked by the construction of the Kariba Dam on
the Zambesi River. Ackerley was appalled by the way arrogant
Westerners brought 'civilization' to 'primitive' people. It struck him as
'interferingness' on a grand scale. One of the few books he chose to
review himself when at *The Listener* had been Nicholas Guppy's
account of the Wai-Wai, who pursued a peacefully 'promiscuous and
polygamous' life in the equatorial forests of South America. They were
particularly commendable in their treatment of animals, for their
numerous pets, like Queenie, were given their freedom and so stayed
with their humans by choice. All had been well until Christian
missionaries arrived: 'Already the diseases of civilization, coming in
with the mouth-organs and safety pins, have decimated the tribes.' A
worse fate greeted those who happened to be in the way when the
Kariba Dam was built. Ackerley describes the persecution and murder
of the indigenous tribe, the Batonkas, and the drowning of forests,
villages and animals as the waters rose. He concludes the review by
itemizing the 'extra compensations' for this loss:

> £3,000,000 are to be spent on turning the lake into the most
> wonderful tourist resort in the world, with 'modern hotels with
> panoramic views . . . luxurious "flotels" . . . pleasure cruising . . .
> pretty uniformed hostesses . . . music and dancing under the tropical
> moon . . . skin-diving and aquaplaning . . . camping, caravan, and
> picnic sites . . .'

K. W. Gransden, his successor at *The Listener*, commissioned him to
write several reviews about conservation, animal life and true crime.

Ackerley continued to turn his gruelling experiences to good
account. His article about the horrors of social security, 'Doleful
News', was written for *Encounter*, went into proof, but was never
published and has since vanished irrecoverably into that magazine's
inaccessible archives. One reason it was never published may have
been that Ackerley was worried that it might make 'a sad story or a
National Issue' out of him. Another reason may have been that, as

Ackerley complained to Gorer, there was 'something very idle or screwy' about *Encounter*. He did a broadcast review of Santha Rama Rau's stage adaptation of *A Passage to India*, a prospect he rather dreaded, but which went very well and pleased Forster. He also took out his Family Memoir once again and tinkered with that.

However, Ackerley's main preoccupation was with *We Think the World of You*, which he had turned to once again in the hope of altering it sufficiently to appease The Bodley Head's lawyers. He had been advised to change the scene from Walthamstow to Hackney and spent afternoons wandering around Victoria Park soaking up the local atmosphere. He disliked making alterations:

> I write by ear as well as by eye, and my finished prose has a kind of rhythm, very easily disturbed. Afterwards I find it hard to alter a single word, the balance of a sentence is liable to get upset. I am not trying to praise myself, only to say how I work. I could never knock off a novel in a few months, like[——]; I abhor slovenliness; a single misprint upsets me; I love a thing to be as perfect as I can make it – and having got as close as I can to personal approval and written the thing off as 'done', find it truly painful to be asked to alter it in the smallest way.

Nonetheless, he was now determined that the book should be published and in December 1959 wrote to David Higham in triumph, outlining nine major changes he had made on legal advice. These included altering the characters' appearances, circumstances and numbers of spouses and offspring, as well as ensuring that at no point is it stated that Evie is an Alsatian (although the physical description leaves the reader in little doubt, as Ackerley pointed out).

> Well, I hope you will now manage to push this thing through for me. Author though I am I must say that I think, on re-reading it, that it is a stunner. Beautifully written, as tight as a drum, I am quite lost in admiration of my own cleverness; it contains at any rate three dialogues of terrific impact, that difficult mixture of strict economy, explosive emotion, and perfect naturalness that it is a triumph to bring off. I have done it, I know. I hope you will think me a good boy.

He was still concerned that The Bodley Head was not offering him good enough terms.

> I fancy [the editor] believes, and I may have given him the impression, that my feeling for the book is a bit tired, and he may be trading on that, but if there is some truth in it, my feeling for cash is not tired at all, and it was primarily in the hope of making some money that I revised the book and let the publishers see it again.

The plan to travel to Japan was still very much in Ackerley's mind, but there were several obstacles to be overcome. The first was financial, but a gift of £500 from Forster took care of that. The second was that he dreaded the eighteen-hour flight that would be required to transport him to Tokyo. The most glaring obstacle, however, was Queenie. She had finally had her troublesome womb removed during a harrowing emergency operation the previous summer. She had also endured a stroke and although she had recovered from this, she was distinctly doddery. Ackerley had gone on extended holidays before and grown accustomed to leaving Queenie in the care of Nancy, but time was clearly running out for the old dog. There appear to be two reasons why Ackerley was able to contemplate leaving her. The first was that he dreaded the prospect of her actual death. He had always regarded himself as something of a coward and he clearly felt that it would be less painful for him not to be there when she died. It seems likely that he also felt that her death would be as much a release for him as for her. No longer in her thrall, would he perhaps turn once again to human relationships? There could be no question of his having another dog, but it was possible that the gap left in his life might be filled, without betrayal, by human beings. In Japan he would be able to discover whether or not he still had this capacity. Francis King certainly thought that the trip was a last-ditch attempt to re-enter the world of human relationships.

Aunt Bunny was in a similarly frail state, but Ackerley was less concerned about leaving her than about escaping the grasp of Nancy. From past experience he knew that she would do everything in her power to prevent his going. As well as money, Forster offered advice:

> Your wisest plan would be to go to Japan without telling Nancy, but she would soon notice your absence, and the next wisest is to tell her

now that you are going, observe whether she (i) collapses (ii) wilts or merely (iii) perks up, and take the next step accordingly. There is of course not the least reason you should go because you have told her you will.

Serious advice is difficult to give, but I do feel that we only live once and ought to see as much of the world as possible while we are alive. And I also feel – though not so certainly – that the ailing ought not to hamper the healthy.

As a first step towards the planned journey, Ackerley underwent a course of inoculations. He appeared to suffer no side effects himself, but Nancy instantly developed palpitations and tremors which the doctors ascribed to blood pressure. This did not augur well for Ackerley's plans, but he was determined to get away on holiday and in June he weathered hysterical scenes with Nancy and set off on a European tour. As a trial run for the longer trip to Japan, this holiday was not propitious. He jokingly told friends that he was hiring a car and that they should therefore watch the obituary columns, a jest that had become rather sour by the end of his time abroad.

He went to Marseilles to join the American novelist, Max White, who was a friend of the Buckinghams. White was crippled by arthritis and in constant pain and so was not the most inspiriting companion. Indeed, dosed with up to twenty-four aspirin a day, he was grouchy and unpredictable, inclined to make scenes in restaurants when service was slow and shout at motorists and pedestrians in the street, often for no discernible reason. Ackerley did his best to assist this tragic figure, but, as he confessed to May Buckingham 'I began to feel rather like Van Gogh and Gauguin in Arles – and maybe he began to feel the same, that his uncontrollable temper might soon flare out at me as well.'

He was not altogether sorry to depart after a fortnight for Athens, and was delighted to meet up with Donald Windham and his friend, Sandy Campbell, who were rather better company than White. He spent a week with them, correcting the proofs of *We Think the World of You*, which had been mailed to him there. He also looked up several of Francis King's friends and was soon happily mixing in the homo-sexual set, doing his best to pick up sailors and waiters. Windham and Campbell recalled that his attempts in this direction were occasionally farcical. He had never grown accustomed to wearing dentures and often carried them in his pocket. At the approach of a likely youth he would hastily insert his teeth and unleash a dazzling smile upon his prey. So alarming was this grimace that young men often hurried by, as if evading a lunatic. He did, however, secure the company of a sixteen-year-old, 'one of a group of naughty boys who operate around the Rex cinema in Venizelos', whom he took to his hotel. He might have seen more of the youth, but was unnerved by one of King's friends who told him that 'there was a law against tampering with the under-aged'. Ackerley now decided that his tastes, reawakened after some years, were for adolescents, who were in genial and plentiful supply in Greece. He later picked up a seventeen-year-old Turkish tourist, but was alarmed by a telephone call which suggested that they were being watched, either by the police or by the hotel management. 'So my Athens life has been ruined,' he complained to King.

He reluctantly returned to Marseilles, where he found White unable to decide whether to travel to Italy to join friends there or to move on somewhere else. Ackerley scouted round for alternatives for him, but to no avail. By this time there had been so many altercations that hardly any restaurants were still willing to serve White. After a particularly violent scene over a bill, White told Ackerley that he wished to be alone in future. With some relief, Ackerley left Marseilles for Paris to stay with his old friend, Georges Duthuit.

After being there for three days, he was standing with Duthuit in the Boulevard St Germain when he was bowled over by a skidding car. He was knocked unconscious and suffered concussion, was cut and bruised about the head and legs, and damaged the vertebrae in his neck. The French doctors stitched him up but failed to X-ray his neck properly, as he discovered when he returned to London. He had in fact 'fractured' several vertebrae and was put in a neck-brace, which gave him the appearance of 'something between a Congo belle and a Regency beau'. He was obliged to undergo radiotherapy three times a week, which meant that he spent a great deal of his time in the corridors of Putney Hospital.

Matters were not much improved by news that Max White had sent May Buckingham a farewell letter, clearly intending to commit suicide. Ackerley was filled with remorse about abandoning White and wrote a long letter to May explaining what had happened. In fact White was still alive and was transported back to America by the Red Cross. Forster insisted that Ackerley should not blame himself, writing to May that White's

later behaviour to Joe was unkind and rude, and I think that no one
but Joe, who possesses both intelligence and sweetness, could have
understood it and put up with it. Not one word of complaint or
criticism, not even a snubbed feeling, which certainly I should have
had if I had been treated like that.

In spite of this inauspicious attempt to leave England, Ackerley was
determined to get to Japan. He was further encouraged by Forster who
had made some money out of the stage adaptation of *A Passage to
India* and pressed £200 of it on his friend. Ackerley announced that he
would leave at the end of August, whereupon Nancy developed heart
murmurs and fainting fits, a recurrence of her blood-pressure symptoms. Queenie was also doing her best to thwart her master's plans,
following him round the flat with a mournful expression. Ackerley
himself developed an 'indolent ulcer' on his ankle as a result of his
Paris accident. These deterrents notwithstanding, he eventually
booked his flight, glad at the prospect of being out of the country when
We Think the World of You was published.

Since correcting the proofs of the book, his old fears about libel had
been rekindled. In spite of what he referred to as the book's 'castra-
tion', he feared that Freddie's family, whom he had not seen since the
early 1950s, might rise in their collective wrath against him. He
consulted a solicitor whom he had met on his walks with Queenie and
was alarmed that this man felt 'disquietude' about the book's publication. Ackerley made some half-hearted attempts to halt publication,
but finished copies of the book were all ready for publication which
was firmly scheduled for 27 September 1960.

On the evening of 13 September, Ackerley crept out of the flat so as
not to disturb Queenie, and travelled with Nancy to a hotel at the air
terminal, since his flight left at six-forty the following morning. Nancy
behaved remarkably well and produced no signs of illness, apart from
returning the oysters her brother had provided for their farewell meal.
On the advice of Forster he had decided that nothing would bring him
back before time, not even the death of Queenie, and certainly not the
death of Aunt Bunny. If either event occurred, as seemed not unlikely,
Nancy would have to cope.

After the gruelling flight, Ackerley was met at Tokyo airport by James
Kirkup. He spent a couple of days in the capital, looked after by Cyril

Eland, a British Council colleague of Francis King, before setting off by train for Kyoto. King was living in a 'large comfortable office-house' which he shared with three servants, four dogs and two cats. He had a car and drove Ackerley round the numerous temples of Kyoto, which had been the country's capital for almost eleven hundred years until in 1868 the government had been moved to Tokyo. Although no one had been prepared to commission him to write an account of his journey (apart from *The Listener*, which had asked for a short article), Ackerley still hoped that he might find material for a book in Japan and kept detailed notebooks of the buildings and customs of the country. Not all of them impressed him. As might be expected, he was less than enthusiastic about a visit to a geisha house:

> What boredom! Two old madams, a plain *maiko* (a seventeen-year-old virgin who has not reached geisha age), a geisha (in informal dress) quite pretty, and a baby-chan of eleven, the daughter of one of the madams . . . The evening was like a sort of Victorian Sunday in the country . . . The girls and madams sat about us, conversing politely (in Japanese, none could speak English) and filling our cups and lighting our cigarettes. The *maiko* entertained us to two dances, one with fans. One of the madams played the *samisen* (a three-stringed instrument, stretched with the skin of a cat, its screws sometimes made of gold: a boring instrument). Then the eleven-year-old played it, insensitively twanging away. Then she brought in a *koto* and twanged away inexpertly on that. The mother, knowledgeable on *Noh*, was then asked to recite a passage from one of the plays. She did so. Though incomprehensible to us, it was nevertheless obviously a mature and honourable artistic performance. Childish fun and games then ensued. Even the 'family album' was produced . . .

Rather more to his taste were the city's thriving gay bars, where twenty-five shillings procured a boy and a bed. The bars were thronged with rapacious Westerners, mostly Americans, whom Ackerley didn't much like, since they spoke of nothing but their conquests and indulged in endless 'sissy-talk'. In nearby Osaka there were further clubs, some little more than bar-brothels, called Slave Markets, where boys cost £1. 'Not really my cup of saké,' Ackerley told Forster. 'Bad breath, I am told, no circumcision. Good torsos, no legs.' Japanese

whisky highballs gave him headaches, he complained, and he preferred to write letters, or receive them, than loll in bars. However, he
was enchanted by the landscape, the gardens, Imperial villas and
pagodas, the monasteries and shrines with their Buddhas, and, of
course, the wildlife. In the Western district outside the city he was
delighted by the Monkey Hill where rhesus and other monkeys ran
wild in a large enclosure on the densely wooded slopes:

> A large grey monkey in a cage got an erection when it saw Francis
> [he recorded]. It had bright blue balls. From the top of this hill the
> panoramic view in the sunshine – the whole of Kyoto, the river
> below, the hills beyond – was magnificent. A urinal which we used
> had windows looking on this view. We gazed at it as we peed. Surely
> the prettiest urinal in the world.

After three or so weeks, Ackerley travelled back through Tokyo to
Sendai to stay with James Kirkup, who was working as a lecturer in
English literature there. Ackerley was inclined to play his two hosts off
against each other, telling each of them that he was far happier with
the other. This may have been the result of a feeling that he was
imposing upon their hospitality. A little flattery, particularly at the
expense of a rival, seemed a way of securing his welcome. In spite of a
determination to like the country he found himself rather bored. This
was largely constitutional, the reaction of a man unused to freedom.
He also missed, amidst the frenetic desire and pursuit which characterized expatriate life, what he considered 'the serious side of life', a
commodity provided for him in England by such friends as Forster. He
confessed himself far too eager to greet the post for a man supposedly
getting away from it all, half-way across the world.

In Sendai he met fewer people than he had in Kyoto, apart from
those boys glimpsed fleetingly as they entered or emerged from
Kirkup's bedroom, and felt that he was not getting to know the
Japanese sufficiently. However, for all his grumbling to Forster in
letters, his notebooks show him taking a far livelier interest in the
experience than he was prepared to admit. He pottered around the
shops, made excursions into the surrounding countryside and flirted
inconclusively with the local greengrocer's boy, ordering quantities of
fruit and vegetables he did not need. A visit to a zoo did little to raise
his spirits, although he returned there often to commune with a tigress

who was confined in a cage measuring some fifteen by ten feet. Her plight made Ackerley sceptical of the Japanese aesthetic sense:

Matsushima is one of the three famous beauty spots in Japan. Perhaps it ranks among the great beauty spots of the world. The Japanese are great nature lovers, we are told, though they do not mind leaving litter all over beauty spots, and to Matsushima they flock in all its changing seasons and boat about among its five hundred islands. They come to it in Cherry Blossom time, in *momoji* [maple] time, at all seasons and to view the full moon in the waters. There are special moon-viewing hotels and moon-viewing rooms. In the autumn a delicious feeling of melancholy descends upon the Japanese, the falling leaves, the reddening *momoji*, fill them with the most agreeable sense of sadness, and they write little haikus on the transience of life.

How feeble they are! To me the tigress in the Zoo (reserved apparently for kids: but why add a zoo to a place which already has a famous attraction?) was as beautiful as Matsushima and all its five hundred islands. And the tiger, and the lioness, and the leopard, and the hobbled elephant were also melancholy this misty rainy day – and had a better reason for dissatisfaction with the business of life than the Japanese. Why don't the Japanese let the moon, the cherry blossom and *momoji* alone for a bit and do a bit of tigress-gazing, elephant-gazing, lioness-and-leopard-gazing for a change – and ask themselves a few questions of an objective nature, such as whether it is fair on wild beasts to keep them in cages – especially small cages - - and whether they hadn't better do something about it?

And why do children have to see a real tiger? Kano-Tanyu did very well in his paintings without – working from hearsay and imagination.

I confess that the animal scene always upsets me, in whatever country I happen to be.

At the beginning of November Ackerley decided to go to Tokyo, where there was an exhibition of Japanese art treasures he particularly wanted to see. He booked into the YMCA and wrote to Francis King:

Why in the world does not everyone come to stay in the YMCA, with its large *va et vient* of young Japanese, its general feeling of something must surely happen soon, its low prices (600, 700 and 800 yen for a room), its naked swimming pool, communal bath rooms, body-building room, constantly changing lift-boys and every other attraction – instead of staying for 1800 yen a night, at lowest, at stuffed shirt hotels, for a little extra comfort.

He spent his sixty-fourth birthday there and 'was given the nicest present anyone could have by being picked up in the communal washplace of my floor by a perfectly charming person'. The perfectly charming person was not a prostitute but a young businessman called Saito, a salesman for the Nippon Beers brewery who spoke some English and seemed genuinely affectionate. Ackerley was smitten. He spent the next couple of evenings loitering expectantly in the corridors of the YMCA, hoping to meet the young man again. Three days later he saw him in the hallway and they went to bed again. The following evening he returned to the YMCA late and left his door open.

At 12.00 I heard the latch click and my name whispered. There he was, the darling, glimmering in his fresh cotton underwear, smelling of bath and soap and perfume. He stayed till 1.30, whispering to me. The Secret Sharer. We live and must live I think in the shadows. I shall never enter his day nor he mine. Saito: out of the shades of my life, into the shades of my death.

In spite of his years of abstinence, his emotions centred entirely upon Queenie, Ackerley had changed little. He wrote to several friends about what he now thought of as an affair and began to arrange his plans around this new companion, deciding to stay on in Tokyo rather than join Francis King in Kyoto as planned. Forster was careful not to send a letter of congratulation by return, fearing that by the time it reached Ackerley the affair might have ended. His pessimism was well-founded, for, like all Ackerley's lovers before him, Saito began to prove unreliable.

I am now puzzled about my little affair, which isn't working out as I hoped [he wrote to King]: that's to say that my romance has not visited me for the last two nights, and I was hoping he would pop in every night. Difficult to contact him by day: he's off to work at 9.0 and though finished at 5.0 returns here all hours. He goes to

cinemas, or plays cribbage with his mates. Seems not to drink . . .
I'm a bit put out over all this, because I don't like to go out of an
evening after about 9.0 in case he thinks to call – so for the last two
nights I've had a very frustrated time, hanging about my room,
beautifully shaved and reeking of scent – all in vain. I slipped a note
under his room door yesterday, asking him to pay a visit, but
nothing happened. I don't like to visit him, afraid he might not like
it. A bore, because I could have gone off to the Shinjiku bars, but
told myself that a bird in the hand was worth two in the bush. Only
the bird is not in the hand. Must waste this evening too, I fear: would
much sooner have him than another. If it flops I shall book a train
for you. I've had enough Deaths in Venice in my time.

There followed an acutely embarrassing scene in the YMCA
washroom, where Ackerley had been lying in wait. Saito had entered
and gone straight into a lavatory stall without acknowledging
Ackerley, who attempted to follow him in in order to ask why he had
not replied to messages. Saito, perhaps misunderstanding his motives,
attempted to shut the door in his face and Ackerley was obliged to
make an apologetic withdrawal. He decided that he had badly mis-
managed the entire affair and so packed his bags for Kyoto:

I had bungled it, I fear: there was nothing left. What did it all mean? I
don't know – except that in bed he was a darling, so affectionate and
sweet and cuddly – loving to be kissed and staying on long after the
climax on both sides had been reached. I'm afraid I was a fool. Love
makes one that. But he didn't give much help. I don't even know his
full name.

The last night in the YMCA ended in further humiliation:

Drank too much whisky last night. Wetted bed and, somehow, one
slipper. Have a notion I peed in it for some reason and emptied it out
of the window. I had fallen into such depression at seeing Saito's
room occupied by someone else – and not even having his name and
address.

The only cheering news was that *We Think the World of You* had been
published and respectfully reviewed, with no sign of a writ. It received

no individual reviews in the newspapers, but a short notice in the *Observer* by Kingsley Amis had been very complimentary, and L. P. Hartley had praised the novel in John Lehmann's *London Magazine*. Further plaudits came from the *TLS* and from Paul Scott in the *New Statesman* ('beautiful and superbly executed . . . What a brilliant book this is!'). Less welcome, but rather what Ackerley had feared, was a queer-bashing review in the *Spectator* by John Coleman:

> Frank's foul selfishness, that of a quasi-tender rock-solid queer, is finally recognized, but it came too late for me. His canophilia . . . is chronic, sad and private; and I don't want to be persuaded of its importance. But as a case history of an obsession, humanly crippling, no one could refuse this tale its mawkish, classically delineated truth.

Worse news was to reach him from Putney. Aunt Bunny had suffered a stroke and had lost her speech and the use of one arm. Fortunately, Nancy had proved remarkably calm and competent and had got the old woman to hospital. Once there, Bunny recovered slightly and, independent to the last, asked why she could not go home. Now that Bunny was in hospital and being taken care of, Nancy did not ask her brother to return home, which was a great relief, as he told Forster:

> I am not anxious to return – the decay and squalor of my life is not the only thing I shrink from having again. I have a feeling of absolute emptiness and uselessness, I don't want ever to write again and I don't want to read, and how to get through another period of Putney life I do not know, nor how, especially if old Bunny returns to that scene, I shall manage to get away from it again.

He wondered whether it would be possible to stay in Japan for a year and his enthusiasm for the country grew when he met a 'pretty young Buddhist priest' with a shaven head called Kinoshita. As Ackerley explained to Forster, being an ordained priest did not prevent a man from taking other jobs and Kinoshita was a student at the University, studying English, Buddhism and comparative religions. Nor did it prevent him from hopping in and out of bed with Westerners like Ackerley. Kinoshita was twenty years old, a Korean who had come to Japan as a small child after his father, a wealthy merchant, had been ruined during the Second World War. His father had gradually built up his business again, but Kinoshita decided that he did not care for money and only wanted a simple life of study and contemplation. His father had paid for him to go to the University of Koyasan and there Kinoshita decided to become a priest. 'He is a sturdy boy,' Ackerley reported, 'the Buddha face, infinitely sweet and very clever: he speaks English better than most people I have met and can read and write the Chinese script. He wants to live with me always.' As preparation for this, Kinoshita invited Ackerley to stay in his monastery, which had guest rooms and acted rather as a Young Men's Buddhist Association hostel.

The Daimyooin Temple at Koyasan was a place of pilgrimage for the Shingon sect and in the summer was thronged with the devout. But in winter it was almost entirely deserted. It was perched a chill 3800 feet up in the mountains beyond Osaka and was reached by cable-car. As a priest, Kinoshita got board and lodging in return for cleaning the rooms and grounds; Ackerley paid £1 a day for a room and three meals. His room had sliding screens painted with landscapes, some cushions, a bronze charcoal-brazier or *hibachi* on which a large kettle steamed, a clothes-rack, an altar, and a vase of chrysanthemums and red-berried twigs. Beneath the floor was the heating system, an ash-pit in which glowing pieces of charcoal were buried. A stool was placed over this *kotatsu* or fire-box and a large quilt draped over the stool. Host and guests sat on the floor around the *kotatsu*, with their legs thrust beneath the quilt – 'a very pleasant companionable idea,' Ackerley thought. As a visitor, he was given first dip in the scalding bath which would later be used by the priests. He was also given Japanese clothes, a cotton wrap and a padded silk robe, and some bedding. After dinner Kinoshita and an even younger novice joined Ackerley around the *kotatsu*. The novice spoke no English and shortly withdrew, leaving Ackerley and Kinoshita alone beneath the quilt. Although perfectly compliant, eager even, Kinoshita was rather nervous about sex, fearful that his fellow priests would be wondering where he had got to, and might even come looking for him. Afterwards, he returned to his own room, which he shared with three other priests.

The following day Ackerley went to morning service where a row of young priests sat chanting in front of an image of Buddha hidden in a cabinet (the statue was exposed only once every fifty years). After breakfast Kinoshita took Ackerley to see the tomb of Kobo Daishi, the ninth-century founder of the Shingon sect. The tomb itself was unimpressive, since it was merely the thatched wooden house in which the saint had lived. His body was not removed when he died, but left there, 'a skeleton sitting in his room'. The house was surrounded by a fenced 'garden' of gilded metal lotus flowers amongst which rhododendrons grew. In the vicinity, amongst the massive pines and ancient cryptomerias or Japanese cedars, were many other tombs, some of famous Japanese figures, set in gardens. There were also humbler wooden grave tablets, Buddhas large and small, shrines piled with pebbles and stones, and twists of fortune-papers attached to the trees and bushes. The bereaved, from the Imperial family downwards, brought the hair, finger-nails, teeth and ashes of the dead in little sacks to place in the priests' care. Even in the depths of winter, pilgrims sauntered amongst the tombs and shrines, bowing, clapping, praying and lighting incense. Stray dogs roamed there too, unmolested because according to legend dogs had helped the saint. When in China he had thrown his *sanko* (a Buddhist implement used for ritual consecrations) into the air, where it disappeared from view. When Kobo arrived in Japan he began searching for somewhere to build his monastery and met a huntsman with two dogs, who told him to look on Mount Koya where a light could be seen. He loaned Kobo his dogs which led the saint up the mountain to a pine-tree in the top of which the *sanko* had lodged. The dogs had been buried with full honours, their tomb becoming a shrine. Ackerley found this shrine but could not get in for it was opened only once a year. However, he realized that here, in the cradle of the Shingon sect, he had found the subject for the article he had promised *The Listener*.[1]

Ackerley was given a tour of the Daimyooin Temple and introduced to its Master, a remote and taciturn figure who was the second highest Shingon priest in Japan. He also met Kinoshita's fellow priests, a jolly

[1] Ackerley was also delighted to discover the existence of Tsunayoshi, who ruled in Yedo from 1680 to 1709 and was known as 'The Dog *Shogun*'. He had 'decreed that all animals, and especially dogs, should be protected and treated with the utmost consideration and courtesy. Elaborate kennels for stray dogs were built, and the dogs were escorted ceremonially to them in palanquins, like noblemen, peeping out through the screens at the bowed heads of the populace. Every canine death had to be reported and was carefully investigated. Punishments of exile, imprisonment, or death for killing any animal were imposed. A court page was beheaded for killing a bird.' Ackerley conceded that: 'Tsunayoshi may be thought to have gone a little too far', but thought the *Shogun* 'was on the right lines'.

collection of youths keen on ping-pong, and his tutor in English, a wise, charming and cultured man who had heard of (but never read) Forster's books. Sex with the little priest had now become far more relaxed and satisfactory – 'How can love be wrong?' Kinoshita had replied when asked about his moral view of their relationship – and Ackerley was extremely happy. His experience coloured his entire feelings about Japan:

> You feel you are among a people who genuinely care for your comfort and happiness, who are gentle, kind, sensitive, considerate and warm-hearted, who never cheat, steal or over-charge, who are always desirous to help, and with whom, in short, you feel perfectly safe.

'Oh dear, why did we not discover Japan before we were so old!?' he asked Forster. The only thing that worried him was that Kinoshita seemed to be so poor and underfed. The young man had no clothes, apart from one shabby suit and his priestly robes, his room had no heating in spite of the snow, and his food was less interesting and nourishing than Ackerley's, largely consisting of plain rice and root vegetables. Ackerley himself had little enough money, but he gave Kinoshita some and shared his meals with him. Each evening was spent beneath the quilt in Ackerley's warm room. Kinoshita begged Ackerley not to return to England or, if he had to, to come back to Japan as soon as possible and live with him.

Ackerley stayed twelve days in all and gave a carefully contrived speech of thanks to the Master before leaving. He thought that the Master did not appreciate his young priest sufficiently, and so emphasized how well Kinoshita had looked after him. The speech was very well received. Kinoshita confessed that he had slept with many people, but that the affair with Ackerley was entirely different. He particularly pleased Ackerley by saying: 'I know that you are serious and good – you have compassion for all animals, dogs, cats, birds – and I know you love me.' It had been agreed that they would meet the following weekend in Kyoto, which they did, but outside the charmed walls of Daimyooin Ackerley suddenly became impotent and felt humiliated.

Kinoshita returned to Koyasan and Ackerley did some intensive sightseeing, making copious notes on the various Buddhist sects in his notebooks. The experience of monastery life had deeply impressed him and he had become genuinely interested in Buddhist beliefs, particularly in the emphasis upon wisdom and compassion, two qualities he had always found lacking in English life. An otherwise useless guidebook to Japan lent to him by Benjamin Britten contained a valuable account of Shinto Buddhist gods, which he absorbed. The only thing that had been missing at Koyasan, stray dogs apart, had been wildlife – even birds had seemed scarce up in the mountains – so Ackerley was delighted to be taken to a park in which deer roamed and nuzzled his outstretched hand.

It had been decided that he and Kinoshita should spend Christmas together, after which they would have a short holiday, travelling around the western part of Honshu. Ackerley returned to Koyasan to collect him and on Christmas Eve they set off for Kurashiki, a town on the south coast where Kinoshita's father lived with his second wife. Ackerley was booked into a local hotel and that evening Kinoshita's father took them out to dinner. Regardless of their own religious beliefs, the Japanese regarded Christmas as a festival and responded with Western gusto, hanging up decorations and playing carols on the radio. Ackerley recalled that on their walks at Koyasan Kinoshita had often sung 'Jingle Bells' to himself as he sauntered amongst the shrines. The carols made Ackerley think guiltily of Nancy and Queenie alone in the Putney flat (Bunny was still in hospital), but Kinoshita's father was determined that they should have an enjoyable time and flirted with the fat jolly women in the bar. On Christmas Day Ackerley was taken to the Kurashiki Museum of Western Art, which to his great surprise contained excellent examples of work by Cézanne, Van Gogh, Renoir and El Greco.

They then took a train right across the island to Kaiki, a hot-spring spa on the north coast. They stayed in the old spa hotel, now mostly patronized by honeymoon couples and students, and bathed in the waters, which were supposed to be good for skin complaints. Unfortunately the bill was rather more than Ackerley had expected and they decided to move on, west along the coast to Izumo-Taicha. They stayed there a couple of nights and inspected the shrines before skirting Lake Shinji and arriving at Matsue, where Lafcadio Hearn had lived. Ackerley did not share the reverence of the Japanese for this Irish-Greek writer who had settled in Japan in 1890, adopting the country's clothes and customs. His house had been maintained as a shrine, in which an assortment of personal items, including his underwear, were reverently displayed. Ackerley was not impressed:

Have the Japs any critical faculty? One really wonders at the veneration in which this man, practically unread, largely unknown in England now, is held here, the more so since I believe his studies of Japan are more sentimental than thorough.[1] Blunden is another case. If he comes here to do anything he is usually asked to write an extempore poem (all poets are) and then it is often carved in stone and set up somewhere as a monument of his visit. The poem may be piddling – it usually is – but no matter.

Ackerley's view of Japan and the Japanese fluctuated with his romance. He was beginning to tire of Kinoshita, who spent far too much time reading, even when they were passing through beautiful country he had never seen before. The young priest was occasionally inconsiderate, in marked contrast to his behaviour at the Temple. When things went wrong he regarded it all as a huge joke, even when it meant that Ackerley had lost or wasted money. What had previously seemed an attractively childlike quality in the Japanese character now struck Ackerley as a national childishness. As so often in his life, lack of funds was also causing loss of temper. He was paying for the entire holiday but really could not afford to do so. The sight of a monkey chained to a table to amuse the customers at a café did little to lighten his spirits. Even a boat trip across the lagoon from Amano-hashidate to Ichinomia disappointed:

> One wonders why it is thought one of the three great beauty spots in Japan. A sheet of water surrounded by mountains and villages. Mountains are nothing new. We have had them all day on both sides of the train.

Ichinomia turned out to be 'as cold as the polar regions which it resembled', and the hotel there was a disaster. Snow drifted in through the screens of the bedroom, the food was cold and the service poor. All in all Ackerley was pleased when they set off south back to Kyoto, even though when he arrived he was obliged to book into a hotel, since Francis King appeared to be unable to accommodate him. The reason for this, King later confessed, was that Ackerley had proved a less than perfect guest:

[1] This information probably came from Plomer who thought Hearn very overrated.

Poor Joe had so little money that he really could not be expected to make any contribution to the household expenses; but he raced through the gin at a furious pace, starting on it long before I got back from the office and continuing for the rest of the evening. Auden used to make him pay for his gin – Joe was obliged to mark the bottle each time he took some and the inches were subsequently measured! – but I really did not feel that I could indulge in that kind of stinginess.

Ackerley further disgraced himself by encouraging King's previously well-trained dogs to sleep on the beds and climb up on to sofas and chairs. By the time he left, the dogs were to be found eating expensive, imported meats from the dining-table.

New Year's Eve ended in a terrible muddle, when Ackerley and Kinoshita lost each other on the way to a homosexual party. Ackerley had not wanted to go in the first place, and angrily shuffled back to his hotel to write letters and warm himself with whisky. He tried to convince himself that Kinoshita's apparent lack of consideration was in fact a good thing, 'more comradely and easy-going than the subordinate or subservient' relationship. However, he was not entirely bereft when it came to the moment of parting:

> I fancy there is something of the self-seeker in Kinoshita's character, to get on, almost at any cost, is his constant thought and ambition, and since Buddhism is a self-searching or self-seeking, thinking about oneself so as to perfect oneself instead of thinking of others, selfishness may well become one's character without one even knowing what was happening. I am not sure that Kinoshita is not already something of a schemer.

It may be that Ackerley knew that a parting was inevitable and that he was attempting to make things easier for himself. The last few pages of his Japanese notebook were ripped out and destroyed,[1] but when he eventually got back to England, he wrote to Francis King:

---

[1] King suspects that the missing pages contained criticisms of his hospitality. Ackerley had been hurt when banished to a hotel and may well have commented upon this. Knowing that, as literary executor, King would inherit the notebook, Ackerley might later have destroyed the offending pages.

If you hear anything of Kinoshita, let me know. I have pulled myself together to write to him. He gave me much happiness, and I was in the mood for it: I shall always be grateful to him, but of his character I cannot make up my mind. I have to learn more of Buddhism first – to him it comes first, I am sure – such hurdles between hearts worry me, I have none myself. I am another Leonard Woolf. I cannot understand religiosity, though I try. I can never see it as anything but fear, and that, in the powerful dominating race, seems to me pusillanimous and shameful.

He had hoped to visit Hong Kong where Edmund Blunden was living and wrote an orientally flattering letter somewhat at odds with his notebook jottings, assuring Blunden that 'in both [Sendai and Kyoto], as you will know – indeed, throughout Japan – you are much spoken of and your name greatly revered'. The ostensible object of the letter was to ask whether Blunden could find him a hotel (which, he emphasized, had to be very cheap, since funds were low), but clearly Ackerley was hoping for an invitation to stay. Resistant to this broad hint, Blunden booked Ackerley into the YMCA, but there was a muddle over dates, and letters went astray. Consequently Ackerley changed his plans and decided to go straight to Thailand, since he had an acquaintance in Bangkok who would accommodate him. This turned out to be a mistake, for in contrast to the bone-penetrating chill of Japan, the temperature in Bangkok was 90°F. He had problems with his visa, was plagued by mosquitoes and instantly developed a bad cold, which was accompanied by vomiting and diarrhoea. 'Make a firm resolution never to come,' he counselled Francis King.

The heat is stunning and humid, the place is a network of mostly stagnant waterways, all breeding mosquitoes galore, the terrain is perfectly flat in all directions, a low skyline, no higher than the length of palms, and banana and rain-trees that hems one in. Moving away from dear Japan towards India, all the disagreeable features of that latter country, as I remember it, begin here: the muddy complexion (often diddy-daddied [i.e. pustuled]), the muddy eye, laziness, stupidity, dishonesty, betel-chewing, dirt and filthy smells, bad and unhygienic food, no hot water, prickly heat, rampant rabies, and wretched mangy dogs, hairless and emaciated, whom no one will kill, and no one will feed. You would *detest* it my dear.

Sex appeared to be freely available, but Ackerley complained that he 'couldn't even raise a finger, let alone anything else, to investigate in this boiling, sweating atmosphere'. His guide was another young monk, a 'large lazy conceited dunderhead' who added to Ackerley's irritation with the country. He insisted upon dragging Ackerley round all the sights and showing him off to his teachers and family. His behaviour was not unlike that of that other bore way back in 1924, Ackerley's Chhatarpur tutor, Abdul Haq. Unaccustomed to the heat, ill and exhausted, Ackerley was not the perfect tourist. He looked at himself in the mirror and saw 'an old boiling-fowl', similar to those inedible birds with which he was confronted in every restaurant. The shrines and temples were pretty but tawdry, with Buddhas wherever one looked. The museums did have a few *lingams*, or phallic images, but were otherwise disappointing:

> Sought high and low for indecencies. Found none. Fear respectable royalty influential – many boring gilt chariots for conveying Royal remains to the burning Royal chairs. Royal collections of *bijouterie* and other rubbish. Royal camp stools and death beds. Cushions on which royal bums had sat.

The whole place appeared to have been geared to American tourists. Only the zoo earned full marks for its spacious enclosures and natural features such as boulders and trees in the shade of which animals could escape the terrible heat. But in the town dogs lay in the streets dying, unheeded by passers-by. One bitch, covered in sores, unable to move and yelping in pain, particularly upset him. He was furious that Buddhist belief prevented a vet from putting the creature out of its misery and vainly attempted to find a chemist who might sell him strychnine.

It was something of a relief after a week to fly home, stopping off briefly in Tehran ('wretched place'), where he was greeted by snow. On 15 January 1961, he arrived in London. Queenie had survived his absence, but Aunt Bunny had died in hospital on 3 January. With Bunny gone and funds low, it was inevitable that Nancy should leave her lodgings and move into Star and Garter Mansions. The entire flat was redecorated and in March Nancy came to live with her brother, permanently. Once there, she promptly fell ill with pleurisy and pneumonia and Ackerley was obliged to nurse her back to health. His care was apparently inadequate and Nancy threatened to throw herself out of the window because she considered him insufficiently attentive. ('So inconsiderate of pedestrians,' Ackerley complained to Geoffrey Gorer.)

> I have to pretend to greater love than I possess: any slackening sets the familiar mechanism going: 'Nobody loves me. I might as well be dead.' And one never knows when one has erred, a thoughtless word, or staying writing in one's room too long without visiting her.

This illness was merely the first of many. Nancy's practice of taking to her bed when things went wrong, established very early on, appears to have created some sort of pattern. As a young woman, she had merely sulked between the sheets; now she developed alarming medical symptoms, often running temperatures of as much as 102°. She took innumerable tranquillizers and sleeping pills in order to keep her life on an even keel, but would occasionally be overwhelmed by waves of depression or screaming rage, which brought physical illness in their wake. Sometimes she had to go into hospital and then spend several expensive weeks recuperating in assorted convalescent homes on the south coast. It seems that no one ever made a firm diagnosis of her illness. The tentative one of schizophrenia, made in 1948, was never confirmed, and it seems highly unlikely that this was the trouble, since her condition did not, as doctors feared, inexorably deteriorate. Aunt Bunny had dismissed the diagnosis on the grounds that, far from having a 'split personality', Nancy was 'the same all the way through'. When Ackerley asked her why her niece had suffered a breakdown, Bunny replied: 'Envy, hatred, malice and all uncharitableness.' 'Very true indeed,' Ackerley commented in his diary. 'Clever Bunny to perceive it'.

Whatever the case, although she occasionally had relapses, Nancy was never again as ill as she had been when incarcerated at Graylingwell.[1] Even so, she never entirely recovered from her suicide

[1] In 1963 Nancy developed disturbing new symptoms, suffering a loss of co-ordination. She fell over twice at a dinner party even though she had had very little to drink. Her condition rapidly worsened: Ackerley reported that she had become an old woman within a fortnight. She was taken into hospital for tests, but nobody could

attempt and her eyes never lost their look of barely suppressed desperation, as if she were permanently haunted by the spectre of her breakdown. Psychiatric treatment was sometimes proposed by her baffled GP, but as Ackerley told Geoffrey Gorer, who had also suggested this treatment,

> She has ... been through the psychiatric machine before, deep insulin and electric-shock treatment; true it did its job, but the 'insanity' (can't remember the right word) out of which it brought her was occasioned by the same psychological pattern that has continued, with ups and downs, ever since.

Another alternative was psychoanalysis, but he felt that this might reawaken the terrors of 1948, which were perhaps best left unexplored:

> The old trouble ... has always been a fright to her, and left a large area of her memory – such as her abominable treatment of my aunt – mercifully blank. Personally I think it would be a mistake to do anything to revive those memories; my aunt and I were always careful to steer her away from that area when we saw that she looked puzzled.

There is no doubt that, as the Graylingwell doctor had said, Nancy suffered from a 'long-standing personality disorder'. Prescribed drugs might help, but the condition was something that she – and her brother – had to live with. He was in no doubt as to what sort of cohabitation this would be. A few years earlier he had been reading a natural-history book and had noted in his journal:

> Symbionts are creatures (of different kinds?) that live together to their mutual advantage. Commensals are creatures that live together without injury and may or may not benefit from the

---

decide what was wrong with her. Whilst talking to the doctors an idea suddenly occurred to Ackerley: 'Would it help you to reach a diagnosis if I told you that our father had died of syphilis?' he asked. It did. Tests were performed and 'spirochetes were found'. This was clearly a moment for truth-telling and Ackerley informed his sister that she had been visited by 'the sins of the fathers', which not unnaturally alarmed her. Although a course of penicillin cured her, she later confessed that she lived in fear of 'crumbling to pieces'.

association (mensa = table); inquilines are creatures that live in the abodes of others and are not parasites; parasites are creatures that live at the expense of their host and harm it.

When he withdrew to his room, Ackerley was not merely avoiding Nancy, he was also attempting to put his recent holiday to good use. Without a great deal of enthusiasm, he reviewed a batch of books on Japan for *The Listener*. He also worked on his article about Kobo Daishi, but wondered whether the magazine would pay well enough, and placed the matter in the hands of David Higham, with whom he enjoyed an increasingly friendly professional relationship. He told Spender that the article contained his 'usual ingredients I fear, boys and dogs, but I think it is rather fun'. It was published in *The Listener* in August 1961 and was a characteristic essay, reminiscent of *Hindoo Holiday*, with Kinoshita fulfilling the Narayan role, the eternally attractive youth whom Ackerley woos. It also contained a 'shocking' detail of the sort he had always enjoyed slipping into the magazine when he was literary editor, a detail which also provided a sly gloss upon his relationship with the 'attractive . . . grave and beautiful' young priest with whom he was linking arms:

> At this point the avenue [to Kobo Daishi's tomb] was embanked and through one of the earth walls a cedar root had forced its way. One could not fail to notice it, it was so huge and obtruded on our path; I could not help but touch it, it was so beautiful in its texture and colour. As smooth as silk, it bulged nakedly out like the scrotum of some fabulous beast. Soft beads of gum had sweated out of it and clung to its stretched, contorted surface. The great tree it had erected drove like a spear into the sky. I laid my hand upon it; it was warm like flesh and seemed to throb.

The reader is left in little doubt as to why Ackerley feels 'at one with the universe'.

In spite of such fun, and further reviews of Japanese and animal books, Ackerley declared himself thoroughly bored. Writing 'Kobo Daishi', and receiving letters from Francis King, Kinoshita and a Japanese air-force boy he had met on a train, made him nostalgic for Japan. He was determined to make some money in order to return there. There was little, it seemed, to be made from *We Think the World of You*, which, in spite of favourable reviews, had not sold particularly well. However, two American publishers had been bidding for the book. Since Ivan Obolensky had offered $1500, twice as much as Alfred Knopf, Ackerley's choice seemed ready-made and, although somewhat disconcerted when he met Obolensky, who studiously avoided any mention of the book, he was delighted to receive the first part of his advance.

Apart from the occasional review Ackerley was unable to concentrate upon writing. By now Queenie, like her master, was old, deaf and decrepit. Ackerley had prayed that she would die whilst he was in Japan, but he had returned to find her 'somewhat wraith-like' and 'almost out of the few wits she has left', but still pottering on. In May she was sixteen and had, Ackerley reported, 'forgotten the difference between indoors and outdoors for an important matter'. The flat stank as badly as it had when Bunny was in decline. She no longer ventured out on walks, but occasionally staggered out on to the terrace, where she attempted to relieve herself, and watched neighbours and birds silently, no longer raising her voice in warning. On good days she would occasionally totter after a pigeon. 'One day a sparrow perched on her rump as she stood looking silently through the balustrade; it seemed almost the final humiliation.' In spite of the advice of friends, Ackerley determined to carry on with her, praying that she would die in her sleep. He would have had her destroyed, but her eyes remained bright, fixed upon him as she gazed from her chair. Her teeth gave her trouble, her breath was appalling and she had developed a benign tumour on her jaw. Geoffrey Gorer felt that she had now reached the end of the line, but Ackerley wrote back crossly: 'I will act firmly when the time comes, and I think it may be near, but it has not come yet.' Would Gorer have hastened the end of his brother, who had recently died after an incurable illness, Ackerley enquired? Shortly after her birthday Queenie had two rooted-abscessed teeth removed and, harrowing though this operation was, she was found by the vet to have a strong heart for her age. This proved a brief reprieve. After a short and not very vigorous new lease of life, she began to deteriorate rapidly. 'I can do no more than read trash and mark time upon the moment when I shall have to summon euthanasia to her release,' he told Higham. 'Beyond that I cannot look.' With grim dedication, Ackerley nursed his geriatric patient. Her circulation was poor and her digestion unreliable, and he stood by with blankets, laxatives, suppositories and a vaselined finger. She could no longer eat unaided.

For three weeks I spoon-fed her with everything, glaxo protein foods, little bits of raw mince steak, water, milk, putting them into the pouch of her jaw. She became weaker and thinner. Now she could not get up at all of her own accord, to walk or change position in her bed; I lifted her for everything, and when she was up she had difficulty in lying down again, slowly, carefully, and awkwardly subsiding as though she had rheumatism. She got very thin; the bones of her bottom stood out, her ribs were visible, her stomach sank in . . . Lying in her bed under her blanket her eyes were fixed always upon me, so loving, so bright still, so beautiful. It made the step I had to take in the end all the more difficult (how I wished she would die, like my aunt, in her sleep), until she did something that upset me even more than her inability to eat, she began to turn her face to the wall, to turn her back on me. Then I had her destroyed.

In fact the vet was summoned twice and then put off. Eventually, on 30 October, Ackerley gave Queenie a heavy dose of sleeping tablets and sat down to write a letter to Geoffrey Gorer. The vet then arrived and gave her a tranquillizing injection. After ten minutes she had entered a profound sleep. Ackerley carried her down the stairs for the last time and put her in the vet's car. He did not accompany her to the surgery where the 'final quietus' would be administered.

I wish I believed in an afterlife [he later wrote], that kind of sweet afterlife believed in by the Hindoos, in which great love brings souls together again. I would have immolated myself as a *suttee* when Queenie died. For no human being would I ever have done such a thing, but by my love for Queenie I would have been irresistibly compelled. I had thrust her behind the curtain and if there was a life of the spirit, there, just upon the other side, she must inevitably wait. What else could she do, she who had no other desire but for my love. She would wait there, where I had pushed her, just behind the curtain, as she had always stopped in the street, patiently until I joined her. If I had believed in such things I would not have kept her waiting. With open arms I would have cast myself through after her and our bright spirits, disencumbered by our aged, hampering bodies, would have bounded off joyfully together over the Elysian Fields.

18

In mourning

ACKERLEY never entirely recovered from the death of Queenie. He described 30 October 1961 as 'the saddest day of my life', and there is no doubt that, like many widowers, he went into a slow decline thereafter. 'I shall never stop missing her,' he told Donald Windham, 'no human being has ever meant so much to me as she meant.' The flat seemed haunted, he told Francis King:

> It is difficult, in this room that we shared, not to think about her all the time, fifteen years and they were the happiest of my life; she provided for it a background of secure, unalterable devotion, which my nature needed: how I am to get on without it I do not know. I don't so much mind being *in* the room as entering it, or indeed entering the flat at all; perhaps the heart of emptiness is a little less cold than the approaches.

Forster wrote to say that he was glad that Ackerley had been 'personally involved' in Queenie's death, but it was this involvement which sharpened Ackerley's misery with the relentless gnawing of remorse. Although he knew that he had done the kindest possible thing in having Queenie destroyed, he also saw this action as a betrayal of her immovable trust in him. 'It was decently done,' he told Benjamin Britten, 'she knew nothing that happened to her; it is I who knew too much.' This guilt informs a poem he wrote about her death:

> Pretty lady, pray forgive,
> I took your loving life away
> I could not bear to see you live

Self-soiled and old, so sickly thin
I let the needle enter in
Pretending it was play.

Unable to mourn Queenie with much sincerity, Forster nonetheless took practical action and decided to pay for Ackerley to travel to America as his emissary when Santha Rama Rau's adaptation of *A Passage to India* opened in New York. Ackerley's view of America and the Americans, like that of many Englishmen, fluctuated violently between genuine admiration and fastidious distaste. In 1951, recommending librettists to Britten, he had written: 'Let the Americans have a shot too. It *is* the sort of thing they do, and they have rare minds, such good standards of taste. I have the most soaring opinion of them.' As it soared, so his opinion plunged and, although he liked most of the Americans he met, and made close friends amongst them, he came more and more to distrust them as a people.

He looked particularly askance at American politics, and the national paranoia about Communism. When, in the 1950s, he had flirted with the idea of encouraging his intellectual friends to join the Communist Party, announcing their move in *The Times,* he had been motivated by a feeling that the world was once more drifting towards war and that it would be better to be Red than dead. He had not thought out his position at all clearly, and after reproofs from his more politically serious friends, like Herbert Read and Stuart Hampshire, he abandoned the idea, remarking:

I saw that it wouldn't work anyway, even if one did manage to create a relatively civilized and attractive Communist party here and start a slide into it, for the US would not stand for that and would blast a Communist England off the map, I suppose; so that we should in any case have the war which it was my sole object to try to avoid. That we should be sacrificed to American fear seems to me intolerable: has not Mr Acheson [President Truman's virulently anti-Communist Secretary of State] lately said 'The British have taken it once and can take it again'. They, of course (the Americans), though they don't seem to think so, will survive relatively cosily in their immense continent; the Russians too; just a few dents and burns here and there: we shall be destroyed.

His unhappy experience of US publishers did little to improve his regard for Americans, and a large number of his letters in the 1960s contain disparaging references to America and its people, as do his notebook entries and journalism. He was pleased, for instance, to insert in one of his articles what he described as a 'jolly gratuitous insult' to American readers. It was, therefore, with mixed feelings that he accepted Forster's offer of a passage to America. At the beginning of 1961 he had told John Wickens that he had never felt any inclination to visit America, but now that the prospect was in view he was rather more enthusiastic, particularly when it became apparent that Forster was prepared to pay for him to visit California where he would have an opportunity to see old friends such as Gerald Heard, Christopher Wood and Christopher Isherwood.

It was Isherwood who reported the unwelcome rumour from America that Ivan Obolensky had, like the Cummington Press before him, gone bust. Ackerley had heard nothing from Obolensky for some six months, despite the fact he had written to him to ask whether it would be possible to restore *We Think the World of You* to its unexpurgated version. All he had received was a request for a photograph from the company's publicity department; he had sent one and received no acknowledgement. He asked Higham to make enquiries:

> The Americans are so arrogant and conscienceless in their behaviour to other people's works that I am greatly worried as to how they are treating mine. Are they setting up afresh in America, or taking pages in photostats from here? If they are setting it up afresh *I ought to have had proofs*. I feel quite anxious.

Ackerley's anxiety was entirely justified. The company had not gone bust, but denied receiving any letter from him. In consequence, they informed him, they had used the original Bodley Head edition. They had omitted to use recommendations supplied by Isherwood and Angus Wilson, but agreed to make up bookmarks using these quotations and insert one in each copy. Galley proofs had been airmailed to Ackerley.

No galleys ever arrived, but finished copies of the book did. Ackerley was appalled. Far from using the unexpurgated version of the novel, as Ackerley had originally hoped, the publishers had used an uncorrected proof of the Bodley Head edition. The book was riddled with errors and omissions and the careful sectional arrangement of the book had been ignored. Both as a craftsman and as an editor Ackerley was extremely angry to see a carefully wrought work of art ruined by carelessness. He sent Higham a copy of the book with its 'stupidities and mistakes' marked:

> I am quite disgusted with it; how do publishers expect things to make sense and sell in so muddled a state? And why did I not have a proof?
>
> Can you sting the bastard for me? I will never let him have another book. And could you make a mental note that in any future contracts of mine in English speaking countries an emphatic clause should be inserted that I must see a proof before publication?

Higham's American associates delivered a rebuke to Obolensky, who replied apologetically that he had been away at the time and had not personally overseen the production. The person who had was no longer with the company.

In England, however, the book had begun to do well, boosted by a long and serious review by Stuart Hampshire in *Encounter*. Hampshire wrote that the book 'set a standard of truthfulness' and that its meticulously narrated story achieved something important and rare: 'This is an eccentric and strange episode of the conversion of love. But a very particular case is turned into a general truth by the art of fiction.' In the Christmas 1961 edition of the *Sunday Times*, three critics selected *We Think the World of You* as one of their Books of the Year (even though the book had been published in 1960): Richard Buckle, Raymond Mortimer and Desmond Shawe-Taylor. Friends had also written to congratulate him. John Gielgud, Stephen Spender and W. H. Auden all agreed upon the book's excellence, and it was bought by an English paperback publisher, Ace Books.

Even so, little could cheer Ackerley during the early months of 1962 and he did not get to the New York première of *A Passage to India*, which took place on 31 January. He was approached by the publisher Paul Elek who wanted him to edit an anthology of animal stories, but depression sapped his will, and nothing ever came of this project. He considered buying a smallholding in Norfolk, where he often stayed with Jack and Velda Sprott, and becoming a 'farmerlet'. Forster thought this an excellent idea, but unsurprisingly it got no further than talk. Eventually, weathering Nancy's predictable bout of illness, Ackerley summoned up the energy to fly to New York.

Sandy Campbell recalled Ackerley's arrival:

> *Vaguely*, I had said to him: 'Joe, if you ever come to America for *A Passage to India*, come and stay with me.' Well, one day I was home and the doorbell rang, and up the stairs, five flights – there was an elevator, but up the *stairs* – came Joe Ackerley. He had got off the plane, he had come to the house, he had rung the doorbell . . . and there he was! How did he know that I would be there? He had his suitcase.

In fact Ackerley had written to Campbell to warn him of his arrival, but had reached the East 80th Street apartment before the letter. Donald Windham was in Italy at the time and so Campbell put Ackerley up for a few days and then found him a rather scruffy hotel in Gramercy Park. There Ackerley whiled away his time feeding the cockroaches, rather as his mother, in her decline, had fed her pet fly. The trip, as he had predicted, was not a success. Most of his friends and contacts were working during the day and although he was entertained in the evenings, he spent the days drifting listlessly around the city. He took his nephew, Paul, whom he hadn't seen since 1945, to see *A Passage to India*, and was glad to visit the Metropolitan Museum of Art and see Sargent's portrait of Roger's first wife, Louise Burckhardt. He was delighted by the tame squirrels in Central Park, but wished that he had a companion with whom to share his experiences. Campbell visited him every day, recalling that on one occasion he arrived at the Irving Hotel at ten a.m. and found Ackerley already well into a tumbler of whisky. 'He was lost . . . I was worried about him, he was not happy; he hadn't found whatever it was that made him happy.' The real trouble, as Ackerley confessed to Gorer, was that with the death of Queenie he had *lost* that which made him happy:

> I carry it with me always, this desolation in my heart. It is a feeling of being quite without purpose, at a loss, at an end. To be boozed up at night is good; to wake in the morning renewed sorrow.

He was, however, pleasantly surprised by the natives, writing to Windham: 'Considering the ill-repute Americans seemed to have earned in Europe and the Far East, I am delighted and surprised to find them so kind and so good-mannered.' He dined with Auden and Chester Kallman, Lincoln Kirstein, Edmund Wilson, Edith Oliver, Paul Cadmus (who introduced him to members of the New York City Ballet), Carl Van Vechten and others, but none of this did much to raise his spirits. 'I feel like a parcel which, though empty, wants to be picked up and taken everywhere until it comes undone,' he wrote.

After a fortnight he flew on to Los Angeles, where he stayed with Noel and Marietta Voge, both of whom taught at UCLA. Ackerley had met Noel when he had been in England during the war, and Forster had stayed with the Voges during American trips. Much as he appreciated the efforts made by his hosts, Ackerley was repelled by Los Angeles, writing dyspeptically to Francis King:

> Almost everything is absurdly expensive, and university lecturers' fees are less than gardeners'. Don't ever come here. I bussed up to the ocean, your Pacific, this morning and mooched along Santa Monica Boulevard. Dogs are not allowed on any green place, not even upon the sands of the vast seashore. Don't ever come here. A long rack on the Boulevard offered free pamphlets and literature, in different receptacles, from no less than fourteen varieties of the Christian Church. Don't ever come here . . .

And so on. Whilst Christopher Wood evoked painful memories since he was preoccupied with Penny, his ageing dachshund, Gerald Heard was 'well worth crossing America to see'.

> He is so gay and mischievous, so affectionate, so learned and beautiful with his visionary gaze. He is a tantric Buddhist, a 'senile optimist', as he calls himself, and believes in the continuance of the spirit and that all children should have their sphincters loosened by penetration and massage at the age of seven to dispel anxiety and tension.

Heard felt that his life's work had been achieved and confessed that he was 'impatiently awaiting death'. His prediction that Ackerley would not survive to see 1964 proved the most cheering aspect of the entire American trip, although Ackerley enjoyed visiting Isherwood and his companion, Don Bachardy. The previous summer Bachardy had been in London and both Ackerley and Nancy had sat for him. The result had been two extremely telling portraits which, in their unblinking representation of decay and defeat, attained the sort of truth Ackerley applauded. These reunions apart, Ackerley was not unhappy, after three weeks, to bid Los Angeles farewell:

> The place was appalling, a nightmare of Western — perhaps ultimately all — civilization, the way that it is going. On one of my last afternoons there, stranded in my host's house in this vast metropolis, a bulldozer arrived and, in a jiffy, pushed down every tree in the extension of our avenue. Within an hour or so, some fifty great trees went down like ninepins, bringing up the side-walks with their roots: another interminable 'freeway' for 65 miles-an-hour traffic was to be added to the maze of freeways already existing. The following morning the road outside the house was crawling with birds and squirrel families, young and adult, who had lost their homes. An endless shuttling of cars, full of empty aimless heads: the American way of life has nothing for me . . .

Neither, it seemed, had the English way of life. He was commissioned to write an article about dogs for *Punch*, but, after struggling for a while, felt unable to produce anything. He also tinkered with his Family Memoir, writing the chapters which deal with his own sexual life. His mood may be gauged by the fact that he destroyed a lot of papers. He told Gorer that he was in a

> low state of mind, self-induced by returning to my autobiography. It is better not to write — or even think — about oneself at all unless one can do so with complacency. But no area of my life affords me, upon scrutiny, a vestige of that. The best I can do is to laugh at myself, but whatever a hollow laugh may be, I fear it is that. However, I have almost finished the autopsy now.

The journeys to Japan and America had confirmed his fears that the world of intimate human relationships was closed to him. Apart from a few close and long-standing friendships, he did not appear to engage with anyone to any great degree. Even those who might reasonably be supposed to be intimates discerned a coldness. Stuart Hampshire felt that Ackerley was 'incapable, in a Freudian sense, of loving anybody', a judgement echoed in a chilling exchange Ackerley had with his half-sister, Diana. Anxious to say something to relieve his depression, she asked whether he would ever consider having another animal. He said no. 'I'm sure you will, you know,' Diana replied. 'Someone like you, so full of love . . .' As she said it, she suddenly realized, for the first time, that 'this was exactly what he was not'.

> He gave me *such* a look – I'll never forget it – and he said: 'Do you really believe that I'm full of love?' And having put one foot in, I had to put the other in and said 'But of course!' He knew that I didn't mean it. There was a dead silence.

Ackerley's depression was little helped by the fact that he had begun to suffer acute pain in his left leg, which meant that he was unable to sit down, and which made his foot numb. He was suffering from sciatica, but after six weeks of intense discomfort he went to see a doctor who sent him to hospital for tests for prostate and kidney disease. Nothing untoward was found. He was obliged to stand or lie down and spent much of his time dosed up with alcohol and pain-killers, neither of which proved any more effective than the physiotherapy and infra-red treatment prescribed by his doctor. He took to his bed for a month and re-read Proust, frustrated and morose.

The only bright light in his existence was provided by a fledgling sparrow he found on the pavement outside Star and Garter Mansions one day. It had damaged its leg and, apart from a few wing-feathers, was entirely bald, but this unprepossessing creature moved Ackerley to pity and he scooped it up and installed it in his room. He fed it with bread and milk, using a pen-nib, and gradually coaxed it back to health. This was a considerable feat, but Ackerley's friends looked on in horror as his room was gradually transformed to accommodate the bird, which he named after the popular television cowboy, Hopalong Cassidy. He spread copies of *The Times* on the floor and gathered cardboard boxes, some old files and the Oxford Atlas in order to make a 'playpen'. He also made a perch, four inches above the ground, and provided an earth-filled flower pot in which Cassidy could enjoy dust baths. In one box he put an old sock, in the woollen folds of which the bird slept. Cassidy flapped ineffectually about the room, hopping about the furniture and covering everything with shit. Although

Ackerley

Ackerley constantly protested that he did not really care for the bird –
'a dirty, tatty, unrewarding little beast, entirely ungrateful' – he took
great pains with it and was deeply upset when he took it out on to the
terrace and it hopped through the balustrade. He spent two hours
hunting along the Lower Richmond Road for the bird, easily identi-
fiable amongst other sparrows because half their size, and eventually
located it in a neighbouring pub. He recaptured it and bore it back to
the flat in triumph, but the rigorous search had done little to ease his
sciatica and by the evening he could hardly move at all. In spite of his
assumed indifference towards the bird, he began to wonder whether it
might not have somehow acquired part of Queenie's spirit, an oriental
notion he took half-seriously.

When Ackerley was in the States, he had been disappointed not to
see Bill Roerick, who had been on tour at the time. Now Roerick came
to England and found Forster 'distressed' by Ackerley's absorption in
Cassidy. Roerick got the impression that Forster missed Ackerley's
frequent trips to Cambridge, which had been curtailed by the sparrow.
Roerick was invited to Star and Garter Mansions and was astonished
by the transformation of Ackerley's room:

> The day-bed, the pictures, the desk, the floor, the chairs, and the
> rows of books were covered with newspapers. A bowl of seed and
> one of water stood on newspapers on the hearth. Joe ushered me in
> to meet his sparrow. But there was no bird in sight. Joe called – no
> answer. Then, sadly, he said, 'He must have gone', and began to
> remove the papers from the bookshelves. From between some books
> came the bird. He nervously flew across the room to the chimney-
> piece, defecating as he flew. 'There you are!' said a pleased Joe. The
> bird paid no attention.
>
> I suggested that it was perhaps short of humane to keep it indoors.
> 'But it can get out if it wants to', and he pointed to the window. It
> was open about an inch and a half. A determined sparrow might
> walk under it if he ducked his head. The bird, Joe claimed, was
> welcome to leave anytime it wished but it *wouldn't* leave his room.

Roerick agreed with Forster that the situation was bad not only for
Ackerley, but also for the bird. Whilst Ackerley was in the kitchen
preparing drinks, Roerick removed the seed and water and placed
them outside the door in the hallway; the bird hopped after them.

When Ackerley saw this he was astonished. Cassidy hopped up the steps and out on to the terrace. He stood for a moment on the balustrade and then flew away. In letters recounting this incident, Ackerley claimed that Roerick had *driven* the bird out of his room and his life. He had intended to return the bird to the wild himself, but insisted that it had shown no inclination to leave him. Roerick was sceptical and suggested that Ackerley was unwilling to acknowledge that the bird could do perfectly well without him. He recalls that

> although the drinks were drunk in a strained but highly civil atmosphere, there was no doubt in my mind that Joe was not best pleased. His politeness, however, kept him from reprimanding me – or even showing annoyance.

In retrospect, Roerick acknowledges that he should have let well alone, but thinks that it was better that Ackerley should have believed that he had driven the bird away rather than have had to face up to its unassisted desertion. Ackerley spent a great deal of time inspecting the local sparrows, hoping to discover Cassidy amongst them, but concluded sadly that it might have fallen victim to the Duke's Head cats. Forster was delighted that the bird had gone, but Ackerley complained that Cassidy's disappearance 'added a new sorrow to my heart, which had enough already'.

He was distracted from these avian concerns by a tragedy which had befallen the Buckinghams. Their son Robin, now married with two sons, had been mysteriously ill for some time. The first symptoms, which appeared at the end of 1960, were of jaundice, but May suspected that the illness was more serious, possibly cancer of the liver. These original fears were kept from Ackerley, who was fond of Rob (as he was known), in order to ensure that he got off to Japan. By now the illness had finally revealed itself as Hodgkin's Disease and it was clearly terminal. Rob had been placed in a health hydro at Weymouth, which, like some smart hotel, did not care to have its patients dying on the premises and was prepared to rush the dying to Weymouth Hospital. Forster, disgusted by this attitude, insisted that if Rob's condition worsened he should be ferried back (by chauffeur-driven car if necessary) to London, where he lived. Ackerley often visited Rob at the hydro and when it became clear that the end was near, he hired a car and drove down to Weymouth himself in order to fetch Rob and his wife, Sylvia, back to their London home. Ackerley's driving was so terrifying that Sylvia became more concerned for their immediate safety than for her husband's long-term prospects.

Shortly afterwards, Rob died. Ackerley went round to see May the next day, a gesture many would have shunned in favour of a carefully composed letter.[1] 'Darling, I know *exactly* what you're going through,' he told her as they sat in Hanger Lane Park. 'I've been through it *all* with Queenie. And *don't* believe people when they tell you that time heals it and that you'll forget. You won't.' Some might have regarded the comparison as tactless, but May was one of the few people who had truly understood Ackerley's relationship with Queenie, and she was deeply touched by this speech.

In August Ackerley was persuaded by Sonia Orwell to take part in a farcical International Writers' Conference at the Edinburgh Festival. He was so flattered to be asked that, rather against his better judgement, he accepted and spent a week in Edinburgh listening to Mary McCarthy, Norman Mailer and William Burroughs, but not, as he put it, opening his own beak, not even when the debate turned to homosexuality in literature. He was still suffering from sciatica and found sitting with the delegation uncomfortable. He was surprised that anyone could consider him distinguished enough to appear as part of the Conference '*galère*', but in fact his literary stock was rising. After *We Think the World of You* received its Christmas boost in the *Sunday Times*, sales had improved to such a degree that The Bodley Head had reprinted it in March 1962. In the wake of the disastrous American edition, Ackerley was glad of the opportunity to make the new English one perfect by correcting its few misprints.

In September, to his immense surprise, he was told that the book was to be given the W. H. Smith Annual [sic] Literary Award for 'the most outstanding contribution to English literature to appear in the two years ending December 1961'. The news was supposed to be a great secret, although it leaked out to such an extent that Nancy overheard it being discussed on a train. The judges were Elizabeth

---

[1] This was something that Ackerley saw as a duty of friendship and Janet Adam Smith recalled her surprise and gratitude when he insisted upon coming to see her when her husband, Michael Roberts, died.

Bowen, Harold Nicolson and Philip Toynbee. Their decision had not been reached without some disagreement, for whilst Bowen and Toynbee were convinced that Ackerley should receive the prize, Nicolson had not entirely recovered from the shock he had been given by *My Dog Tulip*, and was nervous about honouring a novel with a homosexual theme. Toynbee was not prepared to sacrifice Ackerley's right to the prize to Nicolson's concern for his own reputation, and eventually won his fellow judge round. Ackerley felt that Richard Hughes should have won the prize and was sceptical of the entire idea since he had thought little of the two most recent winners, Laurie Lee's *Cider with Rosie* ('second-rate') and Patrick White's *Voss* ('unreadable').

Forster warned him that he could not 'expect to get all that money from a commercial firm without hopping through a hoop'. Ackerley, who disapproved of circuses, literary or otherwise, ruefully acknowledged that the £1,000 prize money would no doubt compensate for the indignities he was to undergo. His only concern was that the publicity might draw Freddie's attention to the book and that he would end up spending the prize-money settling a libel action. 'I look forward to the cheque with pleasure, to the party with the utmost horror,' he told Higham. 'I have to make a speech, a thing I have never done before; take me out to lunch and tell me what to say.' Higham, it appears, had no advice, but Forster, amused that a homosexual novel should be awarded a prize funded by the notoriously prudish firm of booksellers, provided some ribald suggestions:

> It is a surprise as well as a pleasure to receive such a cheque from such a firm, hitherto the very soul of purity. Can it be that a change has occurred? Can it be that after closing time the inner arcana of your directors are visited by guests of brawn and beauty? Can this account for certain unexpected promotions in your junior staff? Can it be that I could be of any further help?
>
> I scarcely dare hope so . . . But I cannot but recall that the founder of your firm was once hailed on the humoursome Victorian stage as the 'ruler of the Queen's Navee' [in Gilbert and Sullivan's *HMS Pinafore*]. If you require any reintroductions there I shall be happy to effect them. My connection has not been inconsiderable. And I should waive my usual fee.
>
> Your generous cheque (for which I thank you) will cover all

incidental expenses, and I accept it in the spirit in which it was no doubt given: as an advance payment on lust.

A large party was arranged at the Savoy on 16 October at which Smiths had proposed that the cheque should be presented to Ackerley by Hugh Carleton Greene, the current DG at the BBC and a director of The Bodley Head. Ackerley threatened to boycott the ceremony if Greene was involved. 'To have someone else's cash handed to me by a Corporation so mean with their own would be the limit,' he told Francis King.[1] A further tactless suggestion was that, since Queenie was dead, a substitute Alsatian could be procured to take her place on the podium beside the winning author. A naked boy would have pleased him rather more, Ackerley told Roy Fuller, but it would scarcely have pleased Lord Longford, whom Smiths had perversely chosen to present the award. At the time Longford had achieved notoriety and the unsuitable sobriquet 'Lord Porn' for his militant campaigning against obscenity. Smiths' next suggestion was that a blown-up photograph of Queenie could act as a backdrop to the proceedings, but Ackerley 'then had to explain that if a libel action were desired it could hardly be better invited than to have the very face of "Johnny's" dog spread all over the press.' In the end Smiths supplied 'a giant copy of the book decorated with golden bay-leaves, standing in front of a sort of slum decor' (in fact an enlarged photograph of a typical working-class London street).

Ackerley was so nervous that he declared himself 'almost a hospital case by the Great Day'. He arrived at the extremely smart and well-attended party with three speeches prepared and listened, faintly appalled, as Lord Longford opened the proceedings. The irony of Longford's being called upon to honour a book which had undergone extensive revision in order to avoid a prosecution for obscenity was lost on no one but the Earl himself. He announced that he had been told that 'there was something dubious about the book, but he had read it twice and didn't see, could it be in the last paragraph (which he

---

[1] To add insult to injury, his successor at *The Listener* had been appointed at a much-increased salary. Although he liked, and approved the appointment of, K. W. Gransden, he deeply resented the fact that the BBC was prepared to pay the new literary editor 'double' the amount he had ever received, whilst at the same time refusing to give the old literary editor a generous pension.

read aloud) and perhaps Mr Ackerley would explain.'[1] Mr Ackerley declined and Longford pronounced the book a 'delicate, beautifully written tale by one of our most distinguished men of letters'. Ackerley then stepped up to receive the cheque, and delivered the shortest of his three speeches, recalled by Fred Warburg as:

> Thank you for the £1,000 – I shall take myself off to Japan with it – couldn't afford to go otherwise – I've always wanted to return.

The indignities were not yet over, however, as he complained to Francis King: 'The press was certainly a pain, photographing me in every disgusting position – waving the cheque above my head – and, after all, not a single one appeared in the papers.'

[1] According to Fred Warburg, Longford later confessed that he had not read the book at all.

19

Ackerley contra mundum

'STUFFED with cash . . . I can go anywhere, do anything I like, if God spares me,' Ackerley told Francis King after winning the Smith Award. Indeed, his plan to revisit Japan was serious enough for him to cast round for accommodation. James Kirkup had left Japan, but King was still there, as were several of the British Council people Ackerley had met during his visit. King suggested that Ackerley should join him for Christmas in Angkor, but then changed his plans since he could not really afford the trip. Ackerley did not want to spend Christmas in Nagasaki, but thought that he might join King in the new year with the prospect of seeing the Naked Festival at Miyazaki Aoshima, during which young men scrabbled unclothed around a cave. This also fell through, as did a plan to travel to Japan by freighter with Kirkup and an invitation to join the Sprotts in Norfolk. Although desperate to get out of England, he eventually failed to do so and thus endured one of the coldest winters on record.

Christmas 1962 was particularly grim. For some time now, Ackerley's half-sister Sally had supplied Star and Garter Mansions with a Christmas turkey. This kind gesture was not always appreciated, since the birds were invariably large and Nancy made a fuss about cooking them. This year they invited for Christmas Eve a couple with whom they had something in common. The woman was 'another schizo, like Nancy, out of her bin for the hols'. Ackerley reported that 'the evening was a little anxious at times, but there was no bloodshed.' The only other visitor was John Morris, and the main highlight of the season, a broadcast on the radio by William Plomer, was missed because of inattention and alcohol. The weather was so cold that

394

Ackerley took to his bed, where he remained, fully dressed in corduroy trousers, three pullovers and bedsocks, reading detective stories and reports of the Tribunal set up to investigate the case of William Vassall, the homosexual spy who had recently been convicted of treason. He occasionally ventured outside in order to deal with hunks of bread that people had thrown out for the birds but had inconsiderately failed to crumble. He did not bother to wash or shave and announced that his chief concern was 'to reduce the hours of consciousness to less than twelve'. It was, he told Plomer, 'a jolly start to a Happy New Year'.

Indeed, the whole of 1963 was fairly disastrous, much of it spent alcoholically comatose. Ackerley always drank a great deal and appeared to have a considerable capacity. Few people recall ever seeing him the worse for drink in company, although there is no doubt that by this stage of his life he was drinking more than was good for him. When going to visit friends he always packed a half-bottle of Scotch for his own consumption in case his hosts' drinks cupboard proved insufficient. Money that might have been spent on trips to the Far East was now released to be spent at the off-licence. As he confessed to Francis King:

> My mother took to the bottle, I am my mother's son, and God bless the Smith Award for enabling one to be careless of expense. This morning as I lay in my bath I noticed with surprise some bruises and abrasions on my carcase and wondered how on earth I had sustained them. Then I vaguely recollected that in bending down to remove my shoes the previous night before going to bed, I had fallen forward on my face among various articles of furniture.

Towards the end of the year he had another and more serious tumble. He claimed that he had only been drinking the usual amount, but after a row with Nancy, who had been accusing the charwoman of using her make-up, Ackerley suffered a blackout and was discovered lying on the floor of his bedroom with a gash in his head that required stitches.

Alcohol was about the only interest that Ackerley and Nancy had in common. Their relationship had slithered into grim parody of marriage, a union held together largely by guilt and gin. Their circumstances reminded some onlookers of a Strindberg play, whilst the novelist Clifford Kitchin, watching from his window as the shabby couple trailed along the street, arm in arm, clutching a bottle from the off-licence, murmured: 'Charles and Mary Lamb'. It was almost worse for Nancy to be allowed to live with her brother than to have been abandoned to solitude, for their life together merely emphasized the unbridgeable gulf between them. She had got what she wanted but, as Ackerley observed, she was one of those 'victors who find their victory dust and ashes in their hands'. The claustrophobic atmosphere of Star and Garter Mansions, from which Nancy rarely emerged except to do the shopping, crackled with tension and bitterness and occasionally erupted into storm. Ackerley would inform Nancy that he was spending the evening with someone else and she would suffer a complete loss of control. Sometimes she screamed so loudly that anxious neighbours would come to investigate. When Ackerley reluctantly asked friends whether Nancy might be invited along, and they (sometimes with equal reluctance), agreed, Nancy was rarely grateful. 'I am too old and ugly to go anywhere!' she would cry. How could she possibly be seen in company when she had no clothes to wear, when her hair needed doing, when her face was blotchy and she could not afford decent make-up?

Her half-sister Diana suspected that Nancy suffered from agoraphobia and simply could not face the outside world. This may well have been true; it was equally true, however, that, in spite of all the anger and cruelty that the relationship engendered, Nancy wanted her brother for herself and resented the fact that he might seek other company than hers. Ackerley sometimes took her to the coast for a week, largely as a peace-offering, so that he could later go on holiday with friends like Jack and Velda Sprott without causing appalling scenes. These breaks were rarely successful, since Nancy required several hours of preparation before she felt she could face the world and never appeared before ten-thirty in the morning, which meant that they missed the morning excursion coaches. 'Her self-consciousness about her appearance has reached the point where she prefers to sit with her back to the light – and the view,' Ackerley told William Plomer. 'Provided with the quietest room in the hotel, facing the sea, she never gets a proper night's rest unless drugged with one of the four different kinds of soporifics she fidgets between; her bowels seldom work.'

'What a boring useless woman she is!' Ackerley exclaimed to Geoffrey Gorer. 'How I wish I could make her vanish away.' But he could not. If they really *had* been married, a divorce might have been arranged. But the tie was more binding than that. Ackerley was still haunted by what he saw as the failure of his relationships within his family; he was still haunted by the fact that his sister had once been so unhappy that she had attempted suicide and had a serious breakdown. In his darker moments he still blamed himself. 'I have always been addicted to remorse,' he admitted, and, however much he may have disliked the idea, Nancy fed his habit.

Whilst Nancy could just about accept that Ackerley's friends might be more interested in him than in her, she was less prepared to accept the partisanship of their half-sisters. Elizabeth had developed lateral sclerosis and, after a grim tour of Europe visiting medical experts, she came back to England to live with Sally and her husband at their home in Cheshire. Although the twins had far less in common with Ackerley than Diana did, Sally sometimes asked her half-brother to come to stay with her. In fact, he only went twice, but this was twice more than Nancy. Sally and Elizabeth met Nancy once, but the meeting was not a great success. In 1957 Elizabeth died.

Ackerley might have visited Sally more often, but quite apart from the problem of going without Nancy, there was the small matter of how he was to be introduced to Sally's friends and neighbours: how was their relationship to be explained? Matters were considerably complicated when Gerald became the fourth Duke of Westminster in 1963.[1] Ackerley was very amused by the idea that he had a half-sister

---

[1] The route by which Gerald became Duke is a tortuous one. When Sally and Gerald married in 1945, the second Duke, 'Bendor', was still alive and it seemed highly unlikely that Gerald would ever inherit the title. Had it not been for the sort of accidents of fortune which can upset the best-laid plans of primogeniture (infant mortality, a preponderance of daughters, a scarcity of sons, the perils of military traditions within a family), Gerald and Sally would have remained minor members of the ducal family. Although twenty-eight years older, Bendor was Gerald's first cousin; both were grandchildren of the first Duke. The first Duke's eldest son had predeceased him, leaving *his* only son, Bendor, to inherit the dukedom in 1899. Since Bendor's only son died in infancy, the heir in 1945 was Robert Arthur, eldest son of the first Duke's second son. Robert had a young son, Hugh Frederick, and so the line seemed assured. Unfortunately, in 1947 Hugh was accidentally killed during army manoeuvres, aged only nineteen. The next in line after Robert would now be his cousin, William, the only son of the first Duke's third son. This raised problems, since William had been 'dropped on his head as a baby', the standard euphemism with which the aristocracy explains mental handicap, and was commonly known as 'Poor Billy'. When his father, Robert, died (a mere five weeks before 'Bendor') in 1953, 'Poor Billy' became the third Duke of Westminster, but in name only. Since the first Duke's fourth and fifth sons had

who was a duchess. 'Does it become me, I wonder, to be writing to such common folk as yourself –' he asked Plomer, 'mere Toms, Bills and Harrys'. Sally was less eager to acknowledge kinship, largely because it would raise questions about her own origins. Illegitimacy was still considered something of a blot upon a ducal escutcheon. Some of the most distinguished dukedoms had, of course, been bestowed upon the by-blows of monarchs, but (*autres temps, autres moeurs*) this counted for little in the early 1960s. An elaborate ploy was devised by Ackerley, whereby it would be claimed that he and Sally shared a mother rather than a father and that this woman had married a Mr Ackerley first, then a Mr Perry.

A further reason Ackerley did not visit Cheshire more often was that although he liked Gerald the two of them held diametrically opposed views on almost every subject. Gerald was highly conventional, of conservative, military background, a keen sportsman and a Tory; a man, Ackerley ruefully acknowledged, whose 'life, when not trying to kill people in the war, was entirely occupied with hunting and killing animals'. Furthermore, Ackerley suspected that Gerald strongly disapproved of homosexuality. He was astonished that Gerald, when asked by his wife what he wanted for Christmas, had asked for the penis-bone of a fox, fashioned into a tie-pin. He felt that the penis-bone of a homosexual, should such a thing have existed, would have pleased Gerald equally. This was grossly unfair, but perhaps Ackerley could not rid himself of the image of the second Duke, the awful 'Bendor', who had blackened the family name by hounding his homosexual brother-in-law out of the country in the 1920s. Predictably, Ackerley and Gerald had clashed over the Suez Crisis. Ackerley had drunk too much and become dogmatic and rude. Gerald was exquisitely polite and acutely embarrassed, particularly when Ackerley, deeply ashamed, attempted to apologize the next morning. Ackerley always appreciated good manners, but it was clear that meetings between the two men were almost bound to end in dissent.

Ackerley nonetheless saw a great deal of Diana, whom he still occasionally attempted to set against Nancy. There would be secret

---

already died without issue, Gerald, who was the oldest son of the first Duke's sixth son (who had been killed in the Great War), became the heir. He had power of attorney and managed the estates on behalf of his incapable cousin. Gerald and Sally had no children and so when Gerald died the dukedom passed to his younger brother, Robert, father of the present, sixth Duke of Westminster.

telephone calls and letters, clandestine meetings and a great deal of mischievous plotting, which annoyed Diana. She had become fond of Nancy and thought that Ackerley treated her badly. To make matters worse, Nancy always rose to the bait, complaining endlessly that Diana was only interested in Joe and not in her. She deeply resented the fact that Ackerley was 'dotty' about Diana, complaining to friends that had she not known her brother was homosexual she would think that he must be in love. Diana was also irritated when Ackerley visited her and made no attempt to make himself presentable. 'I've got my teeth in my pocket,' he announced one day. 'I nearly put them in, but then thought: oh well, Diana won't mind.'

Family matters were inescapable at this period, since Ackerley's main literary preoccupation was with *My Father and Myself*. 'Every now and then I turn, with revulsion, to the family memoir I have been picking at and recoiling from for some thirty years,' he told Francis King. 'It is not an enjoyable task,' he informed David Higham, who was very anxious to see the manuscript, 'reviewing the past and my own unsatisfactory part in it – so far as I can make myself out – and I go on with it only because I have nothing else to do.' In spite of his dissatisfaction with the memoir as a whole, he was persuaded to send one section of it, his account of the Great War, to Sonia Orwell, who was editing a new magazine called *Art and Letters*. 'A doomed mag, I fear,' he told Higham, 'for it has no *raison d'être*. However, I believe it is propped up by some idiot's money.' He was right to suppose that the magazine, which was edited in Paris, would not run to many issues, but it did survive long enough to publish his piece, 'Boom Ravine', in its second number in the summer of 1964.

Other literary projects were mooted, most of them absurd and none more so than a proposal to turn *We Think the World of You* into a 'pop musical'. 'It sounds awfully silly to me, but why not investigate,' he instructed Higham. 'If my novel is to be undignified, the indignity will have to be heavily paid for in advance . . .' In fact this preposterous scheme got quite far, largely because Ackerley needed the money and because there was some suggestion that Cliff Richard, for whom Ackerley entertained an inexplicable passion, was to be approached to take the part of Johnny. Ackerley met and liked the young musician who had proposed the idea, and agreed to collaborate with him. The main obstacle appeared to be the realization of Evie, and a number of options were investigated, amongst them that the dog could be 'evoked by mime, music and sound', by ballet, or by film projected on to the backcloth. Higham said that he could supply the names of a number of actresses admirably suited to the part. There was also the problem of the vile infant who provides some of the novel's best comic scenes. 'The idea of working that ghastly baby by means of an expert ventriloquist had occurred to me . . .' Ackerley wrote without much conviction. Negotiations dragged on for some fifteen months before it was finally agreed to abandon the project.

Another suggestion came from the Indian actor and dancer Ram Gopal, who wanted to film *Hindoo Holiday*. Ackerley was fond of Gopal and encouraged by the fact that he was a rich and generous man. Ackerley would be involved at every stage, not only with the script but also on location in India. This was an enticing prospect but one that relied more on enthusiasm than commitment. Ackerley did in fact work on several of Gopal's scripts, and consumed a quantity of Gopal's champagne, but the project never came to anything.

He continued to do the occasional review, mostly of animal books, and also worked briefly as a publisher's reader. James Michie, a former contributor to *The Listener* who had become an editor at The Bodley Head, recalls that one reader's report was so scandalous that it had to be kept in a safe for fear of offending the secretaries. It has since disappeared, but the single report that does survive gives a flavour of Ackerley's frankness:

> I have now waded through your Indian's book. He has an interesting story to tell and tells it well without being able to write it well. It is fresh and original, very amusing at times, and I quite understand why you are interested in it, this autobiography of a smart young Muslim trickster stowaway, trying to get a fuck among English women and managing at last. A most salutary story.

He was considered distinguished enough to be canvassed for his opinion of American involvement in Vietnam by Cecil Woolf and John Bagguley who, in imitation of the famous Spanish Civil War symposium, were editing a book entitled *Authors Take Sides on Vietnam*. Contributors were asked two questions: 'Are you for, or against, the intervention of the United States in Vietnam?' and 'How, in your opinion, should the conflict in Vietnam be resolved?' Ackerley delivered a characteristic answer:

Some months ago I signed a declaration [published in *The Times* as a full-page advertisement] that although I had voted for the Labour government in the last election, I did not subscribe to Mr Wilson's support of President Johnson's Vietnam policies. I am not therefore 'for' the intervention of the United States in Vietnam. I believe indeed that America's militant anti-Communism is the greatest present menace to world peace. At the same time, after a lifetime of international warfare, I despair of world peace, other menaces abound, and even if the struggle in Vietnam could be resolved, our sigh of relief would be only a momentary one.

I believe with Dr Konrad Lorenz that we have not yet learned how to curb the intraspecific instinct for aggression which many other animals know how to control in order to save their own species from destruction. Hopeless therefore of permanent solutions to uninhibited human aggression, my pity in the Vietnamese war turns first to the inconvenience, worry, fear, pain and death caused to the lower beasts in their peaceful pursuits by all the savage and stupid bombing and chemical poisoning of the country in which they try to live.

Other literary projects appear to have been started, but later abandoned. At some point he began rewriting his diary for the period of Nancy's suicide attempt, copying it out into a new manuscript notebook labelled 'From my notebooks 1948'. This can have done little to alleviate the wretched impression of his life he had gained whilst writing *My Father and Myself*. As he worked, he destroyed the original diaries, but he did not get very far. Out of the nineteen original notebooks, he transcribed three and a half into the new volume. Volume four survives and can be compared with the transcription to show that the changes he made were entirely literary ones: the truth about those dark years was to prevail. Since he bequeathed the notebooks to his literary executor it seems certain that he intended them to be published one day, as indeed they were in part after Nancy's death as *My Sister and Myself* (1982).

He also began typing up the jottings from other and earlier diaries, presumably intending to put together some sort of commonplace book. There was an abortive plan to collect together some of the journalism he had published in the past, adding to it unpublished material, largely about animals, and he also considered assembling a volume of autobiographical essays. Several editors later told Francis

King that had they known Ackerley had been prepared to review for them they would have offered him work. In fact, although Ackerley drafted several uncommissioned reviews and articles, whenever he was approached directly he tended to prevaricate and excuse himself. Roy Fuller twice attempted to secure pieces for *London Magazine* without success. Ackerley might have made a lively if eccentric film critic, since he had always enjoyed the cinema – claiming that he was more saddened by the death of Stan Laurel than by the deaths of T. S. Eliot, Edith Sitwell or Winston Churchill – and now took advantage of the reduced rates he got as an old-age pensioner. Anything with 'dear Cliff Richard' in it delighted him, and he was pleased to recommend Elvis Presley to Forster:

> If his new film *Jailhouse Rock* reaches Cambridge I think you would not find the evening entirely wasted if you got one of your young friends to take you. He is a handsome boy and dances and sings most provocatively. A surprisingly good actor too. And the moral of the story good: love and honour win the day over ambition and the golden calf.

Other films pleased him less. 'Few great men can have done more to bring out the tastelessness and vulgarity of the human race than the late Walt Disney,' he proclaimed. *The Dam Busters*, a 'film about high-minded people obsessed with the need to destroy each other and their grand and painstaking works' was pronounced 'odious', apart from the 'one decent and understandable character, a dog, the Flight Commander's dog', whose devotion to his master Ackerley thought 'a beautiful contrast to the idiocy of human beings.'

Increasingly, it was dogs, and other animals, which engaged Ackerley's attention, frequently compared, in their peaceful lives, with 'murderous humanity'. His attitude was summed up by Mme de Sévigné's observation: *Plus que je vois les hommes plus que j'aime les chiens.* Such an outlook did not appeal to Forster, who in 1934 had dismissed this sentiment as 'one of the most hopeless and ignoble maxims ever uttered'. The death of Queenie had increased rather than dissipated Ackerley's concern for the animal kingdom and there is no doubt that Forster was gravely disappointed by this. 'This is a human world,' he would insist. In fact, Forster was fond of animals, admitting to William Plomer in 1943 after one of his cats had had a stroke: 'I get over-devoted to animals, but it is difficult not to take them seriously in war time, when men are behaving so impossibly.' Acquaintance with Queenie had considerably tempered this excessive devotion, but when in good humour Forster saw the essential goodness of Ackerley's crusade on behalf of the beasts: he would tell him, for instance, that under his influence he had opened a window to let a wasp fly away rather than crushing it. However, the crusade had become a hobby-horse, and the war was long over. 'I can enter no more into the wrongs of animals,' Forster grumbled over the prospect of a visit from Ackerley in 1965. Ackerley would have argued that men were still behaving impossibly, perhaps even more so, and he sometimes gave the impression that in loading the ark he had thrown the human race overboard.

This was not the case, of course. Eric Fletcher, who had first got to know him when he came up to Cambridge as an undergraduate in 1948, insisted that Ackerley loathed cruelty to people quite as much as cruelty to animals and would be the first person to help a fellow human-being. Jack Sprott once accused Ackerley of 'hating the human race'.

> I got quite startled [Ackerley told Geoffrey Gorer]. I know I often speak disrespectfully of it, but I was surprised to be taken all that seriously. Besides, I remember him being pretty misanthropic himself, in spite of all his toilings for the betterment of mankind.

Ackerley would argue that he liked humans but wished that there were fewer of them: 'I am *not* a misanthropist; I like people and get on well with them; I am only a *numerical* misanthropist.' He believed that the rapid rise in population threatened the animals, and that soon there would be insufficient room for the species to co-exist. He was in no doubt as to which of the animals – the human or the non-human – would survive. Those manically hygiene-conscious people who complained about dogs fouling the streets and parks would soon want to tidy up the world and rid it of animals altogether. Many of his pronouncements were deliberately provocative, showing that in spite of a general feeling of lassitude, his propensity for teasing and up-setting had not abated. Indeed, now that the importance of sex had dimmed for him, the plight of animals provided him with a substitute cause to embrace.

Of course, his loathing of censorship remained and he was to be found signing a letter to *The Times* in defence of *Lolita* as well as one protesting at the barbaric export of cats and dogs for vivisection. The two hobby-horses were harnessed together with his suggestion that in order to stem the rising population and thus save the animal kingdom, homosexuality should be encouraged. He would present this argument with a completely straight face, so that those who did not know him imagined that he was attempting to win them over to his master plan. Indeed, there was more than a grain of seriousness in this modest proposal, rather more so than in his equally fervent enthusiasm for developing a strain of human myxomatosis. Oddly enough, he did not read *Gulliver's Travels* until he was sixty-seven:

> It is a joy to find hitherto neglected classics in store for one's old age; in this particular case one appreciates it more when one has had the experience of living. What a savage book, even more appropriate to our own times than to Swift's; it is very much my own view of the world.

He told James Kirkup: 'It is *my* book', and there is something of a Swiftian disrelish about Ackerley's view of the world during the last years of his life. His shock tactics were similar to those of the much-maligned Dean, relying upon grotesque exaggeration and savage irony. 'Road-death statistics rise, so do populations,' he complained to Francis King, '– did you notice that 25 *million* Chinese had been spawned last year? The road accidents are really awfully inadequate. Yet governments never see that, they are always trying to prevent them.'

A chance to explain his position was given him by Kirkup who, in 1961, had been appointed literary editor of *Orient/West*, a bi-monthly scholarly magazine published in Japan, devoted to Far Eastern topics. Kirkup was keen that Ackerley should contribute something, and proposed a piece on Lowes Dickinson (who had travelled in China before the First World War). Ackerley firmly rebuffed this idea, but thought that he might concoct something out of his Japanese notes about the tigress whose plight had so disturbed him at Matsushima Zoo. A visit to Whipsnade, the 'open' zoo on the Chilterns where a tigress had just given birth to twins, rekindled his Japanese memories and he began compiling a 'philosophical article' entitled 'I am a Beast', in which, he warned Georges Duthuit, 'the human race does not come

out well'. Indeed, Ackerley opens in combative mood with the statement: 'I dislike children.' He proceeds with mock apology:

> I didn't mean to begin with that remark. I'm afraid it may pain the
> Japanese, who are fond of them, or at any rate compassionate
> towards them, but it slipped out. Shall I modify it and say that
> Japanese children are the best in the world – well anyway the
> prettiest? Yes, I will allow that. English children are seldom pretty
> and often odious, and as for American children the less said about
> them the better.

He compares the lot of the Matsushima and Whipsnade tigresses,
introduces Queenie and a few Zen notions, and suggests that zoo
enclosures are to protect animals from people and not vice versa.
Perhaps the article's most provocative passage recalls an occasion
when a child which had been tormenting a lion in a zoo had been badly
mauled before a keeper had managed to free him.

> Bulletins about the child's health, as he lay in hospital between life
> and death, were issued daily in the press. Until he died, some days
> later, he was front-page news. No bulletins were issued about the
> health of the lion, who had been struck on the head with an iron bar,
> and no one inquired after him. I myself wrote a letter of inquiry for
> publication but I did not send it. I had not then reached enlighten-
> ment, and in the sacred hush that enveloped this child's sick-bed I
> was as scared as I would be to remain seated while the National
> Anthem is being played.

He sent the first part of the article to Japan without much hope that
it would prove acceptable. Unsurprisingly, Maurice Schneps, the
American editor of the magazine, did not greatly care for it, but Kirkup
asked Ackerley to send the second half. He did so and then was
dismayed to discover that he was not to be sent proofs. He wasn't even
sure the two halves would match up correctly. Recalling the disaster of
the American edition of *We Think the World of You*, Ackerley was
extremely angry, as he told Richard Murphy:

> Americans (Kirkup's Editor is an American) think they can do as
> they like and cheerfully re-write one's articles if they believe they can

improve on them or dislike what the author says. Oh beware of America when you get there! You cannot be too much on your guard! The world is ruled from there, in the American imagination, and everything the world contains. And they stop at nothing. However, my chief grievance is against Kirkup, and I have shot a few searing bolts into his bottom – in so far as one can send searing bolts into the bottom of anyone in so distant a country as Japan. I fear they cool as they pass over the North Pole.

It appears that, cool or not, they found their mark, and Kirkup hastily despatched proofs, thus becoming 'the best of boys once again'. Ackerley felt that his fuss had been justified when he discovered a 'ghastly error'. The article was eventually published in 1964 in the March/April edition of the magazine. Ackerley told William Plomer: 'The editor of *O/W* didn't like my article at all and thought it would "blow the lid off the US", but I have heard no explosion so far.' The article had been partially defused by the removal of a paragraph in which Ackerley reported that the deer and monkeys of the island of Kinkasan in Sendai Bay had been tame until 'it amused the American soldiers to practise their marksmanship upon them, and now, if seen at all, they are glimpsed only as shadows fleeing through the primeval forest at man's approach.' Even so, he was still obliged to parry accusations of misanthropy, complaining to Plomer:

> I don't see why I should be called misanthropic; I expressly said I did not hate people; I only wanted to tease them about the superior attitude they adopt, the distinction they make between themselves and the animals. I make no distinction, and I think if the word 'human' had never been invented we might all be a great deal happier than we are. That is all the article was attempting, and I fear failing, to say.

This attitude was reflected in an article he began writing about the death of Martha, the last surviving Passenger pigeon. This species had once thrived in its native America, but had been laid waste by 'the greed and ruthlessness of men' to such an extent that only one bird remained, solitary in her cage at Cincinnati Zoo:

> In 1914 a tragedy occurred so shocking, so awe-inspiring, so poignant and so irreparable that if all mankind had put on sackcloth

and ashes it would scarcely have seemed an adequate expression of their shame and repentance. Doubtless the First World War springs to your self-important minds. Let it spring off again. The less said about that the better, and the less said about the Second World War the better – and the less done to further the Third World War the better, or you may find yourselves in a case similar to that to which I allude. It was the death of a pigeon. She was a female, and she died of old age on September 1, 1914, at one o'clock in the afternoon.

He redrafted this as a letter, which was rejected by *The Times*, whose 'greylist' he claimed to be on. The Aberfan disaster provided another subject for a sermon, this one in undistinguished verse, in which he compared the accident, in which part of a slag heap engulfed a Welsh school, with the deaths in transit of a consignment of doves and finches which were being transported by aircraft from Kuala Lumpur to London in inadequate crates. 'When we concede/This connection/We shall not need/God's protection//When we can read/This equal sum/ We shall not need/Kingdom come'.

Even friends who were able to understand Ackerley's concerns often failed him in their actions. A weekend at Saltwood Castle was somewhat dampened when Kenneth Clark announced that he was off to gas the moles which ruined his lawns. Similar depredations were made by Sonia Orwell's former husband, Michael Pitt-Rivers, anxious to preserve his Wiltshire plantations from deer, and Geoffrey Gorer, who was concerned about the damage done to his crops by birds. Whilst these men had practical reasons for wishing that there were fewer creatures on the earth, Forster disgraced himself in a rare display of unbridled self-interest:

There is a rowan tree in Bob [Buckingham]'s front garden in Coventry, and when I was last there I was watching, with interest and pleasure, the blackbirds and thrushes eating the berries. They would pluck one, hold it visibly for a moment, like a coral bead, in their beaks, then swallow it at a gulp. I mentioned this to Morgan. He said: 'Yes, aren't they a nuisance.' Astonished I said: 'Why a nuisance?' He said: 'I like to see the berries on the tree.' I still think that human selfishness could hardly go farther; the birds are in trouble enough for eating *our* food without being reproached for eating their own . . .

407

Ackerley recounted this anecdote several times in letters and later incorporated it in his memoir of Forster, adding: 'He was at this time in extreme old age, though I don't see why that should excuse him.' A comparison of the different versions of the anecdote demonstrates how Ackerley polished it in order to emphasize the beauty of the birds' actions and thus strengthen his point.

Other friends shared his concern for animal rights, a topic which was receiving much attention in the press at the period. David Sylvester, who was assistant editor of the *Sunday Times Magazine*, was planning a special issue entitled 'How We Use Animals'. He hoped that he would be able to persuade Ackerley to contribute, but Ackerley replied that he had 'already shot [his] bolt' in 'I Am a Beast', and was unable to write anything else. Sylvester's request nonetheless resulted in letters of advice in which Ackerley suggested aspects of animal abuse which might be considered and in which he clearly states his position on animals and upon life itself. He was particularly exercised by the vast numbers of monkeys imported by the United States and subjected to psychological tests 'in order to study their grief and the deterioration of their faculties, to prove something which any bloody fool could guess for himself.' He also became concerned by the treatment of horses in Western films: how were they made to fall?

> I am always worried by these Westerns, just on the horses' account, and am reminded of the Charge of the Light Brigade, that much lauded and revolting story which earned a popular poem, not of course about the beautiful innocent horses that got blown to bits, but about the mindless oafs who rode them. How the human race does love itself!

He also told Sylvester about Ruskin's remark: 'There is no wealth but life.' Kenneth Clark had sent him a copy of his anthology *Ruskin Today*, drawing his attention to this statement.

> This seems to me a profoundly important remark [Ackerley wrote], profounder, perhaps, than Ruskin himself realized, for he was speaking in his capacity as an economist. But simply and on its face value it seemed to me a good slogan for a new religion out of which all superstition would be drained away, life itself, for its own sake, would become the only serious and valuable thing.

He related an incident he had witnessed in a fishmonger's in which a child had asked to see eels killed, not only the one he was to eat, but also the one his mother had rejected. 'It is a difficult story,' Ackerley wrote.

> All allowances have to be made, and we have to be fed and can we be expected also to *feel* for the lives of the creatures we take away for our pleasure? *I* think yes; there seems to be something profoundly *wrong* with the story; it is more than the arrogance of 'There is no wealth but *human* life', it has callousness also.

He had been impressed by Brigid Brophy's article 'The Rights of Animals', which had been published in the *Sunday Times* in October 1965, and had written to commend it. He believed that she was right in stating that becoming vegetarian was 'the only way', but it was not one he was prepared to take at his advanced age.

> I would like to return to that diet . . . but Nancy, who used to preach it thirty years ago and even fed Queenie on prunes and ground-nuts, has become a carnivore again. Perhaps she thinks meat is good for me. But I keep thinking of the death of the animals, in such vast quantities, to keep the human race going (humanely killed, we are assured, but of that we know and prefer to know nothing), and feel sick. We have a joint of lamb this evening . . . it is difficult even to be a vegetarian without being a bother.

He and Nancy did their best, however: 'We never buy veal and scour the district always for free range eggs, which can be got.' Sally's turkey was viewed with increased dismay:

> I really must stop that annual gift. It is too disgusting to approach with a groan the inexhaustible flesh of an animal that has been deprived of its life for our pleasure. I keep imagining the spirit of the slaughtered creature hovering above us, complaining about the useless loss of its precious life.

Many people shared Forster's disquiet over Ackerley's absorption in animal matters. They had forgotten that Ackerley was by nature a crusader, and had been ever since Arnold Lunn had made him read books about homosexuality. He crusaded on behalf of threatened species, whether it was a young homosexual who had killed himself rather than face ostracism, a writer or artist who was not allowed freedom of expression, a dog threatened with imprisonment or destruction, or animals exploited, abused or driven to extinction by the greed, stupidity or callousness of humans. He was ready to campaign on behalf of Young Holland and the Abergavenny men, the denizens of the Mousehole, the poets and critics of *The Listener*, Queenie and her fellow dogs, the animals of Vietnam and the Zambesi valley, the Wai-Wai, the Batonkas and Martha the Passenger pigeon. He embraced causes with fervour, wit and energy, gradually becoming a sort of Don Quixote figure who, in enforced retirement, was forever on the look-out for new quests. He still kept an eye upon the columns of *The Listener*, delighted, for example, to find the word 'fuck' – 'a word never before seen in these chaste pages' – had been printed in the course of a review. However, the battle over what was or was not permitted in the magazine was no longer his and, increasingly, it was the animals who engaged his attention.

In Walt Whitman's 'Song of Myself' Ackerley discovered some lines which he felt would serve as his epitaph. He frequently quoted (and misquoted) them in letters and copied them into diaries and notebooks. The lines he thought would suit his tombstone were: 'I think I could turn and live with animals . . . They bring me tokens of myself, they evince them plainly in their possession,' but the full version shows how far Ackerley found his own beliefs stated in the poem:

> I think I could turn and live with animals, they're so placid and
>   self-contain'd,
> I stand and look at them and long and long.
>
> They do not sweat and whine about their condition,
> They do not lie awake in the dark and weep for their sins,
> They do not make me sick discussing their duty to God,
> Not one is dissatisfied, not one is demented with the mania of
>   owning things,
> Not one kneels to another, nor to his kind that lived thousands of
>   years ago,
> Not one is respectable or unhappy over the whole earth.
>
> So they show their relations to me and I accept them,

They bring me tokens of myself, they evince them plainly in their
    possession.

If friends felt that Ackerley had withdrawn somewhat from human
affairs, there is no doubt that his energies and his heart were engaged
by their pets. He often went to sit with Anna, the Siamese cat of his
friend Villiers David, when her owner was away. He also fell in love
with Jack Sprott's marmalade cat, a ten-year-old neutered male who
was extremely timid, scarcely daring to venture out of the house in
Nottingham and consequently having no 'cat friends'. When Sprott
went to Ghana he had asked Ackerley to keep an eye on his domestic
affairs. Sprott's former lover, Charles Lovett, now lived with someone
else, but continued to act as 'factotum' and had agreed to feed the cat
during Sprott's absence. Ackerley was appalled to discover that the cat
was left entirely alone apart from the brief daily visits of Lovett to feed
him with frozen stewing-steak. Furthermore, there was no heating in
the house. Ackerley travelled to Nottingham several times, a 'wretch-
edly tedious and dull' four-and-a-half hours' coach journey, in order
to keep the cat company and to ensure that heating should be
provided, 'regardless of cost'. On one visit he discovered that Lovett
had installed his sister and her daughter in the house, against the
express wishes of Sprott. This posed a moral dilemma for Ackerley. By
rights he should have insisted that they left. On the other hand, if they
stayed, the house would remain properly heated and the cat would
have human companionship. He decided in favour of the cat, and
wrote several letters about this to Sonia Orwell, who had recently
acquired a kitten, and to Forster, who was highly entertained by these
accounts of 'Kitty-Cat-Castle'.[1]

Ackerley's undimmed affection for friends and his wish to amuse
them is apparent in the letters he wrote during the 1960s. Whilst there
is no doubt that Ackerley was depressed, he took a sombre relish in
the sheer awfulness of life. Indeed, the horrors of the late-twentieth-
century became one of his grand set pieces, rather as his accident-
prone love affairs had been in the 1920s and '30s. Donald Windham
insisted that:

[1] Lovett had a wire-haired terrier which Ackerley also attempted to befriend. The
dog greeted Ackerley's overtures with bared teeth and bit his hand, which went septic.
'I do see that no more appropriate death than rabies could be devised for me,' Ackerley
told Plomer, 'but I would prefer not to have it nevertheless for I believe it is painful.'

Joe Ackerley in his later years railed at mankind, just as he railed at the 'horrid, tatty, ungrateful little bird' that he rescued and lovingly cared for for months. His tongue was acerbic, not his heart . . . Certainly I remember him as anything but forgetful of all he owed his friends, especially Forster. Arranging frequent meetings, writing frequent letters, he was self-forgetting, self-knowing, self-merciless, and about his own faults one of the funniest men alive.

Ackerley continued in his self-appointed role as lugubrious jester to the circle, something of an Eeyore to Forster's comfortable Pooh Bear. He was written out, he claimed, and most of his literary energies went into letters composed specifically to entertain his friends. Of a letter to Michael Pitt-Rivers Ackerley wrote: 'In my role of comedian I was trying to think up things to amuse him,' and Windham recalled 'Joe's comic self-caricatures in his letters to friends to cheer *them* up when *he* was depressed'. When the mask slipped and genuine misery spilled upon the page he was quick to apologize. 'Yes, I am depressed,' he told David Higham when the agent asked whether lunch might cheer him up, 'but nothing new, I'm sorry I let it show.' Sometimes he managed to create poetry out of his unhappiness, hitting upon phrases or observations which his friends grew to cherish. Lionel Fielden particularly recalled the rhythmic phrase: 'Sadly I wake to each unwanted day', and Forster often gathered friends to listen to extracts from Ackerley's letters. 'The days potter by here much the same,' Ackerley wrote to him once; 'sometimes the sad sound of their ticking gets into my ears as they disappear into history, carrying nothing in their delicate hands but a yawn.' Forster copied this sentence into his commonplace book, remarking: 'Can the day that produced such a sentence be lost?'

But in spite of a genuine disenchantment with life and a considerable sapping of the will, Ackerley was always someone who took a dourly amused view of life and worked constantly at turning its disasters and disappointments to good use. Equally characteristic were letters about animals, about Christmas at Star and Garter Mansions (always an occasion of black comedy), and about the antics of Forster's cousin-by-marriage, Florrie Whichelo, whom Ackerley had befriended at Forster's eightieth birthday party. Forster was enchanted by, and uncharacteristically kept, several of Ackerley's letters from this period which described Florrie wrestling with a burglar and fighting off the amorous advances of the Radio Rentals man.

Ackerley also had momentary enthusiasms which enriched his correspondence, as for example when Stephen Spender presented him with the three-volume Nonesuch edition of the Bible for Christmas in 1963. Eric Fletcher recalls Ackerley's assumed astonishment at the 'obscenity' to be found in the holy book:

> Have you ever *read* the Bible? Well, how do they get away with publishing it? It's absolutely filthy – a Dirty Book! Fornication, incest, bestiality – it's got the lot!

This jest provided much material for letters. 'I am half-way through Genesis,' he informed Veronica Jeppe, a South African fan with whom he exchanged letters about Afghans and Alsatians, 'and quite appalled by the disgraceful behaviour of all the characters involved, including God. I wonder if you have ever read this hair-raising book?' Worse was to come in the New Testament.

> The Gospel of St Mark ought to be explained, it is the question of the character of Christ – old hat, perhaps. But when you come to look into him, was he not a thoroughly nasty man? How can one excuse the barren fig-tree, or the Gadarene swine, or the (to St Peter) 'Get thee behind me, Satan'? If you attend, it is awfully hard to like him.

Anecdotes would be worked upon and adapted for each of his correspondents.

He continued to do odd jobs, briefly becoming a tutor to Villiers David's Swiss boyfriend, for instance, improving his English and introducing him to the theatre. He also continued to proffer advice and assistance to anyone who wanted it. He gave his writer friends guidance about their books and prospective publishers, telling James Kirkup to resist cuts in his autobiography and suggesting that Donald Windham change the proposed title of the novel eventually published as *Two People*. He also read *This Small Cloud*, the memoir Harry Daley was writing, and brought his wide experience of editing and the laws of libel to bear upon the rambling and occasionally acrimonious manuscript. 'How I live in other people's lives!' he exclaimed. 'Well, I much prefer them to my own.'

20

Welcoming the dear dark angel

A real chance to use his creative energies came in September 1965 when Ackerley was summoned back to *The Listener* for a month in the hiatus between the departure of Anthony Thwaite and the arrival of Derwent May. Since Thwaite had taken over from Ackerley's immediate successor, K. W. Gransden, the magazine had carried no reviews of animal books and no poems by James Kirkup. Ackerley was determined to remedy this deplorable state of affairs. He asked Kirkup to send poems immediately and sorted through the shelves of 'ruthlessly discarded' books on birds, beasts and reptiles. He was persuaded to return to his *Listener* vomit, as he put it, because his BBC Security Pay had dried up the previous year and he was now £380 a year worse off. To his surprise the Corporation was willing to pay him well for his month's work. He charged fifty guineas a week, guineas because he thought that more professional: it was how doctors calculated their fees. Roy Fuller was asked for a poem and fulfilled all the requirements by supplying one 'To a Wasp'. Ackerley also accepted Hugh Massingham's poem 'Cow' and two extracts from Kirkup's long 'Japan Marine' sequence, only one of which was eventually published. (The second was set up in proof but by that time Ackerley had departed and it was spiked.)

Old loyalties were honoured during his month in the literary editor's chair. A review of a biography of John Buchan by his old predecessor, Janet Adam Smith, was commissioned from C. V. Wedgwood (whose first reviews anywhere had been commissioned by Ackerley), and in the Autumn Book Supplement there were reviews of Gavin Maxwell's *The House of Elrig*, Desmond Morris's *The*

Mammals and R. K. Murton's *The Wood-pigeon*, which Ackerley reviewed himself. ('Regarded now, since the suppression of the rabbit, as Public Pest No 1 among vertebrates (more and more pests will be added to the list, even dogs and cats, unless we can learn to control our own breeding), what hell the life of wood-pigeons seems to be.') John Lehmann wrote on Julian Maclaren-Ross and Hilary Corke delivered a characteristically ferocious attack upon the *Penguin English Dictionary*. William Trevor was called upon to review Charles Burkhart's account of one of Ackerley's favourite novelists, I. Compton-Burnett.[1] Fuller's poem, Kirkup's 'The Sea Within' and a review of Ian Niall's *The Gamekeeper* were published in subsequent issues. 'So I . . . hope the Fauna Preservation Society will be gratified and that James's persecution mania will take a turn for the better,' Ackerley commented.

He found the work quite hard after six years of enforced idleness. Apologizing to Fuller for not thanking him for sending some poems, he explained:

> I have been so long in the dustbin from which I am now temporarily rag-picked that I find myself mouldy and stale and, with no help of any kind – not even a secretary – to cope with a Book Supplement, Anthony's muddle (so different from my own), and a variously changed scene, I have been at the end of such small wits, if any, that I still possess . . . I am left with an office-boy, aged 14–15, named Keith, a pleasant child, quite safe from me now, who brings me a cup of tea, price 4d, at 3.15 pm when one doesn't want a cup of tea, and adds a score of new books per day to the thousands already encumbering the small office. I fear the paper has gone to the dogs – no not the dear dogs – yes, why not the dear dogs? they piss on it – since Gransden's day. Did you know that contributors are now paid on publication, and there are twenty long book-reviews dating back to the winter of last year? I wonder people write for it any more, waiting a year for their money.

He complained that he could scarcely remember how to paste-up a page for the printers, but some problems were still the same: 'The

---

[1]No doubt Compton-Burnett's brilliantly mannered accounts of illegitimacy, 'secret' families and sexual irregularity struck several chords with Ackerley, and it may be that she was equally struck by the 'plot' of *My Father and Myself*, which she read with interest, remarking that it should have been retitled *Myself and My Father*.

[poem on] Eliot has, I think, too long a line for convenient printing,' he warned Fuller. 'Reaching the very bottom', he considered publishing a poem of his own, an extract from 'Destination D' entitled 'After the blitz, 1941', but after consulting Fuller and King, decided against it.

Once the month was over, he handed the desk on to Derwent May, advising him to get rid of all the old hacks, as he termed them, that Thwaite had brought in and giving him the names of reviewers whose opinions were worth reading. He then settled down to revise *My Father and Myself*, sending chapters to Geoffrey Gorer and to Diana Petre, whose view upon her part in the story he required. Much of Ackerley's depression during the last years of his life was brought about by his determination to complete this book. His self-obsession was as strong as ever, but the reflection in the mirror had darkened. This was less a case of Narcissus gazing enraptured into the depths of the pool than of Dorian Gray confronting the picture in the attic.

Ackerley believed that all the most important relationships in his life (apart from the one with Forster) had been dismal failures. He and his father had been unable to confide in each other; except for a few sentimental memories, he had no real impression of his mother; he never knew or appreciated his brother; his relationship with Nancy was the worst of them all. The family had established a pattern, for Ackerley had been unable to form any sort of balanced, long-lasting relationship with any of his lovers, either. Once he had established that he had failed in love, Ackerley began to believe that he had failed in his career. At about this time he dug out *The Bench of Renunciation*, the short story he had written in 1923 and which contained a dismal self-portrait of himself as a young writer wondering whether he would ever achieve anything in life. It must have been with a certain grim satisfaction that he read the passage in which the young man, observing the elderly painter he had befriended, remarks: 'Standing there he mocked himself with visions, saw himself going gloomily on, getting a little more slovenly, a little more weary, a little more acrimonious and dull, more helpless, more abandoned . . .' This prediction appeared to have come true, or so Ackerley felt in spite of evidence to the contrary. He made notes about his job at *The Listener*, accusing himself of lacking confidence, interest and judgement:

For anyone with the mental equipment I am describing to be a good Literary Editor, which I was sometimes said to be, would be surprising, and of course I was not; I was not sufficiently interested in *The Listener* even to read it — in fact I rather despised it as I despised the BBC . . . I got my own part of the paper done as rapidly as possible, in order, in the last fifteen years of office, to get home to my dog; so easy did the mechanics of it become to me in the course of time that, excepting the five supplements each year, little thought was needed to make up my pages and keep the ball rolling, and little given. The fact that I ran the literary and art side of this paper entirely singlehanded for over twenty years is, perhaps, an achievement in itself and, considering the inadequacies and insecurities of my character, deserves a small burst of compassionate applause; for, without wide knowledge and critical acumen, never sure of my taste and judgement, I had to make decisions all the time by myself, the selection of poems and of art critics, the selection of books for review and of reviewers. How glad I was whenever my problems were forestalled or solved by people writing in for books or for the occasional suggestions made by friends and colleagues; as I have already said, I was ever one of life's subordinates, I have always wanted someone standing at my elbow, throughout life, taking all my responsibilities from my shoulders.

This melancholy self-portrait is so flagrantly at odds with the regard in which Ackerley was held, and knew himself to be held, that it could only have been written in the deepest dejection. It seems inconceivable that Ackerley could in all honesty believe that: 'Ill-read, unmindful, of narrow interest, I often felt too stupid to connect a single book with a suitable reviewer's name.' Apart from anything else, if this were true, the BBC would hardly have invited him back for a month at a cost of fifty guineas a week. In the final analysis, perhaps he did not believe it, for he did not incorporate these pages into *My Father and Myself*. He might also have reflected that, if he had made a mess of his emotional and family life and had wasted his time upon the work of others at *The Listener*, he had also managed to write a handful of very good books. He kept these volumes, a small but impressive stack, beside his bed and sometimes sat in pubs alone, re-reading them and chuckling appreciatively to himself. This was not mere vanity (the books are only mentioned in passing in *My Father and Myself*); it was a craftsman's justifiable satisfaction in a good job well done.

By now David Higham had done everything in his power to prise the manuscript of *My Father and Myself* out of Ackerley's stubborn grasp. The Ackerley files in the Agency's archives largely consist of begging letters in which Higham asks when he can expect to see the book, the first of which is dated February 1963. After another four years of cajoling, Higham had few methods of encouragement and persuasion left to him: 'Just to say that if we are now in 1967 I hope very much that shortly I shall have the New Year's present of the typescript.' When, in April, he eventually saw it he was very excited and determined that it should be published.

Ackerley greatly disliked the onset of old age. As early as 1959, when he was only sixty-three, he was complaining to Geoffrey Gorer of the 'odour of decay, one's own and everyone else's about one'. He still looked extremely distinguished, although his face in repose suggested a certain bemusement, not so much with matters of the moment, but with the whole extraordinary business of life. 'Baffled' was the evocative word that came to James Kirkup when he thought of Ackerley. Convinced that he was a beautiful old man, Ackerley reflected that others had weathered less well. As the years passed, he watched with grim resignation as his friends tumbled into senescence. Gorer himself was more cantankerous than ever. He would spend afternoons on the lawn, watching the public right of way which ran across his land. If a dog or child deviated from the path by an inch, he would interrupt conversation to leap to his feet, wave his stick in the air and bellow. Ackerley thought this sort of behaviour appalling. Herbert Read was reported as 'quite worn out of whatever value he ever had'; John Morris scarcely bothered to keep in contact and was 'looking like a giant panda'; William Plomer had become secretive and remote in his bungalow beside the sea; Colleer Abbott, 'the aged poet', was irascible and friendless, like an 'old turkey-cock' with his 'rosy wattles'; whilst Harold Nicolson was 'positively disgusting'.

Even Forster appeared to be losing his tenacious grip upon life. As he grew older and frailer, his tough constitution undermined by a series of 'turns', Forster would call upon 'Darling Joe' to conduct him across London from station to station, hailing taxis for him and securing him a comfortable seat on trains. Watching this venerable figure negotiating queues, Ackerley would become irritated by what he considered Forster's excessive politeness in allowing women much younger and healthier than he to barge ahead of him. Ackerley may well have felt that such chivalry towards the gentle sex was coming rather late in the day.

In 1961 Forster had paid an Easter visit to Ackerley with Bob Buckingham, and stumbled in the entrance of Star and Garter Mansions, falling flat on his face. He had been badly shaken and had to be put to bed for a while before being driven back to Cambridge. He had in fact broken his wrist, but a more serious legacy of the fall was that a few days later he suffered a mild heart attack. A course of anti-coagulants caused haemorrhaging and a transfusion became necessary. Forster survived, however, and continued to show a zest for life which Ackerley found inexplicable. In November 1964 he was discovered 'wandering about the Buttery regions of King's in his pyjamas in the small hours of the morning, aphasic and incoherent'. He had suffered a mild stroke, and Ackerley was summoned to Cambridge to sort out and cancel various appointments. When, five months later, Forster had a second, more serious, stroke, Ackerley spent 'a dedicated week propping up' his old friend:

> A pleasant week as well [Ackerley told Roy Fuller], for it is always pleasant to be with him. He can't use his pen now, or see or hear very well, and is muddly in his speech and gait. But though feeble and sleepy, how cheerful and interested he keeps.

Forster now needed the services of a secretary. Since Ackerley was eager for something with which to fill the sober hours, he seemed the obvious choice. The only penalty for having Forster as a regular contributor to *The Listener* had been that Ackerley had always had to type up the copy for the printers since nobody at the office was able to decipher the great man's distinctive scrawl. He had also typed up *The Hill of Devi* and draft versions of several stories and of *Maurice*, and so was accustomed to the role of amanuensis. Now Ackerley elected to travel to Cambridge twice a week to sort out his old friend's correspondence, one result of which is the orthographical curiosity that a considerable number of Forster's later letters are in Ackerley's hand. Forster was extremely grateful for this help, but was inclined to tetchy misunderstandings, as Ackerley explained to William Plomer, in the course of a letter about wildlife:

Bufo bufo [the common toad] has no teeth, but the palatine bone
has a sharpened edge, similarly with *Morgan morgan*. He rasped or
bit me by letter on Monday, before my Tuesday visit to him: 'I had
never realized that you loathed Cambridge, and your outburst gave
me quite a shock. It *is* good of you to come out to the hated city and
we must see whether something else can be arranged.' What on
earth was he talking about? When I saw him on Tuesday I said:
'Now explain me to myself, Morgan. How came I to speak disre-
spectfully of Cambridge?' 'You said it was an awful place.' 'How
did I come to make such a remark, so contrary to my belief?' 'You
looked out of the window and said "God, how awful it all is!"' I said
'Do *you* ever look out of your window?' The view is an immense
dirty hole in the ground and a gigantic crane poised over it. Well, we
got that straight, but I felt rather vexed . . .

Such rows were rare and short-lived. In 1958 Forster had written to
Ackerley: 'Unlike Housman I am glad to have been born into the world
and very glad you were at the same time – i.e. some years afterwards.'
In spite of many disagreements during their forty-five-year friendship,
Forster never really changed his mind about this and there was never
any real danger of a serious or long-lasting rupture. As Ackerley wrote
in his tribute to Forster, 'his love once given was never taken away, so
that disappoint him sometimes though I might, our friendship was
firm and safe.' Indeed, Forster believed that: 'As long as one's friends
with people one can, and should, put up with their tiresomeness,' a
maxim both men were to put to the test very thoroughly over the years.
Any criticism Ackerley made of Forster tended to be the result of
momentary irritation and his love and admiration never faded. People
saw the tie between the two men as almost a family one. Usually
Ackerley regarded Forster as a 'much-loved older brother', but occasionally he gave the impression that he was someone who had been
lumbered with an adored but 'difficult' elderly parent. His criticisms
were generally humorous, suggesting that Forster's public persona
was not entirely, one hundred per cent genuine and that he was not
quite the holy sage he appeared to be (a judgement which Forster
would have endorsed). However, if others dared to voice criticisms
Ackerley was quick to repudiate them. When Stuart Hampshire
accused Forster of 'prissiness' he received a long letter which mounted
a vigorous defence of the old man. Any criticism Forster made of

Ackerley he usually qualified with the observation that few of his friends could have put up with what poor Joe had to suffer in the way of family and ill-fortune. Eric Fletcher recalled that Forster was often alarmed by Ackerley's behaviour, but there was no sense of disapproval or moral obloquy. 'Oh well,' he would say resignedly to friends when Ackerley had done something particularly absurd, 'that's Joe.' Fletcher detected 'an unusual and impressive quality of intimacy about their friendship' and it was one that endured.[1]

Ever since Ackerley's letters had helped Forster overcome his block with *A Passage to India*, the older writer had admired and relied upon his friend's literary judgement. Forster had spent a great deal of time encouraging Ackerley, but equally Ackerley was to encourage Forster, not only by commissioning articles and reviews for *The Listener*, but also by taking Forster's homosexual writings seriously. Not everyone did, and Forster had been wary about showing his stories to people ever since Lowes Dickinson had professed himself disgusted by one of them. From the 1930s onwards, Ackerley had often been called upon to read and discuss Forster's stories. In 1939 Forster told Ackerley that he was working upon a 'rollicking' story about a foursome, three men and one woman. The two men discussed this idea and Forster commented:

> When you laughed, I really felt it was worth doing, and I certainly am pleased at turning out something which is rude, clever, and about four nice people, all of whom get their whack.

He said that he was incorporating Ackerley's suggestions into the story which eventually became 'The Obelisk'. Ackerley's contribution to Forster's stories was rather more substantial than the one he had made

---

[1] For instance, when Forster was to be honoured with the *Medaglio d'oro* of the Italian Ministry of Culture in 1966, he accepted it on three conditions: that he would not have to make a speech; that he would not have to dress up; and that he could be accompanied by Ackerley. This meant that the Italian Embassy had to accommodate two guests rather than one, but Ackerley so delighted the Ambassadress that she begged them to stay longer. This was in spite of the fact that Ackerley had managed to get Forster on to the wrong train at Cambridge, with the result that the Ambassador had waited in vain at King's Cross, anxiously scanning the crowds for his two distinguished guests. 'The trouble was that there were two London trains side by side and we noticed only one,' Ackerley explained to May Buckingham. 'One left at 3.35 for Liverpool St., the other at 3.40 for King's Cross. Can you imagine a more mischievous arrangement?'

to *A Passage to India*. There was never what one could strictly call a collaboration, but the younger writer became a sounding board for ideas and often provided solutions to narrative and other problems. 'The Other Boat', for example, part of which had been published in *The Listener* as 'Entrance to an Unwritten Novel', owed much to Ackerley. It was one of the stories that Forster, 'greatly encouraged' by Ackerley, often unearthed, and it underwent considerable revision during the late 1950s. In February 1958 Forster claimed that Ackerley had 'invented . . . one of the biggest as well as the best turns in the story', Lionel March's outburst to Colonel Arbuthnott in defence of Cocoa, after which he murders the boy.[1] Writing of their relationship at the end of his life, Ackerley thought that 'something else besides whatever [Forster] found to like in my personality or character bound me closely to him, my temperament, we shared the same emotional view of life'. It was this bond which led Forster to consult Ackerley not only about his emotional affairs but also about these stories.

Jack Sprott told Oliver Stallybrass, who edited Forster's post-humously published *The Life to Come and other stories*, that Ackerley had helped Forster destroy several stories during a 'grand review'. Forster's own term was a 'smut-scratch' and he enlisted Ackerley's help because, as he put it, 'you and I might find some amusement together', whereas Sprott, who was his literary executor, would not want to deal with them. Sprott was furious that stories had been destroyed, but more might have gone had it not been for Ackerley, who was responsible for persuading Forster to save and complete the frequently threatened 'The Torque'. Unable to publish the stories, Forster needed his friends as an audience, and stories like 'The Torque' were only spared because they had given pleasure. Ackerley had also assisted Forster with 'Arthur Snatchfold', 'Dr Woolacott', 'Little Imber' and, of course, *Maurice*. It was Ackerley and Plomer who suggested that Forster should write the long, explanatory 'Terminal Note' to the novel in September 1960.

When in 1965 Prospect Productions, a Cambridge-based theatre

---

[1] It is interesting to speculate how many of the details of the 'continuation' of the story came from Ackerley. The boat in question is heading for Bombay, and it was on a similar trip that Ackerley had met Giorgio, the sailor whose liaison with Ackerley Forster had been obliged to cover up for in 1924. Similarly, Lionel's initial horror at being obliged to share a cabin with a 'dagoe' recalls the conversation Ackerley had with the man aboard the *Aquileja* on his return from India.

company, wanted to mount a stage adaptation of *Howard's End*, it was natural that Ackerley should be called in to sort out a number of muddles, which arose largely because Forster had become rather vague since his second stroke. Forster had agreed that Prospect could put on a dramatization of the novel, but mentioned in passing that he might have assigned theatrical rights to Lance Sieveking, who had adapted it for radio. It turned out that Sieveking, who had also produced an expanded version of his radio adaptation for the stage, did have rights, but that nothing had been put down on paper. Prospect were not very impressed by Sieveking's adaptation, and negotiations were begun whereby Richard Cotterell and Toby Robertson of Prospect would produce a new version. Forster was not really fit enough to take an active part in these proceedings and so Ackerley was obliged to act as go-between for the interested parties. 'He knows I have been meeting you,' Ackerley told Cotterell,

> and was a little curious, but pressed no questions. I told him nothing at all [about the dispute]. He has not been very well, a pain in his heart, but it had passed when I saw him. As soon as I hear from Lance I will write to you again, and I much hope that an accommodation may be reached. What I am afraid of is that if Morgan knows that his forgetfulness has caused a dispute he may decide to withdraw both permissions to dramatize the book, in spite of contracts. Friendship and veneration would make such an attitude difficult to deal with; we could not bother him further. At present he prefers, it seems, to know nothing and to leave matters in my hands.

Eventually a compromise was reached whereby Cotterell and Robertson produced a version which was credited jointly to them and to Sieveking, with a split in the royalties, and this was put on at the Arts Theatre in July. Although it was not entirely successful, James Lawrie, a theatrical impresario, had decided to take over Prospect's option and put on the play in London's West End. In fact the script required a great deal of work and Forster was happy for Ackerley to continue as his unofficial representative of the novel's interests as it was once more adapted for the stage. 'It's an awful job,' Ackerley told Harry Daley. 'What a plot! It's a wonder he got away with it; all those coincidences.' As he worked away at the script and reread the novel, he came to realize that Forster had 'got away with it' simply because of the quality of his writing. Reduced to mere plot and period dialogue, the story certainly had its absurdities. After a while he began to enjoy rewriting those parts of the play which most risked provoking inappropriate laughter in the stalls. Lawrie recalled that most of Ackerley's suggestions were very helpful, although some were distinctly old-fashioned.

Further confusion occurred when Prospect announced that they would like to mount a production of *A Room with a View*. Forster assumed that Sieveking would be the adapter and so gave his consent. When he discovered that this was not the case, he attempted to withdraw permission. Since, once again, nothing had been put on paper and Forster's memory was by now unreliable, there was considerable dispute as to whether the project should go ahead. Then Sieveking announced that Forster had given him permission to adapt *The Longest Journey*, an unlikely proposition since Forster had repeatedly said that the book, which was his favourite, should not be dramatized. Forster complained that Sieveking was being 'tiresome' and once again Ackerley was obliged to sort matters out, not entirely to Sieveking's satisfaction: 'Our triangular correspondence is weaving a pattern of remarkable complexity,' he complained, 'especially as I never quite know whether you are at Putney or Cambridge.' Both adaptations were eventually abandoned.

A further muddle arose over a projected biography of Forster. The idea was first mooted in the summer of 1960 and it was decided that the appointed biographer should be someone who knew Forster well and had known him for some time. Three names were put forward: Ackerley, P. N. Furbank and William Plomer. Ackerley declined at once on the grounds that his memory was too poor for the task. He suggested that Furbank was at a disadvantage because he had only known Forster as an old man (they had first met in 1947, when Forster was sixty-eight). This left Plomer, who agreed to take on the job when approached by Jack Sprott. There the matter rested for almost seven years. Plomer was far from being the perfect choice, largely because he was a man of considerable discretion. Forster had wanted the biography to contain a full and proper account of his sexual and emotional life, and Plomer was a man who believed that private lives should be private. He also appeared to be reluctant to question Forster too intently in case he became an unwitting and unwelcome *memento mori*. Indeed, he had been so careful that Forster, his memory further eroded by age and ill-health, had entirely forgotten about the project, and subsequently asked Furbank to write a biography. Once again

Ackerley had to sort out the confusion, helping Forster draft a tactful letter to Plomer, explaining that the Furbank book would be 'a *full* biography . . . with access to my private papers and anything else he needs to consult.' He hoped that this 'would not conflict with anything you may be doing or may have done?' Ackerley also wrote to Plomer:

> I am afraid he [Forster] is now much preoccupied with his own importance; it is understandable; the poor old fellow is physically helpless and has nothing to do but sit and receive homage, letter or visitor, from all over the world, and of course he is a great man. If we get forgotten we can't complain. His mind is almost gone. It is very sad.

Plomer was not pleased, and suspected that Ackerley was responsible for Forster's change of plan. There is no evidence for this, but the cause of Plomer's suspicions probably lay in the old quarrel about Jack Sprott's 'banned' broadcast in 1953, which had divided Forster's friends into two camps. Knowing that Ackerley was still a close friend of Sprott, Plomer no doubt imagined that some sort of conspiracy had been hatched.

Ackerley continued to be desperately short of money, so much so that he would salvage cutlery from the Putney towpath for use in Star and Garter Mansions rather than buy new knives and forks. He seemed incapable of earning any money from his writing, although in 1965 *My Dog Tulip* finally found an American publisher, Fleet, and was chosen for the Book of the Month Club. 'A galaxy of famous authors recommend it on the dust-jacket,' he told David Sylvester, including William Plomer whose surname had been misprinted as 'Polmer'. A further blot on the dust-jacket was a 'crude drawing of a male Alsatian' and Ackerley wrote to the publisher complaining about both. He later recanted, since the book itself, unlike Obolensky's edition of *We Think the World of You*, was '*excellent*, not a comma misplaced'. Even so, money was hardly rolling in,[1] and he was obliged

[1] For someone who took such pains with his work, and who is today recognized as one of the most distinguished writers of English prose this century, Ackerley's earnings were pitifully small. In the last six years of his life his income from his writing was £1,225 1s 11d, the bulk of this supplied by the sales from the American edition of *My Dog Tulip*, which did not arrive until the last six months of his life. The previous year, 1966, he earned precisely £2 18s 8d.

to rely upon Forster's occasional cheques for any luxuries, such as holidays or alcohol. Unfortunately, Forster strongly disapproved of drink and had almost dismissed Jack Sprott as his literary executor after word of the professor's indulgence had reached him. Forster rarely spent any money on himself and this frugality earned him in some quarters an entirely undeserved reputation for meanness. As Ackerley pointed out:

> Morgan is a thrifty man. He gives his money lavishly to friends who need it – I have had thousands of pounds from him since my retirement, and he has propped many other friends up too – 'Aren't I lucky to have so much money?' he says – but he won't spend a penny on himself if he can help it.

Nonetheless, it was rather galling when cheques arrived, as they sometimes did, with admonishments not to spend the money on 'drinky-pops'. Ideally Ackerley would have liked Forster to have settled some sort of allowance upon him, rather as he had upon Sprott in the 1920s and, more recently, upon the Buckinghams. Inflation had greatly reduced the value of his BBC pension and by 1966 he worked out that his 'entire income, when the barrel is scraped, including pension, old age pension, and dividends on investments, comes to under £1000 a year'. After tax had been deducted, he was left with around £700 a year to spend upon himself and Nancy, roughly half the amount he actually needed.[1] He discussed the matter with Geoffrey Gorer, who suggested direct action, which Ackerley eventually took with some reluctance in October 1966. He was concerned that he and Forster were not as close as they had been: 'We drift apart a little, I fear. I hardly dare look at a robin, he prefers to talk about human cock-stands.' However, he decided to take the risk and reported to Gorer:

> If Morgan may be called a bull, I have followed your advice and taken him by the horn. A letter asking him if he could settle me in a solid way as he has settled Bob. It might have been better to say it personally, but he seems to get on without me now and I had no

---

[1] Nancy had no income whatsoever, not even an old age pension, since she had never paid any National Insurance.

expectation of being asked down [to Cambridge] again: he would have to buy a bottle of gin. I fear that somehow I have fallen from grace, and hardly expect a generous reply. But it was a straight-forward dignified letter and 40 years of friendship bind us, so we will see. I am glad to have got it off my chest, even if it goes in the wastepaper basket.

The letter did indeed go into the wastepaper basket, along with most of the other letters Forster received from Ackerley, but not before Forster wrote out a cheque for £1,000. In the accompanying letter Forster wrote that it was 'both easy and pleasant' to send the money, but could not resist adding: 'I think if you kept an account of what you and Nancy spent on drink it might help as a check.' Ackerley confessed to Gorer that the sum was 'not as much as I hoped for, of course; but it is most welcome and should keep me from whining again for a year or eighteen months.' He instantly ordered a Soho Wine Supply list, informing Gorer that:

the spirits, especially the gin, are of considerable interest. I know nowhere else where Booths and Gordons can be obtained for 43/6. I don't know what you pay for Gordons, but it may be that a sizable saving could be made with this firm.

Even with Forster's cheque and the Soho Wine Supply's special rates, Ackerley was still on the look out for further financial assistance towards his longed-for goal of semi-permanent, alcohol-induced somnolence. When Forster's life had seemed in danger, Ackerley had been approached by the *Observer* to write an obituary. He had declined to write one then, but, aware that his old friend (who weathered another stroke and 'a touch of pneumonia' in January 1967) could not last forever – and that he too was unlikely to survive very much longer[1] – he now began to attempt to marshal his thoughts about Forster. He did this with some trepidation, recalling his friend's

---

[1] Ackerley had been aware for some time that, as he put it, 'the dear dark angel is close at hand'. 'Although I am nearly 20 years [Forster's] junior, that is no guarantee that I shall not predecease him,' Ackerley wrote to Kirkup in February, '– younger people than I tumble down and off all round me from coronary thrombosis, the new fashionable death'. A heavy smoker for fifty-five years, Ackerley had often been advised by Forster to give up on the grounds of both health and money.

reaction to a woman who had sent Forster a draft of the obituary she had prepared for the morgue of a New Zealand newspaper. Ackerley recognized that this journalist, although somewhat tactless, had been 'inspired by the highest motives; she wished to get him right and to please him beyond the grave.' Forster was not persuaded and tore up the obituary unread. 'I too was actuated by respectable motives,' he told David Sylvester:

> I wanted to know what I thought, the intellectual exercise; the motives for this letter are lower, I want to make out of it as much money as I can. I wonder whether I might send it to you to read, privately, as a friend? It would interest me to know i) if you thought it worthy and ii) how much you thought it worth, and to whom. I wouldn't want you to take any *steps* about it, just to read and return it, if you kindly would, with advice. I am regarding my financial future with some dismay and, as you know, am rarely able to put pen to paper.

Sylvester, suspecting correctly that Ackerley was angling to discover whether the *Sunday Times* had commissioned an obituary, replied that William Plomer had written one, but that he would be happy to comment upon Ackerley's. Ackerley sent it with a note:

> I think you may say 'Balls' at first – and apologize later on, for it builds up. With your present concerns, the zoological part will amuse you. I wonder how it compares with W.P.'s version; he has seen little of the old man in the last ten years and I hope he does not repeat my anecdotes, taken from my letters. That would not be fair, for he knows that I have been working on this.

He also sent a copy to Stuart Hampshire, who felt that it contained insufficient 'warts'. 'I simply can't think of any,' Ackerley told Sylvester. 'You may be sure that they would be there if I could.' He then sent the piece to David Higham, asking him to make discreet enquiries:

> I had qualms about sending it out – to kill an old friend before he is dead seemed so indelicate – but by holding it up I have lost the place for which I intended it, the *Sunday Times* . . . It seems that since

Forster's last illness got into the news, the rat race has already begun, and this rat may now be too late for any of the rewarding Sunday papers. Of course Forster may easily outlast me and his other old friends; he seems quite recovered and doctors are wonderfully clever at keeping the spark of life going. However, in the event of his pre-deceasing me, I would like, as his oldest and closest friend, to say my say, and here it is.

The piece was far too long for a conventional newspaper obituary, even that of someone as distinguished as Forster. Indeed, it was hardly an obituary at all, more of a personal recollection, and it was one delineated with immense care and affection, though never merely misty-eyed; P. N. Furbank acclaimed it as 'a brilliantly written and moving portrait'. No one who reads it could doubt that, however eager Ackerley was to sell it, it was written for love rather than money. Higham sold it to the *Observer* for 100 guineas, a sum which was still owing at Ackerley's death.

Another way of raising money, and one which was much frowned upon, was to sell Forster's letters. Ackerley had kept every one of them and now had 1075, running from 1922 to 1966, a remarkable and valuable collection, not only in literary and biographical, but also in monetary terms. This was an even more delicate matter than the obituary article, for Ackerley was well aware of Forster's views about these letters. Since the major row during the war, when he had been worried that his letters might fall into the hands of burglars and blackmailers, Forster had made a further unsuccessful attempt to wrest his correspondence from Ackerley. In August 1958 the purge Forster had been carrying out upon his 'indecent' stories reminded him that there was further inflammatory material to be found in the letters he had written to Ackerley over the years. On the pretext of tidying things up in the event of his death, Forster had written to Ackerley, informing him that he was:

> collecting such letters written by myself as may be available, and storing them here [i.e. King's College], where they should be safe. I asked you some years ago I remember, about my letters to you, and you said they were stored with Herbert Read.
>
> I would so like everything to be known about me, but one is not oneself, and if one's a writer as well there's always danger of a biography being written which may cause inconvenience.

429

As in 1945, Ackerley had not been taken in by this ruse for an instant:

> The letters I stored with Herbert were returned many years ago and are safe with me (I shall tell him just that). He doesn't want to store them, but go thro' them and destroy the greater part. But they are the map of my life with him and I want to read through them one day and relive it. I am sorry he is nervous. Surely he is not collecting his letters: it is only mine he wants.

He did indeed tell Forster just that and the matter was instantly dropped, not even mentioned in Forster's next letter:

> Not a word about his letters. How good he is. He would have felt safer, even in death, to have had his letters returned, he thinks he is not a good letter-writer and betrays himself and others. It may be that he *is* not a good letter-writer, but whether he is or no, his letters and his friendship have been the major influence on my life from Cambridge onwards, if I gave up his letters I should give up one of the foundations of my life. I expect he knows that, he knows everything; he tried it on, out of nervousness, and has easily let it go. I only said 'The letters are here and I should not care for them to be anywhere else'.

This seems to counter the suggestion that Ackerley may have refused to return the letters because he intended to sell them.[1] Ackerley had

---

[1] The Forster scholar, Mary Lago, floats this idea, but her evidence is not compelling:

> The interesting fact that comes to mind, as one lists the letters from Forster to Ackerley [for her *Calendar of the Letters of E. M. Forster*], is that, about 1961, Ackerley began to *save envelopes*, with far greater consistency than in any previous year. Also in 1961, the manuscript purchases of the University of Texas were beginning to receive wide publicity. In 1962, Forster gave the manuscript of *A Passage to India* to be sold for the benefit of the London Library. It brought £6,000 at Christie's, then a record price for a manuscript by a living author . . . One must wonder, therefore, whether Ackerley had intended since 1961 to sell the letters and whether this was his unacknowledged reason for refusing to return them.

This theory collapses in a welter of dates. Ackerley began collecting envelopes *before* the manuscript of Forster's novel was sold, and his refusal to return the letters can scarcely be a result of anything that happened in 1961 or 1962 since it was made in 1958. Forster frequently failed to date letters and any recipient who wanted to keep track of them would have needed to retain the envelopes for their postmarks.

certainly been looking through the letters during this period and had begun annotating them, partly for the sake of posterity, but principally because they formed a background to his own emotional life, which he was examining in *My Father and Myself*. Several of Forster's letters (unattributed) are quoted in the book. Many of the notes Ackerley made refer to his own life rather than to Forster's.

However, the fact remains that in 1967 Ackerley set about finding a buyer for this vast amount of valuable manuscript material. He had by this time finished *My Father and Myself* and was in need of the money. Although disappointed, as he frankly confessed, Ackerley was not 'irked' by Forster's £1000 and was indeed negotiating the letters' sale in the wake of having written an article which expressed 'unstinted admiration and love for Forster'. Rumours had reached him that the University of Texas, which had been buying a great deal of manuscript material, was 'broke'. 'I am of course entirely ignorant of the *worth* of these letters of mine,' he told Sonia Orwell, 'and am interested not so much in that as in securing for them a sum of money which will enable Nancy and me to drink ourselves carelessly into our graves.' He was conscientious in his dealings and wondered whether he could impose a ten- to twenty-year embargo upon them. 'I do think it would be unconscionable of me to allow my letters, which give a unique and progressive account of Morgan's deeply-felt emotional affairs with people still living and still his close and constant friends as well as my own, to be open to public inspection while they live.' Negotiations were put in the hands of the famous London firm of Bertram Rota, who eventually acquired £6,000 for them.

This sum did not permit Ackerley to drink himself into the grave, carelessly or otherwise. News that the deal had gone through reached him in late May. He had spent a lively weekend in Coventry at the Buckinghams' house with Forster and Christopher Isherwood. Isherwood was returning to America and Forster and the Buckinghams were travelling to Aldeburgh for the Festival. Ackerley returned to London, not intending to see Forster again until late June. On 27 May he informed both Sonia Orwell and Paul Cadmus that he had given up smoking, admitting that this was 'somewhat late in my day', as indeed it was. A week later, at the age of seventy-one, he died in his sleep. On the morning of 4 June he did not appear at breakfast and Nancy assumed that he must be having a lie in. He had in fact had a coronary thrombosis.

431

Epilogue

To everyone's surprise Nancy did not collapse when her brother died. She was calm when she found him and remained so throughout, telephoning Sonia Orwell and Francis King, who both came round to deal with doctors, lawyers and undertakers. News of Ackerley's death was carried to Aldeburgh, where the Buckinghams decided not to tell Forster until just before he went to bed, so that he could sleep off the shock. They all wept a little as they told him. No one was sure whether or not the news had really sunk in until Forster became very cross when a writer whom Ackerley had disliked, and who was also attending the Festival, rushed round to say how sad *he* was to lose such a friend. It was decided that Forster should not attend the funeral, which was held at Putney Vale Crematorium, overlooked by the Common where Ackerley and Queenie had so often walked.

Nancy inherited everything, such as it was, apart from a small bequest to Francis King as literary executor. She was most indignant that her brother's BBC pension could not be carried on in her name and set about selling things in order to have some money. The lease of the flat also expired with Ackerley, and the landlady decided that if Nancy wished to take over the tenancy the rent would have to be increased. Nancy announced that she would wait to see what repairs the landlady was prepared to carry out before coming to any decision about whether she would stay at Star and Garter Mansions or, as friends had suggested, move to Brighton. The flat was once again in a shocking condition, with the bathroom ceiling threatening collapse. A concerned neighbour who looked in to see how Nancy was coping was horrified by the state of disrepair and suggested that a health inspector should be summoned at once. The bathroom apart, there was another reason Nancy felt that she could not bear to stay in the flat: she insisted that it was haunted by too many happy memories.

However, Sonia Orwell arranged for a friend to redecorate the flat entirely when repairs had been carried out and this prospect decided Nancy to stay in Putney. The firm of Bertram Rota was once again summoned and books and letters were sorted and sold. Fortunately, Ackerley had parcelled up his 1948–1949 diaries and marked them as the property of Francis King, so that Nancy never saw that terrible manuscript. Another terrible manuscript, in her view, was that of *My Father and Myself*. She told John Morris that she was shattered by the apparent sadness of her brother's life and disgusted by what she called its 'obscene disclosures'. Even so, she was prepared to be persuaded by Francis King that the book should be published.

Before this could happen, other members of the family had to be consulted. Although she hated the book, Diana did not think this sufficient grounds for suppressing it, and she agreed to obtain a waiver from Sally. A certain amount of secrecy surrounded the preparation of Ackerley's book for the press, and alarmed friends speculated about the nature of a manuscript which, it was alleged, no typist could be asked to copy and which could not even be entrusted to the post. When the book was finally published by The Bodley Head in September 1968, it had undergone very few alterations. The information that S. P. B. Mais had left Rossall 'under a heterosexual cloud' was excised, a couple of names were changed and one (still) libellous sentence was deleted.

My Father and Myself was promoted as a volume in the tradition of Edmund Gosse's *Father and Son*, and further comparisons were made by the reviewers. The author's diligent attempts to uncover the facts of his father's life reminded some of A. J. A. Symons's *The Quest for Corvo*, whilst the iconoclasm and irony recalled Butler's *The Way of All Flesh* (a comparison which would have pleased Ackerley). Angus Wilson placed Ackerley in a tradition of 'ironic mockery', running from Butler, through Forster, to Ackerley and Isherwood:

a powerful, important stream of English literary thought, rejecting first Victorian institutions and Victorian Christianity, then questioning all family life because of its hidden economic foundations, finally in Ackerley and Isherwood standing back in self-accusation from the mockery itself.

433

Wilson might have added that this stream is a homosexual one, temperamentally antipathetic, as it were, to traditional Christian family values. Ackerley's contribution is a comic one, its irony gentle rather than savage, fulfilling Roger's devout wish that people generally would be kind to his memory. The ingenious counterpointing of Ackerley's own 'secret life' with that of his father blurs the customary distinctions between the generations, the rebellious children and their moral elders. The story of his family provides him with a splendidly comic paradigm of bourgeois respectability. The slightest tap exposes its essentially gimcrack nature, the entire edifice crumbling to reveal a rather less admirable but altogether more engaging 'truth'. Both in England and America the book was loudly and widely acclaimed not only as a fitting culmination of Ackerley's career, but also as a masterpiece in its own right. It remains Ackerley's best-known book, the one upon which his reputation rests, and rests secure.

After Ackerley's death, many of his friends were terrified that Nancy would batten on them as she had on her brother, and during the first month or so their telephones rang with disturbing frequency. Francis King, Jack Sprott, Geoffrey Gorer, Colleer Abbott and John Morris were the most repeatedly consulted of friends, whilst her half-sister Diana Petre did her best to help. ('It was like giving a pint of blood every time you went to see her,' she recalled.) However, in her freshly decorated flat Nancy took on a completely new lease of life. She acquired a cat called Clovis on which she doted, but unfortunately it disappeared one day. She replaced it with another one called Nefertiti, which outlived her. She also acquired an entirely new circle of friends, mostly young homosexual men who were interested in her brother, but who soon became fond of her too. Although she was still neurotic, it seemed as if all the poison had suddenly drained out of her; she lost her haunted look and became as gay and lively as she had been as a young woman. 'I don't suppose she had another screaming fit ever again,' Diana Petre said. Nancy's life had been tormented by conflicting emotions over her brother, whom she loved with an intensity that inevitably led to hatred when he appeared to reject her. Now that he was no longer there, she became the keeper of the flame.

It was not, perhaps, a flame from which she could derive much warmth, but she was delighted to oversee the publication of the memoir of Forster, a slim volume of poems and a stout one of letters. She was less delighted by an article in which James Kirkup, repeating a story he had been told by a mutual friend, stated that Ackerley had been in the habit of taking drugs and had been found dead 'amongst his hypodermics', a claim for which there is no evidence whatsoever. Ackerley's books were reprinted, and in 1971 both *My Father and Myself* and *We Think the World of You* were published in paperback editions by Penguin. The royalties from these and the money from the sale of Forster's letters helped support Nancy, and towards the end of her life she added a codicil to her will in which she endowed a literary prize in her brother's name. The J. R. Ackerley Prize is awarded every year to a volume of autobiography by a British writer.

Nancy died of cancer in 1979. She spent the last few weeks in a hospice where she entertained the nurses with fond recollections of her days in Paris in the 1920s, when she was a beautiful mannequin with the world at her feet. Friends who visited her remarked upon her extraordinary serenity. She had never seemed happier.

Source notes

A Note on Sources

Rather than disfigure the text with numbers, I have simply listed references to material quoted by page number and in order. Books are referred to by author or short title; full details may be found in the Bibliography. The majority of Ackerley's papers, including all his diaries and drafts of his books, belong to his executor, Francis King [FK]. Many more are in private hands and uncatalogued. Where sources can be clearly identified – dated diary entries or drafts of books – I have done so, but much of what Ackerley wrote was in undated notebooks or on loose sheets of paper. All unattributed quotations from Ackerley's writings come from the collection of Francis King. Other locations (and abbreviations) are listed in the Acknowledgements and Bibliography. Unless otherwise stated, letters from Ackerley belong to their recipients. Where possible I have gone to the originals, but otherwise I have relied upon Neville Braybrooke's edition of the *Letters*. Occasionally Ackerley kept drafts or copies of the letters he wrote, and I have also made use of these.

Ackerley's books are abbreviated as follows: PBFA (*Poems by Four Authors*); POW (*The Prisoners of War*); HH (*Hindoo Holiday*); EA (*Escapers All*); MDT (*My Dog Tulip*); WTTWOY (*We Think the World of You*); MF&M (*My Father and Myself*); EMFAP (*E. M. Forster: A Portrait*); M&OP (*Micheldever & Other Poems*); Braybrooke (*The Letters of J. R. Ackerley*); MS&M (*My Sister and Myself*). Unless otherwise stated, all references are to the first British edition.

Ackerley is JRA throughout. I refer to myself as PP.

INTRODUCTION
1 Forster – to Duncan Grant, 17.10.68 [*Letters II*, p. 293].
  'I think . . .' – to Donald Windham, 17.5.63.
  Hampshire – to PP, 28.7.88.

The Times – 6.6.67.
2 Howard – *Listener*, 22.5.80.
  'I have been . . .' – Braybrooke, p. 337.
  Spender – to PP, 24.7.87.
  Monteith – to PP, 10.11.88.

3 'Curiosity . . .' – MF&M, p. 140.
Patmore – *The Unknown Eros*,
I xii.
'there is a step' – to Hilary Corke,
n.d. (November 1955).
'Though never untrue . . .' – MF&M
draft.
5 'I am not a good' – diary, 11.9.49.

1: A CHAPTER OF ACCIDENTS
7 'purges' – MF&M, p. 49.
9 'scratching himself' – Roger
Ackerley to PP, 20.12.88.
11 Fullers – note to letter from Forster,
9.2.23.
12 'He was overworked' – diary,
9.7.57.
'a very superior' – note to letter from
Forster, 15.3.23.
14 'a kind of unconscious' – MF&M,
p. 76.
'played with' – MF&M draft.
16 'the prevalent depravities' –
MF&M, p. 80.
'a chaste' – MF&M draft.
Mais – *All the Days*, p. 38.
17 'The best boy' – MF&M, p. 112.
'closest friend' – Mais, op. cit.,
p. 54.
Mais – *From Shakespeare*, pp.
109–110.

2: PRISONER OF WAR
20 'defeated by' – MF&M, p. 101.
'buffoon' – ibid., p. 57.
21 poems – *Rossallian* 16.11.15.
Flatau – note to letter from Forster,
13.6.24.
'Having possessed' – MF&M draft.
23 'Sir Douglas Haig's' – MF&M,
p. 56.
24 'I did not feel' – MF&M, p. 59.
footnote – to C. C. Abbott,
13.12.65.
25 'I never want' – to Anne Beadsmore
Smith, 4.7.16 [IWM].
27 Flataus – note to letter from Forster,
13.6.24.
'The Everlasting Terror' – *English
Review*, November 1916.
28 *Doctor Faustus* – Act I, sc 3.
29 'the coming' – Peter Ackerley to
JRA, 23.6.18 [FK].
30 'Thin soup' – diary, 8.7.17.
'a prison in paradise' – Bulstrode
[IWM].
31 *Walking Round* – [FK].

32 'a recognizable' – MF&M, p. 117.
33 POW – pp. 21, 62, 68.
'He may be in love' – ts draft of
POW (c 1921) [Durham].
'Don't you know' – POW, p. 14.
'To love him' – POW draft.
34 Peter's letter – 23.6.18.

3: BLENHEIM HOUSE
35 'was profoundly shaken' – MF&M,
p. 74.
'shows our differences' – MF&M
draft.
'a more intimate' – ibid.
'Joe isn't' – MF&M, p. 106.
38 Gardiner – to Nancy West, 22.6.67
[FK].
letter to Marsh – 2.6.19.
'He always' – W. J. H. Sprott,
'J. R. Ackerley; an appreciation',
Listener 15.6.67.
39 'I recollect' – MF&M, p. 101.
40 '11 Half Moon' – diary, 27.9.21.
41 Roger's will – dated 30.10.19
[Somerset House].
'an inglorious' – MF&M, p. 102.
Benson – to JRA, 9.6.20.
44 'I used to have' – JRA note on letter
from G. L. Dickinson,
(c. November 1921).
47 JRA on Nancy – diary, 9.1.49.
48 Arundell – to PP, 8.8.87.
Runciman – to PP, 8.6.87.

4: DEAREST MY MORGAN
49 'He did this' – EMFAP, p. 1.
JRA on 'Ghosts' – note to letter from
Forster, 26.4.22.
50 'I want him' – quoted Furbank,
E.M.F. II, p. 108.
M el Adl letter – ibid.
51 'I don't know' – Forster to JRA,
26.4.22, *Letters II*, pp. 24–5.
52 'lisping little artist' – MF&M, p. 123.
54 'Norman Douglas' – MF&M draft.
Douglas letters – 4.10.15, 10.9.16
[HRC].
55 'Hasn't got' – Harry Daley to
P. N. Furbank, 24.11.68.
56 'When they came' – Daley to
Furbank, 24.11.68.
58 'four independent books' – PBFA,
p. 5.
59 'a wretched compilation' – note to
letter from Forster, 16.5.23.
Squire – *London Mercury*, April
1923.

Spectator – 24.3.23.
TLS – 22.2.23.
'fantastic and endearing' – Forster,
Hill, p. 39.
footnote [1] 'ghastly' – JRA to Roger
Senhouse, n.d. (1941).

60 'well suited' – Locked Diary,
14.10.23 [KCC].
'the Prince' – Forster, *Hill*, p. 160.
'the royal flirt' – to JRA, 12.8.23.

61 'parsimonious and havering' – to
JRA, 16.5.23.
'a misfortune' – 25.5.22 [KCC].
Furbank – *EMF I*, pp. 201–2.

62 Forster letter – 28.9.56.
'I was always' – MF&M, p. 65.

63 'It is difficult' – to F. Barger, 17.6.22
[KCC].
'I don't quite' – Locked Diary,
14.10.23 [KCC].
'My mother' – 9.3.23 [*Letters II*, p. 34].
Marianne Thornton – p. 280.
'I've often thought' – to D.
Windham, 2.12.62.
'Dear My© Joe' – Forster to JRA,
6.5.25.
footnote – *Marianne Thornton* –
p. 278.

64 Forster on *POW* – to JRA, 9.5.23.
Forster on Indians – 24.10.23.

65 phrasebook – JRA to Forster,
23.12.23 [KCC].
JRA and Cook's – letter to his
mother, 21.12.23 [Neville
Braybrooke].

5: IN THE SERVICE OF THE MAHARAJAH

66 Maharajah's lineage – Vadivishi.

67 'matters of the greatest' – diary,
1.2.24.

68 Maharajah to Forster – 12.10.21
[KCC].
'antique' – to Forster, 23.12.23
[KCC].
'quadruple bed' – diary, 16.1.24.
JRA to Forster – 23.12.23 [KCC].

69 'the ultimate' – diary, 16.1.24.
'Spencer says' – HH, p. 11.

70 diary – 25.12.23.
Mrs Stoney – diary, 29.12.23.
'What sort' – HH, p. 25.

71 'considerable and dismal' – diary,
16.1.24.
'entirely medieval' – diary, 10.1.24.
'Explanation' – HH, p. ix.

72 'If there were' – HH, p. 120.
footnote – diary, 13.4.24.

73 'and looks it' – to Forster, 23.12.23
[KCC].
'Captain Drood' – diary, 10.2.24.
'I must kiss' – HH [rev. ed.], p. 82.

74 JRA and Mahadeo – diary, 2.4.24.
'I like to see' – ibid, 18.2.24.
'the insupportable Habib' – diary,
caption to sketch.
'I didn't engage' – HH, pp. 175–6.

75 Abdul – ibid, pp. 300, 164.
'crafty-ebbing' – Braybrooke,
p. xxv.
Forster – 1.4.24 [*Letters II*, p. 53].

76 Forster – 29.1.24 [*Letters II*, p. 48].
'In Fatehpur Sikri' – diary, 15.3.24.
'There is something' – diary,
18.2.24.

77 'It was in' – ibid.
customs – diary, 4.4.24.
'What does' – HH [rev. ed.], pp.
246–7.

78 rites – diary, 18.2.24, 4.4.24.
'If I give' – JRA to Forster, 23.4.24
[KCC].

79 'I will not' – diary, 4.4.24.
'endless little' – ibid.
to Forster – 23.4.24 [KCC].
'The man' – diary, n.d.

6: THEATRICALS

81 'Morgan was' – note to letter from
Forster, 29.6.24.
'a great work' – 29.6.24.

82 'an obvious' – to Prentice, 22.8.24
[C&W].
Mahadeo's letter – JRA transcript
[FK].

84 'It may cause' – Locked Diary,
17.10.24 [KCC].
Dickinson – typed note, 23.11.24
[HRC].

85 '61' – Dickinson, *Autobiography*,
p. 128.
'Excitement' – ibid.
Forster to Dickinson – 20.11.24
[KCC].
'He has upset' – note, 23.11.24
[HRC].

87 'I have often' – MF&M draft.
JRA to Kirkup – 19.7.63
[Braybrooke, p. 228].

88 'the peculiar' – note, 23.11.24
[HRC].

89 'scared or bored' – 25.10.24, quoted
MF&M, p. 145.
JRA and Roger – MF&M, p. 147.

90 Roger – MF&M, p. 144.

91 Sassoon – *Diaries*, pp. 234–5.
'good natured' – MF&M, p. 123.
92 Carson and Wilde – Hyde, *Trials*, p. 127.
Sassoon – *Memoirs of an Infantry Officer*, p. 209.
94 *Judcote* – MF&M, pp. 178–9.
95 'physically unresponsive' – MF&M, p. 137.
96 Proctor – Dickinson, *Autobiography*, p. 20.
'Body and Soul' – ibid, p. 280.
97 'dear dead' – diary, 13.11.48.
Dickinson – 2.9.25 [HRC].
98 Mrs Whitworth – Robert Harris to PP, 20.1.87.
'The play' – to JRA, 7.7.25.
Nation – 11.7.25.
Harris – to PP, 20.1.87.
London Mercury – August 1925.
New Statesman – quoted TLS, 16.7.25.
Agate – Agate, pp. 110–11.
99 *Spectator* – 12.9.25.
Dickinson – note to letter from JRA, n.d. (September 1925) [HRC].
Spender – 'The Cult of Joe', *New York Review of Books*, 16.9.76.
Dickinson – n.d. (July 1925) [HRC].
100 Howard – Lancaster, p. 153.
Lawrence – to Forster, 29.11.25 [Lawrence, p. 295].
Bennett – Sassoon, *Diaries*, p. 284.
Dickinson – to JRA, 2.9.25 [HRC]
JRA on POW – to Hugh Walpole, 4.11.25 [Braybrooke, p. 14].
Harris – to PP, 20.1.87.
footnote – *Maurice*, p. 185.

7: PROMISING YOUNG MAN
101 *Vogue* – September 1925.
Mais – From *Shakespeare*, pp. 114–5.
102 Forster – 21.4.26.
103 'Now I am' – Forster to JRA, 29.1.26.
Gielgud – to PP, 17.5.87.
Mitchison – Mitchison, p. 21.
Spender – to PP, 24.7.87.
105 ff Daley – Daley, pp. 78, 119, 90–1, 6.
106 David Daley – to PP, 26.5.87.
107 'a good sexy' – Daley, p. 57.
'overwhelmingly' – to Furbank, 21.3.86.
108 'How irritating' – diary, 11.12.48.
Forster's expense – to JRA, 13.6.30.

JRA to Agate – P. N. Furbank to PP.
109 'contrived to keep' – 'Christmas Carol, 1940' [FK].
Thompson – *The Times*, 11.9.71.
110 Mitchison – Mitchison, p. 107.
motor racing – Daley to Furbank, 4.8.68.
111 Heard to Sprott – 22.1.27 [KCC].
Heard on Daley – to Sprott, 14.7.27 [KCC].
Daley on Sprott – to Furbank, 17.8.70.
112 Charlton on Daley – David Daley to PP, 26.5.87.
113 uniforms – Daley to Furbank, 24.11.68.
Heard on Daley – to Sprott, 1.8.27 [KCC].
114 'garnished' – to Sprott, 4.2.30 [KCC].
Mitchison – to PP, 7.12.87.
Heard on guardsmen – to Sprott, 4.2.30 [KCC].
115 Forster's warning – 18.8.39.
newspapers on West wedding – clippings, n.d. [Diana Petre].
116 *Banana Budget* – 1.9.26.
'Daley's sensitive' – to JRA, 20.6.26.
'vulgar, indiscreet' – Daley to Furbank, 14.12.68.
117 Ideal Friend – MF&M, p. 125.
'sentimental . . . nauseous verses' – MF&M, p. 115.
'neat sentence' – MF&M, p. 123.
footnote – MF&M draft.
119 Daley – to Furbank, 24.11.68.
'I have never' – MF&M, p. 80.
Auden – 'Papa was a wise old slyboots', *New York Review of Books*, 27.3.69.
footnote – Carpenter, p. 48.
121 'I think' – to JRA, 31.1.27 [Diana Petre].
Forster on operation – to JRA, 17.3.27.
JRA note – 3.6.62 [Diana Petre].
Forster on JRA – Locked Diary, 1.1.27 [KCC].

8: TALKS DEPARTMENT
123 'glamour' – Janet Adam Smith to PP, 11.6.87.
125 'the first real' – 'History of Education and Talks Organisation', undated ts by R. Wade [WAC].
JRA to Strachey – c. November 1928 [Braybrooke, p. 15].

'tipsy' – to Strachey, 30.10.29
[WAC].
Mais – *All* pp. 234–5.
126 'Not a Happy One?' – *Listener*,
27.3.29.
'The Policeman on His Beat' – ibid,
13.11.29.
'Workers of Europe' – ibid, 12.4.33.
'booking them in' – Daley to
Furbank, 30.6.68.
'When at last' – *Listener*, 27.3.29.
127 street markets – Harry Firman [sic],
'Peacocks, Pots and Pants', *Listener*
21.8.29.
Reith – 4.12.31, 12.1.32 [WAC].
'took to' – 14.4.30.
128 'The Grim Game of Escape' –
Listener, 10.6.31.
'No doubt' – c. July 1931.
'Introduction' – EA, p. 9.
'since that was' – to Allen Lane,
28.7.32 [BH].
129 Forster's boost – 'Tales of Unrest',
Listener, 14.12.32.
'underpaid and insulted' – 4.8.28.
'One has to' – 30.9.31.
JRA & Macdonell – 26.8.30, 3.9.30,
5.9.30 [WAC; Braybrooke, p. 20].
130 'You see' – Daley to Furbank,
12.4.68.
131 Albert – MF&M, p. 126.
Forster – 12.12.26.
132 Forster – 31.3.29.
Daley – to Furbank, 24.11.68.
Reid – to JRA, 16.6.30 [HRC].
Heard – to Sprott, 3.3.30 [KCC].
133 Forster – 9.4.28 [quoted MF&M,
p. 129], 17.7.28, 27.1.28, 9.4.28,
n.d. (1926?).
134 Roger's claret and 'jumps' –
MF&M, pp. 97, 89.
136 West – 12.5.29, 28.6.29 [Diana
Petre].
137 Forster – 5.5.29.
138 'In fact' – MF&M, pp. 150–51.

9: HOUSE OF CARDS
139 Roger – 21.10.20 [Diana Petre].
140 Roger – 13.12.37 [Diana Petre].
'I see' – MF&M draft.
141 'a tall' – MF&M, p. 152.
142 footnote[2] – clipping, n.d. [Diana
Petre].
143 'slum children' – Petre, p. 91.
144 Diana – to PP, 18.8.87.
The Times – 7.9.29.
145 'like a character' – to Forster,

3.10.29 [KCC].
'The house of cards' – ibid.
147 'Even now' – MF&M, p. 157.

10: HIS FATHER'S SON
149 JRA on Roger – MF&M draft.
150 'a grown man' – 21.10.20 [Diana
Petre].
'Between my father' – MF&M draft.
'troublesome women' – ibid.
'When all' – Patmore, op. cit.
151 Forster – n.d. (late 1929).
'pimps' – Forster to JRA, 17.11.38.
Daley – to Furbank, 24.11.68.
'a small sad' – to William Plomer,
20.12.34.
poems – [FK].
154 'Whitmanesque' – Braybrooke, p. 23.
'Salute one another in passing!' –
The Venture, Vol. I No. 1,
November 1928.
'lovely' – to JRA, 9.4.28.
Redgrave – Redgrave, p. 62.
'There was' – to Plomer, 20.12.34.
155 'My mother' – diary, 9.1.49.
156 'You know' – ibid.
Nancy – Diana Petre to PP.
157 Kipling – 'The Female of the
Species', *The Years Between* (1919).
Forster – n.d. (late 1938) [quoted
Furbank, *EMF II*, p. 217].
'I had been' – diary, 13.7.52.
158 'afraid' – diary, 13.2.49.
Festing Jones – 2.11.27 [HRC].
159 Nicolson – 24.11.31 [HRC].
Prentice – 27.9.28 [C&W].
'Explanation' – HH, pp. x–xi.
160 Prentice – 9.12.31 [C&W].
Forster – n.d. (1929?).
'on the grounds' – JRA to
L. P. Hartley, n.d.
Sackville-West – 9.3.32 [HRC].
161 Waugh – *Spectator*, 16.4.32.
Welby – 'A Glimpse of the Real
India', *Listener*, 20.4.32.
Thompson – *Week-end Review*,
9.4.32.
162 Prentice – 9.12.31 [C&W].
Connolly – Connolly, p. 245.
Hartley – n.d.
Aga Khan – to JRA 2.8.34, 11.8.34
[Neville Braybrooke].
163 Dickinson – to JRA, n.d. (April
1932) [HRC].
Cowasjee – Introduction to HH
(Arnold/Heinemann, India, 1979),
p. 7.

Forster – 10.11.32.
details of Buckingham marriage –
May Buckingham to PP, 19.6.87.
164 Woolf – *Sickle*, p. 262.
footnote – information from David
Daley and Neville Braybrooke.
165 Plomer – *Turbott* (Oxford, 1985),
p. 10; *At Home*, pp. 7, 57.
166 de Gallatin – MF&M, p. 184.
168 footnote – MF&M, p. 195.
169 'to drag' – MF&M, p. 201.
170 'History' – Wade, op. cit. [WAC].
'disappointing' – to JRA, 13.3.33
[WAC].
'I thought' – 13.2.33 [WAC].
172 Fielden – Fielden, p. 119.

11: INSIDE THE MACHINE
173 press release – 'Editing of *The
Listener*', Lambert to S. Tallents
2.2.38 [WAC].
Financial Times and *New Statesman* –
Briggs, pp. 287–8.
174 'The BBC states' – 'Editing of *The
Listener*'
Lambert – ibid.
175 memo – [WAC]
176 JRA on Forster – MF&M, draft.
Braybrooke – Braybrooke, p. xx.
Grigson – Grigson, p. 136.
'specially important' – JRA to
Lambert, 24.2.37 [WAC;
Braybrooke, p. 324].
177 short stories – Lambert to Tallents,
31.10.35 [WAC].
'mainly of' – JRA to Lambert,
24.2.37.
private memo – n.d. [WAC].
178 JRA on Tallents – MF&M draft.
JRA to Douglas – 15.4.35
[Braybrooke, pp. 25–6].
179 Auden – 'Papa was a wise old slyboots'.
JRA on Isherwood – to Siepmann,
24.4.33 [WAC]; Francis King,
Listener, 17.3.66.
'sent out' – JRA to Lambert, 24.2.37
[Braybrooke, p. 325].
Cooper – 4.11.38 [WAC].
Tallents – JRA note to letter from
A. S. Neill, 22.4.37 [HRC].
180 Abbott – *Listener* 12.11.42; JRA to
Abbott, 5.10.42, 6.11.42.
Fuller – 13.11.44.
JRA on Capetanakis – diary,
13.11.48.
'quite remarkable' – *Listener*,
14.12.44.

181 'a lifetime's work' – *Listener*,
2.11.44.
Sitwell – notebook, n.d. [HRC];
quoted Pearson, p. 379.
'There was a great' – Stuart
Hampshire to PP, 28.7.88.
Moon Farm – JRA to Corke, n.d.
(November 1955).
182 Grigson – Grigson, p. 136.
Bell review – JRA to Bell, 7.4.53
[KCC].
footnote – Grigson, p. 136.
183 Fuller – 1.3.45.
Williams – 26.1.37 [Braybrooke,
pp. 36–7].
Forge – to PP, 19.8.87.
'In all' – to Richard Murphy,
14.1.64 [Braybrooke, p. 240].
184 Forge – to PP, 19.8.87.
'often seeking' – MF&M draft.
footnote – Macaulay, pp. 153–4;
Marjorie Redman to Braybrooke,
16.3.72.
185 Lambert – to Tallents, 31.10.35
[WAC].
BBFC – Findlater, p. 121.
Reed – galley with Woolf papers
[Sussex].
186 Ryan – JRA to Leonard Woolf,
4.11.37.
Read – 20.11.35 [WAC].
'if one gets' – to Fuller, 19.12.38.
Fuller – 19.12.38, 1.2.39, 16.3.56.
187 Church – 1.5.44 [HRC].
Fuller – 1.11.44.
188 'A Correct Compassion' – see
Kirkup, pp. 217–223.
Bellerby – *Listener*, 22.6.67.
189 JRA and Lambert – Braybrooke, p.xvi.
JRA and Reith – David Daley to PP,
26.5.87.
190 Reith – 12.6.35 [WAC].
Lambert – to Murray, 3.7.35
[WAC].
191 Tallents – 6.2.36 [WAC].
JRA – memo, 17.2.36; to Bell,
4.3.36; Clark, 31.3.36 [WAC].
192 'Inside the "Queen Mary"' –
Listener, 8.4.36.
'some fun' – to Bell, 1.4.36 [WAC].
'Do we really' – to Tallents, 3.4.36
[WAC].
193 Picasso and jazz – Reith to Tallents,
2.6.36, 14.10.37 [WAC].
Read – n.d. (1937), 5.8.35 [WAC].
Ryan and JRA's response – 22.2.38
[WAC].

194 Read – 28.10.35 [WAC].
195 JRA on 'The Artist Speaks' – to Lambert, 29.10.36, 20.3.37 [WAC].
196 Rouault – 6.7.37 [WAC; Braybrooke, p. 40].
'to conceal' – JRA to Cooper, 9.9.37 [WAC].
Lambert – JRA to Cooper, 9.9.37.
Cooper – ibid.
198 'No Fields' – Urquhart to PP, 2.9.87; JRA to Urquhart, 21.12.36.
'Début' – 19.1.37.
199 'I am always' – 27.9.37.
'unreadable' – 23.6.38.
'Your letter' – 10.7.38.
200 'I think' – 30.11.38.
'No, no' – 6.12.38.
'No, I've' – n.d. (early 1939).
201 'No, I think' – 5.3.39.
Urquhart on JRA – to PP, 10.8.87, 2.9.87.
Fisher – to Reith, n.d. (autumn 1936) [WAC].
202 'very poor' – Fisher to Tallents, 10.11.37 [WAC].
'intelligently done' – to Reith, n.d. (autumn 1936).
'I don't' – 10.9.36 [WAC].
'literary reviews' – to Tallents, 6.1.37 [WAC].
203 Lambert – 31.10.35 [WAC].
'In view' – 1.11.37 [WAC].
204 'art articles' – 1.11.37 [WAC].
205 Clark – 19.11.37 [WAC].
Reith – 22.11.37 [WAC].
206 Woolf's proof and Ryan's memos – [FK].
'I feel' – 3.11.37 [FK].
207 'Your deservedly' – 4.11.37 [Sussex].
'The place' – ibid.
208 Woolf – 6.11.37 [FK].
'The most' – 7.11.37 [Sussex].

12: THE DARK AGES
209 friend – Stuart Hampshire to PP, 28.7.88.
210 Harris – 'Destination D' [FK] and MF&M draft.
212 Dover pubs – JRA to Sprott, n.d. (c. 1936) [KCC].
'a pair' – Cunningham, p. 374.
Forster's bomb – to R. Buckingham, 26.8.36 [KCC].
213 'too trashy' – to JRA, 2.3.37.
'Jo-Jo' – n.d. (c. October 1937).

214 Catkin – to Sprott, n.d. [KCC].
215 Forster – n.d. (July 1938) [Furbank, *EMF II*, p. 226].
'Dame Dora' – 4.11.37 [Sussex].
216 Paul's letters – 15.11.39, n.d. (1940) [Diana Petre].
217 JRA to Spender – Spender: *Letters*, p. 178.
Lambert – memo, 21.2.39 [WAC].
218 'otherwise I' – to Donald Windham, 31.1.52.
'impertinent' – MF&M, p. 120.
'the best' – Braybrooke, p. 61.
Forster – 11.4.39 [KCC].
Sackville-West – 14.1.41 [Berg].
219 Thomas – *The Times*, 13.6.67.
'the erstwhile' – to L. P. Hartley, n.d.
220 Church – December 1937 [Braybrooke, pp. 43–4].
JRA to Sackville-West – 19.1.41, 9.1.41, 8.1.41, n.d. [Berg].
222 JRA memo – 21.1.41 [WAC].
224 Barker – n.d. (1945).
Thomas – 30.1.41 [WAC].
Woolf – n.d. (September 1941).
225 Thomas and JRA – ibid.
Maconachie – 21.5.42 [WAC].
226 DG – n.d. [WAC].
Woolf – n.d.
Reed – *Daily Telegraph*, 3.4.40, 13.4.40.
227 JRA to Reed – 29.4.40 [Braybrooke, pp. 51–3].
228 Abergavenny trial – *News of the World*, 8.11.42.
footnote – *Spectator*, 19.4.40; JRA to Daley, 19.8.64; POW, p. 37.
229 Forster – 3.5.40, n.d.
Spectator letters – *Spectator*, 20.11.42, 27.11.42, 4.12.42, 18.12.42.
230 'My own' – to Demetrios Capetanakis, 29.4.43.
'sable fiddlesticks' – to Plomer, 4.9.39 [Durham].
231 Cook – quoted M&OP, p. 9.
233 Mallalieu – 26.7.40 [Braybrooke, p. 55].
'overlong' – to Capetanakis, 19.8.41 [Braybrooke, p. 59].
234 Forster on Paddy – to JRA, 14.5.41, 23.5.41; to Plomer, 12.6.41 [Durham].
236 Paul – 5.7.41 [Diana Petre].
239 Capetanakis – 18.8.41 [Braybrooke, pp. 59–60].
Senhouse – n.d. (1941).

Source notes

13: A YOUNG MAN MARRED

241 'one of the' – MF&M, p. 140.
Daley – to Furbank, 24.11.68.

242 'Having saved' – diary, 6.2.66.

243 'in compensation' – ibid.
Daley – to Furbank, 24.11.68.

244 Forster – 12.6.43 [Durham; quoted Furbank, *EMF II*, pp. 249–50].
'As for my' – 16.8.43 [quoted ibid, p. 250].
'trivialities' – 18.8.43.
'I saw' – c. 11.11.43 [KCC].
King – MS&M, p. 11.
Morris on Daley – note to letter from Forster, 25.9.43 [KCC].
Forster on Morris – to Plomer, 8.10.60 [Durham].

245 Forster – to Morris, c. 11.11.43, 25.9.43 [KCC]; to Plomer, 10.8.43 [Durham]; to JRA, 25.9.43, 22.9.43, n.d. (c. 27.9.43).

246 Kipling – 'The Story of the Gadsbys'.

247 Donat reports – 22.12.44, 12.9.45, 8.11.45, 30.3.46, 10.11.46, 28.8.45, 10.1.45 [Neville Braybrooke].

248 Daley – to Furbank, 24.11.68.

249 'They hoped' – diary, 6.6.45.

250 Mac and Freddie – ibid.
'He was gentle' – diary, 13.6.45.

251 'Both these' – ibid.

254 'I recollected how' – diary, 1.5.49.

256 Daley – to Furbank, 24.11.68.

14: A DOG'S LIFE

259 MDT – pp. 11–12.

261 'fairy story' – jacket copy
New Statesman – 'Nom d'un chien', 31.12.49.

262 friend – Stuart Hampshire to PP, 28.7.88.
'I saw' – MF&M, p. 139.
'constant, single-' – MF&M, p. 217.
diary – 30.6.50.

263 Forster – quoted MF&M, p. 131;
Time and Tide, 23.6.34.

264 'what could' – diary, 24.12.48.
Woodyear – MDT, p. 22.
Lehmann – jacket of MDT, 2nd ed.

265 letter – [FK].

266 footnote – Daley to Furbank, 21.3.68.

268 glass – diary, n.d. (1953), 12.3.50.

269 'Never a dull' – diary, 4.3.49.

270 Manning – information from Neville Braybrooke.
song – diary, 30.1.44.

271 MF&M – pp. 217–8.

272 Daley – to Furbank, 24.11.68.
Roerick – to PP, April 1988.

271 May Buckingham – to PP, 19.6.87.

274 'some interfering' – Braybrooke, p. 99.
'Fireworks' – *The Times*, 17.10.53.
'Knowing that' – diary, 30.9.49.

275 'It was far' – diary, 9.1.49.

276 'It was one' – ibid.

277 Bunny – Stuart Hampshire to PP, 28.7.88.

278 'fellow-thinker' – diary, 9.1.49.

279 Nancy – diary, 30.12.48.
'It was' – diary, 9.1.49.

280 Plomer – 6.11.47.

281 'On the other' – to Plomer, 17.1.48.

282 puppies – MDT, p. 119.
Bunny – diary, 9.1.49.
JRA on Nancy – diary, 22–26.10.48.

285 'No, no' – diary, 26.12.48.

286 Nancy – diary, 30.12.48.

287 Christmas arrangements – JRA to Nancy, n.d. [FK].

288 'suppose that' – diary, 30.12.48.

289 'rather sweet' – diary, 9.1.49.
Nancy – ibid.

15: MY SISTERS AND MYSELF

291 details of Nancy's suicide bid – diary, 9.1.49.

292 Forster – to Buckinghams, c. 18.1.49 [KCC]; quoted, diary, 13.2.49.
'slobbering' – diary, 22–26.10.48.

294 Nancy on Graylingwell – Braybrooke, p. 80.
ECT and Graylingwell – diary, 9.1.49.

295 Kirkup – diary, 21.2.49.
'Once again' – diary, 14.2.49.

296 'What I am' – diary, 13.2.49.

297 doctor's letter – quoted in diary, 20.2.49.
'dull, acquiescent' – diary, 24.4.49.

298 'I don't mind' – diary, 29.4.49.
'Near the' – diary, 5.6.49.

302 'Not in my' – diary, 18.7.49.
Sassoon – Sassoon's diary, 14.7.49 [Rupert Hart-Davis].
'Siegfried sweet' – diary, 13.7.49.

303 'Dear Siegfried' – ibid.
'You'd better' – diary, 23.7.49.

305 'You don't' – diary, 30.6.50.
Sassoon – Sassoon's diary, 5.7.50 [Rupert Hart-Davis].

306 'S.S.' – diary, 30.6.50.

'When I told' – diary, 6.7.50.

308 Diana – to PP, 25.9.87.

309 JRA on Nancy and Diana – diary,
14.5.49, 4.6.49, 4.7.49.

311 Sylvester – 14.7.63.
friend – Stuart Hampshire to PP,
28.7.88.
'busily engaged' – MDT, p. 24.

312 Forster – to Buckinghams, 25.5.54
[KCC].
'I am very' – to John Raymond,
18.4.37 [C&W].

313 'the James' – to Parsons, 22.1.37
[C&W].
Lothian – Braybrooke, p. 96.
HH negotiations – to Parsons,
4.10.51, 16.11.51 [C&W].

314 Parsons – 29.10.54 [C&W].
'I am *not*' – 15.11.54 [C&W].
'immensely exciting' – 16.11.54
[C&W].

315 'Homosexuality and bestiality' – to
Windham, 3.5.54.

315 Woolf – 3.12.54 [Sussex].
JRA to Woolf – n.d. [Sussex].

316 Woolf – n.d. [Sussex].
'some bits' – to Parsons, 3.12.54
[C&W].
MF&M – p. 11.

317 'to be firmly' – to Warburg, c.
February 1955 [S&W].
Spender – n.d. [Braybrooke, p. 115].
footnote² – Sophocles, p. 140.

318 'the art of' – diary, 30.9.49.
'It is the wrinkled' – to Gorer, n.d.
Forster – 6.3.51.

319 'to cut out' – to Gorer, n.d.
Forster – 7.3.55, n.d. (1956).
'ruthless excisions' – to Parsons,
1.6.55 [C&W].
'never been' – n.d. [S&W].
Warburg – 25.5.55 [S&W].

16: LAST YEARS AT *The Listener*

320 'in view' – Warburg to JRA, 14.9.55
[S&W].
Hogarth – 27.9.55 [S&W].
footnote – MDT, p. 34.

321 printers – Warburg, 17.10.55
[S&W].
alterations – [S&W].
'a full half-hour' – MDT, p. 111.

322 Gorer – n.d.
Holland – *The Times*, 30.6.26.

323 Gorer – n.d. (c. September 1955)
[Braybrooke, p. 109].
Fuller – n.d. (1956).

324 May Buckingham – 17.4.56 [KCC].

325 Forster – c. 15.4.56 [KCC].
Spender – 20.4.56 [Braybrooke,
pp. 119–20].
'to off-set' – to Gorer, n.d.
Forster – jacket copy.

326 Forster – n.d.
Warburg – n.d. [S&W].
King – 16.1.57.

327 *Punch* – 18.7.56.
Listener – 19.7.56.
Spectator – 24.8.56.
Fuller – 28.7.56 [HRC].

328 JRA to Fuller – n.d.
Nicolson – 4.7.56 [Nicolson,
pp. 375–6[.
Sitwell – to James Purdy, 28.12.56
[Elborn, p. 229].
Church – to Braybrooke, 23.2.72.
Strachey – Partridge, pp. 249–50.

329 mattress – to Gorer, n.d. [Sussex].

330 *New Statesman* – 'Hunting in
Africa', 7.12.57.

332 bearskins – *The Times*, 13.3.59.
Sparrow – *The Times*, 2.10.57.
Cooper – to PP, 8.12.87.

333 Cooper's review – *Listener*, 29.5.58.
Bell – to PP, 6.9.87.
Raven – *Shadows*, p. 209; to PP,
2.7.87.

334 Hampshire – to PP, 28.7.88.

335 Windham – 31.1.52, 11.3.55.

336 'The Convenience' – Redman to
Braybrooke, 15.2.73; Findlater,
p. 47.

337 Rockingham and Mousehole –
Raven to PP, 2.7.87; JRA note to
letter from Forster, 5.1.58.
footnote – Forster to JRA, n.d.
(c. 30.11.58); *Listener*, 26.2.59.

338 Forster on Bobbie's – 7.1.58.
'another piece' – note to letter from
Forster, 5.1.56.
'be frisky' – n.d. (Janury 1958).
'I wanted' – note to letter from
Forster, c. 15.1.58.

340 Britten – 6.6.51, 28.7.51, 17.8.61,
19.9.62, 11.1.63 [Britten-Pears
Library].

341 '"Not noisy"' – to Plomer, 15.3.63.

342 Forster at BBC – to Florence Barger,
10.2.53 [KCC].
footnote – Reith, p. 525; diary,
12.8.53.

343 Poetry Book Society – to Fuller,
6.12.57, 5.12.57, 9.12.57, 6.3.58,

9.6.58, 18.6.58; to Plomer, 6.11.59.

345   'stingy' – EMFAP, p. 15.
Plomer – 16.9.59.
Warburg – n.d. (c. January 1958)
[S&W].

346   JRA to Warburg – attached to letter
from Forster, 20.1.58 [HRC].
Warburg to JRA – n.d. [S&W].

347   Forster – enclosed with letter to
JRA, n.d. (February 1958)
Warburg – 17.2.58 [S&W].
'ticked off' – to JRA, c. 31.11.58.

348   Spender – December 1955
[Braybrooke, p. 115].

349   Girodias – JRA to Henry Reed,
2.4.59 [Braybrooke, p. 150].
'absolutely adamant' – Warburg to
King, 8.9.71 [S&W].
Hamilton – to JRA, 2.6.59 [BH].

350   'squatting' – to Herbert Read,
2.4.59.

351   Forster – to Plomer, 20.3.58
[Durham]; to JRA, 7.3.58.
Fuller – 16.9.59.
'sweet end' – to Plomer, 16.9.59.
footnote – Raven to PP, 2.7.87.

352   Sylvester – 6.11.59.

17: A PASSAGE TO JAPAN

353   King – 9.1.60 [Braybrooke, p. 162].
Wickens – 8.11.59 [Braybrooke,
p. 159].
Roerick – to PP.

354   Buckingham – 25.11.59
[Braybrooke, p. 161].
'Ditty' – *Listener*, 17.12.59.

355   Kariba – 'Creation and Destruction',
Listener 3.12.59.
Guppy – 'A Shameful Lot', *Listener*
22.5.58.
'sad story' – to Spender, c. December
1959 [Braybrooke, p. 161].

356   Gorer – 6.2.67.
'I write' – to Higham, 15.9.59.
Higham – 22.12.59.

357   'I fancy' – to Higham, 16.1.60.
Forster – n.d. (c. January 1960).

358   Buckingham – n.d. (July 1960).

359   boys in Athens – to King, 21.6.60
[Braybrooke, pp. 165–6].
'Congo belle' – to Windham, n.d. (c.
July 1960).

360   Forster – c. 19.7.60 [KCC].

361   King's house – to Forster, 21.9.60
[KCC].
Geisha House – diary, 24.11.60.
Forster – 21.9.60.

362   Monkey Hill – diary, 2.10.60.

363   Matsushima – diary, 31.10.60.
YMCA – to King, 5.11.60 [HRC].

364   'At 12.00' – diary, 9.11.60.
King – n.d. (November 1960).

365   'I had bungled' – diary, 16.11.60.
'Drank too much' – diary, 17.11.60.

366   *New Statesman* – 1.10.60.
Spectator – 7.10.60.
Forster – 21.11.60.

367   Kinoshita – to Forster, 1.12.60.
'a very pleasant' – diary, 26.11.60.

368   Kobo-Daishi – diary, 27.11.60.

369   Kinoshita – 4.12.60.
'You feel' – on envelope of letter
from Forster, 9.9.60.
Forster – 1.12.60.
'I know that' – diary, 6.12.60.

371   Hearn – diary, 27.12.60.
lagoon – diary, 28.12.60.

372   King – to PP, 14.12.88.
Kinoshita – diary, 2.1.61.

373   King – n.d. (February 1961).
Blunden – 29.10.60.
King – 9.1.61 [Braybrooke, p. 188].

374   'old boiling-fowl' – diary, 10.1.61.
museums – diary, 11.1.61.
'wretched place' – to King, n.d.
(January 1961).

375   Gorer – 29.4.61.
Bunny – diary, 13.7.52.
footnote – to Gorer, 31.8.63;
MS&M, p. 21.

376   Gorer – n.d. (1961).
'The old trouble' – to Gorer, 24.9.61.
'Symbionts' – diary, 9.7.57.

377   Spender – 19.8.61 [Braybrooke,
p. 195].
'Kobo-Daishi' – *Listener*, 31.8.61.

378   Queenie's state – to Sonia Orwell,
18.1.61; to King, 20.2.61; to Gorer,
24.5.61.
Gorer – 10.6.61.
Higham – 7.9.61.

379   'final quietus' – to Forster, 31.10.61.

18: IN MOURNING

380   'saddest day' – to Windham,
9.11.61.
King – 6.12.61.
Forster – 1.11.61.
Britten – 21.11.61.
poem – Braybrooke, p. 200.

381   Britten – 6.6.51.
Read – n.d. (1951) [FK].

382   'jolly gratuitous' – to Plomer,
13.1.64.

Higham – 24.9.61, 1.1.63 [i.e. 62].

383 *Encounter* – 'Truth in Fiction', May 1961.

384 Campbell – to PP, 4.5.88.
Gorer – 17.3.62.
Windham – 6.3.62.

385 'I feel like' – to Gorer, 17.3.62.
King – 30.3.62.
Heard – to King, 29.3.62.

386 'The place was' – to King, 21.5.62.
Gorer – n.d. (late 1962).

387 Hampshire – to PP, 28.7.88.
Diana Petre – to PP, 25.9.87.

388 'a dirty, tatty' – to Windham, 21.6.62.
Roerick – to PP, 24.5.88.

389 'added a new' – to King, 1.10.62.
Rob Buckingham – May Buckingham to PP, 19.6.87.

390 footnote – Janet Adam Smith to PP, 11.6.87.

391 Smith winners – to King, 1.10.62.
Forster – n.d. (1962).
Higham – 28.9.62.
Forster – 'Joe's Speech', n.d. (1962) [HRC].

392 King – 1.10.62.
'then had to explain' – to Fuller, n.d. (October 1962).
'hospital case' – to Windham, 2.12.62.
Longford's speech – JRA to Fuller, October 1962; *The Times*, 17.10.62.
footnote – Lettice Cooper to PP, 8.12.87.

393 Warburg – Warburg, p. 212.
King – 2.11.61.
footnote – Warburg, p. 212.

19: ACKERLEY *contra mundum*

394 King – 11.10.62.
'another schizo' – to Plomer, 28.12.62.

395 'to reduce' – to Gorer, 29.1.63.
Plomer – 2.1.63.
King – 25.2.63.

396 Kitchin – MS&M, p. 14.
'victors' – diary, 13.2.49.
Nancy – JRA to Plomer, n.d. (c. 5.5.64).
Plomer – 16.5.63.
Gorer – 11.7.64.

397 'I have always' – to Gorer, 1.5.61.
footnote – information from Diana Petre.

398 Plomer – 5.3.63.
JRA on Grosvenor – to Plomer, 28.2.67; to Gorer, 23.12.59.

399 MF&M – to King, 25.2.63; to Higham, 23.2.63.
Higham – 6.9.63.
WTTWOY musical – to Higham, 23.3.63, 8.1.64.

400 reader's report – n.d. [BH].
Authors – Woolf & Bagulley, pp. x, 105.

402 Cliff Richard – to King, 25.2.63.
Forster – n.d. (1958?).
Disney – to Plomer, 30.12.66.
'murderous humanity' – to Gorer, 2.10.66.
Forster – *Time and Tide*, 23.6.34.
'This is a human' – EMFAP, p. 23.
Forster's cats – to Plomer, 22.12.47 [Durham].

403 'I can no more' – to the Buckinghams, 25.8.65 [KCC].
Fletcher – to PP, 21.9.87.
Gorer – 4.4.67.
'I am *not*' – to David Sylvester, 8.1.67.

404 letters to *The Times* – 23.1.59, 13.1.67.
Swift – to Richard Murphy, 14.1.64; to Kirkup, 18.1.64 [Braybroke, pp. 241, 242].
King – 12.1.60.
Duthuit – 22.7.63 [Braybrooke, p. 230].

405 'I am a Beast' – *Orient/West*, March/April 1964.
Murphy – 14.1.64 [Braybrooke, p. 240].

406 Kirkup – 18.1.64, 4.2.64 [Braybrooke, pp. 241–2].
Plomer – 5.8.64.

407 'There is a rowan' – to Plomer, 6.11.66.

408 memoir – EMFAP, p. 24.
Sylvester – 16.1.67, 8.1.67, 16.1.67.

409 vegetarianism – to Plomer, 6.11.60.
turkey – to King, 3.1.67.

410 'a word never' – to Gorer, 30.10.65.

411 Sprott's cat – to Forster, 23.12.63.
footnote – 2.12.65.

412 Windham – to *TLS*, 14.4.78.
'In my role' – to Sonia Orwell, 13.1.65.
Windham – *TLS*.
Higham – 7.5.66.
Fielden – Braybrooke, p. 16.
commonplace book – p. 230.

413 Fletcher – to PP, 21.9.87.
Jeppe – n.d. (December 1963).
'The Gospel' – to King, 11.10.64.
'How I live' – to Gorer, 7.9.66.

20: WELCOMING THE DEAR DARK
ANGEL
414 'ruthlessly discarded' – to Fuller,
20.9.65.
415 Murton – *Listener*, 7.10.65.
'So I . . .' – to Fuller, 21.9.65.
Fuller – 12.9.65, 21.9.65.
416 'For anyone' – MF&M draft.
418 Higham – 23.1.67 [HRC].
Gorer – 23.12.59.
Read – to Gorer, n.d.
Morris – to Plomer, 9.1.64.
Abbott – to Gorer, 7.9.66; to
Plomer, 25.10.63.
Nicolson – to Paul Cadmus, 27.5.67.
419 'wandering about' – to Cadmus,
17.12.64.
Fuller – 16.10.65.
420 Plomer – 2.12.65.
Forster – 7.7.58.
'his love' – EMFAP, pp. 8–9.
Forster – to JRA, 17.1.31.
JRA on Forster – Hilary Corke and
Stuart Hampshire to PP, 7.7.87,
28.7.88.
421 Fletcher – to PP, 21.9.87.
Forster stories – 13.4.39, n.d. (April
1939), 12.11.56, n.d.
(c. February 1958).
footnote – JRA to Abbott, 16.5.66;
to May Buckingham, 26.5.66
[KCC].
422 'something else' – EMFAP, p. 9.
Sprott – Forster: *Life*, p. xiii; Forster
to JRA, 6.4.65.
423 Cotterell – n.d. [FK].
JRA on *Howard's End* – Daley to

Furbank, 4.8.68; JRA to Abbott,
18.6.65.
424 Sieveking – 24.4.66 [KCC].
Forster biography – Sprott to
Plomer, 21.7.60 [Durham].
425 Forster – 29.4.67 [Durham].
Plomer – 6.5.67.
Sylvester – 5.10.65.
'crude drawing' – to Oscar Collier,
29.9.65 [Braybooke p. 271].
426 'Morgan is' – to Herbert Read,
17.7.65 [Braybrooke, p. 266].
'drinky-pops' – n.d. (c. 3.11.66).
'We drift' – to Windham, 5.11.66.
Gorer – n.d. (October 1966).
427 Forster – 14.11.66.
Gorer – 16.11.66.
footnote – to Kirkup, 16.3.65,
16.2.67 [Braybrooke, pp. 261, 317].
428 'inspired by' – to Sylvester, 8.4.67.
Sylvester – 17.4.67.
Higham – 19.4.67.
429 Furbank – *EMF II*, p. 323.
Observer – 'Morgan', 14.6.70.
Forster – 21.8.58.
430 JRA – note to letters from Forster,
21.8.58, 26.8.58.
footnote – Lago, p. x.
431 'irked' – ibid.
'unstinted admiration' – *EMF II*,
p. 323.
Orwell – 27.5.67.

EPILOGUE
432 Forster at Aldeburgh – May
Buckingham to PP, 19.6.87.
433 'obscene disclosures' – Morris to
Plomer, 7.8.67 [Durham].
Wilson – *Observer*, 22.9.68.
434 Diana Petre – to PP.
435 Kirkup – 'Dear Old Joe', *London
Magazine* April/May 1975.

Bibliography

I: Books by J. R. Ackerley

Poems by Four Authors, Bowes & Bowes, 1923
The Prisoners of War: A Play, Chatto and Windus, 1925
Hindoo Holiday: An Indian Journal, Chatto and Windus, 1932; revised ed.
   1952
Escapers All [ed.], The Bodley Head, 1932
Intermède Hindou, trans. Marie Mavraud, Gallimard, Paris, 1935
My Dog Tulip: Life with an Alsatian, Secker and Warburg, 1956; revised ed.
   The Bodley Head, 1966
We Think the World of You, The Bodley Head, 1960
My Father and Myself, The Bodley Head, 1968
E. M. Forster: A Portrait, Ian McKelvie, 1970
Micheldever & Other Poems, Ian McKelvie, 1972
The Letters of J. R. Ackerley, ed. Neville Braybrooke, Duckworth, 1975
My Sister and Myself: The Diaries of J. R. Ackerley, ed. Francis King,
   Hutchinson, 1982

II: Unpublished material

The Ackerley Estate [FK]
Archives of Chatto and Windus, The Bodley Head and Martin Secker &
   Warburg at the University of Reading [C&W, BH, S&W]
The Berg Collection at the New York Public Library [Berg]
King's College, Cambridge [KCC]
The Harry Ransom Humanities Research Center at the University of Texas
   [HRC]

Bibliography

The Imperial War Museum [IWM]
The University of Durham Library [Durham]
The University of Sussex Library [Sussex]
The BBC Written Archives Centre [WAC]

III: Anthologies containing poems by J. R. Ackerley

ADCOCK, ST JOHN, *The Bookman Treasury of Living Poets*, Hodder and Stoughton, n.d.
CHURCH, RICHARD and BOZMAN, M. M., *Poems of Our Time: 1900–1942*, J. M. Dent, 1945
COOTE, STEPHEN, *The Penguin Book of Homosexual Poetry*, Penguin, 1983
DAVISON, EDWARD, *Cambridge Poets, 1914–1920*, W. Heffer and Son, 1920
MOULT, THOMAS, *The Best Poems of 1922*, Jonathan Cape, 1923
NEWBOLT, SIR HENRY, *The Mercury Book of Verse*, Macmillan, 1931
SQUIRE, J. C., *Second Selections from Modern Poets*, Martin Secker, 1924

IV: Newspapers and magazines

The Banana Budget
Encounter
The English Review
Horizon
The Listener
London Magazine
London Mercury
The Nation
News of the World

The Observer
Orient/West
The Rossallian
The Spectator
The Sunday Times
The Times
The Times Literary Supplement
The Venture
The Week-end Review

V: Secondary sources

ADAM SMITH, JANET [ed.], *Poems of Tomorrow*, Chatto and Windus, 1935
AGATE, JAMES, *The Contemporary Theatre, 1925*, Chapman and Hall, 1926
ALEXANDER, PETER F., *William Plomer: A Biography*, Oxford, 1989
ALLEN, WALTER, *As I Walked Down New Grub Street*, Heinemann, 1981
AUDEN, W. H., *Forewords and Afterwords*, Faber and Faber, 1973
BEAVER, PATRICK, *Yes! We Have Some: The Story of Fyffes*, Publications for Companies, 1976
BRIGGS, ASA, *The History of Broadcasting in the United Kingdom, Vol II*, OUP, 1965

BROPHY, BRIGID, *Don't Never Forget*, Jonathan Cape, 1966

BULSTRODE, REVD R., *A Parson in Khaki*, unpublished ts, Imperial War Museum, London

CARPENTER, HUMPHREY, *W. H. Auden: A Biography*, George Allen and Unwin, 1981

CHARLTON, L. E. O., *Charlton*, Faber and Faber, 1931

—, *The Mystery of Cowsole Wood*, Hodder and Stoughton, 1948

CHURCH, RICHARD [ed.], *The Spoken Word*, Collins, 1955

CONNOLLY, CYRIL, *Journals and a Memoir* [ed. D. Pryce-Jones], Collins, 1983

CUNNINGHAM, VALENTINE, *British Writers of the Thirties*, OUP, 1988

DALEY, HARRY, *This Small Cloud*, Weidenfeld and Nicolson, 1987

DAS, G. K. and BEER, J. [eds], *E. M. Forster: A Human Exploration*, Macmillan, 1979

DAUMAS, PHILIPPE [ed.], *Cahiers d'Études et de Recherches Victoriennes et Edouardiennes*, 4 & 5, Université Paul Valery, Montpellier, 1977

DAY-LEWIS, SEAN, *C. Day Lewis: An English Literary Life*, Weidenfeld and Nicolson, 1980

DICKINSON, G. LOWES, *The Autobiography of G. Lowes Dickinson* [ed. Dennis Proctor], Duckworth, 1973

—, *The Greek View of Life*, Methuen, 1896

—, *Plato and His Dialogues*, Allen and Unwin, 1931

ELBORN, GEOFFREY, *Edith Sitwell*, Sheldon Press, 1981

FIELDEN, LIONEL, *The Natural Bent*, André Deutsch, 1960

FINDLATER, RICHARD, *Comic Cuts*, André Deutsch, 1970

FINNEY, BRIAN, *The Inner I*, Faber and Faber, 1985

FORSTER, E. M., *Abinger Harvest*, Edward Arnold, 1936

—, *Arctic Summer & Other Fiction* [ed. O. Stallybrass & E. Heine], Edward Arnold, 1980

—, *Aspects of the Novel*, Edward Arnold, 1927

—, *Commonplace Book* [ed. Philip Garner], Scolar Press, 1979

—, *Goldsworthy Lowes Dickinson*, Edward Arnold, 1934

—, *The Hill of Devi and other Indian writings* [ed. E. Heine], Edward Arnold, 1983

—, *Howard's End*, Edward Arnold, 1910

—, *The Life to Come and Other Stories* [ed. O. Stallybrass], Edward Arnold, 1975

—, *The Longest Journey*, Edward Arnold, 1907

—, *Marianne Thornton. A Domestic Biography, 1879–1887*, Edward Arnold, 1956

—, *Maurice*, Edward Arnold, 1971; Penguin, 1972

—, *A Passage to India*, Edward Arnold, 1924

—, *A Room with a View*, Edward Arnold, 1908

Bibliography

FORSTER, E. M., *Selected Letters* [ed. M. Lago & P. N. Furbank]: *Vol I: 1879–1920*, Collins, 1983; *Vol II: 1921–1970*, Collins, 1985
—, *Two Cheers for Democracy*, Edward Arnold, 1951
—, *Where Angels Fear to Tread*, Edward Arnold, 1905
FRY, PHILLIP LEE, *An Annotated Calendar of the Letters from E. M. Forster to Joe R. Ackerley*, University of Texas at Austin, 1974
FRYER, JONATHAN, *Isherwood*, New English Library, 1977
FULLER, ROY, *Home and Dry*, Alan Ross, 1984
FURBANK, P. N. *E. M. Forster: A Life. Vol I: The Growth of a Novelist 1879–1914*, Secker & Warburg, 1977; *Vol II: Polycrates' Ring 1914–1970*, Secker and Warburg, 1978
GELLERT, ROGER, *Quaint Honour*, Secker and Warburg, 1958
GLENDINNING, VICTORIA, *Edith Sitwell*, Weidenfeld and Nicolson, 1981
—, *Vita: The Life of V. Sackville-West*, Weidenfeld and Nicolson, 1983
GREEN, G. F., *A Skilled Hand*, Macmillan, 1980
GRIGSON, GEOFFREY, *Recollections*, Chatto and Windus, 1985
HERZ, J. S. and MARTIN, R. K., *E. M. Forster: Centenary Revaluations*, University of Toronto Press and Macmillan, 1982
HOLROYD, MICHAEL, *Lytton Strachey: The Years of Achievement*, Heinemann, 1968
HYDE, H. MONTGOMERY, *The Other Love*, Heinemann, 1970
—, *The Trials of Oscar Wilde*, Penguin, 1962; Dover, 1973
ISHERWOOD, CHRISTOPHER, *Christopher and His Kind*, Methuen, 1977
—, *Down There on a Visit*, Methuen, 1962
KING, FRANCIS, *E. M. Forster and His World*, Thames and Hudson, 1978
KIRKUP, JAMES, *I, of all People*, Weidenfeld and Nicolson, 1988
LAGO, MARY, *Calendar of the Letters of E. M. Forster*, Mansell, 1985
LANCASTER, MARIE-JAQUELINE [ed.], *Brian Howard: Portrait of a Failure*, Anthony Blond, 1968
LAWRENCE, T. E., *The Letters of T. E. Lawrence* [ed. M. Brown], Dent, 1988
MACAULAY, ROSE, *Last Letters to a Friend, 1952–1958* [ed. C. Babbington Smith], Collins, 1962.
MAIS, S. P. B., *All the Days of My Life*, Hutchinson, 1937
—, *From Shakespeare to O. Henry*, revised ed., Grant Richards, 1923
—, *The Happiest Days of My Life*, Max Parrish, 1953
MEYERS, JEFFREY, *The Enemy: A Biography of Wyndham Lewis*, Routledge and Kegan Paul, 1980
MISRA, S. B., *20th Annual Administrative Report of the Chhatarpur State, Bundelkhand, C.I. for Sambat 1980*, National Press, Allahabad, 1924
MITCHISON, NAOMI, *You May Well Ask*, Victor Gollancz, 1979; Flamingo, 1986

MOUNT, CHARLES M., *John Singer Sargent: A Biography*, W. W. Norton, NY, 1955

NICHOLS. G. H. F., *The 18th Division in the Great War*, Blackwood, 1922

NICOLSON, HAROLD, *Diaries and Letters 1930–1964* [ed. S. Olson], Collins, 1980

PARTRIDGE, FRANCES, *Julia: A Portrait of Julia Strachey*, Gollancz, 1983

PEARSON, JOHN, *Façades: Edith, Osbert & Sacheverell Sitwell*, Macmillan, 1978

PETRE, DIANA, *The Cruel Month*, Collins, 1955

—, *Portrait of Mellie*, The Bodley Head, 1951

—, *The Secret Orchard of Roger Ackerley*, Hamish Hamilton, 1975

PLOMER, WILLIAM, *At Home: Memoirs*, Jonathan Cape, 1958

—, *Sado*, Hogarth Press, 1931

—, *Turbott Wolfe*, Hogarth Press, 1925

RATCLIFFE, CARTER, *John Singer Sargent*, Abbeville Press, NY, 1982

RAVEN, SIMON, *Boys Will Be Boys: A Miscellany*, Anthony Blond, 1963

—, *Shadows on the Grass*, Blond and Briggs, 1982

REDGRAVE, MICHAEL, *My Mind's Eye*, Viking, 1983

REES, GORONWY, *Brief Encounters*, Chatto and Windus, 1974

The Rossall School Register, 1871–1939, Cambridge University Press, 1940

SASSOON, SIEGFRIED, *Diaries: 1923–25* [ed. R. Hart-Davis], Faber and Faber, 1985

SERPELL, JAMES, *In the Company of Animals*, Blackwell, 1986

SOPHOCLES, *The Theban Plays* [ed. E. F. Watling], Penguin, 1947

A Short History of the 55th Infantry Brigade in the War of 1914–18, privately printed, n.d.

SPENDER, STEPHEN, *Journals: 1939–1983*, Faber and Faber, 1985

—, *Letters to Christopher* [ed. Lee Bartlett], Black Sparrow Press, 1980

STOCKLEY, A. H., *Consciousness of Effort: The Romance of the Banana*, privately printed, 1938

STUART, CHARLES [ed.], *The Reith Diaries*, Collins, 1975

TREVELYAN, RALEIGH, *The Golden Oriole*, Secker & Warburg, 1987

VADIVISHI, A., *The Ruling Chiefs, Nobles and Zamindars of India*, G. C. Longanadham Bros, Madras, 1915

WARBURG, FREDERIC, *All Authors are Equal*, Hutchinson, 1973

WEEKS, JEFFREY, *Coming Out*, Quartet, 1977

WHISTLER, LAWRENCE, *The Laughter and the Urn: The Life of Rex Whistler*, Weidenfeld and Nicolson, 1985

WOOLF, CECIL and BAGGULEY, JOHN, *Authors Take Sides on Vietnam*, Peter Owen, 1967

WOOLF, VIRGINIA, *The Sickle Side of the Moon: Letters, Vol V* [ed. N. Nicolson], The Hogarth Press, 1979

Index

Ackerley's writings are indexed under the entry for Ackerley himself

457

Index

FitzGerald, Edward 306 and n
Flatau, Darota 27
Flatau, Hermione 27
Flatau, Rex 27
Flatau, Theodore 21, 23, 26, 27
Fleet (American publisher) 425
Fletcher, Eric 403, 413, 421
Florence 52, 54–8, 280
Forde, Florrie 42
Forge, Andrew 183–4, 334
Forster, Alice Clara 49, 50, 62, 63 and n, 83, 89, 113n, 157, 158, 160, 212, 326
Forster, E. M. 1, 100, 106, 107, 145, 154, 170, 289, 306n, 334, 337n; beginning of friendship with Ackerley 48, 49–52; depression over love affair 49–50, 61; correspondence with Ackerley 51–2, 62, 63, 75, 79, 102, 131, 133, 157, 229, 235, 244, 245, 263, 325, 326, 357–8, 361, 362, 368, 369, 402, 412, 427–31; growing friendship with Ackerley 58–9, 61–4, 80, 83–4, 94; Indian career 59–60; sexual encounters and friendships 61, 62, 83–4; 85–6, 89, 108, 116, 127, 163–4, 212; and Ackerley family connection 63; on Anglo-Indians 64, 69; as Ackerley's literary mentor 80, 158, 160, 240, 311, 318, 319, 325–6; and Ackerley's play 98, 99, 102; class-consciousness 108, 133; and Ackerley's promiscuity 121, 122, 131, 132–3, 213, 215, 230, 231, 235, 243–5, 338; broadcasting 124, 127–8, 129, 342; 'indecent' writings 131, 197, 422, 429; warns Ackerley against Nancy 137, 154, 288; attitude to women 156–7, 163; as listener 176; contributions to Listener 2, 178, 197, 205; and BBC homosexual purge 182n; seeks return of letters 243, 245, 429–30; and Ackerley's devotion to Queenie 263, 318, 381, 402–3; and Nancy's mental illness 288, 291, 292; as Hon. Fellow of King's College, Cambridge 333; openness of homosexuality 337–8; clash with BBC 342; clash with Warburg 345, 346–7; financial aid for Ackerley 351, 357, 360, 381, 382, 426–7, 431; boycotts Ackerley's farewell party at BBC 352; and Ackerley's absorption in animal matters 388, 389, 409; suggested acceptance speech for Ackerley's W. H. Smith Award 391; attitude to animals 263, 402–3, 407–8, 411; failing powers and succession of strokes 418–20, 423, 424–5, 427, 429; tetchy misunderstandings 419–20, 424; strength of friendship with Ackerley 420–2; homosexual writings 421–2, 429; dependence on Ackerley's literary advice 421–4; projected biography 424–6; disapproval of Ackerley's drinking 426, 427; personal frugality 426; Ackerley's obituary of 427–9; sale of letters 427–31, 435; and Ackerley's death 432
Fowler, Chappell Hodgson 41, 216, 277, 279
Freud, Lucian 322
From Shakespeare to O. Henry (S. P. B. Mais) 17
Fry, Roger 85, 127
Fuller, Dr Charles 11
Fuller, John 189
Fuller, Kate 327
Fuller, Roy: and Listener 180, 183, 186–7, 188, 189, 414; correspondence with Ackerley 180, 183, 186, 323, 327, 351, 392, 415–16, 419; and Poetry Book Society 343–4
Furbank, P. N. 61, 106, 424–5, 429
Furness, W. A. 18

Gallatin, Count James Francis de 103, 166–9
Gallimard 162
Gamekeeper, The (Ian Niall) 415
Gardiner, Rolf 37, 48
Garibaldi (John Drinkwater) 247
Garnett, David 129
Garsington 122
Gascoyne, David 175
Gathorne-Hardy, Edward 114
George VI 217
Georgian Poetry (ed. Marsh) 38, 233n
Gerard Manley Hopkins (John Pick) 180
Gide, André 162, 338
Gielgud, John 98, 103, 113, 383
Giorgio (sailor) 65, 74, 80, 89, 422n
Girodias, Maurice 349
Gloriana (Britten) 340
Gopal, Ram 400
Gorer, Geoffrey 379, 407, 416, 434; friendship with Ackerley 318, 418; correspondence with 322, 323, 375, 376, 378, 384, 386, 396, 403, 426, 427
Graham, Billy 184 and n
Graham, John 9
Graham, Virginia 327
Gransden, K. W. 355, 392n, 414
Grant, Duncan 113, 191, 194
Graves, Robert 27
Graylingwell (mental hospital) 294, 295–7, 375
Greek View of Life, The (Dickinson) 118
Green, G. F. 197
Green Hat, The (Michael Arlen) 99
Greene, Hugh Carleton 392
Grigson, Geoffrey 176, 182 and n, 184, 189
Grosvenor, Gerald see Westminster, Gerald Grosvenor
Grosvenor, Sally see Perry, Sally
Guilty Souls (Robert Nichols) 88
Gulliver's Travels (Swift) 404

459